MANAGEMENT OF FINANCIAL INSTITUTIONS

HOLT, RINEHART AND WINSTON SERIES IN FINANCE

William Beranek, Adviser

Pennsylvania State University

Alexander A. Robichek and Alan B. Coleman

Management of Financial Institutions: Notes and Cases

Donald E. Vaughn

Survey of Investments

MANAGEMENT OF FINANCIAL INSTITUTIONS notes and cases

ALEXANDER A. ROBICHEK

ALAN B. COLEMAN

Graduate School of Business
Stanford University

IN ASSOCIATION WITH

Leonard Marks, Jr.
Professor of Finance

David M. Ehlers
Research Associate

Robert L. Katz
Lecturer in Business Management

Gert von der Linde
Associate Professor of Finance

All of the Graduate School of Business
Stanford University

HOLT, RINEHART AND WINSTON

New York / Chicago / San Francisco / Atlanta
Dallas / Montreal / Toronto / London

Library of Congress Catalog Card Number: 67 – 18882

SBN 03–063740–6

0123 4 9876543

Printed in the United States of America

To our wives Norma and Janet

Preface

The university curriculum in the field of finance has been undergoing radical changes during the past ten years. The teaching emphasis has shifted from a primarily descriptive approach to one using analytical tools and decision-oriented materials. This book is indicative of the change. It represents the results of our efforts to develop an integrated set of teaching materials, designed to stimulate and challenge both the instructor and the student.

The material in this book is currently used in the Management of Financial Institutions course at the Stanford Graduate School of Business. The course emerged in its present form in early 1965 as a result of an amalgamation of the Commercial Banking course and parts of the Financial Markets and Institutions course. The scope of the course is to provide the student with an understanding of the role of the major financial institutions and of the principal financial management problems faced by these institutions.

The emphasis throughout the course—and consequently in this book—is on the application of analytical techniques to the solution of significant financial problems. Thus, all the cases require analysis directed at a particular problem. However, many of the cases in this volume, especially those dealing with institutions other than commercial banks, illustrate an important departure from the traditional finance cases. In addition to raising an issue requiring a decision, these cases provide considerable background material on the industry and about a particular institution within the industry. In a sense, these cases are a combination of text and case material.

The course material is structured in a logical sequence to lead the student to consider a variety of issues that apply uniformly to many of the institutions. The decisional issues were carefully selected and coordinated so that by the end of the course the student will have been exposed not only to all the major financial institutions but also to the broad range of decisional problems faced by these institutions. Each case in this book has been thoroughly tested in the classroom. Also, a number of the cases have been successfully used in executive development programs.

It has been our experience that the preservation of the source material adds to the realism of the cases and aids student motivation. Therefore, regardless of whether the case is disguised or not, we have attempted to present the problems as we found them.

We would like to express our thanks to the many businessmen and their organizations for their willing cooperation in providing the information for the cases presented here. A note of appreciation is due to a number of our colleagues for their helpful criticisms, but especially to Professor Leonard Marks, Jr., who contributed significantly to the development of the teaching materials relating to Commercial Bank Management. In addition we wish to thank Professors Gert von der Linde, Robert L. Katz, and Vincent Jolivet for letting us use cases developed by them.

A number of the cases in this volume were written under our direction by a number of excellent casewriters. While we accept full responsibility for the contents of this volume, our special thanks in this regard go to David M. Ehlers, John G. McDonald, Paul R. Johnson, Lee A Tavis, and Richard H. Terzian.

In conclusion, we wish to acknowledge the long hours spent in typing and frequent retyping of the material by Lola J. Lambert, Helen L. Burgess, Sharon Jones, and June S. Scharfenberg.

A.A.R.
A.B.C.

June 1967
Stanford, California

Contents

MANAGEMENT OF FINANCIAL INSTITUTIONS

FINANCIAL INSTITUTIONS AND MARKETS

Financial Institutions in Perspective: 1900 – 1965

1

The material in this note[1] is designed to give the user a broad perspective on the role of the leading financial institutions in the United States. The statistical and background material presented here is very much abbreviated. The interested reader who wishes a more comprehensive coverage of the subject is encouraged to review one of several available textbooks on the subject.

Exhibit 1 of this note provides a graphical representation of the relative size of the primary financial institutions in 1929 and 1964. Particularly noticeable is the decline in relative importance of commercial banks (from 58 percent to 41 percent of total assets of all institutions) and the increase in relative importance of pension funds, savings and loan associations, and investment companies.

Exhibit 2 is a summary statement of net sources and uses of funds in the financial markets in 1965. Particularly observable is the degree to which financial institutions provide funds to the users – 83.2 percent of all sources were institution-generated. This exhibit also illustrates the relative importance of the various financial institutions and the markets into which the funds are channeled. The reader should note that the amounts in the table of Exhibit 2 are on a net basis; that is, only the net changes in assets and liabilities are taken into account. Thus, for example, the amount of gross mortgage credit extended is considerably in excess of the $31.0 billion shown in the table.

Exhibits 3 through 12 follow the same format. Each exhibit discusses a particular financial institution and consists of four parts:

1. a brief description of the institution;
2. a chart showing the growth in assets and the share of assets of all institutions between 1900 and 1965;
3. comparative balance sheets and funds flow for select years, and
4. a chart showing the distribution of assets and liabilities.

Not all the financial data were available through 1965; thus, the data in the exhibits are those available for the most recent year.

[1]Compiled April 1966.

Exhibit 1

ASSETS OF FINANCIAL INSTITUTIONS

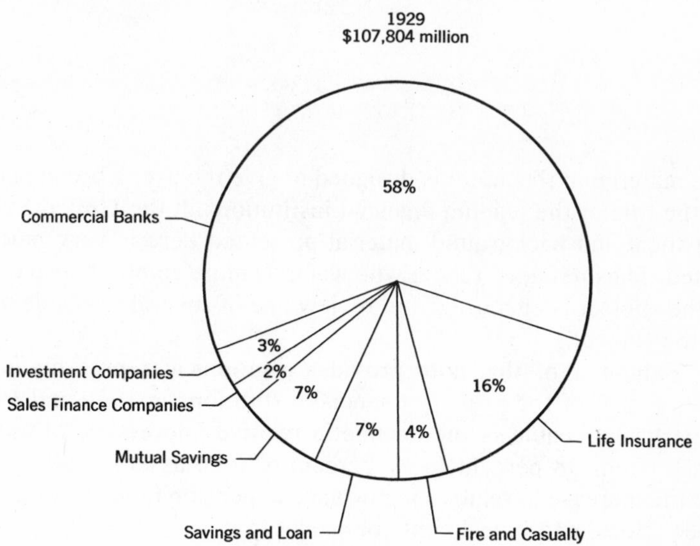

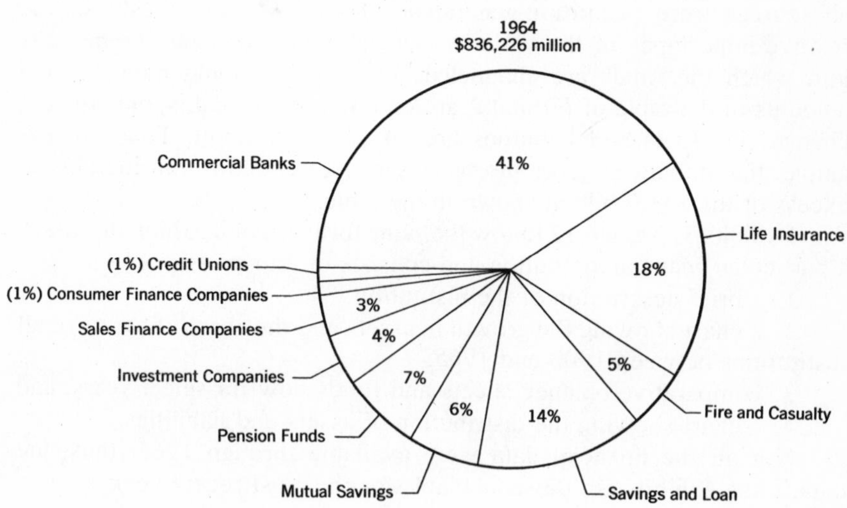

Exhibit 2

SOURCES AND USES AND FUNDS—1965

(billions of dollars)

Sources of Funds (Net)	*Estimated Amount*	*Percent of Total*
Life insurance companies	8.1	10.3
Corporate pension funds	4.8	6.1
State and local government retirement funds	3.1	3.9
Fire and casualty companies	0.9	1.1
Savings and loan associations	9.4	12.0
Mutual savings banks	3.8	4.8
Finance companies	5.3	6.7
Investment companies	1.7	2.2
Credit unions	1.1	1.4
Commercial banks	27.3	34.7
Total—financial institutions	65.5	83.2
Nonfinancial corporations	5.9	7.5
All other	7.3	9.3
	78.7	100.0

Uses of Funds (Net)	*Estimated Amount*	*Percent of Total*
Corporate bonds	8.2	10.4
Term loans by banks to business	2.8	3.6
Short-term loans by banks to business	11.9	15.1
Net trade credit of nonfinancial corporations	5.6	7.1
Finance company loans to business	2.5	3.2
Total business debt	31.0	39.4
Corporate stocks	0.3	0.4
Open market paper	0.7	0.9
Credit for security purchases	1.1	1.4
Consumer credit	9.2	11.7
State and local government securities	7.8	9.9
U.S. government and agency securities	0.4	0.5
Real-estate mortgages	25.3	32.1
All other	2.9	3.7
	78.7	100.0

SOURCE: *The Investment Outlook—1966*, Bankers Trust Company, New York.

Exhibit 3

COMMERCIAL BANKS

Commercial banks are the only institutions that accept demand deposits. Their traditional role was to furnish short-term funds to business, agriculture, and government, but through the years they have become veritable "department stores of finance."

Their functions include substantial activity in the granting of intermediate-term credit through term loans and long-term credit through leasing and the acquisition of government bonds and mortgages. Other services include acceptance of time and savings deposits and the making of consumer loans.

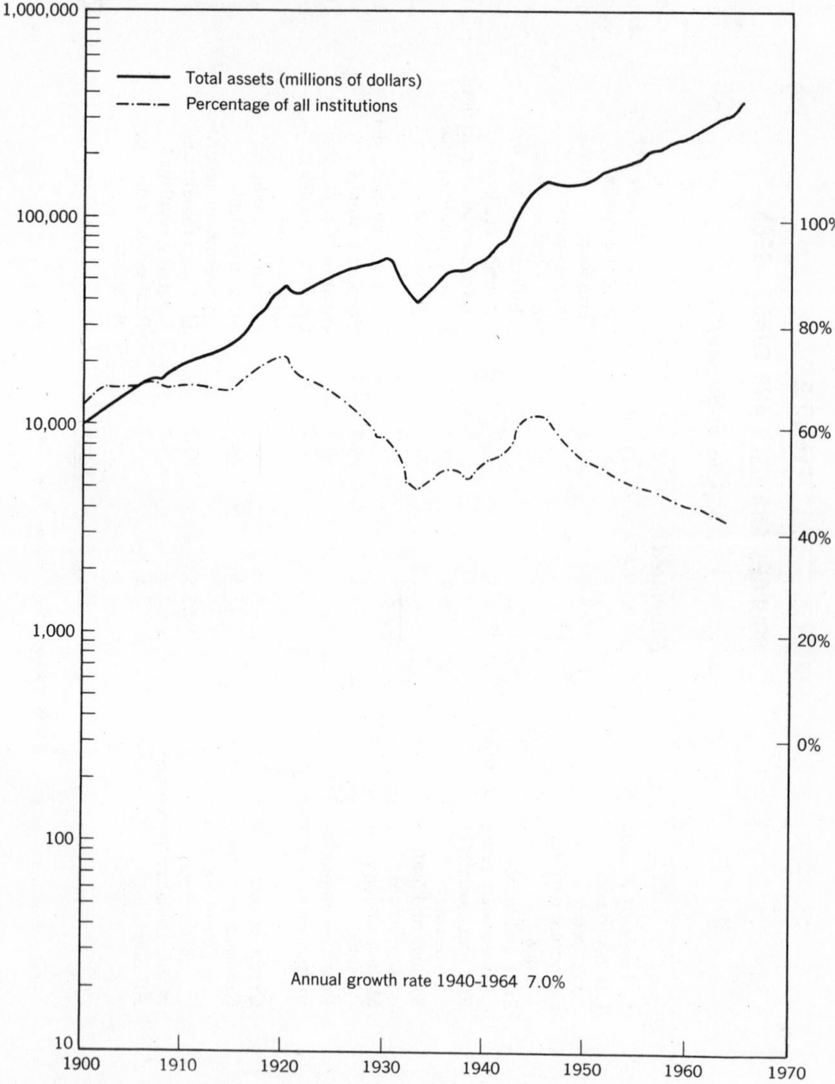

SOURCES: Institute of Life Insurance Fact Book, various issues, New York.
Board of Governors of the Federal Reserve System, Federal Reserve Bulletin, Various issues, Washington, D. C.

Exhibit 3 (Continued)

Funds Flow
(millions of dollars)

	1959	*1965*	*Difference*
Cash	$ 49467	$ 57430	$ 7963
U.S. government securities	58937	$ 57430	(417)
Other securities	20501	44600	24099
Mortgage loans	28145	49323	21178
Other loans	82687	151707	69020
Other assets	4949	9980	5031
	$244686	$371560	$126874
Deposits	$219903	$323770	$103867
Capital and misc. accounts	24783	47790	23007
	$244686	$371560	$126874

Assets and Liabilities

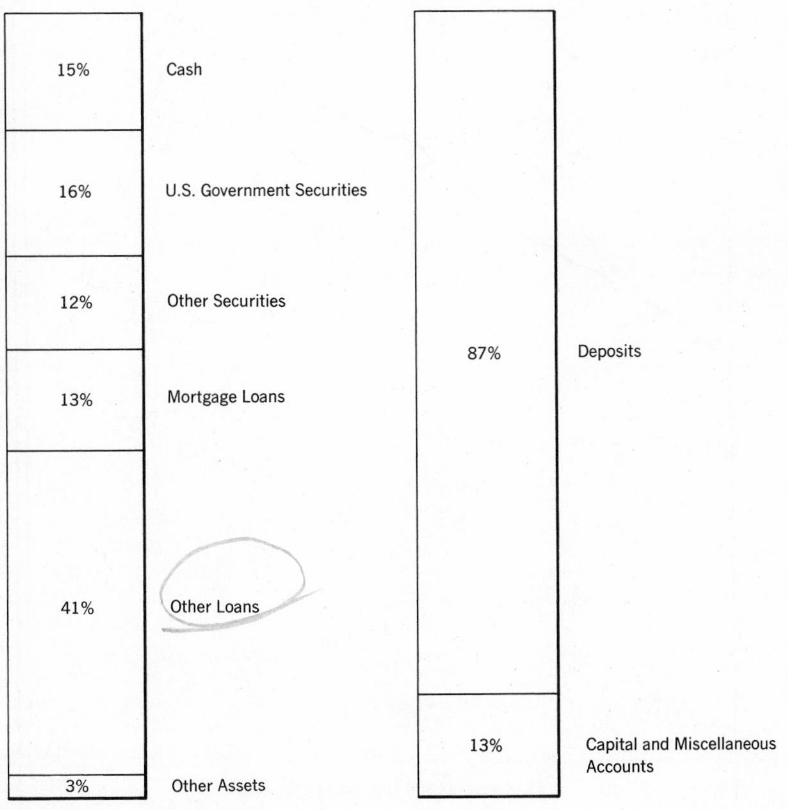

SOURCE: *Monthly Review,* June, 1964, Federal Reserve Bank of New York.

Exhibit 4

LIFE INSURANCE COMPANIES

Life insurance companies sell contractual policies that pledge the company to make installment or lump-sum payments to (a) the policyholder when he reaches a certain age or is disabled, or to (b) the beneficiary of the policyholder should the latter die. In return, the policyholder agrees to make periodic payments (premiums) to the company. These funds are invested in a wide variety of capital-market instruments, such as mortgages and corporate and government securities.

There are two basic types of life insurance companies—mutual and stock. Mutual companies are owned by the policyholders, while stock companies, like the bulk of the nonfinancial corporations, are owned by shareholders.

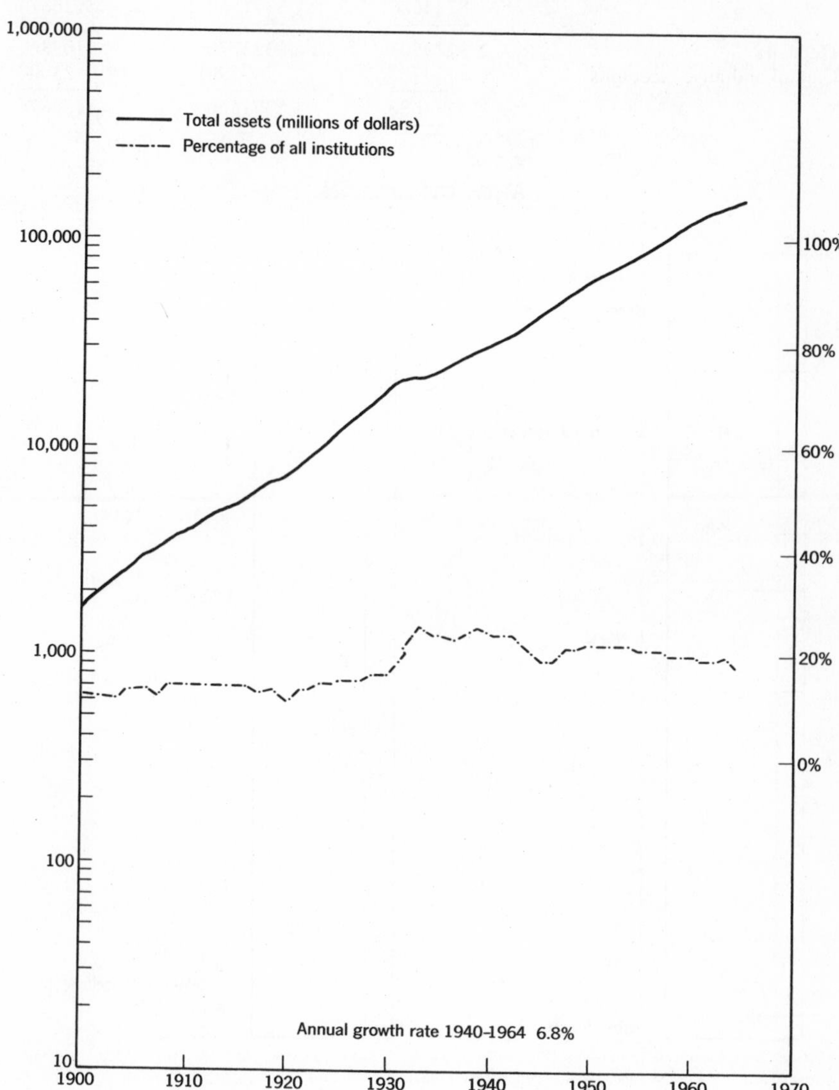

Exhibit 4 (Continued)

Funds Flow
(millions of dollars)

	1959	*1965*	*Difference*
U.S. government securities	$ 6868	$ 5110	$ (1758)
Other government securities	4713	6567	1854
Corporate bonds	45105	58539	13434
Common stocks	4561	7133	2572
Mortgages	39197	59276	20079
Real estate	3651	4695	1044
Policy loans	4618	7623	3005
Other assets	4937	8698	3761
	$113650	$157641	$43991
Policy reserves	$ 93975	$127100	$33125
Other obligations	9117	13520	4403
Capital and surplus	10558	17021	6463
	$113650	$157641	$43991

Assets and Liabilities

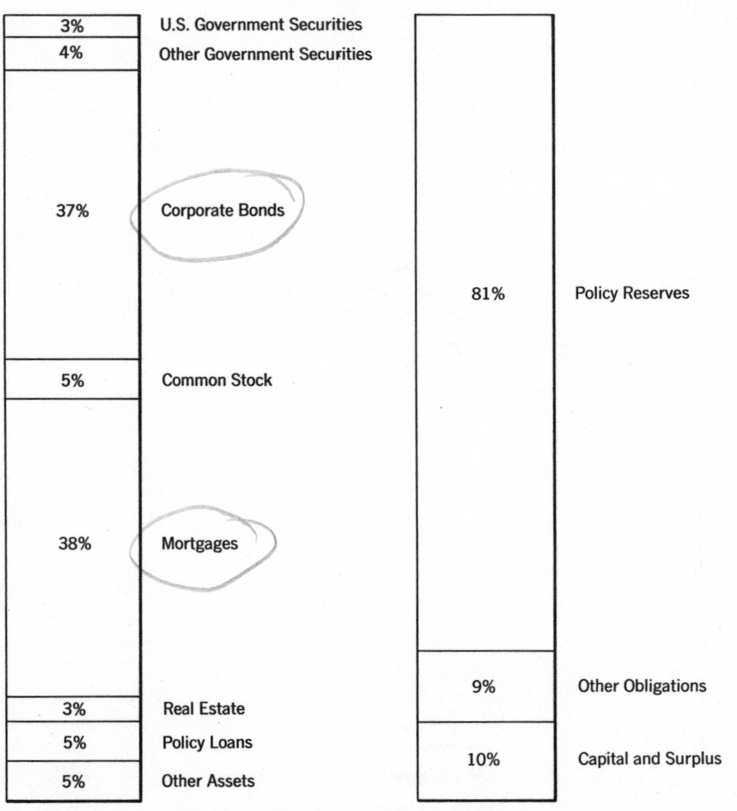

SOURCES: Institute of Life Insurance, *Life Insurance Fact Book,* various issues, New York.
Board of Governors of the Federal Reserve System, *Federal Reserve Bulletin,* various issues, Washington, D. C.

Exhibit 5

FIRE AND CASUALTY COMPANIES

Unlike life insurance companies, fire and casualty companies have no firm dollar obligations to policyholders. Insurers against loss to property from fire and other causes, they sell contracts that provide for indemnification of damage losses up to the limits of the policy. Casualty insurance companies are primarily concerned with losses caused by injuries to persons and by damage to property of others. The net worth of stock companies constitutes protection to policyholders.

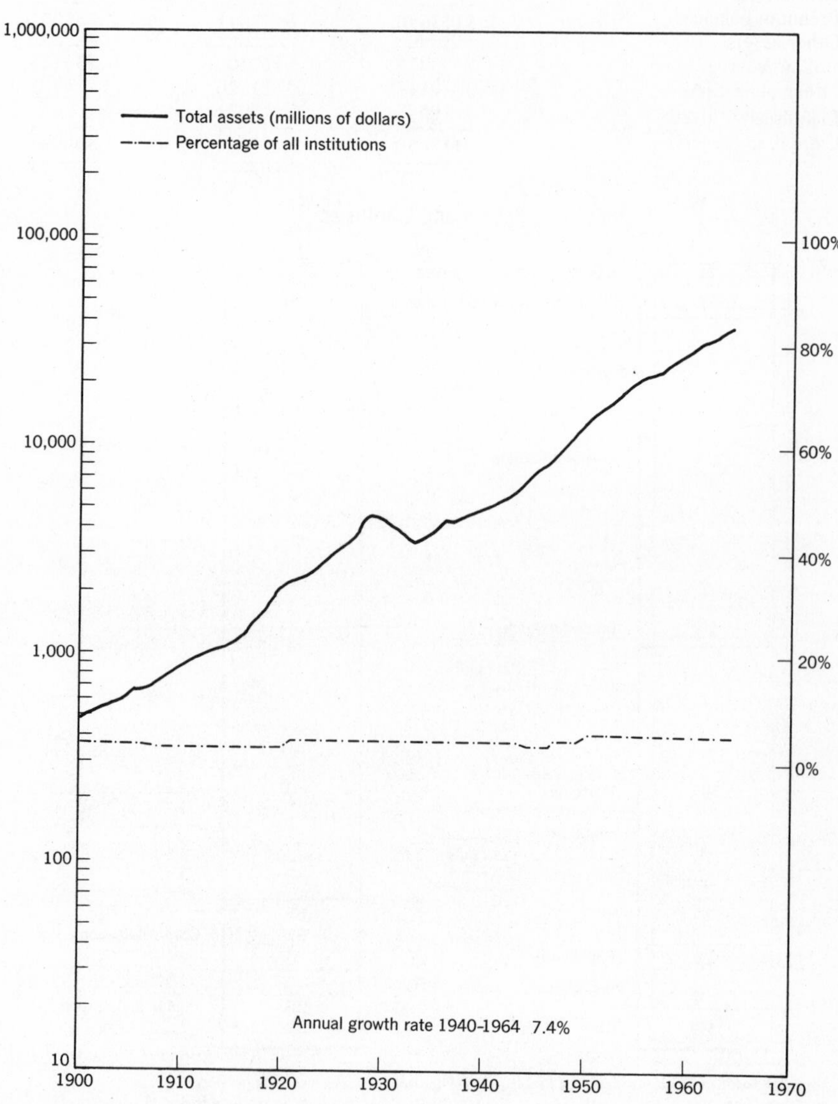

Exhibit 5 (Continued)

Funds Flow
(millions of dollars)

	1958	*1964*	*Difference*
Cash	$ 1389	$ 1379	$ (10)
U.S. government securities	5426	5916	490
Other government securities	6074	10679	4605
Corporate bonds	1609	1965	356
Preferred stocks	826	989	163
Common stocks	7580	13643	6063
Mortgages	154	115	(39)
Real estate	406	560	154
Premium balances	1622	2443	821
Other assets	564	1176	612
	$25654	$38865	$13211
Liabilities	$15240	$22200	$ 6960
Capital and reserves	10414	16665	6251
	$25654	$38865	$13211

Assets and Liabilities

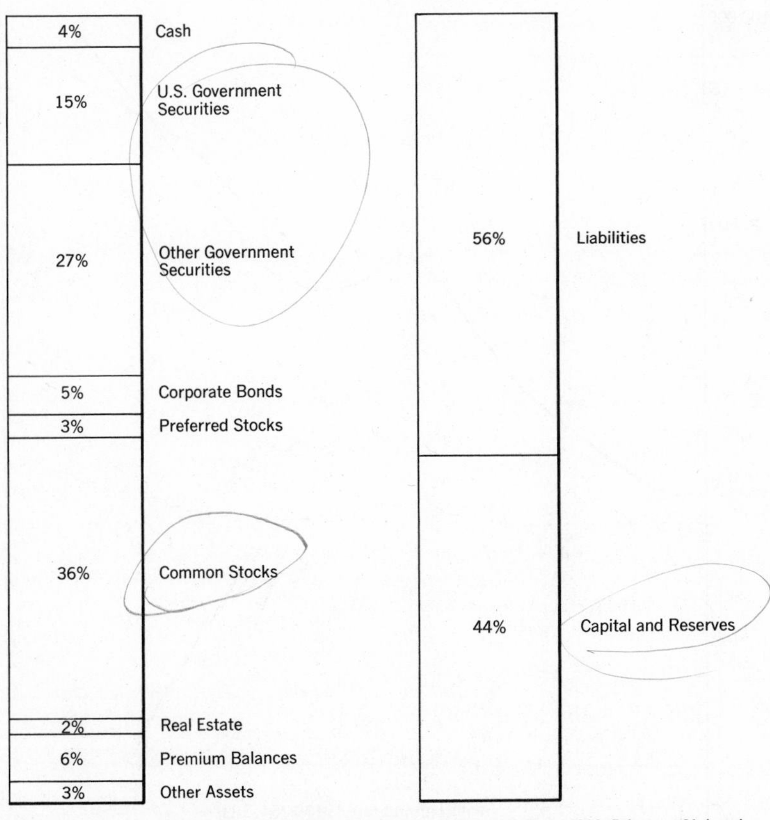

SOURCES: R. W. Goldsmith, *Financial Intermediaries in the American Economy Since 1900*, Princeton University Press, 1958. *Best's Fire and Casualty Aggregates and Averages*, New York: Alfred M. Best, Inc., various issues.

Exhibit 6

SAVINGS AND LOAN ASSOCIATIONS

There are two types of savings and loan associations: mutual and stock. In certain regions of the United States—California is the leading example—a substantial percentage of associations are stock companies.

Savings and loan associations are the only major financial institutions expressly designed to make home-mortgage loans. Associations operate almost exclusively in the long-term markets, with activity mostly confined to local housing finance. They collect savings that technically represent payment for savings and loan shares. Thus, those who have accounts with savings and loan associations are actually stockholders rather than depositors, and they receive dividends rather than interest. The great majority of savings and loan associations are members of the Federal Savings and Loan Insurance Corporation, a government agency insuring accounts up to $15,000.

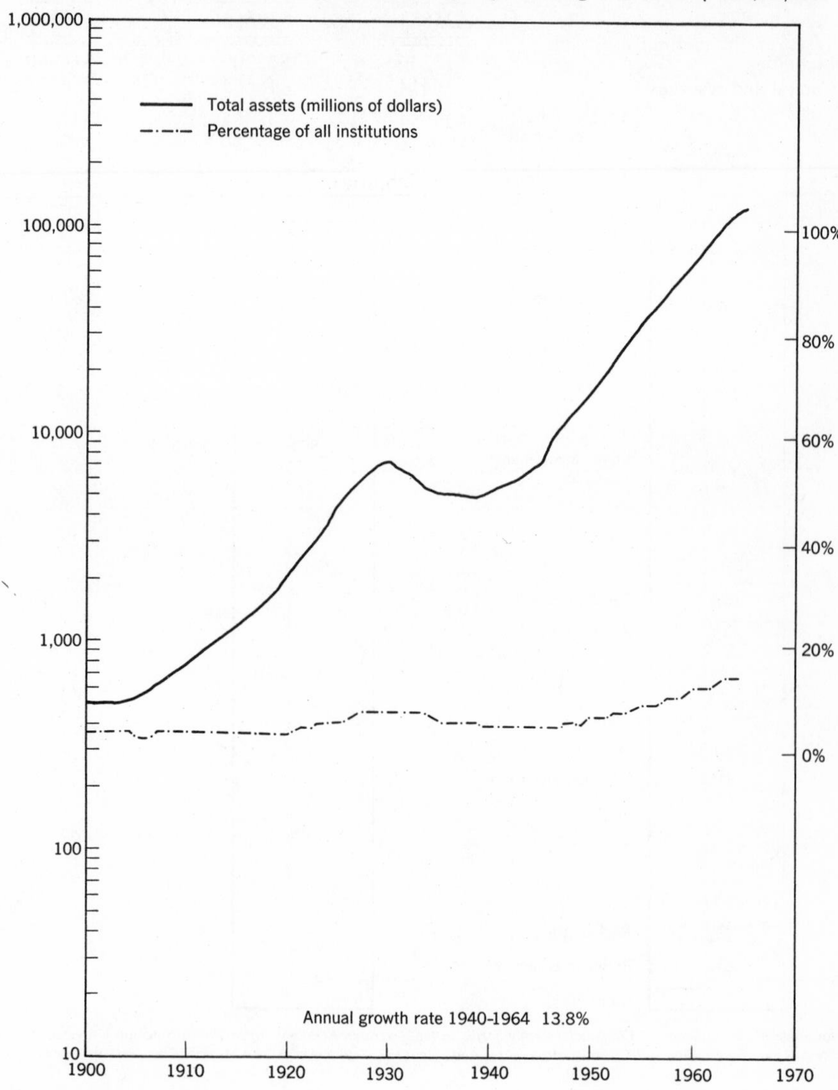

Exhibit 6 (Continued)

Funds Flow
(millions of dollars)

	1959	*1965*	*Difference*
Cash	$ 2183	$ 3899	$ 1716
U.S. government securities	4477	7405	2928
Mortgages	53141	110202	57061
Other assets	3729	7936	4207
	$63530	$129442	$65912
Savings capital	$54583	$110271	$55688
Borrowed money	2387	6440	4053
Loans in process	1293	2189	896
Other liabilities	874	1834	960
Reserves and undivided profits	4393	8708	4315
	$63530	$129442	$65912

Assets and Liabilities

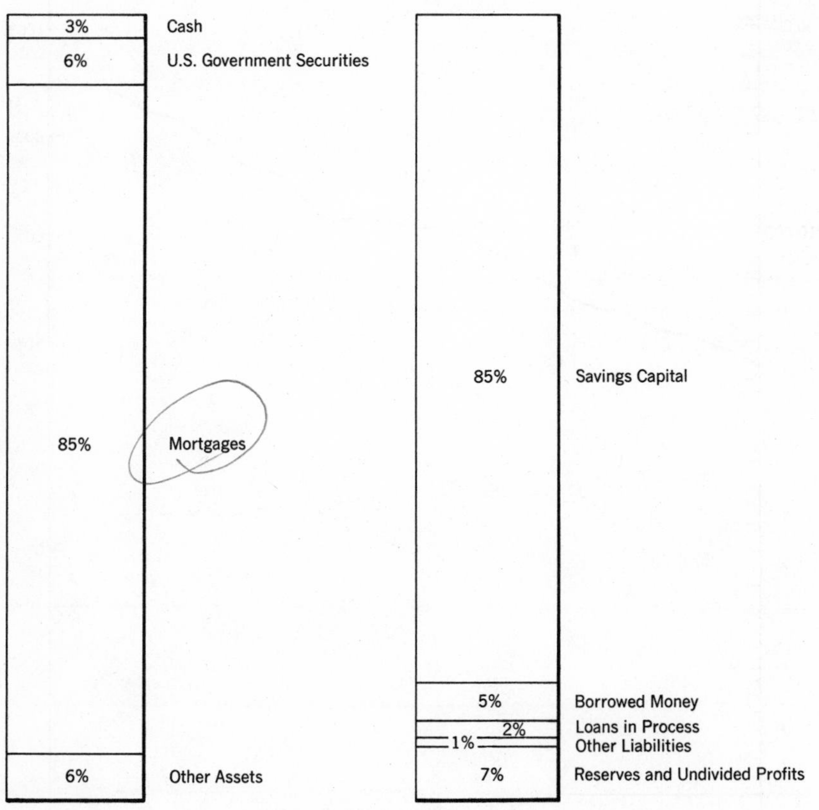

SOURCES: R. W. Goldsmith, *Financial Intermediaries in the American Economy Since 1900*, Princeton University Press, 1958.
Board of Governors of the Federal Reserve System, *Federal Reserve Bulletin*, various issues, Washington, D. C.
United States Savings and Loan League, *Savings and Loan Fact Book*, various issues, Chicago, Illinois.

Exhibit 7

MUTUAL SAVINGS BANKS

Mutual savings banks accept savings deposits and invest them in mortgages, government bonds, and other securities. All mutual savings banks are state-chartered, state-supervised, nonstock institutions owned entirely by their depositors. Earnings are distributed quarterly or semiannually to savers in the form of interest credited to their accounts. Excess earnings are used to build up protective surplus accounts.

Mutuals were first organized in the nineteenth century by public-spirited men who wanted to encourage thrift among people of small means. Policy rests in the hands of a board of trustees whose original members were selected by those who organized the bank.

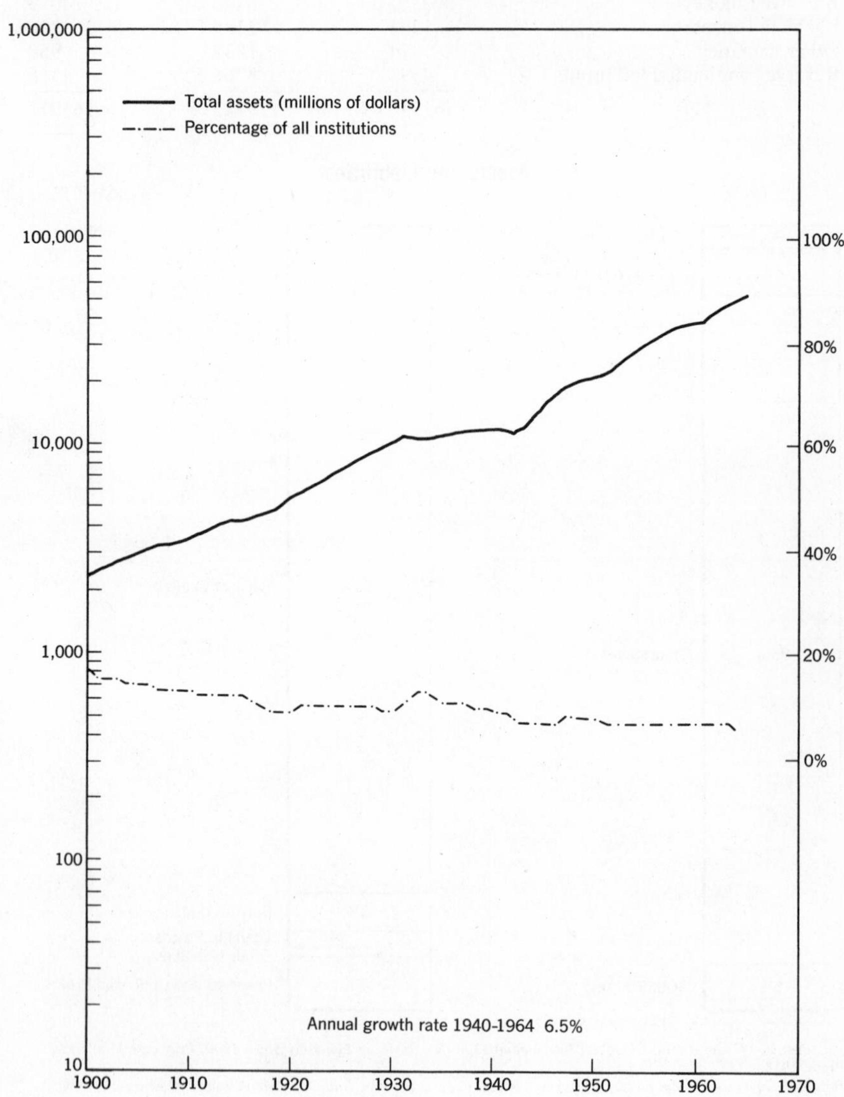

Exhibit 7 (Continued)

Funds Flow
(millions of dollars)

	1959	*1965*	*Difference*
Cash	$ 829	$ 1015	$ 186
U.S. government securities	6871	5179	(1692)
Other government securities	721	319	(404)
Corp. securities	4845	5482	637
Mortgages	24769	44412	19643
Other loans	358	855	497
Other assets	552	943	391
	$38945	$58203	$19258
Deposits	$34977	$52437	$17460
Other liabilities	606	1107	501
General reserve accounts	3362	4657	1297
	$38945	$58203	$19258

Assets and Liabilities

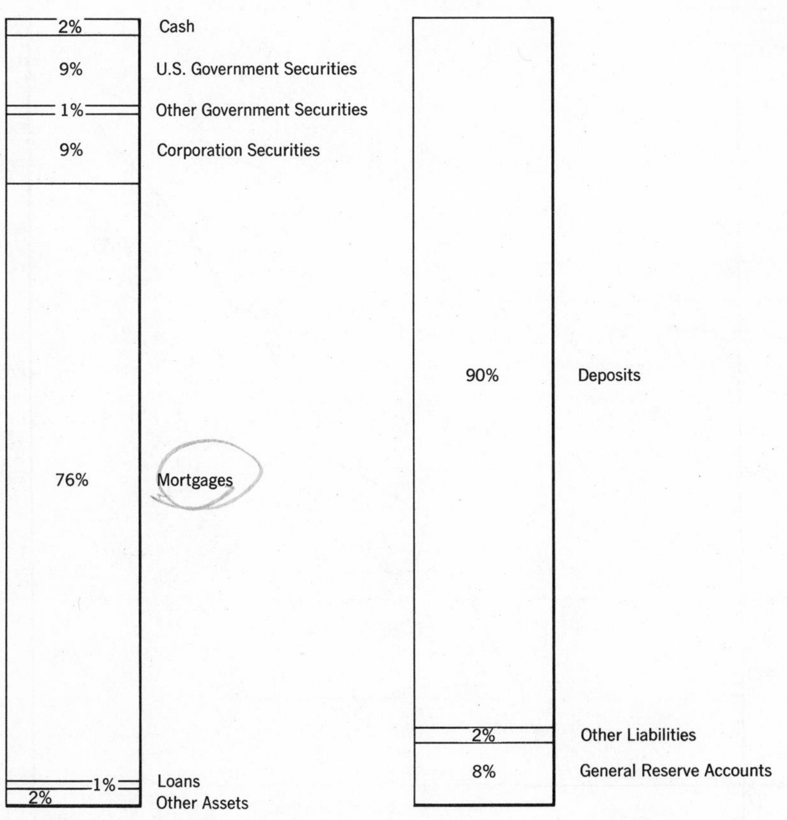

SOURCE: Board of Governors of the Federal Reserve System, *Federal Reserve Bulletin,* various issues, Washington, D. C.

Exhibit 8

PRIVATE PENSION FUNDS

Private pension funds are accumulated out of the contributions of employers and employees and are invested in securities to provide an income for employees upon retirement. Noninsured pension funds are typically individual financial entities with assets separate from those of the parent institution. They are administered by employers and employees. Pension funds are "funded" by setting contributions at levels estimated actuarially to be adequate when combined with expected income on such funds to provide stipulated benefits to participants. In addition to the private pension funds summarized in this exhibit, there are a number of pension funds that are administered by life insurance companies. The assets of these funds are included in Exhibit 4.

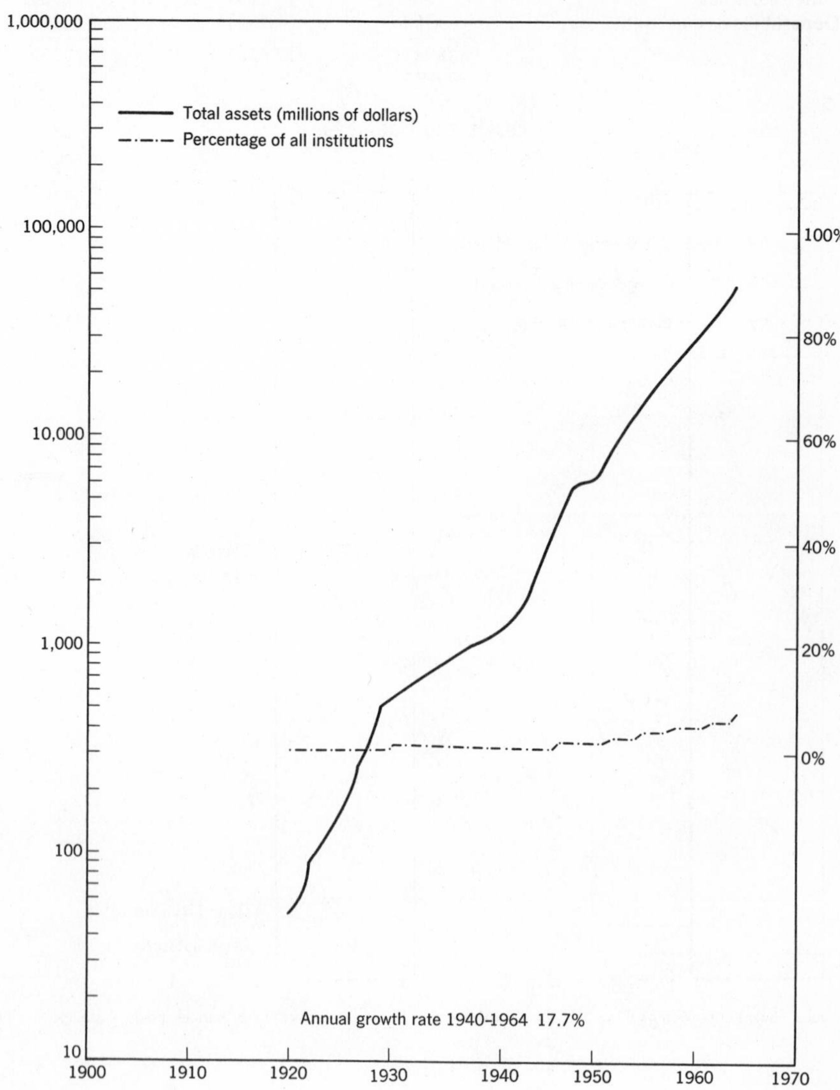

Exhibit 8 (Continued)

Funds Flow
(millions of dollars)

	1958	*1963*	*Difference*
Cash	$ 576	$ 792	$ 216
U.S. government securities	2205	3028	823
Mortgages	273	2238	1965
Corporate bonds	12960	19580	6620
Preferred stock	279	700	421
Common stock	7241	18120	10879
Other assets	266	2142	1876
	$23800	$46600	$22800
Deposits and reserves	$23800	$46600	$22800

Assets and Liabilities

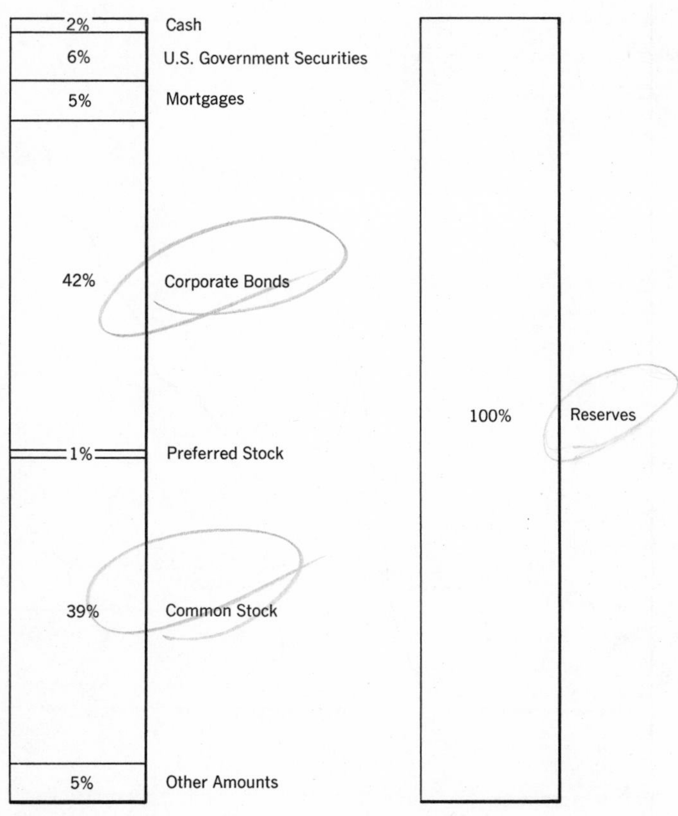

SOURCES: R. W. Goldsmith, *Financial Intermediaries in the American Economy Since 1900,* Princeton University Press, 1958.
Institute of Life Insurance, Life Insurance Fact Book, various issues, New York.
Board of Governors of the Federal Reserve System, *Federal Reserve Bulletin,* various issues, Washington, D. C.

Exhibit 9

INVESTMENT COMPANIES

Investment companies include open-end companies or "mutual funds," closed-end companies, and fixed and semifixed trusts. The largest proportion of the assets are held by open-end investment companies. Investment companies sell stock to individuals, and use the proceeds to purchase the securities of other corporations. Dividends are paid to shareholders out of income received from investments. The main features of investment companies are the professional management of the securities and the diversification afforded. The open-end investment company stands ready to issue and repurchase shares at a value representing the current market value of its security holdings (plus a selling or redemption fee). On the other hand, the shares of closed-end investment companies are traded in a manner similar to that for other stocks; their prices depend on the interaction of demand and supply for the shares.

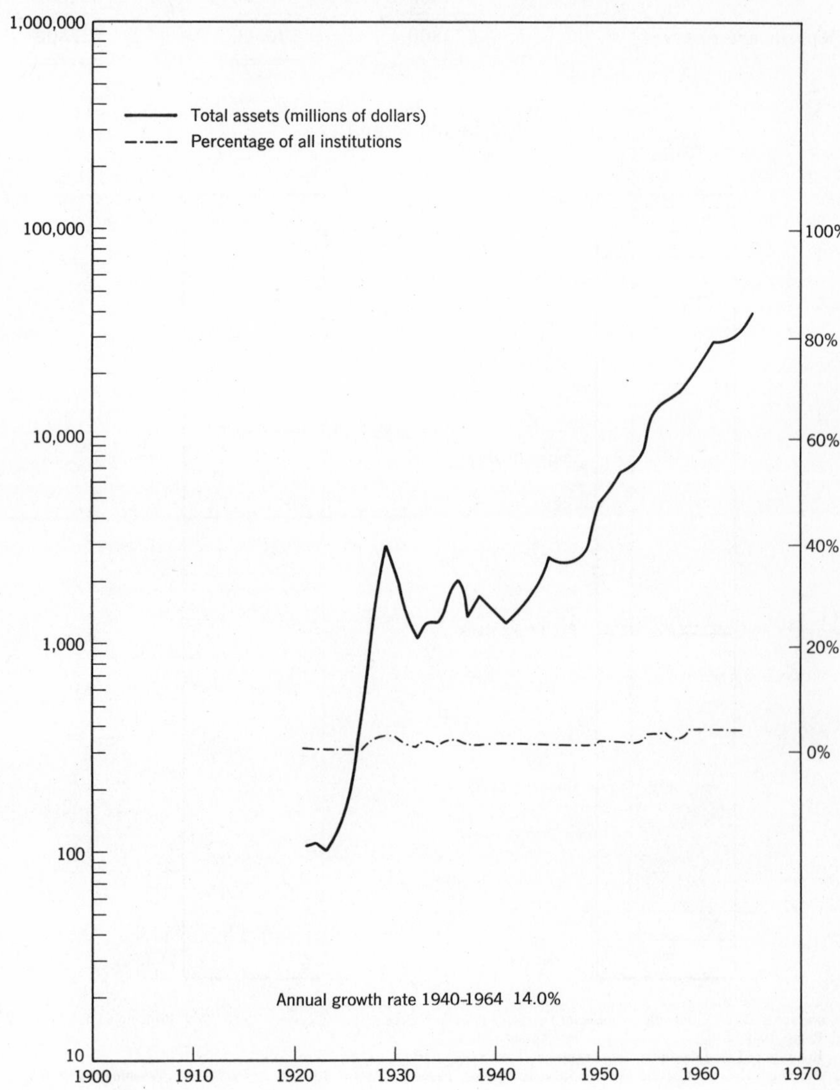

Exhibit 9 (Continued)

Funds Flow
(millions of dollars)

	1959	*1964*	*Difference*
Common stock	$15800	$27460	$11660
Bonds and preferred stock	3600	5560	1960
Other assets	600	1096	496
	$20000	$34116	$14116
Capital and surplus*	$20000	$34116	$14116

*Detail not available

Assets and Liabilities

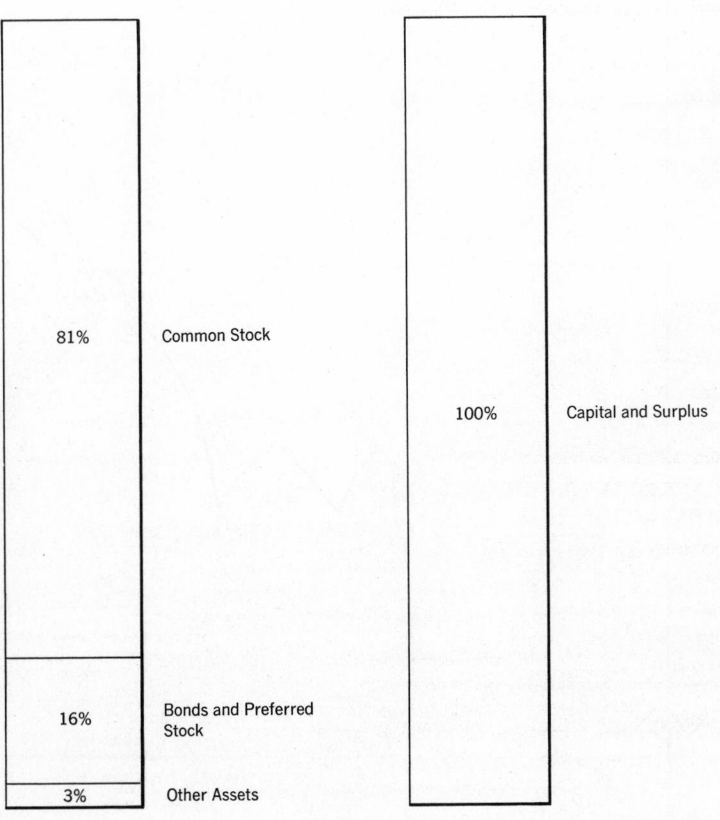

SOURCES: R. W. Goldsmith, *Financial Intermediaries in the American Economy Since 1900*, Princeton University Press, 1958.
Securities and Exchange Commission Estimates, 1950–1963.
Investment Company Institute plus Estimates of Closed-end Investment Companies and Investment Trusts, 1954.
Arthur Wiesenberger, *Investment Companies*, various issues. New York.

Exhibit 10

SALES FINANCE COMPANIES

Sales finance companies are principally engaged in financing the purchase of consumer durables such as automobiles, refrigerators, and television sets. Rather than lending directly to the consumer, these companies usually purchase installment paper from others. In addition, sales finance companies lend to business and agriculture to facilitate the purchase of inventory and equipment. At present, the sales finance company field consists of local companies, regional companies, and large national companies. Typically, sales finance companies have very close relationships with the firms that sell them retail paper. Some finance companies are "captive companies" controlled by a dealer or manufacturer from whom the dealer buys his merchandise. Sales finance companies obtain their funds by selling securities in the open market and by borrowing from commercial banks.

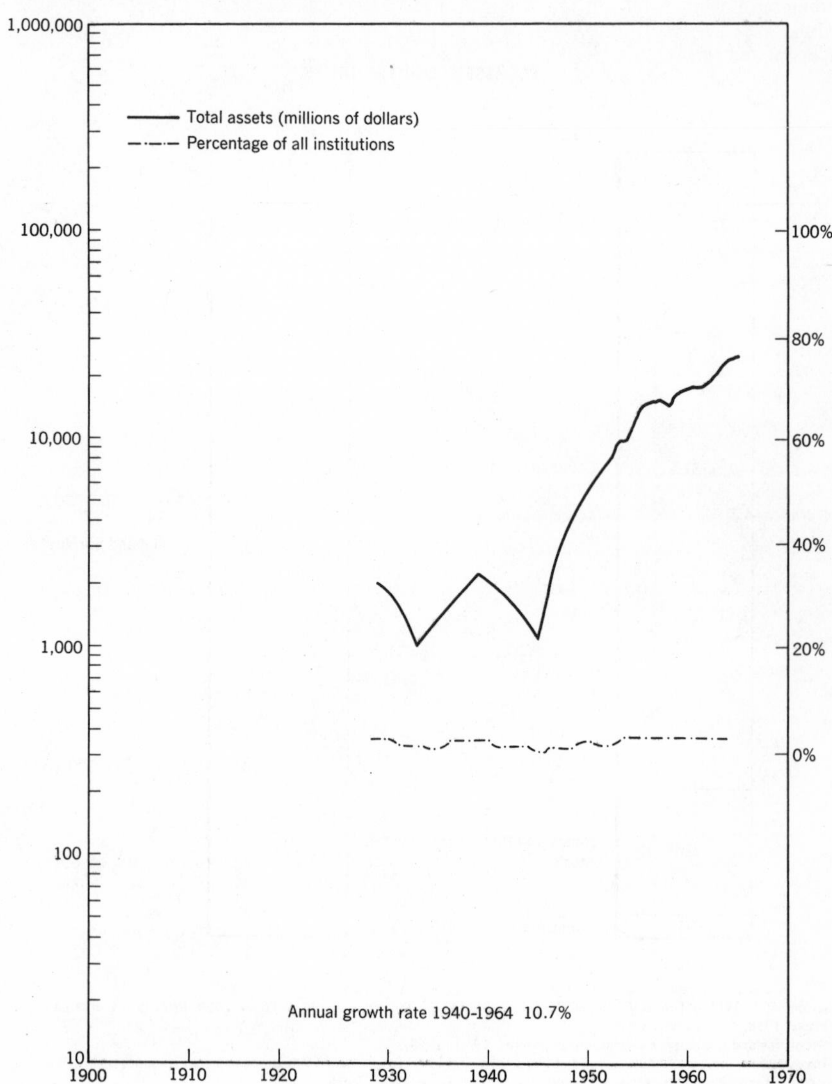

Exhibit 10 (Continued)

Funds Flow
(millions of dollars)

	1960	*1963*	*Difference*
Cash	$ 887	$ 1238	$ 351
Investments	532	859	327
Consumer goods paper	11472	13523	2051
Business credit	354	3166	2812
Other credit	2130	2194	64
	$17720	$20980	$3260
Commercial paper	$ 4340	$ 6080	$1740
Notes payable to banks	3725	3562	(163)
Long-term debt	637	7145	774
Other liabilities	674	1678	1004
Capital and surplus	2610	2515	(95)
	$17720	$20980	$3260

Assets and Liabilities

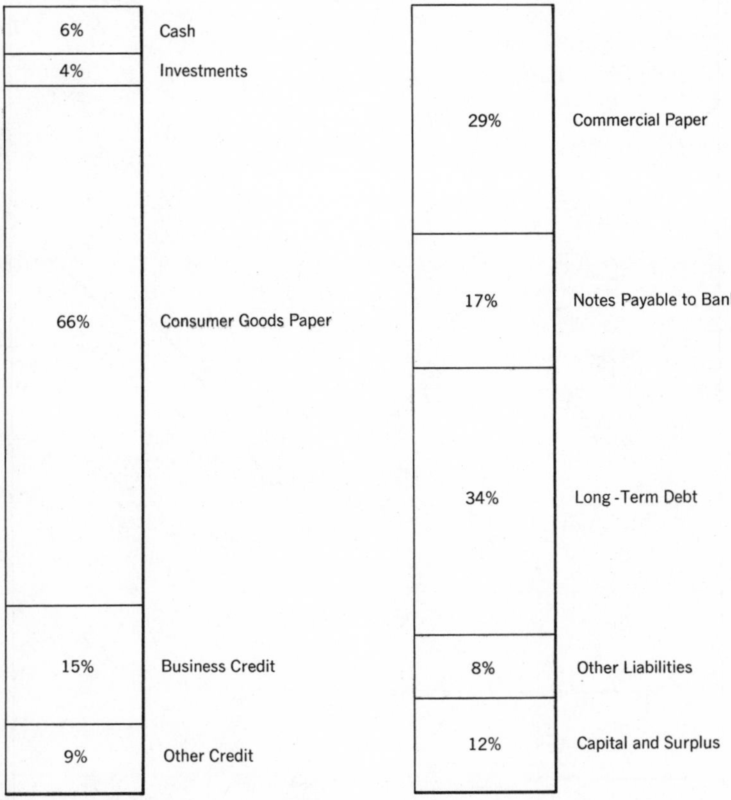

Assets	%	Liabilities	%
Cash	6%	Commercial Paper	29%
Investments	4%	Notes Payable to Banks	17%
Consumer Goods Paper	66%	Long-Term Debt	34%
Business Credit	15%	Other Liabilities	8%
Other Credit	9%	Capital and Surplus	12%

SOURCES: R. W. Goldsmith, *Financial Intermediaries in the American Economy Since 1900,* Princeton University Press, 1958.
Board of Governors of the Federal Reserve System, *Federal Reserve Bulletin,* various issues, Washington, D. C.
Finance Facts Yearbook, various issues.

Exhibit 11

CONSUMER FINANCE COMPANIES

Consumer finance companies, sometimes referred to as personal finance or small-loan companies, are one of the oldest of the group of financial institutions specializing in consumer installment credit. These companies specialize in small personal loans, often on an insecured or signature basis, to buy consumer durable and nondurable goods, to meet household expenses, to consolidate prior debts, and for other purposes. Consumer finance companies make most of their loans directly to consumers, but some companies are expanding into consumer-durables financing, commercial financing, and other types of lending. Consumer finance companies obtain their funds from the sale of securities and by borrowing from other financial institutions. Loan-size limitations and maximum interest rates are prescribed by state laws.

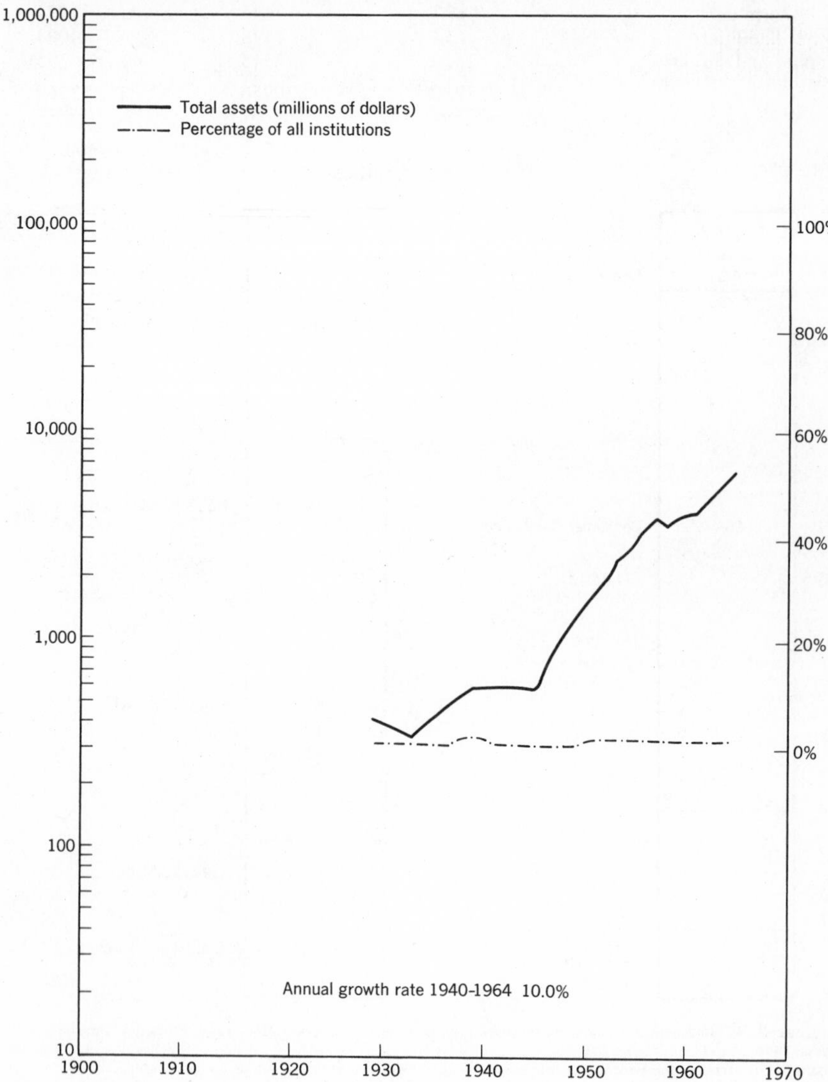

Exhibit 11 (Continued)

Funds Flow
(millions of dollars)

	1960	*1963*	*Difference*
Cash	$ 144	$ 214	$ 50
Securities	206	312	106
Personal loans	3206	4062	856
Consumer goods paper	411	528	117
Other assets	123	164	41
	$4110	$5280	$1170
Commercial paper	$ 219	$ 413	$ 194
Notes payable to banks	765	873	108
Long-term debt	1808	2447	639
Deposit liabilities	227	121	(106)
Other liabilities	182	244	
Capital and surplus	909	1182	273
	$4110	$5280	$1170

Assets and Liabilities

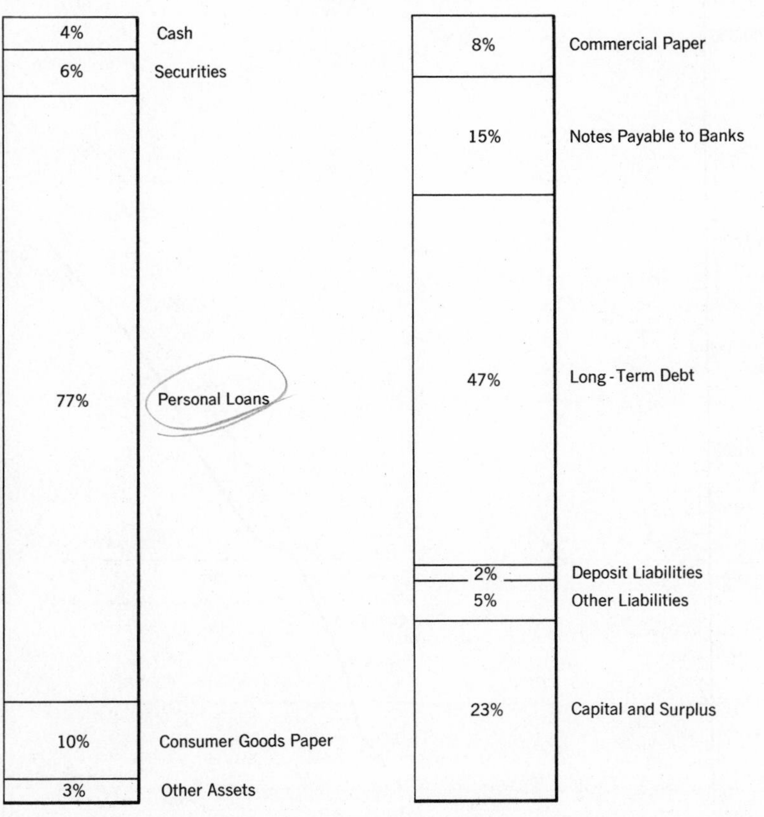

SOURCES: R. W. Goldsmith, *Financial Intermediaries in the American Economy Since 1900*, Princeton University Press, 1958. Board of Governors of the Federal Reserve System, *Federal Reserve Bulletin*, various issues, Washington, D. C. Finance Facts Yearbook, various issues.

Exhibit 12

CREDIT UNIONS

Credit unions are cooperative thrift and loan societies composed of individuals bound together by some tie such as a common employer, membership in a labor union, a church, or a fraternal order. Members purchase ownership shares resembling savings accounts, and each in turn may borrow from the association. Income from these loans and other investments provides funds from which members are paid dividends. They are often managed by members who serve, usually on a part-time basis, without compensation.

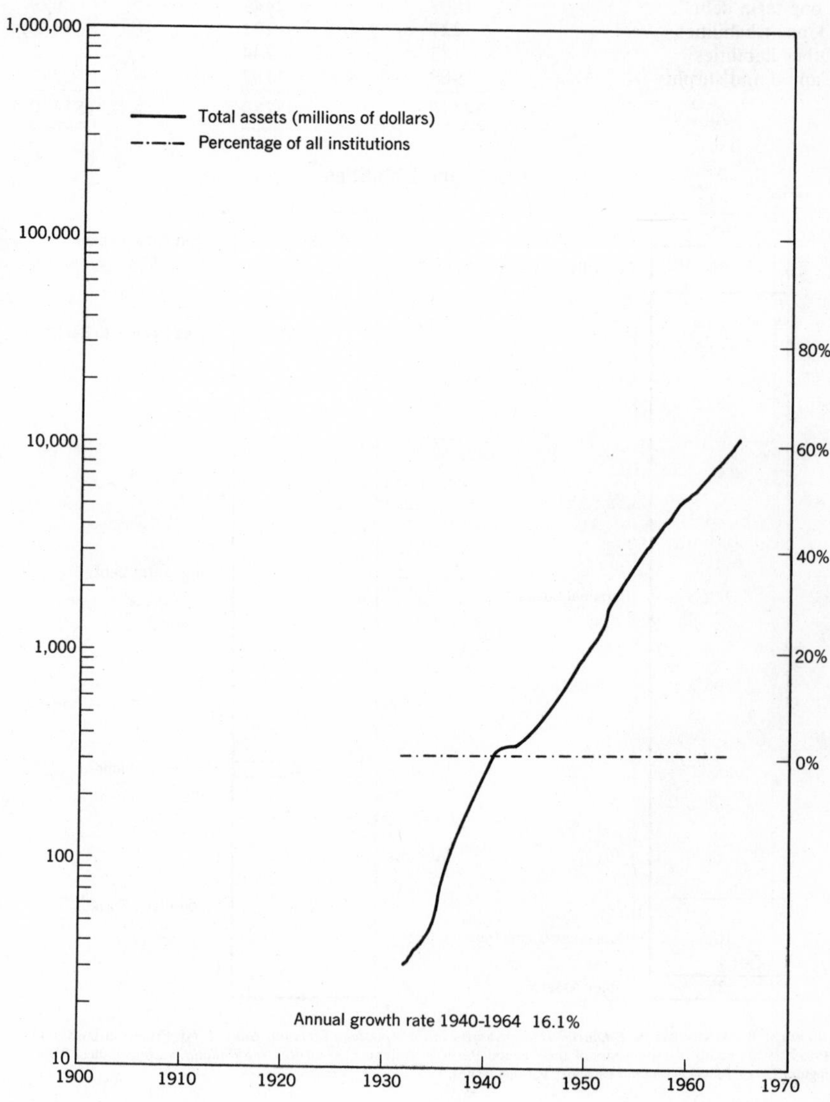

Exhibit 12 (Continued)

Funds Flow
(millions of dollars)

	1959	*1963*	*Difference*
Cash	$ 151	$ 247	$ 96
U.S. government securities	1593	2306	713
Loans outstanding	3280	5622	2342
	$5024	$8175	$3151
Savings deposits	$4410	$7194	$2784
Reserves	614	981	367
	$5024	$8175	$3151

Assets and Liabilities

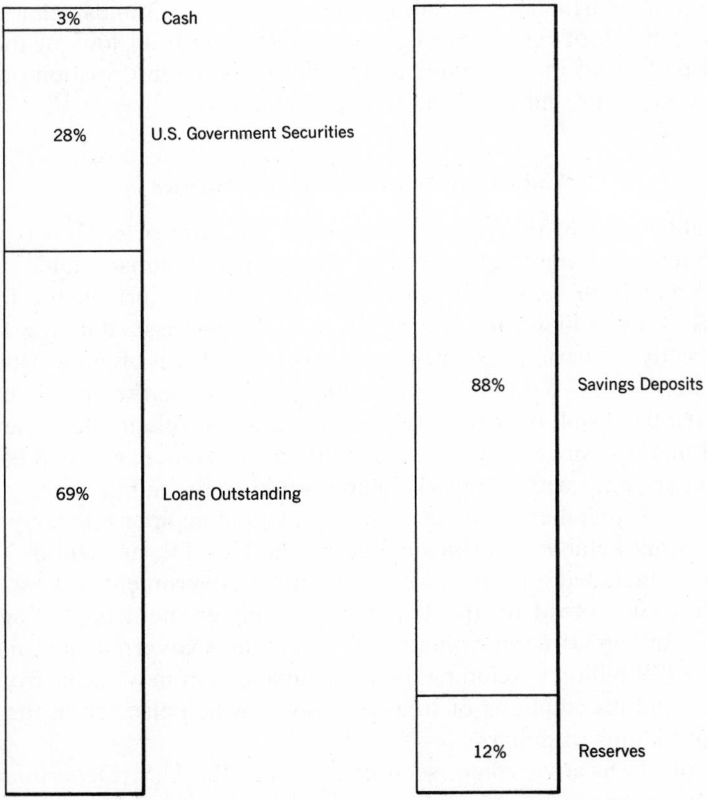

Assets		Liabilities	
3%	Cash	88%	Savings Deposits
28%	U.S. Government Securities	12%	Reserves
69%	Loans Outstanding		

SOURCES: Board of Governors of the Federal Reserve System, ***Federal Reserve Bulletin,*** various issues, Washington, D. C.
Credit Union National Association, ***Credit Union Yearbook,*** various issues, Madison, Wisconsin.

United States Government Securities, Interest Rates, and Monetary Policy 2

This note[1] on government securities has been prepared to provide background information for the study of several cases in this book. It begins with a brief discussion of the components of the United States public debt. The center of attention is focused on that portion of the public debt which is direct debt of the government, marketable and interest bearing. It is this portion that comprises the heart of money and capital markets in the United States. There is a discussion of the four instruments—bills, certificates of indebtedness, notes, and bonds—that make up this portion of the debt. This is followed by a brief look at the historical pattern of interest rates and finally by some information on economic conditions and trends as of September 1964.

United States Government Securities

The public debt of the United States is in the form of several types of marketable and nonmarketable securities. The nonmarketable issues consist mainly of savings bonds, which are designed principally for the savings of individuals, and special issues, which are issued by the Treasury directly to various government agencies and trust funds. Although there were about $100 billion outstanding in nonmarketable issues as of September 1964, they were relegated to a minor role in the money and capital markets since they were nonmarketable. Hence, we shall be concerned here only with the marketable portion of the public debt.

As of September 1964, there were outstanding approximately $208 billion in marketable securities issued by the U.S. Department of Treasury. (This included only the direct debt of the government and excluded securities guaranteed by the United States government or any agency thereof.) In 1963, trading volume in United States government securities totaled $429 billion (excluding direct acquisitions of new issues from the treasury and redemptions of treasury issues, which also ran in the hundreds of billions of dollars).

In the U.S. government securities market the U.S. Department of

[1]Compiled September 1964.

Treasury raises new money for government operations and refinances outstanding securities. The Federal Reserve uses the market for conducting open-market operations, one of the major instruments of monetary policy. The government securities market in the United States is recognized as the largest and perhaps the most important financial market.

Marketable issues consist of bills, certificates of indebtedness, notes, and bonds. They differ mainly in the length of the period to maturity at the time of issuance. Treasury bills are short-term securities with one year or less to maturity when issued. They are issued weekly and have thirteen weeks or twenty-six weeks to maturity. In addition, one-year bills have been issued quarterly since April 1959 and special bills have been issued at irregular intervals. Bills are issued on a discount basis (more on this later) and are usually offered by the auction method. Until 1961 the Federal Reserve System conducted its open-market operations exclusively in treasury bills. Although this policy was modified to "bills preferably" beginning in February 1961, open-market operations still take place in bills more frequently than in any of the other marketable issues.

Certificates—or certificates of indebtedness—are short-term securities with one year or less to maturity when issued. They are usually coupon securities issued at par. A special kind of certificate known as the tax anticipation certificate has been issued at various times since 1953. As of September 1964, there were no certificates of any kind outstanding.

Notes are issued with original maturity of one to five years. Bonds may be issued in any maturity but usually are issued with five or more years to maturity. Both notes and bonds are usually coupon securities issued at par value. Some bonds have an optional call feature that allows the treasury to retire or refund them prior to their final maturity.

Exhibit 1 gives a breakdown of marketable securities by the type of issue. Since the type of issue is largely a function of the length of the period to maturity at the time of issuance, it is not necessarily indicative of the maturity structure of outstanding debt.

A second method of classifying marketable government securities (Exhibit 2) is by maturity date. The short average maturity date of outstanding debt has been of concern to the treasury in the postwar period. Through advance refundings which began in 1960 the treasury has extended a considerable amount of debt into long-term issues. (A computation by the First Boston Corporation shows that the average maturity date in January 1964 was five years one month, whereas it would have been three years two months if there had been no advance refunding.)

Exhibit 3 gives a breakdown for securities outstanding according to ownership.

Exhibit 1

MARKETABLE U.S. GOVERNMENT SECURITIES, BY TYPE (1960–1964)

(dollar figures in billions)

	Bills	*Certificates*	*Notes*	*Bonds*	*Total*
As of:					
June 30, 1964	50.7	–	67.3	88.4	206.5
Percent of total	24.6		32.6	42.8	100.0
Dec. 31, 1963	51.5	10.9	58.7	86.4	207.6
Percent of total	24.8	5.3	28.3	41.6	100.0
Dec. 31, 1962	48.3	22.7	53.7	78.4	203.0
Percent of total	23.8	11.2	26.5	38.6	100.0
Dec. 31, 1961	43.4	5.5	71.5	75.5	196.0
Percent of total	22.1	2.8	36.5	38.5	100.0
Dec. 31, 1960	39.4	18.4	51.3	79.8	189.0
Percent of total	20.8	9.7	27.1	42.2	100.0

SOURCE: *Treasury Bulletin.*

Exhibit 2

MARKETABLE U.S. GOVERNMENT SECURITIES, BY MATURITY (1959–1964)

(dollar figures in billions)

	June 1964	*Dec. 31 1963*	*Dec. 31 1962*	*Dec. 31 1961*	*Dec. 31 1960*
BY MATURITY					
Less than 1 year					
Amount outstanding	81.4	89.4	87.3	85.9	75.3
Percent of total debt	39.4	43.1	43.0	43.8	39.8
1–5 years					
Amount outstanding	65.5	58.5	61.6	64.9	70.8
Percent of total debt	31.7	28.2	30.3	33.1	37.5
5–10 years					
Amount outstanding	34.9	35.7	34.0	19.8	18.7
Percent of total debt	16.9	17.2	16.7	10.1	9.9
Over 10 years					
Amount outstanding	24.7	24.0	20.1	25.4	24.2
Percent of total debt	12.0	11.6	9.9	13.0	12.8
Total debt					
Amount outstanding	206.5	207.6	203.0	196.0	189.0
Percent of total debt	100.0	100.0	100.0	100.0	100.0

Exhibit 2 (Continued)

	June 1964	Dec. 31 1963	Dec. 31 1962	Dec. 31 1961	Dec. 31 1960
BY MATURITY OR EARLIEST CALL DATE					
Less than 1 year					
Amount outstanding	92.3	97.8	90.6	87.4	84.0
Percent of total debt	44.7	47.1	44.6	44.6	44.4
1–5 years					
Amount outstanding	67.0	65.0	75.3	75.7	75.2
Percent of total debt	32.4	31.3	37.1	38.6	39.8
5–10 years					
Amount outstanding	22.6	20.7	17.0	15.5	16.5
Percent of total debt	10.9	10.0	8.4	7.9	8.7
Over 10 years					
Amount outstanding	24.6	24.1	20.1	17.4	13.2
Percent of total debt	11.9	11.6	9.9	8.9	7.0
Total debt					
Amount outstanding	206.5	207.6	203.0	196.0	189.0
Percent of total debt	100.0	100.0	100.0	100.0	100.0

SOURCE: *Treasury Bulletin,* various issues.

Exhibit 3

OWNERSHIP OF MARKETABLE U.S. GOVERNMENT SECURITIES June 30, 1964

(dollar figures in billions)

Maturity Date:	*Within 1 Year*	*1–5 Years*	*5–10 Years*	*Over 10 Years*	*Total*
HELD BY INVESTORS					
Covered in treasury survey					
6039 commercial banks	17.9	24.8	7.4	1.0	51.1
502 mutual savings banks	1.5	1.3	1.3	1.5	5.6
297 life insurance companies	0.5	0.5	0.3	3.3	4.6
488 other insurance companies	1.4	1.6	0.8	0.4	4.2
488 savings and loan associations	0.7	1.1	0.9	0.5	3.2
469 corporations	8.0	2.0	0.1	0.1	10.2
315 state and local government general funds	5.8	2.1	0.6	1.7	10.2
191 state and local government pension and retirement funds	0.7	0.3	0.5	4.3	5.8
U.S. government accounts and Federal Reserve Banks	22.2	16.5	2.7	5.6	46.9
All others	33.6	16.8	8.0	5.9	64.3
TOTAL	92.3	67.0	22.6	24.6	206.5

SOURCE: *Treasury Bulletin,* various issues.

Each treasury certificate of indebtedness, note, and bond bears a specified rate of interest. (Treasury bills do not bear any interest.) This rate is typically stated on interest coupons attached to the security and hence is known as the coupon rate. The coupon rate is to be distinguished, however, from the market rate of interest or yield to maturity. (See Appendix A for a discussion of yield to maturity.)[2]

Market prices of the coupon securities normally are quoted in terms of 32nds. Thus, a price quotation of 100–16 or 100.16 means 100 16/32. Securities are normally bought and sold on full lots. A quotation, such as 100–16 bid to 100–18 asked, usually indicates that on full lots the dealer would pay the bid price and would sell at the asked price.[3] Under normal circumstances price adjustments are made on relatively small transactions. The published yields which appear in various sources including *The Wall Street Journal* are generally computed on the asked side of the market. In case of issues having optional maturity dates, the yield is figured to the optional date when the price is at a premium over par and to the maturity date when the price is at a discount.

Treasury bills do not have a contractual rate of interest specified for the investor. The yield is determined entirely by the discount from par at which the obligation sells. Although treasury bills are widely quoted and traded on a rate basis called "yield," they are actually quoted and figured on a bank discount basis. There are three basic differences between the yield computed with the bank discount method and effective yield:

1. When yield is figured on a bank discount basis, the discount is divided by the par value. When yield is figured on the effective yield method, the discount is divided by price.

2. The bank discount method utilizes a 360-day year. The effective yield method utilizes a 365-day year.

3. The bank discount method ignores compounding effects. The effective yield method takes compounding into account.

See Appendix B for a further discussion of the differences in the two methods of computing yield.

---

[2]It should be noted that yield to maturity is usually given on a before tax basis. It is possible for two securities to have the same before tax yield and yet have different after tax yield. This phenomenon results because ordinary income and capital gains are taxes at different rates. For example, if all the yield from one security were taxable as ordinary income, and some of the yield from the other were taxable as capital gain, the after tax yields would differ. More detailed descriptions of federal taxation of income from government securities will not be included here. Interested readers may see *Securities of the United States Government,* 21th edition, 1964, published by the First Boston Corporation, pp. 144–151.

[3]Accrued interest to the delivery date is added to the price of coupon obligations.

Interest Rates and Monetary Policy

The purpose of this section of the note is to suggest the intricacies of monetary policy, the interpretation of monetary developments, and the impact these policies may have on interest rates. The note reflects conditions as of September 1964 and is not intended to depict monetary conditions as they may exist at the time the reader reads this note.

Historically, market yields on long-term government securities have fluctuated within a much narrower range than those on short-term issues. Nevertheless, the long maturities have fluctuated much more in terms of price. Exhibit 4 provides a graphical picture and Appendix C contains a discussion of this phenomenon.

Exhibit 4

PRICE AND YIELD FLUCTUATIONS ON U.S. GOVERNMENT SECURITIES

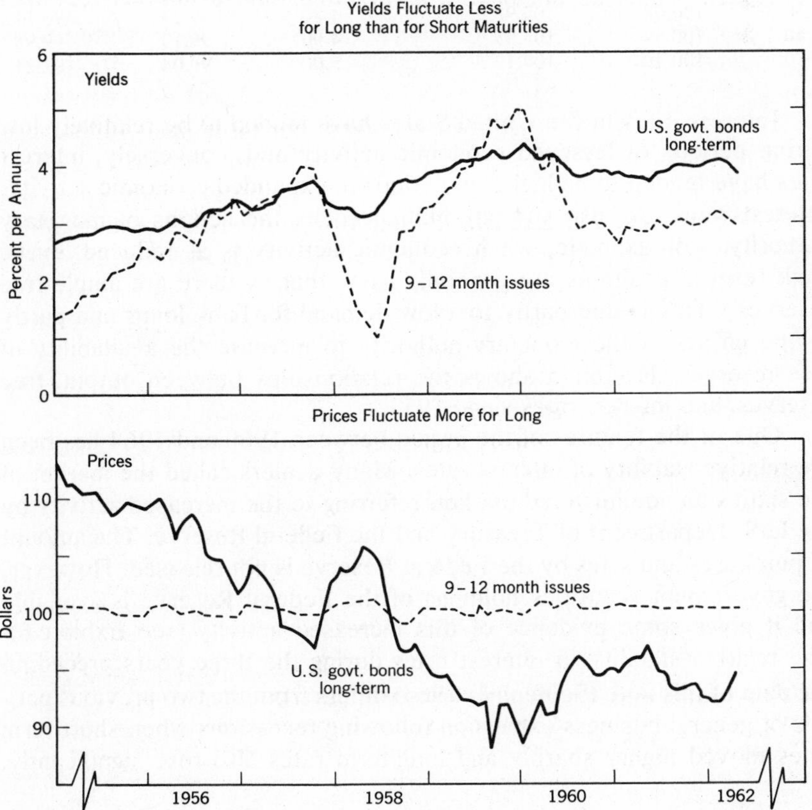

Exhibit 4 (Continued)

PRICES AT VARIOUS YIELDS FOR TWO 4-PERCENT COUPON BONDS

(one matures in 1 year; one matures in 10 years)

Yield	*1 Year*	*10 Years*	*Yield*	*1 Year*	*10 Years*
2.10	101.87	117.06	3.60	100.39	103.33
2.20	101.77	116.08	3.70	100.29	102.49
2.30	101.67	115.11	3.80	100.19	101.65
2.40	101.57	114.15	3.90	100.10	100.82
2.50	101.47	113.20	4.00	100.00	100.00
2.60	101.37	112.26	4.10	99.90	99.19
2.70	101.27	111.33	4.20	99.81	98.38
2.80	101.18	110.40	4.30	99.71	97.58
2.90	101.08	109.49	4.40	99.61	96.79
3.00	100.98	108.58	4.50	99.52	96.01
3.10	100.88	107.69	4.60	99.42	95.23
3.20	100.78	106.80	4.70	99.32	94.47
3.30	100.68	105.92	4.80	99.23	93.71
3.40	100.59	105.05	4.90	99.13	92.95
3.50	100.49	104.19	5.00	99.04	92.21

Interest rates in the United States have tended to be relatively low during periods of lessened economic activity and, conversely, interest rates have tended to be higher in periods of expanded economic activity. Interest rates are also strongly influenced by the actions of monetary authority. For example, when economic activity is at reduced levels, bank reserve positions are generally easy, that is, there are ample free reserves.[4] This is due partly to a low demand for bank loans and partly to the efforts of the monetary authority to increase the availability of free reserves. Exhibit 5 shows the relationships between output, free reserves, and interest rates since 1953.

One of the features of the period between 1960 and 1964 has been the relative stability of interest rates. Many dealers called the market of the sixties an administered market, referring to the increased activity by the U.S. Department of Treasury and the Federal Reserve. The amount of purchases and sales by the Federal Reserve is not released. However, the government securities holdings of the Federal Reserve is available and it gives some evidence of this increased activity (see Exhibit 6). The relative stability in interest rates during the three years preceding the date of this note (September 1964) differs from the two previous periods of general business expansion following recessions when short-term rates moved higher sharply and long-term rates also rose significantly.

[4]Free reserves are equal to the reserves in excess of requirements of member banks less their borrowings from district Federal Reserve Banks.

Exhibit 5

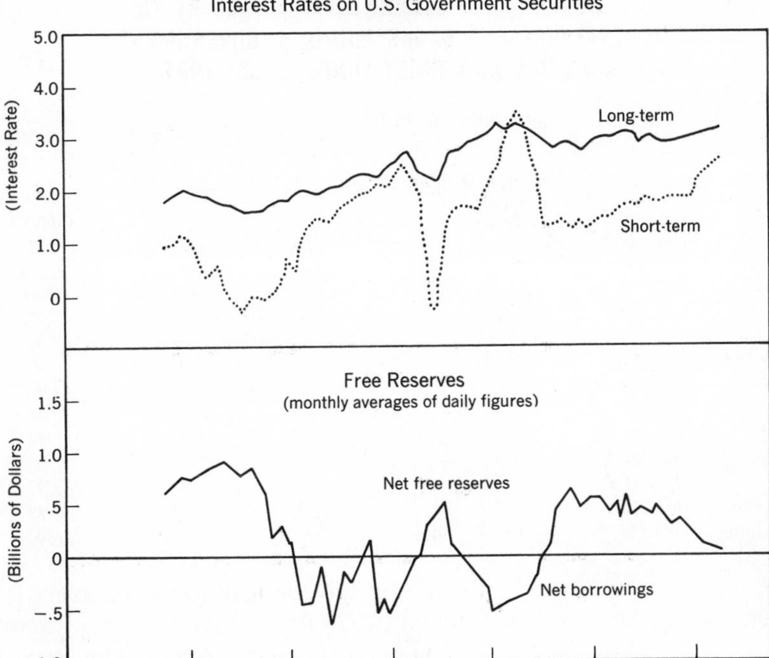

SOURCE: *Federal Reserve Bulletin,* various issues.

Since early 1961, monetary authorities have been pursuing the twin objectives of supporting the recovery while trying to minimize pressures on the balance of payments. These considerations have given rise to what has been termed "Operation Twist" or "Operation Nudge." The objective has been to hold up short-term rates in order to reduce the outflow of short-term capital to other nations, while holding down long-term rates to encourage domestic investment. Continuing unemployment and unused capacity have led the monetary authorities to follow a less restrictive policy since 1961 than would have been the case otherwise. Free reserves in the banking system, for example, have remained at a much higher level for a longer time period than in previous recoveries. On the other hand, balance of payments considerations have influenced monetary policy so that it has not been as easy as purely domestic objectives might have dictated.

Since the enactment of Operation Twist, long-term rates have been relatively stable. The monthly average rates during the four years from mid-1960 to mid-1964 fluctuated between 3.8 percent and 4.2 percent. As of September 1964, yields on long-term government bonds were

Exhibit 6

U.S. GOVERNMENT SECURITIES HOLDINGS BY THE FEDERAL RESERVE BANKS AND U. S. GOVERNMENT AGENCIES AND TRUST FUNDS, 1960–1964

(par value in billions of dollars)

End of Month	Government Agencies and Trust Funds*			
	Special Issues		*Public Issues*	*Federal Reserve Banks*
1960				
March	43.3		10.4	25.3
June	44.9		10.4	26.5
September	45.0		10.6	27.0
December	44.3		10.7	27.4
1961				
March	44.0		10.9	26.7
June	45.0		11.0	27.3
September	45.0		10.9	27.8
December		54.5		28.9
1962				
March		54.5		29.1
June		56.5		29.7
September		56.4		29.8
December		55.6		30.8
1963				
March		55.1		31.0
June		58.4		32.0
September		58.3		32.6
December		58.0		33.6
1964				
March		57.6		33.8
June		61.1		34.8

* Before December 1961 the issues are shown separately under "Special Issues" and "Public Issues"; both of these are under the major heading of "Government Agencies and Trust Funds." After 1961 only one heading is needed.
SOURCE: *Federal Reserve Bulletin.*

averaging close to 4.2 percent. In addition, the economic recovery which had begun in early 1961 continued.

The international phase of Operation Twist was less successful. Although treasury-bill rates which were around 2.4 percent from mid-1960 to mid-1961 moved up by stages to 2.9 percent by late 1962, the international payments deficit continued. To reduce the outflow of both short-term and long-term capital, the government announced two new measures in mid-1963: (1) The Federal Reserve rediscount rate was

Exhibit 7

U.S. BALANCE OF PAYMENTS 1956–1964

(millions of dollars)

Year	*Exports*	*Imports*	*Balance on Goods and Services*	*U.S. Govt. Grants and Capital*	*Private Capital Net*	*Foreign Capital Net*	*Errors and Unrecorded Transactions and Other Items*	*Balance on Regular Transactions*
1956	23,595	19,628	3,967	−2,362	−3,071	653	− 122	− 935
1957	26,481	20,752	5,729	−2,574	−3,577	487	455	520
1958	23,067	20,861	2,206	−2,587	−2,936	22	− 234	−3,529
1959	23,476	23,342	134	−2,421	−2,375	863	− 379	−4,178
1960	27,044	23,193	3,851	−2,781	−3,885	341	−1,444	−3,918
1961	28,438	22,852	5,586	−3,396	−4,180	622	−1,703	−3,071
1962	30,084	25,021	5,063	−3,547	−3,434	162	−1,849	−3,605
1963	32,020	26,335	5,685	−3,785	−4,307	311	−1,165	−3,261
1964*	36,004	27,943	8,061	−3,469	−5,652	420	−1,358	−1,998

*Average of the first three quarters based on seasonally adjusted data.

BALANCE ON REGULAR TRANSACTIONS, BY QUARTERS

(seasonally adjusted annual rates)

	1962	*1963*	*1964*
I	−3,568	−4,680	− 968
II	−1,984	−5,256	−2,764
III	−3,672	−1,516	
IV	−5,196	−1,592	

SOURCE: *Economic Report of the President.*

increased from 3 percent to 3½ percent; (2) A new "interest equalization tax" was proposed to reduce the purchase of foreign securities, new or outstanding, by United States residents from foreigners. In the process treasury-bill rates moved up from 2.9 percent during the first five months to 3.4 percent by the end of 1963. As of September 1964, bill rates had crept up above 3.5 percent, but the balance of payments problem persisted. (Exhibit 7 gives recent balance of payment figures.)

Exhibit 8

FEDERAL RESERVE REPORT

Assets and Liabilities of 11 Weekly
Reporting Member Banks in New York City
(millions of dollars)

ASSETS:	*Sept. 16 1964*	*Sept. 9 1964*	*Sept. 18 1963*
Total loans and investments	35,706	34,714	32,956
Loans and investments adjust. (r)	35,144	33,664	32,382
Loans adjusted (r)	24,224	22,981	21,597
Commercial and industrial loans	12,775	14,426	11,491
Agricultural loans	17	17	14
Loans to brokers and dealers for:			
U.S. gov't. obligations	785	350	661
Other securities	1,938	1,764	1,882
Other loans for purch. or carry:			
U.S. gov't. obligations	8	8	10
Other securities	601	594	540
Loans to nonbank fin. inst.:			
Sales, personal finance, etc.	1,572	1,303	1,636
Other	812	830	609
Loans to foreign banks	657	654	374
Real estate loans	2,124	2,100	1,766
Other loans	3,528	3,509	3,185
Loans to domestic com'l banks	562	1,050	574
U.S. gov't. securities—total	5,461	5,325	5,509
Treasury bills	1,591	1,398	1,160
Treasury certifs. of indebtedness	0	0	157
Treasury notes & bonds maturing:			
Within 1 year	717	746	526
1 to 5 years	1,867	1,860	2,192
After 5 years	1,286	1,321	1,474
Other securities	5,459	5,358	5,276
Reserve with Fed. Res. Bank	3,598	3,152	3,649
Currency and coin	260	275	234
Balances with domestic banks	97	88	86
Other assets—net	2,479	2,520	2,278
Total assets—liabilities	47,898	45,156	44,324

Exhibit 8 (Continued)

LIABILITIES:	*Sept. 16 1964*	*Sept. 9 1964*	*Sept. 18 1963*
Demand deposits – adjusted	16,594	15,507	16,502
Demand deposits – total (e)	26,483	23,893	25,595
Individ., partnerships and crps.	18,192	16,165	17,740
States and political subdivisions	311	296	315
U.S. government	870	725	902
Domestic interbank:			
Commercial	3,261	3,259	3,070
Mutual savings	311	307	310
Foreign:			
Official institutions	554	620	410
Commercial banks	844	844	794
Time and savings deps. – total (v)	12,668	12,916	10,582
Individ., partnerships, and corps.:			
Savings deposits	4,525	4,519	4,360
Other time deposits (z)	4,697	4,939	3,501
State and political subdivisions	418	425	373
Domestic interbank	256	257	119
Foreign:			
Official institutions	2,626	2,632	2,089
Commercial banks	80	78	80
Borrowings:			
From Fed. Res. Banks	0	10	115
From others	1,689	1,228	1,330
Other liabilities	2,825	2,863	2,792
CAPITAL ACCOUNTS	4,233	4,241	3,910

r-Exclusive of loans to domestic commercial banks and after deduction of valuation reserves: individual loan items are shown gross.
e-Includes certified and officers checks not shown separately.
v-Includes time deposits of U.S. government and postal savings not shown separately.
z-Includes Christmas savings and similar accounts which amounted to $72 million for the current week.

Member Bank Reserves and Borrowings of Central Reserve New York City Banks
(millions of dollars)

		Change Since
	Sept. 16 1964	*Sept. 9 1964*
Reserves with Fed. Res. Bank	3,989	+ 441
Required reserves (partly estim.)	4,069	+ 244
Excess reserves	80	+ 197
Daily averages for week:		
Estimated excess reserves	30	+ 23
Borrowings at Fed. Res. Bank	21	− 9
Free reserves	9	+ 32

An analysis of the weekly Federal Reserve Report often yields useful information about current trends in monetary policy. The report for the week ending September 16, 1964 is reproduced in Exhibit 8.

Exhibit 8 (Continued)

Member Bank Reserve Changes

Changes in weekly averages of member bank reserves and related items during the week and the year ended September 16, 1964, were as follows (in millions of dollars):

		Change from week ending	
	Sept. 16 1964	*Sept. 9 1964*	*Sept. 18 1963*
Reserve bank credit			
U.S. Gov't. securities:			
Bought outright—system acc't.	35,262	+ 28	+3,053
Held under repurch. agreemt.	135	− 242	+ 135
Acceptances—bought outright	38	− 1	+ 2
Held under repurch. agreemt.	18	− 8	+ 18
Loans, discounts and advances:			
Member bank borrowings	225	− 253	+ 32
Other			− 32
Float	1,846	+ 283	− 149
Total Reserve Bank credit	37,524	− 192	+3,059
Gold stock	15,462	....	− 120
Treasury currency outstanding	5,564	− 2	− 26
Total	58,550	− 195	+2,914
Money in circulation	38,425	+ 182	+2,409
Treasury cash holdings	435	+ 9	+ 18
Treasury deposits with F.R. Banks	906	+ 49	− 36
Foreign deposits with F.R. Banks	142	+ 11	....
Other deposits with F.R. Banks	194	+ 6	− 15
Other F.R. accounts (net)	1,163	− 57	+ 24
Total	41,265	+ 200	+ 239
Member bank reserves			
With F.R. Banks	17,285	− 394	+ 51
Cash allowed as res. (est.)	3,321	+ 313	+ 191
Total reserves held (est.)	20,606	− 81	+ 706
Required reserves (est.)	20,303	+ 122	+ 751
Excess reserves (est.)	303	− 203	− 45
Member bank reserves Wednesday to Wednesday			
With F.R. Banks	17,013	− 130	....
Currency and coin (est.)	3,632	+ 223	....
Total reserves held (est.)	20,645	+ 93	....
Required reserves	20,664	+ 450	....
Excess reserves	−19	− 357	....
Borrowings at F.R. banks	74	− 68	....

Exhibit 8 (Continued)

Twelve Federal Reserve Banks' Position
(millions of dollars)

	Sept. 16 1964	*Sept. 9 1964*	*Sept. 18 1963*
ASSETS			
Total gold certificate reserves	15,181	15,183	15,283
U.S. Gov't. securities:			
Bought outright:			
Bills	4,910	5,112	2,834
Certificates			10,712
Notes	25,077	25,064	13,990
Bonds	5,126	5,097	4,438
Total bought outright	35,113	35,273	31,974
Held under repurch. agreemt.			
Total U.S. Gov't. securities	35,113	35,633	31,974
Total assets	59,154	56,987	55,861
LIABILITIES			
Federal Reserve Notes	33,128	33,217	30,847
Total deposits	18,429	18,309	18,252
Ratio of gold certificate reserves to deposits and F.R. notes	29.1%	29.2%	30.8%
GOLD RESERVES	15,463	15,463	15,583

On Wednesday, September 16, 1964, the following article appeared in the *Wall Street Journal:*

Despite a recent slight tightening of bank credit supplies, the Federal Reserve Board hasn't altered its views that its policy of monetary "ease" can continue without posing inflationary dangers.

This is the view being expressed privately by Government financial officials, who contend that the much-discussed reduction of bank reserves in the last few weeks is motivated only by temporary balance-of-payment considerations.

This reasoning was buttressed publicly in a speech yesterday by C. Canby Balderston, board vice chairman, who spoke of a "continued absence of general inflationary pressures" on the domestic scene. His speech on credit policy didn't touch on the bank reserves trend or on the Chrysler Corp. labor contract, which has prompted fears among businessmen about a possible inflationary surge.

Analysts interpreted the omissions as indicating the board remains in agreement with key Administration economists that further "orderly" business growth is in prospect and that it will be some months before any solid evidence emerges on whether the auto contract will set off pay hikes in other industries that can't afford them without raising their prices.

Since Board Chairman William McChesney Martin said earlier this year he doesn't think the board should "lead the way" to higher interest rates, the speech strengthened the attitude among other Government men that the slight reduction in reserves isn't an anti-inflationary measure and that the board isn't contemplating measures of that sort soon.

Addressing the Cleveland chapter of the American Marketing Association, Mr. Balderston said "The Federal Reserve has been able to contribute to the ready availability of credit in view of the continued existence of unused resources – manpower and production capacity – and the continued absence of general inflationary pressures."

Following usual board custom, he didn't specifically say whether he thought this condition would continue or, if it did, for how long. Significantly, though, the tone suggested that this favorable condition is still believed to be the dominant one, and he didn't give any hints it may be waning.

In past business expansions, Mr. Balderston said, "credit generally has come to be in short supply and its cost has mounted. But in the current expansion, which has been under way for more than three years, credit has continued to be readily available and its cost has risen very little from the recession lows." This, he said, is because savings have continued "unusually large" and because demand for borrowed funds has "not pressed strongly against the enlarged supplies available."

The nation's central bank, he said, has "accommodated the growth of credit on liberal terms." Unless the system had provided reserves in the quantity that it did "there could not have been so much of an expansion of bank deposits or so full an accommodation of bank credit demands" as in the last few years. Thus, he observed, "monetary policy can be said to have remained 'easy' in furtherance of the national objectives of maximum growth in employment and in the economy, at relatively stable prices."

The continuing large balance-of-payments deficit has prevented any move toward even greater ease, he said, adding that short-term interest rates have been permitted to work upward in order to maintain a reasonable parity with money rates available on short-term investments abroad.

The reduction of cash available for ready lending by banks has been a deliberate policy of the board in the last four to six weeks, it is understood, but money men emphasize that the timing and the smallness of the cut suggest its relation only to a "narrow" money market objective rather than to "broad" economic considerations. For about a year the board has kept the average "free reserves" of banks at around $100 million. More recently, they've averaged under $100 million and for the week ended last Wednesday were estimated at $58 million.

The free reserves figure measures the amount of funds banks have immediately available for lending after setting aside required percentages of the deposits they hold. The Federal Reserve commonly influences their level by its dealings in Government securities, as its net purchases pump newly created money into banks and its net sales drain funds from the commercial banking system.

"Whatever change there has been appears related to short-term interest rates," one Washington economist commented, noting it is short-term rates that the Treasury has been meaning to bolster lately through expanded weekly sales of 13- and 26-week bills. The motive has been to make short-term rates in the U.S. high enough so that private American funds aren't lured abroad by higher rates. The Federal Reserve has reported it was active in late July in foreign currency transactions aimed at this end, and some officials believe the reserve tightening since is an "exploratory" move to see if such outflows can also be curbed that way.

Without such maneuvering by the Treasury and Federal Reserve, officials fear there could be a considerable surge of U.S. funds abroad, deepening the U.S. balance-of-payments deficit. This deficit occurs as dollars leaving the country exceed those returning from all foreign sources. The surplus dollars that pile up in foreign central banks can be used to purchase U.S. gold. If the board intended to curb credit to domestic borrowers generally, it would make a much more marked change in available reserves, some analysts add. And financial men say the decision to start reducing reserves was made well before terms of the Chrysler settlement became known last week. Aside from the possibility that this settlement could cause an inflationary development some time in the future, Administration men say they don't see any inflationary "straws in the wind" at this time.

The September 17, 1964 issue of *The Commercial and Financial Chronicle* contained the following observations:

The picture as to whether the Federal Reserve switched gears to a tighter credit policy still appears murky. Clouding the picture last week were the settlement date occurrence for banks, quarterly income tax payments, and the largest borrowings from banks to meet September 15 tax deadline since March, 1962, by business dealers and finance firms. In the prior week, the Labor Day drain on free reserves, and the Fed's decision to support higher bill rate did not help clear the picture. For three weeks in a row free reserves on average have been below the year's average of about $100 million.[5]

Each year since 1960, free reserves have dropped significantly. But during the course of each year the free reserve average kept a fairly even season pattern. They dropped, nevertheless, from $682 million at the end of 1960 to $419 million a year later; from $268 million at the end of 1962 to $209 million at the end of 1963; and the monthly range this year has been $171 million in January to $78 million in May. Yet the monthly average in November, 1963, was $33 million. The weekly average in July ranged from $196 million to $28 million; in August it fluctuated between $114 million and $86 million.

It could well be that should key commodity prices, such semi and fully manufactured goods prices as steel and autos, consumer credit extension,

[5]Appendix D contains the Federal Reserve Report of September 16, 1964.

investment spending change significantly upward and the savings rate and quality of credit drop, the Fed would send out clearer signals than those discerned in the past three weeks.

The latest official word on the subject, though nothing directly was said, was enunciated by Governor C. Canby Balderston on September 15 in Cleveland, Ohio. His praise for economy's inflationary restraint had a bullish impact on government bond prices. He reviewed generally the Federal Reserve's credit guideposts to date and more than intimated what would trigger the Fed into pulling harder on the credit reins. Forebodings were expressed about the mammoth rise in total savings and credit flows in recent years, and about the too liberal and too readily available credit jeopardizing credit quality in certain areas. Once moderation in pricing, borrowing and investing ceases, and savings and productivity declines, he warned that interest rates would be allowed to go up and credit availability would contract. The question now is, does the Fed believe we have reached that point? Should free reserves stay below $100 million this week, one would surmise another tightening turn was taken.

In commenting on Mr. Balderston's speech, Albert Kraus wrote in the New York *Times* of September 16, 1964, in part:

Mr. Balderston made no mention of the Federal Reserve's recent slight tightening of bank reserves or the Chrysler Corporation wage settlement, which many observers have viewed as inflationary. This lack, however, was interpreted as evidence that the Federal Reserve sees no immediate threat to stability from the Chrysler settlement.

Other monetary students have been less sanguine. While agreeing that the jury may be out for some time on the inflationary consequences of the Chrysler pact, they say that its generous terms are a symptom of what they call an excessively easy monetary policy rather than a cause in themselves of possible price rises.

They cite the newest money supply figures in support of this view.

The nation's money supply has risen at a 7 percent annual rate since May, after rising only 1.3 percent in the previous six months, the Federal Reserve Bank of St. Louis reported.

By way of comparison, the money supply rose at a 4.5 percent annual rate from September, 1962, to November, 1963, and at an 0.3 percent rate in the previous nine months.

In August, the money supply averaged $157.2 billion compared with $156.7 billion in July.

While acknowledging the rapid growth of the money supply since May, the St. Louis Reserve Bank noted that most of the recent growth occurred early in the summer. From late June through early this month, it said, the money supply had grown at a rate of roughly only 3 percent.

The money supply is customarily defined as checking account deposits plus money in circulation. By a broader definition, time and savings deposits at commercial banks are also included. The money supply so defined has risen at an 8.7 percent rate from May to August, after rising at a 5.5 percent rate the previous six months. From September, 1962, to November, 1963, it rose at a 9 percent rate.

On the morning of September 21, 1964, *Moody's* observed:

Broader economic and financial developments that influence monetary policy makers appear to call for some limitations on credit expansion in the coming period. Monetary policy from the early 1961 recession low has permitted a huge credit expansion. And doubtless the Federal Reserve is concerned that further expansion of credit might lay the base for an outcropping of inflation. In the latest Federal Reserve Bulletin, the summary of business conditions notes the upward pressures on sensitive industrial commodity prices. Also the amount of efficient, but unutilized, plant capacity has declined to a point where increased demand for industrial products could exert more widespread upward pressures on prices. And the level of unemployment has declined to a per cent where the remainder is not likely to be reduced significantly by an easy credit policy.

None of this is to suggest that the Federal Reserve is expected to adopt an aggressively restrictive credit policy any time soon. But even if monetary policy were not changed from that of the earlier months this year, it would have significant bearing on the outlook for interest rates. This is a time of the year when interest rates tend to rise seasonally. And it seems very likely that some of this seasonal practice will be shown in market yields over the remainder of the year, unless unexpectedly the Federal Reserve should fail for some reason to supply bank reserves more freely than it has been.

APPENDIX A

Yield to Maturity

Yield to maturity is the rate of interest which the market is prepared to pay or accept in exchanging present for future purchasing power. Or, to put it differently, it is the rate which equates the present value (*PV*) of all present and future cash outflows with the present value (*PV*) of all present and future cash inflows. If we pay $105 for a bond, which pays $5 interest at the end of each year and $100 at maturity at the end of the fifth year, yield to maturity may be found by solving the following equation:

$$PV \text{ of cash outflow} = PV \text{ of cash inflow}$$

$$\text{Purchase price} = \frac{\text{coupon (1)}}{(1 + y)} + \frac{\text{coupon (2)}}{(1 + y)^2} + \frac{\text{coupon (3)}}{(1 + y)^3} + \frac{\text{coupon (4)}}{(1 + y)^4} + \frac{\text{coupon (5)}}{(1 + y)^5} + \frac{\text{principal}}{(1 + y)^5}$$

Equation continued.

$$105 = \frac{5}{(1+y)} + \frac{5}{(1+y)^2} + \frac{5}{(1+y)^3} + \frac{5}{(1+y)^4} + \frac{5}{(1+y)^5} + \frac{100}{(1+y)^5}$$

$y = 3.89$ percent

It is possible to compute an approximate yield to maturity without interest tables by finding the average annual return on the average investment. Average annual return, in the case of a bond, consists of two factors—annual coupon interest and annual change in capital value. A change in capital value will occur in those cases where a bond is purchased at something other than par value (maturity value). In the example with which we are working the purchase price is \$105 and the par value is \$100. Thus, over the five-year life of the bond there will be a decrease in capital value of the bond of \$5. For purposes of simplification we shall amortize this premium equally over the life of the bond. In this example, then, the annual coupon interest is \$5 and the annual change in capital value is \$1. Therefore the average annual return is \$4.

Average investment may be found by averaging the value at purchase and the value at maturity. This utilizes a straight line amortization of any discount or premium. In this example, the purchase price is \$105, the maturity value is \$100, and thus the average investment is \$102.5.

The approximate yield to maturity, then, for the preceding example is as follows:

$$\text{Yield to maturity} = \frac{\text{annual interest} + \text{annual change in capital value}}{\text{average investment}}$$

$$y = \frac{5 + (\text{par value} - \text{price})/\text{years to maturity}}{(\text{price} + \text{par value})/2}$$

$$y = \frac{5 + (100 - 105)/5}{(100 + 105)/2}$$

$y = 3.90$ percent (approximate)

APPENDIX B

A Comparison of Two Methods of Computing Yield: Bank-Discount Method and Effective-Yield Method

There are three basic differences between the bank-discount method and effective-yield method of computing yield:

1. When yield is figured on a bank-discount basis, the discount is

divided by the par value. When yield is figured on the effective-yield method, the discount is divided by price.

2. The bank-discount method utilizes a 360-day year. The effective-yield method utilizes a 365-day year.

3. The bank-discount method ignores compounding effects. The effective-yield method takes compounding into account.

To demonstrate these differences, we shall use an example of a 91-day treasury bill which sells at a yield of 3.50 percent as computed by the bank-discount method. Since the bank-discount method utilizes a 360-day year, in order to find the dollar amount of the discount for the bill with 91 days to maturity we make the following computation:

$$\text{Discount} = \frac{91}{360} \times 3.50 \text{ percent}$$

$$\text{Discount} = 0.88472 \text{ percent}$$

$$\text{Discount} = \$0.88472 \text{ per } \$100 \qquad \text{(for 91-day bill)}$$

The dollar price for a $100 bill with 91 days to maturity on a 3.50 percent discount basis may be found by subtracting the discount from par value:

$$\text{Price} = \$100 - \$0.88472$$

$$\text{Price} = \$99.11528$$

Let us now take this 91-day bill that sells at $99.115 and yields 3.50 percent as computed by the bank-discount method and see what its effective yield is. To do so we shall pass through two intermediate stages as we eliminate each of the three basic differences between the bank-discount method and effective-yield method. Although the terms ascribed to such intermediate stages are relatively unimportant, the differences should be clearly understood.

Let us begin by eliminating the first basic difference that was listed above—the divisor in the "yield" equation. Let the other two conditions of the bank-discount method remain unchanged; that is, use a 360-day year and ignore compounding effects. We can compute a "yield," which we shall call bank yield, by dividing discount by price.

$$\text{Bank yield} = \frac{\text{discount}}{\text{price}} \quad \text{(for 360-day year)}$$

$$\text{Bank yield} = \frac{\$3.50}{\$99.11528}$$

$$\text{Bank yield} = 3.53124 \text{ percent}$$

Now let us modify this result by eliminating the second difference—the number of days in the year. Let the third condition of the bank-discount basis remain unchanged, by continuing to ignore compounding effects.

In order to convert the discount from a 360- to a 365-day year we make the following computation:

$$\text{Discount} = \frac{365}{360} \times 3.50 \text{ percent}$$

$$\text{Discount} = \$3.5486 \qquad \text{(for 365-day year)}$$

We can now compute a new "yield" (which we shall call investment yield) by dividing discount by price.

$$\text{Investment yield} = \frac{\text{discount}}{\text{price}} \quad \text{(for 365-day year)}$$

$$\text{Investment yield} = \frac{\$3.5486}{\$99.11528}$$

$$\text{Investment yield} = 3.580275 \text{ percent}$$

Finally, the effective yield may be obtained by eliminating the third difference, that is, by ceasing to ignore compounding effects. The effective yield on a 91-day basis may be found by dividing the discount for a 91-day bill by the price.

$$\text{Effective yield} = \frac{\$0.88472}{\$99.11528} = 0.892617 \text{ percent} = i$$

The effective yield on an annual basis may be found by annualizing the 91-day figure.

$$\underset{\text{(on an annual basis)}}{\text{Effective yield}} = (1 + i)^{\frac{365}{91}} - 1$$

$$= (1 + 0.00892617)^{\frac{365}{91}} - 1$$

$$\underset{\text{(on an annual basis)}}{\text{Effective yield}} = 3.62 \text{ percent}$$

Thus, a 91-day treasury bill with a yield computed to be 3.50 percent on the bank-discount method has an effective annual yield of 3.62 percent.

APPENDIX C

A Comparison of Price Behavior on Long-Term and Short-Term Securities

The relationship between price and yield is expressed by the following general equation (as given in Appendix A):

$$p = \frac{\text{coupon (1)}}{(1 + y)} + \frac{\text{coupon (2)}}{(1 + y)^2} + \cdot \cdot \cdot + \frac{\text{coupon } (n)}{(1 + y)^n} + \frac{\text{par value}}{(1 + y)^n}$$

where p = price; y = yield to maturity; and n = number of years of interest payments, years to maturity.

Let us take two \$100 securities which pay \$4 interest at the end of each year until maturity. Assume that one matures in one year ($n = 1$) and that the other matures in ten years ($n = 10$). Assume that the yield to maturity is 3.50 on both securities. The price for the security where $n = 1$ is

$$\text{Price} = \frac{4}{(1 + 0.035)} + \frac{100}{(1 + 0.035)}$$

$$\text{Price} = 100.5 \qquad \text{(one-year security)}$$

and the price for the security where $n = 10$ is:

$$\text{Price} = \frac{4}{(1 + 0.035)} + \frac{4}{(1 + 0.035)^2} + \cdot \cdot \cdot + \frac{4}{(1 + 0.035)^{10}} + \frac{100}{(1 + 0.035)^{10}}$$

$$\text{Price} = 104.19 \qquad \text{(ten-year security)}$$

If the yield to maturity drops by 0.20 (to 3.30), the price for the one year security is

$$\text{Price} = \frac{4}{(1 + 0.033)} + \frac{100}{(1 + 0.033)}$$

$$\text{Price} = 100.68 \qquad \text{(one-year security)}$$

and the price for the ten-year security is:

$$\text{Price} = \frac{4}{(1 + 0.033)} + \frac{4}{(1 + 0.033)^2} + \cdot \cdot \cdot + \frac{4}{(1 + 0.033)^{10}} + \frac{100}{(1 + 0.033)^{10}}$$

$$\text{Price} = 105.92 \qquad \text{(ten-year security)}$$

Thus, we can see that for a given change (0.20 in this example) in yield, the change in price is much greater for the ten-year security. (Although not demonstrated here, it is equally true for an increase, as well as a decrease in yield.) This can be proved mathematically from the general equation. However, for our purposes, it is sufficient that the reader get an intuitive understanding for this phenomenon.

Let us begin our discussion by introducing the formula from Appendix A for the approximate yield to maturity:

$$\text{Approximate yield to maturity} = \frac{\text{annual interest} + \text{annual change in capital value}}{\text{average investment}}$$

$$y = \frac{r + (v - p)/n}{(p + v)/2}$$

where n = years to maturity; p = price; v = par value; r = coupon interest; and y= yield to maturity.

In order to explain any difference in price behavior in long-term securities vis-à-vis short-term securities, we must focus our attention on those terms in the above equation which are a function of n (years to maturity) since the securities are identical in all other respects.

By isolating this term, we have shown that a given change in $(v - p)/n$ will require a greater change in p when n is large than when it is small.[1] It is precisely this result which we set out to demonstrate. There is only one term in which n appears—annual change in capital value—or $(v - p)/n$. Any change in this term will have to be brought about by a change in p since v and n are both fixed. For a change in the term of -0.10 where n is 1, the change in price will have to be $+0.10$. For a change in the term of -0.10 where $n = 10$, the change in price will have to be $+1.0$.

APPENDIX D

From *The Wall Street Journal,* September 18, 1964:

> The cash supplies of the nation's banks immediately available for lending and investing in the week ended Wednesday continued at a lower level than in most weeks this year. Figures released by the New York Federal Reserve Bank tended to confirm that the Federal Reserve System has moved toward a slightly tighter credit policy, characterized for months as one of "moderate ease."
>
> The banks' "free reserves"—their pool of uncommitted usable funds—averaged \$78 million in the statement week, compared with an average \$58 million originally estimated for the prior week, since revised to \$28 million. For most weeks this year, average free reserves fluctuated around or above \$100 million.
>
> Government financial officials say privately that the recent slight tightening of bank credit supplies doesn't conflict with what they say is a predominant view of the Federal Reserve Board, that is, that a policy of monetary "ease" can continue without posing inflationary dangers for the domestic economy. They contend that the tightening is motivated only by a temporary balance-of-payments concern, that it is an effort to hold short-term U.S. interest rates firm enough to prevent an outflow of money from this country to higher-yield investments abroad.
>
> The New York Reserve Bank also reported that commercial and industrial loans at leading New York City banks soared in the statement week by \$349 million from the prior week. The sharp rise resulted chiefly from increased borrowings by corporations to meet income tax instalments due

[1]The term $(v - p)/n$ represents the *annual* amortization of premium or discount. The numerator $(v - p)$ represents the *total* amortization. For any given change in annual amortization, the change in total amortization will be greater for the security with the longer maturity because it consists of a greater number of annual amortizations.

in the period. The rise was the largest for any week in such a tax period since March 1962.

Reserves that commercial banks must set aside against customers' deposits may either be held as cash in their own vaults or as deposits at Federal Reserve banks. On any day, some banks' reserves may exceed their requirements while others may have to borrow from Federal Reserve banks. When aggregate excess reserves exceed total borrowings the margin constitutes free reserves, or immediately available cash. When total borrowings are greater than reserves, the banks are said to have "net borrowed reserves."

Factors contributing to a slight increase in the statement week's average reserves from the prior week's estimate were a $283 million average increase in the "float" of checks delayed in collection, for which banks automatically get Federal Reserve credit, and an average $313 million rise in vault cash allowed as reserves.

A key offsetting factor was a $214 million average reduction in Federal Reserve holdings of Government securities. When the agency is a net seller of securities, money is drawn out of the banking system as the buyers withdraw funds from their accounts in payment. Another contracting force in the statement week was an average $182 million increase in currency in circulation, reflecting funds withdrawn from the banks.

On a Wednesday-to-Wednesday basis, the Reserve reduced its holdings of Government securities by about $520 million. It was a net seller of $562 million of securities maturing in a year or less, and it was a net purchaser of $19 million of securities maturing in one to five years, $16 million of securities of five to 10 years and $7 million of securities of over 10 years. The Treasury's monetary gold reserves held unchanged for the 31st successive week at $15,463,000,000, other Federal Reserve figures showed. However, the ratio of the Treasury's gold reserve to Federal Reserve liabilities slipped to a new low of 29.1% from the previous low of 29.2% last week. The drop was due largely to a rise in the liabilities.

By law, the minimum ratio is fixed at 25%, although the Reserve Board can suspend the minimum in emergencies. The ratio has been declining in recent years.

The spurt in commercial and industrial loans at New York banks followed a $10 million decline the previous week and brought the total of such loans outstanding to $12,775,000,000, up $503 million from mid-year. In the like week a year ago, such loans rose $130 million from the prior week but were up only $62 million from mid-year.

Loans of the major New York banks to sales finance and business credit companies rose by $220 million in the latest week. The total, however, was down $205 million from mid-year. A year ago, such loans climbed $345 million in the week and were $267 million above the 1963 mid-year level. In Chicago, commercial and industrial loans increased $63 million in the week, leaving the total $57 million above the mid-year figure. In the year-earlier week, such loans climbed $110 million and were $109 million higher than at mid-year.

Money Market Fundamentals 3

ILLUSTRATIVE EXAMPLES

The exercise presented in this chapter serves to review some of the basic concepts of money and banking economics. It consists of filling in the missing numbers in the balance sheets which appear under all columns headed by a number other than 1.

The exercise has several columns numbered 1. Each of these columns contains identical balance sheets for "All Member Banks Combined" and "All Federal Reserve Banks Combined," and each serves as the starting point for the problems given in the exercise. At this starting point the total deposits of member banks are $81,000 demand and $30,000 time, loans are $45,000, security holdings are $64,000, required reserves are $18,000, and excess reserves are $1000. The required reserves consist of $16,200 representing 20 percent of demand deposits plus $1800 representing 6 percent of time deposits. In working the problems, assume that reserve requirements continue at the rate of 20 percent on demand deposits and 6 percent on time deposits.

The numbers other than 1 that appear above the various columns refer to the particular problem situations described in the exercise. There are thirteen separate problems, but a number of the problems are related in the sense that they represent alternative ways of handling particular situations. For example, problems 4(a) and 4(b) are intended to illustrate the impact of two different courses of action that the Federal Reserve can take in support of the market for United States government securities.

The primary aim of this exercise is to indicate the general direction of the effects of monetary forces. Therefore, in solving the exercise, be sure to identify the possible market causes for the type of situation described by the problem.

The examples presented were prepared by James N. Land, Senior Vice-President (now retired), Mellon National Bank and Trust Company, Pittsburgh, Pennsylvania.

Notes to Exercise

The reader should note that all figures are hypothetical. Figures for nonmember banks have been omitted in the interest of simplifying the illustrations presented. Reserve requirements are assumed to be 20 percent on demand deposits and 6 percent on time deposits. The numbers below refer to the column number in the exercise.

1. Assumed starting point.
2. Member banks increase loans by $5000.
3. Subsequently member banks increase loans by an additional $5000 and adjust their reserve positions
   (a) by selling U.S. government securities to Federal Reserve Banks, or
   (b) by borrowing from Federal Reserve Banks, or
   (c) by selling securities to nonbanks.
4. Federal Reserve Banks buy $1000 U.S. government securities in support of market
   (a) from nonbanks, or
   (b) from member banks.
5. U.S. government finances $1000 deficit
   (a) by selling $1000 new bonds to nonbanks, or
   (b) by selling $1000 new bonds to member banks.
6. Following changes occur in position of member banks:
   (a) loans of member banks decline $3000, and
   (b) subsequently member banks buy $1500 U.S. government securities from Federal Reserve Banks.
7. Federal Reserve Banks sell U.S. government securities to nonbanks
   (a) first in amount of $1000, and
   (b) subsequently in additional amount of $1000, any necessary adjustment of member banks' reserves being accomplished by reducing loans.
8. Federal Reserve Board raises reserve requirements on demand deposits by 1 percent.

All Member Banks Combined	*1*	*2*	*3(a)*	*3(b)*	*3(c)*	*1*	*4(a)*	*4(b)*	*1*	*5(a)*	*5(b)*
ASSETS											
Cash on hand	$ 1,000	$ 1,000	$ 1,000	$ 1,000	$ 1,000	$ 1,000	$ 1,000	$ 1,000	$ 1,000	$ 1,000	$ 1,000
Reserves with Federal Reserve Banks:											
Required	18,000					18,000			18,000		
Excess	1,000					1,000			1,000		
Loans	45,000					45,000	45,000	45,000	45,000	45,000	45,000
Securities	64,000	64,000		64,000		64,000			64,000	64,000	
Other assets	1,000	1,000	1,000	1,000	1,000	1,000	1,000	1,000	1,000	1,000	1,000
Total	130,000					130,000			130,000		
LIABILITIES											
Demand deposits	81,000					81,000			81,000		
Time deposits	30,000	30,000	30,000	30,000	30,000	30,000	30,000	30,000	30,000	30,000	30,000
Borrowings from Federal Reserve Banks	100	100	100		100	100	100	100	100	100	100
Other liabilities	8,900	8,900	8,900	8,900	8,900	8,900	8,900	8,900	8,900	8,900	8,900
Capital accounts	10,000	10,000	10,000	10,000	10,000	10,000	10,000	10,000	10,000	10,000	10,000
Total	130,000					130,000			130,000		

All Federal Reserve Banks Combined	*1*	*2*	*3(a)*	*3(b)*	*3(c)*	*1*	*4(a)*	*4(b)*	*1*	*5(a)*	*5(b)*
ASSETS											
U. S. government securities	23,000	23,000		23,000	23,000	23,000			23,000	23,000	23,000
Discounts and advances to member banks	100	100	100		100	100	100	100	100	100	100
Collection items credited to member bank reserves	900	900	900	900	900	900	900	900	900	900	900
U.S. Treasury gold certificates	20,000	20,000	20,000	20,000	20,000	20,000	20,000	20,000	20,000	20,000	20,000
Total	44,000	44,000	45,000	45,000	44,000	44,000	45,000	45,000	44,000	44,000	44,000
LIABILITIES											
Federal Reserve Notes outstanding	23,000	23,000	23,000	23,000	23,000	23,000	23,000	23,000	23,000	23,000	23,000
Member bank reserves:											
Required	18,000					18,000			18,000		
Excess	1,000	–	–	–	–	1,000			1,000		
U.S. Treasury deposits	1,000	1,000	1,000	1,000	1,000	1,000	1,000	1,000	1,000	1,000	1,000
Capital funds	1,000	1,000	1,000	1,000	1,000	1,000	1,000	1,000	1,000	1,000	1,000
Total	44,000	44,000	45,000	45,000	44,000	44,000	45,000	45,000	44,000	44,000	44,000

All Member Banks Combined	*1*	*6(a)*	*6(b)*	*1*	*7(a)*	*7(b)*	*1*	*8*
ASSETS								
Cash on hand	$ 1,000	$ 1,000	$ 1,000	$ 1,000	$ 1,000	$ 1,000	$ 1,000	$ 1,000
Reserves with Federal Reserve Banks:								
Required	18,000			18,000			18,000	
Excess	1,000			1,000			1,000	
Loans	45,000			45,000	45,000		45,000	45,000
Securities	64,000	64,000		64,000	64,000	64,000	64,000	64,000
Other assets	1,000	1,000	1,000	1,000	1,000	1,000	1,000	1,000
Total	130,000			130,000			130,000	
LIABILITIES								
Demand deposits	81,000			81,000			81,000	
Time deposits	30,000	30,000	30,000	30,000	30,000	30,000	30,000	30,000
Borrowings from Federal Reserve Banks	100	100	100	100	100	100	100	100
Other liabilities	8,900	8,900	8,900	8,900	8,900	8,900	8,900	8,900
Capital accounts	10,000	10,000	10,000	10,000	10,000	10,000	10,000	10,000
Total	130,000			130,000			130,000	

All Federal Reserve Banks Combined	*1*	*6(a)*	*6(b)*	*1*	*7(a)*	*7(b)*	*1*	*8*
ASSETS								
U. S. government securities	23,000	23,000		23,000			23,000	23,000
Discounts and advances to member banks	100	100	100	100	100	100	100	100
Collection items credited to member bank reserves	900	900	900	900	900	900	900	900
U.S. Treasury gold certificates	20,000	20,000	20,000	20,000	20,000	20,000	20,000	20,000
Total	44,000	44,000	42,500	44,000	43,000	42,000	44,000	44,000
LIABILITIES								
Federal Reserve Notes outstanding	23,000	23,000	23,000	23,000	23,000	23,000	23,000	23,000
Member bank reserves:								
Required	18,000			18,000			18,000	
Excess	1,000			1,000		–	1,000	
U.S. Treasury deposits	1,000	1,000	1,000	1,000	1,000	1,000	1,000	1,000
Capital funds	1,000	1,000	1,000	1,000	1,000	1,000	1,000	1,000
Total	44,000	44,000	42,500	44,000	43,000	42,000	44,000	44,000

MANAGEMENT OF COMMERCIAL BANKS

Formation of a Bank 

ESTABLISHING A NEW BANK

Rosario Bank

Mr. Thomas L. Sutton was graduated from the Stanford Business School in June 1949, and accepted a position as a management trainee in the Palm Tree National Bank, a medium-sized commercial bank which operated seventy-eight branches throughout southern California. Palm Tree National's training program lasted two years and consisted of the following: bank operations; installment, real estate, and commercial loan analysis; personnel relations; and the trust and escrow functions. Mr. Sutton worked several months in each of these areas, thereby acquiring an understanding of the main elements of commercial banking.

When Mr. Sutton completed the training period in June 1951, he was transferred to the Ventura branch of the Palm Tree Bank. His principal duties involved the analysis of real estate and installment loan applications. During the next year Mr. Sutton gained considerable experience in analyzing these loans, and he enjoyed the opportunity of meeting a wide variety of local businessmen.

In September 1952, Mr. Sutton learned of the efforts of a few prominent businessmen in nearby Moorpark, California, to organize a new unit bank in their community. At the time there was only one small bank in Moorpark, and frequently local merchants had difficulty in securing the banking services they required. Later in September, a spokesman for the Moorpark merchants invited Mr. Sutton to become an officer in the proposed bank.

The opportunity offered a promotion, greater personal responsibility, an increase in salary, and a chance to gain supervisory experience in a locally managed bank. Mr. Sutton decided to accept the new position, and in October 1952 he was appointed assistant cashier of the First National Bank of Moorpark, a unit bank with capital of $250,000. His new duties included certain lending responsibilities as well as public relations activities in the community. In this position Mr. Sutton believed he could obtain broader banking experience and develop valuable personal friendships.

One afternoon in the spring of 1954, Mr. Sutton called upon William Glynn, a large hay and grain dealer in the small unincorporated area of Rosario, about twenty miles from Moorpark. The purpose of the visit was to try to secure the firm's deposit account and to acquaint Mr. Glynn with the Moorpark Bank's interest in expanding its agricultural loans. Mr. Sutton had learned from trade sources that Mr. Glynn was a successful businessman and that he was highly respected in Rosario. Dun and Bradstreet's reference book rated his firm AAA1.

During the discussion, Mr. Glynn pointed out that Rosario did not have banking facilities for the convenience of local merchants and residents. The nearest bank was about eight miles away. Mr. Glynn suggested that the Moorpark Bank consider the addition of a branch office in Rosario. The area had been growing steadily in population (1940, 1380; 1954, 2256) and an increasing number of small business were being established. Mr. Glynn mentioned that about six months earlier a number of local businessmen signed a petition inviting a large state-wide banking chain to open a branch in Rosario. After investigation, the bank declined the invitation.

Mr. Sutton knew that the directors of the Moorpark Bank did not want to expand their operations at this time. Nevertheless, the possibility of establishing a small independent bank in Rosario interested Mr. Sutton. He decided, therefore, to spend some of his own time investigating the feasibility of such a venture.

Since there were few published statistics or other data covering the Rosario area, most of Mr. Sutton's investigations involved conversations with local businessmen and residents. He learned that most of Rosario's farmers raised citrus fruits, livestock, alfalfa hay, and other grain crops. Mr. Sutton also noted that Dun and Bradstreet's reference book listed seventy-one companies in the town's area, with credit ratings generally ranging from H-4 to D-2. There was, however, no automobile agency in the town, and Rosario residents purchased most important durable consumer items in Oxnard, a town with a population of 30,000 about ten miles from Rosario. An aerial photograph of Rosario and the vicinity revealed the rural character and sparse population of the area.

Mr. Sutton also talked with several large real estate and land development firms. They agreed that new building activity would probably increase in the area because nearby communities were expanding in that direction. Residential construction in Rosario had been held back because of relatively poor drainage and the lack of sewers. Some local real estate men stated that if Oxnard annexed Rosario, the former would probably construct the necessary storm and sewage disposal services. Some of the real estate agents, however, believed that Rosario might incorporate in preference to annexing itself to Oxnard. If Rosario voted to incorporate, there would be some delay in improving the sewer systems because the new town probably would have difficulty raising the necessary funds. Thus, an important part of Rosario's residential and business development hinged on the town's future decision on incorporation or annexation. In his talks with local officials, Mr. Sutton learned only that the town government planned no action in the near future.

Mr. Sutton's preliminary inquiries increased his interest in the possibility of a new bank in Rosario; however he realized that he must devote more time to interviews with local merchants to appraise the need for such a bank. Accordingly, Mr. Sutton made another appointment with Mr. Glynn for the express purpose of having Glynn arrange introductions to several Rosario businessmen.

Mr. Glynn was cordial and cooperative during the meeting and reemphasized his personal interest in a new bank for Rosario. He introduced Mr. Sutton to several merchants during the next few weeks, and based on these discussions Sutton thought that enough capital could be raised locally to start a bank. He noted that the men he talked to were proud of their town and anxious to see it grow. A few of them inquired about establishing a national bank, evidently believing that its prestige would reflect favorably on the community. After a number of these interviews, Mr. Sutton decided that the businessmen in particular and the community in general presented a favorable atmosphere for the establishment of a small unit bank.

Although community service and local support were necessary, Mr. Sutton realized that the success of a new bank depended upon its ability to attract enough depositors and loan customers to return a satisfactory profit to stockholders. He had difficulty, however, preparing a forecast of deposits, because no real estate valuations or other estimates of community wealth were available. For unincorporated areas such as Rosario, Mr. Sutton did not believe that approximate estimates of local wealth based upon the number of gas meters or telephones in the vicinity were applicable in this situation. He finally decided to base his deposit forecast on the rule of thumb employed by the comptroller of the currency in reviewing applications for national bank charters. This rule suggested deposits of $1 million for each one thousand population. Mr. Sutton used the population within Rosario's school district, since he believed this would produce the most conservative deposit estimate. He did not know, however, the number of commercial and personal accounts that the bank might attract from outlying areas. Mr. Sutton tentatively estimated the bank could have $2,500,000 in deposits by the end of the first year.

The lack of factual data about Rosario made it difficult for Mr. Sutton to appraise the amount and types of loan requests which a new bank might receive. In analyzing the area's loan potential, Mr. Sutton thought that real estate lending would provide the most important source of profitable loans. He also anticipated some volume in seasonal agricultural loans plus some commercial and personal loans. If adjacent communities continued their residential expansion toward Rosario, Mr. Sutton reasoned that the bank would also gain some new depositors and loan customers from this source.

Mr. Sutton prepared an income statement for a first year based on the information he had gathered and his knowledge of current bank practice. He used these assumptions:

1. Average deposits for the year, $2,150,000.
2. Initial capital of $350,000.
3. Primary and secondary reserves and vault cash would equal about 30 percent of deposits and capital.
4. The remaining deposits and capital would be invested as follows: 35 percent loan portfolio, 30 percent investment portfolio, and 5 percent fixed assets.

Based on these data, his knowledge of the approximate earning power of loans and investments and an estimate of operating expenses, Mr. Sutton believed that the bank would break even by the end of the first year. He thought that he could expect profits of from $10,000 to $20,000 in the second year. Mr. Sutton realized, however, that these estimates were "rough" because of the lack of reliable information.

As he reviewed these figures, Mr. Sutton wondered whether he should proceed with the idea of establishing a bank in Rosario. Although he thought that the town would continue growing, Mr. Sutton was disturbed that a large state-wide banking chain had declined this apparent opportunity. He knew, however, that he must reach a decision soon, since he could not afford to devote much more of his time investigating the venture without jeopardizing his present position at the Moorpark Bank.

MANAGING A NEW BANK

First National Bank of Rosario

After several weeks of careful thought about the Rosario situation, Mr. Sutton concluded that it presented a good opportunity for a new independent bank. He decided, therefore, to resign his position at the Moorpark Bank to devote full time to organizing the new venture.

Mr. Sutton invited nine influential local businessmen to form a committee to help sponsor and promote the formation of a new bank.

These men earlier had promised to lend financial support to the new enterprise. All of them possessed substantial personal means as well as valuable business and social relationships in Rosario. Mr. Sutton hoped that most of these men might continue to support the new bank through serving on the board of directors. Sutton believed that the selection of an exclusively local board would be an important element in the successful establishment of the bank.

Within a month after the formation of this committee, sufficient capital had been pledged to permit Mr. Sutton to make formal application for a bank charter. One of the most important decisions regarding the formation of the bank involved the question of whether to apply for a national or state charter.

Operating under a national charter, the Rosario Bank would have to join the Federal Reserve System. This requirement would place the bank under the regulatory jurisdiction of the Board of Governors in Washington, D.C. Under a state charter, the bank would be subject to regulation by the California Banking Commission. Mr. Sutton drew up the following arguments concerning membership in the Federal Reserve System.

Advantages of Membership in Federal Reserve System

1. Use of the Federal Reserve's check collection and clearing facilities.
2. Use of the borrowing privilege (at the prevailing discount rate) when additional short-term or seasonal funds are required.
3. Availability of varying denominations of currency and coin for normal or emergency purposes.
4. Receipt of a cumulative dividend of 6 percent on the Federal Reserve capital stock owned by the member bank.
5. Higher public prestige associated with a national charter and membership in the Federal Reserve System.

Disadvantages of Membership in Federal Reserve System

1. Higher reserve requirements must be maintained than those necessary under a state charter. Vault cash and correspondent deposit balances may not be included as a credit against required reserves.[1]
2. Member banks must participate in par collection of checks and refrain from exacting exchange charges on checks presented through the mail.
3. Member banks must purchase Federal Reserve stock in the amount of 3 percent of the member's capital and paid-in surplus and be

[1]Vault cash and correspondent balances now may be included as a credit against required reserves due to a change in Federal Reserve Board regulations.

prepared to purchase an additional 3 percent if so requested by the Federal Reserve.

4. Restrictions are placed on the maximum amount of interest members may pay on time deposits. In 1955 this limitation was 2½ percent.

After thinking about the advantages of a national charter, Mr. Sutton decided that the strongest practical arguments favored applying for a state charter. He reasoned that the higher Federal Reserve requirements might limit the profitability of the new bank, particularly in the early years. Another important advantage of a state charter resulted because in California a nonmember state bank may lend on unimproved farm land whereas a national bank may not. This was an important consideration in Rosario because of the increasing interest in new housing developments and subdivisions in the area. Mr. Sutton also noted that a city correspondent could normally furnish a small country bank with lending and check clearing services approximately similar to those available through the Federal Reserve. This factor became especially important, since the new bank must maintain correspondent relationships in any event, whether it obtained a national or state charter. Even though chartered by the state, the Rosario Bank could still become a member of the Federal Reserve System provided it adhered to the same financial standards and practices as national banks.

In discussing the question of the charter with other members of the committee, Mr. Sutton presented in detail his reasons why a state charter offered the greatest advantages for a new unit bank. Several other members of the committee, however, believed the Rosario Bank should request a national charter. These men stated that the prestige embodied in a national charter remained an extremely important consideration to local businessmen who associated greater financial strength with a national bank.

A minority of the committee members agreed with Mr. Sutton's position regarding the bank's charter. The conflicting arguments thus involved an evaluation of the importance of prestige to a young, untested financial institution versus the opportunity to maximize profit. Mr. Sutton finally agreed reluctantly with the majority opinion. He promised to file as soon as possible the necessary documents formally requesting a national charter.

Since Mr. Sutton had not participated in the preliminary procedures of establishing the Moorpark Bank, he was unfamiliar with the details involved in applying for a banking charter. He knew, however, that applications for a national charter are made through the Comptroller of the Currency in Washington, D.C. Sutton learned that the procedure is as follows:

1. A formal application for a permit to organize must be filed with

the Comptroller of the Currency. This application must present full financial and administrative details regarding the proposed bank.

2. Upon receipt of the application by federal authorities, the chief district national bank examiner conducts an investigation, considering among other criteria the need for additional banking services in the community, adequacy of the proposed capital, future earning prospects, and the character and personal integrity of the proposed management. The chief district examiner also seeks the opinions of officials in the district concerned.

3. A local recommendation is drafted by the chief district examiner's organization division and is forwarded through the offices of the Assistant Chief and Chief National Bank Examiner, each of whom attaches supplementary recommendations. The application then is submitted to the Comptroller of the Currency for the final decision.

4. If the decision is favorable, the applicant is notified and provided with the necessary forms to complete the final application procedures. When the technical legal documents have been executed, and when the new bank has purchased the required amount of Federal Reserve stock, the Comptroller of the Currency issues a charter which authorizes the bank to commence operation. The time required to complete these investigations and the administrative delays in final approval vary with each application.

Mr. Sutton completed and filed with the Comptroller of the Currency the necessary applications for a national charter. On September 3, 1954, he received notification that the Comptroller of the Currency had approved the application.

Shortly after receiving this notice, Mr. Sutton called the first formal meeting of the board of directors to establish operating policies for the First National Bank of Rosario. The initial meeting of the recently appointed board convened on October 12, 1954. The board was composed of nine men, seven of whom were leading members of the business community in Rosario. The remaining two directors were the active officers of the bank, Mr. Sutton, president, and Mr. Treadwell, cashier.

A number of important problems required immediate attention. Mr. Sutton wanted to devote the first directors' meeting to the discussion of these issues: (1) preliminary selection of a location for the bank, (2) bank loan policy, and (3) methods of promoting the bank's services.

The problem of location was quickly settled. Mr. Glynn, who had been elected chairman of the board, proposed that he sell for a modest price a key lot which he owned in the town's main shopping area. The proposal appealed strongly to the other directors and after a short discussion they unanimously accepted the offer. Tentative building plans were in preparation, and Mr. Sutton thought the new facility would be ready for occupancy in about four months.

The board next turned to the discussion of a loan policy consistent with community needs and the initially limited resources of the bank. In preparing for the board meeting, Mr. Sutton had spent considerable time thinking about the most effective method of presenting his views on this subject. He therefore commenced the discussion by reviewing the important operating problems which a unit bank typically encounters in California.

1. A unit bank, unlike a branch bank, cannot easily adjust itself to changes in business conditions in its particular area. Branch banks may readily transfer funds from one area to another to help moderate deposit and loan fluctuations.

2. A unit bank may not be able to diversify adequately its loan portfolio. Hence, the unit bank becomes necessarily more dependent on dominant local industries. This customer concentration requires a more conservative loan policy, particularly for a new bank.

3. Management and personnel resources of a unit bank may be more limited than branch banks, which often can utilize specialists.

4. A unit bank generally offers less complete banking service than a branch bank. In addition, the legal loan limit may represent a more serious handicap to a unit bank.

5. Costs of operation in a unit bank are usually higher since basic services must be spread over a smaller volume of business.

After discussing the above factors, Mr. Sutton emphasized his personal attitude regarding loan policy:

1. The standards of conservatism that the bank should observe in granting loans: Because the profit potential of the bank was limited, its capitalization was necessarily small. A small capital account in turn required conservative operating policies to minimize losses on loans. Accordingly, Mr. Sutton believed that no losses whatsoever in the loan account would represent a desirable goal.

2. The amount of real estate loans in the loan portfolio: Mr. Sutton thought that the bank should emphasize this type of credit since lending on real estate would help contribute to greater loan stability.

3. Loan interest rates: Mr. Sutton personally opposed direct-rate competition. He believed local competitive conditions should determine interest rates. He preferred to place greater competitive emphasis upon improved personal service and convenience to the customer. However, he did favor some rate concessions to the larger, more stable accounts.

The final important topic on the directors' agenda concerned policies relating to promotion of the bank's services. Mr. Sutton had prepared an outline of marketing methods and media which might help publicize the bank and secure new accounts. He knew that the directors' opinions and advice in these matters would be especially valuable since they were well acquainted with the community and with small business promotion and advertising.

Mr. Sutton presented the following alternatives to the other directors for their comments:

Media and Methods

1. Newspaper advertising—ads in the weekly Rosario paper or in the daily Oxnard paper.
2. Radio spot announcements—using the radio station in Oxnard.
3. Direct mail—statement stuffers, brochures, letters, and the like.
4. Door-to-door solicitation by the bank's officers of: (*a*) all business firms in Rosario and (*b*) stockholders (235 stockholders held an interest in the new bank).

Bank Services That Could Be Promoted

1. Savings accounts—should the bank pay more than the prevailing percent interest rate?
2. Home loans—should the bank promote real estate loans?
3. Home improvement loans—repair and modernization?
4. Automobile loans—should the bank offer a lower rate of interest than the 4½ percent currently charged by other commercial banks?

Exhibit 1

FIRST NATIONAL BANK OF ROSARIO

Charter No. 14723—Reserve District No. 12

Report of Condition of the First National Bank of Rosario in the State of California, at the Close of Business on January 4, 1955

ASSETS	
Cash, balances with other banks, including reserve balance and cash items in process of collection	$168,901.50
United States government obligations, direct and guaranteed	99,900.59
Corporate stocks, including $9,750.00 stock of Federal Reserve Bank	9,750.00
Bank premises owned $56,701.42, furniture and fixtures $8,433.77	65,135.19
Other assets	13,812.72
Total assets	$357,500.00
CAPITAL ACCOUNTS	
Capital stock, common stock, par $195,000.00	$195,000.00
Surplus	130,000.00
Undivided profits	32,500.00
Total capital accounts	$357,500.00

I, Thomas L. Sutton, President of the above-named bank, do solemnly swear that the above statement is true to the best of my knowledge and belief.

Exhibit 2

FIRST NATIONAL BANK OF ROSARIO

Comparative Operating Statements
for 1955
from January 5, 1955 to:

Income	*January 31*	*March 31*	*June 30*	*December 30*
Interest securities	$ 881.28	$ 3,495.52	$ 7,888.60	$18,487.40
Dividends stocks	48.75	146.25	292.50	585.00
	$ 930.03	$ 3,641.77	$ 8,181.10	$19,072.40
Interest real estate loans	$ 13.69	$ 826.51	$ 4,111.89	$15,493.56
Interest installment credit loans	14.65	2,100.46	6,150.82	16,231.96
Interest other loans	39.76	535.80	1,927.47	8,265.03
Profit on sale of U.S. securities		125.00	125.00	125.00
Interest on deposits				638.89
Total	$ 998.13	$ 7,229.54	$20,496.28	$59,826.84
Service charges and fees bank loans	$ 30.00	$ 342.00	$ 1,019.15	$ 2,820.22
Service charges deposit accounts	195.00	1,026.18	3,712.77	11,900.01
Other service and miscellaneous charges	0.80	100.17	647.66	2,579.66
Collection charges			13.25	62.75
Exchange charges	14.75	64.10	273.07	852.37
Profit from cashing "E" bonds				130.80
Safe deposit rentals	275.00	402.50	612.50	856.00
Night deposit rental	3.71	20.00	86.00	60.00
Total operating income	$1,517.39	$ 9,184.49	$26,860.68	$79,088.65
Cash overs	23.13	43.78	67.15	110.79
Total operating and other income	$1,540.52	$ 9,228.27	$26,927.83	$79,199.44

Exhibit 2 (Continued)

Expenses	January 31	March 31	June 30	December 30
Interest on deposit accounts	$ 307.91	$ 988.21	$ 2,879.73	$11,749.50
Bond amortization			42.50	93.50
Depreciation bank premises, etc.		499.39	1,620.21	4,342.47
F.D.I.C. assessments	135.00	270.00	630.00	1,530.00
Taxes real estate			73.38	827.59
Social Security and unemployment insurance		73.38	774.57	1,396.57
Expenses, general	7,470.75	14,948.04	27,183.59	56,225.51
Expenses, bank premises		425.95	990.73	2,438.88
Total expenses (excluding interest)	$7,605.75	$16,216.76	$31,314.98	$66,854.52
Total operating expenses	7,913.66	17,204.97	34,194.71	78,604.02
Cash shorts	10.16	114.01	40.59	173.11
Total operating and other expenses	$7,923.82	$17,318.98	$34,235.30	$78,777.13
Net profit (loss) for the periods	($6,383.30)	($8,090.71)	($7,307.47)	$ 422.31

Exhibit 3

FIRST NATIONAL BANK OF ROSARIO

Comparative Balance Sheets

Resources	*1/5/55*	*1/6/55*	*1/10/55*	*1/31/55*	*3/31/55*	*6/30/55*	*12/30/55*
LOANS							
Real estate loans				$ 30,000.00	$ 219,585.81	$ 325,620.85	$ 564,067.56
Veterans guaranteed loans				10,300.00	27,043.12	27,028.85	101,314.49
Mutual mortgage insurance loans				11,357.40	11,295.60	58,202.04	52,683.99
Total real estate loans				$ 51,657.40	$ 257,924.53	$ 410,851.74	$ 718,066.04
Unsecured loans					52,001.08	107,733.47	148,640.20
Installment credit loans				11,565.83	58,744.04	145,288.88	324,218.54
Flooring					4,114.50	1,924.00	2,325.00
Other secured loans	$ 16,740.15	$ 16,740.15	$ 16,740.15	16,740.15	23,000.00	76,400.62	157,955.25
Total other loans	$ 16,740.15	$ 16,740.15	$ 16,740.15	$ 28,305.98	$ 137,859.62	$ 331,346.97	$ 633,138.99
Overdrafts					43.11	62.95	276.87
Total loans and overdrafts	$ 16,740.15	$ 16,740.15	$ 16,740.15	$ 79,963.38	$ 395,827.26	$ 742,261.66	$1,351,481.90
SECURITIES							
Federal Reserve stock	$ 9,750.00	$ 9,750.00	$ 9,750.00	$ 9,750.00	$ 9,750.00	$ 9,750.00	$ 9,750.00
U.S. securities	99,900.59	99,900.59	210,088.10	530,035.66	680,079.64	879,437.69	827,885.01
Other bonds							9,865.30
Total securities	$109,650.59	$109,650.59	$219,838.10	$ 539,785.66	$ 689,829.64	$ 889,187.69	$ 847,500.31
REAL ESTATE AND EQUIPMENT							
Bank premises	$ 56,701.42	$ 56,701.42	$ 56,701.42	$ 81,353.45	$ 82,322.28	$ 82,782.08	$ 97,073.63
Furniture, fixtures, and equipment	8,433.77	8,433.77	8,441.90	26,210.29	41,316.88	44,953.68	49,575.38
Total real estate	$ 65,135.19	$ 65,135.19	$ 65,143.32	$ 107,563.74	$ 123,639.16	$ 127,735.76	$ 146,649.01
Total earning resources	$191,525.93	$191,525.93	$301,721.57	$ 727,312.78	$1,209,296.06	$1,759,185.11	$2,345,631.22
CASH AND DUE FROM BANKS							
Cash	$ 44,117.99	$ 48,517.78	$ 52,048.67	$ 33,520.22	$ 25,098.14	$ 52,264.78	$ 66,315.20
Federal Reserve Bank reserve account	10,018.75	10,491.08	10,737.29	59,728.69	101,210.04	131,556.92	204,971.25
Due from other banks	197,208.69	338,902.12	330,924.04	205,155.41	102,793.89	105,170.20	170,583.18
Total cash	$251,345.43	$397,910.98	$393,710.00	$ 298,404.32	$ 229,102.07	$ 288,991.90	$ 441,869.63
Deferred charges	10,291.31	10,291.31	10,292.31	13,793.24	5,710.76	7,192.36	3,357.35
Accruals			3.15	589.65	5,215.80	4,935.38	9,433.91
Losses	3,435.66	3,366.91	3,564.70	6,383.30	8,090.71	7,307.47	
	$456,598.33	$603,095.13	$709,291.73	$1,046,483.29	$1,457,415.40	$2,067,612.22	$2,800,292.11

Exhibit 3 (Continued)

Liabilities	*1/5/55*	*1/6/55*	*1/10/55*	*1/31/55*	*3/31/55*	*6/30/55*	*12/30/55*
DEMAND DEPOSITS							
Commercial deposits	$ 48,688.30	$ 82,913.54	$149,033.80	$ 332,849.68	$ 598,436.21	$ 770,131.06	$1,053,671.47
Incomplete B/L					800.00		140.00
I.C.L. dealer reserves				69.76	2,372.78	4,917.48	5,176.43
Total demand deposits	$ 48,688.30	$ 82,913.54	$149,033.80	$ 332,919.44	$ 601,608.99	$ 775,048.54	$1,058,987.90
DUE TO BANKS							
Money orders	60.00	227.96	291.96	120.32	644.56	2,216.18	3,782.17
Cashiers checks	20,790.15	20,790.15	30,995.28	25,721.84	11,420.50	21,820.77	31,387.95
Total due to banks	$ 20,850.15	$ 21,018.11	$ 31,287.24	$ 25,842.16	$ 12,065.06	$ 24,036.95	$ 35,170.12
SAVINGS AND TIME DEPOSIT							
Term savings deposit	$ 28,002.88	$ 37,800.36	$ 63,904.27	$ 208,134.20	$ 318,738.92	$ 425,773.21	$ 902,617.27
Christmas savings deposit	137.00	163.00	286.00	848.00	1,415.50	2,126.00	1,790.00
Time deposit open account				7,000.00	7,000.00	7,000.00	7,063.09
Loan trust fund				176.48	221.28	258.82	592.69
Total savings and time deposits	$ 28,139.88	$ 37,963.36	$ 64,190.27	$ 216,158.68	$ 327,375.70	$ 435,158.03	$ 912,063.05
Total public deposits	1,420.00	103,700.12	107,280.42	112,753.06	113,359.80	379,420.69	373,132.57
Gross deposits	$ 99,098.33	$245,595.13	$351,791.73	$ 687,673.34	$1,054,409.55	$1,613,664.21	$2,379,353.64
OTHER LIABILITIES							
Deposits				$ 307.91	$ 844.37	$ 2,735.89	$ 7,879.97
Unearned disc. I.C. loans				867.04	3,335.75	8,414.71	21,749.78
Reserve for taxes, insurance				135.00	825.73	2,250.21	5,277.32
Loan commitments					40,500.00	83,047.20	28,109.09
Total other liabilities				$ 1,309.95	$ 45,505.85	$ 96,448.01	$ 63,016.16
TOTAL LIABILITIES	$ 99,098.33	$245,595.13	$351.791.73	$ 688,983.29	$1,099,915.40	$1,710,112.22	$2,442,369.80
CAPITAL, SURPLUS							
Capital stock – common	$195,000.00	$195,000.00	$195,000.00	$ 195,000.00	$ 195,000.00	$ 195,000.00	$ 195,000.00
Surplus	130,000.00	130,000.00	130,000.00	130,000.00	130,000.00	130,000.00	130,000.00
Undivided profits	32,500.00	32,500.00	32,500.00	32,500.00	32,500.00	32,500.00	32,922.31
Total capital	$357,500.00	$357,500.00	$357,500.00	$ 357,500.00	$ 357,500.00	$ 357,500.00	$ 357,922.31
Total liabilities and capital	$456,598.33	$603,095.13	$709,291.73	$1,046,483.29	$1,457,415.40	$2,067,612.22	$2,800,292.11

Bank Operating Policies 5

THE BANK'S LIQUIDITY POLICY

Grand Canyon National Bank

"Do you think our bank's financial position has become too liquid?" asked one of the Grand Canyon National Bank's directors during the regular monthly board meeting in June 1960. The question, which was addressed to Mr. Nicholas Boyd, the bank's president and founder, had arisen from a discussion among the directors concerning recent competitive developments in commercial banking in Arizona and particularly in Phoenix, where Grand Canyon National Bank was located. Since competition for good quality loans was becoming keener, one of the directors suggested that the bank's income could best be maintained through increasing its investments in short-term United States government securities. After a brief discussion of the current liquidity position, Mr. Boyd agreed that the bank's present cash reserves of approximately $4,300,000 were probably a little high. He agreed, therefore, to consider the suggestion to increase the size of the short-term investment portfolio.

The Grand Canyon National Bank was founded by Mr. Boyd in 1925; it was one of the oldest surviving independent unit banks in Arizona. Mr. Boyd and members of his family owned two thirds of the bank's stock; the remaining shares were held by approximately 75 stockholders, including several of the bank's employees. The personnel of Grand Canyon National was comprised of three officers and twelve clerical employees. The officers included: Mr. Boyd, president; Mr. Henry Sander, 71, vice-president and cashier; and Mr. Paul Kittredge, 35, vice-president. Five members of the staff, including Mr. Boyd and Mr. Sander, had served with the bank for over 30 years; there was no mandatory retirement age for employees. The staff's average length of service was approximately 20 years.

Grand Canyon National was located in downtown Phoenix, a few blocks from the city's commercial center. The bank had occupied the same building since its establishment in 1925. Because of its central downtown location, parking had become a difficult problem. It was often hard for customers to find a parking place within convenient walking distance of the bank. As a result, a substantial portion of Grand Canyon National's customers handled their routine banking business by mail. Mr. Boyd estimated that from 40–50 percent of the bank's total transaction volume was done by mail. This proved particularly economical from the bank's point of view because the clerical staff could be kept to a minimum and the processing of mail could be handled during the day at times most suitable to bank personnel.

Nicholas Boyd, the founder and president, was 70 years old and had spent his entire professional career in the field of commercial banking. Mr. Boyd was fundamentally conservative in his management of the bank and in the judgment and financial advice he gave to his customers. He had consistently applied conservative loan and investment policies in directing the bank's affairs, and as a result the Grand Canyon National had developed a well-deserved reputation within the business community as a sound and highly respected financial institution.

One aspect of banking which Mr. Boyd believed particularly important was a close personal association between a banker and his customers. Mr. Boyd took particular pride in the fact that he was well acquainted with a substantial number of his depositors and therefore he was in a good position to judge their financial requirements and credit worthiness. The highly personal and friendly service which his bank could provide was, in Mr. Boyd's judgment, one of its principal assets. He was determined that this characteristic of Grand Canyon National should be preserved regardless of what course the growth and development of the bank should take in future years.

Investment Policies

Mr. Boyd had developed a number of basic operating policies to guide the Grand Canyon National Bank's investment program. The most fundamental policy was that all bank investments should mature in ten years or less, and that a substantial majority of them should mature in five years or less. In recent years the bank's total resources were generally divided as follows:

	Percent
Cash and equivalent	23
Investments (federal, state, and municipal bonds)	54
Loans	23

Exhibit 1 contains the bank's statements of condition for the years 1955–1959.

Exhibit 1

GRAND CANYON NATIONAL BANK

Statements of Condition
December 31, 1955–1959
(dollar figures in thousands)

Resources	*1955*	*1956*	*1957*	*1958*	*1959*
Loans and discounts	$ 2,441	$ 2,915	$ 3,764	$ 3,674	$ 3,838
U.S. securities	7,753	7,505	6,954	7,726	7,348
Other securities	913	1,014	1,367	1,513	1,448
Fixed assets	81	77	73	69	67
Cash and due from banks	3,317	3,204	3,575	3,784	4,205
Total	$14,505	$14,715	$15,733	$16,766	$16,906
Liabilities					
Capital	$ 193	$ 193	$ 193	$ 193	$ 193
Surplus	346	347	385	385	423
Undivided profits	95	152	143	192	199
Deposits	13,871	14,023	15,012	15,996	16,091
Total	$14,505	$14,715	$15,733	$16,766	$16,906

It had been Mr. Boyd's custom to restrict the maturities of all United States government bonds in the bank's portfolio to five years or less. Approximately one third of the bank's U.S. government bonds matured in two years or less, while the remaining two thirds usually matured in two to five years. In addition to these U.S. government securities, it had been Mr. Boyd's practice to hold approximately $250,000 in U.S. treasury 91-day bills in order to meet any unusual or unanticipated liquidity demands. The bank also invested from time to time in state and municipal bonds; maturities in these obligations were limited to 6–8 years. Exhibit 2 presents a summary of Grand Canyon National's investment portfolio as of June 30, 1960.

Mr. Boyd was proud of the fact that his banking philosophy and policies had attracted a very loyal and stable group of customers. There had been very little turnover in past years among the bank's accounts. In 1960, Grand Canyon National had approximately 5400 customers, divided about equally in both number and deposit volume between savings and commercial accounts. The bank included among its commercial customers many of the oldest and best established business enterprises in Phoenix.

Because of the diversified character of Grand Canyon National's customers, the bank's deposits showed only moderate seasonal or cyclical

Exhibit 2

GRAND CANYON NATIONAL BANK

Investment Portfolio—June 30, 1960
Interest Rates, Maturity, and Principal Amount

U.S. TREASURY NOTES			
4 3/4%	August 1960	$ 744,000	
4%	February 1962	205,000	
4%	May 1962	104,000	
2 5/8%	February 1963	111,000	
4%	May 1963	164,000	
4 7/8%	November 1963	57,000	
3 3/4%	May 1964	1,702,000	
5%	August 1964	28,000	
4 5/8%	May 1965	162,000	$3,277,000
FEDERAL, STATE, AND MUNICIPAL BONDS			
2 1/8%	November 1960	$1,694,000	
2 3/4%	September 1961	300,000	
2 1/2%	November 1961	62,000	
2 1/2%	August 1963	885,000	
3%	February 1964	520,000	
2 5/8%	February 1965	385,000	3,846,000
Total			$7,123,000

movement. There was only a slight seasonal variation throughout the year, and there were seldom any sizable deposit fluctuations from month to month. The maximum annual high to low changes in deposits in recent years had been approximately 20 percent, and Mr. Boyd normally anticipated a fluctuation of no more than 15 percent. The bank had only some half dozen extremely large accounts (with deposits generally ranging from $100,000 to $500,000); hence there was no serious threat of substantial deposit volatility due to unanticipated fund movements in large accounts. The high proportion of deposits represented by savings accounts also added substantially to the bank's stability and to its comparatively low deposit volatility. Finally, the diversified economic character of Arizona and of the Phoenix area had proved favorable insofar as material changes in deposits were concerned. Population growth in recent years had stimulated business and industry throughout the state, thereby helping to dampen the severity of recent post-World War II recessions.

Mr. Boyd's liquidity and investment policies, combined with moderate deposit volatility, had enabled the bank to enjoy a traditionally strong financial position. In its thirty-five-year history, Grand Canyon

National had never found it necessary to borrow from the Federal Reserve Bank to meet its required reserves or any sudden liquidity demands.

Loan Policy

Mr. Boyd's basic philosophy was to attempt to differentiate his bank in terms of customer service and "personality," and, insofar as possible, to avoid direct competition with the large and very rapidly expanding statewide branch banks. Mr. Boyd preferred to avoid or to minimize many of the newly developed "retail" or "department store" banking services such as credit cards and extensive emphasis on consumer installment loans.

In general, Grand Canyon National insisted on higher credit standards than other Phoenix banks in approving commercial loans. As a result of these higher standards, however, the bank was able to offer many of its better customers lower interest rates than those normally available at competing financial institutions. The higher credit standing of Grand Canyon National's customers and the over-all quality of its loan portfolio were indicated by the bank's record of loan charge-offs: only $150 in loans had been written off as noncollectible in the past five years.

The great majority of Grand Canyon National's commercial loans were single payment, secured loans, written on a six-month or a one-year basis. The bank rarely granted term loans; Mr. Boyd generally preferred to restrict loan maturities to one year or less so that reasonably frequent credit reviews could be made on individual accounts.

As a matter of bank policy, Mr. Boyd avoided loan participations. He desired to service an individual customer's entire credit requirement rather than sharing the banking responsibility with another financial institution. For similar reasons, Mr. Boyd also avoided any participation loans with the Small Business Administration. Occasionally, Grand Canyon National's legal lending limit of $61,500 had restricted the bank's ability to meet the total credit requirements of a few large accounts. Under these circumstances, Mr. Boyd referred the customer to larger banks in Phoenix. Mr. Boyd planned to increase the bank's capital from time to time in the future in order to minimize the importance of the legal lending limit in servicing his customers' credit needs. He expected to raise the bank's limit to $75,000 within the next few years. These new capital funds would be provided through the retention of earnings. In recent years the bank had paid approximately one third of its earnings in cash dividends to stockholders. Mr. Boyd expected to continue this dividend policy during the next few years.

There were a few types of commercial loans which Grand Canyon National either did not grant at all or which it did not particularly encourage. For example, it was the bank's policy to avoid granting loans to automobile dealers to finance inventory and sales. The bank also did not solicit loans from enterprises catering primarily to tourists, such as motels and resorts, unless the borrower was strong and well established.

Mr. Boyd had also decided not to emphasize consumer loans, preferring to leave active promotion of this business to the several competitive state-wide branch banks. He reasoned that the Grand Canyon National could better succeed through attempting to distinguish itself from chain banking rather than competing directly with it. As a result, Grand Canyon National had emphasized its personality as a businessman's bank, stressing customer service and reliability. The bank did make some consumer loans, however, to established customers whose credit standing was adequate. To customers who could demonstrate their credit worthiness, the bank offered very attractive interest rates. For example, it granted 5 percent automobile loans provided that the terms of sale were one-third down and twenty-four months to pay. The bank also made a few home improvement loans and single payment personal loans.

On real estate loans, the Grand Canyon National granted its financing on conventional terms. The bank did not make FHA loans. Real estate loan maturities were limited to ten years, and the bank would loan up to 60 percent of its own appraisal of the property value. Mr. Boyd did not use the selling price or other independent valuations in reaching his decisions on real estate loan applications. These lending policies had given the bank an enviable record of success. Grand Canyon National had never been obliged to foreclose on a real estate loan in its entire thirty-five-year history, and Mr. Boyd was proud of the financial service and advice the bank had provided to its real estate customers.

Although Grand Canyon National could legally invest up to 60 percent of its time deposits ($8,100,000 in 1960) in real estate loans, the bank had only accepted approximately $1.5 million of these loans as of June 1960. The total loan portfolio in recent years had been generally divided as follows:

Real estate loans to businesses and individuals	$1.5mm
Automobile loans to individuals	0.4mm
Secured and unsecured commercial loans	1.2mm
Secured loans to individuals	0.7mm
	$3.8mm

In determining his over-all loan policy, and the extent to which Grand Canyon National was "loaned up," one important factor which Mr. Boyd had to consider was the bank's capital structure. While the ratio of capital to total liabilities was somewhat on the low side, the ratio of capital to riskless assets was quite high. Mr. Boyd believed that

Exhibit 3a

GRAND CANYON NATIONAL BANK

Average Operating Ratios of Member Banks
in the Twelfth District—1959*

Arizona,† Idaho, Nevada, and Utah Banks with Total Deposits
(thousands of dollars)

	Twelfth District†	*Under $2,000*	*$2,000 to $5,000*	*$5,000 to $15,000*	*$15,000 to $50,000*	*$50,000 and over*
Number of banks	161	3	11	15	5	11
SUMMARY RATIOS						
Percentage of total capital accounts						
1. Net current earnings before income taxes	19.4%	19.4%	16.3%	22.2%	26.8%	25.8%
2. Profits before income taxes	14.3	16.6	13.3	19.2	17.7	14.2
3. Net profits	9.1	12.8	9.8	13.0	10.5	8.6
4. Cash dividends declared	3.5	3.3	2.3	5.4	3.1	5.7
Percentage of total assets						
5. Total earnings	4.67	5.23	4.53	4.49	4.94	4.69
6. Net current earnings before income taxes	1.33	1.88	1.34	1.42	1.61	1.61
7. Net profits	0.64	1.30	0.82	0.81	0.63	0.54
SOURCES AND DISPOSITION OF EARNINGS						
Percentage of total earnings						
8. Interest on United States government securities	19.8	14.8	21.9	22.5	18.9	15.3
9. Interest and dividends on other securities	5.0	3.4	2.8	4.3	3.6	4.4
10. Earnings on loans	60.2	71.0	65.2	63.0	62.1	66.1
11. Service charges on deposit accounts	8.7	8.1	6.7	6.9	7.2	7.1
12. All other earnings	6.3	2.7	3.4	3.3	8.2	7.1
13. Total earnings	100.0%	100.0%	100.0%	100.0%	100.0%	100.0%
14. Salaries and wages	29.0	28.7	26.2	25.0	27.5	26.5
15. Interest on time deposits	22.3	18.0	26.4	25.7	19.3	20.1
16. All other expenses	19.9	17.5	17.6	17.8	20.9	19.0

17. Total expenses	71.2%	64.2%	70.2%	68.5%	67.7%	65.6%
18. Net current earnings before income taxes	28.8	35.8	29.8	31.5	32.3	34.4
19. Net recoveries and profits (or losses –)‡	–5.7	0.2	–4.9	–3.9	–9.7	–15.9
20. Net increase – (or decrease) in valuation reserves§	–1.3	–4.8	0.0	–0.6	–0.7	0.7
21. Taxes on net income	7.6	6.6	6.6	8.9	8.6	7.7
22. Net profits	14.2	24.6	18.3	18.1	13.3	11.5
RATES OF RETURN ON SECURITIES AND LOANS						
Return on securities						
23. Interest on United States government securities	2.86	3.60	3.01	2.83	2.85	2.79
24. Interest and dividends on other securities	2.94	3.63	3.84	3.08	3.25	2.71
25. Net recoveries and profits (or losses –) on total securities‖	–0.64	0.00	–0.38	–0.43	–1.31	–2.30
Return on loans						
26. Earnings on loans	6.78	7.20	6.82	7.07	7.18	6.44
27. Net recoveries (or losses –) on loans‖	–0.10	0.04	–0.19	–0.06	–0.07	–0.02
DISTRIBUTION OF ASSETS						
Percentage of total assets						
28. United States government securities	30.8	22.3	32.1	33.7	31.7	25.4
29. Other securities	8.0	4.2	4.2	6.9	5.7	7.5
30. Loans	41.7	51.6	43.4	40.4	42.9	48.2
31. Cash assets	17.9	21.0	19.8	18.0	17.8	16.9
32. Real estate assets	1.4	0.9	0.5	0.9	1.8	1.7
Capital and deposit ratios – in percentages						
33. Capital accounts to total assets	7.1	9.9	8.2	6.7	6.2	6.4
34. Capital accounts to total assets less United States government securities and cash assets	14.6	17.3	17.4	14.2	12.3	11.2
35. Capital accounts to total deposits	7.8	11.1	9.0	7.2	6.7	7.0
36. Time deposits to total deposits	42.5	36.3	47.0	45.8	40.9	38.0
37. Interest on time deposits to time deposits	2.58	2.85	2.77	2.65	2.57	2.66

*Adapted from *Operating Ratios of Member Banks Twelfth Federal Reserve District for the Year* 1959, published by the Federal Reserve Bank of San Francisco, February 29, 1960.
†Average ratios for Arizona member banks are not shown separately because they are not comparable with those for other District states or the prior year due to a change in accounting procedures. Twelfth District Arizona member banks only are included in combined totals.
‡Net recoveries or losses on loans, securities, and other assets excluding changes in valuation reserves on loans and securities.
§On loans and securities.
‖Net recoveries or losses excluding changes in valuation reserves.

Exhibit 3b

GRAND CANYON NATIONAL BANK

	Time Deposits As Percentage of Total Deposits			*Loans As Percentage of Total Assets*				
	Under 25%	*25% to 50%*	*50% and over*	*Under 20%*	*20% to 30%*	*30% to 40%*	*40% to 50%*	*50% and over*
Number of banks	6	120	35	4	16	38	75	28
SUMMARY RATIOS								
Percentage of total capital accounts								
1. Net current earnings before income taxes	14.9%	20.2%	17.6%	10.3%	15.1%	20.2%	20.0%	20.5%
2. Profits before income taxes	13.1	14.7	13.3	9.8	13.5	16.0	13.9	14.0
3. Net profits	8.7	9.3	8.3	7.5	9.6	10.6	8.5	8.3
4. Cash dividends declared	2.9	3.4	3.9	3.4	2.7	2.8	3.8	4.1
Percentage of total assets								
5. Total earnings	3.61	4.75	4.58	3.42	3.72	4.57	4.82	5.11
6. Net current earnings before income taxes	1.10	1.39	1.17	0.69	1.07	1.35	1.36	1.49
7. Net profits	0.64	0.67	0.56	0.51	0.70	0.72	0.61	0.62
SOURCES AND DISPOSITION OF EARNINGS								
Percentage of total earnings								
8. Interest on United States government securities	26.6	19.4	20.0	38.1	36.1	22.3	16.9	11.9
9. Interest and dividends on other securities	8.3	4.8	5.2	11.8	6.4	6.1	4.3	3.6
10. Earnings on loans	48.4	59.8	63.6	26.9	44.4	55.0	64.2	70.3
11. Service charges on deposit accounts	11.4	9.2	6.5	11.6	6.3	10.6	8.7	6.9
12. All other earnings	5.3	6.8	4.7	11.6	6.8	6.0	5.9	7.3
13. Total earnings	100.0%	100.0%	100.0%	100.0%	100.0%	100.0%	100.0%	100.0%
14. Salaries and wages	37.4	29.9	24.9	38.5	26.9	29.4	29.1	28.5
15. Interest on time deposits	10.6	19.9	32.4	17.4	27.4	21.9	22.2	20.9
16. All other expenses	22.2	20.5	17.2	23.5	17.3	19.2	20.2	20.8

17. Total expenses	70.2%	70.3%	74.5%	79.4%	71.6%	70.5%	71.5%	70.2%
18. Net current earnings before income taxes	29.8	29.7	25.5	20.6	28.4	29.5	28.5	29.8
19. Net recoveries and profits (or losses –)*	−2.6	−6.5	−3.7	−0.6	−3.3	−4.6	−6.8	−6.7
20. Net increase – (or decrease) in valuation reserves†	−0.7	−1.1	−2.2	−0.4	0.2	−1.5	−1.3	−2.2
21. Taxes on net income	8.7	7.7	7.2	4.7	6.7	7.8	7.4	8.4
22. Net profits	17.8	14.4	12.4	14.9	18.6	15.6	13.0	12.5
RATES OF RETURN ON SECURITIES AND LOANS								
Return on securities								
23. Interest on United States government securities	2.65	2.88	2.84	2.71	2.87	2.90	2.83	2.91
24. Interest and dividends on other securities	2.67	3.00	2.80	3.15	2.65	2.83	2.93	3.28
25. Net recoveries and profits (or losses –) on total securities‡	−0.18	−0.72	−0.48	−0.04	−0.22	−0.41	−0.71	−1.12
Return on loans								
26. Earnings on loans	6.36	6.83	6.69	6.51	6.43	6.95	6.85	6.62
27. Net recoveries (or losses –) on loans‡	−0.01	−0.12	−0.03	−0.03	−0.06	−0.09	−0.13	−0.04
DISTRIBUTION OF ASSETS								
Percentage of total assets								
28. United States government securities	35.4	30.5	30.7	46.7	46.3	34.5	28.4	20.7
29. Other securities	10.4	7.7	8.8	14.4	9.0	9.9	7.3	5.9
30. Loans	28.5	41.7	43.7	13.6	25.4	35.9	45.0	53.8
31. Cash assets	24.6	18.3	15.5	23.9	18.2	18.3	17.4	17.6
32. Real estate assets	1.1	1.5	1.1	1.2	1.0	1.3	1.5	1.5
Capital and deposit ratios – in percentages								
33. Capital accounts to total assets	7.4	7.2	6.8	6.8	7.4	7.0	7.1	7.5
34. Capital accounts to total assets less United States government securities and cash assets	19.3	14.8	13.0	28.8	21.0	14.9	13.1	12.3
35. Capital accounts to total deposits	8.0	7.9	7.4	7.3	8.0	7.6	7.8	8.3
36. Time deposits to total deposits	17.1	39.1	58.5	28.9	41.4	41.7	43.6	43.2
37. Interest on time deposits to time deposits	2.61	2.55	2.68	2.49	2.53	2.51	2.60	2.66

NOTE: Balance sheet figures used as a basis for the ratios are averages of amounts reported for December 31, 1958, and June 10 and October 6, 1959.
*Net recoveries or losses on loans, securities, and other assets excluding changes in valuation reserves on loans and securities.
†On loans and securities. ‡Net recoveries or losses excluding changes in valuation reserves.

the bank's capital structure was one of the important factors determining the appropriate maximum size of Grand Canyon National's loan portfolio.

Competition

In 1959, the three largest chain banks operated a total of forty-six branches in the Phoenix area, as compared with nineteen branches in 1955. As a result of this substantial increase in commercial banking facilities, the competition for new loans and deposits had become very keen.

The large chain banks heavily advertised a wide variety of services (such as automobile loans, trust services, safe deposit boxes, and "drive-in" windows) through the media of direct mail, newspaper, radio, and television. Much of this promotional material stressed specific bank services to consumers, interest rates on loans, as well as convenience to the customer in banking with branch offices located outside of the downtown business district.

In its advertising, Grand Canyon National emphasized personal service and individual attention to customers as well as low interest rates on commercial and personal loans. The bank's appeal was primarily institutional in character; individual bank services or specific interest rates were not featured in advertisements. Grand Canyon National had traditionally relied on newspaper advertising supplemented by occasional spot announcements on radio. No advertising on television had been undertaken.

In addition to the use of public advertising to secure new business, some of the newly established branch banks were, in Mr. Boyd's opinion, lowering their basic standards of credit and accepting marginal commercial and personal loans in order to attract new customers and expand the volume of business. Much of this pressure to accept questionable loan applications had resulted from the very substantial increase in banking competition in Phoenix in recent years.

Grand Canyon National Bank had not aggressively sought any substantial volume of small personal deposit accounts. For example, it was the bank's policy to require a minimum balance of approximately $250 in personal checking accounts. In this manner, Mr. Boyd felt that members of the local business community would have much higher confidence in personal checks drawn on the Grand Canyon National Bank. He believed that this greater public confidence redounded to the benefit of both the bank and its deposit customers. In Mr. Boyd's judgment, small-deposit accounts were costly to administer and were not likely to prove most profitable to the bank. As a result, he preferred to leave such accounts to the large branch bank organizations.

Another beneficial aspect of concentrating on somewhat larger personal and commercial accounts was that the bank's service charges could be kept low. Grand Canyon National's administrative and clerical expenses were comparatively modest, and total costs had remained fairly steady for the past few years. This favorable cost experience permitted the bank to offer to its customers the lowest charges on routine bank services of any competing financial institution in Phoenix.

There were several reasons why Mr. Boyd believed his bank could perform more effective over-all banking services for its customers through the operation of a single downtown office. First, and perhaps most important, was Mr. Boyd's strong feeling about the importance of personal and individual contacts with customers. The addition of branches and the large subsequent expansion in the total number of accounts would lessen the closeness between the bank and its depositors, thereby altering one of the characteristics which had contributed so much to the bank's success.

In addition, there were several administrative objections to a change from unit to branch operations. These included: the uncertain profit outlook for new branches in view of very strong competition; the high marginal tax rates, both corporate and personal which would result if branches did prove profitable; the lack of officers and trained clerical staff to manage new branches; the increase in administrative responsibility at the main office, thereby adding to total operating costs; and finally, the loss of operating flexibility because of the need for branch personnel to refer to the head office for some decisions on credit and loan policy. In short, Mr. Boyd felt he could continue to serve his customers more efficiently at a single main office downtown where speed of decision making and personal service could be maximized while administrative burden and operating costs could be minimized. In this manner, Mr. Boyd believed that the bank could retain a distinctive character and still participate in its fair share of the normal economic and commercial growth in the Phoenix area.

THE BANK'S LOAN POLICY

Bank of E. Chase

Mr. Willard Chipman was appointed president of the Bank of E. Chase in September 1960, upon the death of his uncle, Mr. Solomon Chase. Shortly after assuming his new responsibilities, Mr. Chipman began considering changes in the bank's policies with respect to commercial lending and the proportion of total resources held in cash. In Mr. Chipman's opinion, the bank's policies on these matters had become unduly conservative in recent years. He planned, therefore, to begin modifying liquidity and loan policies in order to improve the Bank of E. Chase's operating income and its competitive position in the community. Mr. Chipman had not decided, however, to what extent these policies should be changed or how the changes could be most effectively administered.

The Bank of E. Chase, a unit bank located in Los Padres, California, was the outgrowth of a private brokerage and banking business established by Mr. Elihu Chase in 1882. Mr. Chase bought and sold agricultural produce of various kinds. In the mid-1880s, his customers began drawing checks and drafts on their accounts at Chase's, and in this manner the banking portion of the brokerage business evolved. In 1902 Mr. Chase established a new office in Los Padres' growing business district; in 1905 the bank was incorporated as the "Bank of E. Chase," continuing under Elihu Chase's management until his death in 1922. At that time the founder's son, Mr. Solomon Chase, was elected president. He had been employed at the bank since his graduation from Stanford University in 1911. Solomon Chase died in 1960 and his nephew, Willard Chipman, was appointed president. Mr. Chipman had served with the bank since 1940.

Exhibit 1

BANK OF E. CHASE

Selected Statistics on
San Jacinto County and the City of Los Padres

Population and Economic Trends, San Jacinto County	*1940*	*1950*	*1953*	*1956*	*1958*
Population estimates	69,685	114,647	135,100	155,000	175,300
Personal income	$49,956	$183,655	$259,943	$314,559	
Per capita income	717	1,602		2,042	$ 2,151
Value of farm products	22,312	60,994	75,846	88,460	
Factory payrolls	1,670	7,290	9,558	26,367	
Taxable sales	26,146	99,664	134,733	169,069	

SOURCE: California State Chamber of Commerce, *Economic Survey Series* and *California Blue Book*, 1958.

Population Growth and Trends, City of Los Padres	*1940*	*1950*	*1953*	*1956*
Population	8,519	21,567	27,000	28,879
No. of occupied dwelling units	2,242	6,128	7,500	7,563

SOURCE: Industrial Plant Location Committee, California State Chamber of Commerce, *Standard Industrial Survey Summary Report*, August, 1958.

The city of Los Padres is located in San Jacinto County in Southern California. The region's economy is heavily dependent upon agriculture. (See Exhibit 1 for more detailed statistics on Los Padres and San Jacinto County.) The most important crops include: citrus fruits, particularly lemons and oranges; walnuts; lima beans and other vegetables; poultry, livestock, and dairy products. According to census figures, Los Padres is one of the most rapidly growing cities in the county. It serves as a central shipping point for farm produce and is also the site of a growing retail trade center. The principal industry in or near the city includes a very large sugar refinery, several frozen-food packing plants, a sizable tractor assembly plant, and an oil refinery. In addition, there is a moderate amount of mining and light manufacturing activity. Los Padres is essentially a "one-industry town," although the relative importance of agriculture has been gradually declining.

Liquidity Policy

Since the end of World War II, the Bank of E. Chase had kept a comparatively high proportion of its assets in liquid form. (See Exhibits 2 and 6.) Cash and equivalents during this time had generally averaged from 25 percent to 45 percent of total resources. It was Mr. Chase's policy to have enough cash on hand January 1 to meet all normal liquidity demands throughout the seasonal crop year. Because of the predominant importance of agriculture in the county, the bank generally anticipated heavy deposit withdrawals beginning early in the year, reaching a peak in midsummer shortly before the crops were harvested and sent to market. In late summer and fall, the bank's deposits and cash balances generally rose as farmers began receiving payments from canners and food processors. Peak liquidity usually occurred in December and January. The cash flow patterns attributable to farm customers had become somewhat less pronounced, however, because of the growth of industry and commerce which had developed in Los Padres after World War II (see Exhibit 5).

Since it had been Mr. Chase's practice to accumulate sufficient cash at the end of the year to meet all anticipated liquidity demands during the following season, the bank did not calculate a secondary reserve requirement, nor did it consider its investment portfolio as available for any but the most pressing financial emergencies. Insofar as investments in U. S. government, state, and municipal bonds were concerned, these would be held until maturity. He preferred not to sell portions of his investment portfolio in order to meet any liquidity demands resulting from deposit or loan fluctuations. These policies had been consistently applied in recent years, and all bonds had been held until maturity (see Exhibit 5).

There were no other special factors affecting the Bank of E. Chase's deposit volatility other than those resulting from the seasonal agricultural cycle described above. The bank had very few extremely large accounts; hence little deposit fluctuation resulted from major fund transfers. Because of the Bank of E. Chase's long-standing and sound banking record in Los Padres, it had attracted an exceptionally loyal and stable group of customers. There was relatively little turnover among the bank's accounts and virtually none among long-established customers. Furthermore, the postwar economic recessions of 1948–1949 and 1953–1954 had comparatively mild effects in San Jacinto County. All these factors helped to moderate the Bank of E. Chase's over-all deposit volatility.

Mr. Chipman believed that some aspects of the bank's liquidity policies had become unduly conservative, although he had not yet decided how or to what extent the existing policies should be altered. Exhibits 2 to 6 contain statements of condition covering the years 1955–1960, a summary of the bank's loan and investment portfolios as of August 8, 1960, and a summary of monthly fluctuations in cash, loans, and other principal bank assets.

Exhibit 2

BANK OF E. CHASE

Statements of Condition
December 31, 1955–1959, and August 8, 1960
(dollar figures in thousands)

Resources	*1955*	*1956*	*1957*	*1958*	*1959*	*1960*
Loans and discounts	$ 2,358	$ 3,077	$ 3,343	$ 3,956	$ 4,243	$ 4,607
Securities	5,898	5,256	5,329	5,506	5,541	5,830
Fixed assets	105	110	114	120	119	131
Cash and in banks	4,412	4,633	6,318	4,780	5,674	3,966
Total	$12,773	$13,076	$15,104	$14,362	$15,577	$14,534
Liabilities						
Capital stock	$ 200	$ 200	$ 200	$ 200	$ 200	$ 200
Surplus	400	900	1,000	1,000	1,000	1,000
Undivided profits	782	334	308	277	290	398
Reserve for losses	35	.....	.....	10	24	.....
Reserve for taxes	.....	.....	.....	.....	37	.....
Deposits	11,356	11,642	13,596	12,875	14,026	12,936
Total	$12,773	$13,076	$15,104	$14,362	$15,577	$14,534

Exhibit 3

BANK OF E. CHASE

Composition of the Loan Portfolio
August 8, 1960
(dollar figures in thousands)

Commercial and industrial	$ 662
Other loans to farmers	1,161
Real estate – secured by farm land	1,498
Real estate – residential	350
Real estate – other than farm and residence	622
Personal – installment	40
Personal – single payment	130
All other loans, including overdrafts	144
Total	$4,607

Exhibit 4

BANK OF E. CHASE

Composition of the Bond Portfolio
August 8, 1960
(dollar figures in thousands)

Maturities	*U.S. Governments*	*Municipals**	*Corporate*
Less than 5 years	$1,531†	$1,087	. . .
5 to 10 years	1,357	993	. . .
10 to 20 years	471	371	$20
Totals	$3,359	$2,451	$20

*There were approximately 185 municipal bond ledger accounts with par values of from $1,000 to $100,000.

†U.S. Government Bonds:

Maturing in less than one year	$ 581
Maturing in one to two years	774
Maturing in two to five years	176
	$1,531

Loan Organization and Policy

The commercial lending function at the Bank of E. Chase always had been flexibly and informally organized. It had never been thought necessary to prepare a written statement of the bank's policy with respect to the organization of commercial lending or the granting of individual credits. At the time of Mr. Chase's death in 1960, there were three officers, in addition to the president, who were responsible for granting loans. These three officers had served with the bank for forty-eight, twenty-eight, and

Exhibit 5

BANK OF E. CHASE

Trends of Principal Bank Assets

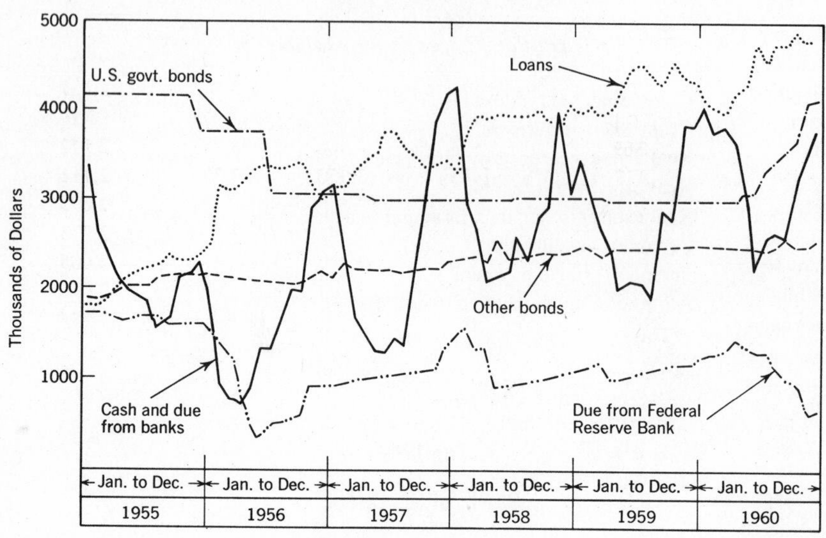

Exhibit 6

BANK OF E. CHASE

Mid-month Summary of Principal Bank Assets, 1955–1960
(dollar figures in thousands)

1955	*Cash and Due from Banks*	*Due from Federal Reserve Bank*	*Loans*	*U.S. Government Bonds*	*Other Bonds*	*Total Resources**
January	$3,373	$1,730	$1,808	$4,172	$1,903	$12,986
February	2,732	1,750	1,791	4,172	1,888	12,333
March	2,431	1,709	1,890	4,172	1,932	12,134
April	2,289	1,676	2,019	4,172	1.979	12,135
May	1,987	1,646	2,132	4,172	2,035	11,972
June	1,928	1,669	2,184	4,172	2,042	11,995
July	1,811	1,690	2,229	4,172	2,027	11,929
August	1,562	1,686	2,229	4,172	2,125	11,774
September	1,667	1,595	2,371	4,172	2,149	11.954
October	2,143	1,602	2,309	4,172	2,186	12,412
November	2,207	1,601	2,315	4,172	2,157	12,452
December	2,318	1,602	2,365	3,771	2,144	12,200

*Excluding bank premises and other miscellaneous fixed assets.

Exhibit continued.

Exhibit 6 (Continued)

1956	*Cash and Due from Banks*	*Due from Federal Reserve Bank*	*Loans*	*U.S. Government Bonds*	*Other Bonds*	*Total Resources*
January	$1,857	$1,666	$2,505	$3,771	$2,180	$11,979
February	935	1,388	3,164	3,771	2,137	11,395
March	795	1,304	3,102	3,771	2,137	11,109
April	728	917	3,156	3,771	2,119	10,691
May	869	526	3,308	3,771	2,112	10,586
June	1,357	485	3,355	3,371	2,111	10,679
July	1,352	506	3,359	3,102	2,095	10,414
August	1,640	522	3,343	3,102	2,073	10,680
September	2,046	574	3,396	3,065	2,065	11,146
October	1.986	603	3,422	3,065	2,055	11,131
November	2,952	929	3,152	3,065	2,134	12,232
December	3,122	925	3,033	3,065	2,207	12,352

1957	*Cash and Due from Banks*	*Due from Federal Reserve Bank*	*Loans*	*U.S. Government Bonds*	*Other Bonds*	*Total Resources*
January	$3,192	$ 951	$3,113	$3,065	$2,178	$12,499
February	2,456	972	3,171	3,065	2,289	11,953
March	1,722	989	3,340	3,065	2,222	11,338
April	1,526	1,017	3,433	3,065	2,243	11,284
May	1,329	1,027	3,509	3,013	2,243	11,121
June	1,298	1,046	3,773	3,013	2,232	11,362
July	1,473	1,066	3,771	3,013	2,212	11,535
August	1,387	1,077	3,578	3,013	2,219	11,474
September	2,361	1,084	3,511	3,013	2,240	12,209
October	3,021	1,104	3,376	3,013	2,257	12,771
November	3,930	1,127	3,410	3,013	2,265	13,745
December	4,230	1,380	3,441	3,013	2,326	14,390

1958	*Cash and Due from Banks*	*Due from Federal Reserve Bank*	*Loans*	*U.S. Government Bonds*	*Other Bonds*	*Total Resources*
January	$4,321	$1,523	$3,338	$3,013	$2,336	$14,531
February	2,970	1,558	3,744	3,013	2,394	13,679
March	2,694	1,372	3,949	3,013	2,404	13,432
April	2,099	1,340	3,933	3,013	2,332	12,717
May	2,149	927	3.973	3,013	2,585	12,647
June	2,192	955	3,980	3,013	2,380	12,520
July	2,606	971	3,976	3,062	2,358	12,973
August	2,367	988	3,955	3,062	2,412	12,784
October	2,977	1,059	3,921	3,062	2,433	13,452
September	2,864	1,025	4,039	3,062	2,436	13,426
November	4,009	1,052	3,822	3,062	2,439	14,384
December	3,113	1,086	4,068	3,062	2,458	13,787

Exhibit continued.

Exhibit 6 (Continued)

1959	*Cash and Due from Banks*	*Due from Federal Reserve Bank*	*Loans*	*U.S. Government Bonds*	*Other Bonds*	*Total Resources*
January	$3,475	$1,117	$4,012	$3,062	$2,491	$14,157
February	3,124	1,165	4,055	3,062	2,495	13,901
March	2,761	1,207	3,967	3,062	2,420	13,417
April	2,543	1,029	4,023	3,012	2,532	13,139
May	2,001	1,047	4,292	3,012	2,532	12,884
June	2,134	1,061	4,510	3,012	2,485	13,202
July	2,102	1,100	4,548	3,012	2,487	13,249
August	1,949	1,138	4,442	3,002	2,497	13,028
September	2,914	1,157	4,319	3,002	2,515	13,907
October	2,824	1,178	4,551	3,002	2,510	14,065
November	3,887	1,189	4,431	3,002	2,522	15,031
December	3,846	1,212	4,351	3,002	2,540	14,951

1960	*Cash and Due from Banks*	*Due from Federal Reserve Bank*	*Loans*	*U.S. Government Bonds*	*Other Bonds*	*Total Resources*
January	$4,107	$1,290	$4,139	$3,002	$2,528	$15,066
February	3,798	1,308	4,063	3,002	2,517	14,688
March	3,874	1,327	3,986	3,042	2,524	14,753
April	3,696	1,464	4,211	2,993	2,514	14,878
May	3,180	1,401	4,280	3,109	2,512	14,482
June	2,242	1,332	4,738	3,109	2,491	13,912
July	2,616	1,303	4,597	3,358	2,463	14,337
August	2,684	1,104	4,760	3,459	2,507	14,514
September	2,611	1,020	4,784	3,558	2,587	14,560
October	3,269	969	4,899	3,657	2,498	15,292
November	3,510	643	4,814	4,117	2,520	15,604
December	3,787	660	4,772	4,137	2,578	15,934

fifteen years, respectively. In 1960 the bank's total staff consisted of seven officers and twenty-five clerical employees.

Primary credit authority had remained under Mr. Chase's discretion. All important credit matters were referred by the other three lending officers to him for final decisions. There was no loan committee established to review jointly any difficult credit decisions; Mr. Chase relied on his own judgment on large and/or marginal loans, and he seldom discussed these decisions in detail with his other officers. No formal lending limits for officers had been agreed upon. As a result, the junior officers would decide when an individual credit application should be referred to Mr. Chase for a final decision. Thus, on some occasions, the officers would approve, without further consultation, credits up to $10,000 to established customers, while at other times they would refer credit applications for as little as $500 to the president.

Mr. Chase based his credit decisions primarily on his personal knowledge and long-standing associations and friendships with customers. He often did not rely importantly on financial statements or credit reports in his judgments on loan applications. He frequently did not require customers who were well known to him to submit any financial statements or proof of ability to repay when applying for loans. Customers were never required to fill out a loan application when they requested accommodation. Many loans granted were based almost entirely on the mutual confidence and close personal association which had developed between the bank and its customers over the years. The bank's files contained very little credit memoranda or credit "dictations" on individual loans or on any current developments with particular accounts.

Although the bank's lending procedures were informally organized, Mr. Chase's judgment had proved excellent. The bank's record of losses on loans had been very low; Mr. Chase had successfully demonstrated the importance of nonfinancial factors, particularly the moral factor, in granting credit. His long acquaintanceship with San Jacinto County and his ability to appraise character and business ability had been among the bank's most important intangible assets.

In recent years, the Bank of E. Chase had not aggressively sought new lending opportunities in order to increase the size of its loan portfolio. Mr. Chase had accepted the normal loan requests which came from established and credit-worthy customers, and, if such loans proved insufficient to utilize the bank's funds, he increased the size of his investment portfolio. There was no policy governing the over-all size or composition of the loan portfolio. In general, the bank's credit standards were high, and Mr. Chase's lending policies, which are summarized in outline form below, were firmly established, and exceptions to them were relatively few.

Summary of Lending Policies

I. General Rules: No loans were made
   - A. Unless the bank was fully satisfied as to the moral character of the borrower, no matter what extenuating circumstances were involved.
   - B. To persons who did not have an account with the bank or who were the borrowing customer of another bank.
   - C. For "capital" purposes (for example, term loans) except in cases of the borrower's superior ability to repay.
   - D. If the proceeds would be used outside the geographic area served by the bank.

E. Which were cosigned unless the cosigner came to the bank and was personally informed that, in event of default, the bank would expect immediate repayment from him.

II. Real Estate Loans

A. For Farm Property: Maximum of 50 percent of appraisal; maximum of ten years, seven years optimum, amortized on an annual basis.

B. Residential and Commercial: Maximum of ten years, 5–7 optimum; maximum loan, 50 percent of appraisal, 40 percent preferred; amortized monthly.

C. No FHA loans granted.

III. Commercial Loans

A. Collateral Loans

1. Loans on dry edible beans (which constituted the majority of the bank's collateral loans) were made to approved customers up to 75 percent of the current market value of the beans while deposited as collateral.
2. Listed securities loans, collateralized by listed securities, could not exceed the lowest price at which the individual stocks had sold in the past eighteen months. In most cases, such loans did not exceed 75 percent of the current market value of top-grade listed stocks; 60 percent for medium-grade listed stock; 50 percent or less on all other unlisted securities on which a quotation was easily obtainable.
3. No loans were granted secured by the assignment of accounts receivable.
4. No loans were granted secured by chattel mortgages on machinery and equipment, except farm loans.
5. No loans to appliance and equipment dealers secured by consumer purchase contracts.

B. Unsecured Loans

1. Loans to farmers were made where production expectations exceeded farm expense by a sufficient margin to justify credit, and where farming ability and customer integrity were well known.
2. Loans to business firms for inventory were made subject to liquidation upon the sale of that inventory; however, no commercial loans were made whose maturity would exceed one year.

IV. Personal Loans

1. Personal loans were made upon presentation of evidence of satisfactory financial strength. The bank did not, however, emphasize or encourage personal loans.

2. Installment loans for the purchase of consumer durables were only granted in exceptional circumstances.
3. No home improvement loans were made, as such. Although some were granted, they were not so classified.

The bank's loan portfolio as of August 8, 1960, is shown in Exhibit 3.

Shortly after his appointment as president, Mr. Chipman decided to draft a written statement outlining the bank's policies with respect to commercial lending, including loan organization, the approximate over-all size of the loan portfolio, and the kinds of loans which the Bank of E. Chase was prepared to grant. Mr. Chipman believed that this formal policy statement should serve as the starting point for the reorganization of the bank's lending program and the introduction of more progressive credit standards.

In addition to considering policy changes with respect to liquidity and commercial lending, Mr. Chipman was also concerned about other aspects of bank management which were important to his institution's competitive position in Los Padres and San Jacinto County. Banking competition was keen in the area, especially in Los Padres. Two of the largest branch banks in California maintained offices in the town.

In spite of this competition, however, the Bank of E. Chase had not undertaken any public advertising or vigorous promotion of bank services. Mr. Chipman thought, however, that an advertising and public relations program would have to be undertaken if the bank was to retain a position of leadership in the community's affairs. This was becoming particularly true as the city of Los Padres grew and new people moved into the area who were unfamiliar with the bank's origin and long association with the farmers and merchants of Los Padres.

Mr. Chipman was also anxious to begin expanding the bank's services to its deposit customers. For example, the bank did not have a trust department. It also did not offer its depositors a "banking by mail" program. This was an especially important factor in Mr. Chipman's opinion, since no branch offices had been established and customers therefore had to come into town in order to transact routine banking business. Mr. Chase had opposed the idea of establishing branch offices; however, Mr. Chipman believed that competitive developments in the county might force the bank to change its single-location policy.

One important aspect of any changes in operating policies concerned their impact upon the bank's stockholders. The descendants of Elihu Chase still owned the controlling interest in the bank; however, upon the death of Solomon Chase the distribution of shares among various members of the family had broadened. In future years, Mr. Chipman anticipated an even wider distribution of the shares. As the bank's stock came

Exhibit 7a

BANK OF E. CHASE

Average Operating Ratios of Member Banks in the Twelfth District—1959*
California Banks with Total Deposits
(thousands of dollars)

	Twelfth District	*Under $5,000*	*$5,000 to $15,000*	*$15,000 to $50,000*	*$50,000 to $275,000*	*$275,000 and over*
Number of banks	161	7	23	13	8	9
SOURCES AND DISPOSITION OF EARNINGS						
Percentage of total earnings						
1. Interest on United States government securities	19.8%	22.3%	18.3%	20.4%	14.1%	15.2%
2. Interest and dividends on other securities	5.0	4.6	4.2	6.4	5.9	3.8
3. Earnings on loans	60.2	58.3	58.1	54.4	66.3	66.5
4. Service charges on deposit accounts	8.7	9.7	11.9	7.9	7.3	6.6
5. All other earnings	6.3	5.1	7.5	10.9	6.4	7.9
6. Total earnings	100.0%	100.0%	100.0%	100.0%	100.0%	100.0%
7. Salaries and wages	29.0	29.7	31.0	28.2	26.5	27.2
8. Interest on time deposits	22.3	29.1	21.2	26.9	23.4	21.7
9. All other expenses	19.9	18.6	22.3	19.6	19.9	18.0
10. Total expenses	71.2%	77.4%	74.5%	74.7%	69.8%	66.9%
11. Net current earnings before income taxes	28.8	22.6	25.5	25.3	30.2	33.1
12. Net recoveries and profits (or losses—)†	−5.7	−2.5	−4.1	−6.3	−6.3	−8.9
13. Net increase—(or decrease) in valuation reserves‡	−1.3	−1.6	−1.6	−1.3	−2.0	−0.9
14. Taxes on net income	7.6	5.4	7.9	8.7	10.1	9.3
15. Net profits	14.2	13.1	11.9	9.0	11.8	14.0

Exhibit 7a (Continued)

	Twelfth District	*Under $5,000*	*$5,000 to $15,000*	*$15,000 to $50,000*	*$50,000 to $275,000*	*$275,000 and over*
RATES OF RETURN ON SECURITIES AND LOANS						
Return on securities						
16. Interest on United States government securities	2.86%	3.05%	2.91%	2.76%	2.83%	2.65%
17. Interest and dividends on other securities	2.94	2.61	3.15	2.89	2.75	2.66
Return on loans						
18. Earnings on loans	6.78	6.90	7.10	6.59	6.55	6.07
DISTRIBUTION OF ASSETS						
Percentage of total assets						
19. United States government securities	30.8	34.8	29.6	33.8	23.6	25.1
20. Other securities	8.0	8.1	6.9	9.4	9.8	6.4
21. Loans	41.7	40.1	42.0	39.2	48.0	48.2
22. Cash assets	17.9	14.9	19.3	16.0	16.4	18.6
23. Real estate assets	1.4	1.8	1.8	1.2	1.6	1.0
Capital and deposit ratios – in percentages						
24. Capital accounts to total assets	7.1	6.6	7.5	6.3	6.2	6.2
25. Capital accounts to total assets less United States government securities and cash assets	14.6	13.2	15.2	13.1	10.5	11.2
26. Capital accounts to total deposits	7.8	7.2	8.3	6.9	6.8	6.9
27. Time deposits to total deposits	42.5	52.8	42.1	50.9	44.3	39.5
28. Interest on time deposits to time deposits	2.58	2.69	2.65	2.56	2.70	2.66

*Based on "Operating Ratios of Member Banks Twelfth Federal Reserve District for the Year 1959," published on February 29, 1960, by the Federal Reserve Bank of San Francisco.
†Net recoveries or losses on loans, securities, and other assets excluding changes in valuation reserves on loans and securities.
‡On loans and securities.

Exhibit 7b

BANK OF E. CHASE

	Time deposits as percentage of total deposits			*Loans as percentage of total assets*				
	Under 25%	*25% to 50%*	*50% and over*	*Under 20%*	*20% to 30%*	*30% to 40%*	*40% to 50%*	*50% and over*
Number of banks	6	120	35	4	16	38	75	28
SUMMARY RATIOS								
Percentage of total capital accounts								
1. Net current earnings before income taxes	14.9%	20.2%	17.6%	10.3%	15.1%	20.2%	20.0%	20.5%
2. Profits before income taxes	13.1	14.7	13.3	9.8	13.5	16.0	13.9	14.0
3. Net profits	8.7	9.3	8.3	7.5	9.6	10.6	8.5	8.3
Percentage of total assets								
4. Total earnings	3.61	4.75	4.58	3.42	3.72	4.57	4.82	5.11
5. Net current earnings before income taxes	1.10	1.39	1.17	0.69	1.07	1.35	1.36	1.49
6. Net profits	0.64	0.67	0.56	0.51	0.70	0.72	0.61	0.62
SOURCES AND DISPOSITION OF EARNINGS								
Percentage of total earnings								
7. Interest on United States government securities	26.6	19.4	20.0	38.1	36.1	22.3	16.9	11.9
8. Interest and dividends on other securities	8.3	4.8	5.2	11.8	6.4	6.1	4.3	3.6
9. Earnings on loans	48.4	59.8	63.6	26.9	44.4	55.0	64.2	70.3
10. Service charges on deposit accounts	11.4	9.2	6.5	11.6	6.3	10.6	8.7	6.9
11. All other earnings	5.3	6.8	4.7	11.6	6.8	6.0	5.9	7.3
12. Total earnings	100.0%	100.0%	100.0%	100.0%	100.0%	100.0%	100.0%	100.0%
13. Salaries and wages	37.4	29.9	24.9	38.5	26.9	29.4	29.1	28.5
14. Interest on time deposits	10.6	19.9	32.4	17.4	27.4	21.9	22.2	20.9
15. All other expenses	22.2	20.5	17.2	23.5	17.3	19.2	20.2	20.8

Exhibit 7b (Continued)

	Time deposits as percentage of total deposits			*Loans as percentage of total assets*				
	Under 25%	*25% to 50%*	*50% and over*	*Under 20%*	*20% to 30%*	*30% to 40%*	*40% to 50%*	*50% and over*
16. Total expenses	70.2%	70.3%	74.5%	79.4%	71.6%	70.5%	71.5%	70.2%
17. Net current earnings before income taxes	29.8	29.7	25.5	20.6	28.4	29.5	28.5	29.8
18. Net recoveries and profits (or losses−)*	−2.6	−6.5	−3.7	−0.6	−3.3	−4.6	−6.8	−6.7
19. Net increase−(or decrease) in valuation reserves†	−0.7	−1.1	−2.2	−0.4	0.2	−1.5	−1.3	−2.2
20. Taxes on net income	8.7	7.7	7.2	4.7	6.7	7.8	7.4	8.4
21. Net profits	17.8	14.4	12.4	14.9	18.6	15.6	13.0	12.5
RATES OF RETURN ON SECURITIES AND LOANS								
Return on securities								
22. Interest on United States government securities	2.65	2.88	2.84	2.71	2.87	2.90	2.83	2.91
Return on loans								
24. Earnings on loans	6.36	6.83	6.69	6.51	6.43	6.95	6.85	6.62
DISTRIBUTION OF ASSETS								
Percentage of total assets								
25. United States government securities	35.4	30.5	30.7	46.7	46.3	34.5	28.4	20.7
26. Other securities	10.4	7.7	8.8	14.4	9.0	9.9	7.3	5.9
27. Loans	28.5	41.7	43.7	13.6	25.4	35.9	45.0	53.8
28. Cash assets	24.6	18.3	15.5	23.9	18.2	18.3	17.4	17.6
29. Real estate assets	1.1	1.5	1.1	1.2	1.0	1.3	1.5	1.5

*Net recoveries or losses on loans, securities, and other assets excluding changes in valuation reserves on loans and securities.
†On loans and securities.

Exhibit 8

BANK OF E. CHASE

Summary of Earnings, Expenses, and Dividends
Years Ending December 31, 1955 and 1956,* 1958–1960

	1955	*1956*	*1958*	*1959*	*1960*
CURRENT OPERATING EARNINGS					
Interest on loans commercial department	$ 59,901.23	$ 83,589.41	$127,360.31	N.A.†	N.A.†
Interest on loans savings department	52,098.92	78,573.49	98,011.71	N.A.†	N.A.†
Total	$112,000.15	$162,162.90	$225,372.02	$256,809.09	$358,970.03
Interest on bonds commercial department	$ 52,890.98	$ 60,067.69	$ 71,658.95	N.A.†	N.A.†
Interest on bonds savings department	70,458.70	70,217.37	48,147.93	N.A.†	N.A.†
Total	$123,349.68	$130,285.06	$119,806.88	$125,049.21	$171,233.54
Discounts, commission, and exchange	$ 9,388.73	$ 10,248.90	$ 27,395.28	$ 30,192.54	$ 45,319.90
Safe deposit rents	2,385.18	2,381.18	2,936.10	3,118.50	3,110.90
Other rents commercial department	16,345.28	2,291.90	33,440.42	21,512.25	22,525.52
Other rents savings department	10,976.61	2,034.88	8,728.35	N.A.†	N.A.†
Total operating earnings	$274,445.63	$309,405.43	$417,679.05	$436,681.59	$601,159.89
CURRENT OPERATING COSTS					
Interest paid commercial department	$ 6,638.86	$ 4,047.65	$ 5,586.45	N.A.†	N.A.†
Interest paid savings department	42,612.87	36,871.63	40,452.55	N.A.†	N.A.†
Total	$ 49,251.73	$ 40,919.28	$ 46,039.00	$ 46,047.66	$ 91,320.77
Bond premium adj. commercial department	$ 8,607.13	$ 11,920.37	$ 7,102.52	N.A.†	N.A.†
Bond premium adj. savings department	8,964.00	4,278.00	3,341.44	N.A.†	N.A.†
Total	$ 17,571.13	$ 16,198.37	$ 10,443.96	$ 8,470.38	$ 5,252.35
Depreciation	$ 3,695.50	$ 4,193.60	$ 7,739.86	$ 8,273.22	$ 9,717.91

Exhibit 8 (Continued)

	1955	*1956*	*1958*	*1959*	*1960*
Expenses paid					
1. Salaries – officers, directors, employees	74,526.19	83,769.05	134,439.26	144,189.38	161,423.96
2. Ranch and other property expense	1,092.56	2,350.74	2,643.83	1,423.66	3,750.46
3. Insurance and bonds	16,175.27	9,095.83	8,586.92	7,985.81	16,208.39
4. Taxes	21,210.69	25,825.79	18,302.88	17,496.99	10,059.88
5. Postage	2,543.71	3,851.82	5,191.25	5,531.20	6,412.35
6. Freight and express	36.22	108.00	142.70	490.06	821.87
7. Stationery and printing	6,284.38	8,635.09	8,133.57	16,175.79	11,324.04
8. Advertising	642.80	644.84	1,477.72	2,530.12	1,772.55
9. Legal expenses	409.60	991.18	4,273.88	1,355.65	2,199.72
10. Telephone and telegraph	828.67	1,050.72	1,431.44	1,525.35	2,066.76
11. Utilities	601.80	561.18	929.23	1,117.97	1,460.96
12. Building maintenance	414.68	2,039.23	2,125.92	2,614.96	2,014.72
13. Work and repairs	1,294.24	2,212.80	1,909.50	1,800.89	2,590.35
14. Dues, donations, subscriptions	4,928.20	2,130.89	3,509.87	4,815.70	6,469.08
15. Miscellaneous	215.11	455.42	2,261.07	942.20	3,014.91
16. Janitor supplies	268.76	277.06	380.67	366.24	666.90
Total	$131,472.88	$143,999.64	$195,739.71	$210,361.97	$232,256.90
Cash short	$ 611.91	$ 885.96	$ 289.43	$ 178.90	$ 401.71
Total operating expenses	$202,603.15	$206,196.85	$260,251.96	$273,332.13	$338,949.64
NET CURRENT EARNINGS	$ 71,842.48	$103,208.58	$157,427.09	$163,349.46	$262,210.25
NONRECURRING EARNINGS	987.29	2,381.95	3,622.29	83,321.49	22,361.02
NONRECURRING EXPENSE	1,961.15	48,170.05	27,150.28	40,402.25	69,997.49
TOTAL NET EARNINGS	70,868.62	57,420.48	133,899.10	206,268.70	214,573.78
DISTRIBUTION OF EARNINGS					
Taxes	N.A.†	N.A.†	37,250.00	39,600.00	N.A.†
Dividends	35,000.00	40,000.00	70,000.00	80,000.00	90,000.00
Balance to reserves and undivided profits	35,868.62	17,420.48	26,649.10	86,668.70	124,573.78

*Comparable data for 1957–1958 not available. †N.A. = not available.

into the hands of younger members of the family, he believed that there would be a keener interest in current income and in the policies and programs of the bank which contributed to that income. Mr. Chipman also realized that the bank's younger shareholders would have a strong desire to maximize the potential market value of their investment. As a result, it was Mr. Chipman's responsibility to direct the bank's affairs in such a manner that the changing investment objectives of the stockholder group could be met most effectively.

Management of Cash and Investments

MANAGEMENT OF SECONDARY RESERVES

Death Valley National Bank

The Death Valley National Bank of Barstow, California, was a unit bank with total resources in 1956 of $14 million. The bank employed eleven people: three officers, four tellers, two bookkeepers, and two secretaries. Death Valley National was controlled and managed by Mr. Elmo T. Patterson, a long-time resident of Barstow, a town situated in the southwestern corner of the Mojave Desert. The Patterson family had controlled the bank since its establishment in 1910.

During recent years Barstow had grown rapidly; in 1956 the town had a population of 11,000. In addition about 2000 military personnel were stationed at nearby Army and Marine bases. The two most important local industries were agriculture and mining. Barstow was the center of an irrigated alfalfa, dairy, cattle, and poultry raising region along the Mojave River. The principal mineral deposits in the area included: borates, clay, feldspar, gypsum, potash, sodium sulphate, and gems.

Elmo Patterson was born in Barstow in 1901; he attended the University of Southern California, receiving a Bachelor of Arts degree in 1923. Shortly thereafter, Mr. Patterson accepted a position in the credit department of the Union Oil Company in Los Angeles. In 1931, Mr. Patterson decided to return to Barstow to work for his father in the Death Valley National Bank. During the ensuing years he gained experience in almost all phases of the bank's operations. With the virtual retirement of his father in 1947, Mr. Patterson assumed major responsibility for managing the bank. Upon the death of his father in 1949, Mr. Patterson became president.

One of his new responsibilities concerned management of the bank's $9 million investment portfolio (see Exhibits 1 and 2). Since his father had always supervised the bank's portfolio, Mr. Patterson had learned comparatively little about the problems of managing the bank's investment funds. He decided, therefore, to take advantage of the investment counseling service offered by the bank's Los Angeles correspondent, the Sierra Bank and Trust Company. This service consisted of an annual written detailed analysis of Death Valley National's investment portfolio, together with interim reports on special situations affecting individual bond issues. From 1950, Elmo Patterson had relied upon these annual investment analyses and interim reports to guide his judgment on the management of the bank's bond portfolio.

The Sierra Bank maintained a correspondent bank division within its investment department to provide investment counseling services to its 265 correspondent banks. Each year, an officer in this department prepared a comprehensive analysis of a correspondent's bond portfolio according to quality, maturity, diversification, capital protection, and provision for liquidity. The correspondent bank division usually completed about twenty-five reviews every month. The reports were scheduled so that a correspondent bank received its annual report at the same time each year.

In preparing an analytical report, the investment officer worked

Exhibit 1

DEATH VALLEY NATIONAL BANK

Statement of Condition
August 15, 1956

RESOURCES		CAPITAL AND LIABILITIES	
Cash	$ 2,039,050	Capital	$ 727,293
U.S. securities, due in one year and less	1,527,500	Deposits	12,710,490
Other bonds, due in one year and less	32,500	Other liabilities	77,243
CCC	81,900		
Loans	2,005,522		
U.S. securities due or callable between 1 and 5 years	2,618,200		
Other bonds, due between 1 and 3 years	48,100		
U.S. savings bonds and other special government issues	2,015,000		
U.S. securities, due or callable over 5 years	1,983,800		
Other long-term bonds	635,982		
Banking house, furniture and fixtures	350,000		
Federal Reserve Bank stock	17,550		
Other resources	159,922		
Total resources	$13,515,026	Total capital and liabilities	$13,515,026

Exhibit 2

DEATH VALLEY NATIONAL BANK

Maturities
(par value)

	U.S. Government Obligations				*Percent of Total Account*	
Year	*Direct and Guaranteed Issues Including Savings and Depositary Bonds*	*Savings and Depositary Bonds at Maturity Value (These amounts also included in 1st column)*	*All Other Bonds*	*Total All Bonds*	*For Each Five-Year Period*	*Cumulative by Five-Year Period*
1954	....	....	....	....		
1955	....	....	....	....		
1956	$1,332,500	$ 260,000	$ 32,500	$1,365,000		
1957	616,200	130,000	48,100	664,300		
1958	799,500		26,000	825,500		
1959	1,170,000		45,500	1,215,500		
1960	487,500		80,600	568,100	52.4%	52.4%
1961	106,600		93,600	200,000		
1962	1,487,200	1,105,000	102,700	1,589,900		
1963	1,300,000		65,000	1,365,000		
1964	195,000		87,100	282,100		
1965			26,000	26,000	39.1	91.5
1966			104,000	104,000		
1967						
1968	650,000	650,000		650,000	8.5	100.0
1969						
1970						
1971						
1972						
1973						
1974						
1975						
1976						
1977						
1978						
After 1978						
Unknown						
Default						
Total	$8,144,500		$711,100	$8,855,600	100.0%	

closely with a senior bond account analyst. There were five senior analysts in Sierra's correspondent bank division. An analyst supervised the preparation of the necessary statistical data for each report and advised the investment officer concerning suggested changes in the correspondent's bond portfolio.

On August 23, 1956, Mr. Patterson received from the Sierra Bank the regular annual review of Death Valley National's portfolio. The text of the investment portfolio analysis and recommendations of August 15, 1956 is presented below:

QUALITY[1]: High-grade securities ($8,660,600) and good-grade securities ($195,000). We have no changes to suggest in your holdings from a quality standpoint.

ADEQUACY OF CAPITAL STRUCTURE: We have used the following ratio[2] to evaluate in general the adequacy of your capital structure:

	Your Bank	*National Average*	*California Average*
1. Capital / Assets at risk (total assets less cash and governments)	21.8%	14.7%	11.3%
2. "Free capital" / Estimated asset risk[3]	71.0%	114.0%	. . . . .

Ratio # 1: According to this ratio your bank measures up well capital-wise. This ratio is frequently used, particularly for rather crude comparisons when a detailed breakdown of the assets is not available. However, it has the serious theoretical disadvantage of treating all risk assets alike, regardless of the character of the asset and the degree of market risk.
Ratio # 2: This ratio shows that your "free capital"[4] is somewhat lower than the national average in relation to estimated asset risk. While ratio #2 is also a crude over-all measure, it does attempt to assign an estimated degree of market risk to each of the risk assets. Since your fixed assets constitute a rather large proportion of total assets, your bank's "free capital" ratio appears a bit low. Fixed assets equal 51.7 percent of capital funds in your bank compared to the national average of 12.6 percent and the California average of 16.9 percent. A "true" evaluation of your capital position probably lies somewhere between the opposite indications of the above two ratios. It appears to us, however, that your capital remains somewhat lower than desirable in relation to asset risk.

Conclusions and Implications of Your Capital Position

Since your bank to some degree is undercapitalized in relation to asset risk, we believe you should be cautious about further increasing that risk. We offer these specific recommendations:

1. Concerning municipal bonds, we would confine any acquisitions

---

[1]As a general guide to estimating the over-all quality of a correspondent's bond holdings, Sierra Bank had established these six bond categories: (1) High Grade, (2) Good Grade, (3) Intermediate Grade, (4) Fair Grade, (5) Poor Grade, (6) Unclassified.

[2]See Exhibit 3.

[3]For an explanation of how this ratio is calculated, see Appendix A.

[4]"Free capital" is defined as total capital less fixed assets.

to moderate proportions. While you need not absolutely discontinue the purchase of municipals, we would recommend confining further acquisitions to small amounts to high-grade names. These could be added when outstandingly attractive offerings come along.

2. Until your capital builds up to higher levels, we believe you might restrict to small proportions the purchase of any medium- and longer-term governments. This will help avoid increasing the weight of market risk against capital.

3. We feel, however, that it would be proper for you to accept additional high-quality loans to build your loan portfolio up to at least $2,600,000.

Since additional loans would serve to increase risk assets, it is not easy to show statistically why it would be advisable for you to assume additional risk in loans and inadvisable to do so in the bond account. Our reason simply is that $2,600,000 in loans would constitute only 20 percent of deposits, a very moderate ratio compared to the national average. We think that a higher proportion of loans to deposits would be desirable because it would improve the diversification of your bank's assets. We further believe that, after you attain the $2,600,000 total, you might consider steadily increasing your loan portfolio on a conservative and selective basis. As long as your capital remains somewhat low, however, we would not suggest that you build up your loan-to-deposit ratio to the national average of about 47 percent.

Maturity Diversification

Your bond account appears reasonably diversified maturity-wise, except for a large concentration in the years 1962–1963 (see Exhibits 2 and 4). (In the maturity-shortening suggestion at the close of this report we shall recommend selling from these 1962 holdings.) Bonds, maturity-certain beyond five years, equal 20 percent of your deposits, compared with only 13 percent for the national average. While averages are not a rigid criterion, it appears that you have a pretty sizable commitment in medium-term governments. This serves to reinforce our recommendation that you avoid increasing market risk by purchasing any medium- and longer-term bonds while your capital remains somewhat low as discussed above.

Adequacy of Provision for Liquidity

You are in the best position to evaluate your probable liquidity requirements. Nevertheless, we believe for the following reasons that you should probably increase your secondary reserve of near-term securities. This will help provide greater liquidity (marketability at minimum risk) than your bond account now possesses.

1. Your ratio of cash and one-year governments to deposits is 28.1 percent—about the same as the national average of 27.6 percent. (The

national average does not necessarily offer a reliable guide, particularly in matters of liquidity.)

2. Your present holdings of securities, maturity-certain within one year, together with a portion of your cash are sufficient to repay $1,878,500 in deposits. This will still allow you to preserve a 16 percent cash ratio against remaining deposits. You thus could repay 14.8 percent of your deposits without having to sell any securities maturing beyond one year. The question arises whether this provision is sufficient, with a reasonable margin of safety, to provide for the deposit and/or loan demands you may receive. An answer to this question requires a consideration of the magnitude of your seasonal and random deposit fluctuations, emergency demands, and the minimum desirable margin of safety.

SEASONAL FLUCTUATIONS: Based on Exhibit 5, it appears that the major fluctuations in deposits during the past five or six years have been due to special circumstances and not to seasonal influences. Since seasonal demands have been relatively mild, we must consider the character of your deposits and local economic conditions in order to appraise any unusual demands for funds.

DEPOSIT ANALYSIS: Your bank's percentage of *time deposits* (26.8 percent of total) compares closely with the national average. These deposits therefore probably afford no more than an average amount of deposit stability. Your *public fund deposits* (27.1 percent of total deposits) are very substantially greater than the national average (10.1 percent). Under certain circumstances such funds could display unusual vulnerability. We agree, however, with your estimate that about one third of these public deposits are highly volatile. We believe that a reasonable amount of liquidity for your bank would be about 20 percent of *total deposits*. You are, however, in a much better position than we to judge the reliability of this estimate. There is a greater incentive at this time to err on the short rather than on the long side because of money market pressure toward firmer interest rates.

Estimate of Desirable Secondary Reserve of Securities, Maturity-Certain in One Year

a. For loan increase (to bring loan portfolio to $2,600,000)	$ 422,500
b. Estimated volatile portion of public funds (one third of $2,691,882)	897,294[5]
c. Estimated volatile portion of "regular" deposits (after deduction of public funds and U.S. government open account)	1,678,300
	$2,998,094
Deduct: 16 percent of items "*b*" and "*c*" (16 percent of these deposit withdrawals could be paid out of cash without reducing your ratio of cash to remaining deposits)	412,095
Net secondary reserve requirement	$2,585,999

[5]U.S. government open account excluded from public fund total in making this calculation.

Present Secondary Reserve (Compare with Estimated Net Requirement Above)

a. Governments maturity-certain in one year or less	$1,527,500
b. U.S. 2 percent Depositary Bonds[6]	260,000
c. Other bonds due in one year or less	32,500
d. CCC Certificates of Interest (now matured)	81,900
Total secondary reserve	$1,901,900

Theoretical Deficiency in Secondary Reserve on the Basis of the Above Assumptions and Calculations

Estimated secondary reserve requirement	$2,585,999
Present secondary reserve	1,901,900
Deficiency	$ 684,099

Conclusions Concerning Your Liquidity

On the basis of the above estimates, it appears that your present secondary reserve is approximately $700,000 below a desirable level. The question now becomes—what should you do about it? This boils down to a consideration of: first, how good are the estimates of your probable requirements; second, a weighing of the relative disadvantage of taking losses on the sale of medium-term bonds against the advantage of a more liquid position.

We believe that despite recent market declines, a fair-sized maturity-shortening operation would be desirable. The figure we have in mind is $325,000. As deposits increase over the period ahead, we would suggest that the inflow be used: either for an increase in loan volume up to a reasonable amount; or to augment your secondary reserve of securities maturity-certain within one year. We specifically recommend the following changes in your portfolio:

1. You should carry out a maturity-shortening sale such as the one set forth above.

2. You should consider another maturity-shortening at some time in the future if secondary reserves need further strengthening. The timing and magnitude of any future bond portfolio maturity change will be largely determined by: (*a*) developments in the economic situation, (*b*) the levels of your deposits and loans, and (*c*) bond-market prices.

The probabilities favor a further weakening of government bond prices over the months just ahead. Hence you should not depend on making further shortening sales at prices as high as present levels. In other words, what really must be done in providing additional liquidity should probably be done *now*. It appears possible that it will require

[6]The excess of Depositary Bonds not needed to cover U.S. government open account.

Par Value	*Issue*	*Market*	*Gross*	*Approximate Current Yield Given-up after Tax*	*Annual Income Given-up[7] after Tax*
Suggested sale:					
$325,000	U.S. Treasury 2 1/2% bonds due Nov. 13, 1962	97 31/32	2.88%	1.38%	$4,485

Par Value	*Issue*	*Market*	*Approximate Current Gross Yield*	*Net Yield*	*Annual Net Yield Income*
Suggested purchase:					
$195,000	U.S. Treasury bills	....	1.88%	0.90%	$1.755[7]
$130,000	U.S. Treasury 2 3/4% bonds due Sept. 13, 1957–1960	101 10/32	1.52%	1.19%	$1.547[8]
$325,000	Average net yield			1.05%	$3,302
	Net annual income losses				$1,183

[7]After 52 percent Federal Income Tax.
[8]After 22 percent surtax (partially tax-exempt issue).

several months before more favorable opportunities will arise for selling medium-term governments.

3. You should retain new funds available for investment in the near-term area until your secondary reserve reaches a comfortable level.

4. Because of your somewhat low capital position, we would suggest that you: (*a*) discontinue almost entirely the purchases of municipal bonds or other bonds in the "risk asset" category, and (*b*) avoid adding to medium- or longer-term governments.

Exhibit 3

DEATH VALLEY NATIONAL BANK

Ratio Sheet

	Your Bank as of 8/15/56	*All Insured Commercial Banks in U.S. as of 6/30/56*	*All Insured Commercial Banks in California as of 6/30/56*
RATIOS BEARING UPON LIQUIDITY			
1. Cash to deposits	16.0%	22.8%	18.1%
2. Cash and one-year governments to deposits	28.1	27.6	....
3. Estimated "unpledged bonds"*—to total deposits less public funds	34.2	30.8	29.3
4. Loans to deposits	15.7	46.8	52.7
CAPITAL RATIOS			
1. Total capital funds to deposits	5.7	8.4	7.1
2. Total capital funds to loans	36.3	18.0	13.5
3. Surplus and undivided profits to loans	20.0	12.5	9.1
4. Total capital funds to "other bonds"	102.2	96.6	83.2
5. Surplus and undivided profits to "other bonds"	60.5	67.2	56.2
6. Total capital funds to total assets less cash and governments	21.8	14.7	11.3
GENERAL RATIOS			
1. Total time deposits to total deposits	26.8	25.4	44.6
2. Total public funds to total deposits	27.1	10.1	9.5
3. "Other bonds" to total bond account	8.0	22.4	23.2
4. Fixed assets to total capital funds	51.7	12.6	16.9
5. Fixed assets to capital stock	128.4	41.3	52.2
6. Fixed assets to total deposits	3.0	1.1	1.2
7. Deposits as of dates indicated are	8.8 times 12/30/39 deposits	3.3 times 12/30/39 deposits	4.4 times 12/30/39 deposits

*"Unpledged bonds" estimated by deducting from total book value of bonds an amount equal to 110 percent of public funds on the assumption that this amount of bonds is required to be pledged to secure public funds.

Exhibit 4

DEATH VALLEY NATIONAL BANK

Maturities as Related to
Total Bond Account and Total Deposits
August 15, 1956
(based on total bond account of $8,855,600 par value and total deposits of $12,710,490)

		Percent of Account		*Percent of Deposits*	
Maturity Category	*Par Value Your Bank*	*Your Bank*	*Average Figures**	*Your Bank*	*Average Figures**
U.S. savings bonds and other special government issues	$2,145,000	24.2%	3.4%	16.9%	1.0%
0–3 months	325,000				
3–6 months	747,500				
6–9 months	325,000				
9–12 months	0				
Total 0–1 year	$1,397,500	15.8	16.0	11.0	4.8
12–15 months	$ 161,200				
15–18 months	0				
18–21 months	669,500				
21–24 months	130,000				
Total 1–2 years	$ 960,700	10.9	13.3	7.6	4.0
2–3 years	$ 633,100	7.1	10.8	5.0	3.3
3–4 years	611,000	6.9	5.7	4.8	1.7
4–5 years	533,000	6.0	8.4	4.2	2.5
5–10 years	2,471,300	27.9	33.2	19.4	10.1
Over 10 years	104,000	1.2	9.2	0.8	2.8
Total	$8,855,600	100.0%	100.0%	69.7%	30.2%

*All insured commercial banks in the United States, governments only, as of 6/30/56.

Exhibit 5

DEATH VALLEY NATIONAL BANK

Seasonal Flow of Funds
(dollar figures in thousands)

Year– First Six Months	*Change in Deposits*	*Change in Loans*	*Net Outflow*	*Net Inflow*
1951	$+ 631	$+174	......	$ 457
1952	+ 285	+113	......	172
1953	+1,106	+356	......	750
1954	−1,232	− 38	$1,194	......
1955	−3,585	+ 40	3,625	......
1956	+1,082	+296	......	786

Exhibit 5 (Continued)

Year— First Six Months	*Change in Deposits*	*Change in Loans*	*Net Outflow*	*Net Inflow*
1951	$+ 447	$− 5	....	$ 452
1952	+ 408	+ 30	....	378
1953	+2,503	−160	....	2,663
1954	+1,136	+ 88	....	1,048
1955	− 148	+ 55	$203	......
1956	....	......	....	......

APPENDIX A

Asset Risk in Relation to Capital Position

Explanation of Our Risk Ratio

There are a number of ratios frequently used by bank supervisory authorities and others as measures of the risk element in a bank's assets relative to the size of its capital accounts. In many of these ratios it is assumed that treasury securities are riskless regardless of their maturity. We are not in accord with this view as we believe there is a risk of interest rate changes with attendant fluctuations in government security prices, which fluctuations will vary in degree depending upon the maturity of the issues involved. To take into account this market risk in bonds and the credit risk in both loans and in bonds other than governments, we use the following ratio which relates so-called free capital of a bank to an estimate of the risk in the assets. The percentage of risk assigned to each asset category is necessarily arbitrary, and others might assign different percentages to the different groups. Nonetheless, we believe the risk percentages we have chosen are reasonable in themselves, and in any case the final ratio, prepared on the same basis for all banks, has a certain validity for purposes of comparison. The calculation of the estimated risk in your assets is shown below with the final ratio derived by dividing the figure for total risk into the amount of your free capital. Free capital is calculated by deducting from total capital funds such fixed assets as bank building, furniture and fixtures, and other real estate. The final ratio in a measure indicates the protection the capital accounts afford depositors against the estimated risk in the assets of the bank.

Assets	*Your Totals*	*Arbitrary Assumption as to Percentage of Risk*	*Estimated Amount of Risk*
CCC	$ 81,900	-0-	$ -0-
Loans	2,005,522	10%	200,552
U.S. savings bonds and other special government issues	2,145,000	-0-	-0-
0–1-year U.S. securities	1,397,500	-0-	-0-
1–5-year U.S. securities	2,618,200	3	78,546
5–10-year U.S. securities	1,983,800	7 1/2	148,785
Over 10-year U.S. securities	-0-	10	-0-
0–3-year "other bonds"	80,600	5	4,030
Over 3-year "other bonds"	630,500	10	63,050
Capital accounts $727,293			Total $494,963
Less (fixed assets) 375,705			
Free capital $351,588			

	Your Bank	*National Average*
Free capital / Estimated asset risk	71.0%	114%

MANAGEMENT OF CASH POSITION

Provident National Bank

The Provident National Bank, a large unit bank located in Houston, Texas, had total resources in July 1960 of over $650 million (see Exhibit 1). Provident National was classified by the Federal Reserve System as a "reserve city bank." Reserve city banks are required to settle their reserve balances with the Federal Reserve Bank on Wednesday of each week. The average cash balances kept at the Federal Reserve during the week must be a prescribed percentage of the bank's average demand and time deposits. In July 1960 the reserve requirements for this group of banks were 16 1/2 percent for demand deposits and 5 percent for time deposits. Exhibit 2 contains a summary of the Provident National's accumulated cash reserve position for a portion of the reserve week ending July 20, 1960.

The Provident National's over-all cash position[1] reflected a great

[1]A commercial bank's "cash position" is defined as the sum of cash in vault and deposits due from correspondent banks and from the Federal Reserve Bank.

Exhibit 1

PROVIDENT NATIONAL BANK

Statement of Condition
June 30, 1959–1960
(dollar figures in thousands)

Resources	*June 30, 1959*	*June 30, 1960*
Cash and due from banks	$130,931	$192,882
U.S. government securities	104,113	115,320
State, county, and municipal bonds	11,887	10,731
Federal Reserve Bank stock	764	1,140
Loans and discounts	284,000	320,478
Accrued interest receivable	1,492	1,579
Customers' liability under letters of credit and acceptances	10,681	10,351
Bank premises, furniture and fixtures	1,851	2,518
Other resources	224	816
Total resources	$545,943	$655,815
Liabilities and Capital		
Deposits	$492,291	$586,165
Other liabilities	23,285	26,625
Capital stock	9,104	15,964
Surplus	16,361	22,044
Undivided profits	4,902	5,017
Total liabilities and capital	$545,943	$655,815

number of individual investment, loan, and liquidity decisions made by the bank's officers throughout the year. As a basis for planning, a staff economist forecast the level of deposits and expected loan demand on a continuous basis for periods of three months, six months, and one year. Once these sources and applications of funds had been estimated, the bank could then determine what should be its investment policy and the composition of its investment portfolio.

Early in 1960, the bank's senior officers concluded that interest rates would probably drift lower for the next six to twelve months. In anticipation of these lower interest rates, it was decided that the bank should remain as fully invested as possible in order to benefit from higher interest income and from the capital appreciation in the bond portfolio which would result as interest rates began to fall.

After the bank's deposit, loan, and investment objectives had been estimated and short-run policies established, it was the responsibility of Mr. George Howes, assistant vice president, to manage the daily cash position in order to adjust for short-run cash fluctuations and to ensure that the bank maintained the required minimum balances with the Fed-

Exhibit 2

PROVIDENT NATIONAL BANK

Minutes
Bond Investment Committee
for Reserve Week Ending July 20, 1960
Reserve Position and Adjustments
(dollar figures in millions)

Reserve Position	*Thursday 7/14*	*Friday 7/15*	*Monday 7/18*
Opening reserve surplus (+) or deficit (−) cumulative over reserve week	......	$ −6.0	$−24.1
Reserve increase (+) or decrease (−) with reversal of borrowing transactions, previous day	$ 19.6	7.6	7.9
Net opening reserve surplus (+) or deficit (−) cumulative over reserve week	19.6	1.6	−16.2
Commercial factors increasing (+) or decreasing (−) reserves	−13.0	0.6	−9.0
Reserve surplus (+) or deficit (−) before adjustments, cumulative for reserve week	6.6	2.2	−25.2
Reserve adjustments			
Sales (+) or purchases (−) of U.S. government securities	−5.0	−6.3	......
Federal funds purchases (+) or sales (−)	−7.6	−7.9	......
Borrowing at Federal Reserve Bank	......	......	......
Closing balance, cumulative surplus (+) or deficit (−)	−6.0	−12.0	......

Trends in Basic Reserve Position
Weekly Averages of Daily Figures
(dollar figures in millions)

	Reserve	*Week Ending*	
	6/29	*7/6*	*7/13*
Total reserves	$64.8	$65.5	$61.3
Required reserves	60.6	65.2	61.2
Surplus (+) or deficit (−)	4.2	0.3	0.1
Federal funds sold (+) or purchased (−)	7.5	30.9	10.9
Borrowing at Federal Reserve Bank (−)	.....	.....	.....
Basic surplus (+) or deficit (−)	11.7	31.2	11.0

eral Reserve Bank. It was Mr. Howes' objective to minimize the cost of meeting the bank's reserve requirements at the "Fed" and to invest any temporarily excess funds as profitable as possible.

Mr. Howes was a member of Provident National's investment department, which was organized as follows:

Investment Division

Bond Portfolio Section	Cash Position Section	Commercial Customer Bond Investment Services Section

During the first two weeks in July, Mr. Howes made the following investment commitments in order to employ excess balances which had accumulated in Provident National's account at the regional Federal Reserve Bank:

Purchase Date	*Amount*	*Issue*	*Cost or Yield Basis*
7/4	$ 730,000	Fed. Intermediate Credit Bank 3.80% due 4/3/61	100
7/13	18,460,000	U.S. treasury bills due 3/22/61	2.84%*
7/14	5,000,000	U.S. treasury bills due 1/12/61	3.17%
	2,000,000	Brokerage participation loan due 7/29/60	4.75%
7/15	5,000,000	U.S. treasury bills due 7/15/61	3.26%
	1,240,000	Federal Home Loan Bank 3.25% due 1/19/61	100
	5,000,000	Brokerage participation loan due 7/29/60	4.00%

*These securities were paid for by crediting the U.S. treasury tax and loan account at the Provident National Bank. The only cost to the bank was 16 1/2 percent of the deposit, the amount which must be kept at the Federal Reserve Bank. Because it was estimated that the treasury would probably leave these funds on deposit for from thirty to forty days, the yield on these bills was some thirty basis points higher, thus making the total effective yield approximately 3.14 percent.

The month of July was usually the Provident National's peak period for accumulating excess funds. The high point in deposits generally occurred during the weekend closest to the middle of the month, after which they declined sharply. In 1960, the weekend closest to the middle of July was Saturday the 16th and Sunday the 17th.

On Friday, July 15, Mr. Howes sold $7.9 million in federal funds, thereby deliberately creating a cumulative deficit reserve position of approximately $20 million for the week.[2] Mr. Howes assumed that a $20 million to $25 million reserve surplus would occur on Monday, thereby canceling the effect of Friday's sale of federal funds. A large part of this reserve surplus was expected to come from immediate credit at the Federal Reserve on one-day items. These items consisted of checks

[2]Federal-fund sales on Friday are for three days; thus the sale of $7.9 million for three days is the equivalent of selling $23.7 million for one day. Federal funds are additional reserves which a commercial bank may either loan to or borrow from other banks in order to adjust its reserve position to the required level. These loans are generally made on a 24-hour basis. The cost is determined by the forces of supply and demand for such funds within the commercial banking system.

drawn on other banks which Provident National forwarded to the Houston Clearing House and to its correspondent banks. When these checks were cleared, the cash became usable funds on deposit in Provident's Federal Reserve account. Mr. Howes further assumed that the bank would experience its typical reserve drain on Tuesday[3]; hence average reserve balances for the week would closely approximate the legal requirements.

By mid-morning on Monday, July 18, Mr. Howes realized that his assumptions were not proving correct. The bank opened on Monday with a cumulative reserve deficit of $24.1 million for the reserve week which would end on Wednesday, July 20. The large immediate credits to the bank's account at the Federal Reserve had not materialized. A number of factors were responsible:

1. Incoming deposits over the weekend were smaller than expected.
2. A larger than normal deficit was incurred at the Houston Clearing House.
3. A large correspondent bank withdrew funds one day earlier than was considered normal.
4. Several important depositors made larger than normal withdrawals.
5. An adverse arithmetical error of $2 million was made in the general books department.

During Monday the bank experienced a further reserve deficit which Mr. Howes thought would approximate $9.0 million for the day. As a result of these developments the bank's cash reserve position required immediate attention. Since the normal Tuesday reserve deficit generally averaged between $7 million and $10 million, Mr. Howes realized that by the close of business Tuesday, the bank could have a cumulative reserve deficit of as high as $35 million. A deficit of this size would be very difficult to overcome through normal adjustments such as borrowing federal funds or selling U.S. Department of Treasury short-term securities.

On Monday afternoon, Mr. Howes decided that some action should be taken before the close of business that day in order to offset at least a substantial portion of the nearly $25 million cumulative deficit which existed at that time (see Exhibit 2). There were several alternatives for Mr. Howes to choose from in order to adjust the bank's reserve position:

[3]The Provident National's proof and transit department worked each Friday and Sunday night in order to process the heavy volume of "banking-by-mail" transactions. As a result, incoming items arriving over the weekend were cleared more promptly than by other banks in the area, and Provident National generally experienced a peak in usable funds on Monday. This peak typically declined on Tuesday and Wednesday as other banks completed the processing of weekend mail.

	Income Lost	Added Expense
1. Purchase of federal funds		3.5%
2. Sale of short-term securities:		
a. $2MM federal agency paper	3.62%	
b. 5MM treasury bills	3.26	
c. 18.5MM treasury bills	3.14	
d. 5MM treasury bills	3.17	
3. Cancellation of $7MM brokerage participation loan with New York correspondent	4.00–4.75%	
4. Borrowing from the Federal Reserve Banks		3.5%
5. Selling part of the permanent portfolio	?	

Discussion of Alternatives

1. PURCHASE OF FEDERAL FUNDS. This was the device most commonly used by Provident National to adjust deficit balances at the Federal Reserve Bank. It was Provident National's policy, however, to limit federal funds purchases to no more than $20 million. As a matter of policy, the bank did not want to be either an excessive seller or buyer of federal funds. Mr. Howes considered the use of federal funds as a "fine adjustment" in the bank's reserve position. Since short-term adjustments in cash reserves usually ranged from $5 million to $10 million, federal funds provided the bank with a convenient means either of profitably employing excess reserves or of offsetting small reserve deficits. The bank's limited use of federal funds sometimes made it necessary either to extend reserve adjustments over a longer period or to make adjustments of a more permanent nature.

2. SALE OF SHORT-TERM SECURITIES. If the adjustment of the cash position required funds for more than a few days, short-term securities could be sold to provide the necessary funds. Mr. Howes was reluctant, however, to sell any securities to meet the present reserve deficit unless absolutely necessary because of the bank's current policy of remaining as fully invested as possible. Mr. Howes hoped to be able to retain until maturity at least $30 million of short-term securities.

3. BROKERAGE COLLATERAL LOANS OR OTHER LOANS CALLABLE ON DEMAND. These loans were usually arranged through the Provident National's correspondent banks in New York. When Provident National negotiated a brokerage collateral loan, it indicated the length of time it wished to employ its funds. Although such loans were callable on demand, the bank normally would not recall the funds until the agreed time had expired.

4. BORROWING FROM THE FEDERAL RESERVE. The accumulated reserve deficit could be made up through borrowing from the Federal Reserve Bank. The Provident National, however, looked upon the use of

Exhibit 3

PROVIDENT NATIONAL BANK

Maturity Distribution of United States Government Securities at Par
(dollar figures in thousands)

Maturity	*June 30, 1959*		*May 31, 1960*		*June 30, 1960*	
1 year	$ 30,737	29.4%	$ 12,500	10.5%	$ 7,500	6.6%
2 years	15,300	14.6	20,483	17.2	19,983	17.5
3 years	30,705	29.3	28,060	23.6	20,060	17.6
4 years	18,060	17.3	22,303	18.7	30,803	27.0
5 years	5,600	5.4	27,798	23.3	27,798	24.3
1–5 year total	$100,402	96.0	$111,144	93.3	$106,144	93.0
6 years	$ 3,000	2.9	$ 6,800	5.7	$ 6,800	6.0
7 years	....	.....	1,230	1.0	1,230	1.0
8 years	1,230	1.1	....	.....	....	.....
9 years	....	.....	....	.....	....	.....
10 years	....	.....	....	.....	.....	.....
6–10 year total	$ 4,230	4.0	$ 8,030	6.7	$ 8,030	7.0
Over 10 years	....	.....	....	.....	....	.....
Grand total	$104,632	100.0	$119,174	100.0	$114,174	100.0
Weighted average	2 years, 2 months		3 years, 0 months		3 years, 2 months	
maturity treasury bills not included in above schedule			$60		$3,260	

Exhibit 4

PROVIDENT NATIONAL BANK

Recapitulation of Bond Portfolio
(dollar figures in thousands)

*As of June 30, 1960**	*U.S. Government Obligations*		*State and Municipal Obligations*		*Federal Reserve Bank Stock*		*Total*	
Par	$114,174		$10,595		......		$124,769	
Cost	112,079		10,736		$1,140		123,955	
Market value	113,963		10,597		1,140		125,700	
Yearly income	4,004		306		68		4,378	
Income after corp. tax	1,975		306		37		2,318	
Yield after tax		1.76%		2.83%		3.27%		1.87%

*Excludes temporary holdings of $3260 treasury bills.

Exhibit 5

PROVIDENT NATIONAL BANK

Total Deposits for the Month of July, 1957–1959, July 1–15, 1960
(dollar figures in millions)

Day of Month	*1957*	*1958*	*1959*	*1960*
1	$337	$397	$471	$531
2	336	401	474	.....
3	330	407	478	.....
4	....	....	....	.....
5	351	....	....	562
6	....	....	467	557
7	....	395	472	554
8	330	404	480	554
9	350	406	489	.....
10	361	417	507	.....
11	362	440	....	565
12	393	....	....	581
13	....	....	496	594
14	....	432	518	597
15	360	427	522	594
16	359	421	503	
17	361	415	521	
18	352	428	....	
19	364	....	....	
20	....	....	495	
21	....	406	497	
22	340	407	490	
23	346	411	481	
24	353	407	495	
25	327	401	....	
26	337	....	....	
27	....	....	483	
28	....	392	491	
29	323	395	486	
30	326	397	478	
31	332	397	491	

such borrowing as a privilege. Provident National had found it necessary to borrow heavily at the Federal Reserve during the month of June in order to meet substantial fund requirements as the bank's customers withdrew deposits in order to make their quarterly income tax payments.

Mr. Howes preferred, therefore, to avoid using the "discount window" for as long thereafter as possible.

5. SELLING A PORTION OF SECONDARY RESERVES. On June 30, 1960, the Provident National's secondary reserves were approximately 20 percent of deposits[4]; in view of the bank's current investment policy, Mr. Howes was reluctant to reduce the portfolio very much below this level.

By mid-afternoon on Monday, July 18, the cumulative reserve deficit for the week remained at approximately $25 million. Mr. Howes had not yet decided, however, which of the several alternatives he should choose in order to reduce or eliminate this deficit. He planned, however, to take some action before the close of business on Monday afternoon.

APPENDIX A

Handling Member Bank Reserve Accounts

A substantial part of the daily work of the reserve banks relates to member bank reserve accounts. Member banks use their reserve accounts much as individuals use their bank accounts, drawing on and replenishing them in day-to-day transactions. The Reserve Banks must record all transactions and strike a daily balance for the reserve account of each member bank. As previously indicated, the average balance that a member bank must maintain with a Federal Reserve Bank as a part of its required reserve is related to the member bank's deposits, which are constantly changing. Reserve requirements are computed by averaging daily deposits over a weekly period for central reserve and reserve city banks and over a biweekly period for country banks. When the reserve account of a member bank falls below its requirement, the bank, in preference to other adjustments of its position, may borrow temporarily from its

[4]The Provident National Bank classified its primary and secondary reserves as follows:

Primary reserves

1. U.S. Treasury obligations maturing in less than one year.
2. Deposits at the Federal Reserve Bank.
3. Deposits in correspondent banks.
4. The ability to borrow in the federal funds market.
5. The privilege of borrowing from the Federal Reserve Bank.

Secondary reserves

1. U.S. Department of Treasury obligations maturing in one to five years.
2. Municipal bonds maturing in less than two years.

The material in this appendix is adapted from *The Federal Reserve System: Purposes and Functions,* published by the Board of Governors of the Federal Reserve System, Washington, D.C., 1961. Chapter XIV, pages 213–223.

Federal Reserve Bank to restore its balance to the required level. With some 6000 member banks, the number of such borrowing transactions in any year may run into the thousands, even when the great majority of member banks do not borrow.

The credit transactions of member banks described in earlier chapters are by no means the only entries in their reserve accounts at the reserve banks. For example, entries are made as member banks obtain currency (paper money and coin) to pay out to their customers or redeposit currency in excess of the amount needed for circulation, checks are collected and cleared, Treasury deposits are transferred from member banks to the Federal Reserve Banks, and funds are transferred by telegraph for various purposes. These transactions are described in subsequent paragraphs. . . .

When the demand for currency increases, banks provide themselves with the amounts and kinds of currency that the people in their communities want. Member banks depend upon the Federal Reserve Banks for replenishment of their supply, ordering what they require and having it charged to their reserve accounts. Nonmember banks generally get their supplies from member banks. . . .

When the demand for currency abates, currency flows back from the public and the nonmember banks to the member banks. The member banks return the currency to the Federal Reserve Banks, where it is credited to member bank reserve accounts. The Federal Reserve adjusts its operations so that the outflow and return flow of currency may take place with minimum tightening or easing effect on the general credit situation. . . .

Collection, Clearing, and Transferring Funds

. . . The use of checking deposits by business and the general public is facilitated by the service of the Federal Reserve Banks in clearing and collecting checks and in providing the mechanism through which commercial banks settle for the checks they clear and collect.

For example, suppose that a manufacturer in Hartford, Connecticut, sells $1000 worth of electrical equipment to a dealer in Sacramento, California, and receives in payment a check on a bank in Sacramento. The Hartford manufacturer deposits the check in his Hartford bank. The Hartford bank does not want currency for the check; it wants credit in its reserve account at the Federal Reserve Bank of Boston. Accordingly, it sends the check (together with other checks) to the Federal Reserve Bank of Boston, which sends it to the Federal Reserve Bank of San Francisco, which in turn sends it to the Sacramento bank. The Sacramento bank charges the check to the account of the depositor who wrote it and has the amount charged to its reserve account at the San Francisco Reserve

Bank. The Federal Reserve Bank of San Francisco thereupon credits the Federal Reserve Bank of Boston, which in turn credits the account of the Hartford bank.

Since promptness is important in collecting checks, the Federal Reserve Banks extend to member banks having a substantial volume of checks payable in other Federal Reserve districts the privilege of sending such checks direct to other Federal Reserve Banks for collection. The Hartford bank, therefore, might have forwarded the $1000 check direct to the Federal Reserve Bank of San Francisco for collection, at the same time informing the Federal Reserve Bank of Boston of its action. Credit would then have been given to the Hartford bank's reserve account by the Federal Reserve Bank of Boston on the basis of this information just as if the check had been sent through Boston. . . .

In addition, many other checks are collected by the city correspondent banks, and local checks are collected by banks through local clearing houses or by direct presentation to one another. In such cases, however, the settlement or payment for checks on member banks is largely made, directly or indirectly, through the member banks' reserve balances with the Federal Reserve Banks. Thus, the facilities of the Reserve Banks aid in check clearing and collection whether or not the checks originate locally or move across the country. . . .

Besides checks, the Federal Reserve Banks also handle other items for collection. These include such items as drafts, promissory notes, and bond coupons. . . .

The Federal Reserve Banks also perform important services for the Treasury in connection with the public debt. When a new issue of Government securities is sold by the Treasury, the Reserve Banks distribute offering announcements, receive the applications of banks, dealers, and others who wish to buy, make allotments of securities in accordance with instructions from the Treasury, deliver the securities to the purchasers, receive payment for them, and credit the amounts received to Treasury accounts. As brought out below, these payments for the most part are initially made to and kept on deposit in tax and loan accounts at member and nonmember banks.

Each Federal Reserve Bank administers for the Treasury the tax and loan deposit accounts of banks in its district. Both member and nonmember banks, by complying with the Treasury's requirements, may become "special depositaries" of the Treasury and carry tax and loan deposit accounts. The principal requirement is the pledge with a Federal Reserve Bank, as fiscal agent of the Treasury, of Government securities or other acceptable collateral that will fully secure the balance in the account.

A bank designated as a special depositary credits to the tax and loan account the proceeds of its customers' and its own subscriptions to Government securities issued by the Treasury from time to time. Taxes withheld at the source are also deposited in these accounts. As the Treasury calls for the funds, they are transferred to a Treasury account at a Federal Reserve Bank and become available for disbursement. Tax and loan deposit accounts are a convenient and practically indispensable device for the sale of Government securities in large volume and, coupled with their use for tax receipts, they provide a means of moderating the effect on member bank reserves of fluctuations in the Treasury's cash receipts. The great bulk of Government deposits is carried by the Treasury in these accounts, pending transfer to the Federal Reserve Banks.

Special Loan Problems 7

LOANS WITH CORRESPONDENT

Sturgess Fuel Company

On March 15, 1958, Mr. Horace Olson, vice president at the Boulevard National Bank, was considering a loan participation with a correspondent, the Farmers State Bank in Sturgess, Iowa, an industrial town on the outskirts of Des Moines.

The Farmers State Bank had received a request for a three-year, $112,500 loan from one of its local customers, the Sturgess Fuel Company. Since Farmers State had a legal lending limit of $65,000, it had written Mr. Olson asking that Boulevard National participate in the loan to the extent of $75,000. The Sturgess Fuel Company planned to use the proceeds as follows:

$ 18,750	for purchase of real estate
56,250	for expanding ready-mix cement plant capacity
37,500	for new cement trucks
$112,500	

Boulevard National, a unit bank located in Chicago, Illinois, had total resources of $970 million, loans of $465 million, and deposits of $905 million as of December 1957. Approximately $150 million of these deposits came from correspondent banks primarily in the northern plains states of Nebraska, Iowa, Minnesota, the Dakotas, Wisconsin, Illinois, and Indiana.

Boulevard National had established a reputation as one of the leading correspondent banks in the Chicago area. By 1958, Boulevard's network of correspondents included more than 400 country banks. During frequent visits throughout the midwest, officers in the banks and bankers department encouraged both existing and potential correspondents to utilize Boulevard National's many services. These included transit service, safekeeping, advice on investments, portfolio management, participation in loans, collections, foreign banking services, personnel assistance, advice on bank operations, and credit information.

Boulevard National suggested that its correspondent banks seek assistance when they received loan requests which exceeded their legal limits or technical capabilities, and the bank generally answered these participation requests within twenty-four hours. The country bank usually retained as much of such loans as it wished, up to its legal limit, and Boulevard provided the remainder. In early 1958 Boulevard's loan participations amounted to slightly less than 1 percent of total loans.

Boulevard National participated with its correspondents in three general loan categories:

1. Loans which would exceed the correspondent's legal lending limit.
2. Loans which would unbalance the correspondent's loan portfolio.
3. Loans in which the technical problems of an industry or company required specialized analysis and advice.

In participation loans, Boulevard National preferred not to handle any collateral since the correspondent bank could supervise secured loans more effectively. In order to simplify its administration of participations, Boulevard National generally tried to avoid loans which required restrictive clauses pertaining to working capital, dividends, or pledged assets.

When a correspondent requested a loan participation, it usually supplied Boulevard National with general credit data, including recent financial statements from the applicant. If Boulevard National approved the participation, it credited the correspondent's deposit account with Boulevard's share of the loan. The correspondent bank then completed the final arrangements with the local customer.

Boulevard National usually avoided contacting directly the correspondent bank's customer before approving a loan participation. The bank normally made its decision based only on the information forwarded by the correspondent. If, however, a visit to the local customer was necessary, the correspondent bank generally arranged and participated in the interviews.

When Boulevard National granted a participation, it usually requested full repayment before the correspondent received any portion of the loan. In this manner the correspondent's part of the loan helped maintain the quality of Boulevard National's participation. At times, however, it was difficult to request prior repayment, and in these cases Boulevard National agreed to accept a proportionate share of each repayment.

In its loan participation request to Boulevard National, the Farmers State Bank supplied the following information about the Sturgess Fuel Company.

The company wholesaled and retailed heating equipment, coal and petroleum products, household appliances, and various building materials such as ready-mix cement, lumber, hardware, and plumbing supplies.

The company's sales were divided:

General building materials	50%
Petroleum products	27
Household appliances	13
Heating equipment and sheet metal work	10

Mr. Earl Winton had served as president of Sturgess Fuel Company from the firm's establishment in 1927 until his death in June 1954. After Earl Winton's death, his brother Jeffrey assumed control of the company. In 1958 Jeffrey Winton was 60 years old and since 1938 had worked as Sturgess Fuel's general manager.

The company owned a centrally located two-story brick building which contained the general office, an appliance show room, and a hardware store. A ready-mix cement plant, lumber yard, and a petroleum bulk plant were located on the northern edge of Sturgess near a mainline railroad. In 1958 the firm employed 120 people.

During Earl Winton's lifetime the Sturgess Fuel Company had expanded rapidly, adding several new product lines. The firm financed this expansion through retained earnings and frequent use of short- and medium-term bank credit. When Jeffrey Winton became president of the company in 1954, he told the Farmers State Bank that he planned to concentrate on expanding sales of the firm's present lines rather than adding new products. He also indicated that he would retain a large part of future earnings in order to strengthen Sturgess Fuel's working capital position.

In his application for the $112,500 three-year loan, Jeffrey Winton stated that the funds would be used to finance a recent expansion in the company's ready-mix cement facilities. Because local demand for this product had increased in the past few years, Mr. Winton believed the newly added cement capacity would materially increase sales of this product.

The day following his visit to the Farmers State Bank, one of the officers informed Mr. Winton that the bank would be willing to accommodate Sturgess up to its legal limit. Since the $112,500 request exceeded the bank's limit, the officer stated he would ask one of the bank's correspondents to participate in the loan. The Farmers State Bank therefore contacted Mr. Olson at Boulevard National, asking for a $75,000 participation. Boulevard National had granted no previous loans to Sturgess Fuel Company.

In order to reach a decision in this participation, Mr. Olson began studying credit information submitted by Farmers State Bank (see Exhibits 1–3). In reviewing a summary of Sturgess Fuel's borrowings, Mr. Olson noted that on May 1, 1957, the company had repaid on schedule its most recent bank loan, a $48,750 90-day credit to finance inventory.

Year	*Maximum Loan Outstanding*	*Low Point*	*Number of Months off Books*
1957	$48,750	....	3
1956	....	....	12
1955	25,205	....	2
1954	35,152	$17,175	...
1953	45,330	11,250	...

Exhibit 1

STURGESS FUEL COMPANY

Comparative Balance Sheets, September 30
(dollar figures in thousands)

Assets	*1954*	*1955*	*1956*	*1957*
Cash	$ 14	$ 24	$ 31	$ 68
Accounts receivable	303	266	281	395
Less: res. for bad debts	(10)	(10)	(10)	(14)
Accounts receivable, net	293	256	271	381
Inventory	166	151	139	156
Cash surrender value – life insurance	1	1	2	3
Total current assets	$474	$432	$443	$ 608
Real estate – land	69	70	64	62
Buildings and equipment	496	526	551	682
Less reserves for depreciation	(220)	(257)	(280)	(359)
Property account, net	345	339	335	385
Sundry accounts receivable	4	....	....	10
Deferred charges and prepaid expenses	8	8	7	12
Goodwill	7	7	7	7
Total assets	$838	$786	$792	$1,022
Liabilities and Net Worth				
Notes payable to banks	$ 34	$ 20	....	$ 15
Notes payable to others	28	21	$ 27	23
Accounts payable	185	166	150	202
Reserves for income taxes	76	40	62	65
Accruals	35	29	32	44
Current portion of long-term debt	28	31	19	11
Total current liabilities	$386	$307	$290	$ 360
Real estate mortgage	64	56	39	20
Other debt	....	....	....	70
Total liabilities	$450	$363	$329	$ 450
Capital stock	188	188	188	188
Surplus	200	235	275	384
Total net worth	$388	$423	$463	$ 572
Total liabilities and net worth	838	786	792	1,022

Exhibit 2

STURGESS FUEL COMPANY

Comparative Profit and Loss Statements
Years Ending September 30
(dollar figures in thousands)

	1954	*1955*	*1956*	*1957*
Net sales	$2,134	$1,850	$1,888	$2,596
Gross profit	626	579	614	750
Operating expenses	582	597	600	739
Bad debts	8	1	6	6
Other income	87	88	101	133
Other charges	7	6	4	1
Income tax	76	27	65	70
Net profit	40	36	40	67
Dividends	......	......	......	8

Exhibit 3

STURGESS FUEL COMPANY

Comparative Analytical Data Based on Exhibits 1 and 2

Operating data	*1954*	*1955*	*1956*	*1957*
Net sales	100.00%	100.00%	100.00%	100.00%
Gross profit	29.33	31.30	32.52	28.89
Operating expenses	27.27	32.27	31.78	28.47
Bad debts	0.37	0.05	0.32	0.23
Other income	4.08	4.76	5.35	5.12
Other charges	0.33	0.32	0.21	0.04
Income tax	3.56	1.46	3.44	2.70
Net profit	1.87	1.94	2.12	2.58
Working capital	$ 88	$125	$153	$248
Tangible net worth	381	416	456	565
Total liabilities	450	363	329	450
Ratios				
Current ratio	1.23	1.41	1.53	1.69
Acid test ratio	0.80	0.92	1.05	1.26
Gross rec. ÷ average months net sales	1.70	1.72	1.79	1.83
Inventory ÷ average months cost of goods sold	1.32	1.43	1.31	1.01
Tangible net worth to total debt	0.85	1.15	1.39	1.26
Tangible net worth to fixed assets	1.10	1.23	1.36	1.47
Net profit to tangible net worth	10.50	8.65	8.77	11.86

In addition, Mr. Olson carefully read the following financial analysis of December 31, 1957, which had been prepared by Boulevard National's credit department:

Current Position and Operation Results: The December 31, 1957 statement showed the company in an improved position compared to the prior year end, the current and acid test ratios going up from 1.53 to 1.69 and from 1.05 to 1.26, respectively. Working capital increased by $95,000 to $248,000 from the following assets and liability changes during the year: sources of funds – increase in long-term debt, $51,000; funds from retained earnings, $59,000; and an increase in surplus of $50,000 (presumably because of additional contributions by shareholders).

These sources of funds were used by the company as follows: increase in net fixed assets, $50,000; increase in other assets, $15,000; resulting in a gain in working capital of $95,000. Net sales of $2,595.750 were significantly higher than the previous year (up 37.5 percent); however, net profit showed only moderate improvement, going from $39,750 or 2.1 percent of sales to $66,750 or 2.6 percent. The outstanding feature of the company's operations continued to be the preponderancy of other income, which was $132,750 or 5.1 percent of sales (compared to net operating profits of $11,250 or 0.43 percent of sales). This "other income" was broken down as follows:

Other operating revenues	$94,500
Discounts earned	30,750
Rental and miscellaneous income	7,500

It would be interesting to ascertain the precise nature of "other operating revenues."

Receivables and Inventories: Net receivables were $381,000, $110,250 greater than at the prior year end or, expressed as a ratio of net sales, they increased from 1.72 to 1.76 months' business.

The reserve for bad debts increased to $14,250 while the bad debt charges for the year were $6000. No aging of receivables was provided, but a Dun and Bradstreet report, dated September 10, 1957, indicated that part of the accounts receivables was slow. In view of this fact, we might consider asking for a breakdown of receivables. Inventories were up from $138,750 or 1.31 months' supply (based on cost of goods sold) to $156,000 or 0.72 month's sales supply at current statement date.

Fixed Assets: Investment in land was reduced from $64,500 to $61,500 while the investment in buildings and equipment increased by $131,250 before depreciation. During the year the company expended: $37,500 on autos and trucks; $56,250 on improvements in buildings, plant, and equipment; $18,750 on a garage; and $18,750 on miscellaneous equipment. The ratio of tangible net worth to fixed assets showed slight improvement, increasing from 1.36 to 1.47.

Liabilities and Net Worth: Current notes payable to bank increased $15,000. Notes payable – Others, decreased $3,750 to $23,250 at year end. Trade payables increased by $52,000 to $201,750; the current portion of long-term debt was reduced $7,500 to $11,250. The company was also contingently liable for $80,250 of installment contracts sold to banks. The tangible net worth to total debt ratio went down from 1.39 to 1.26 as a result of an increase in total debt of $121,000 combined with an increase in net worth of $108,750. Our information indicates this company has been a relatively heavy user of debt in past years. The use of debt to finance expansion was reduced between 1953 and 1956, however results in 1957 may indicate a return to the former policy of using debt to finance some fixed asset expansion.

Conclusion: The company showed a satisfactory financial position at statement date, with a large gain in earnings reported for the year. The large increase in fixed assets indicates that the total plant and equipment is high in relation to the company's sales volume, emphasizing the need for either additional equity capital or a reduction in fixed asset investment. Nevertheless, the company has been able to demonstrate steady progress in sales and profits.

PROBLEM LOANS

Pacific Garment Company

On November 15, 1955, Mr. Roger Nash, assistant vice-president of the Southwestern National Bank, was preparing a report for the loan committee regarding the Pacific Garment Company. Pacific Garment had requested renewal of its accounts receivable line of credit for $240,000, 75 percent advance, 6 3/4 percent interest, to expire February 25, 1956; and renewal of its unsecured line for $60,000, expiring on the same date. These lines originally had been approved for ninety days, effective May 25, 1955, and subsequently renewed for another ninety days on August 25. The present request was the second application for extension of this accommodation.

The Pacific Garment Company, founded in 1901, manufactured men's pajamas, dress and sport shirts, and women's sportswear. The company also produced military uniforms under government contracts; however, after World War II this volume had declined and by 1954 amounted to approximately 10 percent of sales.

Pacific Garment had been a satisfactory customer of the Alhambra branch of Southwestern National for nearly 30 years, usually borrowing seasonally on a secured and unsecured basis. Mr. Nash had become personally familiar with the account while he was branch manager. Although he was now a member of the loan supervision department at the bank's Los Angeles headquarters, Mr. Nash had remained in contact with the Pacific account since many of its loan applications were referred to his department for review.

The company's management, in November, 1955, consisted of four officers: Bruce Perry, president; William G. Forbes, vice president; Howard Olson, secretary-treasurer; Michael Spaulding, production manager. Mr. Perry joined the company as a production worker after graduation from high school in 1928. He later transferred to the sales department and was promoted to sales manager in 1946. Perry was appointed president in March 1955 after the death of the former president. Forbes and Olson were also veteran employees of the company, having been with Pacific for sixteen and twenty-two years, respectively. Mr. Spaulding, the production manager, had recently been hired to replace George Knudsen, who retired after nearly 40 years of service. The company maintained a sales force of eight men who sold Pacific products directly to retailers throughout California. Most of these men had been with the company for many years; no new salesmen had been added since 1948.

Pacific Garment had been profitable in its early years; however, operating losses were sustained during the depression of the 1930s. The company finally earned a profit in 1937 and continued profitable from 1937 to 1941. At that time sales and profits greatly expanded as a result of World War II.

After the war, the company's profits tapered off sharply, and in 1952 operating losses began. Style was an important competitive factor; during the postwar period the company had not been able to keep pace with style changes and trends in the industry. During that year the management decided to embark upon an ambitious expansion program, increasing total plant investment $100,000 over a two-year period.

Early in 1953 the company began negotiating loans with the Southwestern Bank to finance the expansion of plant, installation of new equipment, and additional inventory. The bank granted:

1. $90,000 in April 1953, for eight years, secured by buildings appraised for $156,000; monthly repayments were $960 including interest.

2. $90,000 in March 1954, for three years, secured by a mortgage on equipment appraised at $175,650; quarterly repayments were $7500, and interest was paid monthly.

Sales did not expand to utilize fully this added plant capacity; the company incurred a loss of $2000 in 1953, $3000 in 1954, and $48,600 for the first nine months of 1955. Mr. Reed, president of the company for twenty-two years, died in March 1955, and Mr. Perry was subsequently appointed president.

Borrowing History

On May 14, 1955, an analyst in the bank's credit department prepared the following routine report of the Pacific Garment Company:

Total Bank Debt—May 14, 1955		$283,735
Interest Rate: Unsecured loan	5%	
Mortgage loan	4 3/4%	
Real-estate loan	5%	

Indebtedness to us increased $72,513 since review report of 10/4/54, principally in seasonal line. This borrower has not been out of debt for many years, with unsecured loan reaching a low of $12,000 in March 1954, and since has steadily increased to the $150,000 now outstanding. Debts appear disproportionate to net worth, operations unprofitable last three years. Seasonal liquidation of unsecured line appears highly desirable.

Details of Present Borrowings

$150,000—Owing under a $175,000 unsecured line, which is to revert to a $150,000 line on 5/15/55 and is to expire on 3/1/56.

$ 60,000—Originated on 3/17/54 at $90,000, current quarterly repayment program of $7500 plus interest monthly, with a maturity of 3/17/57. Secured by a mortgage on equipment appraised in January 1954 for an insurable value of $175,650.

$ 73,735—New at $90,000 on 4/12/53 with a repayment program of $960 monthly including interest and a maturity of 4/12/61. Secured by a light industrial building appraised in 1952 for $156,000.

$283,735

Outstandings are under various approvals of the headquarters loan committee, with the unsecured line subject to the following conditions:
Dividends are not to be paid except from profits.
If indebtedness is not paid by maturity, borrower will, if requested by bank, furnish satisfactory security.
Use of our credit facilities shows the following recent range of borrowings:

Year	High		Low	
1955 (to date)	April	$283,735	January	$240,000
1954	August	280,000	January	181,000
1953	April	239,000	January	120,000
1952	April	158,000	January	90,000
1951	November	90,000	October	NIL

On May 23, 1955, Mr. Perry visited the Alhambra branch of Southwestern National to discuss his financial problems with Mr. Peter Hayes, branch manager. Mr. Perry indicated that Pacific temporarily needed additional funds to increase working capital and to pay certain trade invoices which were maturing. Specifically, he requested an increase of $150,000 in the company's current credit line to cover maximum needs during the summer and fall selling season, thus extending the line to $300,000. Mr. Perry requested this accommodation for one year. He stated his willingness to place $240,000 on a secured basis, pledging accounts receivable for that purpose; the remaining $60,000 would be unsecured.

Since this credit request was beyond his authorized lending limit

($25,000), Mr. Hayes drew up the following loan application to the loan committee that he forwarded to Mr. Nash in the Los Angeles office.

Present indebtedness (5/12/55)	
Unsecured—under a $150,000 line	$150,000
Secured, equipment, mortgage	60,000
Secured, real estate	73,735
	$283,735
Average deposit balances—$21,000 (1954)	
Application	
Cancel present unsecured line of	$150,000
Approve—accounts receivable line of with advances of 75 percent	240,000
Interest 6 3/4 percent; Expiration: May 25, 1956	
Approve—unsecured line of	60,000
Interest 5 percent; Expiration: May 25, 1956	

Financial

Company prepared statement as of April 30, 1955 (000 omitted)

Current assets	$590
Current liabilities	359
Working capital	231
Capital and surplus	289
Sales (4 months)	800
Loss	(36)

Recommended by Manager Peter Hayes.

In preparing a recommendation for the loan committee, Mr. Nash reviewed the company's available operating statements, the credit analyst's report dated May 14, 1955 and latest correspondent and memoranda in the company's file. After completing his analysis, Mr. Nash decided to recommend the $240,000 secured and the $60,000 unsecured lines; however, he stated that these lines should expire in ninety days—August 25, 1955. Mr. Nash realized the account was overextended, and he believed that immediate steps should be taken by company officials to reduce bank debt. He sent a memorandum to Peter Hayes, branch manager, advising that he was recommending approval of the loan request but asking Hayes to discuss reductions in outstanding bank debt with Mr. Perry as soon as possible.

On May 25, 1955, the loan committee reviewed and accepted Mr. Nash's recommendation, The excerpt from the following memorandum was dictated to record this decision:

Minutes of the Subcommittee on Loans of the Headquarters Loan Committee—May 25, 1955
Alhambra Branch

. . . On recommendation of Manager Peter Hayes, concurred in by Assist- and Vice-President Roger A. Nash, the Committee approved an unsecured loan of—$60,000 with interest at 5 percent, maturity August 25, 1955; and,

> On recommendation of Manager Peter Hayes, concurred in by Assistant Vice-President Roger Nash, the committee approved an accounts receivable line of credit of $240,000 with interest at prevailing rate but not less than 6 3/4 percent, expiration August 25, 1955. Advances will be at 75 percent. . . .

On August 15, 1955, Mr. Perry returned to the Alhambra branch to request his first extension of these credit lines, from August 25, 1955, to February 25, 1956. He explained to Mr. Hayes that Pacific's working capital position was still tight and the extension would be needed to maintain current production. Perry also indicated that operations continued unprofitable. However, the company had recently hired a firm of management consultants to conduct a comprehensive review. Mr. Hayes prepared the following loan application memorandum dated August 16, 1955, which he forwarded to Mr. Nash requesting approval:

Present indebtedness

Accounts receivable—under a $240,000 line	$ 54,000
Unsecured—under a $60,000 line	60,000
Secured—chattel mortgage	52,600
Real estate	71,500
	$238,700

Average deposit balances—$25,200—(1955 to date)
Application

Renew accounts receivable line of credit for with advances at 75 percent Interest: 6 3/4 percent; Expiration: February 25, 1956	$240,000
Renew unsecured line of credit for Interest: 5 percent; Expiration: February 25, 1956	$ 60,000

Financial
Company statement as of April 30, 1955: (000 omitted)

Current assets	$590
Current liabilities	359
Working capital	231
Net worth	289
Sales (4 months)	800
Loss	(36)

Receivable financing for this account originated in June 1955, and our experience has been satisfactory. Turnover of accounts assigned has averaged thirty-seven days.
Recommended by Manager Peter Hayes.

In discussing this application two days later before the loan committee, Mr. Nash pointed out the financial deterioration which had occurred in recent years. While he believed that the bank's interests probably were adequately protected at this time, Mr. Nash noted that Pacific's financial position was worsening steadily. He thought that additional or extended accommodation could not be justified from the bank's standpoint. The account had not been off the bank's books for five years, and total indebtedness had risen sharply. Mr. Nash recommended extension of the present lines for three months only, expiring November 25, 1955; however, he suggested that a formal understanding be reached at once with Mr. Perry concerning a plan for reduction of bank debt. He proposed that Perry be informed that only a considerable improvement in the company's financial condition would warrant further extension of credit. The loan committee accepted this recommendation, and extended the lines of credit for ninety days.

In early October Mr. Perry came to the bank at Mr. Nash's request to discuss the company's financial problems and plans for the future. Mr. Nash pointed out that he reluctantly recommended the latest extension; he therefore questioned Perry regarding the possibility of immediate reductions in bank credit. Mr. Perry then revealed that the board of directors had decided during the past week to sell or merge the business, since they recognized that the company could not solve current sales and production problems without additional financing and new management. Mr. Perry said that the consultant's report had recommended any of these alternatives:

1. Sell the company.
2. Merge with a stronger company in which Pacific stockholders would retain an interest.
3. Contract out the production facilities to a major manufacturer.

Mr. Perry indicated that the directors favored selling the business on a going concern basis rather than liquidating, since a forced sale of technical production equipment and specialized inventory would result in a lower realization on company assets. Pacific had already hired Frank Ross Associates, a firm which specialized in bringing together buyers and sellers of businesses, and Perry hoped that arrangements could be made to sell the company in the next three or four months. Mr. Nash asked about financial requirements during the time necessary to negotiate a sale, and Mr. Perry stated that Pacific would probably need to continue the present accommodation until a buyer was located or a merger arranged. He stressed the desire of Pacific's directors to sell or merge the firm as a going concern rather than to liquidate. Mr. Perry believed, however, that no increase in the lines would be required and that if Ross Associates located a buyer in the next few weeks the company could commence at once to reduce operations and liquidate bank loans. Perry gave Mr. Nash a copy of the management consultant's report together with a special auditor's report which the directors requested before reaching their decision to sell or merge the company. He promised to keep Mr. Nash closely informed regarding any prospective purchasers of the business.

After Mr. Perry had left the bank Mr. Nash examined the auditor's report of September 30, 1955, extracts from which are presented below:

> A review of your statements indicates that not only does the company's financial position need strengthening but extreme measures are required to improve operating results. Net income for 1950 dropped to $37,624 from $62,287 in 1949, and in 1951 it dropped to $6832. For the three years and nine months ended September 30, 1955, operating losses amounted to $54,584.
>
> In 1952 the company embarked upon an expansion program which increased total plant investment from $200,000 on December 31, 1951, to $300,000 on December 31, 1952. There was no appreciable increase in sales or output following the enlargement of plant capacity. The cost of this expansion program, the operating losses of recent years, and the continuance of dividends during unprofitable years have weakened the company. It is now clear the business cannot continue without additional financial aid and the re-establishment of profitable operations. . . .
>
> While we believe certain past actions of the directors and officers might be subject to criticism, we do not believe that an examination is required unless the directors have reason to question the integrity of the accounting. We believe one might fairly criticize the payment of high officers' salaries without the formal approval of the directors and the continuance of dividends during the loss years. However, the salaries and dividends have been paid. The company is now faced with conditions which require prompt remedial action. . . .
>
> We have reviewed the report of the management consultants and consider sound the alternatives they offer (sell, merge, or contract out your facilities). The rebuilding of the company from within would appear impossible without additional aid of a financial and management character. . . .
>
> While complete liquidation would cause the company to convert its assets into cash, pay off its liabilities, and distribute what remains to the stockholders, we believe it reasonable to consider the possibility of converting only current assets and equipment into cash so that the plant and real estate would remain for the shareholders in final liquidation. . . .
>
> The statements following show certain tentative estimated realizations from liquidation of current assets of the company. Comparative balance sheets and income statements are also shown. . . . (see Exhibits 1, 2, 3, 4)

Mr. Nash questioned the liquidation value assigned to the inventory by the auditor. Therefore, he contacted a textile specialist in the Commodity Loan Section of the bank, asking him to estimate the worth of the stock in the event of a forced liquidation. Mr. Nash received the following reply:

> My original thinking was that this inventory might liquidate for approximately 50 percent of total collateral valuation, although the process might prove both tedious and expensive involving sales in San Francisco and Los Angeles.

Exhibit 1

PACIFIC GARMENT COMPANY

Comparative Balance Sheets
1949 – 1955

	Dec. 31, 1949	*Dec. 31, 1950*	*Dec. 31, 1951*	*Dec. 31, 1952*	*Dec. 31, 1953*	*Dec. 31, 1954*	*Sept. 30, 1955*
Cash	$ 9,856	$ 10,135	$ 9,788	$ 2,648	$ 3,655	$ 4,513	$ 15,660
Accounts receivable	126,774	109,919	97,084	103,372	85,810	106,051	171,023
Inventory	274,740	285,636	302,258	312,258	352,564	435,658	291,661
Prepaid expense	1,226	1,362	1,370	2,306	1,900	2,197	2,964
Cash value – life insurance	11,903	12,394	4,801	5,112	5,341	5,566	974
Total current assets	$424,499	$419,446	$415,497	$425,696	$449,270	$553,985	$482,282
Current liabilities*	154,426	126,112	128,249	244,241	186,937	239,153	230,736
Net current assets	$270,073	$293,334	$287,248	$181,455	$262,333	$314,832	$251,546
Building loan	....	....	$ 9,178	....	$ 83,533	$ 76,020	$ 69,488
Chattel mortgage loan	....	....	....	....	....	67,500	45,000
Total long-term debt	....	....	$ 9,178	....	$ 83,533	$143,520	$114,488
Balance – current assets	$270,073	$293,334	278,070	$181,455	178,800	171,312	137,058
Land	6,498	6,498	6,498	6,498	1,225	1,225	1,225
Warehouse or leased land	....	....	....	2,566	2,566	2,566	2,566
Buildings	32,213	32,213	57,029	140,796	141,216	141,216	141,216
Machinery and fixtures	131,219	139,109	139,109	148,985	157,430	164,095	166,828
Autos	6,044	5,941	5,941	5,813	5,813	5,813	5,813
Total fixed assets	$175,974	$183,761	$208,577	$304,658	$308,250	$314,915	$317,648
Less depreciation	110,559	117,117	126,258	136,613	149,222	160,934	170,535
Net fixed investment	$ 65,415	$ 66,644	$ 82,319	$168,045	$159,028	$153,981	$147,113
Equity of stockholders†	$335,488	$359,978	$360,389	$349,500	$337,828	$325,293	$284,171
Capital of stockholders	161,760	161,760	161,760	161,760	161,760	161,760	161,760
Earned surplus	$173,728	$198,218	$198,629	$187,740	$176,068	$163,533	$122,411

*Current liabilities include outstanding short-term bank debt. †Mrs. Reed, widow of the former president, owned virtually all of the company's stock.

Exhibit 2

PACIFIC GARMENT COMPANY

Comparative Income Statements
Years Ending December 31, 1949–1954
9 Months Ending Sept. 30, 1955

Income and Surplus	*1949*	*1950*	*1951*	*1952*	*1953*	*1954*	*Jan. 1, 1955 to Sept. 30, 1955*
Sales	$1,666,768	$1,513,428	$1,262,218	$1,243,374	$1,372,243	$1,432,826	$1,177,645
Cost of sales	1,258,989	1,166,134	982,516	965,752	1,070,555	1,109,057	958,309
Gross profit	$ 407,870	$ 347,294	$ 279,702	$ 277,622	$ 301,688	$ 323,769	$ 219,336
Percent of gross profit to sales	24.5%	23.0%	22.1%	22.3%	22.0%	22.6%	18.6%
Other income	$ 2,609	$ 2,086	....	$ 1,284	$ 8,693	....	....
Total income	$ 410,479	$ 349,380	$ 279,702	$ 278,906	$ 310,381	$ 323,769	$ 219,336
Depreciation	$ 9,956	$ 10,590	$ 10,130	$ 12,892	$ 12,600	$ 11,984	$ 9,600
Compensation of officers	83,520	73,350	53,400	45,630	51,240	41,040	25,560
Other expenses	216,868	205,732	207,692	221,567	248,507	273,574	232,782
Total expenses	$ 310,344	$ 289,672	$ 271,222	$ 280,089	$ 312,347	$ 326,598	$ 267,942
Percent of expenses to sales	18.6%	19.1%	21.5%	22.5%	22.8%	22.8%	22.8%
Net income before taxes	$ 100,135	$ 59,708	$ 8,480	$ (1,183)	$ (1,966)	$ (2,829)	$ (48,606)
Taxes	37,848	22,084	1,648	....	....	....	....
Net income after taxes	$ 62,287	$ 37,624	$ 6,832	$ (1,183)	$ (1,966)	$ (2,829)	$ (48,606)
Surplus at beginning of year	130,003	173,728	198,218	198,629	187,740	176,068	163,533
Life insurance proceeds	....	....	3,285	....	....	....	7,484
Balance—surplus	$ 192,290	$ 211,352	$ 208,335	$ 197,446	$ 185,774	$ 173,239	$ 122,411
Dividends	18,562	13,134	9,706	9,706	9,706	9,706	$........
Surplus at end of year	$ 173,728	$ 198,218	$ 198,629	$ 187,740	$ 176,068	$ 163,533	$ 122,411

Exhibit 3

PACIFIC GARMENT COMPANY

Estimated Liquidating Values (Current Assets)
September 30, 1955

			Per Books	*Estimated to Realize or Pay*
CURRENT ASSETS				
Cash			$ 15,660	$ 15,660
Accounts receivable			171,023	160,513
Inventory			291,661	240,752
Other			3,938	2,160
Total current assets			$482,282	$419,085
LIABILITIES			345,224	345,224
Trade accounts payable and accrued liabilities		$ 64,679		
Demand notes 3 percent dated July 31, 1955*		24,976		
Notes payable, bank		255,569		
Open account	$60,000			
Secured by acc. rec.	81,081			
Secured by real property	69,488			
Secured by equipment	45,000			
Balance—current assets			$137,058	$ 73,861
Estimated allowance for overhead and continuing expenses				(42,000)
Estimated expenses of liquidation (excluding commissions on sales of fixed assets)				(12,000)
Balance—cash available for distribution to stockholders				$ 19,861

*Demand notes owed to stockholders.

However, friends in the trade uniformly feel that I was too optimistic. The consensus of their thinking is that a forced liquidation would do well to bring 40 percent of total collateral valuation. Sales would have to be predominantly in New York, as neither San Francisco nor Los Angeles could absorb any appreciable amounts of this inventory. Even with a fairly active New York sales program, it would take a year or more to liquidate such an inventory. The type of merchandise and the yardages involved complicate the picture. . . .

Mr. Perry contacted Mr. Nash three times during the next thirty days, reporting that two large nationally known garment manufacturers had visited the plant and that both showed interest. However, as of October 20, no firm offer had been received.

On October 24, Mr. Nash telephoned John Ross Associates to learn of any progress. Nash told Mr. Ross that in another two or three weeks Pacific would have to decide whether to continue in business since the lines of credit would expire November 25 and continuing operations

Exhibit 4

PACIFIC GARMENT COMPANY

Estimated Liquidating Value of Inventory, September 30, 1955

Item	*Physical Inventory Going Concern Value*	*Method of Disposition*	*Estimated Percent of Realization*	*Estimated Realization*
Buttons and thread	$ 22,216	By bulk sale	50%	$ 11,108
Labels	3,816		.....	....
Zippers, other sundries and supplies	13,474	Saleable items totaling $10,054 by bulk sale – 50%	37.3	5,027
Work in process	27,186	By completion and sale to trade	100	27,186
Stock	117,694	By sale to trade at 90% of wholesale prices less shipping allowance of $1,350	116	136,525
Piece goods and linings	92,738	By bulk sale	50	46,369
Piece goods in transit and converters	14,537	By outright sales or open sales order	100	14,537
	$291,661			$240,752

would require purchase of raw materials necessary to produce a spring line. Mr. Nash pointed out that the bank could no longer justify extension of interim credit on this account. Mr. Ross stated that a close down of Pacific at this time would defeat any plan for selling the business at an attractive figure. He asked Mr. Nash to do whatever possible to "keep the doors open" for the next sixty days, since within that time Ross would have definite answers from the two concerns actively interested in buying or merging. He promised to telephone Mr. Nash immediately if he received a positive commitment from the prospective purchasers.

On November 15, Mr. Perry called on Mr. Nash to request the second 90-day extension of the $240,000 secured and $60,000 unsecured lines to finance raw material purchases and production for the spring line. Mr. Perry stated that Mr. Ross was still negotiating with the two garment manufacturers, both of whom had shown considerable interest in purchasing Pacific. Mr. Perry believed that a sale on satisfactory terms would soon be arranged.

Special Bank Services 

SERVICE CHARGE POLICY

GREEN GLEN DAIRY

Early in July 1958, Mr. Oliver Austin, assistant cashier of the Empire National Bank in San Francisco, California, was considering what action he should take regarding an anticipated increase in service charges on several of the bank's larger commercial accounts. The expected increases would result from the introduction of a new schedule of activity charges effective July 1. Although no general announcement of the change in rates had been made, the board of directors had asked Mr. Austin to review any accounts whose service charges would materially increase as a result of the revised plan, and to contact customers who he thought should receive an explanation of the new rates.

The Empire National Bank, founded in 1939, operated thirteen branches in the San Francisco metropolitan area. The bank's main office was centrally located downtown, and nine of the thirteen branches were within 10 miles of the city. The bank had the reputation of being conservative in its operating policies, usually stressing safety and reliability in its advertising copy. In 1957, Empire National had total resources of $132 million and was eighth in size among San Francisco banks. Competition among local banks for commercial and industrial customers had become especially keen in recent years. In addition, a growing number of new savings and loan associations and finance companies had been established in San Francisco, thus increasing competition for deposits and for construction, home improvement, and personal loans.

Mr. Oliver Austin, 33, had been employed at Empire National for seven years. After completing military service he returned to the University of Washington to complete his education. He was graduated in 1949, and in 1951 he moved to San Francisco, accepting a position with Empire National. Mr. Austin spent two years as a teller and three years as assistant manager in the Burlingame branch. In 1956 he was promoted to assistant cashier and transferred to Empire's main office as assistant manager of the cashier's department.

In the spring of 1958, Mr. Austin was assigned to study the bank's methods of assessing service charges on commercial deposit accounts and to offer recommendations on necessary revisions. The schedule of charges currently used by the bank was devised in 1950, and no operating cost adjustments had been made since that time.

The determination of the bank's current handling costs was based on a careful study of the direct and indirect expenses involved in processing individual items in commercial deposit accounts. Mr. Austin and his staff made cost accounting analyses in these departments: proof, bookkeeping, commercial tellers, and statements. The results of these studies enabled Mr. Austin to calculate the item costs of handling (1) checks drawn on the Empire Bank, (2) processing of deposit slips, and (3) deposited checks drawn on other banks.

The study group also examined specific expenses in servicing commercial accounts (for example, telegraphic transfers, armored car service, credit department inquiries) together with bank overhead (for example, public relations, insurance, auditing) and distributed a pro rata share of these expenses to each commercial account. Mr. Austin also reviewed the methods of computing service charges used by Empire's correspondent banks in Eastern cities. Exhibit 1 shows a typical commercial account analysis form used by a large New York City bank.

Exhibit 1

GREEN GLEN DAIRY

Example of a Complete Account Analysis Form
Used by a New York City Bank

A.	Average daily ledger balance for month	$
B.	Less: average daily float	______
C.	Average net collected balance	
D.	Less: reserves percent of (*C*)	______
E.	Investable balance	
F.	Earnings credit at rate of percent of (*E*)	$______
G.	Maintenance factor	$
H.	Deposits at ¢	
I.	Checks paid at ¢	
J.	Clearings at ¢	
K.	Transit items at ¢	
L.	Cash handled at ¢ per minute of handling time	
M.	Checks paid that create or increase an overdraft	
N.	Checks returned (drawn or deposited by customer) because of insufficient or no funds or other reasons at ¢	
O.	Other related services	______
P.	Total amount for services rendered (total of lines *G* to *O*)	$
Q.	Less: earnings credit (from line *F*)	
R.	Net service charge	$

Based upon Empire's earnings record for the past five years, Mr. Austin decided that an earnings credit of 2 percent should be allowed on net loanable balances in commercial accounts. Net loanable balances were defined as ledger balances less uncollected funds (float). Austin learned that a similar 2 percent earnings credit was currently used by several West Coast banks, including two of the larger banks in San Francisco. Empire National had formally allowed its customers an earnings credit of 2 1/2 percent.

After completing his study and evaluating the results, Mr. Austin concluded that for some time Empire National had seriously underestimated its costs in processing individual items in commercial accounts. His data revealed:

	Current Handling Costs to Empire Bank	*Current Charges to Empire Commercial Customers*
1. Checks drawn by commercial customers on deposit accounts at Empire	5¢ each	3¢ each
2. Checks deposited by commercial customers	2 1/2¢ each for the 1st 5,000; 2¢ each for all over 5,000	1 1/2¢ each
3. Time necessary for collection of deposited checks (float)	1.50 days	1 day

The above estimates were based on actual out-of-pocket costs and collection experience and did not allow any profit for the bank. In his report to the board of directors, Mr. Austin included the following sample form together with a brief explanation of how future activity charges should be calculated.

(1)	*(2)*	*(3)*	*(4)*	*(5)*	*(6)*	*(7)*	*(8)*	*(9)*
Average Daily Ledger Balance	Net Loanable Balance	Income 2%	Checks Paid at 5¢ ea.	Items Deposited at 2 1/2¢ each (over 5,000, 2¢ ea.)	Maintenance at 90¢ per account	Misc. Expenses	Total Expenses	Profit or Loss

1. *Ledger Balance*—Add the daily balances shown on the account's ledger card; use Friday balances for Saturday and Sunday. When there is no change, use the previous day's balance. Divide by the number of *calendar* days in the month to get the average daily ledger balance.

2. *Net Loanable Balance*—This figure is the ledger balance *less* "float." Float is computed as follows: Add the total amount of deposits made during the month, counting Friday deposits three times; divide by the number of *calendar* days in the month; and multiply by 1.5 to get the typical one and one-half day's float.

3. *Income*—An income credit of 2 percent per annum is allowed on the net loanable balance.

4. *Checks Paid*—Total the number of checks drawn each month against the account. Note this total on the analysis form and extend at 5¢ per check.

5. *Items Deposited*—Count the number of checks deposited each month. Enter the total on the analysis form and extend at 2 1/2¢ per check up to 5,000 and 2¢ per check over 5,000.

6. *Maintenance Charge*—This is an arbitrary 90¢ per month to cover stationery, mailing, and other costs which are fairly constant whether the account is inactive or very active.

7. *Miscellaneous Expense*—This includes several minor expenses which occur less frequently, such as processing the return of dishonored checks and preparing orders of currency and coin.

8. *Total Expense*—This sum is the total of columns 4, 5, 6, and 7.

9. *Profit or Loss*—This is the net difference between income (column 3) and total expense (column 8).

After reviewing Mr. Austin's recommendations, the board decided to adopt a revised schedule of service charges effective July 1. The directors asked Mr. Austin to assume supervision of the cost analysis phase of bank operations and to continue studying methods for the improvement of the calculation and distribution of service charges. Since the board of directors decided not to notify all customers of the changes in activity charges, they also asked Austin to contact only those accounts whose charges would increase materially as a result of the new plan.

At Mr. Austin's request, Warren Clemens, supervisor of the commercial account department, had compiled a list of companies whose deposit accounts had generally shown higher than average activity. Mr. Austin planned to use this list to determine which customers should be contacted and in what manner the new schedule of charges should be explained.

The Green Glen Dairy, an Empire National customer since 1949, was typical of accounts whose service charges would increase substantially unless the company maintained larger deposit balances. Combined balances in the general and payroll accounts averaged $140,000 for the first six months of 1958. Green Glen's general account was an extremely active one since nearly all payments received from the company's customers were by check, and the billing for one month's residential service averaged $17.00. In the first six months of 1958, Green Glen deposited for collection an average of 21,000 checks per month.

The company had been charged $191.98 for bank services during the month of June; Mr. Austin estimated that with the same deposit balances and a similar volume of activity in July, new service charges would exceed $400. Before deciding what action to take, Mr. Austin

Exhibit 2

GREEN GLEN DAIRY

Month	Ledger Balance	Net Loanable Balance	Income 2%	Checks Paid at 5¢	Items Deposited 2 1/2¢ (over 5,000, 2¢)	Maintenance Charge at 90¢ per Number of Accounts	Misc. Expense	Total Expense	Profit or Loss New Method	Profit or Loss Old* Method
Jan.	$120,360	$ 63,840	$106.42	1172– $58.60	20,528 $435.56	$1.80	$3.26	$499.22	($392.80)	($209.04)
Feb.	115,200	64,200	107.02	1000– 50.00	21,487 454.74	1.80	5.11	511.65	(404.63)	(241.58)
Mar.	157,440	105,360	175.64	1060– 53.00	21,822 461.44	1.80	4.19	520.43	(344.79)	(186.28)
Apr.	170,880	119,880	199.84	1339– 66.95	21,703 459.06	1.80	3.87	531.68	(331.84)	(180.41)
May	121,560	70,680	117.82	1201– 60.05	21,677 458.54	1.80	6.02	526.41	(408.59)	(215.10)
June	137,280	81,960	136.63	976– 48.80	20,695 438.90	1.80	5.40	494.90	(358.27)	(191.98)

*"Old method": The actual service charges levied on the Green Glen account from January through June.

asked Warren Clemens to review Green Glen and several other large accounts commencing January 1, 1958. He asked Clemens to apply the new rates to learn what the service charges would have been if the new system had been in effect since the beginning of the year. In response to Mr. Austin's request, Clemens developed the data concerning Green Glen, as shown in Exhibit 2.

In studying these data, Mr. Austin noted that the service charges under the new system would have been nearly double those charged to the Green Glen account from January through June. Even though the new rates were based on careful cost studies, Mr. Austin realized it might be difficult to justify the sharp increases in charges to Mr. Frank Cole, president of Green Glen.

Mr. Cole, 62, had been president of Green Glen since its inception. In addition to his activities in the dairy business, he participated in civic affairs, having served as president of the San Francisco Chamber of Commerce and as a member of several civic welfare and improvement organizations. He was a capable businessman, and his management of the company was responsible for its continuing profitability and growth.

Mr. Austin was fully aware that certain banks absorbed some service and activity charges for competitive reasons to acquire a large new ac-

Exhibit 3

GREEN GLEN DAIRY

Balance Sheet, December 31, 1957

ASSETS	
Current assets	$1,286,365
Investments	104,294
Plant and equipment	519,704
Ranch land and equipment	180,776
Deferred charges and deposits	41,198
Other assets	293,450
Total assets	$2,425,787
LIABILITIES AND CAPITAL	
Current liabilities	$ 898,694
Fixed liabilities	398,668
Reserves and deposits	13,806
Total liabilities	$1,311,168
Capital stock	606,958
Earned surplus	507,661
Total capital	$1,114,619
Total liabilities and net worth	$2,425,787

count or to retain an important established customer who might be considering a change in banking relations. Accordingly, Mr. Austin was uncertain what approach he should take in explaining to Mr. Cole Empire National's new schedule of activity charges.

Exhibit 4

GREEN GLEN DAIRY

Income Statement, Year Ending December 31, 1957

Sales	$8,876,287
Cost of sales	8,593,421
Gross profit	282,866
Miscellaneous expenses	88,241
Miscellaneous income	21,517
Net profit before taxes	216,142
Federal income tax	111,144
Net profit	$ 104,998

Record of 1958 Borrowings at Empire National

	Maximum Loan	*Interest Rate*
Jan. 1956	$ 25,000	5%
Feb. 1956	20,000	5
Mar. 1956	162,000	5
Apr. 1956	156,600	5
May 1956	151,200	5
June 1956	145,800	

SERVICE CHARGE POLICY: A MODEL FOR BANK DECISIONS

A recent survey revealed that four out of five small banks base their demand deposit service charges on "competition."[1] Many banks have advertised low service charges with the expectation of attracting new accounts.[2] It is well known, however, that increased volume does *not*

[1]Survey of 106 small banks (assets less than $50 million) in the Twelfth Federal Reserve District, February 1965. See the appendix to this note.

[2]A. A. Robichek and C. W. Haley, "Bank Service Charges: A Comparative Analysis," *Burroughs Clearing House*, January 1965.

A condensed version of this note written by Alexander A. Robichek and John G. McDonald appeared in *The Bankers Magazine*, Autumn 1966.

always result in increased profit. The prevailing emphasis in banking appears to be on competition and growth of volume; few banks have attempted to estimate the effect of possible changes in service charges on the expected *profit* of the bank.

This note presents a framework for analyzing the impact of alternative service charge schedules on bank profits. First, a decision model is presented which examines the relationship between the level of service charges and bank profit attributable to demand deposits. Then, an example is used to evaluate the possible impact of one decision variable—charge per check—on the demand deposit volume and profit in a hypothetical bank. Finally, in a general application of the model, a number of service charge strategies are evaluated to determine the expected impact of various levels of service charges and earnings credits on profit.

Determination of Profit on Demand Deposits

In order to evaluate alternative financial decisions, it is necessary to specify an objective. For purposes of this note, it is assumed that the bank wishes to maximize the profit attributable to demand deposits. But how does one define "profit attributable to demand deposits"? If funds are transmitted from demand deposits to investment and lending activities at a centrally determined transfer price, one can then attempt to maximize profit in each activity, given the transfer price and operating costs.[3] However, in the absence of a transfer-price procedure, profit is not maximized solely in one activity, but rather in a set of related activities, including demand deposits and the associated investment and lending operations. A number of simplifying assumptions will be made in this paper in regard to the interrelationship between various banking activities. These assumptions are necessary to help us concentrate at the central issue: the expected impact of alternative service charge strategies on bank profit.

The first task is to describe the general relationship between service charges and bank profit attributable to demand deposits. Demand deposits provide funds which are committed to loans, securities, and nonearning assets such as reserve cash and float. Associated with demand deposit activities are a variety of operating costs. A change in service charges may have an impact on both the level (number and size of accounts) and the activity (number of checks per month, and so forth) of demand deposits which, in turn, affect the level of costs and revenues

[3]If one activity in the bank furnishes funds to another activity, a transfer price may be established to determine independently the profit of each activity. The assigned "price" of funds supplied from demand deposits to the investment activity, for example, may be expressed in terms of a rate of return—used by the receiving department as a "cost" of funds and by the supplying department as a "return" on transferred funds.

Exhibit 1

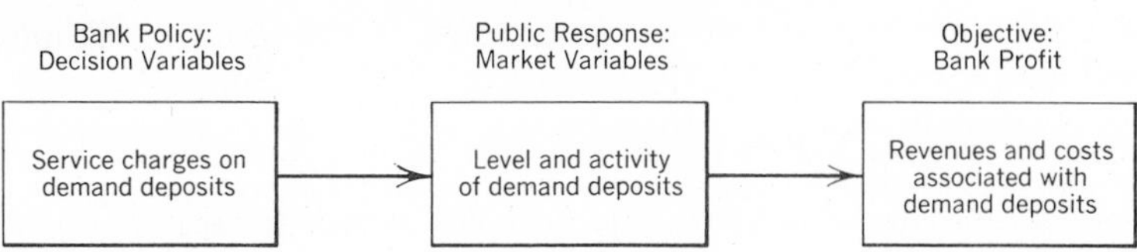

that determine the bank's total profit from demand deposits. This relationship is represented in Exhibit 1.

The bank must consider a number of *decision variables* which comprise its service charge policy—monthly maintenance charge, charge per check, earnings credit, and the like. These decision variables represent the "prices" that the bank places on its demand deposit services. Faced with these prices, consumers respond by determining a number of *market variables* which represent the level of market demand—number of accounts, average balance per account, average number of checks drawn per month, and the like. The bank has a number of *structural variables* pertaining to operating costs and earnings opportunities available in securities and loans. It is the public's response, together with the bank's processing cost and earnings parameters, which will determine the level of profit from funds provided by demand deposits.

The service charge policy which will lead to the highest expected profit is often not intuitively obvious. The highest possible volume of deposits or the largest number of accounts may not be associated with maximum profits. A model is a useful device to state these relationships explicitly and to make them operationally useful.

Defining Profit

Profit attributable to demand deposits is defined here as net revenues from service charges plus net bank earnings on funds provided by demand deposits minus the bank's costs of processing demand deposits. Thus, in general

$$P = S + E - C \tag{1}$$

where P = profit attributable to demand deposits

S = service charge revenue from demand deposits

E = earnings on bank assets provided by demand deposits, net or operating costs associated with investments and loans

C = costs of operations associated with demand deposits

For purposes of analysis, it is convenient to define profit in terms of service charge revenue, net earnings, and cost *per demand deposit account*. As discussed later, the bank may segment its accounts by type, and this framework may be applied separately to each group of accounts. Initially, however, we will consider profit in terms of average figures for a relatively homogeneous group of accounts. Total profit in (1) may be restated as follows:

$$P = S + E - C$$

$$= m_1 s + m_1 e - (m_1 c + F)$$

$$P = m_1 (s + e - c) - F \qquad (2)$$

where m_1 = number of demand deposit accounts

s = average net service charge per account

e = average net earnings per account

c = average variable cost per account

F = fixed costs associated with demand deposits

As a simplifying assumption, fixed costs will be considered constant over the range of service charges being analyzed. "Profit before fixed costs," P^*, may be expressed as follows:

$$P^* = P + F$$

$$P^* = m_1 (s + e - c) \qquad (3)$$

In other words, "profit before fixed costs" depends on the number of accounts and on the service charge revenue, net earnings, and variable cost per average account. "Profit before fixed cost," P^*, may be used in place of the usual profit definition, P, only because it is assumed that fixed costs are constant over the range of analysis. Obviously, fixed costs per se cannot be ignored; but in comparing *alternative* service charge strategies, fixed costs have no effect in determining the best (highest profit) strategy. A banker who finds that his level of fixed costs, as he defines them, changes appreciably with incremental volume should use profit as defined in (2) rather than (3).

Existing use of low service charges as a competitive "weapon" concentrates on increasing the number of accounts and, hopefully, the total level of demand deposits. That is, by decreasing or eliminating service charges, small banks have tended to attract new accounts, raising m_1, while decreasing the service charge revenue per accounts. The heart of the problem lies in determining the net effect of these opposing changes on profit. The objective of a change in service charge policy should *not* be to increase m_1 but to *increase profit,* the product of m_1 and $(s + e - c)$.

Developing the Variables

Decision and Market Variables

Service charge revenue, s, depends (1) on the service charge policy of the bank, as defined by the bank's service charge decision variables, and (2) on the public's market response to bank policy, as expressed by several market variables. In this formulation, it is assumed that an earnings credit is given each account based on average monthly balance. It is also assumed that the bank has one schedule of charges applicable to all accounts; the distinction between business and personal accounts is temporarily omitted in the interest of clarity. Later, this framework may be applied separately to different types of account, grouped by size, nature of customer, and so forth. Thus, monthly revenue per account from service charges on demand deposits, s, may be expressed as follows:

$$s = d_1 + d_2 m_2 + d_3 m_3 + d_4 m_4 + d_5 m_5 - d_6 m_6 m_7 \quad (4)$$

Since aggregate service charge revenue, S, is equal to s times the number of accounts, m_1, service charge revenue depends on these *decision variables* in service charge policy:

d_1 = monthly maintenance charge per account

d_2 = charge per check

d_3 = charge per deposit

d_4 = charge per item deposited

d_5 = flat monthly service charge if minimum balance is less than a specified balance (used by banks levying no other service charges if a specified minimum balance is maintained)

d_6 = earnings credit per $100 of "average balance"[4]

These *market variables* reflect the level and activity of demand deposits:

m_1 = total number of accounts

m_2 = number of checks drawn (average, per account per month)

m_3 = number of deposits (average, per account per month)

m_4 = number of items deposited (average, per account per month)

m_5 = fraction of total number of accounts which fall below required minimum balance (used by banks cited with d_5 above)

m_6 = average balance per account

m_7 = fraction of average account balance to which the earnings credit applies

(Note that the earnings credit can be no larger than the gross service charge in any account.)

In other words, the expected level of s will depend on the d's, as *set by policy*, and on management's *expectations* of the m's, as deter-

[4]In practice, a number of banks now have service charge policies in which a number of d's are zero; for example, service charges d_3 and d_4 are not used in many west coast banks.

mined by market demand. The task of this note is to illustrate an approach that management can use to select a service charge policy (by assigning values to the service charge decision variables d_1 through d_6) so as to maximize expected profit.

Structural Variables

A major portion of demand deposit funds will be invested by the bank in securities or committed to loans. The remaining portion of demand deposit funds must be committed to nonearning assets. Average earnings per account may be expressed as follows:

$$e = m_6 (f_1 r_1 + f_2 r_2 + f_3 r_3)$$

where f_1 = fraction of demand deposit funds invested in securities

r_1 = average rate of return available on securities, net of all costs associated with these investments

f_2 = fraction of demand deposit funds in loans

r_2 = average rate of return available on loans, net of all costs associated with these loans

f_3 = fraction of demand deposit funds in nonearning assets, that is, those assets not committed to investments or loans

r_3 = return on nonearning assets

Since it is assumed that r_3 is zero, the nonearning asset item may be deleted, so that,

$$e = m_6 (f_1 r_1 + f_2 r_2) \tag{5}$$

It should be emphasized that e represents an earnings level (dollars per account per month) after deduction of operating costs of loans and investments.

Finally, the variable costs of processing demand deposit accounts must be considered. Average variable cost per account is as follows:

$$c = c_1 + c_2 m_2 + c_3 m_3 + c_4 m_4 \tag{6}$$

where c_1 = maintenance cost per account per month

c_2 = variable cost of processing each check

c_3 = variable cost per deposit (which may include costs of mail deposits)

c_4 = variable cost per item deposited

The difficulty of ascertaining market demand figures and bank costs is not to be underestimated. In practice, the identification of specific costs and revenues associated with demand deposits is an imposing task, particularly for the small bank with few staff officers. The fact remains that market demand estimates and data on variable costs and revenues are needed if service charge decisions are to be based on expected impact of profits.[5] In this note, only the general framework for estimating the market variables is presented.

Assumptions in the Model

The purpose of this model is to isolate the effects of service charge policy on bank profit. It is clear that one can only achieve this isolation at the expense of a number of restrictive assumptions. John Hicks, the well-known English economist, once remarked that abstraction is usually the condition of clear thinking. As long as one is aware of the assumptions made, the model may be of considerable usefulness in evaluating complicated decisions.

This model abstracts from the effect of demand deposit service charges on other aspects of the bank's activities. For example, changes in service charges policy may be expected to have some effect on other areas of the bank's business. A new customer who is induced to open a checking account may also be a prospective customer for loans or time deposits.

As discussed earlier, fixed costs were assumed to be constant over the relevant range of analysis. Also, increasing levels of demand deposits will at some point create a need for additional capital—a consideration subsumed in this analysis. It was assumed that all demand deposit funds can be invested at the rates implicit in the earnings function, e, and that the operating costs are invariant with deposit volume. In practice, variable costs may be subject to economies of scale; for example, variable costs of machine processing of checks may decrease with increasing volume.[6] Over a narrow range, however, variable costs are often approximately constant.

Most simple models are static, whereas the business situations that the models describe are dynamic. Any effects of revised service charges —in particular, growth in demand deposits—will be superimposed on the bank's existing growth pattern. For example, the president of one independent west coast bank, who raised his bank's service charges on checking accounts, emphasized that it is often difficult to determine cause and effect:

[5]Some statistical data on costs of bank operations are now available. For example, see G. J. Benston, "Economies of Scale and Marginal Costs in Banking Operations," in *The National Banking Review*, June 1965.

[6]There is evidence of increasing economies of scale in processing demand deposits over the period 1959–1961, with marginal cost per account decreasing as a function of number of accounts. See Benston, "Economies of Scale and Marginal Costs in Banking Operations."

> In the twelve months prior to our announcement of higher service charges, our demand deposits increased by 15 percent. In the past year (since the announcement) our total demand deposits rose another 15 percent. We don't know whether they rose *because* of the change or *in spite* of it.

The time dimension is ignored in this model, as it is in many widely used techniques such as cost-volume-profit analysis.

In applying the model, it may be desirable to classify demand deposit accounts into major groups, for example, personal checking accounts, small business accounts, and large corporate accounts. Many of the critical variables may differ considerably among these groups of accounts; service charges may then be evaluated separately for each major group of accounts by using the basic model.

Finally, defining the goal in terms of profit-maximization may not be thoroughly satisfactory to a bank which may have other objectives. Often, however, this profit criterion is consistent with other financial objectives set forth by bank management.

Applying the Model

Estimation of the market variables presents a difficult but essential task. In short, a profit-maximizing model requires a prediction of the effect of various alternative service charges on the level and activity of demand deposits. The most critical market variable is m_1, the number of accounts. Empirical evidence may be found on the relationship between decision and market variables. For example, a bank may experiment with service charges at a number of branches to determine the sensitivity of market demand to various decision variables. It may be possible to raise certain elements of service charges (for example, charge per deposit) with relatively little market reaction, whereas the market may be highly sensitive to changes in other service charges (for example, charge per check). That is, the elasticity of demand may differ significantly with respect to various decision variables.

In the absence of empirical evidence, the assessment must be based on bank management's expectations in each specific situation. For a relatively large bank a change in service charge policy often has a significant impact on the service charge policies of other banks. For many smaller banks the problem is somewhat easier, if it is expected that policy changes will not affect the general level of competitive service charges in the area. In either case, a shift from a follow-the-competition criterion to one based on expected profits necessitates the task of estimating the market's reaction to alternative service charge policies by assigning values to the market variables.

In the determination of earnings rates (r_1, r_2), it may be found that the bank's average yields on investments and loans vary considerably from currently available market rates. Since the relevant rates are those which will be available on future investments and loans, judgment must be exercised in the assignment of values to the structural variables.

An Example: Effect of Service Charge per Check on Profits

In this section we will illustrate the possible impact on profit of one decision variable, service charge per check. Consider a hypothetical bank whose existing service charge schedule includes the following: monthly maintenance charge of \$0.75 (d_1); service charge per check of \$0.04 (d_2); an earnings credit of \$0.10 per \$100 average balance (d_0); all other service charge variables are zero. The bank wishes to assess the expected effect on profit of various alternative levels of charge per check, assuming all other elements of service charge policy are unchanged.

Assume that the applicable structural variables pertaining to costs and earnings are as shown in Exhibit 2.

Exhibit 2

Structural Variables

c_1 = \$0.80	f_1 = 0.30	r_1 = 0.041%
c_2 = 0.04	f_2 = 0.50	r_2 = 0.058
c_3 = 0.15		
c_4 = 0.02		

Management has estimated the impact of different service charges per check on each of the market variables. In this case, it is felt that increasing the charge per check would in some "reasonable" period of time lead to a decreased number of accounts (m_1) and a decreased average number of checks per account per month (m_2). For ease of exposition, the market variables m_3, m_4, m_6, and m_7 are held unchanged. These estimates of the market variables are shown in Exhibit 3.

Exhibit 3

Expected Values of Market Variables as a Function of Charge Per Check (d_2)

Given: Charge Per Check	*Expected Value of Market Variables*						
d_2	m_1	m_2	m_3	m_4	m_5	m_6	m_7
\$0.03	7,850	45.0	1.80	2.50	0	\$1,340	0.80
0.04 (present)	7,650	44.5	1.80	2.50	0	1,340	0.80
0.05	7,300	44.0	1.80	2.50	0	1,340	0.80
0.06	6,850	43.5	1.80	2.50	0	1,340	0.80
0.07	6,350	42.5	1.80	2.50	0	1,340	0.80
0.08	5,750	41.5	1.80	2.50	0	1,340	0.80
0.10	4,850	41.5	1.80	2.50	0	1,340	0.80

Exhibit 4

Computing Expected Profit for Each Value of Charge per Check (d_2)

Charge per Check d_2	*Service Charge per Account* s	*Bank Earnings per Account* e	*Variable Cost per Account* c	*Profit per Account* $s + e - c$	*Number of Accounts* m_1	*Expected Profit per Month* P^*
$0.03	$1.03	$4.61	$2.92	$2.72	7,850	$21,400
0.04 (present)	1.46	4.61	2.90	3.17	8,650	24,300
0.05	1.88	4.61	2.88	3.61	7,300	26,400
0.06	2.29	4.61	2.85	4.05	6,850	27,700
0.07	2.66	4.61	2.82	4.45	6,350	28,300 (max)
0.08	3.00	4.61	2.78	4.83	5,750	27,800
0.10	3.83	4.61	2.78	5.66	4,850	27,500

Expected profit may now be calculated for each value of d_2, based on the relationships defined in equations (4), (5), and (6), and in profit equation (3). These figures are given in Exhibit 4. The second line in Exhibit 4 represents the existing service charge policy and existing profit. In this example the optimum charge per check if \$0.07, resulting in the highest expected profit despite an appreciable expected drop in the volume of deposits.

A Comprehensive Example: Evaluating Alternative Service Charge Strategies

A service charge *strategy* represents a complete service charge schedule or set of values assigned to the decision variables d_1 through d_6. In the previous example, only one decision variable, charge per check, was allowed to vary. We will now consider the expected impact on profit of a number of alternative strategies, allowing changes in all of the decision variables.

In Exhibit 5 strategy *S*-1 represents a hypothetical bank's existing policy; the other five strategies represent alternatives which the bank desires to analyze. Strategy *S*-2 suggests that service charges be set high enough to cover the bank's variable processing costs plus a contribution to fixed costs and that the monthly earnings credit be doubled to \$0.20 per \$100 average deposit. Strategies *S*-3, *S*-4, and *S*-5 present various other possibilities for raising service charges above the bank's present levels. Strategy *S*-6 represents a "no service charge" policy, as long as an account's minimum monthly balance exceeds some specified amount. All of the market variables must be evaluated for each strategy. One may start by determining the values of market variables associated with the bank's existing strategy, *S*-1: the bank currently has 7650 accounts (m_1); each account averages 44.5 checks per month (m_2); the average monthly balance per account is \$1340 (m_6). With this base of existing values, expected values must be assigned to the market variables under each alternative strategy, as shown in Exhibit 6. Assessment of the market's reaction, in terms of expected values of the market variables, represents the heart of this decision-making process. If different values were assigned to the market variables in Exhibit 6, our final conclusion as to the most profitable strategy in this case obviously might be different than the one reached below. The specific results of this set of values are ancillary to the *method* of analysis. While the assessment of market demand often presents a thorny problem, it is an essential step in considering the areas of service charge policy in which the most profitable changes might be made.

With the cost and earnings values given in Exhibit 2, and with the data in Exhibits 5 and 6, we may calculate service charge revenue, bank

Exhibit 5

Alternative Service Charge Strategies

Service Charge Strategy	*Service Charge Decision Variables* d_1	d_2	d_3	d_4	d_5	d_6
S-1 (present)	\$0.75	\$0.04	\$ 0	\$ 0	\$ 0	\$0.10
S-2	0.95	0.05	0.18	0.025	0	0.20
S-3	1.00	0.08	0.10	0.04	0	0.10
S-4	0.75	0.07	0	0	0	0.14
S-5	0.75	0.06	0.15	0.03	0	0.10
S-6	0	0	0	0	\$2.00	0

Exhibit 6

Expected Values of Market Variables under Alternative Strategies

Service Charge Strategy	*Expected Value of Market Variables* m_1	m_2	m_3	m_4	m_5	m_6	m_7
S-1 (present)	7,650	44.5	1.80	2.50	0	\$1,340	0.80
S-2	7,850	44.0	1.65	2.45	0	1,475	0.72
S-3	4,800	41.5	1.70	2.40	0	1,340	0.80
S-4	6,600	42.5	1.80	2.50	0	1,400	0.78
S-5	6,400	43.5	1.65	2.45	0	1,340	0.80
S-6	12,000	53.0	1.80	2.50	0.15	1,250	N.A.

earnings, and variable costs per account under each strategy using equations (4), (5), and (6). Finally, expected profit as defined in (3) may be computed and the strategies may be ranked in order of profitability, as shown in Exhibit 7.[7] The "no service charge" strategy, *S*-6, is expected to attract the largest number of new accounts, bringing the total to 12,000 accounts; however, owing to decreased service charge revenue (s) and increased variables costs (c) from the larger number of checks per account, this alternative has the lowest expected profit. For strategy *S*-2, raising service charges to cover variable costs and doubling the earnings credit is expected to result in a lower average net service charge, s, and to attract new accounts; in this case, higher profit per account, owing to increased bank earnings on higher average balances, and a greater number of accounts leads to the largest expected monthly profit of the six strategies. Note that strategy *S*-5 ranks second in terms of expected profit;

[7]As a practical matter, it should be noted that it is often easier to estimate values of market variables m_2 through m_7 and to calculate average net service charge per account, s, before estimating the critical variable m_1, number of accounts, under each strategy. It is convenient to think of s as the average "price" per month facing the consumer, so that higher values of s may often be associated with the lower values of m_1. Prior computation of s may facilitate the estimating of m_1.

Exhibit 7

Computing Expected Profit under Alternative Strategies

Strategy	*Service Charge per Account* s	*Bank Earnings per Account* e	*Variable Cost per Account* c	*Profit per Account* $s + e - c$	*Number of Accounts* m_1	*Expected Profit per Month* P^*	*Ranking by Expected Profit* P^*
S-1 (present)	$1.46	$4.61	$2.90	$3.17	7,650	$24,300	No. 5
S-2	1.39	5.07	2.86	3.60	7,850	28,300	No. 1
S-3	3.52	4.61	2.77	5.36	4,800	25,700	No. 4
S-4	2.20	4.82	2.82	4.20	6,600	27,700	No. 3
S-5	2.61	4.61	2.84	4.38	6,400	28,000	No. 2
S-6	0.30	4.30	3.24	1.36	12,000	16,300	No. 6

however, it ranks next-to-highest in expected loss of volume with an anticipated loss of 1250 demand deposit accounts, relative to the current level under *S*-1. The model emphasizes the potential difference between the impact of a policy change on expected *volume* of deposits and the concomitant impact on *profits*.

Conclusion

In planning service charge policy, it is essential to evaluate the expected impact of alternative strategies on bank profit. Past emphasis on "following the competition" or on increasing the volume of deposits through low service charges has reflected the lack of a systematic approach to evaluating the profitability of proposed alternatives to an existing service charge policy.

The model presented in this note indicates the expected profitability of alternative service charge strategies based on management's assessments of three sets of variables: decision variables (service charges and earnings credit), market variables (demand response to the bank's service charges), and structural variables (bank's marginal costs and revenues). In any model to be used in business decisions, there is a trade-off between the reality of its assumptions, on one hand, and the complexity of the model and the difficulty of implementing it, on the other. At the core of the problem in this case is the necessity of evaluating the market's reaction (by existing and potential demand deposit customers) to a change in the bank's service charges. In addition, the bank's marginal costs and revenues must be ascertained—in itself a difficult problem of measurement. Principal assumptions in this analysis include the supposition that marginal costs are constant over the range of analysis and that a simplified profit function is satisfactory for decision-making purposes. Granting the problems—both practical and theoretical—in applying analytical tools to complex decisional areas, we foresee a marked trend toward increasing utilization of new financial techniques in internal bank management.

APPENDIX

Service Charge Survey

The information in this appendix was obtained in a survey, conducted in February 1965 of 106 independent banks, each with assets less than $50 million, in the Twelfth Federal Reserve District.

For purposes of analysis, the sample was divided into three groups:

Group	*Size of Bank (assets)*	*Number of Banks*
A	Less than $5 million	40
B	$5 million to $10 million	40
C	$10 million to $50 million	26

1. Charge per check on regular personal checking accounts:

	Number of Banks			
Charge per Check	*A*	*B*	*C*	*Total*
No service charge*	7	9	4	20
$0.03	2	1	–	3
0.04	3	1	1	5
0.05	9	6	2	17
0.06	9	7	10	26
0.07	7	5	8	20
0.08	–	1	2	3
0.15	1	1	–	2
No reply				10

*Specified minimum balance required for no service charge.

	Number of Banks			
Minimum Balance Required	*A*	*B*	*C*	*Total*
$100	–	–	–	0
200	3	3	2	8
250	–	3	1	4
300	1	–	–	1
400	–	1	–	1
500	1	1	1	3
No minimum balance required	2	1	–	3

2. Charge per deposit:

	Number of Banks			
Charge per Deposit	*A*	*B*	*C*	*Total*
$0.05	1	–	–	1
0.06	3	1	4	8
0.07	1	1	2	4
No charge	35	38	20	93

3. Charge per item deposited:

	Number of Banks			
Charge per Item	*A*	*B*	*C*	*Total*
$0.01	–	1	–	1
0.02	1	1	–	2
0.05	1	–	–	1
0.06	–	1	4	5
0.07	–	–	2	2
No charge	38	37	20	95

4. Monthly maintenance charge:

Maintenance Charge	*Number of Banks* A	B	C	*Total*
$0.50	10	6	3	19
0.60	1	1	–	2
0.65	2	4	4	10
0.70	1	–	1	2
0.75	16	18	11	45
0.85	–	1	–	1
1.00*	1	2	–	3
2.00*	4	1	1	6
2.50*	–	–	1	1
No reply				17

*Used by some banks which offer "no service charge" on accounts which maintain a specified minimum balance; accounts which do not maintain the specified balance must pay this monthly maintenance charge.

5. Earnings rate per month:

	Earnings per $100 Balance A	B	C
Group average	$0.11	$0.12	$0.11
Range	0–$0.20	$0.03–$0.25	$0.025–$0.20

Is the minimum balance or average balance used?

	Number of Banks A	B	C	*Total*
Minimum balance	14	19	12	45
Average balance	9	7	4	20
No reply				41

6. Charge for NSF checks:

Charge per NSF Check	*Number of Banks* A	B	C	*Total*
$0.25	1	1	–	2
0.50	3	1	–	4
1.00	9	13	6	28
1.50	8	3	1	12
1.75	–	–	1	1
2.00	12	17	13	42
2.50	1	1	–	2
3.00	–	2	2	4
No reply				11

7. Charge for counter checks processed:

Charge per Check Processed	Number of Banks A	B	C	Total
$0.05	1	1	–	2
0.06	–	1	–	1
0.07	–	–	1	1
0.20	–	1	–	1
0.25	–	2	1	3
0.50*	–	1	2	3
1.00*	–	1	1	2
No charge	39	32	22	93

*Applicable to special (thrifty) checking accounts.

8. How does your bank determine the charges listed above? (Check one or more.)

	Number of Banks A	B	C	Total
Competition	31	29	21	81
What traffic will bear	1	4	2	7
Direct cost	3	7	5	15
Allocated cost	2	4	2	8
Analysis of past results	6	8	5	19
Other	3	1	–	4

9. Are the charges on regular business checking accounts the same as on regular personal checking accounts?

	Number of Banks A	B	C	Total
Yes	24	25	19	68
No	16	15	7	38

10. Does your bank provide special (thrifty) accounts?

	Number of Banks A	B	C	Total
Yes	28	26	21	75
No	12	14	5	31

If so, what are the charges per paid check:

	Charge per Check A	B	C
Group average	$0.11	$0.11	$0.12
Range	$0.08 – $0.15	$0.08 – $0.15	$0.09 – $0.15

MONEY MANAGEMENT SERVICES

Union Bank

The Union Bank is a large southern California bank with headquarters in Los Angeles. The bank's advertising emphasizes the slogan—"The bank of personal service—complete banking service under one roof"—and the Union Bank prides itself in having preserved a close personal and professional association with its customers. Union Bank's total resources were more than $650 million in 1960; it was primarily a businessman's bank, with a substantial portion of its loans to business and industry in Los Angeles County.

Union Bank maintained an active business development department which solicited new accounts and lending opportunities. To assist in acquiring new customers and increasing deposit balances in established accounts, the Union Bank designed a service called "money engineering." Money engineering, featured in much of the bank's advertising, is a careful analysis of the flow of cash within a company, the methods used by the firm in collecting and processing cash, and the firm's use of bank services. The bank's analysts frequently found that they could recommend superior methods of handling cash receipts and deposits of checks; these new methods often permitted the "creation" of larger bank balances as well as some important operating economies. The findings and recommendations resulting from the money engineering analysis were generally presented in a written report to the management of the company studied. There was no obligation attached to the study or the report.

Mr. Dwight Chamberlin, vice president and manager of the Research Department, was responsible for supervising Union Bank's money engineering program. In June 1960 Mr. Chamberlin received a telephone call from Mr. Marshall Staunton, comptroller of the Universal Life Insurance Company in Los Angeles. Mr. Staunton had read a number of recent Union Bank advertisements which featured money engineering and he was interested in learning how this type of research could benefit his company. Mr. Chamberlin arranged an appointment with Staunton for the following week to discuss the design of specialized banking services for Universal.

As a result of this meeting and several subsequent interviews with other financial officers at Universal, Mr. Chamberlin was authorized to conduct a study of the company's methods of processing insurance premium payments. The study included analyses of current routines in handling incoming payments, cash balances on deposit in local banks, and clerical procedures in processing payments which might be performed more economically by the Union Bank. The study was conducted in collaboration with Mr. Roy Tomkins, manager of Universal's systems analysis department.

The research was completed on August 10, 1960. After evaluating the findings, Mr. Chamberlin wrote the following report which he submitted to Mr. Tomkins. It was Mr. Chamberlin's understanding that the report would be examined in detail by the systems analysis department and then forwarded for review by the company's senior financial and administrative officers.

Direct Depositing and "Lock Box" Banking for Universal Life Insurance Company

The Union Bank has successfully designed and operated several plans under which customers' payments of accounts are received and given initial processing by the bank. Remittance checks are banked immediately, and posted records for each transaction are furnished to the customer. The principal benefits of these plans result from increased available funds and decreased operating costs to the customer. Union Bank is compensated for the cost of these services by its earnings on deposits maintained at the bank.

The Universal Life Insurance Company receives income from several sources. The three principal sources have been analyzed, and the following report has been prepared recommending the introduction of certain new banking procedures. A detailed analysis is presented below concerning improvement in the flow of cash and methods of processing these types of income:

I. Ordinary life insurance premium payments.
II. Group insurance premium payments.
III. Mortgage loan payments.

A tabular summary is included at the end of this report, indicating the new balances created and the economies achieved from these recommendations.

I. Ordinary Life Premiums

In the ordinary life premium processing operation, the principal benefits of Union Bank money engineering are achieved through *new economies* for Universal. The following cost schedule for this operation has been prepared. It is believed that all of these costs could be either eliminated or transferred to Union Bank.

Universal's Present Costs	*Monthly Cost*
Mail room—3.1 hours per day, 60 hours per month	$ 180.00
Examining envelopes	62.00
Inspecting payments at 400 per hour, 390 hours per month	1,170.00
Listing checks at 1,500 per hour, 104 hours per month	312.00
Listing notices at 1,500 per hour, 104 hours per month	312.00
Balancing and recapping	156.00
Machine accounting	1,162.00

Universal's Present Costs	*Monthly Cost*
Microfilming and endorsing	315.00
Cards and supplies	234.00
Delivery of deposits	33.00
Miscellaneous	104.00
Total	$4,040.00

Operation of Union Bank Plan for Processing Ordinary Life Premium Payments

Universal would supply policyholders with return envelopes addressed to a Terminal Annex Post Office box to which Union Bank would have authorized access. Throughout the day and night Union Bank messengers would pick up the contents of the box and make deliveries to the bank's special processing department. The bank would then perform these services:

A. Mail would be sorted into current payments and delinquent payments by means of a code number printed on the return envelope.

B. Envelopes would be opened on an electric slicer, taking care to shift contents to avoid mutilating premium notices.

C. Contents would be separated from envelopes and inspected.

D. Exceptions – Any payments involving the following would be returned to the envelope and delivered intact to Universal:

1. Envelopes bearing incorrect number code.
2. Irregular checks.
3. Premium notices over 51 days past due.
4. Disagreement between checks and premium notices.

E. Premium notices and checks would be bundled separately in batches of approximately 100 payments.

F. IBM Machine Processing.

Premium notices, which are 51-column punched cards, would be reproduced into 80-column IBM cards, and the following information would be tabulated:

1. Policy number
2. Month due
3. How paid
4. Life premium
5. Loan interest
6. Dividend debits
7. Batch number

G. Tabulated batches and all checks would be microfilmed.

H. All checks would be endorsed. Batch numbers would appear in the endorsement.

I. Proofing:

1. The IBM cards and corresponding checks would be sent to the bank's Proof Department.
2. The checks would be sorted to the paying banks. At the same time, totals would be proven correct.

J. The Special Processing Department would prepare a deposit slip for the total amount of checks.

K. IBM cards would be sorted by date due and policy number.

L. All IBM cards and tabulations would be delivered to Universal with a duplicate deposit slip.

Benefits of the "Lock Box" Banking Plan for Ordinary Life Insurance Premiums

A. Economies for Universal.
Universal's present costs of cashiering routine premium payments would be eliminated or transferred to Union Bank. It is estimated that these costs approximate $4,040 per month, or $48,480 per year.
B. Increased Available Funds.
Checks in payment of life insurance premiums would be deposited at least one day earlier. This earlier deposit of approximately $234,000 per day increases available funds by $234,000.
C. There would be an earlier knowledge of returned checks.

II. Group Insurance Premiums

New money can be created for Universal through Union Bank money engineering of group insurance premium payments. At present there is a six- to seven-day delay in depositing average daily receipts of $468,000. It is estimated that this delay averaged five days during the past six months, with a delay of three days existing under ideal conditions.

Group insurance premium payments involve an unusual amount of correspondence and use of business envelopes instead of return envelopes. Because of this, a "lock box" arrangement is not advisable. Therefore, an alternative plan which utilizes *direct deposits* has been prepared. This plan eliminates the delay in depositing checks heretofore experienced.

Operation of Union Bank Plan for Processing Group Insurance Premiums

A. Universal would code daily receipts of group insurance premium checks with the number of the account to be credited.
B. A company messenger would deliver these checks to the bank daily. Union Bank would then perform the following services:

1. IBM cards would be punched for each check showing the account number and amount received.
2. Cards would be verified and interpreted.
3. Cards would be machine tabulated showing the account number and amount.
4. Checks would be endorsed.
5. Checks and cards would be microfilmed.
6. Checks would be sorted to paying banks and the total of checks processed would be balanced to the tabulated listing.
7. A deposit slip would be created in duplicate for the amount of total checks processed.
8. IBM cards, a copy of the tabulated listing, and a duplicate deposit slip would be delivered daily to Universal.
9. Microfilm would be delivered to Universal as soon as developed.

Benefits of the Group Insurance "Direct Deposits" Plan

A. Increased Available Funds.
Checks in payment of group insurance premiums would be deposited at least three days earlier. This earlier deposit of approximately $468,000 per day increases available funds by $1,404,00.
B. There would be an earlier knowledge of returned checks.
C. Some reduction in operating costs would be achieved through elimination of listing and proving deposits, endorsing checks, and microfilming (about $50 per month).

III. Mortgage Loan Payments

New money and new economies are available through Union Bank's processing of mortgage loan payments. The economies would result from a "lock box" arrangement whereby, similar to ordinary life premiums, payments would be mailed to a post office box to which Union Bank would have access. New money would be "created" by depositing checks on an average of two to three days earlier.

The mortgage loan department receives payments on mortgage loans from two sources: servicing organizations (for example, mortgage loan companies) and directly from the borrower. Only mortgage payments received directly from borrowers would be processed through a "lock box" arrangement. Remittances from servicing organizations are not recommended for "lock box" methods, since these payments are often accompanied by correspondence.

Loan Payments Received from Loan Servicing Organizations

Because these payments are not readily adaptable to the "lock box" system, we advise a direct depositing procedure via messenger similar to that described above for group premium payments. It is expected that the same methods followed in the processing of group insurance premium payments could be applied to the banking of remittances from servicing organizations.

Loan Payments Received Direct from Borrowers

"Lock box" deposit of mortgage loan payments is recommended for funds received from individual borrowers. As in the processing of ordinary life premium payments, this plan involves:

1. A post office box to which Union Bank has access.
2. Segregation and delivery of irregular payments to Universal.
3. Deposit of regular payments to Universal's account.
4. Delivery to Universal of information describing each transaction.

Volume	*Items*	*Dollar Amount*
Daily	445	$ 39,000
Monthly	9,360	780,000
Annual	112,320	9,400,000

Fluctuations—peak volume occurs from the 10th to 20th of each month.

Universal's Costs	*Monthly Cost*
Mail room—13 min. per day or 4.0 hr per month	12.00
Examining envelopes	4.00
Inspecting payments at 400 per hr. 23 hr per month	70.00
Listing checks at 1560 per hr. 6 hr per month	18.00
Listing notices	20.00
Microfilming and endorsing	16.00
Supervision and miscellaneous	25.00
Total	$165.00

Benefits of the Lock Box and Direct Deposit Plans for Processing Mortgage Loan Payments

A. Earlier deposits of servicing organization remittances (2 days times $234,000 per day)	$468,000
Earlier deposits of payments direct from borrowers (3 days times $39,000 per day)	117,000
Total new balances created	$585,000

B. Economies for Universal.
Annual economies totaling approximately $2000 would result from the reduction of clerical handling costs.
C. There would be an earlier knowledge of returned checks.

Exhibit 1

Comparison of Bank Balances and Bank Services under the Present Basis and the Proposed System

The following exhibit analyzes bank balances in relation to the bank services which they support under both present and proposed systems.

*Application of Bank Balances to Bank Services under Present and Proposed Systems**

Bank Balances Needed to Offset Cost of Services	*Present*	*New Money Created by "Money Engineering"*	*Proposed*
Deposit of ordinary life premiums	$ 936,000	$ 234,000	$3,650,400
Deposit of group premiums	28,080	1,404,000	109,590
Deposit of serviced mortgage loan payments	7,410	468,000	29,250
Deposit of direct mortgage loan payments	56,160	117,000	196,560
Processing withdrawal items	2,059,200	. . . . . .	2,340,000
	$3,086,850		$6,325,800
Surplus bank balances	2,217,150†		1,201,200‡
Average total balances	$5,304,000	$2,223,000	$7,527,000

*All balances referred to are collected balances.
†Unusable balance (see explanation below).
‡Usable balance (see explanation below).

Clarification of Exhibit 1

Bank Services—These services have been described earlier in this report with the exception of "processing withdrawal items." This refers to checks and drafts drawn against the company's bank account.

Bank Balances (Present Basis)—These figures were developed through a three-month study of Universal's banking activity and bank balances over a representative period. The Union Bank Account Analysis Department has estimated that an average collected balance of $3,086,850 would have supported normal banking services.

Surplus (Unusable)—Even though balances on Universal's books were kept at a minimum, average collected balances on the bank's books were $5,304,000 ($2,217,150 more than necessary) during the period studied. This condition exists because while checks are outstanding, they continue to reflect balances on the bank's books which do not appear on Universal's books. Since businesses do not normally draw on balances which no longer exist on their books, this "outstanding check balance" is unavailable for investment by Universal.

New Money Created—Through the earlier deposit of checks now held until completion of bookkeeping transactions, new money will be created. Since checks do not become money until they have been deposited and collected, the speed-up in processing actually "creates" new usable funds.

Bank Balances (Proposed Basis)—These figures refer to balances necessary to support the new services as well as normal banking functions. Of the $6,325,800 necessary, $5,304,000 exists in present bank balances. Operation of the systems can create $2,223,000, leaving a surplus of $1,201,200.

Surplus (Usable)—Through earlier deposit of checks, $2,223,000 can be added to bank balances. Since this increase would show on Universal's books as well as on the bank's, it is in a usable form. Of this amount, $1,201,200 is in excess of the balances required to support total bank services under the proposed plan. This excess therefore becomes available to Universal for investment or other corporate purposes.

Conclusion

By adopting the proposed plan, Universal would enjoy the following benefits:

1. Operating economies of approximately $51,000 per year.
2. Increase in investable funds of $1,201,200.

ALTERNATIVE CONSUMER CREDIT PLANS

Wolverine State Bank

In March 1960, the management of the Wolverine State Bank of Lansing, Michigan, learned that the largest bank in the Lansing area, the Spartan National Bank, was planning to introduce a credit card plan in the near future. Accordingly, in April 1960, Wolverine's executive committee launched a study of recent action by other banking institutions in the field of consumer credit. It was expected that the study would lead to a recommendation that some form of consumer credit financing be made available to the bank's commercial customers. As of 1960, the Wolverine bank did not directly assist local merchants in the financing of consumer credit.

Wolverine State, one of fifteen banks in the city of Lansing, was a large unit bank established in 1919 and built on the philosophy: "Growth through service and security." The bank's total 1959 resources exceeded $200 million. Although not pioneers of change in the local area, Wolverine management was nevertheless desirous of adopting those new banking services which could be shown to offer reasonable benefits to both the bank and its customers. The bank's 1959 loan portfolio totaled $95 million, with $12.4 million represented by consumer loans. By far the largest part of these were automobile loans; other consumer credits involved repair and modernization loans and personal loans.

By April 1960, no Lansing bank had publicly announced the introduction of a new consumer credit plan. The Wolverine management understood, however, that the Spartan National plan would be in operation by the first of July and that several other banks in the area were studying the feasibility of adopting one of the new plans.

BANK OPERATED CONSUMER CREDIT PLANS. Consumer credit plans, designed to provide quick credit for qualified customers, were a recent development in bank lending that had spread from coast to coast within a relatively short period of time. The plans fell into two basic categories: bank credit cards and personal lines of credit (revolving credit).

Bank credit cards were in use as early as 1950, but the real growth of this banking service occurred in 1959 when several large West Coast banking institutions joined their eastern counterparts in offering this service. The first line of credit plan was introduced in 1956 by the First National Bank of Boston. The *American Banker* estimated that some 200 to 250 consumer credit plans were in operation in 1959.

ACCEPTANCE BY BANKERS. The banking community became interested in these new credit plans for several reasons; among them were potential profitability, a means of attracting new business from other types of financial institutions and, of course, competitive pressures.

Not all bankers agreed, however, on the merits of these new plans. Some bankers regarded the new credit plans as "gimmicks." One prominent banker explained that his institution had no such program because "We believe banks are the ones who should be stabilizing the economy rather than adding to inflation." On the other hand, another executive explained his bank's adoption of a credit plan as follows: "Our thinking was to get credit back into the banks. Under our plan, we act as a clearing house on all credit. A customer, in effect, has one charge account at the bank, instead of a number of accounts at various stores."

OPERATING DATA. There were few operating data available on the plans in use. The Bank of America in San Francisco reported that over 80 percent of its credit card users were paying their bills within twenty-five days and thereby avoiding interest charges. Bank of America stated further that delinquencies amounted to about 1.25 percent of volume. It was still too early to determine a trend in loss rates. The First National Bank of Boston reported that its revolving credit plan netted 5.12 percent (before taxes) on the average outstanding loan balance in 1958.[1] Experienced men in the field estimated that one to two years would be required before a new credit plan would begin contributing to profits.

DETAILS OF THE VARIOUS PLANS. The various consumer credit plans fell into two basic categories, and most plans differed only in minor details. Wolverine's executive committee concentrated its efforts on a study of a "typical" plan in each category. In addition, the committee studied a new credit card plan sponsored by International Charge, Inc., a subsidiary of the Seaboard Finance Company. This plan was designed to permit individual banks to offer a credit card with nationwide acceptance. Details of the three plans follow.

Credit Card Plan

Bank credit card plans are a means by which the sponsoring bank finances purchases made by authorized credit card holders at bank affiliated retail outlets. The plans offer the card holders the conveniences of established credit with all affiliated merchants, single statement monthly billing for all credit purchases so made, and long-term credit when desired. For affiliated merchants, the plans provide the means for offering credit to customers, immediate dollar credits from the bank for all sales to card holders, and freedom from the burden and the risks of a credit department operation. The bank handles all the operating details of the plan in return for a fee calculated as a percentage of net sales.

CUSTOMER PARTICIPATION. Banks normally initiate credit card plans by mailing credit cards to all of their customers who meet the bank's credit requirements.[2] Affiliated merchants are provided with a supply of application blanks (Exhibit 1) for their customers, and the banks usually advertise the plan widely to stimulate further customer applications.

Upon receipt of an application, the bank investigates the applicant's credit standing and issues cards to qualified applicants. The card entitles its holder to charge his purchases from those merchants who display the bank's emblem. Each card bears a code which tells the merchant the amount that the card holder can charge on one sale without clearance from the bank.

The bank mails each customer an itemized statement once a month. The customer has twenty-five days in which to pay after receipt of his

[1]Additional information on this plan and on several others appears in Appendix A.

[2]One bank found that one out of five of its customers qualified for its credit card and that, of the people receiving credit cards, approximately 20 percent filled out the agreement indicating that they planned to use the cards.

Exhibit 1

WOLVERINE STATE BANK

Charge Account Application

Last Name (Please Print) | First Name | Initial

Mr.
Mrs.
Miss

If under 21 years of age check box ☐ | Telephone No. | Spouse's First Name | Initial

Address | How long at this address Years Months | Own ☐ Rent ☐ With Parents ☐ | City | Zone | State

If at above address less than 1 year, give former home address | How Long | Years | Months

Applicant's Occupation | Employed By | How Long | Years | Months

Business Address | Telephone Number

Spouse Employed By | Address

Bank With

Checking ____________________
(Bank) (Branch)

Savings ____________________
(Bank) (Branch)

Loan ____________________
(Bank) (Branch)

Credit Established at
(List all oil companies, stores, etc.):

1) ____________________
2) ____________________
3) ____________________
4) ____________________

The following authorized purchasers may charge to this account:

____
____
____
____

Check box if additional cards are requested. ☐

Amount of maximum credit requested (check one) ☐$300 ☐$700 ☐$500 ______ Insert higher amount if desired

I HAVE READ and agree to all of the terms and conditions of the agreement.

__________ Date __________ Signature

monthly statement, with no charge made for the credit service. Should the customer desire to take longer than the normal twenty-five days, he has the option to budget payments over several months. Under this option, the customer must pay a part of the outstanding balance each month (see Exhibit 2) together with interest at the rate of 1 1/2 percent per month on the unpaid balance. All payments are made directly to the bank.

Exhibit 2

Flexible Payment Chart*

Outstanding balance	0–49	50–99	100–149	150–249	250–299	300–349
Minimum monthly payment	10	15	20	25	30	40
Outstanding balance	350–399	400–499	500–599	600–699	700–799	800 and over
Minimum monthly payment	50	65	75	90	100	15% of balance

*All figures are expressed in dollars.

MERCHANT PARTICIPATION. Merchants may join the plan by paying an initial membership fee of $25 and agreeing to comply with specified operating procedures. A copy of the merchant agreement appears in Exhibit. 3.

Exhibit 3

WOLVERINE STATE BANK

Charge Account Plan

Merchant Agreement

1. Merchant agrees to honor all effective CREDIT CARDS subject to such dollar limits for any single sales draft as are imposed by the Bank, provided that the Merchant may with Bank's consent tender sales drafts in excess of said amount on a full recourse basis.

2. Merchant agrees to sell to Bank and Bank agrees to purchase from Merchant at face amount less a 6 percent discount, all accounts created by such honoring and use of Bank sales draft properly completed.

3. Merchant warrants that all such accounts will be bona fide, newly created sales of merchandise and/or services. Merchant will neither make any extra or special charge nor extract any special agreement, condition or security in connection with any sales draft executed hereunder.

4. Bank assumes the credit risk on all sales drafts sold to it within three days of origin. Merchant agrees that any dispute between Merchant and customer will be settled by Merchant without liability to Bank and Merchant agrees to refund to Bank on demand (and Bank has the right to charge to Merchant's account therefor) the amount involved in any disputed account.

Exhibit 3 (Continued)

5. Merchant will immediately remit to Bank any payment made to Merchant on any account sold to Bank.

6. Merchant agrees to maintain a commercial checking account with Bank subject to Bank's usual commercial account service charges.

7. Merchant will pay Bank an initial fee of $25 and will rent from Bank, at a rate of $1 per month each, as many sales draft imprinters as are necessary.

8. The preparation, attachment and delivery to the Bank by the Merchant of the deposit envelopes and the sales drafts enclosed therein shall constitute an endorsement and assignment to the Bank of each of the sales drafts enclosed in said envelope. The Bank will audit and verify the amount shown, and has the right to correct any errors which are found.

9. Upon receipt of promotional material, the Merchant will actively promote the use of the Bank's Charge Account Plan, by prominently displaying the Plan emblem on the Merchant's premises, by recommending the Plan to customers, by making account applications and literature available to customers, and by regularly incorporating invitations in the Merchant's advertisements to open and use the Plan accounts. Applications for issuance of CREDIT CARDS will be on forms provided by the Bank.

10. This instrument and the accompanying Refund Chart [Exhibit 4] constitute the entire agreement between Bank and Merchant.

(Merchant)________________________
Address________________________
By________________________
(owner or his authorized agent)
(Title)________________________

Accepted
THE BANK
By________________________
Date________________________

Merchants rent sales draft imprinters (as many as needed) from the bank for $1 a month each. All other supplies such as sales drafts, credit vouchers, deposit envelopes, customer application blanks, and window decals are supplied by the bank free of charge to the merchant.

Upon presentation of a credit card by a customer, the merchant records the transaction on a special sales draft, imprints the customer's identification on the draft, and obtains the customer's signature. A similar procedure is followed by the merchant when a customer returns any merchandise.

Upon receipt of the sales drafts, the bank credits the merchant's account for 94 percent of the net sales reported. A portion of the 6 percent charge to the merchant is refunded quarterly by the bank according to a prescribed schedule based on total dollar volume and size of the average transaction. A typical rebate schedule appears in Exhibit 4.

THE BANK'S ROLE. The bank handles all the operating details of the plan: credit investigations, issuance of cards, record keeping, customer collections, provision of supplies to merchants, and promotion of the program. In return, the bank receives a fee based on the net credit sales of affiliated merchants and interest on all customer balances not paid within twenty-five days.

Exhibit 4

WOLVERINE STATE BANK

Merchant Refund Chart and Fee Schedule

Quarterly Average Transaction Amount	*Original Percentage Withheld*	*Percentage of Allowable Refund*	*Percentage of Basic Fee*
$ 3.50–$ 4.99	6.00	0.00	6.00
5.00– 5.99	6.00	0.25	5.75
6.00– 6.99	6.00	0.50	5.50
7.00– 7.99	6.00	0.75	5.25
8.00– 8.99	6.00	1.00	5.00
9.00– 9.99	6.00	1.25	4.75
10.00– 12.49	6.00	1.50	4.50
12.50– 14.99	6.00	1.75	4.25
15.00– 19.99	6.00	2.00	4.00
20.00– 24.99	6.00	2.50	3.50
25.00– 34.99	6.00	3.00	3.00
35.00– 49.99	6.00	3.50	2.50
50.00– 99.99	6.00	4.00	2.00
over– 100.00	6.00	4.25	1.75

No refund in event quarterly average transaction amount is less than $3.50, the equivalent of the minimum sales draft charge of 21¢.

When you deposit the sales drafts and credit vouchers at your local branch your account will be credited with 94 percent of the net amount. The total dollar amount of all sales drafts less credit vouchers deposited during the calendar quarter (net sales) will be divided by the total number of sales drafts less credit vouchers to determine the quarterly average transaction amount. The resulting quarterly average transaction amount will determine the percentage of allowable refund. The dollar amount of refund is then computed by applying the percentage of allowable refund to net sales.

An additional volume refund will be made according to the total number of sales drafts submitted per quarter as follows:

	Number of Net Sales Drafts	*Refund/Sales Draft*
First	1,000	0
Next	24,000	1¢
Over	25,000	2¢

NOTE: In no case shall the volume refund reduce the charge/sales draft below 21¢.

Initial Fee: $25 fee per location will be required when contract is signed.

Imprinter Fee: Sales draft imprinters rent for $1 each/month, payable quarterly in advance.

Credit Vouchers: No charge for credit vouchers unless the number of such vouchers exceeds 10 percent of the number of all sales drafts submitted per quarter. A 10¢ fee each will be charged for all vouchers over the 10 percent figures as above.

Personal Line of Credit

This plan offers to qualified individuals a "cash reserve" that can be drawn upon at will—and for any purpose. The plan offers a service to individuals only; commercial establishments are in no way involved in the plan's operation. However, as a service to retailers, a number of banks which offer consumers a personal line of credit complement this plan by offering retailers an accounts receivable financing plan. This latter plan will be discussed separately below.

The personal line of credit differs significantly in purpose as well as in operation from the credit card plan. It was conceived as a means for providing individuals with an emergency cash reserve which could be drawn upon on those special occasions when the ability to pay cash is important. Suggested uses include taxes, medical and dental expenses, home improvements, appliance and furniture purchases, vacations, and so forth. The user, however, is not required to indicate the purpose of his borrowing.

OPERATION OF THE PLAN. Individuals who desire to establish a line of credit apply directly to the bank. Upon approval of an individual's credit, the applicant becomes a member of the plan. The amount of credit extended to each customer is determined by the size of the monthly payments which the customer's family budget can afford. These payments typically range from a minimum of $25 to a maximum of $100 a month. Maximum lines of credit, therefore, would vary from a low of $300 over a one-year period to a high of $2400 over a two-year period. Exhibit 5 presents a typical borrowing and repayment schedule used under this plan. Exhibit 6 contains suggested minimum requirements for approved applications.

Exhibit 5

Monthly Payment	*Borrowing Limit for 12 Months*	*Borrowing Limit for 24 Months*	*Monthly Payment*	*Borrowing Limit for 12 Months*	*Borrowing Limit for 24 Months*
$25	$300	$600	$50	$600	$1,200
30	360	720	60	720	1,440
40	480	960	70	840	1,680

Monthly Payment	*Borrowing Limit for 12 Months*	*Borrowing Limit for 24 Months*
$ 80	$ 960	$1,920
90	1,080	2,160
100	1,200	2,400

Exhibit 6

WOLVERINE STATE BANK

Suggested Minimum Requirements
to Qualify for Personal Line of Credit

A. Stability
  1. Employment
    (*a*) Two years in present occupation
    (*b*) Employed in an acceptable occupation
    (*c*) Salary must be adequate to meet ability standards
  2. Residence
    (*a*) Three years in the community
    (*b*) Home ownership preferable
  3. Personal
    (*a*) Must conform to legal age requirements
    (*b*) Must be of reliable personal habits

B. Ability
  1. Income
    (*a*) Only take-home pay considered
    (*b*) Income from part-time work, overtime, alimony payments, and other similar sources of questionable reliability should be excluded
    (*c*) Consideration of spouse's income should be eliminated in income to debt analysis unless it is permanent; that is, career woman or professional
  2. Obligation
    (*a*) All debts disclosed by the applicant must be considered
    (*b*) Any undisclosed debts preclude credit consideration
  3. Risk Analysis
    (*a*) Monthly payments should not exceed 50 percent of the applicant's net income after deducting all fixed monthly obligations and ample allowance for living expenses
    (*b*) The applicant's total revolving credit limit should not exceed twice his gross monthly income

C. Willingness
  1. Credit References
    (*a*) Three references are required of which two need to be installment debt within the past three years
    (*b*) Any derogatory credit experience precludes credit consideration

A customer can use his line of credit in two ways: (1) He can request that the bank add a part or the whole of his credit line to the balance of his checking account and then write checks against this or, (2) if he prefers to maintain his checking account with another institution, the bank provides him with a small number of special borrowing drafts which are similar (in both appearance and use) to normal checks.

Each month the bank sends the customer a statement showing the condition of his account. The customer is expected to make monthly payments as long as his account shows a debit balance. Interest accrues on the unpaid balance at the rate of 1 1/2 percent per month. Customers who clean up their account before the next billing date receive, in effect, a thirty-day interest-free loan.

Advocates of the personal line of credit say that the plan is well suited to the individual family for three reasons: (1) it provides a single source of credit for all purchases; (2) it is both flexible and convenient;

(3) it enables families to plan their financial affairs more effectively and with greater thrift.

Fluctuations in outstanding loan balances and the flexible maturity of final payments require careful evaluation by a bank of the applicant's ability to manage his financial affairs. The plan is not intended as a debt consolidation loan or merely as an additional loan account. Rather, it is meant as a convenience for the prudent customer who had already demonstrated his knowledgeable use of credit.

Accounts Receivable Financing

This plan enables merchants to assign their accounts receivable to the bank in return for an advance of from 60 percent to 80 percent of the total receivables on a thirty-day note. The assignment is on a non-notification, full recourse basis. Collections are deposited by the merchants in cash collateral accounts which are periodically deducted from the outstanding loans. The plan must be flexible enough to handle several different types of billing. Exhibit 7 describes how the plan worked in another bank for a merchant of medium size with monthly billings. A typical rate schedule for accounts receivable loans is shown in Exhibit 8.

Exhibit 7

WOLVERINE STATE BANK

Assignment of Receivables Transaction
for a Merchant of Medium Size (Monthly Billings)
(the experience of another Michigan bank)

This retail merchant, selling apparel soft goods and housewares (no furniture and appliances), offers credit terms of thirty days, ninety days, and six-month revolving charges. Statements are rendered to customers on the first of each month, with a cut-off date of the 25th of the previous month. This merchant, because of his sizeable receivable volume, finds it necessary to borrow weekly on receivables generated since the 25th of the month. Briefly, the procedure would be as follows:

A. Initial procedure to set up credit:

1. Merchant submits financial data and accounts receivable financing is approved.
2. Accounts Receivable Agreement setting forth procedure and bank requirements is signed.
3. Notice of Intention to Assign Accounts Receivable is filed.

B. Initial borrowing procedure:

1. Merchant prepares initial assignment and certification form which incorporates the total amount of all accounts receivable as of the close of business the last business day prior to its initial borrowing and warrants that they represent bona fide indebtedness due him.
2. Attached to this and referred to in the assignment and certification is a microfilm spool of all customer ledgers.
3. Of the amount of receivables so certified and assigned, 80 percent is loaned to the merchant taking an "add-on" form of note.

Exhibit continued.

Exhibit 7 (Continued)

C. Processing of payments, additional loans, and determination of collateral base:

1. As collections on accounts are made by the merchant, either in the form of cash or check, they are deposited in kind into a cash collateral account maintained at the bank.
2. Once a week, whether new borrowings are requested or not, a certification form is received from the merchant which reconciles the borrowing base which should agree to the bank's collateral ledger card. Such certification indicates the balance of receivables at the beginning of the week, *less* collections and merchandise credits paid by the merchant, *plus* new charge sales during the week, thus resulting in the new borrowing base. Accompanying such certificate is a microfilm of all customer charge slips representing sales made during the week.
3. Once a week, or less frequently as is required, a combined application and certification form for borrowing is presented by the merchant which again recapitulates the borrowing base. An adjustment to the cash collateral account to cover the requested borrowing is made at that time.
4. Once a month merchant prepares a new assignment and certification form (as in initial borrowing procedure) which incorporates the total amount of accounts receivable as of the 25th of the month accompanied by a microfilm spool of its customers' ledgers.

In none of the above procedures is the merchant required to write on separate schedules or on certifications names of individual account holders involved as this is contained on the microfilm of his ledgers and charge slips.

NOTE: In calculating the borrowing base it is usual to deduct an allowance from the face amount of receivables to compensate for probable charge-offs. The amount is based on the merchant's loss experience. In this case, it is less than 1 percent per annum and a 3 percent deduction from our collateral base has been agreed to by merchant.

Exhibit 8

Percent per Month on Average Loan Outstanding	*Amount of Maximum Advance*
3/4	Up to $ 100,000
5/8	$100,000 to 250,000
9/16	250,000 to 600,000
1/2	600,000 to 1,000,000

International Credit Card Plan

This plan offers consumers and merchants the opportunity to participate in a program which is nationwide. Consumers who are issued International Credit Cards may use the cards in a variety of retail establishments throughout the United States and Canada.

The plan is operated by International Charge, Inc., a subsidiary of Seaboard Finance Company. In public advertising, however, Seaboard Finance is not mentioned.

METHOD OF OPERATION. For the consumer and the merchant this plan is similar to the bank credit card plan previously described, with two exceptions: (1) there is no charge to the retailer who joins the plan, (2) the use of imprinters is optional instead of mandatory.

From the bank's standpoint, the International Charge plan is radically different from the plan previously described. International Charge operates this plan; the bank merely acts as the company's local representative.

A bank which affiliates with International Charge contacts local retailers and enrolls them as members of the plan. The bank supplies International Charge with the names of customers who meet the credit requirements of card holders.[3] International Charge issues credit cards and directories of affiliated merchants to these customers. Both items bear the bank's name. At the time that the credit cards are mailed, the bank delivers the necessary supplies to the merchant members and International Charge then launches its local advertising program. The bank may choose to supplement this program with its own local advertising. International Charge also agrees to address and mail to credit customers any direct mail promotional material prepared by the bank.

Once the plan is in operation, the bank clears the merchants' drafts for International Charge and processes any credit card applications which are made directly to the bank. International Charge does all the billing and bookkeeping, furnishes the consumer credit, and delivers supplies to the merchants.

The bank incurs the expenses of establishing the plan. Once it is in operation, the bank receives 1/4 of 1 percent of all charges made with credit cards bearing the bank's name. This 1/4 of 1 percent applies only to the initial billing and does not apply after charges go on a deferred billing. The bank incurs no legal liability of any kind from its participation in the plan.

A bank may, by choice, perform some clerical operations after the plan is under way. These operations could include enrolling new merchants, and acting as the local agent for distributing supplies. Such service enables the bank to maintain a relationship with all of the retail outlets since some of them continue their principal accounts with other banks.

Proponents of the International Charge plan state that it permits many banks to provide a service which they could not undertake alone. In addition, once the plan is under way the bank's work is practically finished; yet, the customers and the merchants will continue to "advertise" the bank's name.

APPENDIX A

Because many consumer credit plans are relatively new, little published information about them is currently available. The following quotations may not, therefore, be fully representative of bank experience with these plans.

---

[3]International Charge provides the bank with a signed statement that the names provided will not be used for any purpose other than in connection with the credit cards.

Credit Card

New Jersey Bank and Trust Company – Passaic, N.J.
Operates sixteen branches; resources as of December 31, 1958, $286,875,000

The plan was started in 1950 and dropped in December 1959. It never did develop substantial volume.

The larger stores in the area retained their own accounts. The smaller stores tended to retain the best accounts for themselves and to send the bank the smaller ticket items or accounts on which they did not wish to assume the credit risk. For the twelve months ending April 30, 1959, the average credit card sale was $14.70.

During 1959, credit cards accounted for 2 1/2 percent of the bank's Consumer Credit Department gross income, and employed 10 percent of the department's staff.

SOURCE: *Burroughs Clearing House.* March 1960.

City Bank and Trust Company – Milwaukee, Wis.
A unit bank; resources as of December 31, 1958, $30,873,000

The bank announced plans to abandon its credit card operation on March 31, 1950. Lack of interest by the merchants was the principal reason for abandonment. The plan had been in operation since June, 1953.

Merchant participation in the plan fell from a peak of 200 members to 84 members. Dollar volume also fell – from $2 million to less than $1 million – the break-even point.

On December 31, 1959, there were 20,000 card holders; but only 13,145 of these cards were used during the previous quarter. The average billing for the quarter was $10.08.

The original charge to retailers was 5 percent. This was increased as costs rose until finally it was too expensive for the smaller stores.

SOURCE: *Burroughs Clearing House.* March 1960.

Chase Manhattan Bank – New York City
Operates 102 local branches; resources as of December 31, 1958, $8,329,982,000

In December 1959, the plan had 5300 member merchants with 6000 stores, and 360,000 card holders representing 320,000 families.

During the fourth quarter of 1959, sales totaled over $5 million. The effective service charge to merchants was 3.53 percent (refund 2.47 percent). The average transaction was $23.

Total sales for 1959 were $11 million. 1960 sales were forecast as $25 million.

Original plans called for the operation to be in the black in two years, but it appears that this objective can be achieved a little sooner than that.

62 percent of the merchant members represent new business.

SOURCE: *Burroughs Clearing House*. March 1960.

Line of Credit

First National Bank of Boston
Operates 25 local branches; resources as of December 31, 1958, $1,885,424,000

The bank has approved lines of credit ranging from $120 up to $6000. The average line is $460. The rejection rate on applications is 20 percent.

There are 17,000 accounts—96 percent of which have outstanding balances. The total outstanding on those accounts is $5,300,000; unused credit available totals $3,000,000.

The average person keeps 2/3 of his line in use at all times; he writes about 9 checks per year. The average check is for about $60.

Delinquencies over thirty days amount to 1.3 percent. Charge-offs are comparable to those on personal loans. The net yield is 50 percent higher than that on personal loans.

SOURCE: *Burroughs Clearing House*. March 1959.

For the first 4 1/2 years of operation, the bank [First National Bank of Boston] approved 80 percent of all applications. However, after an extensive advertising campaign, the bank was able to approve only 54 percent of the applications received.

The bank spends about $10 in advertising for each account that is opened. It now has 24,000 accounts with an outstanding balance of $9,300,000 and available credit of $5,100,000.

About 15 percent of the accounts are "riding the top," but the vast majority of these are holding smaller credit lines.

Charge-offs are running at about 1/3 of 1 percent of the total amount advanced which is slightly better than the experience on personal loans.

SOURCE: *Banking*. February 1960.

Branch Management

SELECTING BRANCH LOCATION

Citizens National Trust & Savings Bank

In the fall of 1955, Lawrence Johnson, head of Citizens National Trust & Savings Bank's research department, was considering the location of a new branch in Redlands, California (see map, Exhibit 1). It was the task of Mr. Johnson and his staff of two part-time employees from another department to gather and analyze data on potential bank sites and to report their findings and recommendations to the board of directors. Mr. Johnson concluded that he and his staff had gathered sufficient information concerning Redlands as a potential bank site to enable them to proceed with an evaluation of their findings.

The Citizens Bank began in 1903 as a small southern California unit bank located in Riverside. By the end of World War II, the bank had begun to expand rapidly as the area in which it operated changed from a largely agricultural region to a diversified industrial center. To keep pace with the resulting surge of population into southern California, Citizens' management adopted a policy of aggressive branch expansion. The number of its branches increased from nine in 1948 to twenty-three in 1955.

Citizens followed no formal procedure in making branch surveys. Mr. Johnson maintained files, covering the San Bernardino–Riverside County areas, containing information derived from many sources, such as officers of the bank, local business organizations, and the bank's customers. In cases where public information concerning population, wealth, and commercial development was not available, Mr. Johnson conducted surveys to obtain the necessary information.

The branch location procedure at Citizens Bank started with a complete report prepared by Mr. Johnson after consultation with the executive vice-president. The report was then submitted to the board of directors. If the directors approved the site and concluded that the bank's financial position warranted the addition of a branch, a formal

Exhibit 1

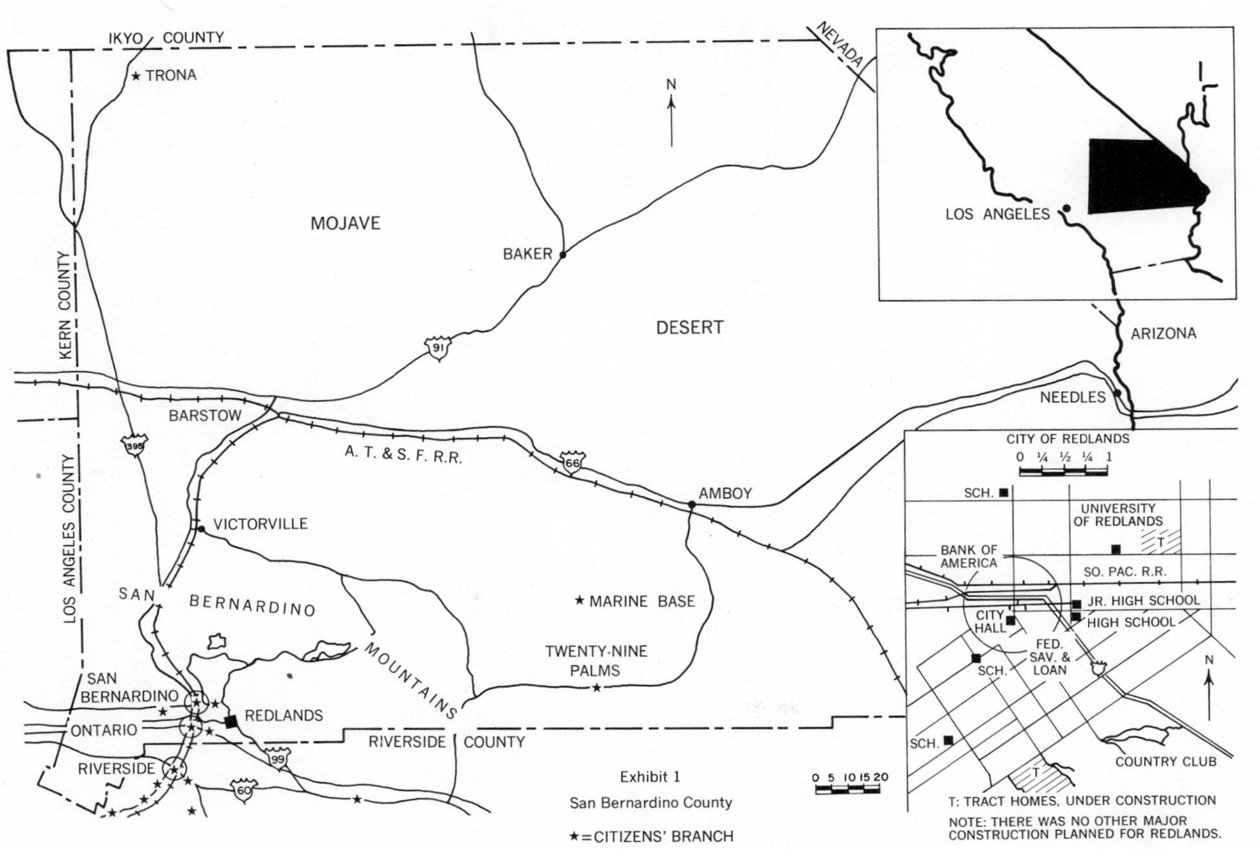

Exhibit 1
San Bernardino County
★=CITIZENS' BRANCH

Exhibit 2

CITIZENS NATIONAL TRUST & SAVINGS BANK

Treasury Department
Office of the Comptroller of the Currency
November 1950

APPLICATION OF

.... Charter No. ....
(Name of Bank) (County) (State)

FOR PERMISSION TO ESTABLISH A BRANCH

Comptroller of the Currency
Washington 25, D.C.

Sir:

Application is hereby made for permission to establish a branch of this bank at the following location:

Street Address City or Town County
(Population)

A certified copy of a resolution of the bank's board of directors authorizing the filing of the aforesaid application is enclosed. A current statement of condition of this bank and a copy of the pertinent State statutes reflecting whether a State bank could be authorized to establish a branch in the location applied for are also enclosed.

The area to be served by the proposed branch has an estimated population of . The following are the banking units now operating nearest to the location of the proposed branch:

Name of Bank	Head Office or Branch	Street Address	Distance from Location of Proposed Branch

The following is a brief summary of the board's reasons for believing that establishment of the branch would be in the interests of the bank.

Additional details concerning the proposal may be obtained by communicating with

......................................, (Telephone No. ......).
(Name) (Title)

It is understood that the cost of any necessary investigation in relation to the application will be borne by this bank.

Date President or Cashier

INSTRUCTIONS

An original and one copy of the application should be filed with the Comptroller of the Currency.

If the establishment of more than one branch is being considered at the same time, a separate application should be filed for each proposed branch.

If the proposal involved the take-over of another bank, with or without branches, a statement to that effect, with the name of the bank, should be included in the summary of the board's reasons for believing that establishment of the branch would be in the bank's interests.

If there is doubt about the adequacy or construction of State statutes relating to branches for State banks, a copy of opinion of counsel for the bank supported by court decisions, an opinion of the Attorney General, or other authority upon which counsel relies should accompany the application.

application was drawn up. Following receipt of this application, national bank examiners from the regional head office conducted their own independent investigation and then recommended either for or against the proposed site. If the chief national bank examiner for the region approved the application, he sent his recommendation to the Comptroller of the Currency in Washington for what usually amounted to a "rubber stamp" approval.

Mr. Johnson generally made available to the examiners the detailed report summarizing the results of his staff's survey of the area. When the national bank examiners and the Comptroller of the Currency reviewed an application for a new branch, they were primarily interested in whether the proposed branch would (1) promote the public convenience and advantage and (2) be desirable from the bank's standpoint. In preparing a bank survey summary for the examiners, Johnson tried, therefore, to emphasize one or more of the following points:

1. The proposed branch would provide needed service in an area with no banking facilities.

2. The proposed branch would provide needed service in an area which had inadequate banking facilities, that is, adequate and convenient banking service was not being provided by existing banks.

3. The service area of the proposed branch had sufficient population and business development to justify a bank or an additional bank.

4. The proposed branch was necessary if the bank was to maintain its competitive position in the area.

5. The proposed branch would be able to obtain sufficient business to put it on a profitable basis within a reasonable period of time.

6. Local groups of businessmen, residents, the Chamber of Commerce, or service clubs had requested the bank to establish a branch in the area.

Mr. Johnson and his staff began a branch survey by preparing a map of the area, generally covering 20 square miles. All banking offices and places of business were marked on this map. The boundaries of the potential branch's service area were then drawn taking into account: (1) the extent and quality of the business center and its pulling power on the surrounding population, (2) the location of existing banks, (3) the location of various barriers (such as railroad lines or major highways) that would limit the bank's drawing power in certain directions, and (4) parking facilities in the area compared with those in adjacent regions.

Once the service area of the projected branch was outlined, the staff next estimated the business potential in the region. Population data were vitally important. If adequate figures were not available, the staff made a field count of single-family homes as well as apartment houses and other multiple-family dwellings. From this field survey a satisfactory population estimate was made by applying to the dwelling unit count the

Exhibit 3

CITIZENS NATIONAL TRUST & SAVINGS BANK

Survey of Redlands Area for Branch Location

TO: L. P. Johnson September 7, 1955
FROM: R. P. Williamson

SERVICE AREA

Primary—Includes incorporated city of Redlands (incorporated November 26, 1888), an area of 17.2 square miles, located in San Bernardino County, on transcontinental highways #99 and #70—approximately fourteen miles northeast of main office, Citizens National, Riverside.

Secondary—Redlands branch would also serve unincorporated areas of Loma Linda, Mentone, Bryn Mawr, and Green Spot, all located within a radius of 5 miles.

POPULATION

Population of Redlands (incorporated) has increased an estimated 16.2 percent since the 1950 census. Population figures for the principal service area are as follows:

	April 1940	*April 1950*	*April 1953**	*April 1955*
Redlands City	14,325	18,429	20,022	21,266
Redlands Township	16,137	21,357	32,124	34,000†
Shopping area (est.)	n.a.	n.a.	42,000	45,000

*Special Census.
†Estimates from utility connections.

School enrollment—As an indication of population growth and future development, the following public school enrollment figures are detailed:

	1950	*1951*	*1952*	*1953*	*1954*
Grades 1–8	3,024	No	3,257	3,519	No
Grades 9–12	1,869	break-down	2,336	2,530	break-down
Total	4,893	5,247	5,593	6,049	6,229

average number of persons per dwelling unit in the general area. The 1950 census data were of limited value in making these surveys because they were out of date and often unavailable for the exact area desired.

While current population figures were significant, the staff also attempted to develop data on possible future growth. Census tract data[1] for 1940 and 1950, when combined with current survey statistics, usually provided the basis for population projections.

The over-all quality and character of the region was another important consideration. These factors were best appraised by analyzing infor-

[1]Census tracts are small areas, having a population generally between 3000 and 6000, into which certain large cities have been subdivided for statistical purposes.

Exhibit 3 (Continued)

Characteristics of City Population and Labor Force, 1950 Census

By Race	*Male*	*Female*	*Total*	*By Age*	*Male*	*Female*	*Total*
Total population	8,701	9,728	18,429	Total	8,701	9,728	18,429
White	8,578	9,581	18,159	Under 5	877	823	1,700
Native	7,899	8,912	16,811	5–14	1,481	1,368	2,849
Foreign	679	669	1,348	15–24	1,397	1,529	2,926
Nonwhite	123	147	270	25–44	2,236	2,510	4,746
Negro	101	131	232	45–64	1,688	1,996	3,684
Other	22	16	38	65 or over	1,022	1,502	2,524

Sources of foreign born: Mexico 437; Canada 176; Netherlands 147; England and Wales 122. Of the total 7675 females 14 years of age or older, 2330 or 30.4 percent were in the labor force, 2242 were employed, and 88 were unemployed in April 1950. One thousand six hundred and eighty women were employed as private wage and salary workers and 347 were government workers. Manufacturing employed 382 men and 156 women, a total of 538 or 8.2 percent of all employed. Median school years completed by persons 25 years or older was 12. There were 7450 families and unrelated individuals in the city with a median income during 1949 of $2113. There were 110 with incomes of $10,000 or more, or 1.5 percent.

At present, public schools include nine elementary schools, two junior high schools, and one high school.

AREA DEVELOPMENT

Residential—Redlands is primarily a residential city for people employed in the citrus industry, nearby military installations, service establishments, and retired people. Housing follows the normal pattern of a medium-sized city, with the minority section in the northwest section of town, older housing closer in, and the luxury, custom class homes in the south hills (adjoining and surrounding the golf course).

Housing availability, prices, and rentals: The housing census as of April 1950 showed 6364 dwelling units, of which 20.1 percent were in structures built since 1940, and 6032 were occupied. Of these 3656 were owner-occupied, or 60.6 percent, and had a median value of $7991. Of the rent or occupied dwellings, 16.7 percent rented for less than $20 per month, 53.5 percent for $20 to $39 per month, 21.5 percent for $40 to $59 per month, and 4.5 percent from $60 to $74 per month, with 3.8 percent in excess of $75 per month. Median monthly rental was $31.67. There are eight hotels in Redlands, with 219 rooms, and thirteen motels in the area with 135 rooms.

Climate: Temperature—Mean average temperature 56.6° to 69°
Rainfall—14.79-inch yearly average.
Altitude—1200 to 2100 feet.

Exhibit continued.

mation on the type of housing in the area, the approximate rental and sale price brackets, and the percentage of home ownership; the type of resident population classified by sources of income, approximate income brackets, and types and stability of employment. From these data the bank's analysts tried to determine answers to critical questions: Is the population composed primarily of wage earners, clerical workers, or professional people? Is the region heavily dependent upon one or two industries? Is the area particularly vulnerable to economic setbacks?

Exhibit 3 (Continued)

CITY STATISTICS

City Government—Sixth class California city, city manager and five elected trustees. 29-man police department, 20-man fire department.

	1950	*1951*	*1952*	*1953*	*1954*
Assessed valuation	$17,835,570	$18,621,240	$19,165,610	$19,906,640	$20,063,070
Total bonded indebtedness	292,000	250,000	210,000	195,000	182,000
Tax rate (per $100)	6.28	6.28	6.79	6.71	7.58
Building permits	2,432,208	3,025,886	3,135,124	3,136,853	5,477,810

UTILITIES

Water—From deep wells and streams (city of Redlands). Cost $1.65 per 1400 cu. ft. used. *Light, Heat, and Power*—Power and light from California Edison Co. Cost 80¢ customer charge plus energy charge ranging from 4.3¢ to 1.3¢ per KWH. Meters—6346. Natural gas from Southern California Gas Co. minimum rate $1.35. Meters—6872. Telephones—7245 within city.

SERVICES

Financial—Bank of America, Security-First National Bank of Los Angeles, Redlands Federal Savings and Loan.

Newspaper—Redlands Daily Facts (circulation 4658).

Hospitals—Loma Linda Hospital, 166-bed capacity; Community Hospital, 76-bed capacity.

COLLEGE

University of Redlands—Four-year liberal arts college. Enrollment fiscal year 1953–1954, 1309; summer school, 927. Valuation of U. of R. property, $5 million.

There are thirty-seven churches, one library, one newspaper, and two banks. Recreational facilities include two theaters, six parks, four playgrounds, and two swimming pools. Nearby are recreations in the mountains, Palm Springs, desert resorts, beach resorts, all within a two-hour drive.

AGRICULTURAL

Agriculture remains one of the leading, if not the leading, factor in the Redlands area economy, representing a total valuation in 1954 of $12,718,197. Citrus remains the leading agricultural product, accounting for approximately two thirds of the total valuation. The other principal agricultural product is livestock (primarily poultry and dairy products).

Total valuation of agricultural products produced in the Redlands district for 1953 and 1954 is detailed below:

The bank used several "rules of thumb" in its branch location studies. The minimum population for a branch in a quality suburban district, largely residential in character but with a good shopping center, was 5000 persons. In a residential area of average quality, a population of 10,000 or over was regarded as satisfactory. Two percent was a minimum for bank deposits as a percentage of annual retail sales; $250.00 was the minimum for bank deposits per capita.

Other items which the staff carefully weighed to measure the wealth of the area included consumer goods purchases; per capita deposits in existing banks; average account balances if known; the general appear-

Exhibit 3 (Continued)

Crop	*1953* *Valuation*	*1953* *Percent of Total*	*1954* *Valuation*	*1954* *Percent of Total*
Citrus*	$12,900,223	80%	$ 9,799,297	77%
Subtropicals, deciduous, grapes, berries, and nuts	6,617	.....	6,959	.....
Vegetable crops	6,470	.....	2,271	.....
Field crops	136,083	1	183,050	2
Livestock	3,010,415	19	2,726,620	21
Total	$16,059,808	100%	$12,718,197	100%

*Total citrus acreage in district includes 7438 acres Navels; 4092 acres Valencias; 508 acres grapefruit; 207 acres miscellaneous.

Industrial—Redlands is still primarily a one-industry city—the citrus industry. In this connection, there are fourteen packing houses in the area, processing and shipping the equivalent of 6135 cars of fruit in the 1953 to 1954 season.

The Redlands Chamber of Commerce, in cooperation with the San Bernardino County industrial director, has started an active campaign of attracting desirable industry to the area. At the present time there are 126 acres within the city limits zoned M-1 for light industry, of which about twenty five percent is vacant and available in parcels ranging in size from ½ to 4 acres. Typical sale prices during 1953 to 1954 have ranged from $2000 to $4000 per acre. There is also considerable land available outside the city for light industry to the northeast and east and west of the city on land owned by the railroad if industries use rail facilities.

There are currently thirty-four industrial concerns (excluding citrus packing houses) within the surrounding area. The six largest manufacturing firms in the area are:

Name of Company	*Employment*	*Products*
Norton Air Force Base	750	Aircraft repair
Universal-Rundle Corporation	250	Sanitary pottery
Big Bear Timber Company	110	Lumber cutting, milling
Redlands Dye & Finishing Company	80	Ladies' nylon hosiery
Robinhood Sportswear	90	Boys' clothing
Grand Central Rocket Company	80	Solid rocket fuel, research

Commercial—Redlands is the major shopping and business center for one of the largest remaining concentrations of citrus acreage in the southern California area. *Combined payrolls of Redlands City labor force* is estimated at approximately $20 million. Shopping area population is estimated at 45,000.

Exhibit continued.

ance of neighborhoods; utility meters and telephone installations; extent of commercial development, and community factors such as type of government, master zoning, and tax burden.

The availability of qualified personnel in an area was not considered a limiting factor in the bank's expansion program; as new branches were added, the employee relations department assumed the responsibility for hiring and training the necessary personnel to operate the branches.

One of the most important elements in the decision to establish a new

Exhibit 3 (Continued)

PRIMARY BUSINESS AREA

DOWNTOWN BUSINESS DISTRICT. *Business licenses:* 1953–786; 1954–729. *Post Office receipts:* 1953–$226,094; 1954–$245,730.

Retail Sales	*1950*	*1951*	*1952*	*1953*	*1954*
City sales tax	$11,429	$13,202	$13,381	$15,370	$16,218

Based on estimates of percentage of taxable sales to total city sales, the above figures indicate *annual retail sales* of approximately $20 million to $22 million.

SECONDARY BUSINESS AREA

Businesses—twenty-seven retail stores; including three markets, five filling stations, three cafes, drygoods store, variety store, and various other general retail or service outlets.

LOMA LINDA. *Businesses*—Eighteen retail stores; including one market, two hardware and appliance stores, three filling stations, three church-owned businesses, and other general retail or service outlets.

BANKING SERVICE

Present banking facilities in Redlands include two banks—branch offices of the Bank of America and Security-First National Bank—handling a service area with a population of approximately 34,000. Although no breakdown is available, it is understood that the Bank of America accounts for over 50 percent of the total deposits and a considerably higher portion of the total loan volume.

In addition, there is one savings and loan association in the area— the Redlands Federal Savings & Loan. This office is an old, established firm with an excellent reputation for customer relations and management. The firm opened a branch office in Fontana in late 1953 and a new branch in Yucaipa in April 1955.

Statistics on bank deposits in the area have been obtained and are detailed below:

Deposits (in millions)	*1950*	*1951*	*1952*	*1953*	*1954*
Banks	$24,329	$25,683	$27,169	$28,215*	$31,810
Redlands Federal	3,928	5,291	6,952	8,404*	9,055
Total	$28,257	$30,974	$34,121	$36,619	$40,865

*Fontana Branch of Redlands Federal Savings opened during 1953—totals consolidated.

Bank debits (in millions)	$224,091	$252,295	$177,574	$213,101	$205,165

From the above statistics, it would appear that total loan volume of the banks in Redlands might range from $15 million to $20 million.

branch was the threat of competition. The branch objective of Citizens' management was to hold and improve the bank's competitive position against the larger state-wide institutions. In order to assure its participation in the growth anticipated for the various communities it served, Citizens had decided on several occasions to locate a branch in a community which was then adequately serviced by existing banking facilities. This action, taken in order to discourage rival banks from entering the area, generally resulted in unprofitable operation for more than the usual period of six to nine months. If a branch did not expect to show a profit within eighteen months, however, the Comptroller of the Currency would not grant the branch a charter.

Redlands, the branch site under consideration by Mr. Johnson, was an attractive residential community in the center of southern California's citrus belt (see Exhibits 1 and 3 for detailed information about Redlands). The city was first brought to the attention of the Citizens Bank when a group of prominent Redlands businessmen, substantial customers of the bank, suggested that a branch in their town would be a great convenience to them.[2] The largest of these customers, together with their loan commitments and deposit totals for the month of August 1955 are shown below:

Customer	*Deposit Account*	*Loan Commitment*
Cajon Fruit Packing Company	$225,000	$500,000
Hill Electric Manufacturing Corp.	50,000	50,000*
Larsen Appliances	10,000	150,000†
		25,000‡

*Accounts receivable line of credit.
†Conditional contract line of credit.
‡Flooring line.

Two other factors which had prompted Mr. Johnson to study Redlands as a potential bank site were (1) the discovery that the Big Valley Savings and Loan Association was considering the location of a branch office there, and (2) the proximity of Redlands to Citizens' head office in Riverside. Mr. Johnson was hesitant, however, to recommend the establishment of a new branch for competitive or geographic reasons alone, since he believed there were many other potentially good bank sites in the same general region in which competition was not a problem.

An appraisal of an area's deposit and loan potential was a vital element in every branch location survey. The first step involved an estimate of the area's total deposits and loans, using information derived from the bank's experience in similar regions; accounts presently maintained with the bank in the proposed service area; the experience of competitive financial institutions; and an analysis of local wealth, commercial development, and shopping patterns. Next, the bank's analysts estimated the proportion of total loans and deposits that the Citizens' Bank might

[2]In 1953, at the request of a valued customer, General Potash and Borax Corporation, the bank had established a branch in the town of Crafton on the Mojave Desert. Crafton, with a population of 2450 was the production center for General Potash.

Exhibit 4

CITIZENS NATIONAL TRUST & SAVINGS BANK

Selected Economic Indicators for San Bernardino County, Riverside County, and the State of California

Indicator	*San Bernardino County*			*Riverside County*			*State of California*		
	Base Year	*Recent Year*	*Percent Change*	*Base Year*	*Recent Year*	*Percent Change*	*Base Year*	*Recent Year*	*Percent Change*
Population (000) (April 1, 1940; July 1, 1954)	161	362	124.9	106	204	92.5	6,907	12,450	80.0
Personal income (000,000) (1940; 1952)	$ 86	$467	448.2	$ 53	$239	337.7	$5,549	$22,496	309.0
Retail sales (000,000) (1939; 1953)	60	393	555.5	39	247	533.3	3,187	15,444	382.8
Value of agricultural production (000,000) (1940; 1950)	15	50	233.3	12	52	333.3	452	1,742	288.8
Value of mine products (000,000) (1940; 1950)	16	53	231.3	4	22	550.0	343	1,219	252.9
Bank deposits (000,000)	35	163	363.9	26	124	370.3	4,256	12,684	198.0
Auto registration (000) (1940; 1953)	60	132	120.0	40	79	104.0	2,573	4,800	85.7
Assessed valuation of property (000,000) (1939–1940; 1953–1954)	140	386	175.8	88	308	250.0	7,094	17,170	136.3
Value added by manufacturing (000,000) (1939; 1947)	14	76	442.8	7	28	400.0	1,123	3,995	255.7

SOURCE: *Reprinted from California Blue Book, 1954.*

expect to attract. The deposit and loan totals for the proposed Redlands branch were estimated as follows:

Period	*Deposits*	*Loans*
Present Redlands customers	$ 300,000	$ 250,000
End of first year	1,750,000	650,000
End of second year	5,000,000	1,600,000

Mr. Johnson felt that one very favorable aspect of Redlands was the anticipated population and commercial growth in the region. Favorable growth prospects are vitally important to a new branch; upon entering an area the new bank may capture only 10 percent to 15 percent of existing deposits since most people do not readily change banks without a compelling reason. On the other hand, a new branch has an equal opportunity when competing for accounts new to the area.

Finally, Mr. Johnson was particularly concerned about two aspects of establishing a branch bank in Redlands:

1. Should a relatively small bank enter a fairly large city which already had two large, well-established banks?

2. Could the Citizens Bank adequately service the very heavy seasonal loans of agricultural industry in Redlands?

Exhibit 5

CITIZENS NATIONAL TRUST & SAVINGS BANK

Statements of Financial Condition

Income Statement, Years Ended December 31	*1949*	*1954*
EARNINGS		
Loan interest	$ 1,635	$ 3,467
Securities dividends and interest	569	1,111
Other operating earnings	289	1,189
Total operating earnings	2,493	5,767
Salaries and wages	719	1,826
Federal income tax	340	966
Other operating expenses	792	1,960
Net operating earnings	642	1,015
Recoveries, etc.	171	662
Losses, etc	214	801
Net recoveries	43 Dr.	139 Dr.
Net profit	599	876

Exhibit continued.

Exhibit 5 (Continued)

Balance Sheet, December 31

RESOURCES		
Loans and discounts	$28,907	$ 62,758
U.S. government securities	28,404	52,521
Other securities	5,399	6,994
Banking premises	484	1,342
Cash and in banks	12,445	23,131
Total	$75,639	$146,746
LIABILITIES		
Capital stock	$ 1,500	$ 3,600
Surplus	1,500	3,600
Undivided profits	1,140	1,986
Contingency reserve	257	2,195
Deposits	71,242	135,324
Other liabilities		41
Total	$75,639	$146,746

EVALUATION OF BRANCH PERFORMANCE

Imperial First National Bank

In the late summer of 1961, the president of Imperial First National Bank appointed Charles Holman as manager of the bank's Oasis branch. Mr. Holman had been a member of the business development department at the San Diego headquarters and was, at one time, an assistant manager of another Imperial branch. With this appointment, Holman inherited a branch whose recent operating results had been disappointing to the bank's branch supervisor.

The Community

The town of Oasis, with a population of 3500, was located 75 miles from San Diego. Irrigation had transformed this area into an important producer of celery, lettuce, and cotton. Over the years, the economic growth rate of the county had been slow but steady as a result of improvements in farming methods and equipment. Census data appear in Exhibit 1.

During the 1930s, Oasis became the major shopping center for farmers in the area. It replaced many smaller communities that lacked its transportation facilities and merchandise selection. After the Korean conflict, however, Oasis began to lose its position as a marketing center

Exhibit 1

IMPERIAL FIRST NATIONAL BANK

Census Data on Vista County

A. POPULATION

	1950	*1960*
Vista County	11,651	11,962
Oasis	3,031	3,491
Alexandria	1,134	1,364

B. PERSONAL INCOME—Vista County (000 omitted)

1955	$34,262	1958	$35,732
1956	37,867	1959	36,841
1957	35,787	1960	37,500

C. EFFECTIVE BUYING INCOME PER HOUSEHOLD—Vista County

1958	$ 6,474
1959	6,839
1960	7,000

D. RETAIL SALES PER HOUSEHOLD—Vista County

1958	$ 5,269
1959	5,361
1960	5,427

E. RETAIL TRADE

		Vista County	*Oasis*
Number of establishments	1959	177	67
	1960	187	73
Total retail sales	1959	$16,731	$7,755
(000 omitted)	1960	17,902	8,163

F. RESIDENTIAL BUILDING PERMITS—City of Oasis

1955	55	1958	10
1956	21	1959	17
1957	19	1960	15

as farmers in the region began trading in other communities. By 1961, Alexandria, a town one third the size of Oasis located 10 miles away, and Desert Springs, with a population of nearly 20,000 located 35 miles to the east, were threatening to replace Oasis as the major shopping areas for farm families. Perhaps the most important reasons for this change were the generally poor physical condition of the town and a growing apathy of the businessmen. From the start of World War II up to 1958 no new construction had taken place in the business section of Oasis. It was not until fire destroyed the Sears Roebuck store that a new building was erected on the main street. Rather than improve the street, however, the modern, attractive design of the structure emphasized the poor condition of the surrounding stores. The local merchants appeared to have lost much of the aggressiveness which once characterized their manner of seeking business.

The Bank

The Imperial First National Bank headquartered in San Diego had sixty-eight branches located in southern California as far north as Los Angeles on the coast and Bakersfield in the valley. Most of the operations, however, took place south and east of Los Angeles in the cities of Long Beach, Ontario, San Bernardino, San Diego, Palm Springs, Brawley, El Centro, and other communities of the Imperial Valley.

During the 1950s the Imperial Bank had experienced the greatest growth of its sixty-five-year history, following the trend of the general economic growth of southern California. Since 1950 the bank had doubled its number of offices through mergers and new branches. The bank was continuing to expand its branch operations, with nine new branches scheduled for 1961. Exhibit 2 presents financial and other statistical data for Imperial First National during this period.

Imperial provided most of the traditional banking services for its customers. A trust department was maintained in San Diego, with similar smaller facilities at Bakersfield, Long Beach, and El Centro. In addi-

Exhibit 2

IMPERIAL FIRST NATIONAL BANK

Statistical Data for the Entire Bank
Year End
(dollar figures in thousands)

	1950	*1952*	*1954*	*1956*	*1958*	*1960*
Total assets	$745,490	$845,671	$1,007,341	$1,087,299	$1,218,179	$1,355,162
Total deposits	680,417	770,119	918,005	985,865	1,099,432	1,214,465
Cash and due from banks	153,687	175,851	192,071	213,263	203,682	220,051
U.S. government securities	283,823	265,089	356,361	233,811	322,699	308,990
Other securities	39,374	46,498	59,034	68,391	70,698	68,823
Loans and discounts	243,688	337,775	375,047	540,991	586,730	704,691
Number of deposit accounts	235,674	261,122	285,582	338,676	370,904	430,276
Number of offices	22	26	31	43	54	68
Number of employees	1,455	1,747	2,022	2,478	2,568	3,220
Net operating income after tax	$ 3,798	$ 4,116	$ 5,187	$ 7,460	$ 8,335	$ 11,385
Earnings per share*	$ 1.02	$ 1.04	$ 1.09	$ 1.48	$ 1.66	$ 2.15

*Based on number of shares outstanding at the end of each year.

tion, an international section was included in the headquarters with active correspondent relationships throughout Latin America, the Far East, and Europe.

Bank officers were hesitant to classify their institution as either a "wholesale" or "retail" bank. They pointed out that, even though commercial loans were the largest single item in the bank's portfolio, the bank was very active in real estate lending and among the leaders in southern California automobile financing. At the close of 1959, Imperial's loan portfolio was divided in the following proportions:

Commercial	42%
Real estate	38%
Automotive	11%
Personal	9%

The deposit structure of Imperial First National was:

Demand deposits	48%
Time deposits	40%
Government deposits	12%

The Bank's Organization

Theoretically, the branch managers (of whom 40 percent were vice-presidents) reported directly to the president. In actual practice, however, the activities of the branches were coordinated by a branch supervisor, whose staff made frequent visits to each office and received periodic reports. The supervisor also aided the personnel officer in the selection of branch managers and their assistants.

The bank's top management attempted to grant each office a considerable degree of autonomy to provide the flexibility necessary for effective competition in lending, personnel recruitment, and general business development. In the area of personnel, for example, the assistant manager in charge of operations hired all the clerical workers in the branch after the central office authorized the number of people and their salary grades. In addition, senior credit officials established loan limits which were generous, so that lending officers could readily handle most customer requirements without reference to the headquarters loan committee.

The Oasis Branch

Two of the fifteen people employed in the Oasis office had been with Imperial for over twenty years and seven less than two years. Exhibit 3 presents information on the salary, employment date, and age of the branch personnel.

Exhibit 3

IMPERIAL FIRST NATIONAL BANK

Oasis Branch Personnel—6/30/61

Name	*Title*	*Grade*	*Monthly Salary*	*Employment Date*	*Birth Date*
Charles Holman	Manager	13	$900	6/1/52	11/12/25
George Stone	Assistant Manager	10	625	2/1/33	9/3/08
Jon Winters	Note, Exchange and Collection teller	6	415	4/1/36	6/28/14
Thelma Witter	Secretary	5	380	5/1/42	9/9/19
Jane MacFarland	Exchange and Collection Teller	5	340	2/1/52	10/7/25
William Burton	Utility Clerk-Teller	5	345	11/1/58	2/6/29
Roger Malthas	Commercial and Savings Teller	4	320	9/9/59	6/6/16
James Perez	Commercial and Savings Teller	4	290	5/11/60	10/10/31
June Whitfield	Commercial and Savings Teller	4	275	1/21/61	8/20/28
Maria Gomez	Commercial and Savings Teller	4	260	3/1/61	3/3/38
Helen Troy	Senior Bookkeeper	4	320	10/1/58	4/14/18
Alicia Romero	Bookkeeper	3	265	11/2/60	3/29/39
Margo Alexander	Bookkeeper	3	230	4/18/61	7/16/40
Mable Burgess	Safe Deposit Attendant-Statement Clerk	3	230	6/1/61	5/15/40
Willie Charles	Custodian		115	3/15/55	1/6/06

The salary ranges for this office:

	Minimum	Average	Maximum
Grade 3	$230	$280	$325
Grade 4	260	315	370
Grade 5	295	355	415
Grade 6	330	400	465

Holman's predecessor at Oasis, recently retired at the age of 65, had been forced to curtail many of his civic activities for several years because of ill health. His lending philosophy had been conservative. He believed that personal and automotive loan business belonged to finance companies rather than to commercial banks.

Until 1957 this conservatism had been modified to some extent by an active assistant manager, Richard McIntyre, who had conducted most of the bank's lending activities. In that year he had been promoted to manager of another branch, leaving the Oasis branch without a second assistant manager.

George Stone, the remaining assistant manager, had been with Imperial longer than any other person at the branch. Over the years, his duties had become primarily concerned with operations. In 1960 he had taken charge of cash shipments, supervision of the bookkeepers and tellers, and maintenance of the general ledger. Stone had virtually no lending experience, although he had once attended a three-month course given by the credit department at the headquarters office.

The Oasis branch was located in the center of town, in a one story wooden frame structure which was old but well maintained. There was one other bank in Oasis, a branch of the state-wide California Trust Company. This office was directly across the street from Imperial in quarters that were little better than Imperial's. Mr. Holman had observed that the personnel across the street appeared younger and more aggressive and the banking floor was a busier place. Officers of Imperial had obtained, on a confidential exchange of information, the following data concerning the Oasis branch of the California Trust Company:

	6/30/59	*12/31/59*	*6/30/60*	*12/31/60*	*6/30/61*
Deposits	$7,286	$8,919	$7,819	$9,987	$8,529
Loans	3,807	3,612	4,130	3,746	4,277

This compared with Imperial's experience of:

	6/30/59	*12/31/59*	*6/30/60*	*12/31/60*	*6/30/61*
Deposits	$9,190	$9,588	$8,384	$9,996	$8,677
Loans	2,733	2,253	2,640	2,664	2,164

Complete financial statements for the Oasis branch of the Imperial First National for the first six months of 1959–1961 are presented in Exhibits 4 through 8.

Branch Evaluation

The management of Imperial First National used a five-point program for evaluating the work of each branch office and its manager. Holman was familiar with this program through his previous branch work and discussions with the branch supervisor. Appraisals were made periodically in the following areas although no formal report was prepared: (1) personnel turnover, (2) real-estate loans, (3) commercial loans, (4) operations, and (5) business development activities.

PERSONNEL TURNOVER: Imperial's personnel officer periodically examined each branch's record of appointments and resignations. An annual turnover rate of between 25 percent and 30 percent among clerical

Exhibit 4

IMPERIAL FIRST NATIONAL BANK

Oasis Branch Balance Sheets

Resources	*6/30/59*	*6/30/60*	*6/30/61*
Loans and discounts secured by stocks/bonds	$ 237,142.72	$ 115,058.37	$ 118,100.37
Loans and discounts unsecured or secured by collections	993,113.10	996,388.16	670,530.45
Cons. loans – secured and unsecured	236,477.02	160,405.20	124,578.51
Cons. loans – installments	41,260.92	20,563.02	5,703.37
Installment loans – auto and other – discounted	33,687.76		
Loans on real estate – city	828,576.01	835,815.20	852,161.63
Loans on real estate – farm	356,022.46	504,489.56	329,360.86
Loans on real estate – FHA Title II	6,999.67	7,322.49	7,631.12
State and local warrants	....	....	56,081.98
Total loans and discounts	$2,733,279.66	$2,640,053.01	$2,164,148.29
Individual overdrafts	$ 4,061.33	$ 11,529.45	$ 4,269.08
Items in transit – other checks	1,127.98	29,056.44	6,299.25
City cash collections	5,693.56	1,582.29	2,756.70
Exchange for clearing house	31,436.45	84,749.97	56,024.18
Cash in vault	44,024.38	62,914.55	40,797.29
Total cash and due from banks	$ 82,282.37	$ 178,303.25	$ 105,877.42
Suspense resources	12.39	9.30	....
Total other assets	12.39	9.30	....
Headquarters debit	$6,369,566.91	$5,554,074.56	$6,403,048.92
Total resources	$9,189,202.66	$8,383,969.57	$8,677,343.71

Liabilities	*6/30/59*	*6/30/60*	*6/30/61*
Cashier's checks	$ 101,284.89	$ 88,125.69	$ 135,187.15
Total due to banks and bankers	$ 101,284.89	$ 88,125.69	$ 135,187.15
Commercial deposits under attachment	$3,006,720.05	$2,796,577.73	$2,820,274.73
Inactive commercial deposits	20,821.66	41,536.54	17,578.61
Com. dep. under attachment	....	....	192.13
State, county, and municipal demand deposits	683,410.15	522,759.64	548,730.52
Demand certificates of deposit	....	....	537.00
Special reserves – dealers	4,350.35	754.19	21.26
Suspense liabilities	221.01	269.25	331.43
Key deposit account	244.00	220.00	174.00
U S. deposits – postmasters, other officers, and agencies	2,636.26	6,598.26	28,452.34
Total demand deposits	$3,819,688.37	$3,456,841.30	$3,551,479.17
Christmas club deposits	$ 10,545.00	$ 8,363.00	$ 9,481.50
Dormant savings deposits	....	369.23	414.52
Savings deposits – active	4,755,664.17	4,531,669.49	4,597,658.09
State, county, and municipal time deposits	603,305.12	386,725.55	518,310.43
Total time deposits	$5,369,514.29	$4,927,128.27	$5,125,864.54
Total liabilities	$9,189,202.66	$8,383,969.57	$8,677,343.71

Exhibit 5

IMPERIAL FIRST NATIONAL BANK

Comparative Statement of Income and Expense
Oasis Branch

Description	*Six Months Ending 6/30/59*	*Six Months Ending 6/30/60*	*Six Months Ending 6/30/61*
Direct operating income			
Interest—commercial loans	$ 34,808	$ 28,280	$ 20,242
Interest—real estate loans	35,014	36,139	30,711
Discount and interest—auto and other loans	936		
Discount and interest—consumer loans	17,281	10,095	8,254
Interest—miscellaneous	3		263
Safe deposit department	1,706	1,613	1,454
Service charges, regular	11,486	10,267	9,451
Service charges, special checking	1,115	1,086	1,156
Service charges and other fees on bank loans	647	601	
Exchange and commission	608	535	425
Sundry recoveries—cash overages	323	114	214
Total direct operating income	$103,927	$ 88,730	$ 72,170
Direct operating expense			
Operating expense—banking department (see Exhibit 7)	$ 52,957	$ 48,095	$ 52,727
Operating expense—consumer loan department	620	352	265
Interest on time deposits	75,017	67,620	70,920
Sundry losses—cash shortages	734	593	69
Total direct operating expense	$129,328	$116,660	$123,981
Direct net operating income	$ (25,401)	$ (27,930)	$ (51,811)
Loans and auto contracts charged off	$ (1,098)	$ (100)	$ (671)
Recoveries on charged-off assets	363	223	253
Net income before headquarters credit	$ (26,136)	$ (27,607)	$ (52,229)
Headquarters credit (see Exhibit 6)	$ 95,887	$ 79,146	$ 63,848
Net income before taxes	$ 69,751	$ 51,539	$ 11,619
Provision for income taxes	$ 39,141	$ 29,198	$ 5,810
Net income after taxes	$ 30,610	$ 22,341	$ 5,809

personnel under grade 6 was considered acceptable.[1] If the figure was above 30 percent, the personnel officer would visit the branch to review the situation. In the case of the Oasis branch, all but one of the tellers

[1]Figured on the number of employees who left the bank divided by the average number employed during the period.

Exhibit 6

IMPERIAL FIRST NATIONAL BANK

Computation of Headquarters Credit
Oasis Branch

Description	*Six Months Ending 6/30/59*	*Six Months Ending 6/30/60*	*Six Months Ending 6/30/61*
INCOME CREDITS			
Central office	$ 60,259	$58,263	$77,325
Area automotive finance department	51,198	36,720	....
	$111,457	$94,983	$77,325
EXPENSE CHARGES			
General administrative overhead	$15,008	$15,541	$13,248
Consumer loan administration	562	296	229
	$15,570	$15,837	$13,477
Net amount credited	$95,887	$79,146	$63,848

The Headquarters Credit was used to credit a branch with income on earning assets of the entire bank from funds supplied by a particular branch's deposits. Should a branch be able to lend, say, $1 million but it loaned only $500,000, the remaining funds could be used by the headquarters and other branches. After subtracting a portion for reserve requirements, the headquarters would credit a branch with an income on the remaining funds. The rate varied as interest rates changed, but it was always less than the amount which the branch could obtain on a moderate-risk loan. This was intended to encourage each branch to lend as much of its available funds as possible.

and bookkeepers who were hired by the bank since 1959 were replacements. Turnover in this office had run about 33 percent a year for several years.

REAL-ESTATE LOANS: At the start of every year, each branch in the Imperial system was given a budget for real estate lending. Oasis had been authorized $187,000 in new loans for 1961, with a $25,000 limit for each loan. Any loan request in excess of the loan limit had to be approved at headquarters. By midyear, $45,000 of the total authorization had been placed by Oasis; Imperial's other branches showed average utilization of over 60 percent of their funds.

The headquarters was concerned with the quality of real estate loans as well as their amount. Through periodic audits of each office, the real estate department appraised the loans which had been made and the payment record of previous loans. The last audit of the Oasis office had been satisfactory.

COMMERCIAL LOANS: No budget was established for the commercial loans of a branch, although each branch was expected to maintain its

Exhibit 7

IMPERIAL FIRST NATIONAL BANK

Comparative Statement of Operating Expense
Banking Department of Oasis Branch

Account	*Six Months Ended 6/30/59*	*Six Months Ended 6/30/60*	*Six Months Ended 6/30/61*
Salaries, staff and official	$31,525.66	$28,352.00	$29,410.50
Christmas bonus	1,232.00	1,134.00	1,160.13
Overtime	183.32	27.17	....
Current service payment pension plan	1,170.00	1,265.00	1,383.31
Insurance, life, health, accident	696.00	589.00	623.46
Federal and state unemployment taxes	524.42	561.37	558.40
Federal old age insurance contribution	966.25	724.99	811.71
Telephone and telegraph	386.50	442.67	517.41
Postage and mail insurance	1,059.59	939.77	685.50
Stationery and supplies	1,940.76	881.17	1,208.69
Imprinting customer checks, rubber stamps	66.12	138.54	66.70
Light, heat, water, power	778.89	693.42	712.68
Rent	8,400.00	9,300.00	9,900.00
Insurance	216.00	246.00	172.23
Legal expense	....	2.92	60.35
Advertising	....	....	1,337.21
Public relations information, expenses, etc.	183.47	140.42	249.21
Travel, entertainment, and other—staff	....	68.01	507.71
Travel, entertainment, and other—officers	160.52	193.79	253.84
Automobile	277.24	93.81	184.89
Clearing house assessment—examination fees	....	....	311.67
Association dues and subscriptions	....	81.50	180.63
Credit reports	366.00	81.10	....
Donations	140.00	35.00	30.00
Upkeep furniture and fixtures, bank premises	615.20	518.00	1,203.67
Janitor, patrol and watchman	1,525.34	1,273.10	904.45
Miscellaneous expense	171.67	188.13	190.23
Taxes—other	41.58	45.87	56.02
Rentals—mechanical equipment	30.69	48.22	45.42
Total	$52,957.31	$48,095.05	$52,726.69

share of the loans in its community. The Oasis office loan limit was $15,000 in unsecured loans and $25,000 in secured loans. The reporting limit of the Oasis branch of the bank was $10,000. Oasis had received satisfactory ratings on the quality and payment record of its loan portfolio. However, the confidential exchange of information with the Cali-

Exhibit 8

IMPERIAL FIRST NATIONAL BANK

Comparative Statistical Report
Oasis Branch

	Period Ending 6/30/59	*Period Ending* 6/30/60	*Period Ending* 6/30/61
DESCRIPTION DEPOSITS			
Number of commercial accounts	1,722	1,708	1,645
Amount of demand deposits	$3,820,000	$3,457,000	$3,551,000
Number of savings accounts	1,897	1,815	1,747
Amount of time deposits	$5,370,000	$4,927,000	$5,126,000
Total number of deposit accounts	3,619	3,523	3,392
LOANS			
Number of commercial loans	267	265	221
Amount	$1,230,256	$1,111,457	$ 788,631
Number of real estate loans	167	170	184
Amount	$1,191,598	$1,347,627	$1,189,154
Number of auto and other loans	26	....	....
Amount	$ 33,688	....	....
Number of consumer loans	527	360	329
Amount	$ 277,738	$ 180,969	$ 130,282
Total number of loans	987	795	734
Total amount of loans	$2,743,280	$2,640,053	$2,108,066
NUMBER OF STAFF			
Banking department	16	14	15
Automotive finance department	0	0	0
Consumer loan department	0	0	0
Total number of staff	16	14	15

fornia Trust Company's branch had shown that the decline in Imperial loans was due to a loss of share rather than a decline of business in the community.

OPERATIONS: The fourth area of branch evaluation was the efficiency of the staff. By means of the national bank examinations (conducted three times every two years) and the semiannual audit by the bank's own staff, the branch supervisor received indications of this efficiency. The branch had been cited on several occasions for inadequate controls and procedures.

BUSINESS DEVELOPMENT ACTIVITIES: The final phase of the evaluation program was conducted entirely through personal visits by the branch supervisor and his staff, or by the officer in charge of the bank's business development. The purpose of these visits was to review the business development activities of the branch manager and to evaluate the effect of these activities on deposits and loan demand. Branch managers were expected to be active in the local Chamber of Commerce and the Community Chest or the Red Cross, and to join at least one civic service club. In addition to these activities the managers made personal calls on established and potential customers. Due to his long illness, the previous manager had been rated poorly in this phase of his operation over the past four years.

Revitalizing the Oasis Branch

As he assumed his duties, Mr. Holman planned his approach to managing the branch. He knew he must study the strengths and weaknesses of the branch and the market it served; concentrate his efforts in those areas over which he could expect to exercise reasonable control; and channel the efforts of the branch staff. Holman considered whether to ask for another assistant branch manager, a position already authorized but unfilled since 1957.

Having observed in other branches the effective use of staff committees in organizing branch activities, Holman thought he should consider this approach. Those committees typically employed were:

EXPENSE COMMITTEE—to approve all expenditures for routine supplies and equipment that were purchased locally, and to watch for needless waste of supplies.

INCOME AND SERVICE CHARGE COMMITTEE—to study the sources of income and recommend methods for increasing it; to insure that service charges were properly assessed.

BUSINESS DEVELOPMENT COMMITTEE—to review the advertising, public relations, and customer service activities. It typically reviewed any major accounts that were closed and assigned members of the committee to take personal charge of customer relations on accounts with substantial average balances.

STAFF RELATIONS COMMITTEE—to evaluate methods for maximum use of available personnel and to study any problems relating to the staff.

Finally, Mr. Holman knew he could call on the branch supervisor or any of the headquarters staff for whatever assistance he might need.

General Policy Problems 10

MARKETING CONCEPT IN BANKING

Bank of California

On the afternoon of January 26, 1966, Mr. Glenn K. Mowry, the executive vice-president of the Bank of California, was going over a report referred to him by the bank's corporate planning division. According to Mr. Paul Erickson, director of corporate planning, the report had been written by Mr. Thomas J. Cunningham, a recent business school graduate who had been working as a trainee under Mr. Erickson. This report (reproduced in the appendix) was concerned with the organizational implications of the adoption of a marketing concept in commercial banking. Mr. Mowry had scheduled a meeting for the next morning with Mr. Erickson and Mr. Herbert Foedisch, senior vice-president and head of the marketing division, to discuss the report and to determine what action, if any, should be taken concerning Mr. Cunningham's suggestions. Mr. Mowry wanted to assess the report's value in light of the bank's present strategy and organization.

Background of the Bank of California

The Bank of California was founded in San Francisco in 1864 by Mr. D. O. Mills and Mr. William C. Ralson. The bank grew steadily and played an important role in the early economic growth of northern California. The early financing activities of the bank included the granting of loans to mining companies in the Comstock Lode and to the Central Pacific Railroad for its drive eastward to meet the Union Pacific. With the acquisition of the London & San Francisco Bank, Ltd. in 1905, the Bank of California acquired offices in Portland, Tacoma, and Seattle. Five years later, the bank received a unique national charter allowing it to continue its operations in California, Oregon, and Washington. It still has the distinction of being the only bank in the country chartered by the federal government to do business in more than one state.

Exhibit 1

BANK OF CALIFORNIA

Organization Nomenclature Chart

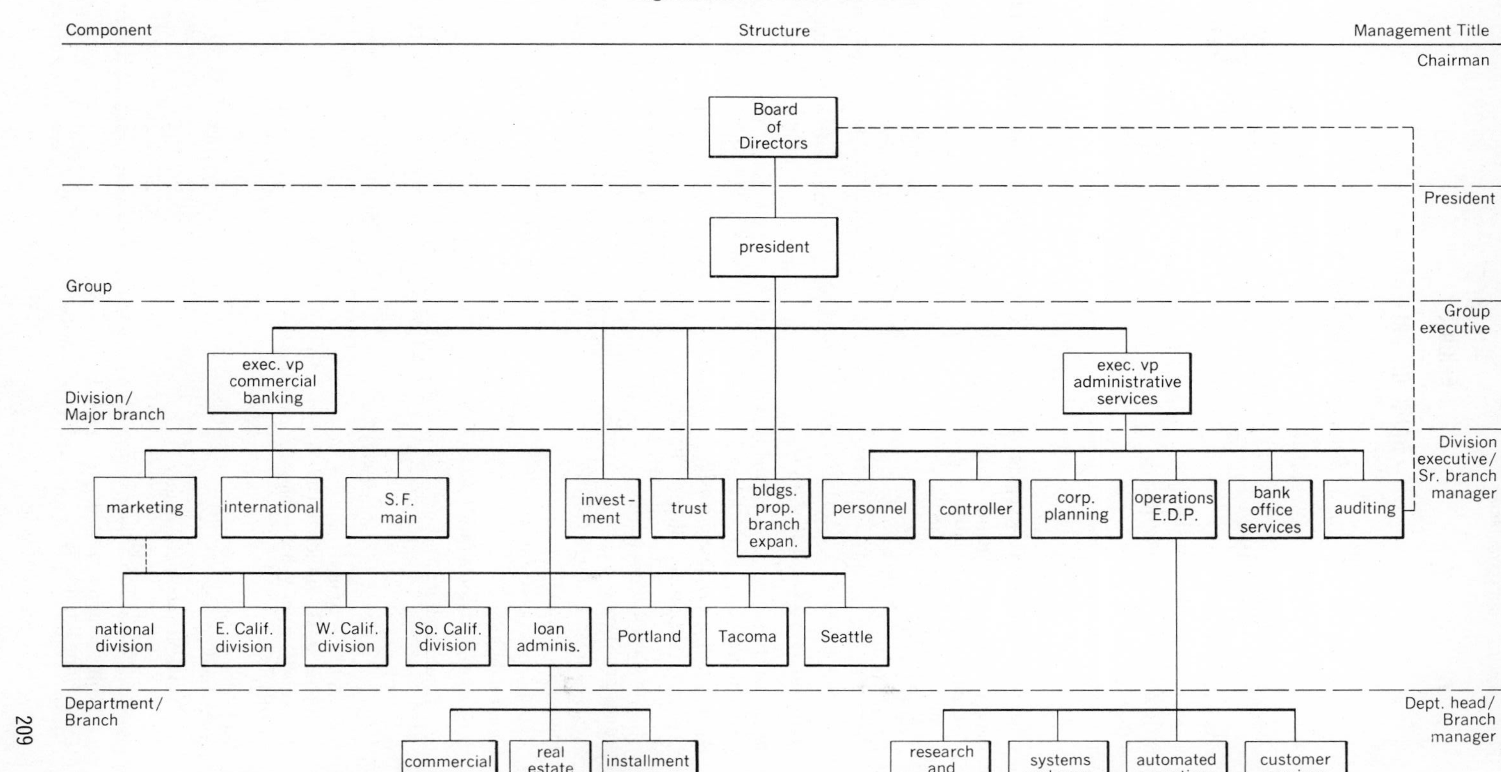

SOURCE: Personnel Department, August 1965.

Exhibit 2

BANK OF CALIFORNIA

Comparative Balance Sheet

	December 31	
Assets	*1965*	*1955*
Cash and due from banks	$188,091,496	$104,823,007
U.S. government securities	195,435,908	149,547,587
State and municipal securities	132,256,553	31,718,650
Other securities	16,429,988	4,630,000
Loans and discounts, less reserve for possible loan losses, 1965 – $12,329,917	763,766,763	215,050,267
Customers' liability on acceptances	14,536,464	13,452,478
Bank premises and equipment, at cost, less accumulated depreciation and amortization, 1965 – $8,081,549	25,693,532	4,934,260
Accrued interest	7,193,262	1,240,201
Other assets	3,348,547	163,401
Total assets	$1,346,752,513	$525,559,851
Liabilities and Capital Funds		
Demand deposits	$ 581,798,782	$310,663,570
Savings and other time deposits	616,838,280	104,646,795
U.S. government and other public deposits	–	59,106,626
Total deposits	1,198,637,062	474,416,991
Funds borrowed	5,000,000	–
Accrued taxes and other expenses	8,565,975	2,883,792
Dividends payable	836,631	344,520
Acceptances outstanding	14,761,928	13,614,155
Other liabilities	9,353,755	1,296,274
First mortgage notes (4.6% due 1993)	20,000,000	–
Total liabilities	1,257,155,351	492,555,732
Capital funds		
Capital notes (4.55% due 1989)	20,000,000	–
Shareholders' equity:		
Capital stock, authorized 1,959,180 shares $10 per value – shares outstanding 1,859,180	18,591,800	11,484,000
Surplus	38,408,200	18,516,000
Undivided profits	12,597,162	3,004,119
Total shareholders' equity	69,597,162	33,004,119
Total capital funds	89,597,162	33,004,119
Total liabilities and capital funds	$1,346,752,513	$525,559,851

During the first half of this century the bank continued to place primary emphasis on traditional banking services to commercial customers. In late 1954, however, the Bank of California acquired the Bank of Martinez and entered the retail banking field. This initial move was followed by other acquisitions and by the establishment of regional-type branch banks. The charter of the bank did not permit branching in Oregon or Washington, and, in the 1950s, all new offices were located in northern California.

In 1962 Charles de Bretteville, who had been a director of the bank and the president of Spreckles Sugar Company, became president of the Bank of California. Under Mr. de Bretteville's direction a number of changes were introduced. A new organization was developed with added emphasis on personnel development, corporate planning, and marketing. (An organization chart is shown in Exhibit 1.) Increased emphasis was placed on developing international business. International offices were opened in nearly all of the bank's port city locations, and in 1964 a branch was established in Manila. Also, in the same year the bank opened an Edge Act subsidiary, which would permit the bank to make foreign investments of a more risky nature. Prior to 1963, the bank had not had offices in southern California. In 1963, a major office was opened in Los Angeles. In 1964, the bank expanded its operations in southern California with the acquisition of the nine-branch American National Bank of San Bernardino. During the 1960s the policy of the Bank of California would be characterized as maintaining the position as a strong wholesale bank while continuing to develop a competitive position in the retail banking industry. Comparative financial data for 1955 and 1965 are shown in Exhibit 2, and a breakdown of loans by types as of the end of 1965.

Exhibit 3

BANK OF CALIFORNIA

By Type of Loans
December 31, 1965

Real-estate loans	23.6%
Loans to banks and financial institutions	13.0
Loans for purchasing or carrying securities	4.9
Loans to farmers	1.1
Commercial and industrial loans	34.8
Loans to individuals for personal expenditures	21.5
All other loans	1.1
	100.0%

Marketing Responsibilities in the Bank's Organization

The responsibility for marketing the banks services was given to several units within its organization.

There were several staff groups which were concerned with business development problems. The marketing division, whose organization is shown in Exhibit 4, developed advertising and promotional programs. Their work included both coordination of branch marketing programs and planning of bank-wide promotions. For example, this group had recently arranged for the Bank of California to sponsor the televised broadcasts of San Francisco Giants' games during the coming season. Another promotion program that had been developed by "marketing" was the Customer-Call Plan. This was a centrally controlled program by which officers and managers called on present and potential commercial customers to promote the bank's services. In planning these promotions, some marketing research was done by this division.

Mr. Foedisch also headed the bank's national division, which handled the development of national accounts. As shown in Exhibit 5, the national division was organized on a geographic basis. The efforts of this group were oriented toward promoting the bank's wholesale services to national companies.

The corporate planning division's work included projects concerned

Exhibit 4

BANK OF CALIFORNIA

Marketing Division

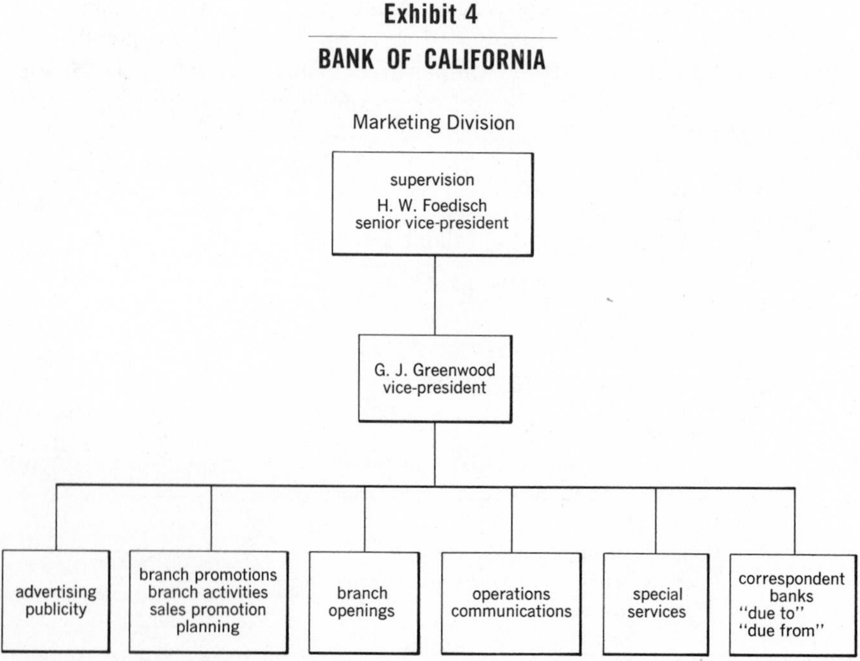

Exhibit 5

BANK OF CALIFORNIA

National Division

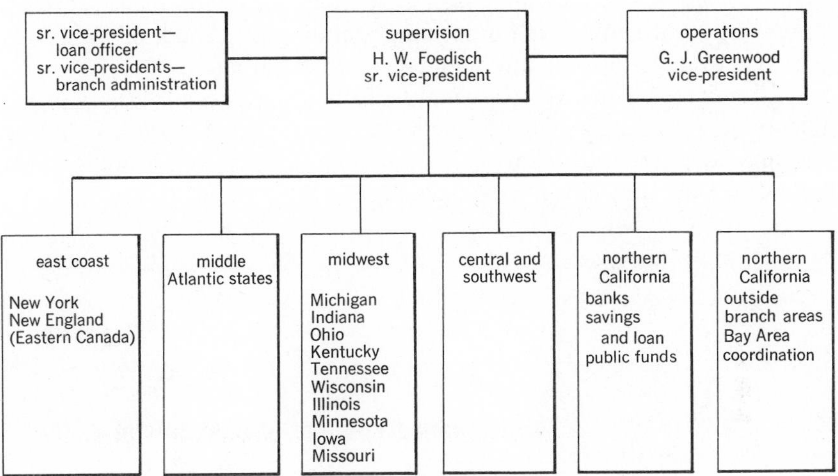

Exhibit 6

BANK OF CALIFORNIA

Organization Planning

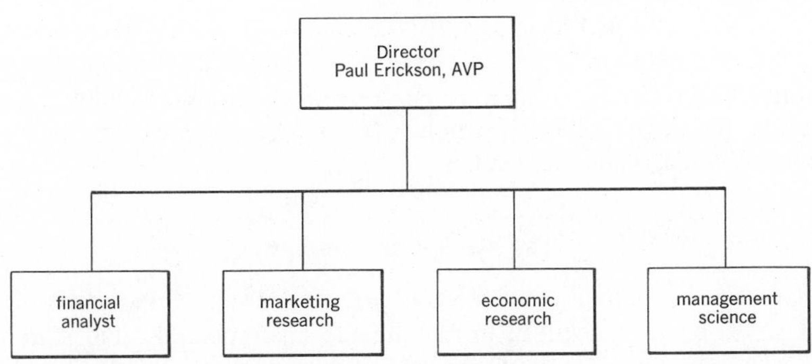

with the bank's marketing policies, especially when the program under study had strategic implications. These studies often involved marketing research activities. The activities and specializations of the men in this group are shown in Exhibit 6. Recently the group was trying to determine the primary factors which influence branch growth and to develop a mathematical model to estimate size of deposits and loans for prospective branch locations. (The actual selection of new branch sites is done by the branch expansion division.) The corporate planning division also worked with the EDP operations department in developing new EDP services to attract and hold customers for other bank services. However, as one officer in corporate planning said, "Bank of California does not want to become a (computer) service bureau."

The direct business development efforts are the responsibility of the officers and managers of the branches within the bank's system. These men are expected to develop business within their respective areas, using the aid of staff specialists when needed.

APPENDIX

The Marketing Concept in Commercial Banking[1]

Commercial banking is currently facing strong competitive pressure. It is facing this pressure because it has failed to adapt to the changing needs of its market. The failure to find and implement new and better ways to fill consumers' needs for financial services reflects a shortcoming in the commercial banking industry; the lack of *the marketing concept.* It is the purpose of this report to show the broad implications of the marketing concept for commercial banking. Specifically, we will concentrate on the implications for organizational structure.

The first step will be to identify the major elements of the marketing concept. We will then apply this concept to commercial banking, showing its implications for the proper conduct of this business. Finally, we will describe the organizational structure of a hypothetical bank that has adopted the marketing concept.

The Marketing Concept

Under the marketing concept, the principal task of management is "not so much to be skillful in making the customer do what suits the interest of the business, as to be skillful in conceiving and then making the business do what suits the interests of the customer."[2] Essentially,

[1]Prepared by T. J. Cunningham.

[2]J. B. McKitterick, "What Is the Marketing Management Concept," American Marketing Association, 1957.

the business becomes an organization to fill customer needs, not an organization to produce and sell its products and services to whichever customer it can convince to buy them. A business which adopts this concept —one which becomes oriented towards the customer rather than towards its products, focuses its major efforts on introducing new products and services, and seeks out new classes of customers who heretofore have not used the existing products—will be the business that will compete successfully in today's highly competitive markets.

The marketing concept implies working backward from consumer's needs, not forward from the company's product or service. It implies developing an organization which will thrive on continual change. It stresses the firm's distinctive competence in developing products and services that meet the needs of specific market segments.

The Marketing Concept As It Relates to Commercial Banking

The commercial banking industry is one which can benefit greatly from adoption of the marketing concept. Commercial banks *sell financial service*. Lending is a means to meet consumers' need for financing. Trust administration is a means for meeting consumers' needs for financial security and investment. Financial counseling is a means for meeting consumers' needs for proper financial planning. Automated services are a means to meet consumers' needs for financial record keeping. In short, it is financial service that a commercial bank offers to the market place.

What is the true criterion for success in this industry? The answer lies in the ability of a bank to determine consumers' needs for financial services, to determine how these needs may be segmented, and to determine the ways in which it may organize to meet these needs most effectively. The answer lies in the adoption of the marketing concept. What are the implications of the marketing concept for the commercial bank?

1. The commercial bank should thrive on accepting change, rather than resisting it. It should implement new technological developments and continually strive to develop new and better ways of meeting consumers' needs.

2. The main focus of the creative search for improved performance should be on optimizing the financial service provided to customers, rather than defending against competition.

3. The over-all marketing effort should add "consumable value," not merely cost, to the bank's financial services. The commercial bank should use the tools of marketing to improve the "need-satisfying ability" of its products. New products (services) should be developed which will better serve consumer needs. They should be packaged in a way which will further improve their ability to fill consumer demands (repayment

flexibility, justifiable deviation from financial restrictions, compensating balance flexibility, and so forth), they should be promoted in such a way as to inform a customer of the ways in which they can fill his needs. They should be distributed in a manner (personal call, mail, telephone, or a branch office), and at the time (when he needs it) most optimal to him. If this is done, the marketing effort will add value to the product, further increasing the bank's competitive advantage.

4. The commercial bank should recognize and meet the needs of market segments in order to maximize its ability to solve their unique problems. Commercial banks face many segments. The financial needs of individuals are different than the financial needs of corporations, the needs of domestic corporations are different than the needs of international corporations, the needs of electronic firms are different than the needs of chemical firms, the needs of the wealthy are different than the needs of the poor. A commercial bank should decide which of these segments it wishes to serve, and then should develop products that will do this optimally. It must ignore the desire to suppress the differences between these market segments, a desire which is often couched in the philosophy that a dollar is a dollar, no matter who uses it. Instead, recognize that the needs for financial service (which is really its product) will be vastly different for each market segment. It must choose the segments it wishes to deal with, and then tailor its facilities, services, and policies to meet the needs of those segments. If this is done, no competitor who tries to compete by straddling one of these segments will ever be successful. If it is not done, the bank in question will be perpetually vulnerable to any competitor who sets out to specifically serve the segment it was trying to straddle.

5. The employees of a commercial bank should be "customer's men" rather than "company men." Every employee of a commercial bank who meets the public is a salesman. Tellers, platform officers, and callmen are all salesmen. As such they should direct their efforts toward serving the customer, not the company. Their sole concern should be with mobilizing the total resources of the bank toward filling their customer's financial needs. Its efforts should be directed toward discovering customer needs ("Could we set up an automatic savings account for you, sir, in order to save you trips to the bank?"), toward informing management of new ways to solve these needs ("Perhaps we should seriously investigate the establishment of an Edge Act corporation so we can meet the equity needs of our foreign customers?"), and toward tailoring the resources of the bank to meet the particular financial needs of its customers.

6. The commercial bank should focus on its distinctive competence, using its distinctive resources and skills to optimize its ability to serve specific segments of consumer needs. This competence may be in the areas of wholesale banking, or retail banking, or international banking,

or trust, and the like. The bank should focus on a limited number of areas, ignoring the temptation to enter into every possible market segment. The bank that focuses on its areas of distinctive competence succeeds because it is more capable of serving the needs of its customers. The bank that does not do so—the bank that straddles all markets—remains vulnerable because it does not optimally serve any specific customer.

In summary, adoption of the marketing concept by commercial banks would require a great change in present attitudes, procedures, and policies. It would require that the bank thrive on the dynamic change which its market has undergone, rather than resist or refuse to recognize it. It would demand that the bank orient itself totally toward consumers' financial needs, rather than simply meeting its competition and selling its traditional products. It would place the marketing function in a position of overriding importance in the bank's power structure. It would mean that the bank would have to segment its markets, spinning off those which it could not serve in an optimal manner, and keeping those which it is uniquely capable of serving.

The author does not mean to imply that nowhere in the field of commercial banking are elements of the marketing concept to be found. Many enlightened bank officials have been able to "sell" certain elements of this concept to their policy makers. The results have been significant. Bank of America's concept of retail banking has resulted in a level of performance that is unmatched across the country and around the world. Morgan Guaranty's market segmentation (wholesale banking only) has been most successful, giving Morgan a distinct advantage over its market-straddling competitors in this area (Chase, City Bank, Manufacturers' Hanover).

Implications of the Marketing Concept for the Bank's Organizational Structure

An organizational structure may be defined as the vehicle for implementing corporate strategy. It is the set of relationships, the allocation of responsibility and authority, which will carry the stated corporate strategy into effect, thus enabling the corporation to achieve its objectives. From this standpoint, each organizational structure must be unique, for it will reflect the particular objectives and strategic choices of each firm. Thus there is no "right" or "wrong" structure for any firm. On the contrary, the correct structure will be that which will enable the firm to implement its unique strategy and achieve its individual objectives.

Because this writer does not wish to assume the bank's own area of distinctive competence and its own concept of consumers' needs, the best organizational structure for the Bank of California cannot be recommended. However, we can examine some of the implications of the adoption of this concept for the organizational structure of the bank, whatever choices it makes. And we can show what form organizational structure might take, given a hypothetical set of these choices.

Selling Financial Service

The first requirement of the adoption of the marketing concept is that individuals throughout all levels of the organization realize that the bank sells financial service, not money, trust, automated services, or the like. It sells specialized financial services to its customers, providing them with a means to satisfy their financial needs. It is particularly because of "marketing myopia" that some commercial banks have been less progressive than other financial intermediaries. Once bank management accepts the general premise that they are selling financial service to meet specific consumers' needs, they may seriously question certain aspects of the bank's organizational structure.

Marketing and Top Management

Another crucial implication of the marketing concept for the organizational structure of this bank is the fact that the marketing function must assume a commanding role in the organizational hierarchy. Top management must have a marketing orientation and must perceive the total market for financial services, so that the bank can foresee and creatively adapt to change. The adoption of the marketing concept means that the marketing function—sales, research, new product analysis, planning, service, and sales training—will assume a role of primary importance in the organizational structure.

The Marketing Function: Management, Services, Operations

The adoption of the marketing concept requires that the marketing function be broken down into three basic segments: management, service, and operations. This is done so that marketing management, divorced from the details of operations, and the specifics of service, devotes its time to the broader implications of new product analysis, organizational planning, management training, and marketing policy. Marketing services —such as advertising, promotion, research, forecasting, and public relations—are indirect selling tools and require a special expertise for their proper utilization. Marketing operations—such as field sales, sales training, customer service, product service, and sales administration —are direct selling tools. The separation of the three functions, therefore, insures that each is handled most capably, that each is evaluated in light of its own responsibility, and that each contributes to over-all marketing effort.

Segmentation

Inherent in the marketing concept is the belief in segmentation. Segmentation is the division of the total market into certain *need* categories, categories that can be identified by some sort of empirical measure. If it adopts the marketing concept, a bank must engage in some sort of market segmentation and structure its organization to reflect the market segments on which it is concentrating. It makes no difference whether it segments by product, by customer type, by geography, or by size of checking account. The important thing is that the method of segmentation give recognition to *differing consumer needs* for financial services.

But even more important is the fact that the bank cannot properly serve all segments. It cannot force its package of financial services to straddle every part of the market. The bank must choose these segments which it can serve better than anyone else and organize to serve them better.

We emphasize the importance of segmentation in the marketing concept without specifying a procedure by which a bank can determine its "optimal" segments of the market. In general, we urge that bankers examine their total market for financial services, that they try to segment it in the best way possible, and that they then utilize this information to build up a service package which will optimally satisfy those segments that they choose to serve. Finally, they must organize in such a way that this package will be most effectively presented to the segment for which it was produced.

Market Research

The adoption of the marketing concept implies that the firm will focus its efforts on a creative search for new and better ways to meet their market's needs for financial services. The tool for this effort is market research. Thus market research must play an important role in the organizational structure of this bank. It must be staffed by a professional who is well versed in the techniques of the field. It must be given proper recognition in all marketing analysis and planning. It must be directed toward continually evaluating the effectiveness of the bank's current package of financial services and toward the complete analysis of creative proposals to improve this package. It must be directed toward determining new and better ways to segment markets and new and better ways to serve them. Its findings will be the cornerstones for the dynamic development of the marketing concept.

Sales Training: Creating Customers' Men

We have seen the importance of salesmen for the implementation of the marketing concept. We have seen that these men must be customers' men, capable of mobilizing the total resources of the bank toward meeting a customer's financial needs. Thus, the adoption of the marketing concept requires that the commercial bank train and develop its employees so that they may have this capability. Training must assume an important position in the organizational structure. It must be centralized so that the program will focus on the total resources of the bank, not just on particular functions or products. It must be complete so that no man will leave the program without the total picture of the bank in his mind. It must be continual as the bank aggressively adapts to its changing market.

Planning: Insurance for Success

The adoption of the marketing concept implies that the planning function assume a great deal of importance in the organizational structure. Planning insures that the organization is continually equipped to meet the dynamic needs of its market, that the firm goes where it wants to go, and that the total organization and its objectives are the guiding principles, not the fragmented objectives of each department or function. Thus the marketing concept, which implies adaptability to change, market innovation, selective segmentation, and corporate direction dictates that the planning function be placed in a position of great influence and recognition; the very functions that planning fulfills are the means to the successful adoption of this concept. Thus the commercial bank that adopts the marketing concept must place the planning function in a commanding position within the organization.

We have touched on a few of the more important implications of the marketing concept, showing how the commercial bank which adopts it must, in determining its organizational structure, give proper recognition to these facts: that the bank is selling financial service; that marketing is a three-pronged tool consisting of management, service, and operations; that the marketing function must assume a commanding role in the organizational power hierarchy, while operations moves into the background; that segmentation must be practiced; that market research will be the key to success; that salesmen must be trained to sell the total package of the bank's financial services; and that planning should be given all the respect and authority due the importance of its responsibility.

Organizational Structure: An Example

We will describe briefly the organizational structure of a hypothetical bank. This example incorporates the organizational implications of the marketing concept described above. Our primary assumption is that the bank has decided to concentrate on two primary areas: retail banking and wholesale banking.

The following comments apply to the organization chart shown in Exhibit 7.

Groups

Two major operating groups, retail and wholesale, correspond to the two primary market segments on which the bank will concentrate.

Exhibit 7

Bank of California

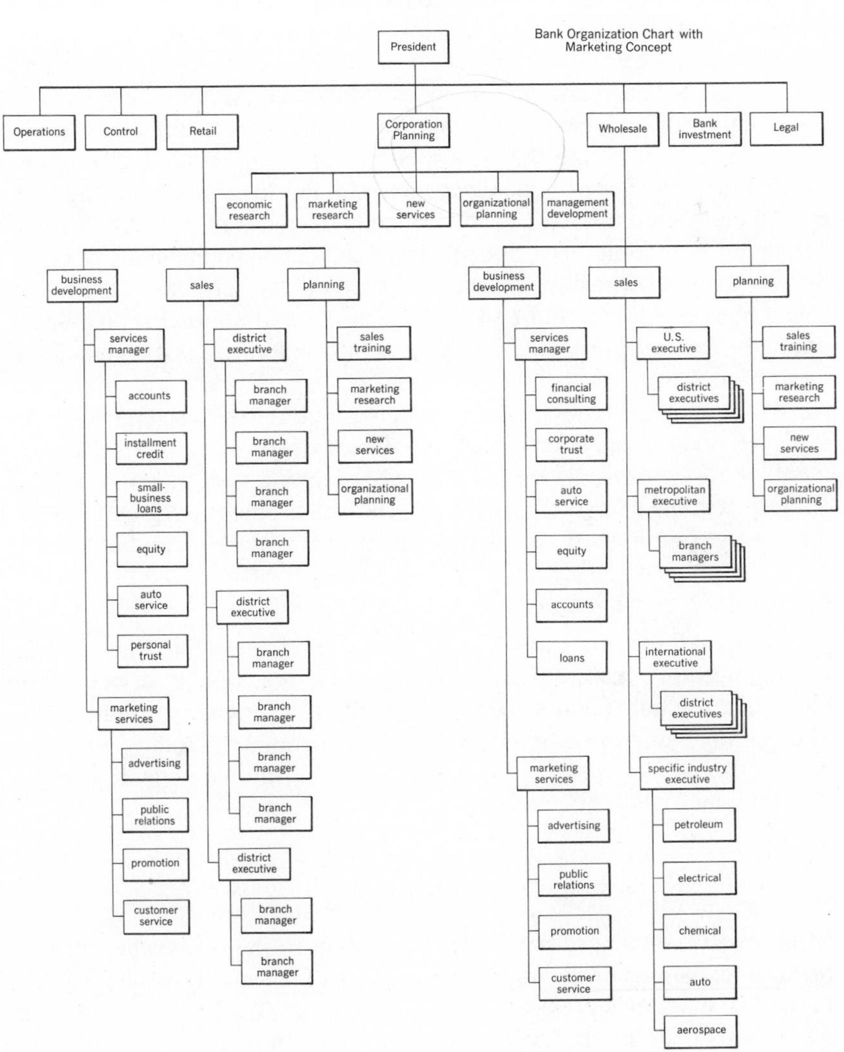

The major group managers have total responsibility for development of their respective markets, including "sales" of financial assets (gaining new deposits) and "sales" of financing services (gaining new loans).

Divisions

The retail and wholesale groups each have three divisions: sales, business development, and planning.

SALES DIVISION is segmented geographically for purposes of decentralized control. In the retail group, district executives supervise branch managers. The wholesale group also is organized with the goal of specialization, with specific-industry departments and geographical segmentation (United States, metropolitan, international).

BUSINESS DEVELOPMENT DIVISION includes two departments: service managers and marketing services. Marketing services include staff coordination of advertisement and public relations—sometimes called "indirect selling." Note that so-called direct selling is done through the sales divisions. Service managers are similar to product managers in manufacturing companies; each service manager is responsible for marketing coordination of a specific service, such as installment credit. Service managers insure that each "product" or service that the bank sells receives coordinated emphasis in direct and indirect selling operations, *for example,* provides service and information on installment credit to all branches.

PLANNING DIVISION includes training, market research, new service analysis, and organizational planning departments. Each of these departments works closely with the corporate planning staff function. Each is directly responsible to the retail or wholesale operating group, so that the special requirements of that segment of the market can be satisfied.

Corporate Staff Functions

Five staff functions assist in corporate-level operations and decision-making but are separate from the line groups that sell the services of the bank. These staff functions are legal, bank investments, corporate planning, control, and operations. The head of corporate planning, for example, will have as assistants his counterparts in the planning divisions of the retail and wholesale groups.

Conclusion

It has been the hope of the author to present to the reader the organizational implications of the marketing concepts for banking, analyzing them in light of banking's present attitudes and concepts. Specifically, the implications of the marketing concept for the organizational structure of a bank like the Bank of California were examined. "Organizational truths" or platitudes could not be presented, for each organization structure must reflect the unique objectives and strategy of the firm. However, the relevant considerations that the bank would have to recognize if it desired to adopt the marketing concept were raised.

It was shown how the elements of customer orientation, marketing management, market segmentation, creative innovation, marketing planning, and the like would be reflected in the organizational structure. The concept of the product manager was also introduced in an effort to separate the vested influence of products from the primary purpose of customer service. In short, it was shown how the bank might organize to reflect the commanding implications of the fully adopted marketing concept.

Above all, the reader must realize that this paper is but a rough beginning to a very complex problem; it handled but a few of the relevant issues, in a manner which barely did them justice. But this does not deny the importance of the marketing concept. Commercial banks have hidden behind their cloaks of conservatism and traditionalism far too long. Their market, their customers' demands, and their competitors all have changed. The commercial bank of the future must adopt a marketing concept dictated by the nature of the market, the nature of the product, and the nature of the competition.

FORMULATING BANK STRATEGY: BRANCH REPORTING

Bear State Bank

In early 1964, Mr. Robert W. Andrews, president of Bear State Bank, was reviewing the bank's progress and charting its future strategy. Although he considered setting specific growth objectives to be a difficult task, as well as one of questionable value, he was looking forward to the day that Bear State Bank would have $100 million in deposits. Annual growth estimates were prepared by an extrapolation of past growth figures modified by plans for business development as well as by changes in the competitive environment. Mr. Andrews felt, however, that no fixed goal should be established for the bank's size because conditions were constantly changing and, therefore, what might be desirable at the present time might not be desirable at some later point. For the same reason he felt that other fixed policies—for example, a policy never to merge—were unrealistic. He felt that the future course of the bank should be dictated by the environmental conditions of the future and not by any hard and fast rules or policy objectives.

Mr. Andrews did not expect the board of directors of the bank to take an active part in outlining future strategy. The board of directors was composed of eight men; two were officers of the bank and six were outside members. In his opinion, the six outside members of the board did not know much about banking, nor did they plan to learn. He felt that they merely approved what the officers of the bank had already done. In his opinion the only benefits that the bank derived from its outside board members were in the areas of public relations and business development. Since three of the outside members of the board were retired, Mr. Andrews felt that only three board members were helpful in the aforementioned areas and that the amount of assistance which they provided was limited. However, one director was chairman of the business development committee and very active in solicitation of new accounts.

Bear State Bank had been founded as a unit bank in 1956, with capital accounts of about $400,000. In the ensuing years it had experienced a considerable amount of growth (see Exhibit 1). During this period it had opened four additional branches. Mr. Andrews, who had been president of the bank since it was founded, felt that the nature of the area had made branching desirable. He noted that there was no great concentration of population or business activity in the area. Thus, it seemed to him that since the sources of potential business were spread out, the bank should also be spread out. In addition, several other banks in the area were opening new branches and Mr. Andrews did not feel that Bear State Bank could afford to stand still in light of this.

The bank did not have a set schedule for the establishment of new branches in the future. Rather than opening one every other year, for example, Mr. Andrews preferred to open branches whenever it seemed appropriate. He had not established the specific number of branches he thought Bear State Bank should have ultimately. He believed, however, that one of the most important limitations on branch expansions was the servicing distance. Bear State Bank employed central posting and he concluded that any new branch should be within easy servicing distance of the main branch. He noted that one of the large state-wide banks was experimenting with a system which might make it economically feasible to process checks for all of California at a single location.

Mr. Andrews thought that the chief advantage which a small bank, such as Bear State, had over the large banks was flexibility. He considered communication and delegation of authority to branches to be the key factors in determining the amount of flexibility which a bank had. The effectiveness of communication was influenced by the distance between branches and the number of branches as well as the personnel involved. Mr. Andrews noted that as a bank grew, a more formal pattern

Exhibit 1

BEAR STATE BANK

Year-End Data
(dollar figures in millions)

December 31	*Total Resources*	*Cash and Due From Banks*	*U.S. Government Securities*	*Other Securities*	*Loans (Less Reserves)*	*Deposits*	*Capital Funds*	*Number of Deposit Accounts*
1963	34.7	4.9	3.5	5.8	19.1	30.0	2.9	20,931
1962	25.2	4.9	3.7	2.3	12.2	21.9	1.9	17,912
1961	17.8	3.7	1.7	2.3	9.1	16.0	1.2	14,366
1960	12.4	2.1	3.2	1.0	5.3	11.1	0.9	10,187
1959	10.5	1.7	2.8	1.1	4.1	9.2	0.9	9,146
1958	7.3	1.2	2.0	0.7	3.2	6.6	0.6	6,707
1957	5.4	0.9	1.1	0.5	2.7	4.9	0.5	5,879
1956	4.8	0.7	1.6	0.0	2.2	4.3	0.5	n.a.

of management generally evolved and an increased amount of delegation of authority became necessary. Typically, this was codified and reduced to regulations in the form of manuals. In the case of Bear State Bank, Mr. Andrews felt that by personally making the principal policy decisions and delegating other decisional authority, the bank achieved a desirable degree of flexibility. Branch lending officers could lend or commit $20,000 unsecured and $40,000 secured. In his opinion, a large organization needed much more rigid policies and therefore was unable to act on such short notice and with such flexibility.

Mr. Andrews noted that in recent years new banks had been chartered in almost every principal city in California. Typically these were unit banks at their inception and were locally owned. In his opinion, they were founded in numerous cases with little reference to earning potential. One reason he felt such banks had been founded was for speculation in their stocks. A second and related reason was that being connected with a new bank was a style of the day. In early 1964, Mr. Andrews felt that banking was considered a "growth" industry and possessed glamour similar to that which the electronics industry had enjoyed several years earlier. Thus, in his opinion, many individuals were eager to be connected with a new bank without any regard to its potential. Mr. Andrews also thought that many of these new banks were poorly managed once they were established. It seemed extremely unlikely that all of these banks would be sufficiently profitable to continue independent operations for any length of time. In short, he expected the glamour connected with such independent banks to diminish gradually and that many would sell, stagnate, or merge.

It seemed to Mr. Andrews that a bank had to give better service in some way in order to be successful. He observed that some banks attempted to compete by convenience of location and others by lower charges, for example reduction or omission of service charges on checking accounts. At least one bank had offered customers time on its computer at low rates. Mr. Andrews though the strength of Bear State Bank was in being close to the customer's requirements, and therefore, being better equipped to adapt to his needs. He considered the larger banks to be relatively inflexible and believed that they required the customer to adapt to them. Mr. Andrews thought that construction loans provided a good example of this. Whereas a large bank might require a customer to take his loan in specified amounts at specified time intervals as well as to repay it on a rigid schedule, Bear State Bank had no fixed policy toward construction loans and tailored-loan terms to meet the particular needs of each customer.

Mr. Andrews thought that Bear State Bank should be responsive to the requirements of the customer. He wanted the bank to make "customized loans" of the exact type that the customer desired. He felt that many individuals were willing to pay a higher rate to get exactly what they wanted. In short, he operated the bank on the idea, "We'll give you what you want, but you must pay for it." Service charges were considerably higher than competitors and generated significant income.

It was Mr. Andrews' opinion that the public had built up an immunity to advertising over the years. He felt that in addition to being ineffective, advertising was very expensive. Billboard advertising along the main roads where the branches were located accounted for 20 percent of the $15,000 spent on advertising in 1963. The remaining 80 percent was devoted to newspaper advertising. During most of 1963, Bear State Bank had run an advertisement twice weekly in the financial section of the local newspaper. In addition, the bank ran a full-page advertisement before opening its fifth branch in 1963. In its newspaper advertising, the bank publicized its extended hours with the slogan: "Bear State Does Not Hibernate! Open 8–5 Monday-Thursday and 8–6 Friday."

The bank did not use spot commercials on local radio and television, because of Mr. Andrews' philosophy regarding ineffectiveness of advertising. He was contemplating a drastic cut in the advertising budget, that is, limiting advertising to local newspapers only and reducing this to the minimum amount sufficient to insure good coverage of news events involving the bank. Specifically, he was considering a 90 percent reduction from the amount spent on advertising in 1963.

Mr. Andrews firmly believed that direct contact and demonstrated competence, rather than advertising and gimmicks, were the most effective ways of selling the bank's services. He was resolved that the bank should continue to do the best possible job for its clients. This, he was convinced, would lead to success in the long run. The branch managers, as well as the president and one board member, made a number of business development calls each week. Travel and entertainment expenses were approximately $17,000 in 1963. Although there was no prescribed number of calls, Mr. Andrews estimated that each man averaged about two calls per week. Every three months the men drew up a list of the "ten most wanted accounts." At the end of the quarter each man reported on his progress toward obtaining these accounts. The accounts that the bank was most actively seeking were those of the larger businesses that had good credit standings.

The Bear State Bank had five branches. Although all the branches were located in the same metropolitan area, the type of depositor and borrower varied greatly from branch to branch. Thus, there were no easy solutions to the problems of determining the specific approach to the community and determining the adequacy of operating results. Mr. Andrews thought that this phenomenon could be illustrated most clearly by comparing two of the branches in some detail (see Exhibits 2 and 3).

Exhibit 2

BEAR STATE BANK

Balance Sheets for Two Branches
at December 31, 1963

Resources	*Branch #1*	*Branch #2*
Real estate loans	$ 466,887.60	$ 752,414.61
Unsecured loans	33,315.09	189,797.92
Secured loans	237,026.50	268,175.53
Installment credit loans	2,957,331.20	77,912.20
Other loans	41,729.92	1,878.25
	3,736,290.31	1,290,178.51
Cash and due from banks	83,621.97	58,888.17
Other assets	31,837.59	25,874.24
Interbranch account		1,225,451.97
	$3,851,749.87	$2,600,392.89
Liabilities		
Demand deposits	$1,208,328.67	$ 871,428.68
Savings and time deposits	807,558.01	1,535,855.01
Other liabilities	321,982.00	193,109.20
Interbranch account	1,513,881.19	
	$3,851,749.87	$2,600,392.89

Exhibit 3

BEAR STATE BANK

Income Statements for Two Branches
for Year Ended December 31, 1963
(in thousands of dollars)

	Branch #1	*Branch #2*
Interest—real estate loans	$ 27.6	$ 69.3
Interest—installment loans	228.0	12.1
Interest—other loans	25.4	28.2
Other operating income	63.7	35.8
Total operating income	$344.7	$145.4
Operating expenses	132.6	125.2
Net operating profit	$212.1	$ 20.2
Other profits and losses	(1.6)	(0.2)
Fixed charges (allocated)	(61.3)	(32.6)
Interbranch interest income (allocated)		29.0
Interbranch interest charge (allocated)	(66.4)	
Net income before taxes	$ 82.8	$ 16.4

Branch #1 was in an area of relatively high population density and below average per capita income. The area immediately surrounding it was a mixture of residential and commercial. The branch had a staff of ten employees. The loans that branch #1 made were predominantly installment loans. At the end of 1963, it had 1874 checking accounts and 1374 savings accounts. The average account size was $650 for checking accounts and $590 for savings accounts.

Branch #1 was in an area which had high per capita income and low population density. The area surrounding this branch of Bear State Bank was almost entirely residential. It had an extremely light loan demand; the loans that it did make were predominantly real-estate loans. The branch had a staff of five employees. At the end of 1963, it had 970 checking accounts and 1188 savings accounts. Based on the balance at the end of 1963, the average account size was $900 for checking accounts and $1300 for savings accounts.

Each month a profit and loss figure was computed for the bank as a whole as well as for each branch. In order to arrive at a profit figure for individual branches some allocations were necessary. The administrative expenses were allocated to branches on the basis of the number of employees. For example, if branch #1 had five employees and the five branches together had thirty employees (not including administrative personnel), then branch #1 would absorb one sixth of total administrative expenses.

The other major adjustment necessary to arrive at a profit figure for each branch involved the balance of interbank clearings. The balance of interbank clearings consisted essentially of the difference between deposits and loans. Each branch was either a net provider or net user of loanable funds. The theory was that if a branch provided funds for other branches, it should receive credit for performing this function, and if it used funds which other branches provided, the branch should pay something for these funds. At the branches where deposits exceeded loans, income at the rate of 3 percent of the average balance of interbank clearings was added to the branch's other income. At the branches where loans exceeded deposits, a charge at the rate of 4 1/2 percent of the average balance of interbank clearings was subtracted from the income of the branch. Branch #2 fell into the former category and branch #1 was in the latter group.

Mr. Andrews felt that the monthly profit figures let him know if a branch was profitable. He did not think that branches or branch managers should be compared or evaluated on the basis of the net profit figures. The bank had no formal rating scheme for branches or branch managers. Mr. Andrews concluded that he was close enough to each situation to evaluate the performance of each branch manager and each branch on an individual basis.

Mr. Andrews expected that the rapid growth which Bear State had been enjoying would continue. He thought that the recent passage of the bill reducing income taxes coupled with existing conditions made the general economic outlook for 1964 quite favorable. He considered the maintenance of good community relations essential to a successful operation, yet he knew no simple method of achieving this. Thus, with numerous considerations in mind, he was wondering what program of action the bank should follow in the future months.

EVALUATION OF PROSPECTIVE MERGER

Southern Hills Bank

"Damn it all, Ray!" exploded Cyrus Higbee, a long-time director of Southern Hills Bank, "you can't be serious about selling the bank. Why, after all the years of effort you've put into this shop—yes, and into the Independent Bankers Association, too,—you just can't turn around overnight and sell out to the chains."

"Well, Cy, you and the other board members can tromp all over me if you want, but I've done a lot of thinking since the convention. I'm not saying we should sell or merge or what, but I do say we owe it to the stockholders to let 'em know how the cards are stacked and what the bets are."

Thus began the liveliest and longest board meeting ever of the Southern Hills Bank. Actually, the situation had been brewing for some time, but Raymond C. Owens, president of the bank, brought the matter to a head at the director's meeting in October 1960, shortly after he had returned from the state bankers' convention. George Walston, president of Planters and Citizens Bank, a state chartered branch bank and correspondent of Southern Hills, had broached the subject of a merger during the annual convention. This marked the fifth or sixth time he had asked Owens about a possible sale or merger; however, on this occasion Walston indicated the seriousness of his intent by adding, "You know, Ray, if we can't at least come to some firm understanding or formal agreement about your joining us, I feel we'll have to begin serious planning for offices in your area. I honestly don't want to push you to the wall; you're too good a friend and associate, but we've got to protect ourselves in your area. What if the Peachtree starts branching out further, or if you decide, for whatever reason, to link up with the Dixie National, of if any other competitor decides to invade your territory? Where would we be? I tell you, Ray, we can't afford to let any of these moves catch us flat-footed. We've got to get off the dime and I'd like to see you get the dime."

Walston's comments were not wholly unexpected, yet Owens was quite surprised at the force with which they were delivered. Owens responded that he'd talk with his directors and inform Walston of their conclusions at an early date. That night was a long one for Ray Owens; he lay awake pondering the history of the bank and the course he should chart for the future.

The Southern Hills Bank had served the town of Exline for seventy-three years. In 1952 Mr. Owens established the bank's only branch in Lakeville, some eight miles away. The decision to set up the branch had been the first departure from the bank's unit character, but the officers had convinced the board that such a move was essential to maintain the bank's dominant position in the Exline area.

Exline was the active trading center of a prosperous rural area where dairy, fruit, and vegetable products were the principal sources of income. Located on the main road of the Seacoast Railroad and U.S. Route 10, a heavily traveled truck route, the town had grown from 11,200 population in 1950 to 16,320 in 1960. Lakeville had experienced slower growth, maintaining a population of about 3000 over the ten-year period. Adding together Exline, Lakeville, a few country towns, and rural residents, the Southern Hills area comprised a total population of nearly 35,000. Farming, food processing and canning, and light industry were the region's important economic activities (see Exhibit 1).

Exhibit 1

SOUTHERN HILLS BANK

Selected Economic Indicators for Exline County and the State

Indicator	*Base Year*	*Recent Year*	*Percent Change in County*	*Percent Change in State*
Population (000) 1950–1960	66	85	28.8%	48.7%
Personal income (000,000) 1950–1959	$94	$182	93.6%	108.2
Retail sales (000,000) 1950–1960	$82	$127	55.8	73.9
Value of mineral products (000,000) 1950–1960	$ 5	$ 11	120.0	32.7
Bank deposits (000,000) 1947–1960	$74	$128	73.0	96.1
Auto registration (000) 1954–1960	40	54	35.0	39.9
Farm acreage (000) 1954–1959	129	109	(15.5)	(2.5)

Exhibit 2

SOUTHERN HILLS BANK

Statements of Condition
December 31, 1958–1960
(dollar figures in thousands)

Resources	*1958*	*1959*	*1960*
Total cash and due from banks	$ 2,838	$ 2,876	$ 2,593
Treasury bills	1,310	1,414	1,541
U.S. bonds	9,191	9,397	9,448
State, county, municipal bonds	4,020	4,417	3,883
Real estate loans	9,995	11,635	11,542
Commercial loans	8,396	9,460	10,099
Fixed assets	394	388	364
Other assets	83	73	63
	$36,227	$39,660	$39,839

Liabilities			
Capital stock and surplus	$ 2,196	$ 2,196	$ 2,106
Undivided profits	684	805	964
Total capital	$ 2,880	$ 3,001	$ 3,160
Reserves	510	623	592
Demand deposits	12,322	14,610	15,100
Time deposits	20,206	21,077	20,597
Discount collected, unearned	309	349	390
	$36,227	$39,660	$39,839

Until 1935 Southern Hills was the only financial institution in the area. But by 1940 a production credit association[1] had been set up, a savings and loan established, and a branch of Peachtree National, the largest state-wide bank, had opened. From time to time there had been rumors that new banks or branches of established banks would be located in or near Southern Hills, but only once (in 1948) was an application actually filed. The charter was denied by the state banking authority; many believed the decision was made because the promoters were reported to be acting for an out-of-state bank holding group. The only

[1]A production credit association (PCA) is a local cooperative association of farmers, organized to provide themselves a source of short- and intermediate-term credit. Each PCA is part of a nation-wide system chartered under an act of Congress. Any person or organization whose principal source of income derives from farming is eligible to borrow, but must become a member of a PCA and purchase one $5.00 share of stock for each $100 borrowed. The stock may be included as part of the loan. Production credit associations obtain their funds from federal intermediate credit banks, owned in part by the associations and in part by the United States government.

Exhibit 3

SOUTHERN HILLS BANK

Profit and Loss Statement
Years ending December 31, 1958–1960
(dollar figures in thousands)

	1958	*1959*	*1960*
Operating income	$1,589	$1,818	$1,961
Bond profits	14	5	8
	$1,603	$1,823	$1,969
Operating expenses	$1,160	$1,242	$1,292
Reserve for losses on loans	58	67	71
Bond losses	-0-	25	-0-
Profit sharing contribution	17	25	29
Miscellaneous	2	19	12
Total expenses	$1,237	$1,378	$1,404
Profit before taxes	366	445	565
Less: reserve for taxes	158	204	263
Net profit	$ 208	$ 241	$ 302
Distribution of net profit:			
Dividends declared	$ 104	$ 120	$ 145
Retained profit	104	121	157
Transfer to surplus	138	-0-	-0-

other apparent threat was the persistent rumor in 1951 that Peachtree would expand its foothold in the area. Early in 1952 the Lakeville branch of Southern Hills Bank was chartered to head off this possible new competition.

Ray Owens was the son of a prosperous farmer whose family had settled in the area about 1860. Starting with the bank shortly after high school, Ray had given thirty-six years of his life to the bank and to the Exline community. During his twelve years as the bank's president, Owens had been active in the Independent Bankers Association as well as in several local and state civic organizations. He worked hard at everything he undertook and would not seek or accept a task unless he was confident that he could handle it.

The bank's success was evidence of Owens' capacities (see Exhibits 2–6). He firmly believed that Southern Hills Bank achieved its success because of its local character. He was fond of saying, "You know, we hill people are a sort of clan and we don't cotton to outsiders much. This bank is locally owned and operated. I know most everyone who comes in here; we're neighbors. Sure, because of their heavy advertising, special gimmicks, and just plain size, the Peachtree grabs off a lot of new customers who move into the area. But every time they change managers we get some of their good customers who know I'm gonna be at this desk day in and day out, ready to discuss their problems with 'em. We've got better than 60 percent of the business in this area and we don't have to offer new fangled services or gimmicks to get or keep the business. We simply provide good, conventional bank services on a personal, friendly basis."

At meetings of the Independent Bankers Association, Owens had stressed the importance of being flexible in bank policies to meet special local needs. He spoke frequently of "beating the giants by outmaneuvering them, that is, being on the spot to anticipate opportunities, seeing problems, and servicing the community while the branch organizations are still talking with their headquarters." Owens also had em-

Exhibit 4

SOUTHERN HILLS BANK

Composition of Loan Accounts
December 31, 1958–1960
(dollar figures in thousands)

Real Estate	*1958*	*1959*	*1960*
Regular	$7,369	$ 9,200	$ 9,374
FHA	1,679	1,708	1,556
Veterans	947	727	612
Total real estate loans	$9,995	$11,635	$11,542
Commercial Department			
Commercial loans	5,065	5,903	6,312
Order bills of lading	13	22	12
Trade acceptances	170	217	246
Business loans	67	56	50
Automobile loans	2,002	2,236	2,419
Equipment loans	602	568	541
FHA title I loans	23	18	12
Property improvement loans	71	61	79
Personal loans	352	366	403
Overdrafts	31	13	25
Total commercial department loans	$8,396	$9,460	$10,099
Total loans and discounts	$18,391	$21,095	$21,641

Exhibit 5

SOUTHERN HILLS BANK

Comparative Statistics
December 31, 1951–1960
(dollar figures in thousands)

Date: Dec. 31	*Total Deposits*	*Loans*	*Net Profit After Taxes*	*Dividends*
1951	$21,072	$11,764	$192	$52
1952	23,001	12,915	204	90
1953	24,752	14,088	206	96
1954	27,553	14,198	229	115
1955	28,083	16,475	267	89
1956	28,616	17,535	293	89
1957	30,704	18,673	211	88
1958	32,528	18,391	208	104
1959	35,687	21,095	241	120
1960	35,697	21,641	302	145

Exhibit 6

SOUTHERN HILLS BANK

Distribution of Stock Ownership
December 31, 1960

Groupings of Shares	*Numbers of Shareholders*	*Number of Shares*
1–9	5	24
10–49	44	1,079
50–99	43	2,747
100–500	83	20,832
over 500	48	66,818
Total	223	91,500

phasized the necessity of developing personnel; Southern Hills Bank was acknowledged to have an excellent staff and officer group.

Following his conversation with Walston at the state bankers' convention, Owens reluctantly concluded that some action had to be taken quickly by the Southern Hills Bank before other banks pre-empted its flexibility. The alternatives were clear: maintain but one branch and continue to compete on terms of local service; expand with new branches; or merge. Because the holdings of the board members represented only

15 percent of the bank's outstanding stock, Owens believed that the shareholders must be told of the increased interest expressed in the Southern Hills area by the state's large banking institutions. Despite his own strong personal feelings about the matter of merger, he argued persuasively for full disclosure of Planters and Citizens position expressed by Walston and for a survey of stockholder reaction. After a heated debate of the issue, a group of five prominent shareholders were chosen to work with the nine directors on the survey.

Owens provided the committee with the following data he had received from the Federal Reserve Bank:

Exhibit 7

SOUTHERN HILLS BANK

Comparison of State-Wide Growth of Unit and Branch Banks 1951–1960
(dollar figures in millions)

Date: Dec. 31	*Number of Unit Banks*	*Number of Branch Systems*	*Number of Branches*	*Total Unit Bank Assets*	*Total Branch Bank Assets*
1951	103	18	159	458	$2,010
1952	103	18	160	507	2,123
1953	93	23	172	471	2,293
1954	87	24	185	361	2,467
1955	84	23	207	342	2,601
1956	75	22	230	311	2,731
1957	71	21	245	329	2,750
1958	71	22	254	322	2,967
1959	68	23	269	317	3,079
1960	64	27	294	285	3,164

After contacting Southern Hills shareholders representing about 50,000 of the 91,500 outstanding shares, the committee determined that most were not anxious to sell. Nevertheless, the shareholders expressed keen interest in learning the answers to three questions:

1. How much would the bank be worth to a state-wide system?

2. What would happen to the personnel currently working at the bank?

3. Would the loan policies of a large banking system be compatible with the needs of the Exline area?

According to the committee, the consensus of owner opinion indicated a price of approximately $90 per share might be required before shareholders would be willing to sell or merge the bank. Since the stock had never sold for more than $46,[2] Owens took this price to mean that the bank "was not for sale."

Owens contacted George Walston, as promised, to report the directors' reactions to the merger interest of Planters and Citizens Bank. He also told him the results of the shareholder survey. Walston was not deterred; he asked that his bank be permitted to make a bid. Owens replied that he was free to do so; but, in view of the shareholders' apparent attitude regarding the value of their stock, he thought Walston would go through much wasted motion.

On learning that Planters and Citizens Bank would make an offer to Southern Hills shareholders, Owens informed other noncompeting banks of the action and invited their expressions of interest.

Two other banks, Farmers and Merchants and Dixie National, indicated interest. Each bank was allowed to make a preliminary examination of the Southern Hills Bank. Owens indicated that Southern Hills would accept formal bids for merger and provided each with a list of questions which he wanted to discuss with them. (See Exhibit 8.)

Exhibit 8

SOUTHERN HILLS BANK

Questions you will be asked to answer with reference to your bank's policies when being interviewed by our board of directors and members of our shareholders committee.

I. LOAN POLICIES

1. Reveal deposits and loans in areas comparable to the Southern Hills.
2. Do advisory boards or loan committees collaborate with management?
3. How are large credit lines and limits established?
4. On what basis are officer's loaning limits established?
5. What are your commodity and accounts receivable loan policies?
6. Employee loans, existing and contemplated home loans, collateral loans, and so forth.

II. PERSONNEL POLICIES

1. Salaries, base pay, bonus policy.
2. Fringe benefits, hospital, medical, surgery, life insurance plan.
3. Retirement plan, eligibility, contributory or noncontributory.
4. Policy re: transfer of personnel.
5. Outside business affiliations of employees.
6. Vacation policies.
7. Officer expense allowances, mileage, and so forth.

III. BID FORMULA

1. How will Southern Hills Bank data be obtained?
2. How will bidding bank and Southern Hills Bank book values be determined?
3. Would state banking department be acceptable source for Southern Hills Bank data?

---

[2]The stock price averaged $42 in 1959–1960, $36 during 1957–1959, $30 during 1955–1956, and $24 in 1953–1954. In most sales the bank put the buyers and sellers in contact with each other.

The Farmers and Merchants Bank subsequently decided not to make a bid. Separate meetings were held in late September with each of the two remaining banks. Owens and the board were basically satisfied with the answers given to the questions presented. Each bidding bank offered essentially the same answers. These included:

The Southern Hills office would be permitted an unsecured commercial loan limit of $50,000 and a maximum of $25,000 on long-term or industrial loans secured by first deeds of trust. The branch management would be independent of the head office and probably could make final decisions on 90 percent of the loan volume. The Lakeville office would have separate lending limits and would report to headquarters through the Southern Hills office. In the event branches were established

Exhibit 9

SOUTHERN HILLS BANK

Comparison of Dixie National Bank
and Planters and Citizens Bank
December 31, 1951–1960
(dollar figures in millions)

	Branches		*Total Resources*		*Deposits*		*Loans*	
	DN	*P & C*	*DN*	*P & C*	*DN*	*P & C*	*DN*	*P & C*
1951	6	16	$222	$335	$202	$316	$ 82	$122
1953	7	17	259	358	218	335	97	137
1955	10	20	299	426	272	393	129	196
1957	14	21	306	464	278	426	159	229
1958	15	22	338	504	305	464	163	236
1959	17	23	366	519	331	477	195	265
1960	19	24	374	540	337	490	196	282

	Investments		*Cash*		*Total Capital*		*Net Profits*	
	DN	*P & C*	*DN*	*P & C*	*DN*	*P & C*	*DN*	*P & C*
1951	$ 83	$129	$50	$79	$14	$15	$1.0	$1.2
1953	84	138	52	75	15	19	1.3	1.4
1955	107	147	55	77	19	26	1.7	2.1
1957	84	143	54	85	21	30	2.2	2.4
1958	109	171	57	90	24	31	2.4	2.7
1959	98	146	64	100	25	33	2.6	3.2
1960	105	160	61	86	26	38	3.2	3.8

Exhibit 10

SOUTHERN HILLS BANK

Dixie National, Planters and Citizens, and Southern Hills
December 31, 1958–1960

		1958	*1959*	*1960*
1. Book value per share	DN	$28.05	$28.38	$28.98
	P&C	40.55	42.10	47.04
	SH	31.48	32.92	34.66
2. Market bid price range per share	DN	$48–35	$46–38	$49–38
	P&C	59–35	69–54	66–52
	SH	36–36	42–36	46–42
3. Earnings per share	DN	$ 2.76	$ 3.00	$ 3.58
	P&C	3.41	4.01	4.67
	SH	2.28	2.64	3.30
4. Return on book value	DN	9.8%	10.6%	12.4%
	P&C	8.4	9.5	9.9
	SH	7.2	8.0	9.5
5. Price-earnings ratio*	DN	14.9	13.9	12.2
	P&C	13.7	15.4	12.6
	SH	15.8	14.7	13.3
6. Dividends per share	DN	$ 1.45	$ 1.45	$ 1.45
	P&C	1.54	1.59	2.04
	SH	1.14	1.32	1.58
7. Dividend yield on book value	DN	5.2%	5.1%	5.0%
	P&C	3.8	3.8	4.3
	SH	3.6	4.0	4.6
8. Dividend yield on market price*	DN	3.5%	3.5%	3.3%
	P&C	3.3	2.6	3.5
	SH	3.2	3.4	3.6
9. Dividend payout percentage	DN	52.5%	48.4%	40.5%
	P&C	45.2	39.7	43.7
	SH	50.0	50.0	47.9
10. Before tax:	DN	66.7%	65.8%	64.1%
Operating expense	P&C	70.0	68.1	66.2
Operating income	SH	77.1	75.5	71.5
11. After tax:	DN	82.8%	83.3%	82.0%
Operating expense	P&C	84.8	84.0	83.3
Operating income	SH	87.0	86.7	84.5

*Market price taken as the average between the high and low price range.

in Chester and Howard (two small communities in the Exline area), they too would report through the Southern Hills office. Since each bidding bank had within 40 miles of Exline large branches with specialized real estate appraisal groups, the Southern Hills appraisers would be consolidated into one of these offices.

2. The board of directors would continue to serve as an advisory board to the management of the Southern Hills office. This advisory

board would report the conditions in the community to the branch management and evaluate the condition of the branch as a unit.

3. The employees of Southern Hills would continue their existing salary structure and would be entitled to a bonus equal to that which they currently received. Moreover, employees who qualified in length of service would be eligible for a pension plan in either of the respective purchasing banks. In 1960, Southern Hills did not have a private pension plan for any of its employees. Other fringe benefits offered were equal or superior to those of Southern Hills Bank and about on a par between the two bidding banks.

In the past five years Dixie National Bank had acquired two branches through merger and had established seven new branches. During the same period Planters and Citizens Bank increased its branch offices by merging with one bank and opening three new branches.

Two recent bank mergers in the state had brought premiums of 4 percent and 9 percent on deposits.[3] At a price of 90 (the value suggested by some shareholders) the Southern Hills Bank would realize a 14.2 percent premium on its deposits.

On January 2, Mr. Owens learned that firm bids from the two interested banks would be received by the end of the week.[4]

CAPITAL ADEQUACY: ISSUANCE OF NEW STOCK

American National Bank

"Have you seen the *Citizen-Journal* this morning? Our stock is being bid at $88.25 and the ask is over $93. That makes a $3 per share increase in the past month on top of the big jump the stock made in early November," commented Mr. Ralph Holbrook, vice-president, at the conclusion of the weekly executive meeting.

The bank's president, Mr. Chester Woodruff, then responded: "Ralph, maybe we should think seriously about selling more stock now while the price is so attractive. We'll probably need more capital before too long and the highest price we've ever gotten in past offerings has been about $59 per share. Let's talk about this a little more at another meeting the beginning of January. Ralph, will you pull together some

[3]This figure is determined by subtracting the selling bank's net worth from the aggregate bid price and then computing the remaining amount of the bid as a percentage of the bank's deposits.

[4]Dixie National Bank stock is selling at $42.50. Planters and Citizens Bank stock is selling at $65.50.

data summarizing our present capital situation? Questions that come to my mind are: Do we need additional capital now? If so, how much? If, on the other hand, we don't require capital at present, should we sell stock anyway in view of the attractive price for our stock?"

In this manner, American National Bank's executive committee ended its monthly meeting. Mr. Holbrook began gathering information which could be used by the committee to discuss the issue of capital adequacy at the meeting on Friday, January 12, 1962.

The American National bank was chartered in Central City, Ohio, April 10, 1926. It was one of the largest unit banks in the area, but in comparison with the large regional and state-wide branch banking systems, American National was moderate in size. The greater Central City population was just under three quarters of a million in 1960, and was a leading business center in mid-Ohio. A number of branch bank offices, savings and loan associations, and finance companies were located near American National in the downtown business district.

In spite of extremely keen banking competition in the metropolitan area, American National had prospered and grown rapidly (see Exhibits 1 and 2). In the last three years deposits had increased nearly 50 percent. The bank had established a reputation as a "businessman's bank," catering primarily to the needs of commerce and industry. The bank's management believed that American National had become large enough (with a lending limit of $1.4 million) to help finance a diversified segment of the business community while remaining sufficiently flexible to serve customers quickly and completely. The officers' numerous personal contacts in the community had facilitated the bank's growth. In particular they had made every effort to eliminate "red tape" and to give each platform officer broad authority to deal with customers. These efforts had been successful in attracting accounts dissatisfied with branch banks where only limited decisional authority had been delegated to the branch. One officer described American National Bank's fundamental philosophy as follows: "With all of our operations at one location, we provide the ultimate in personal banking service to our customers; the creation of an atmosphere of highly personalized service is one of our management's basic objectives."

American National aggressively sought time and savings deposits by keeping interest payments as high as possible under Federal Reserve Board regulations. American National was the first bank in its area to increase the interest rate offered on time deposits when the Federal Reserve Board raised the permissible interest rate ceiling in 1956, from 2 1/2 percent to 3 percent. In the summer of 1960, American National began paying "daily interest" on savings accounts; other Central City banks adopted this plan about nine months later. At the time, local savings and loan associations were aggressively advertising rates up to 4 per-

Exhibit 1

AMERICAN NATIONAL BANK

Statements of Condition
December 31, 1957 – 1961
(dollar figures in thousands)

	1957		1958		1959		1960		1961	
Resources	*Dollars*	*Percent*	*Dollars*	*Percent*	*Dollars*	*Percent*	*Dollars*	*Percent*	*Dollars*	*Percent*
Cash and due from banks	$32,728	22.3	$32,473	19.0	$36,070	19.5	$39,021	17.6	$38,364	15.1
U.S. securities	38,168	26.0	37,528	22.0	39,101	21.2	62,238	28.1	66,452	26.2
Other securities	5,445	3.7	11,375	6.6	10,682	5.8	11,824	5.3	16,640	6.5
Loans and discounts (net)	68,614	46.9	88,369	51.7	97,307	52.8	105,459	47.8	130,386	51.3
Real estate and other assets	1,603	1.1	1,219	0.7	1,357	0.7	2,719	1.2	2,206	0.9
Total resources	$146,559	100.1	$170,964	100.0	$184,517	100.0	$221,261	100.0	$254,048	100.0
Liabilities										
Demand deposits	$73,318	49.3	$85,261	49.9	$97,504	52.9	$99,549	42.7	$105,876	41.7
Time deposits	56,227	38.4	61,862	36.2	57,859	31.4	94,268	42.6	113,443	44.7
U.S. and other public deposits	7,120	4.9	10,676	6.2	11,028	6.0	12,446	5.6	14,277	5.6
Total deposits	$135,665	92.6	$157,799	92.3	$166,391	90.3	$201,263	90.9	$233,596	91.9
Reserve for taxes	757	0.5	885	0.5	993	0.5	1,275	0.6	1,439	0.6
Other liabilities	1,233	0.8	682	0.4	970	0.5	2,118	1.0	1,695	0.7
Common stock	5,008	3.5	6,259	3.7	8,345	4.5	8,345	3.8	8,345	3.3
Surplus	2,541	1.7	3,655	2.1	5,921	3.2	6,051	2.7	6,201	2.4
Undivided profits	1,355	0.9	1,684	1.0	1,897	1.0	2,209	1.0	2,772	1.0
Total capital	$ 8,904	6.1	$ 11,598	6.8	$ 16,163	8.7	$ 16,605	7.5	$ 17,318	6.8
Total liabilities	$146,559	100.0	$170,964	100.0	$184,517	100.0	$221,261	100.0	$254,048	100.0

Exhibit 2

AMERICAN NATIONAL BANK

Comparative Statements of Income and Expense
Years Ended December 31, 1957–1961
(dollar figures in thousands)

	1957	*1958*	*1959*	*1960*	*1961*
OPERATING INCOME					
Interest on loans and discounts	$3,791	$4,231	$5,230	$6,105	$ 7,134
Interest and dividends on securities	1,053	1,261	1,365	1,579	2,569
Other income	729	535	567	631	714
Total	$5,573	$6,027	$7,162	$8,315	$10,417
OPERATING EXPENSE					
Salaries	1,036	1,116	1,254	1,459	1,676
Interest on time deposits	1,632	1,753	1,742	2,005	3,478
Other expenses	805	865	1,015	1,186	1,309
Total	$3,473	$3,734	$4,011	$4,650	$ 6,463
Net operating income before taxes	2,100	2,293	3,151	3,665	3,954
Allocation for federal and state taxes	875	1,000	1,232	1,525	1,749
Net operating earnings after taxes	$1,225	$1,293	$1,919	$2,140	$ 2,205
Operating earnings per share	3.42	2.88	3.22	3.60	3.70
Other income	30	293	38	98	230
Losses and addition to loan reserve	433	431	862	879	721
Net income	$ 822	$1,010	$1,095	$1,359	$ 1,714
Net income per share	$ 2.30	$ 2.25	$ 1.83	$ 2.28	$ 2.87
Dividends per share	$ 1.26	$ 1.40	$ 1.40	$ 1.54	$ 1.68

cent. American National's time and savings deposits had almost doubled since 1959; however, these increased deposits carrying higher interest rates appreciably increased the bank's total interest expense, and, hence, reduced net profit. The newer deposits also proved more volatile, thereby requiring the bank to invest a somewhat higher proportion in securities and shorter maturity loans. The newer time deposits evidently resulted directly from American National's well-publicized policy of paying higher rates of interest. As other banks in the area raised their rates to American's level, many new depositors returned their savings balances to the banks where they maintained their commercial accounts.

The majority of American National's loans were to industrial and commercial customers. Since 1954, loan demand had been strong, and the bank's loan to deposits ratio consistently ranged above 50 percent. In referring to the bank's policy, a loan officer stated: "Personal loans are made primarily as an accommodation to our customers and do not represent an important part of our operation due to our emphasis on business credits." As an example of the bank's desire to meet the continuing needs of its business customers, American National deliberately curtailed its lending on real estate during the period 1958 – 1960 in order to assure the availability of funds to meet the growing demand for commercial loans.

American National's management desired to have as much freedom as possible when making important decisions. Accordingly, the executive committee attempted to anticipate the requests or demands that the national bank examiners might make with respect to the bank's operations. Through taking corrective actions promptly, and in reaching decisions before being pressed by supervisory authorities, the management had been able "to beat them to the punch." It was believed that this basic philosophy would, over the years, help to preserve amicable relations with the comptroller's office, and would, in fact, contribute toward creating "a valuable reservoir of goodwill."

As a result of American's significant growth in loans and deposits, the bank had found it necessary to raise additional capital on several occasions. Earnings simply had not proved adequate to keep pace with rapid growth, even though the bank retained a larger proportion of its earnings than did other competing banks (see Exhibit 3). Accordingly, American National had sold stock on five occasions during the past eight years with the proceeds totalling over $11.5 million. On each of the occasions when stock had been sold, the bank had initiated the action before any suggestions had been made by the examiners.

Since stockholders of nationally chartered banks are guaranteed pre-emptive rights (unless they vote to waive them), all of American's stock was sold to shareholders under rights offerings. From the bank's point of view, the primary disadvantage of a priviledged subscription was that it became more difficult to broaden the stockholder base, since nearly all shares were absorbed by existing owners. As a result, the total number of stockholders had grown less rapidly than desired in recent years, even though the capital account had been substantially expanded. The management was anxious to enlarge the number of stockholders for two reasons. First, there was the belief that shareholders would probably become (if they were not already) customers of the bank, and that they could also influence their friends to do business with American National. Second, a larger number of shareholders would also help make possible a broader and more active market for the stock.

Exhibit 3

AMERICAN NATIONAL BANK

Statistical Comparison of Four Banks*
December 31, 1959–1960
(Index: 1959 = 100)

	Year	*A*	*B*	*C*	*ANB*
Deposits, total	1959	100	100	100	100
	1960	102	102	123	121
	1961	104	118	151	140
Loans, net	1959	100	100	100	100
	1960	102	101	126	107
	1961	103	110	152	133
Capital, total	1959	100	100	100	100
	1960	105	102	110	103
	1961	124	114	121	107
Capital to net loans (capital: loans)	1959	1:10.5	1:7.8	1:6.9	1:6.0
	1960	1:10.2	1:7.6	1:7.9	1:6.4
	1961	1:8.8	1:7.5	1:8.6	1:7.5
Operating earnings after tax	1959	100	100	100	100
	1960	108	120	165	112
	1961	102	124	176	115
Operating earnings per share	1959	100	100	100	100
	1960	108	116	162	112
	1961	96	100	163	115
Dividends per share	1959	100	100	100	100
	1960	103	100	160	110
	1961	105	117	160	120
Dividends as percentage of operating earnings	1959	56.5%	46.9%	46.0%	43.5%
	1960	53.7	40.2	45.4	42.8
	1961	61.6	54.5	45.1	45.5
Market "bid" range	1959	$51–42	$38–32	$64–44	$53–35
	1960	50–42	41–32	58–45	57–46
	1961	72–47	79–41	104–53	87–56
Price-earnings ratio (based on average price and operating earnings)	1959	14.1X	13.7X	31.0X	13.7X
	1960	12.6	12.2	18.3	14.4
	1961	18.3	23.4	27.6	19.7
Book value per share	1959	$24.71	$20.23	$19.86	$30.37
	1960	25.92	20.66	21.47	32.09
	1961	27.57	21.66	22.56	33.47

*Banks A and B are large institutions with many branches. These banks are "retailers" as well as making business loans. Bank C has fewer but larger branches. It tends to be a businessmen's bank.

American National's last common stock offering took place in January 1959, when over $4.2 million was sold (see Exhibit 4). Loans in 1958 were increasing at a rate of $2.8 million per month; however, deposits had expanded more slowly. New capital was needed, therefore, to support the growing loan demand.

Exhibit 4

AMERICAN NATIONAL BANK

Summary of Common Stock and Stockholder Expansion
1953–1961

	Number of Shares Issued During Year	*Price to Stockholders*	*Total Size of Offering (000)*	*Under-writing Expense (000)*	*Basis for Stock Rights*	*Market Bid Price at Time of Sale*	*Market Bid Price Range**	*Maximum Legal Loan Limit at Years end (000)*	*Stock-holders at Year End*
1953	37,400	$35 00	$1,309	N.A.	2 for 3	N.A.	N.A.	$410	550
1954	47,685	39.90	1,903	$86.	1 for 2	$43	N.A.	560	872
1955	35,770	49.00	1,753	33.	1 for 4	61	$70–66	700	1,044
1956	None issued	---	---		---	---	74–57	700	1,075
1957	None issued	---	---		---	---	64–54	750	1,124
1958	44,708	52.50	2,347	67	1 for 4	59	72–56	990	1,638
1959	74,511	58.80	4,381	127	1 for 3	73	106–70	1,430	2,292
1960	None issued	(stock split 2 for 1)*	---		---	---	57–46	1,440	2,534
1961	None issued	---	---	---	---	---	87–56	1,450	2,807

*No adjustment for the 1960 stock split has been made throughout this table.

With respect to adequacy of the bank's capital, Mr. Holbrook noted: "There are serious limitations in using ratios to evaluate capital position. Nonetheless, we use the relationship of capital to net loans, that is, total loans minus reserve for loan losses." By the end of 1958, this ratio stood at 1:7.6, which, while acceptable, did not leave room for future growth. The January 1959 issue of capital helped provide funds for loans, increase the bank's cushion of equity, and raise the legal loan limit.

The market price for the stock in January 1959 was $73, and stockholders exercising their rights (one right for each three shares held) purchased $4.4 million of stock at $58.80 per share. The shares were quickly sold, as 82 percent of the existing stockholders subscribed to the issue. "Our only regret was that many of the bank's customers interested in becoming stockholders could not acquire the shares they wished, due to the heavy oversubscription," recalled Holbrook. The additional equity increased the legal lending limit to slightly over $1.4 million. Since the 1959 sale, the stock was split two-for-one (1960) in an attempt to increase the number of shareholders through doubling the shares outstanding, while at the same time bringing the price into a more popular trading range.

As he began gathering information for the executive committee's review of the capital position, Mr. Holbrook realized that the bank's continuing expansion again had begun to create pressure against the capital account.

By December 1961, loans had increased more than $20 million since the beginning of the year. The latter part of 1961 was a period of growing loan demand and "tight money" in Central City. For example, in addition to American National's growth in loans noted above, the bank still had nearly $15 million in previously approved credit lines which could be drawn down at any time. In some cases during the year, the bank requested customers to defer utilizing the full amount of credits previously authorized.

As American National's regular loan demand continued to grow, the legal lending limit proved an increasing competitive handicap. The bank currently had seven "overline" customers whose total credit needs could not be satisfied by American National because the $1.4 million legal limit was insufficient to handle approximately $10 million of these customers' total needs. The amount of a loan required over the legal limit (the overline) had to be placed by American National with other banks. These "overlines" would constitute additional profitable lending volume to American National, as increased capital raised the legal limit.

The legal lending limit affected American National's operations in still other ways. As the bank had grown larger there were opportunities, not available previously, to participate in loans to very large businesses. These nationally organized companies required more funds than any single bank could provide. Hence, a group of banks would jointly participate in making sizeable credits available. As American National approached a loan limit of $1.5 to $2 million, the bank became sufficiently large to "qualify" for participation in these large multibank lending agreements. The bank's management believed that further increases in legal lending limits would substantially increase these opportunities.

Mr. Holbrook also thought that further deposit growth could be facilitated with additional capital since an increased equity investment would lessen a depositor's risk of loss. In particular, the financial officers of large corporations often requested American National to send them supplementary financial information, such as interim statements, in order to remain closely in touch with the bank's over-all financial position. Since Federal Deposit Insurance Corporation insurance did not cover the bulk of large corporate deposits, financial officers expressed continuing interest in the bank's invested capital which would serve as a buffer to protect depositors.

American National's total size was also competitively important from other points of view. Frequently, important deposit customers, such as large public utilities, distributed deposits broadly in the area served among banks of a "reasonable size." Public agencies frequently established deposit accounts in a similar manner. Since American National was still bordering on the "reasonable size" criterion, further growth in capital, loans, and deposits might enable the bank to begin attracting a larger proportion of private and public deposits.

In deciding whether American National was adequately capitalized at its current level of operations, Mr. Holbrook relied upon the capital-to-loans relationship together with his estimate of future growth projections in loans and deposits. Mr. Holbrook felt that the ratio of capital to loans for American National should be approximately as follows: a 1:6 ratio indicated a large amount of capital; a 1:7 ratio implied a comfortable range; and a 1:9 ratio suggested a rather risky position. After the 1959 sale of stock, the capital-to-loans relationship for American National was 1:5.6. However, by the end of the year it had already declined to 1:6.

American National had materially underestimated its growth in the past and, on one occasion, had sold stock three times during a two-year period (November 1953 to August 1955). It had become increasingly important, therefore, to anticipate the bank's future need for capital more realistically in order to avoid too many small and costly public offerings. For example, the underwriting cost of the 1959 sale was $127,400.

Mr. Holbrook had estimated that American National's deposits would probably increase at an average rate of $2.8 million per month and that one half of these funds would be invested in the loan portfolio. He further assumed that the current proportion of demand deposits to total deposits would remain approximately constant. Recent rates of earnings on total resources had been used in the past when making estimates of future capital needs. Finally, Mr. Holbrook believed that the board of directors and the executive committee wanted to see a moderate dividend increase in the near future.

The executive committee had expressed concern about the dilution in earnings per share which might result from repeated sales of stock. Management was worried that the sale of too much stock before additional earnings were generated to support the new shares could be harmful to the owner's interests.

The stock market generally, and bank stocks in particular, had done well in the latter part of 1961 (see Exhibit 5). American National's stock had scored an impressive gain. Nonetheless, the question of whether to sell a large equity issue while the price was still rising presented a dilemma. Opinions expressed regarding bank stocks in November and December of 1961 read as follows:

> 1) The normal staid and slow-moving bank stock market went on a tear this week. The American Banker's Index of New York City bank stocks jumped over 141—compared to a 1961 low of 98—and currently is at its highest level since 1929.
>
> Traders in the market say that the demand for bank shares—in the past confined to insurance companies and mutual savings banks—has broadened considerably in recent years. For the first time, mutual funds are big buyers of bank stocks. For example, United Accumulative Fund took an initial position of 40,000 shares in Wells Fargo Bank. This institutional demand has attracted individual investors. In fact, the climb in bank stocks, which has come in the face of a drop in bank earnings this year, has been so fast that many traders are worried about the possibility of a serious shake out. Morgan Guaranty, for instance, was up more than ten points in a week.
>
> 2) The sharp rise in bank stocks, which have enjoyed a bull market all their own, shows little sign of letting up.

Mr. Holbrook's report to the executive committee on the question of the bank's capital adequacy was scheduled for January 12th. However, a further problem became apparent at the beginning of the new year as bank stock prices suddenly fell sharply. American National's stock lost ten points in two weeks. Some observers believed a recent ruling of the Federal Reserve Board partially caused the declining market values for bank shares. Early in December 1961, the nation's commercial banks were authorized to pay 3 1/2 percent on time deposits left in the bank six months and 4 percent on time deposits if left on deposit twelve months or more. The action was taken jointly by the Federal Reserve Board and the Federal Deposit Insurance Corporation. Banks could make the new rates effective January 1, 1962. American National immediately an-

Exhibit 5

American National Bank

Summary of Stock-Price Movements
August 31, 1961–January 11, 1962

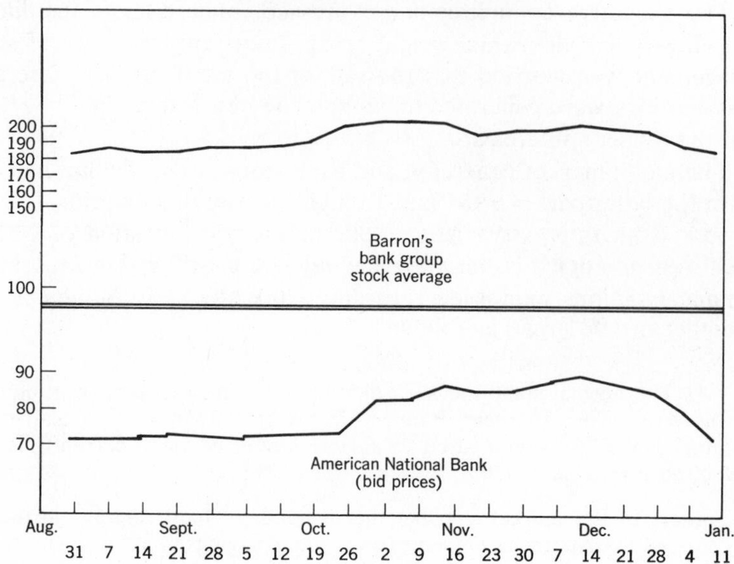

nounced that the bank would raise its interest rates on deposits beginning with the near year.

Mr. Holbrook realized that in his report at the executive meeting he should outline his own opinions on the bank's capital position, including a recommendation on whether or not to sell stock. In the past he had generally suggested to the committee (1) how much capital would be needed in the future, and (2) how the capital should be raised, including an opinion on desirable market timing and price. Mr. Holbrook felt responsible to insure that the bank's future capital requirements were provided in the least expensive manner possible while still allowing American National to meet its objective of profitable growth and service to the business community.

MANAGEMENT OF FINANCIAL INSTITUTIONS OTHER THAN COMMERCIAL BANKS

EVALUATING MONEY MARKET CONDITIONS AND THE BASIC INVESTMENT POLICY FOR A CASUALTY COMPANY

Fireman's Fund Insurance Company

In early January 1964, Mr. Bartlett T. Grimes, treasurer of Fireman's Fund, was reviewing the maturity composition of the commercial paper and government securities which the company owned. He undertook this project to see whether it might be possible to increase the total amount of capital gains and interest income. He was wondering if any changes should be made in the maturities of the present holdings of commercial paper and government securities. Mr. Grimes intended to submit his findings in the form of a specific recommendation to the executive committee.

Company Background

Fireman's Fund began in 1863 as a venture to provide fire insurance to the city of San Francisco. The company's founders called it Fireman's Fund Insurance Company because 10 percent of its yearly profits were contributed to a charitable fund for the city's volunteer fire fighters. In the years that followed, Fireman's Fund grew into a nation-wide multiple line insurance company. Exhibit 1 contains a balance sheet for December 31, 1962. In January 1964, the company was writing insurance policies in seven different lines: fire, inland marine, ocean marine, fidelity and burglary, automobile, casualty, and accident and health.

The business of Fireman's Fund was intangible in the sense that the product which the company provided had real value to the policyholder only after a loss occurred. On the basis of a contract, the company agreed to pay losses sustained from accidental or unforeseen causes, in return for the premium. The coverage period of the contract might vary considerably. For example, most casualty contracts were written on an annual basis, whereas many fire contracts were written for terms up to three or five years.

Exhibit 1

FIREMAN'S FUND INSURANCE COMPANY AND SUBSIDIARIES

Consolidated Balance Sheet
December 31, 1962

ADMITTED ASSETS	
Bonds	
U.S. government	$123,839
Commercial paper	34,077
Canadian	23,010
State and municipal	160,323
Corporate	1,500
	$342,749
Stocks	181,846
Real estate	5,386
Cash	17,923
Premiums in course of collection	97,394
Reinsurance recoverable on paid losses	2,833
Other admitted assets	15,201
Total admitted assets	$663,332
LIABILITIES, CAPITAL STOCK, AND SURPLUS	
Unearned premiums	$239,328
Losses and loss expenses	162,399
Income tax	924
Expenses and other taxes	10,654
Funds held under reinsurance treaties	20,599
Other liabilities	9,866
Total liabilities	443,770
Capital stock	9,513
Retained earnings and surplus	210,049
Total liabilities, capital stock, and surplus	$663,332

By definition, the basic task of a company like Fireman's Fund was to indemnify or guarantee its customers against loss or liability by contingent events. The company performed its job by accepting a large number of risks and charging premiums which would indemnify those who suffered loss and yet provide a return to its stockholders.

To operate, therefore, the company needed (1) a means of selling its services to those in need of insurance, (2) the ability to evaluate risks and determine appropriate rates, (3) the capacity to process the vast amount of paper work that is generated, (4) a method of settling the claims of the insured, and (5) the skill to invest profitably the reserve funds that must be maintained. Mr. Grimes was mainly concerned with this fifth activity.

Reserves and Investment Policy

Fireman's Fund executives believed that their first obligation was to consider the security of policyholders. Since insurance premiums were paid in advance, Fireman's Fund set up an unearned premium reserve. The reserve for unearned premiums represented the money that policyholders had paid for protection they would receive in the future. It is the amount that would have to be returned to the policyholders if all policies were cancelled or terminated.

Fireman's Fund also set up a second liability to its policyholders, namely, the loss reserve. This included an amount sufficient to provide for claims in the course of investigation and settlement, as well as claims not yet reported.

Management of Fireman's Fund felt that it was, in effect, the trustee of the moneys in the amount of these policyholders' reserves and that the stockholders were the beneficiaries of this trust. In other words, no interest or appreciation was attributed to these funds in computing premiums. Based on the source and nature of these policyholders' reserves, company executives had established the following element in their investment policy: "The company's primary liabilities to its policyholders, which are 100 percent of the loss and loss expense reserve and 65 percent of the unearned premium,[1] less the reserve on deferred premium payments, shall be covered 100 percent by cash, premiums in the course of collection, United States and Canadian government obligations and obligations guaranteed by the United States, high-grade commercial paper and other short-term obligations, and State and Municipal bonds rated Moody's 'Baa' or the equivalent or better."[2] Exhibit 2 contains a current breakdown of that portion of these investments with which Mr. Grimes was concerning in making his recommendation.

Management thought that the company was confronted essentially with two separate investment problems. The first was the aforementioned reserve investments, and the second was investing the shareholders' equity. While management felt that the reserves should be offset by high-grade fixed income investments as defined in Appendix A, it thought

[1]Company executives reasoned that acquisition costs, including commissions and clerical expenses, equal to 35 percent of the unearned premiums had already been paid and therefore losses and remaining expenses should be about 65 percent of the premiums. Fireman's Fund reflected this viewpoint in its annual report by adding 35 percent of the accumulated unearned premium reserve to the net worth of the company in estimating the liquidating value of the capital stock.

[2]Appendix A contains some additional excerpts from the basic investment policy.

Exhibit 2

FIREMAN'S FUND INSURANCE COMPANY AND SUBSIDIARIES

Holdings of U.S. Government Securities and Commercial Paper
December 31, 1963

Maturity	*Amount (000s)*	*Percent*
Within 1 year	$47,690*	33.0
Within 1–2 years	21,190	14.6
Within 2–3 years	20,380	14.1
Within 3–4 years	42,927	29.7
Within 4–5 years	–	–
Within 5 years	132,187	91.4
Within 5–10 years	12,500	8.6
Total	$144,687	100.0

*Includes $34,075,000 commercial paper.

that the company had a great deal more freedom with respect to the amount equal to the shareholder's equity. Since these funds were not exposed to the same potential short-term demands, they were regarded as being available for longer-term investments.

Historical Pattern of Interest Rates

Mr. Grimes thought that particular attention should be given to three facts about short-term and long-term interest rates. First, observation of changes in the maturity structure of rates over a period of time showed that interest rates on long maturities fluctuated within a narrower range than did those on short maturities. Second, in terms of price, the long maturities fluctuated more (see Exhibit 3). This was due to the phenomenon of discounting. Third, for much of the time short-term and long-term interest rates fell together, so that the whole spectrum of rates tended to move together in a fairly systematic fashion. Since the behavior of short-term interest rates on federal obligations at times differed substantially from that of long-term rates, however, he concluded that these differences in rates were due to what is known as the term structure —or maturity pattern—of interest rates.

In the past, Fireman's Fund had attempted to take advantage of the price swings caused by changes in interest rates by shifting between bonds of short maturity and long maturity. An example of this type of shifting is shown in Exhibit 4.

Exhibit 3

PRICE AND YIELD FLUCTUATIONS ON U.S. GOVERNMENT SECURITIES

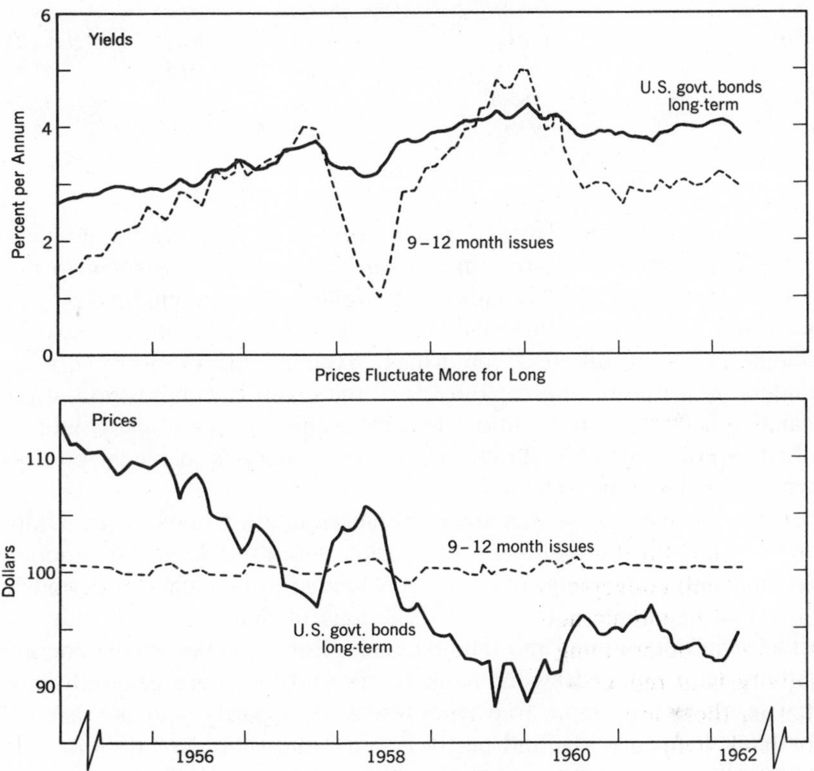

Prices at Various Yields for Two 4% Coupon Bonds
(One matures in one year; one matures in ten years)

Yield	*1 Year*	*10 Years*	*Yield*	*1 Year*	*10 Years*
2.10	101.87	117.06	2.90	101.08	109.49
2.20	101.77	116.08	3.00	100.98	108.58
2.30	101.67	115.11	3.10	100.88	107.69
2.40	101.57	114.15	3.20	100.78	106.80
2.50	101.47	113.20	3.30	100.68	105.92
2.60	101.37	112.26	3.40	100.59	105.05
2.70	101.27	111.33	3.50	100.49	104.19
2.80	101.18	110.40	3.60	100.39	103.33

Exhibit 3 (Continued)

Yield	*1 Year*	*10 Years*	*Yield*	*1 Year*	*10 Years*
3.70	100.29	102.49	4.40	99.61	96.79
3.80	100.19	101.65	4.50	99.52	96.01
3.90	100.10	100.82	4.60	99.42	95.23
4.00	100.00	100.00	4.70	99.32	94.47
4.10	99.90	99.19	4.80	99.23	93.71
4.20	99.81	98.38	4.90	99.13	92.95
4.30	99.71	97.58	5.00	99.04	92.21

Different theories have been advanced as to what are the dominant influences on the term structure of interest rates. There seem to be a number of factors which condition the relationship among interest rates according to maturity. Included among them are the liquidity differences among debts of different maturities, expectations of borrowers and lenders as to future interest rates, and the maturity composition of outstanding securities. In addition, general credit and economic conditions affect interest rates.[3] Yield curves for select periods in recent business cycles are shown in Exhibit 5.

Mr. Grimes knew that over the years interest rates in the United States tended to be relatively low during periods of lessened economic activity and, conversely, interest rates tended to be higher in periods of expanded economic activity. Also, actions of monetary authorities are a factor in determining the interest rates. For example, when economic activity is at reduced levels, bank reserve positions are generally easy, that is, there are ample free reserves. This is partly because demands for bank loans are low and partly because the actions of the monetary authorities are working to increase the availability of bank reserves. Exhibit 6 shows the relationships between movements in output, free reserves, and interest rates since 1953.

Recent Pattern of Interest Rates

One of the features of the past three years noted by Mr. Grimes was the relative stability of interest rates. This was in direct contrast with the two previous periods of general business expansion following a recession, when short-term interest rates moved sharply higher and long-term

[3]No comprehensive review of the literature is attempted here. Interested readers are referred to Joseph W. Conard, *Introduction to the Theory of Interest* (Berkeley: University of California Press, 1959); J. M. Culbertson, "Term Structure of Interest Rates" (*Quarterly Journal of Economics,* November 1957, pp. 485–517); David Meiselman, *The Term Structure of Interest Rates* (Englewood Cliffs: Prentice-Hall, Inc., 1962).

Exhibit 4

FIREMAN'S FUND INSURANCE COMPANY

1961 U.S. Government Bond Program
(Evaluation at August 9, 1961)

*Sold**	*Par Value (000)*	*1961 High*	*Sales Price*	*Proceeds*	*Aug 9, 1961 Close (Bid)*	*Market Value*	*Market Differential*
2 1/2% 6-15-69/64	$15,305	$92.50	$90.55	$13,858,000	$88.5625	$13,554,000	
2 1/2% 12-15-69/64	14,775	92.06	90.75	13,407,000	87.875	12,984,000	
	$30,080			$27,265,000		$26,538,000	
							$727,000

*Purchased**		*1961 Low*	*Purchase Price*	*Cost*	*Aug 9, 1961 Close (Asked)*		
4% 2-15-62	$ 1,800		$101.28	$ 1,823,000	$100.65625	$ 1,812,000	
2 1/4% 6-15-62/59	4,600		99.14	4,561,000	99.53125	4,578,000	
2 1/4% 12-15-62/59	13,900	$98.41	98.92	13,750,000	99.15625	13,783,000	
2 5/8% 2-15-63	7,350	98.50	98.95	7,273,000	99.25	7,295,000	
	$27,650			$27,407,000		$27,468,000	
							$ 61,000
						Net gain	$788,000

*The purchases and sales were carried out in December 1960, and in January and February 1961.

Exhibit 5

YIELD CURVES FOR U.S. GOVERNMENT SECURITIES

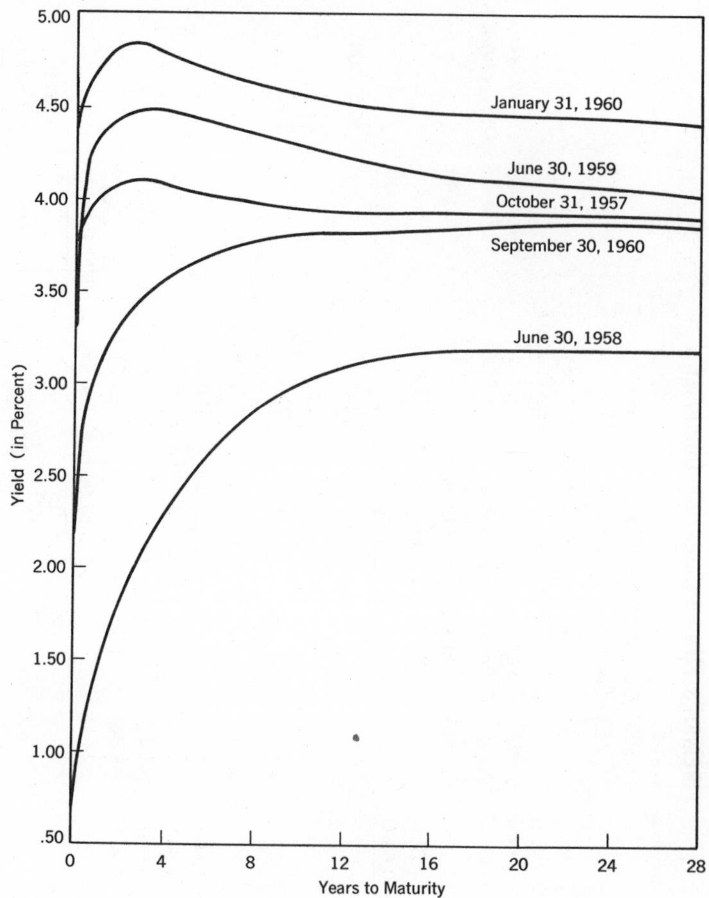

SOURCE: *Treasury Bulletin*, various issues.

rates also rose significantly. Since early 1961, monetary authorities had been pursuing the two objectives of supporting the recovery while trying to minimize pressures on the balance of payments. These considerations gave rise to what has been termed "operation twist." This phrase describes the attempt to hold up short-term interest rates in order to reduce the outflow of short-term capital to other nations, while holding down long-term interest rates to encourage domestic investment. Between 1961 and December 1963 continuing unemployment and unused capacity led the monetary authorities to pursue a less restrictive policy than would

Exhibit 6

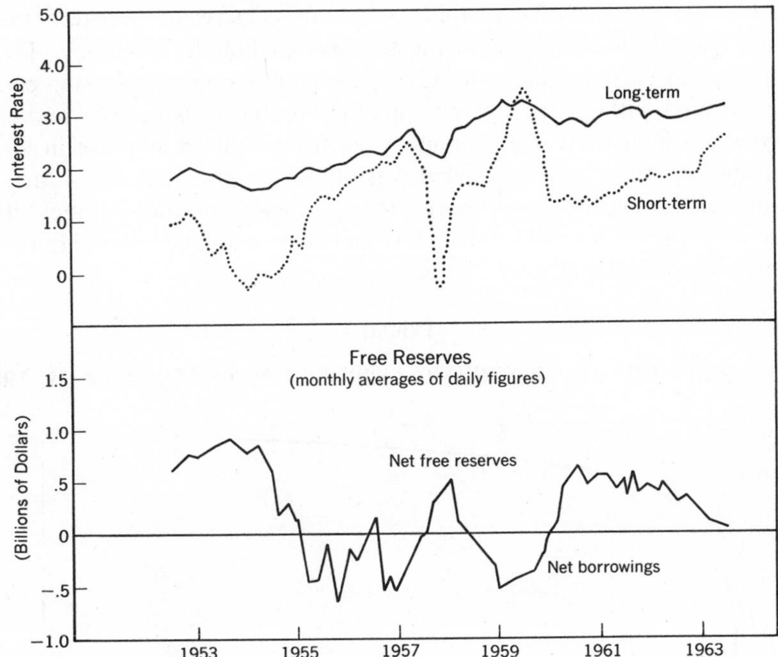

SOURCE: *Federal Reserve Bulletin,* various issues.

have otherwise been the case. Free reserves in the banking system, for example, remained at a much higher level for a longer time period than in previous recoveries. On the other hand, balance of payments considerations have influenced monetary policy so that it has not been as easy as purely domestic objectives might have dictated.

One phase of operation twist met with some success. Most long-term interest rates increased only slightly during much of the business recovery. This was particularly true during 1962. But the international phase of operation twist was less successful during this period. Although Treasury bill rates which were around 2.4 percent from late 1960 to late 1961, moved up by stages to 2.9 percent early in 1962, the international payments deficit continued.

To reduce the outflow of both short-term and long-term capital, the government announced two new measures in mid-1963: (1) The Federal Reserve rediscount rate was increased from 3 percent to 3 1/2 percent; (2) a new "interest equalization tax" was proposed to reduce the purchase of foreign securities, new or outstanding, by United States residents from foreigners. In the process, Treasury bill rates have moved up from 2.9 percent during the first five months to 3.4 percent. The international payments deficit dropped from an annual rate of $5 billion reached in the second quarter of 1963 to an annual rate of $1 billion in the third quarter.

At the time the measures were adopted it was the view of Treasury and Federal Reserve officials that the actions to increase short-term rates would have little effect in raising the cost of long-term money. Thus, according to these officials, the U.S. balance of payments position could be improved without the dampening effect on business activity and employment which they feared might stem from a sharp increase in long-term interest rates. In brief, what was obviously intended was a further closing of the gap between short-term and long-term interest rates, that is, a flattening of the yield curve. The yield curve of December 31, 1963, is shown as Exhibit 7.

Exhibit 7

YIELD CURVE FOR U.S. GOVERNMENT SECURITIES AS OF DECEMBER 31, 1963

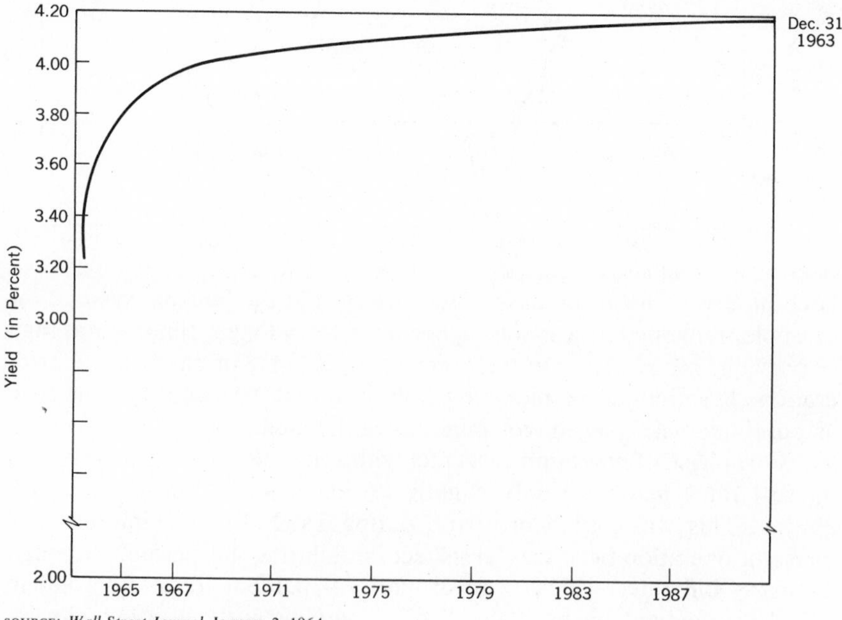

SOURCE: *Wall Street Journal*, January 2, 1964.

Mr. Grimes was particularly interested in the following article by George Shea which had appeared in *The Wall Street Journal* of December 23, 1963:

> Trends in interest rates on borrowed money appear to be resuming their traditional relationship with trends in general business, after almost two years during which the link was partially cut.
>
> The normal relation is for the cost of borrowing to rise when business improves, and to decline when business weakens. The reason, obviously,

is that when business gets better there is increased borrowing for expansion and lenders are able to charge more; whereas when business activity falls repayments on previous borrowings exceed the demand for new loans, and lenders compete with each other by offering lower rates.

The trends were normal in the last recession in business, which started in the spring of 1960, and ended in February, 1961. In January, 1960, before the recession started, the yield on U.S. Government bonds maturing or callable in ten years or more averaged 4.37%. A year and two months later, in March 1961, this average yield had fallen to 3.78%—the equivalent of a price rise of 13.5%.

Bond yields and prices also moved normally in the first year of the subsequent business recovery. From 3.78% in March 1961 the average rose to 4.09% in February 1962.

But then the normal link was broken. The monthly average slipped back to 4.01% in two months, then remained at or slightly under that level through August of this year. Yet business improved substantially in those 18 months, with the industrial production index rising from 116% of the 1957-59 average to about 126%.

The trends were similar during the past three years in other long-term securities, except that in the case of state and local issues yields did not rise but actually declined in the first year of the current business recovery. On short-term borrowings rates moved normally a little longer, rising through the first 17 months of the recovery before leveling off like the long-term rates. The reason for the longer-lasting rise in short-term rates was that the Government made special efforts to push these rates up to induce owners of short-term funds to keep them invested here rather than abroad. Shipment of funds abroad tends to worsen the deficit in the nation's balance of payments. The method of pushing these particular rates up was mainly to add substantially to the open-market supply of U.S. Treasury bills maturing in six months or less.

For the same reason short-term rates resumed their rise a little earlier this year than long-term rates. The short-term yields started moving up in June from their 1962–63 narrow range, while long-term Government bonds didn't get above their corresponding range until September. But since then the trend of rates has continued principally upward, though the short rates have leveled off again because the Government is now trying to hold them steady instead of pushing them up. They've been a bit above 3.5% in most recent weeks.

But the yields on long-term U.S. bonds last week got back up to their late February 1962 level of above 4.1%. They did so in response to a flat prediction by Chairman Martin of the Federal Reserve Board that if the tax cut now before the Senate Finance Committee is enacted and stimulates business further, interest rates will go up.

Mr. Martin's words on this subject are taken seriously because the Reserve Board, within limits, has the power to influence interest rates. He is saying, in effect, that if business improved and tends to push rates up, the Board will not try to prevent them from rising, but will probably follow its normal policy of raising its own discount rate in step with market rates.

> Whether the Board would also move specifically to restrict the supply of credit and thus promote rising interest rates, as it has done during the later stages of business booms in the past, is another question. It is a question that depends on many things, particularly the trends of employment and prices. If unemployment falls and prices of goods and services rise, the Board will almost surely restrict credit, but if unemployment and prices remain at current levels it probably would be reluctant to do so.
>
> However, the market has been put on notice that the policies of 1961–63 —when, broadly speaking, the Reserve Board has actively refilled available supplies of credit as they were used up by new borrowings—are now subject to change. The early weeks of the new year may provide some evidence on this score.
>
> At the turn of each year the Board has to switch its operations from supplying credit to taking up a possible slack in credit. December with its big holiday business is always a month of heavy demands for bank credit and the Reserve Board normally makes sure there is no credit squeeze late in the year; it conducts its operations so as to make credit readily available. But January is always a month when November and December borrowings are repaid, and the Reserve System reabsorbs part or all of the lendable cash with which it has supplied the banks in December. The test lies in whether the lendable cash supplies of the banks remain about unchanged. If they do, it would mean that the Board is satisfied for the time being to continue its 1961–63 policies.
>
> Besides employment and the course of prices, one other factor governs policies on interest rates. It is the deficit in the nation's balance of payments, mentioned earlier. This deficit has diminished in recent months, but it is by no means wiped out and will not be for a long time. As long as it continues, efforts will be made by the Government to keep short-term rates firm.
>
> Nevertheless, if business activity should slacken and unemployment should rise the Reserve Board would unquestionably pursue a generous credit policy. Such a policy probably would be reflected in declining interest rates not only on long-term securities but even in the short-term category, regardless of official efforts to keep these short rates firm. On the other hand, if current economic forecasts of further expansion in business are borne out, borrowers almost surely will face increasing interest charges.

On January 1, 1964, the following appeared in *Moody's Bond Survey:*

> Looking to 1964, we believe that investors can expect a further liberalization of interest rates generally. This trend cannot be expected to unfold along a straight line—trends never do—and it cannot be certain that it will persist for the full year. The current favorable economic outlook is a basic consideration. We expect that the Gross National Product for this year will exceed 1963's by more than 5%. This would generate a sufficient demand for funds to maintain the current uptrend of yields.
>
> Bank credit is not likely to be so freely available this year. In 1962, total loans and investments of all commercial banks expanded by $20.4 billion, or 9.5%. This prompted the Federal Reserve to move, starting near the end of that year and throughout 1963, away from a policy of active credit ease to a more or less neutral policy. Even so, the 1963 expansion of commercial bank credit was about $19 billion, or 8%. Recently, Federal Reserve officials have publicly expressed concern that such an expansion of bank

credit might be laying the base for inflation. A lesser rate of expansion in 1964, say 5%, would mean about $13 billion in additional bank credit. Since loan demand might exceed that amount, the coming Federal deficits probably would then be financed outside the banking system, in line with Chairman Martin's desires. This, of course, would exert upward pressure on Treasury yields.

Balance of payments deficits continued to plague our economy throughout 1963. However, substantial improvement was made toward preventing a run on the dollar. This was done through a build-up of foreign currency holdings, the entrance of the Federal Reserve into international exchange markets, the arrangement of currency swap agreements with other countries, and the sale of foreign central banks of special Treasury issues that were denominated in their currencies. Despite these arrangements, however, international financial relationships will continue as a major concern in shaping official policies.

Although Mr. Grimes used various forecasts such as *Moody's*, he remembered with interest a recent statement by George Shea in the *Wall Street Journal* on the subject of economic forecasts:

There are two noticeable features about these forecasts. One is, of course, the extent to which they tended to fail far more often than they succeeded. However, this finding may be somewhat unfair because no complete search has been made. No doubt many instances could be found where the outcome paralleled the predictions reasonably well.

The other feature is that almost every one of these forecasts, whether it turned out poorly, indifferently or pretty well, was mainly a projection of conditions as they existed when the forecasts were made. Only two mentioned the possibility of changes in the direction of business, and both were made during recessions, those of 1957–58 and 1960–61. Also both of these, like most of the others, assumed then existing conditions would continue for six months or more; yet in one instance the upturn was even then about to take place and in the other it came in four months.

The moral of all this is that bullish forecasts for general business are more likely to be right when they're made in periods of recession than when they're made in times of growing prosperity.

APPENDIX A

Excerpts from Fireman's Fund Insurance Company Basic Investment Policy[4]

Pursuant to the authority vested in the executive committee by resolution of the board of directors, the executive committee hereby establishes the following investment policy and guide:

[4]As amended June 14, 1963.

1. The primary function of an insurance company is the writing of insurance. The assets of the company are to be invested in a way which will contribute in the maximum degree possible.

2. The first obligation of an insurance company is to consider the security of its policyholders. As a consequence, the policy hereby established requires that the company's primary liabilities to its policyholders, which are 100 percent of the loss and loss expense reserve and 65 percent of the unearned premium reserve, less the reserve on deferred premium payments, shall be covered 100 percent by cash, premiums in the course of collection, United States and Canadian government obligations and obligations guaranteed by the United States, high-grade commercial paper and other short-term obligations, and state and municipal bonds rated Moody's "Baa" or the equivalent or better.

3. Bond investments shall consist of United States and Canadian government obligations and obligations guaranteed by the United States and state and municipal obligations rated Moody's "Baa" or the equivalent or better by recognized financial rating services and high-grade Canadian provincial, municipal, and corporate bonds.

4. Bond maturities should be in keeping with the requirements of the insurance business of the company, with the average maturity of governments not to exceed five to ten years and state and municipals not to exceed twenty years, with a maximum maturity on any bond of thirty years.

REAL-ESTATE INVESTMENT POLICY FOR A LIFE INSURANCE COMPANY

Occidental Life Insurance Company of California

In early December 1963, Mr. N. V. Martin, assistant manager of the mortgage loan department, had to make a recommendation to the investment committee of Occidental Life Insurance Company of California on a loan request which a mortgage-loan correspondent had submitted on an apartment house.

The Mortgage Loan Request

In November 1963, Mr. Martin had received a telephone call from Mr. Ed Haynes of the Harris Mortgage Company, a mortgage-loan correspondent in Wichita, Kansas. Mr. Haynes had outlined a proposed mortgage loan in general terms. Mr. Martin had thought that it sounded like one which might interest Occidental Life, and therefore had told Mr. Haynes that he would be interested in examining the loan proposal in more detail.

The Harris Mortgage Company had been a mortgage-loan correspondent of Occidental Life since 1957. Mr. Martin thought that Harris Mortgage had been one of Occidental's better mortgage-loan correspondents during these years. In his opinion, the terms of the loan proposals submitted by Harris Mortgage were usually in line with the general conditions of the mortgage market. As of the end of 1962, Harris Mortgage was servicing a total of $90 million in mortgage loans – $8.5 million of which were owned by Occidental Life.

About two weeks after the initial telephone call from Mr. Haynes, Mr. Martin received the following mortgage-loan request from the Harris Mortgage Company:

Mortgage Loan Request Submitted by Harris Mortgage Company

Consideration

Loan of $350,000 – 6 percent – 20 years – repayable $2,507.50 monthly for interest and principal, plus reserves for taxes and insurance. The note will include the privilege of making payments in addition to those required on thirty days notice on any installment payment date, as follows: (a) up to 10 percent of the original principal amount each loan year, noncumulatively, and without premium and (b) in excess of such amount upon the payment of a premium of 3 percent of such excess during the first five years, 2 percent of such excess during the second five loan years, and 1 percent of such excess thereafter.

Security

Lot 100 feet × 150 feet to be improved with six-story brick apartment building containing thirty-five one-bedroom apartments – each suite averaging 850 square feet. All apartments will have drapes, carpeting, refrigeration, and built-in ranges and ovens. The building will have central heating and air conditioning for all units and will be serviced by one elevator.

Improvements include on-site parking for fifty cars.

Location

1705 Magnolia Avenue, Wichita, Kansas

This is approximately three miles south of the center of the city. There are a number of apartments in this area – the majority are two-story garden type containing two and three bedrooms. Rents generally range from $120 to $135 per month. There are also a few apartments in the area similar to the ones in this proposal. Rents on these range up to $175 per month. This district is populated with families mainly in the medium income bracket ($6000–$8000).

There is a large shopping center two blocks to the east. A grade school and a high school are within a few blocks radius. Public transportation to the downtown area is available on Temple Street, one block east.

Appraisal

This property was appraised December 9, 1963, by Thomas Webb, M.A.I., as follows:

Land	$105,000
Improvements	420,000
	$525,000

The above value was based on reproduction cost. This physical value was supported by capitalizing the net income before depreciation at 8 percent, giving an indicated value of $536,250.

Applicant

John H. Johnston and Mary Johnston, his wife. Mr. Johnston–age 48–is a builder and land developer. He has an annual income of $20,000 and a net worth of $150,000–made up primarily of property equities.

Loan Purpose

Long-term financing of major part of construction cost.

Statistical

Projected monthly rent per suite		$170
Number of suites–35		
Loans per suite–$10,000		
Ratio of loan to appraised value–66 2/3%		
Gross income	$71,400	
Estimated cash expenses	28,500	
Net income before depreciation	$42,900	
Annual debt service	30,090	
Cushion	$12,810	
Cushion ratio[1]	17.9%	
Loan balance end of five years		$297,150
Loan balance end of ten years		225,750
Loan balance end of fifteen years		128,850

[1]The cushion ratio is the relation of the remainder (after annual operating expenses and debt service have been deducted from annual income) to the gross annual income. It expresses as a percentage the shrinkage that can be experienced in gross income (either by vacancies or rent reductions) before payment of principal and/or that interest may be jeopardized.

Insurance

The applicant carries $100,000 ordinary life insurance with this company.

Commitment Fee

Occidental Life will collect a 1 percent commitment fee—to be refunded if the loan is consummated within the eight-month commitment period—or, alternatively, Occidental Life will obtain a guarantee from Harris Mortgage Company that they will pay us a 1 percent fee if the loan is not delivered to us within the commitment period.

Background on Occidental Life

The Occidental Life Insurance Company of California began business on August 14, 1906, with paid-in capital of $200,000 and contributed surplus of $25,000. By December of 1963, the company had assets in excess of $1 billion. Exhibits 1 and 2 contain a balance sheet and income statement respectively for Occidental Life for the year ending December 31, 1962.[2]

At the end of 1962, Occidental Life had some 37,000 licensed representatives in 229 general agencies, 78 branch offices, and 44 group insurance sales and services offices. The company did business in all states of the United States (except New York), all provinces of Canada (except Newfoundland), the Philippine Republic, Hong Kong, and Japan. During 1962, 50 new agencies were established, and it appeared that an additional 50 would be established in 1963. Company representatives wrote a wide variety of ordinary life, group life, pension trust, salary allotment life, annuities, accident and health insurance, and group accident and health policies. Life insurance was written on both participating and nonparticipating plans; other business was nonparticipating.

An increase in 1962 of over $1 billion in life insurance in force brought Occidental Life's total of life insurance outstanding to more than $12.4 billion at the end of 1962. In this respect, at the end of 1962 the company stood in ninth position among the more than 1500 life insurance companies in the United States and Canada. Over the years Occidental Life had consistently moved up this list—ranking thirty-first in 1940, seventeenth in 1950, and eleventh in 1960.

[2]Occidental Life was wholly owned by Transamerica Corporation, whose family of related companies was largely engaged in the field of financial services. The majority of Transamerica's revenues were from insurance operations, including those of Occidental Life, as well as several small property, casualty, security, and fidelity insurance companies. Other subsidiaries of Transamerica included Pacific Finance, a large installment finance company; several title insurance companies; a real estate development company; and a small industrial manufacturing company.

Exhibit 1

OCCIDENTAL LIFE INSURANCE COMPANY OF CALIFORNIA

Statement of Financial Condition
December 31, 1962

Assets

BONDS AND STOCKS This item consists of U. S. government, Dominion of Canada, state, provincial, municipal, and corporation bonds together with carefully selected stocks	$423,618,664.61
MORTGAGE LOANS Mortgages on real estate located in various states and the Dominion of Canada, including loans made under Federal Housing and Veterans Administration	386,930,445.36
LOANS ON POLICIES This is the amount our policyowners have borrowed from the company, pledging as collateral the accumulated reserves on their policies	55,442,602.46
HOME OFFICE BUILDINGS AND OTHER REAL ESTATE HELD FOR INVESTMENT Investments in income-producing real estate, including company-occupied properties ($7,829,348.41)	22,255,486.78
CASH Cash on hand in the home office and branch offices and on deposit in various banks, sufficient to pay all claims promptly and meet the ordinary expenses of the company	14,876,526.73
PREMIUMS DEFERRED AND IN COURSE OF COLLECTION Unpaid premiums and deferred monthly, quarterly, and semiannual installments of premiums including those collected by branch offices but not yet reported to home office	46,525,962.07
ASSETS OF WESTERN MUTUAL LIFE FUND Assets held and kept separate for the benefits of policyowners of the former Western Mutual Life Association. The fund is administered by Occidental under the terms of a management agreement	844,376.87
OTHER ASSETS Assets owned by the company not falling within any of the above classifications but conforming to the laws of the states and provinces in which the company is licensed	8,366,422.02
Total assets	$958,860,486.90

Liabilities

RESERVES ON POLICIES REQUIRED BY LAW This amount, together with interest and future premiums, insures the payment of the benefits under outstanding policies. Reserves are determined in accordance with the standards of the jurisdictions in which the company operates		$673,396,900.21
POLICY CLAIMS AND LOSSES OUTSTANDING Claims under adjustment or adjusted but not yet due and estimated net losses incurred but not yet reported		33,159,567.48
DEPOSIT FUNDS Dividends, coupons, and miscellaneous values left with the company to accumulate at interest		60,251,536.09
DIVIDENDS TO POLICYOWNERS AND EXPERIENCE RATING REFUNDS Amounts unpaid or apportioned but not yet due		15,893,254.74
PREMIUMS AND INTEREST PAID BEFORE DUE This represents premiums and interest paid in advance by policyowners and borrowers		7,713,335.85
U.S. GOVERNMENT, STATE, AND OTHER TAXES ACCRUED This item represents the amount the company has set aside to pay premium, income, and other taxes to federal, state, and other governments		11,075,011.17
MANDATORY SECURITIES VALUATION RESERVES The reserve held to absorb variations in values of stocks and bonds		19,349,469.00
LIABILITIES OF WESTERN MUTUAL LIFE FUND The amount set aside to meet the obligations to policyowners of the Western Mutual Life Fund according to the terms of the agreement under which it is being administered by Occidental		844,376.87
ALL OTHER LIABILITIES The amount set aside to meet future obligations of the company not falling within any of the above classifications		20,520,197.43
Total liabilities		$842,203,648.84
SPECIAL SURPLUS FUNDS Reserves set up for morbidity fluctuation and for general contingencies	$15,654,439.00	
CAPITAL STOCK The amount invested in the company by the stockholders as an additional safeguard over the legal reserve and surplus funds	25,000,000.00	
SURPLUS UNASSIGNED This figure is the amount of the company's surplus over and above all known reserves and other liabilities	76,002,399.06	
Total capital and surplus		$116,656,838.06
Total liabilities, capital, and surplus		$958,860,486.90

Sales of accident and health insurance policies, both individual and group, had also increased at a rapid rate. In 1962, premiums paid to Occidental Life to provide accident and health insurance coverage of all types exceeded $100 million for the first time.

Exhibit 2

OCCIDENTAL LIFE INSURANCE COMPANY OF CALIFORNIA

Statement of Income
Years ended December 31, 1962 and 1961

	1962	*1961*
Premiums and other insurance income	$280,602,247	$269,074,645
Investment income		
Interest	$ 36,129,987	$ 32,541,132
Dividends	2,747,445	2,568,128
Real-estate income	1,970,223	2,071,514
	$ 40,847,655	$ 37,180,774
Less investment expense	2,839,758	2,581,801
	$ 38,007,897	$ 34,598,973
Other income	50,462	111,835
	$318,660,606	$303,785,453
Benefits paid or provided for		
Death claims and other benefits under policies and contracts	$190,648,676	$173,468,329
Increase in reserves for future benefits	51,841,200	60,728,219
	$242,489,876	$234,196,548
	$ 76,170,730	$ 69,588,905
Expenses		
Commissions and agency expenses	$ 26,662,438	$ 26,424,397
Salaries	13,506,888	12,909,447
Taxes and license fees	6,586,556	6,225,479
Other expenses (including depreciation of $557,973 in 1962 and $603,281 in 1961)	8,697,250	6,723,034
	$ 55,453,132	$ 52,282,357
Less expense deducted from investment income	2,839,758	2,581,801
	$ 52,613,374	$ 49,700,556
	$ 23,557,356	$ 19,888,349
Provision for federal taxes on income from insurance operations	7,137,354	7,209,435
Income from operations as reported to state insurance departments	$ 16,420,002	$ 12,678,914
Net realized gain on sale of investments, less provision for federal taxes on income of $554,144 in 1962 and $515,848 in 1961	1,706,801	2,368,633
Net income	$ 18,126,803	$ 15,047,547

Exhibit 3

OCCIDENTAL LIFE INSURANCE COMPANY OF CALIFORNIA

Ten-year Summary of Comparative Financial Data
As of December 31, 1953–1962
(dollar amounts in millions)

Assets	*1962*	*1961*	*1960*	*1959*	*1958*	*1957*	*1956*	*1955*	*1954*	*1953*
Securities										
Bonds	$ 350	$ 317	$ 309	$ 299	$ 276	$ 236	$ 184	$ 152	$ 137	$ 115
Preferred stocks	16	37	33	14	—	—	—	—	2	2
Common stocks	57	44	18	30	24	25	32	44	41	32
Total securities	$ 423	$ 398	$ 360	$ 343	$ 300	$ 261	$ 216	$ 196	$ 180	$ 149
Mortgage loans	387	362	330	298	290	277	275	252	217	196
Other assets	149	139	127	109	100	87	79	69	64	60
Total assets	$ 959	$ 899	$ 817	$ 750	$ 690	$ 625	$ 570	$ 517	$ 461	$ 405
Securities										
Bonds	36%	35%	38%	40%	40%	38%	32%	29%	30%	29%
Preferred stocks	2	4	4	2	—	—	—	—	1	1
Common stocks	6	5	2	4	4	4	6	9	9	8
Total securities	44%	44%	44%	46%	44%	42%	38%	38%	40%	38%
Mortgage loans	40	40	40	40	42	44	48	49	47	48
Other assets	16	16	16	14	14	14	14	13	13	14
Total assets	100%	100%	100%	100%	100%	100%	100%	100%	100%	100%
Liabilities, Capital, and Surplus										
Liabilities	$ 842	$ 791	$ 719	$ 654	$ 595	$ 544	$ 495	$ 449	$ 404	$ 361
Capital and surplus	117	108	98	96	95	81	75	68	57	44
Total	$ 959	$ 899	$ 817	$ 750	$ 690	$ 625	$ 570	$ 517	$ 461	$ 405
Life insurance in force	$12,455	$11,356	$10,206	$9,049	$7,999	$7,222	$6,707	$6,094	$5,262	$4,582
Insurance written	$ 2,270	$ 2,267	$ 2,206	$1,932	$1,517	$1,375	$1,302	$1,325	$1,095	$1,015

Basic Investment Policy of Occidental Life

The great growth in the business of Occidental Life over the past ten years had brought about a substantial increase in Company assets (see Exhibit 3). The basic investment policy of Occidental Life was to invest its assets:

Safely: To insure protection of principal.

Productively: To realize maximum income consistent with safety.

Effectively: To assist in financing those things which contributed most to employment opportunities, the general welfare of the area served, and the improvement of American and Canadian economic standards.

The distribution of assets of Occidental Life differed from the average of all life insurance companies in the United States by several percentage points in some categories—notably bonds and mortgages. The breakdown at the end of 1962 is shown in Exhibit 4.

Exhibit 4

OCCIDENTAL LIFE INSURANCE COMPANY OF CALIFORNIA

	Percentage Distribution of Assets of U.S. Life Insurance Companies 1962		*of Occidental Life 1962*	
Bonds				
U.S. government	4.6		3.9	
Foreign government	0.5		3.6	
State provincial and local	4.0		3.4	
Railroad	2.6		1.2	
Public utility	13.0		14.1	
Industrial and miscellaneous	23.1	47.8	10.3	36.5
Stocks		4.7		7.7
Mortgages		35.2		40.4
Policy loans		4.7		5.8
Real estate		3.1		2.3
Miscellaneous		4.5		7.3
		100.0		100.0

Mortgage Investments of Occidental Life

As of December 1963, the company had about 40 percent of total assets, or $400 million, in mortgage investments. Exhibits 5 and 6 give breakdowns of the mortgage investments by type of mortgage for Occidental Life and for all United States life insurance companies respectively.

Exhibit 5

OCCIDENTAL LIFE INSURANCE COMPANY OF CALIFORNIA

Mortgage Loans
(in thousands of dollars)

	By Type of Loan				By Type of Real Estate				
Year	*Conventional*	*FHA*	*VA*	*Total*	*1–5 Family Units*	*Apartments*	*Commercial*	*Industrial*	*Farm*
1955	$93,102	$ 88,770	$71,637	$253,509	$235,244	$4,066	$ 7,838	$4,242	$2,119
1956	88,501	97,987	90,147	276,636	258,994	1,969	12,390	1,561	1,721
1957	84,659	101,924	92,358	278,941	260,715	1,831	12,869	2,052	1,474
1958	85,626	118,888	87,479	291,993	271,610	3,352	12,982	2,830	1,218
1959	82,140	135,087	82,859	300,086	282,578	2,706	11,429	2,424	949
1960	82,287	170,937	79,260	332,485	315,356	3,299	10,667	2,393	770
1961	89,682	201,144	73,753	364,579	345,275	3,797	11,143	3,752	611
1962	99,589	220,551	69,647	389,787	367,906	4,961	12,845	3,576	498
				(as a percent of the total)					
1955	36.7	35.0	28.3	100.0	92.8	1.6	3.1	1.7	0.8
1956	32.0	35.4	32.6	100.0	93.6	0.7	4.5	0.6	0.6
1957	30.4	36.5	33.1	100.0	93.5	0.7	4.6	0.7	0.5
1958	29.3	40.7	30.0	100.0	93.0	1.1	4.4	1.0	0.5
1959	27.4	45.0	27.6	100.0	94.2	0.9	3.8	0.8	0.3
1960	24.8	51.4	23.8	100.0	94.8	1.0	3.2	0.8	0.2
1961	24.6	55.2	20.2	100.0	94.7	1.0	3.1	1.0	0.2
1962	25.5	56.6	17.9	100.0	94.4	1.3	3.3	0.9	0.1

Exhibit 6

OCCIDENTAL LIFE INSURANCE COMPANY OF CALIFORNIA

Types of Mortgages
Owned by United States Life Insurance Companies
(in millions of dollars)

Year	*Total*	*Farm*	*Nonfarm FHA**	*Nonfarm VA*	*Nonfarm Conventional*
1955	$29,445	$2,273	$ 6,530	$6,074	$14,568
1956	32,989	2,481	6,813	7,304	16,391
1957	35,236	2,584	6,964	7,721	17,967
1958	37,062	2,667	7,671	7,433	19,291
1959	39,197	2,827	8,523	7,086	20,761
1960	41,771	2,982	9,290	6,901	22,598
1961	44,203	3,170	9,949	6,553	24,531
1962	46,902	3,400	10,518	6,395	26,589
			(as a percent of the total)		
1955	100.0	7.7	22.2	20.6	49.5
1956	100.0	7.5	20.7	22.1	49.7
1957	100.0	7.3	19.8	21.9	51.0
1958	100.0	7.2	20.7	20.1	52.0
1959	100.0	7.2	21.7	18.1	53.0
1960	100.0	7.1	22.2	16.5	54.1
1961	100.0	7.2	22.5	14.8	55.5
1962	100.0	7.2	22.4	13.6	56.7

*Includes mortgages insured under the Canadian National Housing Act; in 1962, these amounted to $342 million.

SOURCE: *Life Insurance Fact Book 1963.*

Company Policies Affecting Mortgage Investments

1. AMOUNT TO BE INVESTED IN MORTGAGES. The consensus of the finance committee of Occidental Life was that the investment program should maintain about a 40 percent ratio of mortgages to total assets. As of December 1963, the company was making loan commitments of about $5 million each month. Management believed that commitments of as much as $7 or 8 million could be made in a single month if particularly attractive opportunities turned up. It felt that Occidental Life could adjust for such fluctuations over a longer period of time. In general, management thought it was desirable to maintain the total of outstanding commitments at $30 to $35 million. (Exhibit 7 lists the outstanding commitments at November 30, 1963, by month of expiration.)

Exhibit 7

OCCIDENTAL LIFE INSURANCE COMPANY OF CALIFORNIA

Commitment Expirations
November 30, 1963

December 1963	$ 2,004,500
January 1964	4,061,007
February	5,724,055
March	5,195,206
April	3,651,148
May	3,934,925
June	4,930,783
July	4,030,618
August	115,700
November	30,000
	$33,677,942

2. GEOGRAPHIC DIVERSIFICATION. Geographic diversification of mortgages was influenced to a considerable degree by the volume of insurance underwritings in the various states. Company executives believed that it was desirable to invest funds in the areas from which they were derived. They felt that this policy was beneficial to agents from a public-relations standpoint. (Exhibit 8 gives a comparison of premium income to mortgage investment by states.) At the same time, they wanted their mortgages to be secured by real estate which was located in sound economic areas experiencing healthy growth.

3. RESIDENTIAL LOANS. As shown by Exhibit 5, over 90 percent of the outstanding mortgage loans of Occidental Life were on single-family residential properties. It was the opinion of management that this type of mortgage loan had the least chance of default. Management also felt that the smaller size of these loans enabled the company to spread its investments over more communities and thus the name of Occidental Life was brought to the attention of potential policyholders.

More than 80 percent of the mortgages which Occidental Life held on single-family residential properties were insured by the Federal Housing Administration or guaranteed by the Veterans Administration. Company executives thought that a high proportion of insured and guaranteed mortgages was desirable because Occidental Life made loans all over the country. By having insured and guaranteed mortgages, management believed that (a) the risk of loss of principal was eliminated; (b) the company could invest over wider areas, that is, it was not restricted to

Exhibit 8

OCCIDENTAL LIFE INSURANCE COMPANY OF CALIFORNIA

Comparison of Premium Income to Mortgage Investment
December 31, 1962

State	*Total Insurance Premiums Schedule T*	*Percent of Premium Income*	*Total Mortgages*	*Percent of Mortgage Investments*
Alabama	$ 1,290,787	0.54%	$ 13,152,625	3.37%
Alaska	567,086	0.24%	–	–
Arizona	2,856,685	1.21	9,302,106	2.39
Arkansas	533,218	0.23	5,408,754	1.39
California	122,556,336	52.07	127,152,789	32.62
Colorado	2,541,828	1.08	13,770,851	3.53
Connecticut	1,051,880	0.45	–	–
Delaware	162,776	0.07	916,846	0.24
District of Columbia	704,204	0.30	–	–
Florida	1,908,923	0.81	5,291,574	1.36
Georgia	1,017,506	0.43	8,583,883	2.20
Hawaii	4,891,786	2.08	12,673,198	3.25
Idaho	1,212,676	0.52	2,683,792	0.69
Illinois	11,609,002	4.93	10,109,003	2.59
Indiana	1,752,388	0.74	602,408	0.15
Iowa	2,310,466	0.98	4,846,850	1.24
Kansas	1,370,603	0.58	7,183,847	1.84
Kentucky	616,085	0.26	190,471	0.05
Louisiana	3,082,773	1.31	14,209,562	3.65
Maine	36,537	0.02	–	–
Maryland	1,794,111	0.76	3,846,766	0.99
Massachusetts	1,551,225	0.66	–	–
Michigan	4,102,468	1.74	11,383,692	2.92
Minnesota	2,107,472	0.90	4,815,364	1.24

Exhibit 8 (Continued)

State	*Total Insurance Premiums Schedule*	*Percent of Premium Income*	*Total Mortgages*	*Percent of Mortgage Investments*
Mississippi	1,183,832	0.50	188,154	0.05
Missouri	2,839,091	1.21	16,589,205	4.26
Montana	1,342,326	0.57	2,097,811	0.54
Nebraska	875,306	0.37	1,665,462	0.51
Nevada	1,812,680	0.77	2,003,459	0.43
New Hampshire	119,207	0.05	–	–
New Jersey	1,796,527	0.76	252,728	0.06
New Mexico	1,836,714	0.78	5,548,872	1.42
New York	1,730,674	0.74	–	–
North Carolina	274,479	0.12	–	–
North Dakota	534,774	0.23	–	–
Ohio	9,457,486	4.02	5,818,646	1.49
Oklahoma	1,466,104	0.62	9,069,388	2.33
Oregon	4,401,734	1.87	7,638,634	1.95
Pennsylvania	5,706,290	2.42	689,405	0.18
Rhode Island	564,393	0.24	–	–
South Carolina	221,296	0.09	–	–
South Dakota	406,970	0.17	436,339	0.11
Tennessee	820,792	0.35	5,066,267	1.30
Texas	5,755,243	2.45	28,107,502	7.21
Utah	1,740,998	0.74	11,251,076	2.90
Vermont	52,556	0.02	–	–
Virginia	1,292,589	0.55	138,563	0.04
Washington	6,415,446	2.73	10,052,117	2.58
West Virginia	728,298	0.32	2,972	–
Wisconsin	1,111,200	0.47	2,082,229	0.53
Wyoming	455,297	0.19	5,482,656	1.40
Canada	8,791,744	3.74	19,480,653	5.00
	$235,362,867	100.00%	$389,786,519	100.00%

making loans only in those areas (usually large cities) which had been inspected and approved by a mortgage loan officer or home office appraiser; and (c) the investments were more liquid, since there was a secondary market for insured and guaranteed mortgages.

4. COMMERCIAL AND INDUSTRIAL LOANS. Occidental Life made commercial and industrial loans to well established companies or individuals with high credit standing. The properties securing such loans were required to be well located, and the business of the borrower or lessee had to be competently operated. A recent change in the law by the California state legislature[3] permitted the company to make loans up to 75 percent of fair market value on all types of properties. This had been limited previously to a 66 2/3 percent ratio except on single-family home loans. The existing policy of Occidental Life was to limit commercial and industrial loans to 66 2/3 percent of appraised value. (Details on Occidental Life's Commercial and Industrial Loan Program with regard to loans on apartment houses are contained in Exhibit 9.)

Exhibit 9

OCCIDENTAL LIFE INSURANCE COMPANY OF CALIFORNIA

Excerpts from Present Commercial and Industrial Mortgage Program

APARTMENTS

Limited interest up to ⅔ of fair-market value. Close-in locations only in the larger metropolitan centers. Prefer 20–40 unit apartment buildings, unfurnished. Efficiency apartments – minimum 500 square feet. One-bedroom apartments – minimum 625 square feet. Two-bedroom apartments – minimum 750 square feet.

Rents – medium – $30 to $50 per room (20¢ per square foot). Loan per unit – $5000 to $8000 (may run somewhat higher in the more expensive construction areas in the midwest and northeast). We recognize there is a demand for upgrading in accommodations by renters – more rooms, modern kitchen facilities, second bathroom, air conditioning, and the like that will have a decided effect on occupancy and the successful operation of new apartment projects over the years ahead. While we are not considering luxury type apartments, we look for something better than average in new apartment developments submitted for mortgage financing. Sponsors of such projects must present strong financial statements and personally guarantee the note.

Cushion Ratio – minimum of 25 percent before vacancy allowance and after deducting operating expenses and debt charges on the mortgage.

LOANS TERMS

Loans on commercial, industrial, and residential income properties are limited to 66 2/3 percent of the fair market value of the property. Such value must be determined by a qualified M.A.I. appraiser acceptable to the company. We prefer loans ranging

[3]Life insurance companies in the United States were regulated by the insurance code of the state in which they were incorporated. Each state code of the state had a number of sections setting out the investments that were eligible and any restrictions or reservations on these. Occidental Life Insurance Company of California, being a California-domiciled company, was governed by the California Insurance Code.

Exhibit 9 (Continued)

LOAN TERMS (CONTINUED)

$100,000 to $1,500,000 amortized over ten to twenty years, depending on the age of the security and credit of the owner and/or tenant. Loans of $1,000,000 and over require two independent appraisals. With regard to prepayments, we generally require a lockout for three to five years depending on the term of the loan. Thereafter, the borrower may have the right to pay additional payments not exceeding 10 percent of the original loan in any one year, noncumulatively, and the further privilege of paying the loan in full with a bonus of 3 percent to 5 percent for a series of years, gradually reducing to 1 percent in the final years of the loan.

Interest rates move with the market and are determined to a large degree by the general interest rates prevailing in the area, but considerable weight is also given to the type and location of the property and, to a large degree, to the underlying credit of the owner and/or tenant under long-term lease.

Sources of Mortgage Loans

Occidental Life Insurance Company of California obtained its mortgages from three main sources—directly from the borrowers, through mortgage brokers, and through mortgage loan correspondents. In the southern California area mortgage investments were made either directly or through mortgage brokers. Typically, mortgage loans that Occidental Life made directly to the borrower came through referrals from banks and other financial institutions (including other insurance companies) that were not interested in the loans because of legal restrictions, company policy, or some other reason. The company's insurance customers provided a second source of direct loans. Mortgage brokers, serving as intermediaries between borrowers and Occidental Life, had sold the company a significant portion of the mortgages which it held on properties in southern California. Regardless of whether the loan was made directly or acquired through mortgage brokers, the servicing of mortgage investments in the southern California area was maintained by a division of the mortgage loan department at the head office in Los Angeles.

Outside the southern California area, loans were obtained from mortgage loan correspondents.[4] Occidental Life had always used mortgage correspondents; however, it was not until after World War II when the company began to move heavily into mortgages that it made significant use of them.

Relationships with Mortgage Loan Correspondents

By using mortgage loan correspondents, Occidental Life's management felt that it retained a great deal of flexibility. Since the company had not established branch offices to service its mortgages, it was felt

[4]Occidental Life did make a small number of direct loans to borrowers located outside of southern California. Loans made in this manner generally went to borrowers with outstanding credit ratings.

that mortgage investments easily could be expanded or contracted in any geographical area.

The cost of establishing relationships with mortgage loan correspondents was relatively small. The usual procedure was for a representative of Occidental Life to go to the area where the company desired a mortgage loan correspondent. He would interview several prospects and examine their financial statements before making a final decision. As of December 1963, the company had eighty-nine mortgage loan correspondents, who were located throughout the United States and the provinces of Canada. (Exhibit 10 groups these correspondents according to the total amount of loans which they serviced for Occidental Life.) With few exceptions, these mortgage loan correspondents were banks, mortgage bankers, or other financial institutions which had been handling loans for Occidental Life as well as for other investors for a number of years.

Exhibit 10

OCCIDENTAL LIFE INSURANCE COMPANY OF CALIFORNIA

Servicing of Mortgage Loans

Mortgage Loan Correspondents (Grouped in Order of Servicing Volume)	*Total Serviced at 12/31/62 (In 000's)*	*(Percent of Total)*
1–10	$103,880	26.7%
11–20	60,714	15.6
21–30	45,090	11.6
31–40	32,602	8.4
41–50	22,600	5.8
51–60	17,127	4.3
61–70	10,255	2.6
71–80	5,471	1.4
81–89	1,713	0.4
Total serviced by 89 correspondents	$299,452	76.9%
Home office	89,956	23.1%
Total mortgage loans	$389,408	100.0%

Occidental Life has contracts with each of its mortgage loan correspondents. The contract set out the basis on which new loans would be acquired and established the responsibilities of the correspondent in servicing these loans. Servicing included such things as collecting and remitting monthly payments of principal and interest, verifying that taxes and insurance premiums were properly paid, and carrying out foreclosure proceedings when necessary. The typical servicing fee was ½ percent a year, for residential mortgages; the rate was subject to negotiation on other types of mortgages ranging between ½ percent and 1/10 percent.

Before submitting a detailed loan proposal, a mortgage loan correspondent usually informed Occidental Life of the general nature of the loan (that is, type of loan, approximate size, and interest rate of loan). If Occidental Life then expressed an interest in making the loan, a formal loan proposal was submitted. When Occidental Life decided to accept a loan submitted by a mortgage loan correspondent, it sent a letter of commitment to the correspondent. Exhibit 11 gives a listing of Occidental Life's mortgage loan correspondents in groups of ten according to the amount of new commitment activity which they originated for Occidental Life in 1962. Commitments were generally made for an eight-month period, with delivery at Occidental Life's option during the commitment period. In the interim period before Occidental Life acquired the mortgage, the mortgage loan correspondent financed the mortgage. Typically this was accomplished by taking the commitment letter to a bank and borrowing against it. Occidental Life executives believed that commercial banks had accepted this type of intermediate-term loan on the strength of the commitment of Occidental Life to take over the mortgage in the future. This type of arrangement was known as mortgage warehousing.

Exhibit 11

OCCIDENTAL LIFE INSURANCE COMPANY OF CALIFORNIA

1962 New Commitment Activity

Mortgage Loan Correspondents (Grouped in Order of 1962 New Commitment Activity)	*Amount (In 000's)*	*Amount (Percent of Total)*
1–10	$22,606	32.1%
11–20	12,343	17.5
21–30	7,321	10.4
31–40	4,512	6.4
41–50	2,779	3.9
51–60	755	1.1
61–66	131	0.2
Total new commitments by correspondents in 1962	$50,447	71.5
Home office	20,061	28.5
Total new commitments in 1962	$70,508	100.0%

Current Outlook in the Mortgage Market

Each month the mortgage loan division of Occidental Life prepared a review of the mortgage market. Mr. Martin had on hand the two most recent reviews (November 1963 and December 1963):

Residential Loans, November 1963

Housing starts in September were at a seasonally adjusted rate of 1,687,000 units, exceeding the previous high of last May. September starts where 17 percent above August and 24 percent higher than September 1962. Present indications are that the number of private housing starts for 1963 will be about 1.53 million. Starts of multifamily buildings are now estimated at 37 percent of total residential building starts. It appears, however, that the rapid growth in multifamily starts is slowing down, primarily because of an unfavorable vacancy situation in many areas.

Economists are far from unanimous in their forecasts of expected private housing starts in 1964. The consensus is that there will be some decline due to the expected slowdown in construction of larger multiunit buildings. Various adverse factors in the over-all picture are overbuilding, soft demand, election year uncertainties, delay of the pending tax reduction bill. These may be offset by such favorable conditions as a rise in one–four-family units, the continued ample supply of mortgage funds, increased family formations, and such demand as may be generated from the demolition of existing units.

In regard to the soft demand referred to above, it has been reported that home sales in some areas are so slow that builders have been advertising FHA and VA mortgages loans available at 4 3/4 percent interest instead of at the rate of 5 1/4 percent. These builders must believe that such action will spur sales sufficiently to offset the added discount required in the marketing of such loans.

The National Association of Real Estate Boards, according to its fall 1963 mortgage market analysis, expects the next six months to show a large supply of mortgage funds available for loans, keen competition, and rates remaining at the present level. This analysis reports that mortgage originators are pushing hard for loans by cutting originating fees, servicing fees, and loan costs in order to get business. Lender competition in FHA and VA loans is exceptionally strong and has led to minimum downpayments, longer terms, and lower discounts. The report further reports lower interest rates on conventional loans to buyers with credit worthiness who make substantial downpayments.

FHA AND VA LOAN YIELDS Prices and yields on FHA and VA loans remain stable in a range of 98 to 99 1/2 on spot loans. More FHA and VA loans are being made with minimum downpayments and 35-year terms. Although such loans normally call for lower prices, more and more of them are based solely on the government insurance with no apparent regard to other underwriting requirements.

CONVENTIONAL LOAN YIELD Savings and loan associations still dominate the conventional mortgage field. Insurance companies, in order to obtain residential conventional loans, are under increasing pressure to lengthen maturities and decrease yields. Thirty-year terms are readily available on new properties in most areas. Interest rates generally run 5 1/2 percent to 5 3/4 percent, with 5 1/4 percent available on prime loans in many areas. Prepayment conditions are being eased considerably, with most loans entirely free of prepayment restrictions after the fifth year. An abundance of funds in savings and loan associations is prompting some to make riskier mortgages than they would otherwise consider. Such has been cited by Joseph P. McMurray, chairman of the Federal Home Loan Bank Board, as a danger which may weaken the entire industry.

Commercial and Industrial Loans, November 1963

Forward investment commitments of life insurance companies continue to reflect strong interest in commercial and industrial mortgages. New commitments of this type totaled $227.6 million in September, or 28.5 percent of the month's total commitments in new investments of all classes. This brought the outstanding commitments in commercial and industrial mortgages to an all-time high of $1.787 million at the end of the third quarter of 1963.

This strong competition for commercial and industrial mortgages by life insurance companies continues to exert strong pressures on rates and terms available. "Shopping" has become much more the order of the day by brokers and developers seeking commitments. Gross rates on such loans secured by prime properties and top credits are generally 5 percent – 5 1/2 percent with servicing fees and commissions making a net return somewhat below this. With lesser credits gross rates generally are 5 1/2 percent and 5 3/4 percent. The competition also is making itself felt in other areas, such as higher ratio loans, longer terms, and more generous prepayment privileges.

Savings and loan association assets on August 30 totaled $102.5 billion, up 15 percent from a year earlier and double the amount of only five years ago. To invest these large deposits, these associations are turning more and more from single-family residential loans to commercial and industrial mortgages. In 1962, 30.1 percent of the new loans made by savings and loan associations were for purposes other than single-family financing as against 20.5 percent of new loans made in 1957. This trend is continuing in 1963 with large investments being made in shopping centers, large apartments, motels, and commercial buildings. While they are obtaining favorable rates on such loans, they are accepting much greater risks than are acceptable to life insurance companies and other institutional investors.

Residential Loans, December 1963

It may be too early to draw conclusions, but it presently appears that President Johnson will continue the Kennedy housing program for at least the next year. Any differences between the two presidents in this area are not expected to be significant in this pre-election period. During both the Eisenhower and Kennedy administrations, President Johnson strongly supported housing and community development programs, and rejection or tempering of these programs would be interpreted unfavorably at this time.

Forecasts of expected private housing starts in 1964 are far from consistent but regardless of the volume of starts, it appears certain that competition for mortgages will be even more severe than in 1963. Savings and loan associations are expected to continue their aggressive mortgage programs that will, in many instances, be enlarged by the use of private mortgage insurance with the Mortgage Guaranty Insurance Company and other mortgage insurers.

To meet savings and loan competition, national banks (already extremely active in the mortgage lending field) are seeking legislation authorizing loans up to 80 percent of valuation and for terms of thirty years. If such legislation is enacted, there may be similar legislation applicable to state banks in many areas.

The year 1963 has seen an accelerating growth of mergers, consolidations, and outright sales involving mortgage banking companies. There are many reasons for this development. The intense competition for mortgages is a factor, but of importance also is the use of automation. With the decreasing supply of government-insured and guaranteed home loans and with savings and loan associations taking over the preponderant share of the conventional residential loan market, many mortgage bankers with limited capitalization or in need of sources for new loans have found it necessary to merge or sell. It is estimated that 90 percent of the mortgage bankers and loan brokers are competing for 15 percent to 18 percent of the available mortgages—a very thin spread for an industry. Life insurance company investors who operate through these loan correspondents find these mergers and consolidations a continuing problem in their operations and are apprehensive as to the future of the small- or medium-sized mortgage companies.

Commercial and Industrial Loans, December 1963

Commercial and industrial loans continue in great demand by life insurance companies and other investors. The demand is expected to continue through 1964. Commercial banks are exerting strong pressure by offering interim financing loans for periods up to three years, thereby limiting the volume of available long-term mortgages on commercial and industrial properties.

The trend with respect to interest rates on prime national credits is downward, that is, the rate now is from 5 percent to 5 1/4 percent. This type of credit generally requires loans in excess of two thirds of valuation.

With strong local credits, the interest rate is generally 5 1/4 percent to 5 3/4 percent. During the past year pension funds have come into the mortgage field with sizeable funds seeking top commercial and industrial mortgages and are exerting strong pressure on terms and interest rates.

SETTING RATES ON DEPOSIT ACCOUNTS

Citizens Federal Savings and Loan Association

In late September 1963, Mr. F. Marion Donahoe, president of Citizens Federal Savings and Loan Association, had to make a recommendation to the board of directors regarding the dividend rate to be paid on savings accounts[1] for the next quarter. He felt that recent events which had left the industry in an unsettled condition made this a particularly complex decision.

History of Citizens Federal

Founded on January 14, 1885, Citizens Federal Savings and Loan Association was, in 1963, one of the largest associations in the savings and loan industry. It was started under a state charter and converted to a federal charter in 1935—three years after Congress established the Federal Home Loan Bank System. Citizens Federal was the oldest savings and loan association in California with a federal charter and had always been a mutual association.[2]

At the end of its first 45 years (1885–1930), Citizens Federal had total assets of $1,750,000; by the end of 1962 its assets had passed the

[1]When one puts money in a savings and loan association technically he is purchasing withdrawable savings shares under the association's charter; the saver is thus a shareholder in the association. On the other hand, a savings account depositor in a bank is a creditor of the bank—it owes him the money he put in.

[2]All federally chartered associations are mutual. Mutual associations have no stockholders; voting rights are held by the savers and borrowers. Each savings account holder of Citizens Federal has one vote for each $100, or portion thereof, in his account, subject to a maximum of fifty votes each. Each borrower has one vote.

Exhibit 1

CITIZENS FEDERAL SAVINGS AND LOAN ASSOCIATION

Balance Sheets

Assets	*6/30/62*	*12/31/62*	*6/30/63*	*7/31/63*	*8/31/63*
First-lien real estate loans	$168,582,267.22	$182,558,299.05	$218,272,256.51	$224,193,803.20	$233,441,958.72
Loans on savings	159,852.41	200,873.58	401,967.54	339,995.00	704,565.61
Real estate owned	66,253.08	36,241.23	35,185.31	–	16,989.94
Investments and securities	19,796,711.14	22,807,367.90	20,751,669.35	21,681,625.03	21,176,978.99
Cash on hand and in banks	2,061,248.90	3,815,119.67	4,484,475.87	877,636.21	940,505.27
Office building (net)	2,604,912.95	2,917,669.76	3,270,319.02	3,333,864.14	3,569,042.91
Office equipment (net)	621,423.51	687,010.47	724,076.49	730,016.19	721,400.04
Other assets	561,816.77	570,576.89	1,335,825.93	1,349,484.01	1,335,025.47
Expenses to date	–	–	–	248,585.35	541,909.86
	$194,454,485.98	$213,593,158.55	$249,275,776.02	$252,755,009.13	$262,448,376.81
Liabilities					
Total savings	$163,232,011.73	$185,232,779.64	$212,986,561.67	$208,271,354.14	$210,077,086.76
Advance payments by borrowers	400,672.51	422,763.56	409,211.82	500,403.01	569,493.80
Borrowed money	7,500,000.00	2,000,000.00	4,000,000.00	10,320,000.00	15,820,000.00
Notes payable—office building	1,000,000.00	1,000,000.00	1,000,000.00	1,000,000.00	1,000,000.00
Loans in process*	9,298,333.05	9,726,924.77	15,332,608.43	16,311,386.52	17,235,382.66
Other liabilities	871,056.85	460,561.80	524,814.17	333,891.18	430,568.94
Reserves and surplus	12,152,411.84	14,750,128.78	15,022,579.93	15,012,505.26	15,004,826.14
Income to date	–	–	–	1,005,469.02	2,311,018.51
	$194,454,485.98	$213,593,158.55	$249,275,776.02	$252,755,009.13	$262,448,376.81

*Commitments made to loan money at some future date. No interest is currently being charged. The *loans in process* must be deducted from *first-lien real estate loans* to find the amount of loans currently earning interest.

Exhibit 2

CITIZENS FEDERAL SAVINGS AND LOAN ASSOCIATION

Operating Statements

Income	*Budget, Second Half of 1962*	*Actual, Second Half of 1962**	*Budget, First Half of 1963*	*Actual, First Half of 1963*	*Budget, Second Half of 1963*	*Actual, July, Aug., 1963 Income and Expense*	*July, Aug., 1963 Percent to Budget*
Interest—loans	$5,579,500	$6,215,494	$5,337,850	$5,714,392	$6,606,095	$1,829,703	83
—investments	309,930	404,111	343,870	315,225	323,800	107,563	100
Loan fees	762,000	756,689	543,000	867,680	750,875	353,483	141
Loan service fees	83,500	85,529	92,750	86,907	84,000	27,975	100
Miscellaneous operating	40,500	51,764	31,100	40,344	39,500	7,103	54
Rental income	47,400	46,198	32,850	36,453	22,590	6,456	86
Nonoperating	–	341,936	–	4,184	–	134	–
Gross income	6,822,830	7,901,721	6,381,420	7,065,185	7,826,860	2,232,417	89
Operating expenses	1,391,760	1,160,256	1,896,050	1,856,474	1,654,660	415,952	75
Net (before interest)	5,431,070	6,741,465	4,485,370	5,208,711	6,172,200	1,916,465	93
Less: interest on advance	152,662	52,127	24,550	33,304	290,000	61,563	64
Net (before dividend)	5,278,408	6,689,338	4,460,820	5,175,407	5,882,200	1,854,902	95
Estimated dividend	4,000,331	4,091,621	4,638,848	4,820,668	4,779,731	1,509,399	95
Net income	1,278,077	2,597,717	(178,028)	354,739	1,102,469	345,503	94
Estimated federal income tax	–	–	–	73,786	229,313	71,865	94
Allocation to reserves	$1,278,077	$2,597,717	$ (178,028)	$ 280,953	$ 873,156	$ 273,638	94

*See Exhibit 3.

$213,000,000 mark. (Exhibits 1, 2, and 3 contain recent financial statements of Citizens Federal.) Much of this growth was internal, although mergers did take place in 1953, 1956, and 1962. The April 1, 1962, merger with First Federal Savings and Loan Association of San Jose was the most significant of the mergers in terms of size. The total assets of First Federal were approximately $50 million at the time of the merger. According to Mr. Donahoe, "This merger marked a consolidation of two associations with similar policies. Competition prompted the merger; it was growing increasingly difficult to compete with the large savings and loan holding companies."[3]

Exhibit 3

CITIZENS FEDERAL SAVINGS AND LOAN ASSOCIATION

Adjusted Operating Statement
Second Half of 1962

	Actual, Second Half of 1962	*Tax Transaction Adjustment*	*Adjusted, Second Half of 1962*
Interest – loans	$6,215,494	$–768,871*	$5,446,623
– investments	404,111	– 80,000†	324,111
Loan fees	756,689		756,689
Loan service fees	85,529		85,529
Miscellaneous operating	51,764		51,764
Rental income	46,198		46,198
Nonoperating	341,936	–237,473‡	104,463
Gross income	7,901,721		6,815,377
Operating expenses	1,160,256	+234,089§	1,394,345
Net (before interest)	6,741,465		5,421,032
Less: interest on advance	52,127		52,127
Net (before dividend)	6,689,338		5,368,905
Dividend	4,091,621		4,091,621
Net income	2,597,717		1,277,284
Estimated federal income tax	0		0
Allocation to reserves	$2,597,717		$1,277,284

*Sale of December loan interest billings.
†Interest from exchange of government bonds.
‡Earned discounts from sale of GI and FHA loans.
§Expenses normally paid in December deferred to January 1963.

NOTE: Net income of savings and loan associations became more fully taxable as of January 1, 1963. Tax transaction adjustments similar to those on this exhibit – increasing 1962 income and minimizing 1962 expenses – were commonly made by associations in anticipation of the new federal tax law.

[3]According to Preston Silbaugh, California savings and loan commissioner, in 1962 the ten largest savings and loan holding companies in California controlled 40 percent of the savings and loans assets in the state.

Development Pattern of the Savings and Loan Industry

The phenomenal growth of the savings and loan industry (see Exhibit 4) had many causes. These included insurance of accounts by the Federal Savings and Loan Insurance Corporation, friendly informal service, aggressive advertising and promotion, and the convenience of branch locations and new offices. Many experts thought that the factor contributing most to the industry's growth record was the dividend rate paid for savings. The average dividend rate had risen steadily since World War II (see Exhibit 5).

In a recent article written for the July 3, 1963, issue of *Financial World,* Joseph P. McMurray, chairman of the Federal Home Loan Bank Board, summarized some of the new and perplexing problems which savings and loan managers faced in 1963. These problems, as he saw them, had grown out of major changes in the economic environment.

> First, the public has demonstrated its intention to maintain a greater proportion of savings than ever before in liquid form.
>
> Second, what otherwise would have been a satisfactory demand for mortgage loans has been outstripped by the unprecedented growth of savings available for mortgage investment during the past two years.
>
> Third, the combined effect of the first two developments has been some decline in interest rates, with yields on mortgages offering one of the more conspicuous examples.
>
> This decline has not been large, but the application of even mild downward pressure on mortgage rates causes a critical stress on earnings under the operation of a fourth factor. This has been the heightened competition for liquid savings, with resultant increases in interest rates on time deposits with the banks and in dividend rates on savings capital placed with savings and loan associations.
>
> The cost of funds is, of course, the largest part of the associations' business expense, currently amounting to 75% of mortgage yield.
> To argue that the current level of dividends must be maintained to meet the competition for savings, when savings flows are abundant, is like saying that one must keep up with the Joneses, and hang the cost!

Savings and loan associations contended with two sets of competitors. For savings, they competed with savings departments of the commercial banks, the industrial thrift companies, the life insurance companies, the securities and bond houses, the mutual funds, and the mutual savings banks in some states. On the loan side, savings and loan associations again competed with the commercial banks and the life insurance companies as well as with mutual savings banks, mortgage companies, pension funds, and with individuals.

During the ten-year period ending December 31, 1962, assets of all

Exhibit 4

CITIZENS FEDERAL SAVINGS AND LOAN ASSOCIATION

Savings in Selected Media, by Years
(in billions of dollars)

Year End	*Savings Associations‡*	*Mutual Savings Banks§*	*Commercial Banks‖*	*Credit Unions#*	*Mutual Funds***	*U.S. Savings Bonds††*	*Postal Savings‡‡*	*Total*
1920	$ 1.7	$ 4.8	$10.5	$*	$. . . .	$. . . .	$ 0.2	$ 17.2
1921	2.0	5.5	11.1	*	. . . .	. . . .	0.1	18.7
1922	2.2	6.0	12.3	*	. . . .	. . . .	0.1	20.6
1923	2.6	6.5	13.7	*	. . . .	. . . .	0.1	22.9
1924	3.2	6.9	15.0	*	. . . .	. . . .	0.1	25.2
1925	3.8	7.3	16.3	*	. . . .	. . . .	0.1	27.5
1926	4.4	7.8	17.2	*	. . . .	. . . .	0.1	29.5
1927	5.0	8.4	18.7	*	. . . .	. . . .	0.1	32.2
1928	5.8	8.7	19.3	*	. . . .	. . . .	0.2	34.0
1929	6.2	8.8	19.2	*	. . . .	. . . .	0.2	34.4
1930	6.3	9.4	18.6	*	. . . .	. . . .	0.2	34.5
1931	5.9	9.9	16.0	*	. . . .	. . . .	0.6	32.4
1932	5.3	9.9	12.1	*	. . . .	. . . .	0.9	28.2
1933	4.8	9.5	11.0	*	. . . .	. . . .	1.2	26.5
1934	4.5	9.7	12.0	*	. . . .	. . . .	1.2	27.4
1935	4.3	9.8	12.9	*	. . . .	0.2	1.2	28.4
1936	4.2	10.0	13.7	0.1	. . . .	0.5	1.3	29.8
1937	4.1	10.1	14.4	0.1	. . . .	1.0	1.3	31.0
1938	4.1	10.2	14.4	0.1	. . . .	1.4	1.3	31.5
1939	4.1	10.5	14.9	0.2	. . . .	1.9	1.3	32.9
1940	4.3	10.6	15.4	0.2	1.1	2.8	1.3	35.7
1941	4.7	10.5	15.5	0.3	0.9	5.4	1.4	38.7
1942	4.9	10.6	16.1	0.3	1.0	13.4	1.5	47.8

Exhibit 4 (Continued)

Year End	*Savings Associ-ations‡*	*Mutual Savings Banks§*	*Commer-cial Banks‖*	*Credit Unions#*	*Mutual Funds***	*U.S. Savings Bonds††*	*Postal Savings‡‡*	*Total*
1943	5.5	11.7	19.0	0.3	1.4	24.7	1.8	64.4
1944	6.3	13.3	23.9	0.4	1.6	36.2	2.4	84.1
1945	7.4	15.3	29.9	0.4	2.3	42.9	3.0	101.2
1946	8.5	16.8	33.4	0.5	2.2	44.2	3.4	109.0
1947	9.8	17.7	34.7	0.5	2.2	46.2	3.5	114.6
1948	11.0	18.4	35.0	0.6	2.3	47.8	3.4	118.5
1949	12.5	19.3	35.1	0.7	2.8	49.3	3.3	123.0
1950	14.0	20.0	35.2	0.9	3.4	49.6	3.0	126.1
1951	16.1	20.9	36.6	1.1	4.1	49.1	2.8	130.7
1952	19.2	22.6	39.3	1.4	4.9	49.2	2.7	139.3
1953	22.8	24.3	42.0	1.7	5.1	49.4	2.5	147.8
1954	27.3	26.3	44.7	2.0	7.3	50.0	2.2	159.8
1955	32.2	28.1	46.3	2.4	9.0	50.2	2.0	170.2
1956	37.1	30.0	48.5	2.9	10.3	50.1	1.7	180.6
1957	41.9	31.7	53.7	3.4	9.9	48.2	1.4	190.2
1958	48.0	34.0	60.0	3.9	14.8	47.7	1.2	209.6
1959	54.6	34.9	62.9	4.4	17.5	45.9	1.0	221.2
1960	62.1	36.3	67.1	5.0	18.2	45.7	0.8	235.2
1961	70.9	38.3	74.8	5.7	24.9	46.4	0.7	261.7
1962†	80.4	41.3	88.1	6.3	23.1	46.9	0.5	286.6

*Less than $100 million.
†Preliminary.
‡Savings accounts, deposits, and investment certificates, exclusive of shares of pledges against mortgage loans and investments of U.S. government.
§Regular and special savings accounts.
‖Time and savings deposits of individuals, partnerships, and corporations.
#Shares and members' deposits.
**Net assets of closed- and open-end investment companies.
††Current redemption value of bonds held by individuals.
‡‡Outstanding principal and accrued interest on certificates of deposit.

SOURCE: *Fact Book, 1963*, United States Savings and Loan League, Chicago, Illinois.

Exhibit 5

CITIZENS FEDERAL SAVINGS AND LOAN ASSOCIATION

Average Annual Yield on Selected Types of Investments

Year	*Savings Accounts in Savings Associations*	*Savings Deposits in Mutual Savings Banks*	*Time and Savings Deposits in Commercial Banks*	*United States Government Bonds*	*State and Local Bonds*	*Corporate (Aaa) Bonds*
1930	5.3%	4.5%	3.9%	3.3%	4.1%	4.5%
1931	5.1	4.4	3.8	3.3	4.0	4.6
1932	4.1	4.0	3.4	3.7	4.6	5.0
1933	3.4	3.4	3.4	3.3	4.7	5.5
1934	3.5	3.1	3.0	3.1	4.0	4.0
1935	3.1	2.7	2.6	2.7	3.4	3.6
1936	3.2	2.5	2.0	2.5	3.1	3.2
1937	3.5	2.4	1.8	2.6	3.1	3.3
1938	3.5	2.3	1.7	2.6	2.9	3.2
1939	3.4	2.2	1.6	2.4	2.8	3.0
1940	3.3	2.0	1.3	2.2	2.5	2.8
1941	3.1	1.9	1.3	2.0	2.1	2.8
1942	3.0	1.9	1.1	2.5	2.4	2.8
1943	2.9	1.9	0.9	2.5	2.1	2.7
1944	2.8	1.8	0.9	2.5	1.8	2.6
1945	2.5	1.7	0.8	2.4	1.7	2.5
1946	2.4	1.7	0.8	2.2	1.6	2.4
1947	2.3	1.7	0.9	2.3	2.3	2.9
1948	2.3	1.8	0.9	2.4	2.3	2.8
1949	2.3	1.9	0.9	2.3	2.1	2.6
1950	2.5	2.0	0.9	2.3	2.0	2.6
1951	2.6	2.1	1.1	2.6	2.0	2.9
1952	2.7	2.4	1.1	2.7	2.2	2.9
1953	2.8	2.5	1.1	2.9	2.8	3.2
1954	2.9	2.6	1.3	2.5	2.4	2.9
1955	2.9	2.7	1.4	2.8	2.6	3.1
1956	3.0	2.8	1.6	3.1	2.9	3.4
1957	3.3	3.0	2.1	3.5	3.6	3.9
1958	3.37	3.17	2.21	3.43	3.36	3.79
1959	3.53	3.53	2.36	4.07	3.74	4.38
1960	3.84	3.63	2.56	4.01	3.69	4.41
1961	3.90	3.74	2.71	3.90	3.60	4.35
1962	4.11*	4.07	3.18	3.95	3.30	4.33

*Estimated.

SOURCE: *Fact Book, 1963,* United States Savings and Loan League, Chicago, Illinois.

savings and loan associations in the United States increased at an average rate of better than 15 percent per year. During this same period, California savings and loan associations grew at an average rate of 23 percent per year. By the middle of 1963, the assets of California associations amounted to $16.5 billion of the $100 billion total for all United States associations.

Following World War II the pent-up demand for housing and the related opportunity to finance housing had prompted California associations, including Citizens Federal, to promote the acquisition of savings in unprecedented amounts. The dividend rates paid by California associations typically had been higher than those in other states. Citizens' management noted that it had always been possible in the past to lend out its money profitably.

By 1963, company executives believed that the supply of housing was becoming more in balance with demand, and therefore, they believed that the emphasis in the future would be devoted to increasing the penetration of the loan market. It seemed to Citizens' management that this could be done by giving better service, lending for longer terms, and lending higher percentages of value. But there were limits! Price was an extremely important factor. Historically, savings and loan associations had charged more for their loans, on the average, than had their principal competitors—the banks, the life insurance companies, and the mortgage companies. In the long run, Citizens' executives believed that the savings and loan industry could increase its penetration of the loan market substantially only at lower rates of interest—rates closer to those of outside competitors.

By September 1963, management of Citizens had noted the following signs of a shift of emphasis from attracting savings to expanding the loan side of the business:

1. Lowering of dividend rates paid to savers by most associations in the San Francisco Bay Area and San Diego and by several associations throughout other sections of the country.
2. Changes in laws and regulations to permit
   a. loans meeting certain restrictive qualifications up to 90 percent of value on single-family houses;
   b. a greater percent of an association's assets to be invested in multiple units—buildings with more than the traditional one to four family units:
   c. land development loans;
   d. loans, to a limited extent, more than fifty miles from the home office of an association;
   e. broader authority for making loans on senior citizens and urban-renewal developments.
3. Discussions of changes that would allow savings and loan associ-

ations to make home appliance loans and personal loans and to buy municipal bonds.

The management of Citizens was convinced that in the long run the savings and loan associations in California and in the rest of the country as well would have to adjust to the new economic facts of life, pay less for savings, charge less for loans, and accept a slower growth rate.

Factors Affecting Rate Decision

The management team thought that setting dividend rates involved more than merely deciding what rate was justified by the net earnings of the association. It felt that an association must try to guess what its competitors would do. It had to consider the association's reserve position and its effectiveness in attracting new loan business and new savings accounts. The executives of the association also felt an attempt should be made to estimate how good business would be in the future and

Exhibit 6

CITIZENS FEDERAL SAVINGS AND LOAN ASSOCIATION

Dividend Rates

	First Quarter 1962	*Second Quarter 1962*	*Third Quarter 1962*	*Fourth Quarter 1962*	*First Quarter 1963*	*Second Quarter 1963*	*Third Quarter 1963*
Berkeley S&L (Berkeley)	4.6%	4.75%	4.75%	4.75%	4.8%	4.8%	4.5%
California Savings (S.F.)	4.6%	4.75%	4.75%	4.75%	4.8%	4.8%	4.8%
Citizens Federal (S.F.)	4.6%	4.6%	4.75%	4.75%	4.8%	4.8%	4.5%
First S&L (Oakland)	4.6%	4.75%	4.75%	4.75%	4.8%	4.8%	4.5%
Guaranty S&L (San Jose)	4.6%	4.75%	4.75%	4.75%	4.8%	4.8%	4.5%
Home Mutual (S.F.)	4.6%	4.75%	4.75%	4.75%	4.8%	4.8%	4.5%
Lytton (Palo Alto)	4.6%	4.6%	4.8%	4.8%	4.8%	4.8%	4.85%
Pioneer Investors (San Jose)	4.6%	4.75%	4.75%	4.75%	4.8%	4.8%	4.5%
Security S&L (S.F)	4.6%	4.75%	4.75%	4.75%	4.8%	4.8%	4.8%

SOURCE: Individual institutions.

Exhibit 6 (Continued)

Savings Accounts
(in millions of dollars)

	March 31 1962	*June 30 1962*	*Sept. 30 1962*	*Dec. 31 1962*	*March 31 1963*	*June 30 1963*	*Sept. 30 1963**
Berkeley S&L (Berkeley)	$105.2	$112.6	$121.5	$128.9	$143.6	$151.7	$154.0
California Savings (S.F.)	46.2	48.7	52.1	54.8	58.7	61.1	66.0
Citizens Federal (S.F.)	159.8	163.2	174.7	185.2	204.3	213.0	213.0
First S&L (Oakland)	140.0	147.0	156.2	165.8	178.9	183.6	183.6
Guaranty S&L (San Jose)	101.4	107.5	114.3	122.4	132.6	137.8	137.8
Home Mutual (S.F.)	126.2	139.0	149.1	156.4	167.6	177.7	177.7
Lytton (Palo Alto)	28.8	30.0	38.5	45.2	55.4	65.5	85.0
Pioneer Investors (San Jose)	278.9	294.7	317.7	334.9	366.7	383.3	390.0
Security S&L (S.F.)	89.4	94.1	100.0	107.5	118.2	124.0	135.0

*Estimated by Citizens Federal.

SOURCE: California State Divison of Savings and Loan.

whether interest rates were rising or falling. Some elaboration on these factors follows.

Competition

Citizens' management believed that the most important short-run factor in setting savings dividend rates was the action of competitors. It believed that a rate of 4.5 percent should be high enough to attract adequate savings in competition with banks and other traditional competitors for savings. In the opinion of the management at Citizens Federal, the higher rates now paid by savings and loan associations could not and need not continue in relation to traditional competitors. At the same time, it noted that the California savings and loan industry was experiencing now, more than ever, intra-industry competition – especially rate competition on savings.

Recent dividend rates paid and the corresponding amounts of savings accounts are shown in Exhibits 6 and 7 for the major savings and loan associations in the San Francisco Bay Area. Company executives were condering what conclusions might be drawn from these figures regarding the elasticity of the total savings of an association.

Exhibit 7

CITIZENS FEDERAL SAVINGS AND LOAN ASSOCIATION

Change in Savings Accounts
(in millions of dollars)

	3/31/62 to 6/30/62	*6/30/62 to 9/30/62*	*9/30/62 to 12/31/62*	*12/31/62 to 3/31/63*	*3/31/63 to 6/30/63*	*6/30/63 to 9/30/63**
Berkeley S&L (Berkeley)	$7.4	$8.9	$7.4	$14.7	$8.1	$2.3
California Savings (S.F.)	2.5	3.4	2.7	3.9	2.4	4.9
Citizens Federal (S.F.)	3.4	11.5	10.5	19.1	8.7	–
First S&L (Oakland)	7.0	9.2	9.6	13.1	4.7	–
Guaranty S&L (San Jose)	6.1	6.8	8.1	10.2	5.2	–
Home Mutual (S.F.)	12.8	10.1	7.3	11.2	10.1	–
Lytton (Palo Alto)	1.2	8.5	6.7	10.2	10.1	19.5
Pioneer Investors (San Jose)	15.8	23.0	17.2	31.8	16.6	6.7
Security S&L (S.F.)	4.7	5.9	7.5	10.7	5.8	11.0

Change in Savings Accounts
(in percentage)

	3/31/62 to 6/30/62	*6/30/62 to 9/30/62*	*9/30/62 to 12/31/62*	*12/31/62 to 3/31/63*	*3/31/63 to 6/30/63*	*6/30/63 to 9/30/63**
Berkeley S&L (Berkeley)	7.0%	7.9%	6.1%	11.4%	5.6%	1.5%
California Savings (S.F.)	5.4	7.0	5.2	7.1	4.1	8.0
Citizens Federal (S.F.)	2.1	7.0	6.0	10.3	4.3	–
First S&L (Oakland)	5.0	6.3	6.1	7.9	2.6	–
Guaranty S&L (San Jose)	6.0	6.3	7.1	8.3	3.9	–
Home Mutual (S.F.)	10.1	7.3	4.9	7.2	6.0	–
Lytton (Palo Alto)	4.2	28.3	17.4	22.6	18.2	29.8
Pioneer Investors (San Jose)	5.7	7.8	5.4	9.5	4.5	1.7
Security S&L (S.F.)	5.3	6.3	7.5	10.0	4.9	8.9

*Estimated by Citizens Federal.

General Reserves and Liquidity Requirements

All savings and loan associations had to maintain adequate reserves against possible losses. Under federal and state regulations the minimum amount of reserves plus earned surplus (for all but new associations) was 5 percent of savings. There was no maximum, but few associations allowed their reserves to approach 12 percent of savings, because above this point drastically higher federal income taxes were payable. Citizens Federal had a policy of maintaining general reserves and surplus at a minimum of 7 percent of savings.

All members of the Federal Home Loan Bank system were required to maintain liquid assets at a minimum of 7 percent of savings accounts. The definition of liquid assets included cash and unpledged obligations of the United States.

Advances from the Federal Home Loan Bank

Advances from the Federal Home Loan Bank were available to member institutions. As of September 1963, the FHLB Board limited advances of general use to 17 1/2 percent of savings accounts. Advances could be obtained on either a short-term or long-term basis; terms ranged from a period of less than thirty days up to a maximum of five years. As of September 1963, the interest charge on advances was 3.75 percent. This rate was subject to change at the discretion of the FHLB Board. The declared policy of the FHLB was to base the rate on its own borrowing cost in the open market. The present policy of the FHLB allowed a member to repay advances before they were due with, at most, only a nominal charge.

Citizens' management felt that there was an evolution in attitudes with respect to borrowing from the FHLB. It held the opinion that in the past advances were looked upon solely as a borrowing device to get out of a tight corner, but that now advances were beginning to be seen as a source of permanent capital. Although Citizens Federal had not been a big user of advances in the past, management wanted to make more use of them. The present policy was to borrow an amount between 10 and 15 percent of savings accounts.

Over recent months the amount of advances has fluctuated widely. For example, in July 1963, following the lowering of dividend rates by Citizens Federal, there was a net reduction in the amount of savings accounts. Citizens Federal took up the slack with additional advances from the FHLB (see Exhibit 1). Since Citizens Federal had a substantial amount of unused borrowing capacity as of September 1963, the association would be able to obtain additional advances if necessary.

Supervisory Opinion

Citizens Federal, like other federally chartered associations, was examined and supervised by the officers of the Federal Home Loan Bank.

The supervisors were directly concerned with the safety, solvency, and liquidity of the associations they supervised. Joseph McMurray, chairman of the Federal Home Loan Bank Board, for several months had been personally spearheading a drive to get savings and loan associations to cut the dividends they paid. He argued that this would lessen the temptation for associations to make risky, high-interest loans that could jeopardize their soundness. His theory was that if savings and loan associations paid less for savings, the associations would be inclined to charge less for loans, helping more people buy better homes and giving the economy a boost too.

Quality of Loans

The management of Citizens Federal felt that the borrower's character, his ability to pay, and his past credit record were important factors upon which the quality of a mortgage loan depended. It noted that, in the recent years of rising property values and stable employment, loans were made by some lenders despite below average credit standing or uncertain prospects on the part of the borrower.

Delinquency ratios often provided early indications of the quality of recent loans. Exhibit 8 shows the percentage of mortgage loans which were delinquent six months or longer as of 1959, among the 221 reporting associations in the Stanford Research Institute survey. As shown by Exhibits 8 and 9, the experience of Citizens Federal compared very

Exhibit 8

CITIZENS FEDERAL SAVINGS AND LOAN ASSOCIATION

Trends in Loan Delinquencies by Area and Type of Charter

	California Total	*Southern California State*	*Southern California Federal*	*Northern California State*	*Northern California Federal*
Number of reporting associations	221	91	40	75	15
Total balance due on mortgage loans that were delinquent 6 months or longer at the end of 1959 (thousands)	$12,686	$5,447	$4,347	$2,178	$714
Total balance due on all mortgage loans at end of 1959 (millions)	$ 7,202	$3,149	$2,559	$1,124	$370
Delinquent loan balances as a percent of total loan balances at the end of 1959	0.18%	0.17%	0.17%	0.19%	0.19%

SOURCE: *The Savings and Loan Industry in California*, Stanford Research Institute.

Exhibit 9

CITIZENS FEDERAL SAVINGS AND LOAN ASSOCIATION

Report of Delinquent Loans of Citizens Federal

	July 1962	*Oct. 1962*	*Jan. 1963*	*Feb. 1963*	*March 1963*	*April 1963*	*May 1963*	*June 1963*	*July 1963*	*Aug. 1963*
BY PERCENT OF TOTAL NUMBER OF LOAN										
Two months or less	1.05	0.59	0.92	0.96	0.92	0.95	0.94	1.11	0.78	0.98
Three months	0.12	0.09	0.08	0.05	0.11	0.06	0.06	0.08	0.06	0.04
Over three months	0.08	0.21	0.12	0.14	0.14	0.15	0.09	0.14	0.11	0.08
Total	1.25	0.89	1.12	1.15	1.17	1.16	1.09	1.33	0.95	1.10
BY PERCENT OF TOTAL LOAN BALANCE										
Three months	0.12	0.09	0.10	0.07	0.30	0.06	0.08	0.18	0.07	0.04
Over three months	0.07	0.16	0.10	0.15	0.14	0.18	0.06	0.13	0.23	0.21

favorably with the industry figures and management was pleased with Citizens' unusually low rate of loan delinquencies. It felt that it was directly attributable to the conservative loan policies which Citizens Federal had followed.

One of the most important elements of risk in mortgage lending, according to authorities in the field, may be expressed in the *loan to appraised value* ratio. This ratio may be defined as the amount of money loaned on a first mortgage as a percent of the appraised value of the property securing the loan.

The degree of potential risk to a lender was generally greater with high loan to value ratios than it was with low ratios for two major reasons. First, when the mortgage loan balance was close to the appraised value of the property, the borrower's equity in the property was usually small. He had less money to lose in the case of foreclosure, and therefore, had less incentive to keep up his payments in time of personal difficulty and/or declining property values. Second, as the loan approached the value of the property, the lender had less of a safety cushion against declining real estate prices. In the event he had to foreclose and sell the property, the risk increased that the unpaid balance on the loan would be higher than the selling price.

A study conducted by the Stanford Research Institute indicated that the amount loaned to appraised market value for state-chartered associations in California ran at a fairly constant level between 68 and 70 percent from 1956 through 1959. No later state-wide statistics were available, but it was generally agreed that loan to appraisal ratios had increased considerably since 1959. The recent experience of Citizens Federal is shown in Exhibit 10.

Exhibit 10

CITIZENS FEDERAL SAVINGS AND LOAN ASSOCIATION

Recapitulation of Loans Made by Percent of Appraisal
(rounded to nearest thousand)

Dollars	*July 1962*	*Oct. 1962*	*Jan. 1963*	*Feb. 1963*	*March 1963*	*April 1963*	*May 1963*	*June 1963*	*July 1963*	*Aug. 1963*
PERCENT TO APPRAISAL										
Under 66%	$ 316	$1,506	$ 407	$2,264	$ 400	$ 411	$ 356	$ 318	$ 2,558	$ 570
66%–75%	359	430	889	1,416	1,708	2,113	3,266	1,601	1,662	2,139
71%–75%	3,326	2,778	3,768	2,895	3,880	1,967	1,752	3,088	1,883	2,828
76%–80%	4,179	2,208	2,767	2,651	4,077	5,540	4,231	4,249	5,354	7,521
VA, FHA over 80%	203	242	4,675	–	45	435	247	193	196	118
Conventional over 80%	389	224	201	132	57	96	64	107	60	64
Total	$8,772	$7,388	$12,707	$9,358	$10,167	$10,562	$9,916	$9,556	$11,713	$13,240

Percent	*July 1962*	*Oct. 1962*	*Jan. 1963*	*Feb. 1963*	*March 1963*	*April 1963*	*May 1963*	*June 1963*	*July 1963*	*Aug. 1963*
PERCENT TO APPRAISAL										
Under 66%	3.6	20.3	3.2	24.2	3.9	3.9	3.6	3.3	21.8	4.3
66%–70%	4.1	5.8	7.0	15.1	16.8	20.0	32.9	16.7	14.2	16.2
61%–75%	37.9	37.6	29.7	30.9	38.2	18.6	17.7	32.3	16.1	21.4
76%–80%	47.7	29.9	21.8	28.3	40.1	52.4	42.7	44.5	45.7	56.8
VA, FHA over 80%	2.3	3.3	36.8	–	0.4	4.1	2.5	2.0	1.7	0.9
Conventional over 80%	4.4	3.0	1.6	1.4	0.6	0.9	0.6	1.1	0.5	0.5
Total*	100.0	100.0	100.0	100.0	100.0	100.0	100.0	100.0	100.0	100.0

*Variation from 100 due to rounding.

General Conditions

Citizens' management felt that dividend rates in the long run necessarily depended upon loan rates. Selected loan rates for the past year in the San Francisco area are shown in Exhibit 11. Management was anticipating that general business would continue good into 1964 and that interest rates on loans would gradually rise in the next several months. It also felt that Citizens Federal had most of its assets working and was in a good position to put new money to work promptly in loans of good quality.

Recent Events

Recent events had left the savings and loan business in California in an unsettled condition. On May 24, 1963, Donald White, financial editor of the *San Francisco Examiner*, had written:

> It seems to be a foregone conclusion that several, if not all, of the savings and loan associations will lower their dividend rate on investments from the current 4.8 percent to something less by July.
>
> The question is, which one will make the first move to the lower rates, obviously an unpleasant decision since associations like to make loud noises when they raise but prefer to lower rates quietly.
>
> The associations are caught in a bind between the high rates they pay for money left with them and the rate at which they are able to invest that money in mortgages. Something has to give and in this case it will be the investors in the California associations who have been getting the highest rates for the savings in the U.S.
>
> A trend to lower dividend rates on savings accounts has already started in other parts of the country and is headed this way. One of the big associations in Phoenix, First Federal Savings and Loan, earlier this week announced plans to cut its dividend rate to 4 percent from 4.5 percent effective July 1.

The question of which institution would be the first in California to lower rates was answered in short order. On May 27, 1963, Beverly Hills Federal Savings and Loan Association announced it would cut its dividend rate on savings accounts from 4.8 percent to 4.6 percent. According to *The Wall Street Journal:*

> Bart Lytton, Chairman of Beverly Hills Federal, said the institution is making the cut "to trigger a general downward rate move in Los Angeles." He said the association announced its intention well in advance "to give others a chance to follow. If we had waited until right before the end of the quarter, our cut couldn't have any effect because the others would be locked into their positions, with advertising and policies, etc." While conceding the association, in making the cut, "is fully motivated by the desire to make more profit," Mr. Lytton added another reason for the reduction is "to

Exhibit 11

CITIZENS FEDERAL SAVINGS AND LOAN ASSOCIATION

Mortage Market Quotations for San Francisco Area

	Construction Loans (Interest + Fees)				*Conventional Loans*	
	Commercial Banks, Insurance Companies	*S & L's*	*Banks, Insurance, Mortgage Companies*	*S & L's*	*FHA 5 1/4s*	*VA 5 1/4s*
May 11, 1962	6 + 1–1 1/2	6–6.6 + 2–3	5 3/4–6	6–6 3/4	97	97
August 10, 1962	6 + 1 1/2	6–6.6 + 2–3	5 3/4–6	6–6.6	97–97 1/2	97 1/2–98
November 9, 1962	6 + 1–1 1/2	6–6.6 + 2–3	5 3/4–6	6–6.6	97 1/2–98	98–98 1/2
March 8, 1963	6 + 1–1 1/2	6–6.6 + 2–3	5 1/2–6	6–6.6	98–98 1/2	98 1/2–99
June 7, 1963	5 3/4–6 + 1–1 1/2	6–6.6 + 1 1/2–2 1/2	5 1/2–6	5 3/4–6.5	98–98 1/2	98 1/2–99
September 6, 1963	5 3/4–6 + 1–1 1/2	6–6.6 + 1 1/2–3	5 1/2–6	5 3/4–6.5	98–98 1/2	98 1/2

SOURCE: *House & Home.*

cooperate with the chairman of the Federal Home Loan Bank board, who is urgent and vigorous in persuading the industry to bring savings rates down." Joseph P. McMurray, bank board chairman, "feels high California rates have competitively forced other associations in the country to pay more than they can afford now that they have to pay taxes, and he's been nudging us all to recast our rate approach," Mr. Lytton said.

San Francisco associations also have indicated they are anxious to cut rates from the 4.8% level, but have been waiting for large Los Angeles associations to give impetus to the move.

The management at Citizens Federal Savings had considered three actions on interest rates in June: (1) continue the present policy of paying 4.8 percent interest on all savings accounts; (2) continue the 4.8 percent rate, but restrict the acceptance of new accounts; (3) reduce the rate to 4.5 percent on all savings. On June 21, 1963, the *San Francisco Chronicle* reported their decision:

Four of the Bay Area's largest savings and loan associations (including Citizens Federal) yesterday reduced their dividend (interest) rates on savings accounts from 4.8 to 4.5 percent for the third quarter of the year.

Other leading S & L's throughout the area—though not all—are expected to follow.

The *San Francisco Examiner* reported the rate reduction as follows:

For more than a month now indications were that the rate would be reduced to either 4.5 percent of 4.6 percent. As recently as last April 27, a member of the Federal Home Loan Bank Board urged member associations to "consider rate reductions."

The move to lower rates here was prompted for the most part by the reduction of at least 1% in the interest rate on good quality home mortgage loans. "We used to get 6-3/4% and 7% for prime loans," an industry spokesman said, adding; "now it's down to 5 3/4 and 6%."

On June 25, 1963, Mr. Bart Lytton announced a boost in dividend rates from 4.8 to 4.85 percent at Lytton Savings of northern California, which had offices in Palo Alto and Oakland. He also reported that Beverly Hills Federal was rescinding its reduction announced the previous month and would pay 4.8 percent. Mr. Lytton had explained, "We found ourselves in a rate war and we mean to protect our own substantial savings gains from rate raids." He was referring to the fact that in the previous week southern California subsidiaries of two holding companies had announced increases. In addition, several smaller southern California savings and loans had raised their rates. In effect, the Lytton boost established a triple rate in the San Francisco Bay Area for the third quarter of 1963, with some S&L's paying 4.85 percent, some 4.8 percent, and some 4.5 percent.

Shortly after the Lytton announcement, Mr. Donahoe was quoted in San Francisco newspapers, reaffirming the decision of Citizens Federal to reduce rates. "Those going down are convinced they are doing the right thing. We think our rate is the only sound one based on the present savings and home loan picture in the Bay Area."

In mid-September an article that appeared in the *San Francisco News Call Bulletin* reflected some of the most current news and gossip in the industry:

> It looks like 4.8 or 4.85 pct. might become the prevailing savings and loan dividend rate in San Francisco for the quarter beginning October 1. It's now mixed, starting with 4.5 pct.
>
> This seems to be the dominant thinking of the leaders in the industry attending an annual 3-day California Savings & Loan League convention here.
>
> This seems to be the dominant thinking of the leaders in the industry attending an annual 3-day California Savings & Loan League convention here.
>
> With the final quarter close at hand, an undercurrent of dividend jitters permeates the confab with everyone wondering what the other fellow is going to do.
>
> In many instances, board meetings usually held about now to decide the crucial issue have been postponed until next week.
>
> "It looks like another cliff-hanger," one executive said.
>
> Some associations in San Francisco which wanted to be "statesmen" by going to 4.5 pct. July 1 took a terrific beating.
>
> The scuttlebutt has it that one S&L already has decided to move back to 4.8—or possibly even 4.85 pct.
>
> That would trigger a general increase, probably to the higher figure, leaders in the industry believe.
>
> The Los Angeles situation became volatile when State Mutual SmL went to 5 pct. July 1 while authorities were trying to sell the virtues of cutting from 4.8 to 4.5 pct.
>
> They laughed at first. But State Mutual is reported to have taken in some $60 million in new savings, pushing its assets up from around $120 million to about $200 million in a few months.
>
> "They got money coming out of their ears and can't get it out fast enough," one competitor complained.
>
> "They got a lion by the tail and can't let go," he observed.

As he pondered over the local dividend rate situation, Mr. Donahoe realized that selecting a dividend rate to recommend to his board was unusually difficult.

According to the grapevine, all of the other associations that cut their dividend rates from 4.8 percent to 4.5 percent on July 1, 1963, were probably going back up to a higher rate. In fact, it seemed that 4.85 percent would be the most common rate in the last quarter. He suspected that one or more of the smaller, marginal associations would announce 5 percent, to retain the rate advantage they had enjoyed during the third quarter. Mr. Donahoe believed, from past experience, that the majority of the larger, better-known associations could "live with" the situation if they all paid a rate slightly below that of the smaller associations. Their growth would be slow, but it would be steady. On the other hand, he felt that one association, trying to stand alone at a lower rate, would suffer constant net withdrawals, at an unknown, and possibly disasterous, rate.

Mr. Donahoe knew that Citizens had almost no foreclosed real estate on its books. Although reliable and complete information was hard to come by, he believed that Citizens' delinquency rate was running around one tenth that of several principal competitors. He knew that Citizens not only had all of its available money working in loans, but had developed a considerable momentum in producing new loans. He believed earnings of the next quarter would permit the higher rate, even though in his opinion the 4.5 percent-rate was more sound for the business.

Supervisory authorities had threatened action—possibly a dividend rate ceiling or stiffer reserve requirements—but Mr. Donahoe also knew such threats had been made before at various critical times, but without action. Even if action were initiated, it would take months to eventuate into new regulations.

Mr. Donahoe, as manager of a mutual association, wondered just where his primary obligation lay in recommending a dividend rate for the last quarter. Shareholders wanted maximum returns, with complete safety, complete availability. The general public, too, wanted high returns on their money, along with low rates on mortgages. Supervisors wanted completely safe, trouble-free operations. Other government departments wanted ample real-estate credit, but at low interest rates to stimulate business. Employees wanted good pay, security, pleasant working conditions. Mr. Donahoe reflected that he and his directors were in a position of trusteeship—trusteeship not only toward the savers, whose money they used, but toward the Federal Savings and Loan Insurance Corporation, which assumed the ultimate risk for all insured associations. The rate of associations' growth affected all these claimants, one way or another. With all these conflicting needs and desires by interested groups, Mr. Donahoe knew he had a tough decision to make.

ACQUIRING CONTROL OF A MUTUAL ASSOCIATION

Evergreen Savings & Loan Association

In March 1955, Mr. R. H. Taylor was faced with the necessity of making an immediate decision on whether to invest $18,000 (and subsequently much of his time) to obtain control of Evergreen Savings & Loan Association, an almost defunct mutual association which after 39 years of operation had total assets of only $240,000.

Background on Mr. Taylor

Mr. Taylor was a native of Dunster, Washington, where Evergreen was located: he was 33 years old, hence 6 years younger than Evergreen. His father was a prominent businessman, building contractor, and owner of the city's largest hardware store. R. H. Taylor's education at the University of Washington was interrupted by service in the U.S. Navy during World War II; later (in 1947) he earned an M.B.A. from a well-known eastern school of business administration. He returned to work for his father for a year, then, with his father's financial backing, Mr. Taylor started Falmouth Finance Co., a small-loan firm in a nearby city. This venture was successful, and the business was expanded to include the financing of installment sales. In 1951 a second office was opened in Dunster. In 1954, Mr. Taylor and a partner formed the Far West Mortgage Company, a mortgage brokerage which Mr. Taylor hoped one day would cover the entire Northwest: in the meantime, Far West's profitability was just enough to support the partner who worked there full-time.

For several years Mr. Taylor had been interested in managing a savings and loan association. In 1951 his attempt to open a savings and loan association in a new shopping center in Seattle had been thwarted by the establishment there of a branch of a large mutual savings bank. Since 1952 Mr. Taylor had been negotiating to obtain control of Evergreen; in 1953 he had begun attempts to charter a new S & L in a Seattle suburb, without definite results.

In describing himself, Mr. Taylor wrote:

> . . . the writer is a strong advocate of the free enterprise, private capitalistic profit-seeking economy. Should he associate with Evergreen, it will not be in a philanthropic role. Rather, his performance will be motivated by completely responsible and enlightened objectives for personal gain, as well as his desire to establish and develop a strong business entity in the savings industry.

Background on Evergreen

Evergreen Savings & Loan Association was a state mutual S & L chartered in 1916 in Dunster, Washington. From its inception until 1948, Evergreen was managed by Adam Falk, who controlled the shareholders' proxies. Described by a friend as a "reprobate reactionary," Mr. Falk had strong opinions on the role of government in business. He refused to have Evergreen join either the Federal Home Loan Bank or the Federal S & L Insurance Corp. Mr. Falk had other business interests, and he managed the Association in his spare time with the part-time assistance of Mrs. Mary Reing. Evergreen had an unusual third floor office approximately 10 feet wide and 50 feet long, located far from the center of town. When Adam Falk died in 1948, Evergreen had total assets of only $135,000.

Upon Adam's death, his son David returned to Dunster and assumed his father's positions of director, secretary-treasurer, and manager of Evergreen. David also carried on his father's none-too-successful real estate and insurance business in an office next door. Under David Falk's management Evergreen began to grow in 1951, and by the end of 1954 total assets had risen to $240,000 (see Exhibit 1).

Exhibit 1

EVERGREEN SAVINGS & LOAN ASSOCIATION

December 31 Balance Sheets, 1951 – 1954

Assets	*1951*	*1952*	*1953*	*1954*
First mortgage loans	$111,559	$149,659	$170,121	$182,487
Passbook loans	624	200	730	0
Real-estate contracts	150	2,584	2,440	8,805
FHLB stock	1,600	2,300	3,100	3,600
U.S. government bonds	25,000	25,000	25,000	25,000
Cash	19,951	9,698	18,216	15,553
Leasehold equipment, furniture and fixtures, less depreciation	1,818	3,887*	4,074*	4,113*
	$160,702	$193,328	$223,681	$239,558

Liabilities				
Savings of members	$149,940	$179,202	$215,944	$220,484
Borrowed money	0	7,000	0	10,000
Loans and contracts in process	6,532	1,375	1,298	1,082
Contingent fund and undivided profit	4,239	5,751	6,369	7,759
Other liabilities	0	0	70	233
	$160,702	$193,328	$223,681	$239,558

*Net of depreciation amount to $200.

David did not entirely share his late father's philosophy, and soon after taking over Evergreen he did affiliate with the Federal Home Loan Bank. In early 1952, he put out a "feeler" on the possibilities of insuring the association's savings. The FSLIC's informal reply held out no hope of insurance for the following reasons:

1. The ratio of expenses to gross operating income of 54% in 1951 was too high (see Exhibit 2),

Exhibit 2

EVERGREEN SAVINGS & LOAN ASSOCIATION

Statements of Operation, 1951–1954

Gross Operating Income	*1951*	*1952*	*1953*	*1954*
Interest				
Mortgage loans	$5,843	$ 8,304	$ 9,553	$11,020
Passbook loans	24	26	3	18
Real-estate contracts	4	45	158	210
U.S. bonds	625	625	625	625
Appraisal and legal fees and service charges	720	1,275	895	1,653
Other fees and fines	50	158	99	93
FHLB dividends	19	31	43	63
Miscellaneous income	109	9	80	152
	$7,394	$10,473	$11,456	$13,834

Operating Expenses				
Compensation to directors, officers, and employees	$1,375	$1,743	$1,872	$2,187
Rent, light, and heat	1,179	921	1,198	1,927
Advertising	531	1,398	1,273	1,224
Equipment and furniture, repairs, etc.	20	284	196	250
Stationery, printing, office supplies	151	59	260	430
Telephone, postage, and express	272	217	496	542
Insurance and bond premiums	95	30	296	335
Supervisory examinations and assessments	94	106	142	120
Organization dues, donations, subscriptions	124	193	259	170
Other expenses	151	258	107	180
Interest on borrowed money	0	0	142	0
	$3,992	$5,209	$6,241	$7,365
Net income for year	$3,402	$5,264	$5,215	$6,469
Dividends on savings		$3,752	$4,597	$5,080
Reserves and undivided profits		1,512	618	1,389
		$5,264	$5,215	$6,469

2. reserves and undivided profits were only 2.8% of savings (see Exhibit 1),

3. slow loans comprised 11.2% of the mortgage portfolio,

4. expenses exceeded the 2 1/2%-of-gross-assets legal limitation by $320 during 1951,

5. 10 new loans made in 1951 each exceeded the 2%-of-total assets limitation (approximately $3 thousand maximum),

6. The "leniency" which could sometimes be shown with regard to newly chartered associations would be inappropriate in the case of an association which had shown so little progress in 36 years of existence.

As the result of an April examination, the State Supervisor of the Division of S & L in early May 1954 wrote Mr. Falk a fairly strongly worded letter pointing out the following weaknesses in Evergreen:

1. Expenses were running 54% of gross operating income compared to a national average[1] of 32%.

2. Advertising expense ($1273) equal to 11.1% of operating income in 1953 was much too high compared to the national average[1] of 1.6%.

3. Slow loans had increased by $6494 to a new total of $32,093, and equaled 14.2% of net assets.

4. Operating expenses exceeded the statutory maximum of 2 1/2%, of the first million dollars of assets by $1017. Further, operating expenses did not even include any depreciation on furniture, fixtures, and leasehold improvements.

5. The association needed $120 more of FHLB stock.

Mr. Falk did not immediately reply and in mid-July the State Supervisor wrote him a rather angry letter. Mr. Falk thereupon answered, writing that the FHLB stock had been bought, advertising had already been cut back, and every effort was being made to correct the other undesirable conditions.

Preliminary Negotiations

In 1952 Mr. Taylor had approached Mr. Falk on the possibility of transferring the latter's control of Evergreen S & L Association to Mr. Taylor. Mr. Falk expressed interest in such a transaction but could not be "pinned down" on an asking price. In late 1953, Mr. Taylor offered Falk $3000 if the latter would obtain sufficient shareholder proxies made out to Taylor to give him control. Mr. Falk expressed interest in the offer but made no move to accept it. In March 1954, Mr. Taylor raised the offer to $3000 in cash, plus $75 a month for 30 months to be paid to Falk by Evergreen for past services and consultations (total: $5250).

[1]Based on associations with total assets of under $500,000.

Again Falk's interest did not result in any decision, but he did give Mr. Taylor permission to discuss his offer with the other members of the board of directors.

In a final attempt to get control of Evergreen, Mr. Taylor in December 1954 drew up an agreement calling for a cash payment of $10,000 to Mr. Falk if the following conditions were met:

a. Mr. Falk was to give up his proxies and obtain new ones made out to Mr. Taylor sufficient for control.

b. Mr. Falk was to resign all his positions with Evergreen.

c. Five directors named by Mr. Taylor and 4 of the existing directors were to be elected to the board at the next shareholders' meeting (January 18, 1955).

d. A written statement was to be obtained from the lessor of Evergreen's office releasing the Association from any obligation extending beyond February 1, 1955.

e. Mr. Taylor was to be allowed access to all the Association's books and records.

f. All mortgages held by the Association were to be current and meet the requirements of the State statutes and regulations, unless defects (if any) were waived by Mr. Taylor.

Mr. Falk's interest in the offer was clear, but his inability to sign an agreement persisted.

Offer from the Evergreen Board

On March 21, 1955 Mr. Taylor received an urgent telephone call from Mr. Douglas Owens, president and director of Evergreen, asking if Mr. Taylor was still interested in obtaining control. Mr. Owens advised Mr. Taylor that the board had strong reason to believe that Mr. Falk had embezzled about $25,000 and he invited Mr. Taylor to assist in putting Evergreen back on its feet.

Shortly thereafter, Mr. Taylor and a State Examiner reviewed the Association's books and ascertained that Mr. Falk had embezzled $24,621.60. Mr. Falk admitted his wrongdoing. The situation was kept out of the newspapers.[2]

Mr. Falk agreed to turn over all his personal assets (house, car, etc.) to a trustee to be liquidated to repay the Association. The possibilities of recovery were as follows:

Total embezzlement	$24,622
minus Falk's own account	−1,360
	$23,262
minus insurance bond	−5,000
	$18,262

[2]The FHLB regional office was notified of the situation but nothing had been heard from them.

Of the remaining $18,252, it was estimated that at least $2000 and perhaps as much as $5000 might be realized from Falk's assets.

The remaining 4 directors of Evergreen[3] were willing to put a few thousand dollars into the Association on a temporary basis, but they were hopeful that Mr. Taylor would make up the permanent shortage in return for control of the Association. They proposed that an "expense fund" be created to cover the embezzlement as follows:

Mr. Taylor's contribution	$18,000.00
4 directors @ $1,315.59	5,262.36
Recovery form Falk's account	1,359.24
	$24,621.60

All concerned were quite sure that the exact amount of the defalcation had been determined, but it was suggested that if any additional shortages were discovered, the first $5000 should come out of the expected proceeds from the insurance bond. Beyond that, the 4 directors were willing to assume responsibility individually to make up 10% of any additional losses between $5000 and $20,000 (i.e., a maximum liability of $1500 per man).

The directors' contributions would be the first repaid from any recoveries. Hence, assuming no further losses, their $5262 would be quickly repaid from the insurance bond proceeds and liquidation of Falk's assets. Further recoveries then would be applied to Mr. Taylor's $18,000 contribution. Since Falk's net assets were expected to bring in less than $5000, it appeared that Mr. Taylor's ultimate net "investment" would exceed $14,000.

This "investment" would *not* be a liability of the Association, but the directors agreed that once the Association's earnings were sufficient to pay declared dividends, contribute 25% of earnings to reserves, and maintain a ratio of expenses to gross income not in excess of 35%, then Mr. Taylor's contribution would be refunded, "but without dividends or earnings."

The 4 directors assured Mr. Taylor that if he accepted their offer, his slate of 5 directors would be elected to the board and he would be elected manager and secretary-treasurer. The board also undertook to obtain shareholder proxies in favor of Mr. Taylor (and 2 other nominees chosen by Mr. Taylor) to give him control: 25 such proxies already obtained by Mr. Falk were found in the office.

Other Considerations

In weighing the directors' offer, Mr. Taylor considered a number of other factors. First, he realized that the initial $18,000 would not be all that

[3]State regulations required 7 directors, but 2 had resigned a few months earlier and had not yet been replaced, and Mr. Falk had just resigned also. The president was the mayor of a neighboring small town and the other 3 directors were a local druggist, a car dealer, and a retired manufacturer.

he would have to contribute if he decided to "take the plunge." State law restricted Evergreen's operating expenses to 2 1/2% of total assets (on the first million dollars). In order to build up some momentum in Evergreen S & L, he would be forced to spend more than the 2 1/2%, and the excess would have to come from his own pocket. It was extremely difficult to estimate how much might be needed: the out-of-pocket amount might easily run to several thousand dollars, plus time spent by Mr. Taylor and employees from his other endeavors without compensation from Evergreen.

Another major problem was obtaining coverage from the Federal S & L Insurance Corp. Mr. Taylor felt strongly that insurance was a prerequisite to future growth of the association. Informal inquiries revealed that under the circumstances, obtaining coverage would take at least one year and perhaps two. The FSLIC would no doubt insist upon a full-time manager for Evergreen.

Exhibit 3

EVERGREEN SAVINGS & LOAN ASSOCIATION

S & L Dividend Rates, Dunster and Rest of State – 1948 – 1955

		*Number of Associations Paying Rate Indicated in Rest of State**						
	Dunster Rate	*2%*	*2 1/4%*	*2 1/2%*	*3%*	*3 1/4%*	*3 1/2%*	*Over 3 1/2%*
June 1948	2 %	45	2	7	5	–	–	–
Dec. 1948	2 %	31	3	19	5	–	–	–
June 1949	2 %	28	3	18	12	–	–	–
Dec. 1949	2 %	26	2	18	14	–	–	–
June 1950	2 %	15	–	28	13	–	–	–
Dec. 1950	2½%	11	–	33	14	–	–	–
June 1951	2½%	2	–	41	14	–	–	–
Dec. 1951	2½%	1	–	38	17	–	–	–
June 1952	2½%	1	–	35	19	–	–	–
Dec. 1952	2½%	1	–	23	30	1	–	–
June 1953	2½%	–	–	13	40	2	–	–
Dec. 1953	2½%	–	–	9	44	2	–	–
June 1954	2½%	–	–	8	46	2	–	–
Dec. 1954	2½%	–	–	9	44	2	1	–
June 1955*	2 @ 2½% 1 @ 3 %	–	–	4	48	1	2	1

*Anticipated rate.

SOURCE: Evergreen records. Total number of associations included apparently varied from 55 to 61.

Another expected requirement was that a dividend agreement be signed limiting Evergreen's dividends to the rate paid by "the majority" of the other S & L's in Dunster for a period of 5 years. There were actually only two other S & L's in Dunster, and they had traditionally paid as low or lower rates than prevailed in surrounding areas (see Exhibit 3). Mr. Taylor was of the opinion that local savings were not fully tapped by the local S & L's because similar cities in the state had per capita S & L savings of as much as 160% of Dunster's. The dividend agreement would tie him down as far as rates were concerned, although he thought perhaps the other two S & L's might be convinced of the wisdom of paying more competitive rates.

A further possibility that Mr. Taylor was warned about was that he might have to give up his interest in Far West Mortgage Co. to avoid any possible conflict of interest as far as FSLIC was concerned.

Mr. Taylor, in the short time available to him, had obtained the economic information on Dunster and Shonagan County shown in Exhibit 4. Mr. Taylor was optimistic about the future of the area and about the economy in general.

Mr. Taylor had also reviewed the composition of the 194 savings accounts and found that the largest was for $11,000, the next two largest accounts were for $10,000, and the fourth largest was for only $6500. The average account contained slightly less than $1140. The defalcation had been based on non-recorded savings but corrections had since been made in all cases (with Mr. Falk's help). The defalcation had not been made public, but to cover the possibility of a "run" on Evergreen should the news leak out, Mr. Taylor had discussed the matter with his commercial banker. The banker had agreed that if Mr. Taylor "took over" the Association, the bank would stand ready to loan Evergreen up to $35,000 in an emergency.

On the asset side of the balance sheet (see Exhibit 1), Mr. Taylor estimated that about $30,000's worth of mortgages were slow, but all were collectable. Only two mortgages totalling $2622 were six months or more behind. The largest single mortgage on the books was for $8000; the longest maturity was for 12 years; most of the interest rates ranged between five and seven percent. The other assets were properly valued on the balance sheet.

The Problem

Mr. Taylor had to decide very quickly whether to "take the plunge." The investment of $18,000 immediately would give Mr. Taylor control of a chartered and started association, but one that had little to begin with. Evergreen's "public image" was largely non-existent and it might easily be tarnished if the news of the defalcation became generally known.

Exhibit 4

EVERGREEN SAVINGS & LOAN ASSOCIATION

Economic Data on Dunster and Competiton

1954 population of Dunster: 35,000
1954 metropolitan population: 66,000

	Shonagan County	
	Number Employed	*Gross Payrolls*
June 30, 1954	21,278	$82.2 million
1953	21,175	$80.6 million
1952	19,500	$69.1 million
1951	19,400	$65.0 million

COMPETITION

- 26 S & L offices within 50 mile radius of Dunster, most of which advertise in the Seattle papers which have wide circulation in Dunster.
- 9 mutual savings bank offices within 50 mile radius of Dunster; none of these in Dunster.
- 2 S & L's in Dunster, the Dunster Federal S & L and the Shonagan Federal.

COMPARISON OF S & L'S IN DUNSTER

	Savings		
	1954	1953	1946
Evergreen	$ 220,484	$ 215,944	$ 136,330
Dunster Federal	$5,289,466	$4,745,281	$2,490,281
Shonagan Federal	$6,360,288	$5,605,993	$2,007,327

	Annual Percent Change in Savings							
	1954	1953	1952	1951	1950	1949	1948	1947
Evergreen	2.1	20.5	20.3	27.4	−5.0	0.1	−2.2	−5.1
Dunster Federal	11.4	9.5	12.1	24.5	9.0	8.8	7.4	6.5
Shonagan Federal	13.5	17.8	30.0	32.6	11.0	16.7	13.9	5.8

SOURCES: State S & L Statistics, Evergreen S & L records, U.S. Census, State Employment Statistics.

The Association's 194 savings accounts amounted to only $220,000 and were not insured: savings insurance would take some time to obtain. The Association's quarters were shoddy and would have to be changed: it had no employees, because with Mr. Falk's departure Mrs. Reing decided to quit her part-time job.

On the other hand, Mr. Taylor was interested in the Savings & Loan business, and this opportunity would enable him to get started right away. . . .

SELECTING HEAD OFFICE LOCATION

Central Federal Savings and Loan Association

The July 1964 meeting of the Board of Directors of the Central Federal Savings and Loan Association was the scene of a spirited discussion on whether Central should move to a new building or remain in its rented quarters. For 34 years Central had occupied the fourth (sometimes the third or fifth) story of the Walker Building in the heart of downtown St. Louis. Since 1949 it had also owned the Dempsey Building located two blocks away on a choice corner location, but this building had been leased to others. These long-term leases were all scheduled to expire in 6 months' time (January 1, 1965) and a decision would have to be made soon as to whether Central should take this opportunity to move into a ground floor location in its own building.

Mr. N. L. Knowles, Central's president, was strongly in favor of the move because he felt that the new quarters, once the building was renovated, would be much more in keeping with Central's position as a leading savings and loan association, and would improve its "image" in the eyes of the public. Central's staff needed more room anyway; the concurrent expiration of all the tenants' leases in the Dempsey Building was another favorable factor. An important consideration was Central's strong financial condition (see Exhibit 1), with a surplus of 11.4% of savings. Mr. Knowles looked forward to a near doubling of Central's savings in the next 5 years, and to the possibility of opening Central's first branch offices.

Mr. D. David Greiner, the secretary-treasurer and general manager, opposed the move with equal fervor. To begin with, he saw no need to accelerate Central's growth rate, which he felt was already doing fine. The financial condition of Central was indeed excellent, and Mr. Greiner wanted to keep it that way: in addition, good mortgages were getting scarcer. The floor below the current location was available for rental, so additional space was no problem. Central had done well at its fourth floor location over the years, and sometimes even "bragged" about it in its advertising. Even if the rent rose to $64,000 as a result of renting another floor, this would be considerably less than Mr. Greiner's

---

Exhibit 1

CENTRAL FEDERAL SAVINGS AND LOAN ASSOCIATION

Financial Statements—1959–1964
(in thousands)

Assets	*Dec. 31 1959*	*Dec. 30 1960*	*Dec. 31 1961*	*Dec. 31 1962*	*Dec. 31 1963*	*June 30 1964*
Cash and U.S. government securities	$ 5,048	$ 4,567	$ 4,465	$ 4,750	$ 4,833	$ 4,781
FHLB stock	540	620	697	697	697	697
Prepaid FSLIC premiums	–	–	–	58	162	284
First mortgage loans and contracts	32,051	35,294	40,563	47,355	56,158	59,764
Loans secured by savings	92	67	77	68	52	59
Real estate owned	–	30	18	–	–	149
Future home office property	781	781	800	800	804	832
Furniture, fixtures, other	100	93	66	73	39	52
	$38,612	$41,452	$46,686	$53,801	$62,745	$66,618

Liabilities	*Dec. 31 1959*	*Dec. 30 1960*	*Dec. 31 1961*	*Dec. 31 1962*	*Dec. 31 1963*	*June 30 1964*
Savings	$34,359	$36,683	$39,573	$44,517	$50,610	$53,390
Surplus	3,220	3,701	4,314	5,162	5,766	6,128
Accrued federal income tax	–	–	–	–	150	78
Advance payments by borrower	193	38	43	93	132	95
Advances—FHLB	360	700	2,208	3,367	5,394	6,327
Other liabilities	38	55	54	62	53	45
Loans in process	442	275	494	600	640	555
	$38,612	$41,452	$46,686	$53,801	$62,745	$66,618

Exhibit continued.

$156,000 estimate of the annual cost of occupancy of the new location. Central was currently paying (but not advertising) 1/4 of 1% more than its competitors, and Mr. Greiner did concede that the extra occupancy cost could be more than recovered by cutting out the extra 1/4 of 1% from the

Exhibit 1 (Continued)

Miscellaneous	*Dec. 31 1959*	*Dec. 30 1960*	*Dec. 31 1961*	*Dec. 31 1962*	*Dec. 31 1963*	*June 30 1964*
Surplus as percent of savings	9.4%	10.1%	10.9%	11.6%	11.4%	11.4%
Cash and U.S. government securities as percent of total	13.1%	11.0%	9.6%	8.8%	7.7%	7.2%
Percent increase in savings	–	6.8%	7.9%	12.5%	13.7%	5.5%*
Total S & L savings in state:						
In millions	$ 1,191	$ 1,358	$ 1,535	$ 1,721	$ 1,930	$ 2,019
Percent increase	–	14.0%	13.1%	12.1%	12.1%	4.6%*

*Half-year only.

dividend rate. Such a step might also offset the growth pressures of the new and better location, but Mr. Greiner felt that there were few better uses for the Association's income than the payment of good dividends to the savers, while at the same time maintaining a strong financial position.

Current Location

Central had been founded in 1920 as a state-chartered association and switched to a federal charter in 1934. At first it had been located in a ground floor location on Locust Street, then on North Broadway. It had moved to the fifth floor of the Walker Building in late 1930 as a cost-cutting measure. Later, Central had moved to the third floor for a few years, then to the fourth story where it obtained the entire floor. The Walker Building was approximately fifty years old, but new automatic elevators had been installed. In 1964 Central occupied the fourth floor plus a small portion of the third floor, totalling 8900 square feet. Rental cost, including heat, maintenance and light, was $3.80 per square foot, a total of $33,800 a year. Central's fifty-three employees were somewhat crowded and it was anticipated that if Central stayed there, the rest of the third floor (which was available) would be leased at the same rental charge. This would then give Central approximately 16,800 square feet at an annual cost of $64,000, including heat, light, and maintenance.

Proposed New Location

In 1949 Central had purchased the ground under the Dempsey Building for $720,000, subject to a fifty year ground lease for the building which expired on January 1, 1965. The owners of the building paid all expenses such as property taxes, insurance and maintenance, and in addition paid Central an annual lease payment of $37,600; on January 1, 1965 the ownership of the building would automatically revert to Central. Central's management expected that one day the association would move into the Dempsey Building. In 1956 the owners of the building sold it to Central for $55,000 (in other words, they accepted $55,000 in exchange for the difference between their net rental income and the ground lease payments through 1964). The Dempsey Building was managed by a real estate firm and its net income rose to a high of $77,040 in 1960, dropping to $59,583 in 1963 (see Exhibit 2). Since the longest of tenants' leases had been scheduled to expire simultaneously with the ground lease, all lease renewals for the lower floors were made to terminate January 1, 1965

Exhibit 2

CENTRAL FEDERAL SAVINGS AND LOAN ASSOCIATION

Income Statements—1959–1964
(in thousands)

	1959	*1960*	*1961*	*1962*	*1963*	*6 Months 1964*
Gross income*	$2,080	$2,415	$2,716	$3,493	$3,725	$2,061
Expenses†	494	538	555	612	834	456
	1,586	1,877	2,161	2,881	2,891	1,605
Dividends	1,220	1,396	1,544	2,033	2,136	1,165
	366	481	617	848	755	440
Federal income tax	–	–	–	–	150	78
To reserves and undivided profit	$ 366	$ 481	$ 617	$ 848	$ 605	$ 362
*Including net income from office building	41	77	73	73	60	28
†Including:						
Rent paid	22	22	22	22	29	14
Advertising	64	81	64	55	70	24
Expenses as percent of gross income	24.8%	22.3%	20.5%	17.5%+	22.4%+	22.1%
Annual gross income as percent of average total assets	–	6.0%	6.2%	7.0%+	6.4%+	6.4%+

In anticipation of the new income tax laws, Central, in 1962, had maximized its income and minimized its expenses, thus affecting both the 1962 and 1963 income statements.

(or earlier). Well over a year before that date, an investigation of the desirability of moving into the Dempsey Building was begun.

First, it was determined that if Central moved, it would use 19,000 square feet in the basement, ground floor, mezzanine, and second floor of the Dempsey Building. The 6720 square feet of usable space in the basement would be used for the employees' lounge and lunchroom, telephone equipment, machines, and some clerks; the lobby and tellers would be on the 5400 square foot ground floor: the officers would use 1500 square feet of mezzanine, and other offices would occupy the 5400 square feet on the second floor. The remaining five floors would continue to be rented to others. The outside of the entire building would be modernized completely; the inside part to be occupied by Central would also be thoroughly renovated, with air conditioning and a pneumatic tube system installed. By June of 1964 the property was carried on the books for $832,000, although it was expected that the sale of the property might net around $1,000,000. The contemplated improvements were estimated to cost a further $1,100,000.

Mr. Greiner calculated that the annual occupancy cost of Central's new office would amount to $156,000, or $8.20 per square foot: included in this cost was an allowance of 4 1/2% on the investment. Since the upper five floors were to be leased to others, an allocation of expenses had been made by Mr. Greiner to arrive at the $156,000 figure: in calculating the 4 1/2% return on investment he estimated the investment in the upper five floors to be $300,000, hence the investment in Central's quarters would be $1,632,000 ($832,000 + $1,100,000 − $300,000). Mr. Greiner estimated that the rental revenue from the five upper floors would just cover the allocated expenses plus the $13,500 expected return on investment (4 1/2% × $300,000). The remaining expenses (heating, increased property taxes, maintenance, etc.) allocated to Central's space came to $82,500, which when added to the $73,500 implied return on investment (4 1/2% × $1,632,000) gave Mr. Greiner the $156,000 per year figure.

Dividend Rate and Advertising

In the early 1940's Central had on occasion paid extra dividends. This practice was resumed in 1961. From the beginning of 1962, Central paid the normal rate prevailing in St. Louis of 4 1/4%, plus an extra ¼ of 1% (see Exhibit 3). Although Central was effectively paying 4 1/2%, it did not advertise this point; as a matter of fact, Central's advertising prominently mentioned a 4 1/4% rate without any reference to the extra ¼ of 1%. This strategy was aimed at retaining existing savings and getting new depositors through word-of-mouth advertising, without pushing competing S & L's to meet the unadvertised rate. It was felt that if necessary, the extra dividend could be dropped without any significant loss of savings because Central would still be paying the prevailing dividend rate.

Exhibit 3

CENTRAL FEDERAL SAVINGS AND LOAN ASSOCIATION

Dividend Rates – 1959 – 1964
(in percentage per annum)

Year	*Quarter*	*Central*	*Missouri First*	*Sterling*	*Builders*	*Broadway*
1959	1	3½	3½	3½	4	3½
	2	3½	3½	3½	4	3½
	3	4	3½	3½	4	3½
	4	4*	3½	3½	4	3½
1960	1	4	4*	4	4*	4*
	2	4	4	4	4	4
	3	4	4	4*	4	4
	4	4	4	4	4	4
1961	1	4	4	4	4	4
	2	4	4	4	4	4
	3	4 + 0.4 extra	4	4	4¼	4
	4	4 + 0.4 extra	4	4	4¼	4
1962	1	4¼ + ¼ extra	4¼	4¼	4¼	4¼
	2	4¼ + ¼ extra	4¼	4¼	4¼	4¼
	3	4¼ + ¼ extra	4¼	4¼	4¼	4¼
	4	4¼ + ¼ extra	4¼	4¼	4¼	4¼
1963	1	4¼ + ¼ extra	4¼	4¼	4¼	4¼
	2	4¼ + ¼ extra	4¼	4¼	4¼	4¼
	3	4¼ + ¼ extra	4¼	4¼	4¼	4¼
	4	4¼ + ¼ extra	4¼	4¼	4¼	4¼
1964	1	4¼ + ¼ extra	4¼	4¼	4¼	4¼
	2	4¼ + ¼ extra	4¼	4	4.3	4¼

All associations paid dividends on savings deposited by the 10th of the month as though deposited on the first.

*Switched from semiannual dividend payments to quarterly.

As it was, Central was growing as fast as the General Manager thought to be desirable, and as a result he had cut back advertising expense (see Exhibit 2). In the first half of 1964, $51,000 had been budgeted for advertising but only $23,786 was spent. During this period, Central's savings increased by 5.5 percent (see Exhibit 1) as compared to an increase of 4.6 percent for all St. Louis S & L's.

Mortgages

Mr. Greiner feared that good mortgages at prevailing interest rates were becoming more difficult to obtain, although the general economy was very buoyant. His expectation was fairly widespread as evidenced by the results of a U.S. League Committee on Trends and Economic Policies survey (see Exhibit 4).

Exhibit 4

CENTRAL FEDERAL SAVINGS AND LOAN ASSOCIATION

Selected Statistics from Preliminary Results of Semiannual Survey of Economic Conditions—June 1963

(Survey conducted by U.S. League Committee on Trends and Economic Policies; based on the return of 100 out of 201 questionnaires sent.)

A. Compare conditions today and early last fall in your area regarding:

	Better Now	*Worse Now*	*Same*
Employment	50%	14%	36%
Income	56%	3%	41%
Retail Sales	55%	12%	33%
Home Building	32%	23%	45%

B. What is your chief management problem today?

	Spring 1964	*Fall 1963*
Intensified competition for loans	32%	37%
Growing competition for savings	14%	20%
Maintaining earnings and reserves	31%	20%
Personnel—adequate staffing	4%	6%
Government regulations and taxes	19%	17%

C. How does the competition in your mortgage market now compare with the situation early last fall?

	Keener	*Easier*	*Same*
Banks and Trust Companies	61%	6%	33%
Insurance Companies, Mortgage Bankers	41%	7%	52%
Savings Banks	45%	5%	50%
Other S & L's	62%	3%	35%

D. Rate of interest on the typical conventional home mortgage loans made:

	Less than 6.0%	*6.0%*	*6.1–6.4%*	*6.5% and over*
Fall 1963	33%	54%	5%	8%
Now	48%	42%	4%	6%

E. Do you expect interest rates during the second half of 1964 to be:

Higher	9%
Lower	7%
Same	84%

Exhibit 4 (Continued)

F. Dividend rates on an annual basis (actual or anticipated):

	Your Association				*Your Trading Area*			
	Under 4.0%	*4.0%*	*4.1%–4.4%*	*4.5% and over*	*Under 4.0%*	*4.0%*	*4.1%–4.4%*	*4.5% and over*
2d Half 1963	1%	64%	16%	19%	2%	49%	25%	24%
1st Half 1964	1%	54%	28%	17%	2%	41%	37%	20%
2d Half 1964	0%	53%	31%	16%	2%	41%	35%	22%

SOURCE: *Savings and Loan News*, July 1964, page 29.

During June 1964, Central's new loans had been almost entirely conventional loans on single residences; interest rates ranged from 5 3/4% to 6 3/4%, with an average of 6.2%; loans averaged 60% of appraisal (all appraisals were conducted by outside appraisers); the average loan was for $10,000 on a 20 year maturity. The relatively small number of contracts, apartment loans and business mortgages were for similar terms.

A breakdown of Central's existing loan portfolio on June 30, 1964 was as follows:

Conventional mortgages, 1–4 family homes	$42,834 thousand
Apartment mortgages	4,264 thousand
Contracts: homes	5,149 thousand
apartments	1,000 thousand
business properties	314 thousand
Business mortgages	1,728 thousand
FHA (homes)	1,172 thousand
VA (homes)	2,088 thousand
Church loans	1,002 thousand
Land improvement loans	67 thousand
Home improvement loans	36 thousand
	$59,644 thousand

New Regulations

Mr. Greiner's concern with Central's rate of growth stemmed in part from new and amended regulations governing insurance reserves and issued by the Federal Home Loan Bank in the first half of 1964. Pertinent parts of these regulations and Central's situation vis-a-vis these requirements are shown in Exhibits 5, 6, 7 and 8.[1]

[1]The U.S. Savings and Loan League's *Special Management Bulletin* #98 (July 2, 1964) describes the regulations in detail.

Exhibit 5

CENTRAL FEDERAL SAVINGS AND LOAN ASSOCIATION

Scheduled Items—June 30, 1964

Definitions of "scheduled items" and "slow loans" passed on May 26, 1964 and issued by FHLB on June 15, 1964:

561.15 SCHEDULED ITEMS
The term "scheduled items" means slow loans (other than insured or guaranteed loans), 20 percent of slow loans which are insured or guaranteed, real estate owned as a result of foreclosure, or acquired by deed in lieu of foreclosure, and such real estate sold on contract, or by a loan, where the unpaid principal balance exceeds that permitted under otherwise applicable lending limitations or exceeds 90 percent of the value of the security, and any investment securities upon which one or more interest payments due has not been paid.

561.16 SLOW LOANS
The term "slow loans" means:

a. Any loan or land contract less than 1 year old which is the equivalent of 60 days (2 months) or more contractually delinquent; or

b. Any loan or land contract that is from 1 year to 7 years old which is the equivalent of 90 days (3 months) or more contractually delinquent; or

c. Any loan or land contract more than 7 years old which is the equivalent of 90 days (3 months) or more contractually delinquent unless 10 out of the last 12 contractually required payments have been made; or

d. Any mortgage loan, deed of trust, or land contract on which taxes on the security are due and unpaid for the equivalent of two or more years; or

e. Any loan or land contract that has been modified or refinanced within the preceding 12 months while contractually delinquent.

Provided, That any mortgage loan, deed of trust, or land contract on which the total indebtedness is less than 60 percent of the original amount, any loan on which all contractually required payments have been made during the preceding 12 months and any loan on which payments are being deferred by law shall not be considered to be a slow loan under this section.

Central's "scheduled items" on June 30, 1964

Slow loans—less than 1 year old, 60 days or more delinquent	$ 226,492
—1 to 7 years old, 90 days or more delinquent	832,730
—over 7 years old, 90 days or more delinquent, unless 10 out of last 12 payments made	21,773
Loans where taxes delinquent 2 years or more	0
Real estate owned (124), in judgment (55); loans in litigation (105); contracts in litigation (39)	387,694
Real estate sold where loan exceeds normal limitations	11,406
Total	$1,480,095

NOTE: Since the scheduled items as calculated above were small in relation to Central's net worth, it had not been deemed necessary to take advantage of the provision that only 20% of insured or guaranteed slow loans need to be included. The overall proportion of insured or guaranteed loans was small anyway, amounting to only $3.26 million out of $59.64 million of loans (5.5%).

In addition, the reduction in slow loans allowed by the last paragraph of the FHLB definition (see above) had not been taken into account because management did not think it worth the trouble.

Exhibit 6

CENTRAL FEDERAL SAVINGS AND LOAN ASSOCIATION

Specified Assets

Definition of "specified assets" established on May 26, 1964 by the Federal Home Loan Bank:

561.17 SPECIFIED ASSETS

a. The term "specified assets" means the total assets of an insured institution less the institution's cash, Government obligations and accrued interest thereon, Federal Home Loan Bank stock, prepaid Federal Savings and Loan Insurance Corporation premiums, loans in process, loans on the security of the institution's share accounts, investments of up to $10,000 per institution in other institutions insured by the Federal Savings and Loan Insurance Corporation, and less 30 percent of the institution's actual investments in insured and guaranteed loans.

b. In computing specified assets at the close of any semiannual period, any asset which is sold or disposed of in one semiannual period and then repurchased or reacquired in the next semiannual period shall be computed as if it had not been sold or disposed of during such initial semiannual period.

Central's "specified assets" on June 30, 1964

Total assets	$66,618,371
Minus deductions as above	9,006,565
Specified assets	$57,611,806

Exhibit 7

CENTRAL FEDERAL SAVINGS AND LOAN ASSOCIATION

Minumum Reserves and Net Worth

(Condensed from FHLB rules and regulations in effect June 15, 1964.)

a. Federal insurance reserve for an institution which has been insured 20 years or more must equal at least 5.0 percent of its savings accounts.

b. Net worth of the institution must be at least equal to the Federal insurance reserve requirement plus 15 percent of its scheduled items in 1964 and 20 percent of its scheduled items thereafter.

c. If at any semiannual closing date either of the above requirements is not met, the insured institution must credit to its insurance reserve 25 percent of its net income (or any lesser amount sufficient to meet the requirements).

Central's Requirements as of June 30, 1964

a. Federal insurance reserve:	
5.0% × $53,390,413	$2,669,521
Actual insurance reserve	$5,589,600
b. Minimum net worth:	
15% of scheduled items	$ 222,014
+ required insurance reserve	$2,669,520
	$2,891,534
Actual net worth	$5,878,909

Exhibit 8

CENTRAL FEDERAL SAVINGS AND LOAN ASSOCIATION

Semiannual Credits to Insurance Reserve

Central's Adjusted Net Worth on June 30, 1964

Federal insurance reserves	$5,589,924
Surplus and undivided profits	288,985
	$5,878,909
Minus 15% of scheduled items	$ 222,014
Adjusted net worth	$5,656,895

(Condensed from FHLB rules and regulations in effect on June 15, 1964):

a. No credit to Federal insurance reserves is required if adjusted net worth is at least 12% of specified assets.

b. If adjusted net worth is at least 8% of specified assets (but not 12%), the insured institution must credit (from net income, undivided profits, or earned surplus) at least 10% of its net income to the insurance reserve.

Central's Percentage on June 30, 1964

$$\frac{\text{Adjusted net worth}}{\text{Specified assets}} \quad \frac{\$\ 5{,}656{,}895}{\$57{,}611{,}806} \times 100 = 9.8\%$$

c. If adjusted net worth is below 8% of specified assets, an institution which has been insured 20 years or more and has over $10,000,000 in specified assets must credit to the insurance reserve an amount equal to 10% of net income for the period or an amount equal to 6% of the growth in specified assets during the period, whichever is greater.

Only a few months remained to decide whether Central should move to the Dempsey Building (the existing downstairs tenants wanted to renew their leases soon), and 6 out of the 8 directors had to decide whether to agree with Mr. Knowles or with Mr. Greiner.

COMMON STOCKS AS PENSION FUND INVESTMENTS

Lodi Pension Trust Fund

Late in January 1966, the trustee for the Lodi Pension Trust Fund (LPTF) of the Lodi Wine Company (Lodi) presented the annual report for the pension fund operations in the year 1965 to the Lodi board of directors. At that meeting a board member, Mr. Irwin Wiley, raised a question about the company's policies regarding common stock investments by the pension fund. Several directors had been concerned for some time about the company's investment policy regarding fund assets. Among the directors, there had been considerable difference of opinion as to what the basic financial objectives of LPTF should be.

The existing Lodi policy permitted the trustee, a large bank with headquarters in San Francisco, to invest up to 25 percent of LPTF assets in common stocks. Mr. Wiley questioned the bank officers on the advisability of raising this limitation to permit a substantially greater investment in common stocks. One of the trust officers, Mr. Allen Bacon, stated that the bank, as trustee, managed a number of trust funds with a higher proportion of common stocks than the Lodi fund. In some cases, according to Mr. Bacon, the bank was not formally restricted by trust agreement to a specific limit on investment in common stock. Mr. Wiley suggested that the directors discuss the matter of pension fund objectives and policies in privacy after the conclusion of the trustee's presentation.

Background of Lodi Pension Trust Fund

Founded in 1922, the Lodi Wine Company operated four wineries in the San Joaquin Valley in California. In 1938 the company had established the Lodi Pension Trust Fund and had appointed as trustee a San Francisco bank. Initially, Lodi management had adopted a pension plan to gain the goodwill of its employees and to forestall unionization of company workers. Lodi payments into LPTF had been substantially increased in 1942, after the Revenue Act of that year established the tax-deductibility of all payments to the fund.

The original trust agreement had provided that "LPTF shall be invested and kept invested by the trustee in such a manner as the company shall direct." A resolution by the Lodi board in 1938 had stipulated that LPTF assets could be invested only in bank deposits, corporate bonds, and government obligations. In 1955 a resolution had been passed which permitted the trustee to invest up to 10 percent (by book value) of fund assets in common stocks. A board resolution in 1961, currently in effect, had given the trustee discretionary powers to act in the investment of LPTF assets without any further directions from the company, subject to the limitation that 25 percent was the maximum allowable proportion of common stock. Given this latitude, the trustee had begun limited investment in FHA mortgages in 1961 and had increased the investment in common stock to 15 percent of assets.

The obligations of the trustee included the preparation of a written report on fund transactions and assets at the end of each calendar year. In addition, trust officers of the bank annually had discussed their management of LPTF with the Lodi board of directors at their January meeting. The LPTF was noncontributory, that is, the plan was financed solely by employer payments. In December 1965, Lodi had 770 full time employees. Since 1949, LPTF had been fully funded.[1]

[1]The term "fully funded" is discussed in the appendix.

Exhibit 1

LODI PENSION TRUST FUND

Total Assets and Cash Flows, 1956–1965
(thousands of dollars)

	1956	*1957*	*1958*	*1959*	*1960*	*1961*	*1962*	*1963*	*1964*	*1965*
Total assets in fund at beginning of year (book value)	1,055	1,136	1,258	1,453	1,677	1,993	2,248	2,607	2,965	3,406
RECEIPTS										
Contributions	120	161	225	241	270	306	341	339	408	519
Earnings on assets in fund	37	43	56	65	77	89	103	118	136	163
Net realized gain (loss)	1	1	(1)	2	10	1	11	1	10	3
Total receipts	158	205	280	308	357	396	455	458	554	685
DISBURSEMENTS										
Distributed benefits	72	77	78	76	82	80	84	86	98	132
Management expenses	5	6	7	8	9	11	12	14	15	18
Total disbursements	77	83	85	84	91	91	96	100	113	150
Excess of receipts over disbursements	81	122	195	224	266	305	359	358	441	535
Total assets in fund at year end	1,136	1,258	1,453	1,677	1,993	2,248	2,607	2,965	3,406	3,941

Exhibit 2

LODI PENSION TRUST FUND

Yield on Book Value, 1956–1965
(dollar figures in thousands)

	1956	*1957*	*1958*	*1959*	*1960*	*1961*	*1962*	*1963*	*1964*	*1965*
1. INCOME										
a. Earnings from interest	$ 37	$ 43	$ 56	$ 65	$ 77	$ 89	$ 103	$ 118	$ 136	$ 163
b. Net realized gain (loss) on sale or redemption of assets	1	1	(1)	2	10	1	11	1	10	3
c. Net amount realized	$ 38	$ 44	$ 55	$ 67	$ 87	$ 90	$ 114	$ 119	$ 146	$ 166
2. INVESTMENT										
Weighted mean book value of trust assets during the year	$1,096	$1,198	$1,356	$1,570	$1,835	$2,121	$2,428	$2,786	$3,186	$3,674
3. YIELD										
a. Current book yield: Yield on mean book value, based on current earnings (1a/2)	3.4%	3.6%	4.1%	4.1%	4.2%	4.2%	4.2%	4.2%	4.3%	4.4%
b. Realized book yield: Yield on mean book value, based on net amount realized (1c/2)	3.5%	3.7%	4.0%	4.3%	4.7%	4.2%	4.7%	4.3%	4.6%	4.5%

By the end of 1965, assets in the pension fund had reached nearly $4 million (Exhibit 1). All assets were carried in LPTF accounts at book value until their sale or redemption. Investment yield was calculated by the trustee in two ways: current book yield, the ratio of current earnings (from interest and dividends) to book value; and realized book yield, the ratio of current earnings plus realized gains to book value. In 1965 current and realized book yields were approximately 4.4 percent and 4.5 percent, respectively. Yields on LPTF assets for the years 1956–1965 are shown in Exhibit 2. Generally increasing yields reflect rising interest rates and the changing composition of assets in the LPTF portfolio, as illustrated in Exhibit 3.

Exhibit 3

LODI PENSION TRUST FUND

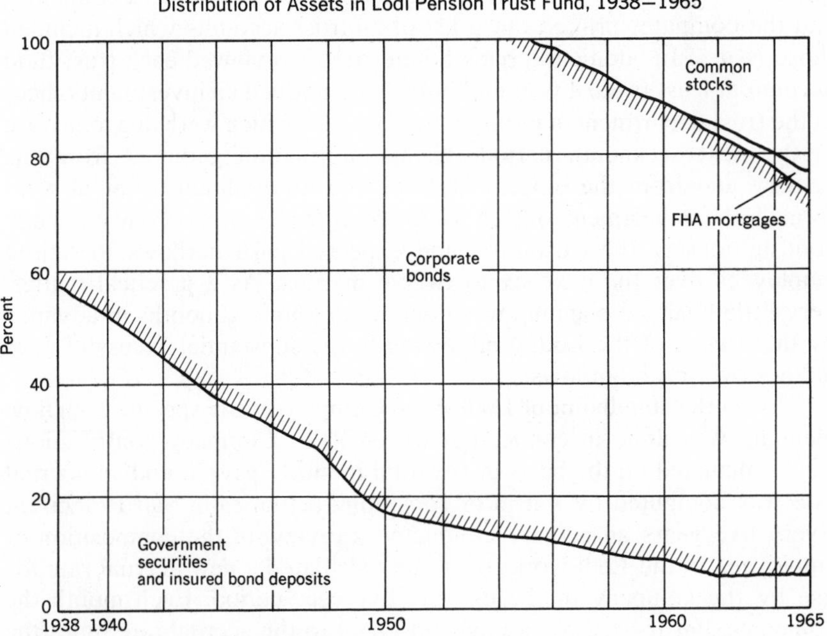

Portfolio distribution is based on book value at year end.

Cash Flow Management

From the standpoint of the trustee, there were four principal sources of cash inflows to LPTF. First, Lodi made regular monthly contributions to the pension fund, based on an "accrual rate" established by a consulting actuary. Second, the trustee received earnings on the assets in the pension fund portfolio. Third, as bonds in the LPTF portfolio matured or were recalled, the principal was received by the trustee. Finally, the trustee from time to time received cash flows from the sale of portfolio securities. Payments of pension fund benefits to retired employees constituted the largest operating cash outflow from LPTF. In addition the trustee received an annual management fee equal to one half of 1 percent of the average book value of trust assets during the year. In the past, cash inflows had exceeded by far cash outflows from the fund. Since 1962, portfolio earnings alone had been greater than total disbursements from the pension fund. All earnings of the pension fund were nontaxable. A summary of cash receipts and disbursements for the years 1956–1965 is shown in Exhibit 1.

A computer information system was of considerable assistance to the trustee in planning the receipt of cash from called or maturing bond issues. At least thirty days in advance of maturity or call, data from Standard and Poor's publications were fed into the trustee's computer, and the computer printed out a list of all trust accounts which included those issues. In addition, a bank administrator reviewed each trust fund account at least twice a year and informally notified an investment officer in the trust department of issues in that account which were due to mature in the next six-month period. Using information gathered from the actuary and from the officers at Lodi, the fund administrator also informed the investment officer as to expected receipts from company contributions to the trust fund and expected cash outflows to retired employees over the next six to twelve months. As a practical matter, very little financial planning was done more than six months in advance by the trustee of the Lodi fund, owing to the substantial excess of cash inflows over cash outflows.

From the standpoint of Lodi Wine Company, little specific cash flow planning was done in connection with LPTF. Company contributions were calculated on the basis of the total monthly payroll and an accrual rate was computed by a firm of consulting actuaries in San Francisco. Every five years an actuary conducted a review of the composition of employees in the Lodi work force and calculated a new accrual rate for use by the company in the ensuing five-year period. Each month the company sent the trustee a payment equal to the accrual rate times the total company payroll for that month. In formulating the accrual rate, the actuary considered the composition of employees by sex, age, and so forth; the benefit and eligibility provisions of the retirement plan; and expected rate of earnings on the assets in the pension fund. The assumed earnings rate was of considerable importance in the determination of the accrual rate. In general, a low earnings rate tended to result in a higher required accrual rate and, as a result, higher company contributions to the pension fund. Owing to the tax deductability of pension fund contributions, the Internal Revenue Service (IRS) has taken a strong interest in earnings rates used by actuaries in calculating accrual rates. Although assumed earnings rates of 2 percent were common in the 1950s, the IRS currently required that an earnings rate of at least 3 percent be used; in 1965, Lodi's consulting actuary used an earnings rate of 3 1/2 percent in calculating an accrual rate of 7.35 percent for LPTF.

Pension Fund Objectives and Investment Policy

Following the trustee's presentation to the January board meeting, several directors expressed divergent opinions regarding the objectives by which investment performance should be measured. A number of board members felt that the existing investment policy regarding common stock restrictions should be reconsidered in light of the pension fund's objectives.

The following excerpts are from the discussion by five Lodi directors: Mr. Wiley, Mr. Ronald Harper, Mr. Wesley Addison, Mr. Richard McNally, and Mr. Alfred Holt.

HARPER: As I see it, the trustee's performance has been pretty good. Why, the average yield on balanced mutual funds was only a little over 3 percent last year. Our big objective has to be safety in preserving asset value in the fund. After all, our employees and their families depend on their pensions, and I'm frankly not willing to subject these people to a lot of market risk. If anything, the 25 percent limit on common stocks is too high.

WILEY: Do you realize how far out of step we are, Ron? I was looking at an SEC survey the other day. It showed that over one half of all corporate pension fund assets are invested in common stocks now (Exhibit 4).

HARPER: Yes, yes, I know that. But look at AT&T and all its affiliated companies. They have a 20 percent limit on common stock in their pension funds. And when it comes to good management, it is mighty hard to beat AT&T.

ADDISON: If you ask me, our pension fund is like any other project that we invest in. We should look at the fund as a "profit center," just like our regular departments. Our other proposed investments have to show a 10 percent expected return after taxes, right? So we should expect to meet that objective in the pension fund. In fact, you can always invest in some other company like IBM; they have a 15 percent return on their book equity. Let's face it: we have at least a 10 percent opportunity cost. Why not put the money into our own plant and equipment? Everybody would be better off in the long run. You talk about avoiding risk. What could be less risky than investing in our own business? The kind of wine we make sells in good times and bad. As a matter of fact, Lodi wine sales sometimes go *up* in a recession.

McNALLY: We might have some legal problems there, Wes. But I agree that our objective should be to get the highest possible yield on the

Exhibit 4

LODI PENSION TRUST FUND

Distribution of Assets on the Basis of Book Value and Market Value—Dec. 31, 1956–1965
(thousands of dollars)

	1956	*1957*	*1958*	*1959*	*1960*	*1961*	*1962*	*1963*	*1964*	*1965*
BOOK VALUE										
Bonds	1,061	1,114	1,171	1,359	1,587	1,709	1,999	2,179	2,381	2,676
Stocks	26	63	103	164	219	310	373	504	681	883
Other assets	49	81	179	154	187	229	235	282	344	382
Total book value	1,136	1,258	1,453	1,677	1,993	2,248	2,607	2,965	3,406	3,941
PERCENT OF INVESTMENTS —BOOK VALUE BASIS										
Bonds	93.4	88.6	80.6	81.0	79.6	76.0	76.7	73.5	69.9	67.9
Stocks	2.3	5.0	7.1	9.8	11.0	13.8	14.3	17.0	20.0	22.4
Other assets	4.3	6.4	12.3	9.2	9.4	10.2	9.0	9.5	10.1	9.7
Total	100.0	100.0	100.0	100.0	100.0	100.0	100.0	100.0	100.0	100.0
MARKET VALUE										
Bonds	1,009	1,104	1,110	1,242	1,508	1,632	1,975	2,109	2,324	2,569
Stocks	27	60	115	197	263	412	442	604	858	1,168
Other assets	49	81	179	154	187	229	235	282	344	382
Total market value	1,085	1,245	1,404	1,593	1,958	2,273	2,652	2,995	3,526	4,119
Market value less book value	(51)	(13)	(49)	(84)	(35)	25	45	30	120	178

pension fund—but for a little different reason. Our basic job, as I see it, is to maximize profits for the stockholders. Now, our employee-retirement benefits are pretty well set. The big variables in this pension fund program are current earnings and asset growth of the fund and the amount of company contributions. To the extent that fund earnings cover retirement benefits, company contributions can be cut down or maybe even eliminated some day. In fact, an increase in pension fund yield of 1 percent, say from 4.5 percent to 5.5 percent, would decrease our contributions about 20 percent. In short, higher fund earnings mean lower fringe-benefit costs for Lodi and better profits for our stockholders. So why not take *all* the limitations off the trustee? Knowing bankers, I'd expect them to be prudent in any case, so why tie their hands with a lot of restrictions.

HOLT: Last year we paid the trustee some $18,000 in management fees, and the results are not too impressive, if you ask me. After all, we're paying over 5 percent interest on the company's new bond issue. But with all these high-paid professionals managing our pension fund, it's yielding less than 5 percent. For the most part it's due to this ridiculous 25 percent restriction on common stock. I'm all for 100 percent common stock. Stocks give a hedge against inflation, and stock yields are higher than bond yields —if you include appreciation along with dividends in the rate of return.

HARPER: Now wait a minute. We're not talking about maximizing anything. These trust fund assets already belong to our employees and we have no business taking unwarranted risks with them. As far as safety of principal is concerned, there is no doubt that bonds offer better protection than stocks. Sure, stocks have done well in the past ten or fifteen years, but sooner or later history will repeat itself. A lot of people think that the Dow-Jones average is 200 points too high. When price-earnings ratios drop back to their old, sound levels, who's going to tell our employees about what a good job we've been doing for them? Some big New York banks are offering 5 percent on CD's now, with no risk at all. With this kind of safe return available, common stocks just don't make sense for our pension fund. And all this talk about big inflation problems just doesn't apply anymore. I was opposed before to the 25 percent limit on common stocks, and I still think it's too high.

APPENDIX

The Growing Importance of Pension Funds in the United States

Pension plans fall into three broad categories: private plans (noninsured or insured), government plans,[1] and OASDI[2] (social security). From the standpoint of number of employees covered, OASDI (covering 130 million individuals in 1962) is much larger than either private plans (25

[1]Government plans include state and local government, U.S. Civil Service, Foreign Service, Railroad Retirement, TVA, and Federal Reserve.

[2]Old-Age, Survivors, and Disability Insurance.

million people) or government plans (10 million people). However, as shown in Exhibit 5, the financial strength of private pension funds ($70 billion in 1963) exceeds both government plans ($46 billion) and OASDI ($22 billion). Furthermore, the impact on capital markets of private, state, and local pension funds is of paramount importance: among all financial institutions, corporate pension funds are the largest net pur-

Exhibit 5

LODI PENSION TRUST FUND

SEC Survey of Private Noninsured Pension Funds
Distribution of Assets, December 31, 1964
(dollar figures in billions)

	Book Value	*Percent*	*Market Value*	*Percent*
U.S. governments	$ 3.1	6.0	$ 3.0	4.7
Corporate bonds	21.2	40.8	20.5	32.4
Preferred stocks	0.7	1.3	0.7	1.1
Common stocks	20.8	40.1	32.9	51.9
Mortgages	2.7	5.2	2.8	4.4
Cash and other assets	3.4	6.6	3.5	5.5
	$51.9	100.0	$63.4	100.0

Distribution of Assets (Book Value), 1954 and 1964

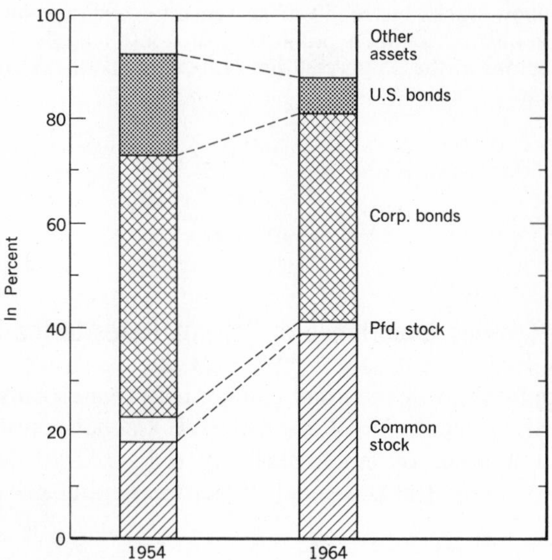

SOURCE: SEC, Statistical Bulletin, June 1965.

chasers of common stocks; and corporate, state, and local pension funds are collectively the largest purchasers of new corporate bond issues.

Pension Fund Terminology

Private pension plans are of two major types: *noninsured* (trusteed) and *insured.* Noninsured plans are usually administered by a bank trustee. Contributions to the pension fund are paid to the trustee, who invests fund assets in income-producing securities in order that funds may be accumulated for payment of retirement benefits. The trust agreement may stipulate specific investment restrictions or may provide complete investment freedom, subject only to "prudent-man" limitations on the trustee. Relative to insured plans, trusteed pension plans often have advantages of greater investment freedom—with the possibility of higher earnings—and generally have greater flexibility in changing economic conditions.

Insured plans provide for contributions by the employer to an insurance company, which is then responsible for payment of benefits under a master contract. Proponents of insured plans point to advantages of relatively fixed costs, ease of administration, and security of future benefits. Combinations of insured and trusteed plans are sometimes used.

Under *contributory* plans, employees bear part of the cost through payroll deductions. In *noncontributory* plans, the employer pays the whole cost of the plan. In time, the employees may acquire an equity in accumulated contributions through "vesting" provisions of the plan. Employers now pay approximately 85 percent of the total annual contributions to private pension funds in the United States.

With regard to financing provisions, pension plans range from *full-funded* to *pay-as-you-go.* A fund is considered to be fully funded if the assets set aside at a given time are sufficient to cover all future pension payment obligations (on an actuarial basis) attributable to employees as of that time. In a pay-as-you-go plan, assets are not set aside in advance of expected benefit payments; benefits are paid, as they come due, out of current operating funds.

For example, the OASDI (social security) pension plan more closely resembles a pay-as-you-go than a fully funded plan. As is shown in Exhibit 5, OASDI trust fund assets totalled approximately $23 billion at the end of 1961. At that time, these assets represented 7 percent of the total liability of $343 billion for future benefits owed to those persons already retired or eligible for benefits. On a discounted cash flow basis, existing fund assets equalled one fifth of the present value of future pension benefits already owed to individuals under OASDI. To be fully funded, existing fund assets equal to 100 percent of the present value of future benefits in "current payment" status would be required.

Growth of Pension Plans

As recently as 1940, total assets of private pension funds amounted to only $4 billion, and private plans covered only one fifth of all workers in industry and commerce. By 1963, private pension fund assets had grown to $70 billion, and the coverage of private plans had been extended to over one half of all employees in industry and commerce.

Since World War II, uninsured private pension funds have been by far the fastest growing segment of the pension fund "financial institution." The assets of uninsured private pension funds grew at a rate of approximately 17 percent per year in the period 1951–1963. Relative to other financial institutions, this rate of growth was second only to that of

Exhibit 6

LODI PENSION TRUST FUND

Growth of Pension Plans in the United States
Number of Persons Covered
(in millions of individuals)

Year	*Private Noninsured*	*Private Insured*	*Government**	*OASDI†*
1930	2.7	0.1	2.6	–
1940	3.6	0.7	3.6	45.0
1950	7.5	2.8	6.6	85.9
1960	17.9	5.5	9.5	123.8
1961	18.8	5.6	9.8	127.4
1962	19.7	5.8	10.3	130.8

Assets and Reserves at Book Value
(in billions of dollars)

Year	*Private Noninsured*	*Private Insured*	*Government**	*OASDI†*
1930	$ 0.7	$ 0.1	$ 0.7	$ –
1940	1.4	1.0	2.4	2.0
1950	6.1	5.6	12.1	13.7
1960	31.1	18.9	34.2	22.6
1961	35.1	20.3	37.7	22.7
1962	39.0	21.6	41.7	20.7
1963	46.5	23.3	46.0 (est.)	22.0 (est.)
1963: Total private	$69.9			

*Government plans include state and local government, U.S. Civil Service, Foreign Service, Railroad Retirement (government-administered), TVA, and Federal Reserve.
†OASDI includes all individuals with wage credits or receiving benefits under Old-Age, Survivors, and Disability Insurance (in the Social Security System).

SOURCE: *Private and Public Pension Funds in the U.S.*, Insurance Company Institute.

savings and loan associations. The growth of private pension funds is illustrated in Exhibit 6.

The expansion of private pension funds since 1940 has reflected a number of underlying forces. There has been great pressure from organized labor since 1949, when the Supreme Court ruled that pension plans were subject to mandatory collective bargaining. The tax-exempt status of employer contributions and the desire to increase the motivation and productivity of employees have been important in employer adoption of pension plans. In particular, pension provisions have been used increasingly to attract and to hold management and supervisory personnel. Finally, the aggregate growth in employment and changing social attitudes (for example, increasing importance of "security" to many people) have spurred the growth in pension funds.

Pension Funds in the Capital Markets

The importance of pension funds in the markets for corporate stocks and bonds is shown in Exhibit 7. In 1963 corporate pension funds were

Exhibit 7

LODI PENSION TRUST FUND

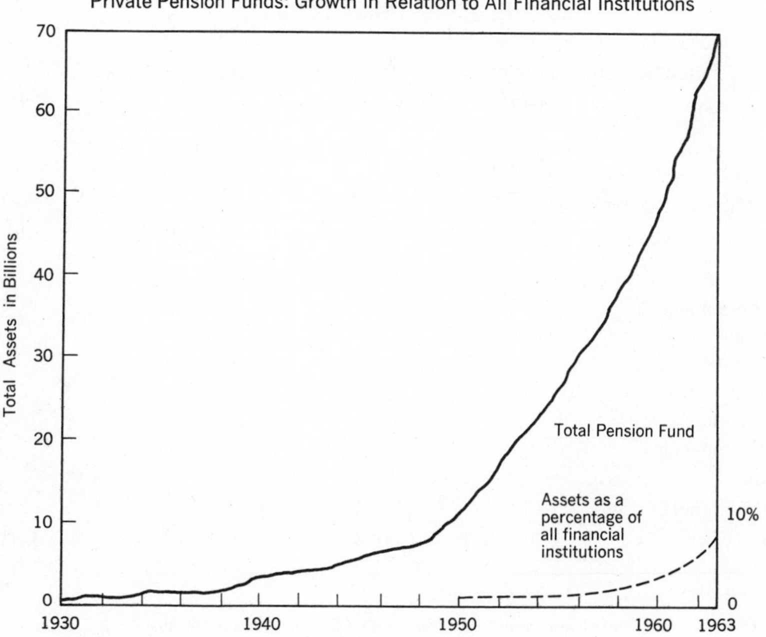

by far the largest net buyers of common stocks with net purchases of $2.2 billion—nearly three times the purchases of the second largest buyers, mutual funds. Net purchases of stock by private pension funds have tripled in the last decade. Corporate pension funds also own more common stock (market value of $26 billion in 1963) than any other financial institution.

Corporate and state-local pension funds purchased nearly two thirds of the net increase in outstanding corporate bonds in 1963. In that year, corporate pension fund trustees bought $1.3 billion in bonds, and state-local funds bought $2.1 billion out of a total of $5.3 billion net additions to outstanding corporate bonds. Corporate pension funds were second only to life insurance companies in ownership of corporate bonds at the end of 1963.

Despite the dramatic growth of private pension funds since 1950, their holdings of U.S. government securities have remained constant in absolute terms (about $2 billion); as a result, the proportion of corporate pension fund assets invested in U.S. government securities had declined (from 32 percent in 1951 to 5 percent in 1964), as trustees seek higher yields in common stocks. The influence of private pension funds in government securities markets has been negligible in recent years.

Exhibit 8

LODI PENSION TRUST FUND

Purchases and Holdings of Common Stocks and Corporate Bonds
(dollar figures in billions)

	Common Stock		*Corporate Bonds*	
	Net Purchases 1963	*Holdings* 12/31/63*	*Net Purchases 1963*	*Holdings 12/31/63*
Corporate pension funds (trusteed)	$ 2.2	$ 25.5	$1.3	$ 16.8
State-local government pension funds	0.2	0.9	2.1	11.5
Commercial banks	—	—	−0.1	0.8
Mutual savings banks	0.1	0.8	−0.3	3.2
Life insurance companies	0.4	4.8	2.1	53.8
Fire-casualty companies	0.6	12.3	−0.1	1.7
Mutual funds	0.7	21.4	0.1	1.8
Individuals and others	−4.5	482.3	0.2	10.4
Total	$−0.3	$548.0	$5.3	$100.0

*Holdings at market value.

SOURCE: H. E. Dougall, *Capital Markets and Institutions* (Englewood Cliffs, N.J.: Prentice-Hall, 1965).

CHANGE IN INVESTMENT POLICY FOR A MUTUAL FUND

Commonwealth International and General Fund

Early in 1965, officials of the Commonwealth International and General Fund (CIG) were considering the possibility of changing the fundamental investment policies of the fund. Despite their high expectations at the time of the fund's formation in 1961, CIG had not been as successful —in terms of public acceptance—as the other funds in the Commonwealth Group. The performance of the fund had been adversely affected by a number of unforeseen developments in foreign and domestic markets during the period 1961 through 1964.

Background of the Commonwealth Group

The Commonwealth Group is composed of one closed-end investment company,[1] a wholly owned management company, and four mutual funds (Exhibit 1). The founder and present chairman of the board, Mr. S. Waldo Coleman, had been one of the first members of the business community in California to recognize the potential of the closed-end investment company and, later, the mutual fund. Several years after his graduation from the University of California at Berkeley in 1903, Mr. Coleman began work with the Coast Counties Gas and Electric Company (CCG&E). In 1914 Mr. Coleman, then 32 years old, was named president of CCG&E. During a vacation in London in 1924 he heard about the closed-end investment companies that had prospered in England since early in the nineteenth century. Only ten investment companies had been formed in the U.S. prior to 1921, and the size and influence of these early companies had been small. Following his return to San Francisco, Mr. Coleman hired a graduate of the Harvard Business School as an investment advisor. In 1925, with an initial investment of $8000, he established a closed-end investment company, the North American Investment Corp-

[1]Closed-end investment companies, much like industrial corporations, issue a fixed number of shares at one time. Once issued, the securities are traded on the open market and are not redeemable. Mutual funds, or open-end investment companies, continuously offer to sell new shares to, and redeem outstanding shares from, the public. The selling price is based on the net asset value of the investment portfolio plus a sales charge or "load" that varies from zero (no load) to 8.9 percent of net asset value per share. All mutual funds will redeem their outstanding shares at current net asset value (minus a nominal redemption fee, in some cases) at the discretion of the shareholder. A mutual fund may be organized as a corporation or as a trust.

Exhibit 1

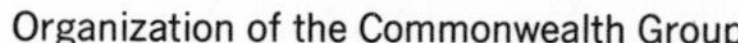

Organization of the Commonwealth Group

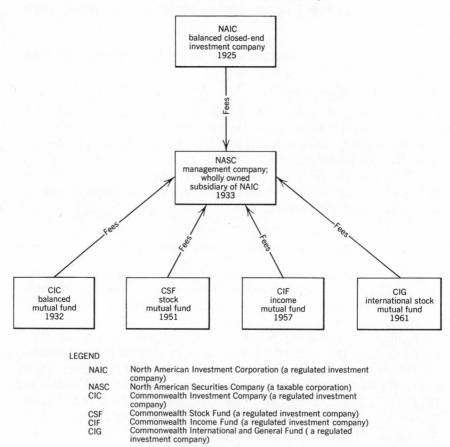

NAIC
balanced closed-end
investment company
1925

Fees

NASC
management company;
wholly owned
subsidiary of NAIC
1933

Fees

Fees

Fees

Fees

CIC
balanced
mutual fund
1932

CSF
stock
mutual fund
1951

CIF
income
mutual fund
1957

CIG
international stock
mutual fund
1961

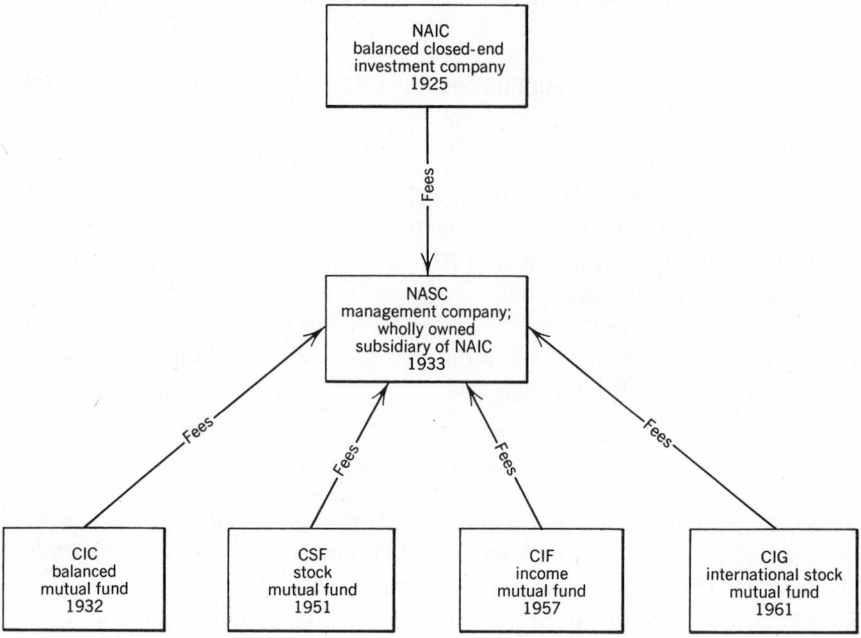

LEGEND

NAIC	North American Investment Corporation (a regulated investment company)
NASC	North American Securities Company (a taxable corporation)
CIC	Commonwealth Investment Company (a regulated investment company)
CSF	Commonwealth Stock Fund (a regulated investment company)
CIF	Commonwealth Income Fund (a regulated investment company)
CIG	Commonwealth International and General Fund (a regulated investment company)

—— Fees ——→ : Payment of management fees

*The operating expenses of all companies in the Commonwealth group are paid be NASC.
†The same corporate officers serve NASC, NAIC, and the four mutual funds.

oration (NAIC). Several months earlier, the first U.S. open-end investment company, or mutual fund, had come into existence when Massachusetts Investors Trust granted its shareholders the right to redeem their shares at net asset value less a specified discount.

Following the market collapse of 1929, Mr. Coleman noted several shortcomings of the closed-end structure. He had observed that many people were unable to sell their shares in a closed-end company at current net asset value. For example, in 1930 it was often possible to buy shares in a closed-end fund managed by a New York investment banking firm at 70 percent of current asset value.[2] Mr. Coleman felt that the redemption feature of mutual fund shares, which enabled the owner to sell his shares at net asset value, would make these shares relatively more attractive to the investing public following the depression. In the period 1929 through 1932, many closed-end investment companies were liquidated, and the value of total net assets in mutual funds declined to $75 million. Of approximately four closed-end investment companies operating in San Francisco in 1929, NAIC was the only one to survive the depression.

Anticipating the growing public interest in mutual funds during the next decade, Mr. Coleman established in 1932 the Commonwealth Investment Company (CIC), a mutual fund with initial capital of $41,500. CIC had the dual objectives of a *balanced* mutual fund: reasonable current income and long-term growth. In the following year, North American Securities Company (NASC) was organized as a subsidiary of NAIC; NASC was to act as underwriter and selling agent for CIC, with the immediate task of introducing the shares of the newly formed mutual fund on the national market through investment dealers. Initially the parent company, NAIC, acted as investment advisor for the new fund. Between 1932 and 1936 total assets in the mutual fund industry grew from $75 million to $500 million; in the same period CIC's net assets grew from $41,500 to $1,900,000. Following the recession of 1937–1938, CIC and the mutual fund industry experienced a period of rapid growth during World War II, with CIC assets reaching $6 million and industry assets totalling $1.2 billion in 1945.

The period 1946–1952 produced the most significant growth to date for the Commonwealth Investment Company, as CIC assets increased more than tenfold while mutual fund industry assets tripled. In 1945 Mr. Coleman initiated the Commonwealth Investing Plan, a voluntary plan for systematic investment patterned on a similar plan he had tried in 1936. The plan called for an initial investment by the investor of at least $100, with scheduled additions to the account in any amount. Investors retained the right to interrupt or terminate their participation in the plan without penalty. Under the plan, all dividends were to be accumulated along with the periodic investments, and investment certificates were to be issued to the investor at regular intervals. Initially, Mr. Coleman had difficulty in getting dealers to sell his new plan to the public. Finally, Kidder, Peabody and Company of New York City started selling the plan, and many other dealers soon followed. The systematic investment plan gained widespread public acceptance, and other funds

[2]Mr. Coleman recalled, as an example of trading difficulties during the depression, that during a four-hour period one day in 1931, it was impossible to get a single bid for a share of duPont stock on the NYSE.

started similar plans. Mr. Coleman felt that the popularity of the Commonwealth Investing Plan was a major factor in CIC's rapid growth following World War II.

In 1950, NAIC delegated all management advisory responsibilities to its subsidiary, NASC, which previously had acted only as a selling agent. Company officials wanted NAIC to retain its tax status as a regulated investment company and, as such, NAIC was allowed to receive no more than 10 percent of its total income from "nondividend-interest sources," such as management advisory fees. As a result, it was decided to pay all management fees to NASC, a taxable corporation.

Two new mutual funds were established in the Commonwealth Group in the 1950s. The Commonwealth Stock Fund was formed in 1952, and by 1965 its assets had grown to $24 million. In November 1957, the Commonwealth Income Fund was started, and over the following seven years the assets of this fund reached $52 million. The market value of net assets in the parent company, NAIC, was $5.4 million at the end of 1964. Commonwealth's first mutual fund, CIC, had a net asset value of $179 million in 1965. Early in 1965 the aggregate net asset value of all the funds managed by NASC (including the CIG fund) was approximately $262 million. It was the second largest mutual fund portfolio managed from a San Francisco headquarters.

Organization of the Commonwealth Group

NASC is a wholly owned subsidiary of NAIC, the original closed-end investment company of which Mr. Coleman (13 percent) and his sister Janet D. Coleman (11 percent) are the principal shareholders.[3] NASC is a taxable corporation that acts as portfolio manager and principal underwriter for five regulated investment companies: the parent company (NAIC) and the four mutual funds in the Commonwealth Group. The same nine corporate officers serve NASC and the five investment companies. NASC receives management fees from each of the investment companies in the amount of one half of 1 percent of each company's net assets, computed daily.[4] In 1964 these fees totalled $1.3 million (Exhibit 2). In turn, NASC pays all officer salaries and all general administrative and operating expenses of the parent company and the mutual funds. During 1964, compensation to sixty-five officers and other employees totalled $689,943; included in this total is an aggregate compensation of $156,636 received by the nine corporate officers (Exhibit 3).

In addition to management fees, a second major source of income to NASC is the portion of sales commission on new shares retained by

[3]NAIC shares are traded on the Pacific Coast Stock Exchange.

[4]CIC pays management fees in the amount of four tenths of 1 percent of those assets in excess of $150 million.

Exhibit 2

COMMONWEALTH INTERNATIONAL AND GENERAL FUND

North American Securities Company
(Subsidiary of North American Investment Corporation)
Income Statement for Year Ended December 31, 1964

INCOME	
Management and other service fees	$1,355,706
Net commissions retained on sales after dealer concessions	307,729
Interest	20,855
Total	$1,684,290
EXPENSES	
Compensation to officers and employees (including officers of parent company and the mutual funds)*	$ 689,943
Sales literature, prospectuses, advertising	186,793
General administrative and operating expenses	302,740
Taxes, other than income taxes	22,115
Total	1,201,591
Income before taxes	$ 482,699
Provision for federal income and state franchise taxes	240,000
Net income	$ 242,699
DIVIDENDS	
Dividends paid to parent company	$ 115,000

*During 1964, the aggregate compensation of the officers of NASC, who are also officers of the parent company and the mutual funds sponsored by NASC, was $156,636.

NASC; these commissions accounted for approximately $308,000 of NASC's total income of $1.68 million in 1963. NASC employs twelve "wholesalers" who are located in major U.S. cities. Each wholesaler contacts investment dealers in his area and encourages them to sell shares of the Commonwealth funds. The wholesaler is compensated by a salary plus a fraction of NASC's share of the commissions on sales in his area.

NASC's profit after taxes in 1964 totalled $242,699, of which $115,000 was paid in dividends to the parent company, NAIC; this $115,000 was in turn paid out by NAIC to its stockholders (Exhibit 4). The prospectuses of NAIC and the four mutual funds all contain the following statement: "It is the policy of the fund to meet the requirements of Section 851 of the Internal Revenue Code by distributing to

Exhibit 3

COMMONWEALTH INTERNATIONAL AND GENERAL FUND

North American Securities Company
(Subsidiary of North American Investment Corporation)
Balance Sheet as of December 31, 1964

ASSETS	
Cash	$ 195,176
Marketable securities at cost (market value: $815,927)	817,196
Receivable for investment companies' shares sold and repurchased	794,660
Receivable for services and advances	148,038
Interest receivable	6,998
Prepaid insurance and expenses	18,492
Furniture, equipment, and leasehold improvements	39,382
Total assets	$2,019,942
LIABILITIES	
Payable for investment companies' shares purchased and repurchases	$ 786,398
Accounts payable	58,277
Payable for profit-sharing plan	100,991
Accrued taxes	184,787
Total liabilities	$1,130,453
SHAREHOLDERS' EQUITY	
Common capital stock (par $100; 1,000 shares authorized; 250 shares issued)	$ 25,000
Paid in surplus	151,802
Retained earnings	712,687
Shareholders' equity	889,489
Total liabilities and shareholders' equity	$2,019,942

shareholders all or substantially all of its net income as defined in the code. When all income is distributed, the fund is not subject to Federal income taxes."

The lists of directors of the four Commonwealth mutual funds are identical. Three of the seven directors are officers of the funds, and four directors are "outsiders." The Investment Company Act of 1940 stipulates that no more than 60 percent of the directors of a mutual fund may be affiliated with the fund or its investment advisor. Each year the directors of the fund must approve the management contract with the investment advisor. A majority vote of the independent directors is suffi-

Exhibit 4

COMMONWEALTH INTERNATIONAL AND GENERAL FUND

North American Investment Corporation
Income Statement for Year Ended December 31, 1964

INCOME	
Cash dividends (including $115,000 from subsidiary company, NASC)	$255,722
Interest	7,928
Total	$263,650
EXPENSES	
Management fee	$ 22,816
Stock transfer and dividend disbursement fee	2,011
Directors' fees	3,700
Custodian and registrar fees	500
Legal, audit, and association fees	2,400
Printing and postage	3,982
Taxes	269
Miscellaneous	310
Total	35,988
Net Income	$227,662
DIVIDENDS	
Cash dividends on preferred shares	$ 92,288
Cash dividends on common shares	137,262
Total	$229,550
CAPITAL GAINS DISTRIBUTION	
Net realized from sale of investments	$213,290
Capital gains distribution to common shareholders	$204,869

cient to renew an existing contract; however, a majority of the shareholders must approve a new management contract.

The Commonwealth International and General Fund

In 1960 Mr. Coleman and other Commonwealth officers began to consider the possibilities of participating in the dramatic expansion taking place in the international economy. He had noted with interest that the Eurofund, started by a group of prominent New York businessmen including a former president of Bankers Trust Company, was investing its funds entirely abroad. Early in 1961, the prospects for foreign investment was indeed promising.

The record of industrial growth in Europe during the 1950s had considerable influence on the rising expectations of United States investors in 1961. In the years 1953 through 1959, the industrial production of many European countries had increased at a faster rate than that of the United States, as indicated in Exhibit 5.

Exhibit 5

COMMONWEALTH INTERNATIONAL AND GENERAL FUND

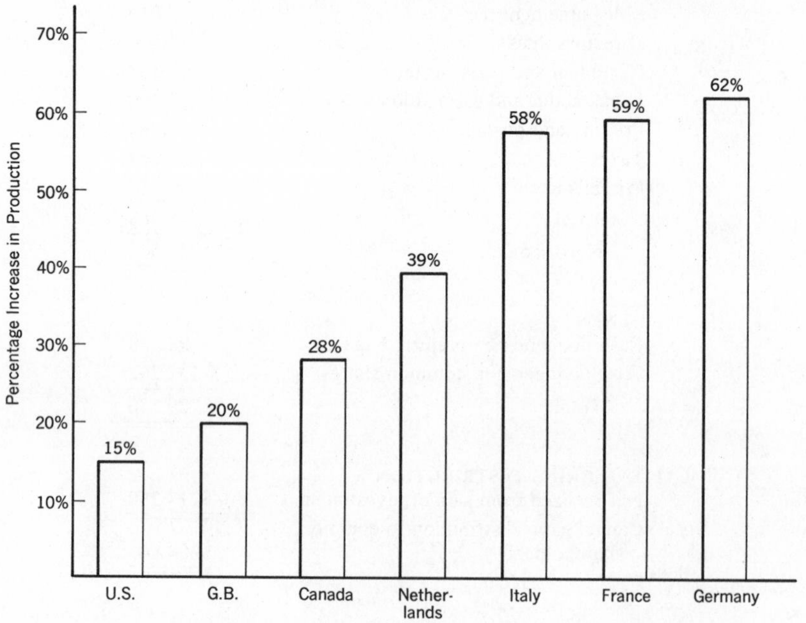

SOURCE: United Nations Monthly Bulletin, January 1961.

In may 1961, *Barron's* noted that stock prices were reaching new highs in many foreign countries:

> During the first quarter of 1961, as most investors know, U.S. stock prices approached an all-time high. More than recouping the moderate loss it suffered during 1960, the Dow Jones Industrial Average spurted more than 10% for the (first) quarter, from 610 to 679, before going on to eclipse all previous peaks early in April. Not so widely recognized, however, is the performance of stock markets in at least five other nations, which scored even greater advances. As the accompanying table makes clear, in the first

three months of this year, leading market indices in Belgium, Britain, Japan, France, and the Netherlands outpaced the Dow Jones Industrials. Stock prices in six out of nine nations shown in the table, it will be noted, also had outstripped those in the U.S. for the year 1960.[5]

Stock Market Index	*Years 1953–1959*	*Year 1960*	*First Quarter 1961*
Dow Jones Industrials	124%	(9%)	10%
Belgian Ensemble	28	(22)	12
British Financial Times	119	(10)	12
Canadian Toronto*	70	(2)	7
Australian #15	96	(10)	4
French Revised	96	6	21
Italian 24 Ore	152	29	5
Dutch ANP-CBS	115	25	30*
German Herstatt	211†	33	2*
Japanese "DJ"	113	49	17

*Corrected for currency premiums.
†Excluding 1953.
Parentheses indicate loss.

SOURCE: *Barron's*, May 1, 1961.

Against this background of general optimism about the opportunities abroad, Commonwealth officials planned the formation of the Commonwealth International and General Fund (CIG). The stated objective of the new fund would be "to pursue, on behalf of its shareholders, the possibilities for capital appreciation that are available in the dramatic industrial expansion taking place overseas, with current income as a secondary consideration."

Once the basic decisions had been made as to the fundamental investment policies of the new fund, it was necessary to draft three basic legal documents: The corporate charter (Certificate of Incorporation)[6]; the registration statement required by the Investment Company Act of 1940; and the Prospectus for the new fund.

The "house counsel" did as much of the legal work as time permitted, including the basic drafting of the legal documents; since only the fees paid to outside law firms are listed below, total legal costs are substantially understated.

The Investment Company Act requires that, in the formation of a new fund, initial capital of $100,000 be obtained from no more than twenty-five people within ninety days after registration statement becomes effective. Early in 1961 this requirement was met, and on April 11,

[5]Robert A. Gilbert, "From London to Tokyo, Stock Prices Have Hit New Highs Throughout the Free World," *Barron's*, May 1, 1961, p. 9.

[6]All of the investment companies in the Commonwealth Group are incorporated in Delaware.

Exhibit 7

COMMONWEALTH INTERNATIONAL AND GENERAL FUND

Approximate Expenses Incurred in the Start-Up of Business

Sales literature	$12,500
Legal and audit fees	3,000
Registration fees	4,500
Prospectus	2,500
Stationery and supplies (including stock certificates)	2,200
Advertising	2,500
Postage	1,000
Direct mail service	500
Miscellaneous	500
	$29,200

1961, CIG shares were offered to the general public at $12.50 a share.

During the first twenty-one days of the offering, a special concession was offered to investment dealers as an additional inducement to introduce the shares to the investing public.

Exhibit 8

COMMONWEALTH INTERNATIONAL AND GENERAL FUND

Sales Charge and Dealer Terms

Amount of Single Transaction	*Regular Sales Charge*	*Dealer Concession*		
		Regular	*Additional**	*Total**
Less than $10,000	8.50%	6.50%	1.50%	8.00%
$10,000–24,999	7.50	6.00	1.25	7.25
$25,000–49,999	5.75	4.50	1.00	5.50
$50,000–99,999	4.00	3.20	0.55	3.75
$100,000–249,999	2.75	2.20	0.30	2.50
$250,000–499,999	2.00	1.60	0.15	1.75
$500,000 or more	1.00	0.80	—	0.80

*These terms applied only to the first twenty-one days of the offering.

The initial offering was successful; as of May 1, nearly two million dollars in shares had been sold. Early in May, the fund began investing in common stocks. By the end of August, net assets had risen to $2.7 million.

As of August 31, 1961, CIG had invested approximately $1.9 million in common stocks; the remaining $800,000 of the initial capital was at that time still invested in short-term government securities. Of this initial investment in common stocks, 35 percent was invested in U.S. companies having substantial international interests, 14 percent in French firms, 12 percent in German corporations, and the remainder in various European, Canadian, and Australian companies.

During 1961 the net asset value of CIG fund shares declined from the initial offering price of $12.50 to $11.29. With the weakness in stock prices in U.S. and foreign markets in 1962, CIG's per-share value fell to $9.78 by the end of November 1962.

An important development of 1963 was the "interest equalization tax" proposed in July and designed to restrain the flow of American investment money to foreign countries. The proposed bill, to be in effect from the summer of 1963 until the end of 1965, levied a tax of up to 15 percent of the value of new or existing foreign stocks and bonds bought by Americans from foreigners. To avoid the tax, the managers of CIG restricted their purchases of foreign securities to those shares which were available in U.S. markets and hence not subject to the tax. The CIG annual report of 1963 stated: "Purchases of your fund's shares would not be subject to the tax because these shares are not foreign securities." In effect, the tax reduced the supply of foreign securities in the U.S. and, in turn, reduced CIG's flexibility. CIG officials often found that foreign securities which they desired to buy were not readily available in this country. Furthermore, the tax exerted a depressing effect on stock prices in foreign markets, as a result of the decrease in purchase orders from investors in the United States.

During 1963 and 1964, CIG's net asset value per share increased, reaching $10.54 in November 1964; however, this market value was still considerably below the initial issue price of $12.50 (Exhibit 10). At the end of November 1964, the composition of CIG's portfolio reflected increasing emphasis on the shares of U.S. corporations. Still a heavy commitment existed in the common stocks of European companies (Exhibit 12). The performance of the fifteen U.S. mutual funds investing abroad during the period 1962 to 1964 is shown in Exhibit 13.

The Future of the Commonwealth International and General Fund

Late in 1964, Mr. Coleman and other officials of the Commonwealth Group felt that several alternatives were available with respect to their management policies on the CIG Fund. The actual performance of CIG, and of the other funds investing abroad, had not matched their expectations during the previous three year period. Mr. Coleman stated late in 1964, "We did not grasp how the American people interpreted an 'international company.' They think of an international company as a foreign firm, but actually some of the biggest companies doing business abroad

Exhibit 9

COMMONWEALTH INTERNATIONAL AND GENERAL FUND

North American Investment Corporation
Balance Sheet as of December 31, 1964

ASSETS	
Investments at market quotations (identified cost, $2,277,341)	$4,654,865
Cash – demand deposits	100,193
Receivable for investments gold	54,898
Dividends receivable	6,417
Investment in subsidiary company (book value, $179,808)*	888,220
Total assets	$5,704,493
LIABILITIES	
Accounts payable	$ 4,889
Payable for investments purchased	33,088
Capital gain distribution payable Jan. 14, 1965	204,869
Total liabilities	$242,846
Net assets at market value applicable to outstanding capital shares, December 31, 1964†	$5,461,647

	6% Cumulative Preferred	Common
CAPITAL SHARES		
Number of shares outstanding	61,196	204,869
Par value per share	$25.00	$1.00
Total preference in involuntary liquidation	$1,537,575	
Asset coverage per share	$89.25	
Net asset value:		
Aggregate amount		$3,924,072
Per-share value		$19.15

*The investment in North American Securities Company is stated at $888,220. That amount includes unrealized depreciation on marketable securities of $1269. The balance sheet of North American Securities Company reflects the marketable securities at cost and the shareholders' equity at $889,489.

†No provision has been made for federal income tax on net income, net realized gains from sales of investments, or unrealized appreciation of investments, since it is the policy of the company to comply with the special provisions of the Internal Revenue Code available to investment companies and to make distributions from net income and realized gains sufficient to relieve the company from all or substantially all such tax.

are U.S. corporations. Of CIG's current investment in common stocks, nearly one half is invested in such U.S. companies."

As one alternative, there existed the possibility of continuing to operate the CIG fund under the existing fundamental policy. In the past, CIG's portfolio of foreign securities had reflected a heavy commitment in the stocks of European companies, and European stock prices had been adversely affected by the Berlin crisis of 1962 and the interest

Exhibit 10

COMMONWEALTH INTERNATIONAL AND GENERAL FUND

Balance Sheets, 1961 – 1964

	November 30, 1961	*November 30, 1962*	*November 30, 1963*	*November 30, 1964*
ASSETS				
Investments in common stocks at market quotation*	$2,287,359	$2,009,418	$1,969,962	$1,399,971
U.S. government obligations	596,838	348,526	149,688	–
Corporate short-term notes at cost	–	102,960	29,806	–
Cash on deposit with custodian	349,070	33,896	19,950	112,965
Receivable for shares sold	19,750	4,935	–	–
Receivable for investments sold	–	22,308	14,712	203,737
Dividends and interest receivable	8,826	7,031	5,584	4,254
Total assets	$3,261,843	$2,529,074	$2,189,702	$1,720,927
LIABILITIES				
Accounts payable	$ 3,998	$ 3,253	$ 2,956	$ 2,243
Payable for shares repurchased	23,780	16,271	32,548	13,724
Payable for investments purchased	385,088	5,017	–	222,945
Total liabilities	$ 412,866	$ 24,541	$ 35,504	$ 238,912
NET ASSETS				
Net assets at market value	$2,848,977	$2,504,533	$2,154,198	$1,482,015
Net asset value per share	$ 11.29	$ 9.78	$ 10.10	$ 10.54
*Identified cost of investments in common stocks.	$2,311,745	$2,438,035	$2,320,225	$1,467,448

Exhibit 11

COMMONWEALTH INTERNATIONAL AND GENERAL FUND

Income Statements, 1961–1964

	Six Months Ended November 30, 1961	*Year Ended November 30, 1962*	*Year Ended November 30, 1963*	*Year Ended November 30, 1964*
INCOME				
Cash dividends net of foreign income taxes	$17,757	$45,325	$48,233	$41,582
Interest	11,296	15,422	11,748	1,226
Total	$29,053	$60,747	$59,981	$42,808
EXPENSES				
Management fee	$ 7,496	$13,126	$11,948	$ 8,972
Custodian and registrar fees	926	525	525	200
Legal and audit fees	1,750	2,366	2,834	2,450
Printing and postage	350	2,306	2,117	1,744
Taxes	–	–	703	–
Miscellaneous	111	460	493	526
Total	$10,632	$18,783	$18,620	$13,892
NET INCOME	$18,421	$41,964	$41,361	$29,768
DIVIDENDS				
Dividends paid to shareholders	$14,990	$36,252	$39,117	$27,768

Exhibit 12

COMMONWEALTH INTERNATIONAL AND GENERAL FUND

Common Stock Investments by Country

	Aug. 31, 1961	*Nov. 30, 1961*	*Nov. 30, 1962*	*Nov. 30, 1963*	*Nov. 30, 1964*
United States	35.1%	31.6%	27.8%	29.2%	42.6%
France	14.0	12.4	10.9	7.0	4.6
Germany	12.6	14.6	15.6	16.9	14.9
Canada	10.2	10.2	10.9	9.5	9.1
United Kingdom	9.8	11.1	13.8	15.3	7.2
Netherlands	5.3	6.5	7.4	9.4	2.4
Australia	3.9	4.2	4.1	3.7	2.6
Sweden	3.7	3.9	3.6	3.9	2.9
Italy	3.2	3.1	3.8	2.8	1.4
Belgium	2.2	2.4	2.1	2.1	–
Japan	–	–	–	0.2	4.1
Spain	–	–	–	–	4.3
Mexico	–	–	–	–	3.9
	100.0%	100.0%	100.0%	100.0%	100.0%

Exhibit 13

COMMONWEALTH INTERNATIONAL AND GENERAL FUND

Comparative Appreciation in Market Price, 1953–1964 and 1962–1964

	Assets (Millions)	Sales Charge	Dividend Return	Appreciation: From 1953 to 1964	Appreciation: From 1962 to 1964
				$100 Investment Ended as. . .	
FUNDS INVESTING ABROAD					
Commonwealth International and General Fund (started 5/61)	$ 1.7	8.5%	1.7%	–	$114.96
Canada General Fund (started 8/54)	54.4	8.5	2.3	–	140.56
Canadian Fund	33.8	7.5	2.5	$238.90	132.39
Channing International Growth Fund (started 6/56)	5.0	8.5	0.6	–	118.18
International Investors (started 8/55)	1.4	8.0	2.4	–	109.39
International Resources Fund	18.3	8.5	1.7	313.72	136.92
Investors Inter-Continental Fund (started 5/55)	49.5	7.5	3.4	–	129.35
Keystone International Fund (started 10/54)	8.5	7.5	1.4	–	117.84
Loomis-Sayles Canadian & International Fund (started 4/61)	18.2	none	1.6	–	128.73
Scudder International Investments (started 6/54)	37.9	*	1.8	–	126.30
Stein Roe & Farnham International Fund (started 8/54)	22.7	none	2.0	–	122.96
Templeton Growth Fund of Canada (started 10/54)	3.7	8.5	1.3	–	126.93
UBS Fund of Canada (started 11/60)	3.7	*	1.3	–	139.49
United Funds of Canada (started 8/54)	9.4	8.5	0.8	–	141.47
United International Fund (started 4/61)	9.3	*	1.1	–	97.18
MARKET INDICES					
Standard & Poor's 500 Stock Average	–	–	3.4	$349.85	$149.21
Forbes Index of 10 Stock Mutual Funds	–	–	2.5	372.38	144.72
Forbes Index of 10 Balanced Mutual Funds	–	–	3.3	233.55	128.23

*Indicates funds not offering shares as of June 20, 1964; existing shares were traded over-the-counter. "From 1953 to 1964" covers the period from September 20, 1953 to June 30, 1964. "From 1962 to 1964" covers the period from June 30, 1962 to June 30, 1964. All capital gains distributions have been reinvested but income dividends have not. "Dividend return" is based on June 30, 1963 prices and succeeding twelve-month income dividend payout. SOURCE: *Forbes*, August 15, 1964.

equalization tax. Under this alternative it would be possible to de-emphase European issues and explore opportunities for investment in the stocks of companies in the Far East and in Central and South America.

Liquidation of the fund, as a second alternative, was not considered practicable. Liquidation at the current market value of $10.54 would be unfair to the investors who had purchased CIG shares at the initial offering price at $12.50.

The third alternative available to Commonwealth officials was to continue to operate CIG under its present charter, which could be amended to reflect a change in fundamental policy. To meet the "market," that is, the desires of the investing public, the existing CIG structure might be used as a basis for a "growth fund," with the new objective of seeking growth opportunities in common stocks both at home and abroad, with primary emphasis on United States companies.

As a fourth alternative, CIG's assets could be merged into another Commonwealth fund. This would leave three funds in the Commonwealth family which, with a stock fund (CSF), an income fund (CIF), and a balanced fund (CIC), might present an adequate spectrum of mutual funds to the investing public. CIG shareholders who received shares of another fund in such a merger would do so without realizing a capital gain or loss on the transaction.

FINANCIAL STRUCTURE FOR A FINANCE COMPANY

Associates Investment Company

In January 1963, Mr. George C. Coquillard, vice-president and treasurer of Associates Investment Company, received a copy of operating projections for the Company for 1963 (see Exhibit 9). One of Mr. Coquillard's responsibilities was to prepare recommendations to the management committee concerning the company's financial structure. In this regard, he was facing two basic questions as of January 1963: (1) How should Associates meet its needs for funds in 1963? (2) What should be the company's financial structure over the long run?

Management of Associates Investment Company had given a great deal of attention to its financial structure in past years. Appendix A contains an excerpt from a study performed by Lehman Brothers for Associates. The study, entitled "Analysis of Capital Structure," was dated May 25, 1953. Mr. Coquillard noted that there was a great deal of similarity between the findings in the 1953 study and his present thoughts on the subject. He believed that there were many factors which should affect the company's financial structure. Those factors that he considered most important included the types of business that the company was in, the sources of financing available, the projected needs of the company, and the outlook for money and capital markets.

History of Associates Investment Company

Associates Investment Company was organized in South Bend, Indiana, in May 1918. During its first year, it operated as a real estate company, but in 1919 entered the automobile finance field by undertaking to finance three automobile dealers in the city of South Bend. At the end of its first year of operation, the company had total assets of $125,000 and was doing business only in South Bend.

By 1941, the Company had seventy-two branch offices, and the vol-

Exhibit 1

ASSOCIATES INVESTMENT COMPANY

Consolidated Balance Sheet
December 31, 1962
(In 000s)

ASSETS		
Cash		$ 72,415
Marketable securities*		23,239
Finance receivables:		
Retail installment receivables	$ 892,256	
Wholesale short-term loans	145,109	
Personal installment loans	189,094	
Commercial loans and other	192,148	
	$1,418,607	
Collateral held for resale	3,393	
Less—Unearned discounts	(107,896)	
Reserve for losses	(34,902)	
Receivables, net		1,279,202
Investment in life insurance subsidiaries		12,909
Property (net)		5,281
Other assets		6,382
		$1,399,428
LIABILITIES		
Commercial paper		$ 428,131
Notes payable—bank		138,700
Miscellaneous liabilities and accruals		104,532
Current portion of long-term debt		42,153
Total current liabilities		$ 713,516
Long-term debt:		
Senior notes		$ 366,897
Subordinated notes		81,367
Capital notes		65,400
		$ 513,664
Capital stock and surplus:		
Cumulative preferred stock		$ 9,000
Common stock		36,034
Paid-in surplus		11,599
Earned surplus		117,174
Less treasury stock		(1,559)
		$ 172,248
		$1,399,428

*All of the marketable securities belong to the consolidated insurance subsidiaries.

ume of receivables purchased during the year reached $251,000,000. Volume declined sharply during the war years as a result of government restrictions on installment financing. As a consequence, the company reduced the number of its branch offices to thirty-six in the interests of economy as the liquidation of receivables continued during this period. In 1942, two manufacturing plants were acquired. During the war years these facilities were devoted to production of war materials. One of the plants was sold immediately following the war, and the remaining plant was sold in 1960.

With the resumption of installment financing following the end of the war, Associates again increased the number of its branch offices. By the end of 1962, the company had total assets of $1.4 billion and with its related organizations had 590 offices in 429 cities in forty-five states and Canada (see Exhibit 1). For the year ended December 31, 1962, the financing business of Associates and its subsidiaries contributed 73 percent of consolidated net income; life insurance business, 15 percent; and insurance business other than life, 12 percent (see Exhibit 2).

Exhibit 2

ASSOCIATES INVESTMENT COMPANY

Consolidated Income Statement
Year Ended December 31, 1962
(In 000s)

INCOME:	
Finance discounts, interest, and other finance income	$137,411
Premium earned and investment income of casualty insurance subsidiaries	21,776
Other income	408
Total income	$159,595
EXPENSES:	
Operating expenses	51,774
Casualty insurance underwriting losses and expenses	18,727
Provision for losses on finance receivables	19,232
Interest on notes payable	42,662
Total expenses	$132,395
Net income before federal income taxes	$ 27,200
Provision for federal income taxes	13,116
Net income excluding wholly owned life insurance subsidiaries	$ 14,084
Net income of wholly owned life insurance subsidiaries not consolidated	2,427
Net income of the company and all subsidiaries	$ 16,511

Financing Business of Associates Investment Company

The financing business could be classified into four types, namely (1) purchase of retail installment contracts; (2) wholesale financing; (3) direct and personal loans; and (4) industrial and commercial loans. Exhibit 3 shows the volume of finance receivables purchased and the amount of finance receivables held at year end for recent years.

Retail Installment Financing

This business consisted of the purchase of secured retail installment obligations – principally retail automobile obligations that arose from the sale of new and used automobiles and, in addition, other retail obligations which arose from the sale of mobile homes, heavy-duty trucks, farm equipment, and miscellaneous consumer goods.

Associates purchased from dealers the retail installation obligations given by the purchasers, whose down payment and credit had to be satisfactory to Associates. The majority of retail automobile obligations were purchased without recourse against the dealer. In some cases of retail automobile obligations, and in practically all cases of other retail obligations, Associates received a guarantee or repurchase agreement from the dealer.

During 1962, automobile obligations accounted for about four fifths of all Associates' retail installment financing. Although Associates was still heavily dependent on automobile financing, the volume of other retail obligations had grown rapidly in recent years. Company executives believed that such a diversification program was desirable and planned to continue it.

Wholesale Financing

The business of wholesale financing, or "floor planning," consisted principally of secured advances to automobile dealers to permit them to carry automobile inventories. The company also did a small amount of wholesale financing of dealers in mobile homes, trucks, farm machinery and equipment, and other products. The average length of time that wholesale receivables remained outstanding during the year ended December 31, 1962 was less than forty days. The average unpaid balance of these receivables outstanding at December 31, 1962 was $58,577 per dealer and ranged up to a high of $1,101,985. While not profitable of itself, management considered wholesale financing to be of major importance to Associates because good dealer relationships were necessary to insure continued large volumes of retail installment receivables being made available to Associates.

Exhibit 3

ASSOCIATES INVESTMENT COMPANY

Finance Receivables Purchased and Held
($000 omitted)

The following tables set forth the volume of finance receivables purchased and the amount of finance receivables held as of the close of the periods indicated:

Finance Receivables Purchased During Period

	Retail Installment Receivables	*Wholesale Receivables*	*Commercial Loans and Other Installment Receivables*	*Personal Installment Loans*	*Total*
1957	$785,830	$815,889	$103,971	$138,104	$1,843,794
	42.6%	44.2%	5.6%	7.6%	100.0%
1958	$599,538	$611,873	$113,822	$152,079	$1,477,312
	40.6%	41.4%	7.7%	10.3%	100.0%
1959	$743,627	$839,591	$163,612	$181,536	$1,928,366
	38.6%	43.5%	8.5%	9.4%	100.0%
1960	$702,733	$912,614	$172,569	$199,946	$1,987,862
	35.4%	45.9%	8.7%	10.0%	100.0%
1961	$652,823	$723,222	$169,654	$215,941	$1,761,640
	37.1%	41.0%	9.6%	12.3%	100.0%
1962	$805,458	$942,091	$248,883	$244,609	$2,241,041
	36.0%	42.0%	11.1%	10.9%	100.0%

Finance Receivables Held At End Of Period

	Retail Installment Receivables	*Wholesale Receivables*	*Commercial Loans and Other Installment Receivables*	*Personal Installment Loans*	*Total*
1957	$762,457	$120,760	$ 50,376	$ 93,989	$1,027,582
	74.2%	11.7%	4.9%	9.2%	100.0%
1958	$648,201	$ 93,825	$ 67,937	$109,639	$ 919,602
	70.5%	10.2%	7.4%	11.9%	100.0%
1959	$752,831	$109,215	$ 89,543	$130,379	$1,081,968
	69.6%	10.1%	8.3%	12.0%	100.0%
1960	$785,907	$150,873	$110,168	$147,319	$1,194,267
	65.8%	12.6%	9.2%	12.4%	100.0%
1961	$777,378	$138,763	$131,943	$166,349	$1,214,433
	64.0%	11.4%	10.9%	13.7%	100.0%
1962	$892,256	$145,109	$192,148	$189,094	$1,418,607
	62.9%	10.2%	13.6%	13.3%	100.0%

Personal Installment Loans

Personal installment loans made to individuals were in the majority of instances secured by liens on personal property. Most of these installment loans were subject to governmental regulations that, among other things, limited the maximum amount of the loan and the maximum charges. The unpaid balances of Associates' personal loans averaged $480 each. Associates' personal loan business had been expanded in recent years, and management anticipated a further growth of this segment of the business.

Commercial Loans and Other Installment Receivables

The commercial loan business consisted of secured short- and medium-term loans made to business interests such as manufacturers, wholesalers, and retailers and of rediscount credit extended to other finance companies. The commercial loans were secured by current accounts receivable, by inventories, or by fixed assets. Advances to other finance companies were secured by a pledge of installment notes and contracts owned by such companies and were secured principally by automobiles. Other commercial installment receivables consisted of time sales obligations purchased at a discount from manufacturers, distributors, and dealers engaged in the selling of communications equipment, steel buildings, construction and industrial equipment, and other income-producing property. In most cases, the guaranty or repurchase agreement of the seller of the goods was obtained. These receivables were usually secured by liens on the property being financed. The unpaid balances on these accounts averaged $7328 at December 31, 1962, and the account balances ranged up to $5,854,639. Beyond this, the company had recently set up a leasing subsidiary, but outstandings were of very modest proportion at the time.

Rates

The rates charged for the various classes of Associates' business varied with the type of risk and the maturity of the receivables and were also affected by other factors including competition, governmental regulation, and current money rates.

The discount rate[1] on retail installment contracts purchased from dealers generally ranged from 4 percent to 6 percent per annum of the original amount of the note in the case of new automobiles; from 5 percent to 15 percent in the case of used automobiles; and from 4 1/2 percent to 12 percent in the case of other products.

[1]Whereas automobile dealers discount (sell) their retail installment contracts to finance companies, the retail purchaser ordinarily pays an "add-on" rate. The determining characteristic of an "add-on" rate is the addition of the finance charge in advance to the unpaid balance at time of purchase. As an example, assume a new car transaction with an unpaid balance of $2000 to be financed at a 6 percent "add-on" rate for a period of one year. The face amount of the installment contract would be drawn for $2120 with eleven monthly installments at $176.66 and one of $176.74.

The rate with respect to wholesale financing of new automobiles for dealers was generally 5 percent simple interest per annum on the average daily balance owed by the dealers, plus a flat charge per vehicle for each ninety days to cover insurance and handling. In the case of used automobiles, the rate was generally 6 percent simple interest per annum, plus a flat charge per vehicle for each sixty days.

Rates on personal installment loans ranged from 5 percent "add-on" to 3 1/2 percent simple interest per month on the unpaid balance.

Rates on commercial loans ranged as follows: Advances against accounts receivable, inventory loans, and fixed asset loans, 10 percent to 13 percent simple interest per annum. The purchase of other installment receivables was at rates ranging from 4 3/4 percent to 6 percent "add-on."

Insurance Business of Associates

Life Insurance

The Capitol Life Insurance Company ("Capitol"), a Colorado corporation, acquired as a wholly owned subsidiary in 1958, operated as a legal reserve life insurance company providing ordinary life, group life, credit life, and accident and sickness insurance. Capitol was licensed to do business in thirty-nine states.

Protective Life Insurance Company, a Nebraska corporation and a wholly owned subsidiary, commenced business operations on October 1, 1954, to provide credit life, health, and accident insurance relating to installment receivables and to reinsure such business.

Alinco Life Insurance Company (which was completely liquidated on December 31, 1962) limited its operation to the reinsuring of credit life risks relating to installment receivables. Between December 1959, when Alinco was placed in voluntary liquidation, and December 13, 1962, the insurance in force gradually matured and all outstanding insurance risks were reinsured in December 1962, prior to completion of its liquidation. Income taxes were paid by Alinco at rates applicable to life insurance companies. The Internal Revenue Service has issued deficiency notices proposing that the entire net income of Alinco for the years 1954 through 1959 be taxed to Associates and Alinco at the general corporation rates. If the government should ultimately be successful in its claims, company executives computed that the total maximum additional liability for taxes for the years 1954 through 1959, together with interest to December 31, 1962, would be $15,600,000. Associates, contending that it was not liable for these taxes, had taken preliminary steps to obtain a court review of these proposed assessments.

Insurance Other Than Life

Associates was represented in the fire, theft, and collision insurance business by Emmco Insurance Company ("Emmco") and its wholly owned subsidiary, Excel Insurance Company ("Excel"). Emmco entered the insurance business in 1936 and was licensed in forty-nine states, the District of Columbia, and Canada. Excel was licensed in thirty-three states and additional licenses were pending for approval. During 1962, almost all of the insurance written by Emmco and Excel was upon motor vehicles and mobile homes financed by the company and its subsidiaries. Thus, the volume of insurance written by Emmco and Excel has tended to fluctuate with the volume of installment paper financed by Associates. As of early 1963, Emmco and Excel were broadening their services to provide inland marine coverage and were expanding their reinsurance activities. They were also soliciting business from other finance companies and banks.

Sources of Financing

Associates Investment Company used various sources of financing. These included bank borrowings and commercial paper as short-term sources and senior notes, subordinated notes, and capital notes as long-term sources. For tax and other reasons, the company was loathe to resort to the sale of additional preferred or common stock as a source of funds. The last sale of common stock was in 1947. Exhibit 4 contains a schedule of the maturity structure of debt outstanding. The categories of senior borrowings, that is, bank borrowings, commercial paper, and senior notes, ranked equally among each other and were superior in rights to the other securities. The other securities ranked in the following order: subordinated notes, capital notes, preferred stock, and common stock.

Senior Borrowings

1. BANK LINES OF CREDIT. Over the years, Associates Investment Company had built up its credit lines. As of the end of 1962, Associates had lines of credit outstanding of $523,350,000 with 492 banks. Each line was used a minimum of twice each year. Management preferred to borrow from the larger banks and noted that two thirds of the company's bank borrowings came from banks which had one half of the lines of credit. In the opinion of Associates' management, the larger banks offered several advantages including (1) the convenience of larger individual loans; (2) the opportunity to borrow faster (via telephone instead of mail); and (3) demand notes which could be repaid at any time rather than time notes which matured on a specified date.

Exhibit 4

ASSOCIATES INVESTMENT COMPANY

Debt Outstanding at December 31, 1962
($000 omitted)

Maturity	*Unsecured Term Notes*	*Subordinated Unsecured Term Notes*	*Capital Debentures*	*Bank Borrowings and Commercial Paper*	*Total*
1963	$ 35.453	$ 4,600	$ 2,100	$566,831	$ 608,984
1964	35,186	5,933	2,160		43,279
1965	10,186	5,933	1,760		17,879
1966	9,686	5,933	1,810		17,429
1967	19,666	6,233	2,210		28,109
1968	4,671	11,307	410		16,388
1969	4,333	2,267	910		7,510
1970	28,833	2,275	410		31,518
1971	3,833	1,783	310		5,926
1972	3,833	1,833	160		5,826
1973	8,333	1,633	160		10.126
1974	3,333	1,633	100		5,066
1975	3,333	1,633	–		4,966
1976	58,333	1,633	–		59,966
1977	3,338	1,338	–		4,676
1978	–	–	–		–
1979	50,000	–	–		50.000
1980	70,000	30,000	–		100,000
1981	–	–	–		–
1982	–	–	30,000		30,000
1983	50,000	–	–		50,000
1984	–	–	25,000		25,000
Subtotal	$366,897	$81,367	$65,400	0	$ 513,664
Total	$402,350	$85,967	$67,500	$566,831	$1,122,648

In early 1963, Associates borrowed from its banks at the prime rate, then 4 1/2 percent, with compensating balances on a "ten and ten" basis, that is, the company must maintain a minimum compensating balance equal to 10 percent of the line commitment plus 10 percent of any amount actually borrowed. Mr. Coquillard was well aware that the true cost of bank borrowings varied with line usage. Given even the most favorable circumstances – no payout period – bank borrowings under any given line cost the company about 5.7 percent annually. When Associates was a very small company, all its borrowings had been from banks under lines of credit. At this stage in the company's development, Mr. Coquillard noted that Associates had to comply with the wishes of the banks for fear of damaging this important relationship. As the company grew, it began tapping another source of short-term financing, namely, commercial paper. In recent years, as a matter of fact, commercial paper notes had come to provide the bulk of Associates' short-term funds. As a national company, Mr. Coquillard felt that Associates could continue to be economical in the use of its lines, but he still considered maintenance of good banking relations essential. In both 1961 and 1962, bank borrowings represented approximately 20 percent of short-term debt.

Some years ago, it was generally thought by the financial community that bank lines of finance companies should be maintained at a level greater than that of short-term debt (commercial paper plus bank borrowings). Gradually this industry norm had eroded and management thought that Associates, like other national finance companies, could run a certain excess of short-term debt over lines. (Exhibit 5 shows short-term debt as a percent of bank lines for major sales finance companies.) For the time being, Associates had set its own limit at 125 percent, or, in other words, bank lines should equal at least 80 percent of short-term debt. On the other hand, it did not feel that this was a riskless activity, particularly in the light of its new compensating balance program. In June of 1962, Associates changed its compensating balance program from a flat 15 percent of the line. Mr. Coquillard had heard that one well-known regional bank, although consenting to go along with the 10 percent plus 10 percent basis, felt that Associates had taken advantage of market conditions. Because of this, Mr. Coquillard believed that Associates could be a likely candidate in the eyes of that bank for a line cancellation during the next tight money period. How prevalent this type of thinking was, he did not know. He did not think it widespread, but nonetheless found its presence in a key bank somewhat disturbing. No evidence for concern on this score had been found among any of the major New York or Chicago banks, however.

Exhibit 5

ASSOCIATES INVESTMENT COMPANY

Short-Term Borrowings of Major Sales Finance Companies
(Dollar figures in millions)

	December 31				
	1958	*1959*	*1960*	*1961*	*1962*
ASSOCIATES*					
Bank borrowings	$175	$245	$175	$198	$139
Commercial paper	226	233	306	278	428
Total	$401	$478	$481	$476	$567
Bank lines	547	571	572	521	523
3 ÷ 4 (percent)	73.3%	83.7%	84.1%	91.4%	108.4%

Exhibit continued.

Exhibit 5 (Continued)

	December 31				
	1958	1959	1960	1961	1962
COMMERCIAL					
Bank borrowings	$192	$301	$203	$177	$324
Commercial paper	363	560	632	523	605
Total	$555	$861	$835	$700	$929
Bank lines	641	689	708	726	681
3 ÷ 4 (percent)	86.6%	125.0%	117.9%	96.4%	136.4%
CIT					
Bank borrowings	$150	N.A.	N.A.	$172	$311
Commercial paper	431	N.A.	N.A.	492	546
Total	$581	$712	$751	$664	$857
Bank lines	650	690	680	680	680
3 ÷ 4 (percent)	89.4%	103.2%	110.4%	97.6%	126.0%
GMAC					
Bank borrowings	$178	$123	$ 511	$ 76	$ 161
Commercial paper	635	868	1,090	787	951
Total	$813	$991	$1,601	$863	$1,112
Bank lines	872	912	905	947	1,068
3 ÷ 4 (percent)	93.2%	108.7%	176.9%	91.1%	104.1%

*Adjusted for acquisition of Securities Acceptance Corporation in January 1962.

A second standard that the banking community had developed over a period of years was the rule that senior debt must not exceed four times a company's borrowing base.[2] Mr. Coquillard considered this debt limit to be very important among bankers and noted that only a few of the largest sales finance companies had exceeded it (see Exhibit 6). He recalled that on those occasions in the 1955–1957 period when Associates broke through this limit several of the company's lead banks inquired as to its plans to correct the situation.

Since 1957, Associates had grown both in size and stature, but company officials were uncertain as to what extent they were still bound by this limitation. In early 1962, Associates served notice to its principal banks that, should circumstances warrant, it would henceforth expect to run its senior debt beyond 4 to 1. Management felt this matter was almost

[2]Senior debt, as defined, consisted of all liabilities not expressly subordinated. It included among other things accounts payable, reserve for taxes, dealer reserve, and so forth. Borrowing base consisted of all subordinate debt plus adjusted net worth. (Noncurrent assets, such as investment in insurance subsidiaries, plant and equipment, furniture and fixtures, other nonfinance assets, and the like were deducted from net worth for purposes of determining adjusted net worth.)

Exhibit 6

ASSOCIATES INVESTMENT COMPANY

Senior Borrowing Ratio of Major Sales Finance Companies

	December 31				
Company	*1958*	*1959*	*1960*	*1961*	*1962*
Associates Investment Company	3.55	3.56	3.25	3.40	3.62
Commercial Credit Corporation	5.13	5.28	5.19	4.69	5.51
CIT Financial Corporation	3.47	4.00	4.11	3.76	4.26
General Motors Acceptance Corporation	5.16	5.13	5.27	4.72	4.94
Pacific Finance Corporation	3.52	3.87	3.96	2.94	4.13
General Finance Company	3.05	3.12	2.89	2.61	2.94
General Acceptance Corporation	3.08	2.54	3.21	3.43	3.57
Ford Motor Credit Company	–	–	–	0.79	3.29

academic at the time, since its ratio was well below 3.5 and banks needed loans, and noted that only limited comment was received.

As of early 1963, Mr. Coquillard did not expect any serious complaint if Associates should run senior debt in the general area of 4.5 to 1. However, he felt that a problem might arise with the advent of more stringent credit conditions and/or worse loss and delinquency experience. In other words, he thought under less favorable economic circumstances the risk of bank censure might reasonably be expected to increase in direct proportion to the extent to which Associates exceeded the 4 to 1 ratio. At what point it would become critical, then, would depend upon the conditions existing at the time.

Management was concerned about losing a major bank line. It did not feel that Associates could stand the loss of a major bank line without throwing open to question the Company's position in the financial community. Because of high loan levels during the tight money period of 1959, one major bank almost cancelled its line to Associates and another reduced its commitment from $10 to $5 million. Company officials were assured by the banks in both instances that in neither case was there any question of the credit worthiness of Associates.

2. COMMERCIAL PAPER. Associates sold commercial paper for periods of 5 to 270 days. Since the time period never exceeded 270 days, the Company avoided registration of the commercial paper under the Securities Act of 1933. Initially, Associates Investment Company sold its commercial paper through brokers. Brokers typically charged ¼ percent commission on a per annum basis on all commercial paper which they sold. In recent years, the company had sold its commercial paper directly. Currently, management estimated the selling cost of placing its

paper directly at $250,000 per year. Roughly, half of this consisted of the salaries of those people involved in this operation.

To hold its customers, Associates had followed a policy of selling a modest amount of commercial paper even when the company did not need the funds. The excess funds were placed into repurchase agreements.[3] Mr. Coquillard noted that the interest paid on commercial paper was usually somewhat greater than the interest earned on repurchase agreements. However, he believed this policy was necessary to maintain the good will of commercial paper customers.

Associates' executives thought that once a company had established its credit rating, the sale of commercial paper was largely a matter of rates. Over the years, they thought that Associates Investment Company had done an effective job of establishing a good credit rating. Therefore, company executives were convinced that the financial officers of large corporations would buy the commercial paper of Associates Investment Company provided the rates were competitive with those on other money market instruments. Typically, the yield on commercial paper was slightly above that available on treasury bills of comparable maturity.

Mr. Coquillard had in the past expressed the view that Associates' short-term debt should be maintained at a level approximately equal to long-term debt. (Comparative capitalizations for the four major sales finance companies are shown in Exhibit 7.) He thought that such a division would afford Associates the debt flexibility that a consumer finance company demanded while providing it reasonable protection against the hazards of a tight money period, namely, high short-term rates and/or a stringency of funds. At the same time, he felt that a large proportion of short-term debt was ordinarily necessary to provide the company an opportunity to obtain the savings which was generally available in short maturities. While short-term money was generally cheaper than long-term money, such was not always the case with all forms. For example, the bank lines were presently on a "ten and ten" compensating balance basis and the prime rate was 4.5 percent. Thus, the marginal cost of additional borrowings at any time was 5.0 percent. Average commercial paper costs in 1961 and 1962 were 2.73 percent and 3.01 percent, respectively. Although Associates had in recent years been successful in obtaining ample commercial paper, Mr. Coquillard could not be certain that this would always be the case. In such an event, Associates might

[3]Under repurchase agreements, government bond dealers or banks sell federal obligations to holders of temporarily idle balances and agree at the same time to buy back the securities at specified future dates, ranging from one to a few days, at specified future prices equal to the sales price plus a predetermined fixed rate of interest. From the point of view of the owner of the federal obligations, repurchase agreements are a form of borrowing money; from the point of view of the grantors of repurchase agreements, the transactions are a form of short-term investment.

have to fall back on a greater proportion of the more expensive bank money.

3. SENIOR NOTES. The third category of senior borrowings – senior notes – ranked equally, as to a claim on the company's assets, with bank borrowings and commercial paper and was superior in rights to the subordinated and capital debt of the company. It was the only form

Exhibit 7

ASSOCIATES INVESTMENT COMPANY

Comparative Capitalizations of Major Sales Finance Companies
December 31, 1962
(In thousands of dollars)

	Associates	*Commercial Credit*	*CIT*	*GMAC*
Short-term – banks, etc.	$ 139	$ 436	$ 311	$ 161
Short-term – commercial paper	428	605	546	951
Term loans	409	513	753	2,220
Senior debt	$ 976	$1,554	$1,610	$3,332
Subordinated loans	81	125	100	258
Junior subordinated loans	65	75	100	242
Subordinated debt	$ 146	$ 200	$ 200	$ 500
Net worth – Preferred	9	37	-	-
– Common and surplus	163	265	362	384
Total net worth	$ 172	$ 302	$ 362	$ 384
Total capitalization	$1,294	$2,056	$2,172	$4,216

(By percentage)

	Associates	*Commercial Credit*	*CIT*	*GMAC*
Short-term – banks, etc.	10.7	21.2	14.3	3.8
Short-term – commercial paper	33.1	29.4	25.1	22.6
Term loans	31.6	25.0	34.7	52.7
Senior debt	75.4	75.6	74.1	79.1
Subordinated loans	6.3	6.1	4.6	6.1
Junior subordinated loans	5.0	3.6	4.6	5.7
Subordinated debt	11.3	9.7	9.2	11.8
Net worth – Preferred	0.7	1.8	-	-
– Common and surplus	12.6	12.9	16.7	9.1
Total net worth	13.3	14.7	16.7	9.1
Total capitalization	100.0	100.0	100.0	100.0

of senior debt which was of a long-term nature. A covenant in the senior notes restricted cash dividend payments if more than 5/6 of the financial structure were senior debt. Thus, a maximum of 5/6 of the financial structure could be made up of bank borrowings, commercial paper, long-term senior notes, and other miscellaneous senior liabilities, and a minimum of 1/6 had to be in the various categories that made up the borrowing base of the company.

Borrowing Base

1. SUBORDINATED NOTES AND CAPITAL NOTES. The capital notes were subordinated notes. Certain other companies had termed capital notes "junior subordinated," which was perhaps more descriptive of their nature. The basic restrictions of the various issues of capital and subordinated debt were similar. They included (1) the total of capital notes and stock equity[4] must be not less than 200 percent of outstanding subordinated indebtedness; (2) stock equity must be not less than 200 percent of capital notes; and (3) the same restriction on payment of dividends as mentioned above under senior notes.

Mr. Coquillard thought that as long as the restrictions were observed the cost of long-term borrowing increased in steps of approximately 1/4 percent as a function of the ranking of the debt. For example, if the market rate on senior long-term debt was 4 3/4 percent, it would be about 5 percent for subordinated debt and 5 1/4 percent for capital notes. Ex-

Exhibit 8

ASSOCIATES INVESTMENT COMPANY

Weighted Average Interest Rates on Long-Term Borrowings
Major Sales Finance Companies
December 31, 1962

	Senior		*Subordinated*	*Combined*
	U.S.	*Canada*	*and Capital*	*Average*
Associates	4.60%	–	5.28%	4.79%
Commercial Credit	4.35%	5.00%	3.76%	4.49%
CIT Financial	4.20%	5.41%	3.76%	4.14%
GMAC	4.07%	5.23%	4.60%	4.23%

The above figures have been prepared from the schedules of long-term borrowings due after one year appearing in the 1962 annual report of each of the companies.

[4]Stock equity is the sum of the capital stock and surplus of the company less certain nonfinance assets such as inventories, land, buildings and equipment, nonmarketable investments, and the like.

hibit 8 shows the weighted average interest rates on long-term borrowings of major sales finance companies at the end of 1962.

2. PREFERRED STOCK. At the end of 1962, Associates had outstanding portions of two issues of cumulative preferred stock with a combined par value of $9 million. It was all privately held. Both issues were being retired through a sinking fund at a combined rate of $2,250,000 per year. At this rate, all of the preferred stock would be retired by 1966.

3. COMMON STOCK. The common stock of Associates Investment Company was listed on the New York Stock Exchange and had a trading range of 80–52 in 1962. At the end of 1962, there were slightly over three and one-half million shares outstanding. The earnings per share in 1962 were $4.49 and the dividends paid amounted to $2.60. Since management was extremely conscious of dilution of stockholders' equity, Mr. Coquillard believed that the only way that the amount of common stock outstanding might be increased would be through the issuance of shares in connection with an acquisition.

Projected Needs of Associates

Exhibit 9, the 1963 Profit Plan (operating projections), provided Mr. Coquillard with an estimate of the aggregate financial needs for the year. He recalled that the 1960 forecast had been grossly inaccurate and had led Associates into an amount of high cost long-term borrowing which subsequent events proved not fully necessary (see Exhibit 6).

The Profit Plan was prepared outside the treasurer's department. The figures for assets and net worth were based on projections of operations. The figures for long-term debt took into account maturing debt but reflected no additional issuance of securities. Thus, figures for short-term debt were used to balance the changes in the other items on the balance sheet. In other words, the Profit Plan as submitted to Mr. Coquillard assumed that all funds which the projection showed to be needed in 1963 would be obtained through short-term borrowings. This was a simple rule of thumb that Mr. Coquillard had suggested for use in the preparation of the Profit Plan. It had no influence on the preparation of his recommendations.

The 1963 Profit Plan projected net receivables at $1.45 billion at December 31, 1963. The pattern of receivables over recent years is shown in Exhibit 3. Mr. Coquillard thought that some figures on the maturity composition of receivables might be useful in analyzing the capital structure problem. He believed that the figures shown in Exhibit 10 approximated the maturity composition of receivables under normal economic conditions.

Exhibit 9

ASSOCIATES INVESTMENT COMPANY

Parent Corporation and Finance Subsidiaries Only 1963 Preliminary Profit Plan (Prepared 1/7/63)

Estimated Balance Sheets—By Months

(in thousands of dollars)

	1962 November Actual	*1962 December Estimated*	*1963 January*	*February*	*March*	*April*	*May*	*June*
ASSETS:								
Cash	$ 52,597	$ 58,500	$ 60,100	$ 61,800	$ 63,300	$ 65,100	$ 66,500	$ 68,300
Receivables:								
Motor vehicle and other retail installment receivables	$ 887,857	$ 896,830	$ 897,241	$ 897,081	$ 911,666	$ 918,234	$ 937,150	$ 963,999
Wholesale—short-term notes	130,312	138,005	159,623	159,947	161,478	160,867	160,868	151,194
Direct and personal inst. loans	183,855	188,000	190,500	193,500	195,500	198,000	200,500	203,000
Commercial loans and other inst. recs.	195,982	202,256	204,214	206,173	208,130	210,555	212,980	215,414
Total receivables	$1,398,006	$1,425,091	$1,451,578	$1,456,201	$1,476,774	$1,487,656	$1,511,498	$1,533,607
Repossessions	3,212	3,000	3,000	3,000	3,000	3,000	3,000	3,000
Less: unearned discounts	(107,078)	(108,223)	(108,593)	(108,898)	(110,743)	(111,925)	(114,350)	(117,139)
reserve for losses	(34,892)	(35,838)	(36,377)	(36,916)	(37,455)	(37,994)	(38,533)	(39,072)
Total receivables and repossessions	$1,259,248	$1,284,030	$1,309,608	$1,313,387	$1,331,576	$1,340,737	$1,361,615	$1,380,396
Investment in wholly owned nonfinance subs.	26,896	26,500	26,600	26,700	26,800	26,900	27,000	27,150
Land, buildings, equipment, prepaid expenses, and other assets	10,301	10,000	10,300	10,600	10,900	11,200	11,500	11,800
Total assets	$1,349,042	$1,379,030	$1,406,608	$1,412,487	$1,432,576	$1,443,937	$1,466,615	$1,487,646

Exhibit 9 (Continued)

	1962 November Actual	1962 December Estimated	1963 January	February	March	April	May	June
LIABILITIES:								
Short-term notes payable:								
Bank borrowings	$ 114,400	$ 180,000	$ 183,347	$ 185,445	$ 193,307	$ 199,008	$ 207,128	$ 214,350
Commercial paper	426,777	391,331	427,810	432,705	451,051	464,353	483,297	500,152
Total short-term notes payable	$ 541,177	$ 571,331	$ 611,157	$ 618,150	$ 644,358	$ 663,361	$ 690,425	$ 714,502
Reserves and accruals	52,662	51,585	50,973	49,859	51,740	51,082	50,446	54,600
Wholesale in transit	24,511	27,000	25,000	25,000	25,000	25,000	25,000	25,000
Long-term notes – not subordinates	402,575	405,466	395,330	393,830	386,830	378,730	373,730	370,730
Long-term notes – subordinates and capital debt	154,467	150,351	149,351	149,351	149,351	148,967	148,717	147,767
Total liabilities	$1,175,392	$1,205,733	$1,231,811	$1,236,190	$1,257,279	$1,267,140	$1,288,318	$1,312,599
NET WORTH:								
Preferred stock	$ 9,000	$ 9,000	$ 9,000	$ 9,000	$ 9,000	$ 9,000	$ 9,000	$ 6,750
Common stock	36,034	36,034	36,034	36,034	36,034	36,034	36,034	36,034
Paid-in surplus	11,599	11,599	11,599	11,599	11,599	11,599	11,599	11,599
Earned and equity surplus	118,296	116,664	118,164	119,664	118,664	120,164	121,664	120,664
Treasury stock – 21,400 shares (at cost)	(1,279)							
Total net worth	$ 173,650	$ 173,297	$ 174,797	$ 176,297	$ 175,297	$ 176,797	$ 178,297	$ 175,047
Total liabilities and net worth	$1,349,042	$1,379,030	$1,406,608	$1,412,487	$1,432,576	$1,443,937	$1,466,615	$1,487,646

Exhibit continued.

Exhibit 9 (Continued)

	1963						1963
	July	*August*	*September*	*October*	*November*	*December*	*Increase (Decrease)*
ASSETS:							
Cash	$ 69,800	$ 70,700	$ 71,700	$ 73,300	$ 74,900	$ 76,770	$ 18,270
Receivables:							
Motor vehicle and other retail installment receivables	$ 969,300	$ 983,509	$ 985,058	$ 996,553	$1,000,363	$1,002,982	$106,152
Wholesale–short-term notes	150,893	117,791	126,721	132,506	139,030	158,072	20,067
Direct and personal inst. loans	205,500	208,000	210,500	212,500	214,500	218,000	30,000
Commercial loans and other inst. recs.	218,090	220,706	223,441	226,841	230,241	233,643	31,387
Total receivables	$1,543,783	$1,530,006	$1,545,720	$1,568,400	$1,584,134	$1,612,697	$187,606
Repossessions	3,000	3,000	3,000	3,000	3,000	3,000	–
Less: unearned discounts	(118,538)	(120,565)	(120,927)	(122,516)	(123,486)	(123,831)	(15,608)
reserve for losses	(39,611)	(40,150)	(40,689)	(41,228)	(41,766)	(42,304)	(6,466)
Total receivables and repossessions	$1,388,634	$1,372,291	$1,387,104	$1,407,656	$1,421,882	$1,449,562	$165,532
Investment in wholly owned nonfinance subs.	27,250	27,350	27,450	27,550	27,650	27,800	1,300
Land, buildings, equipment, prepaid expenses, and other assets	12,100	12,400	12,700	13,000	13,200	13,500	3,500
Total assets	$1,497,784	$1,482,741	$1,492,954	$1,521,506	$1,537,632	$1,567,632	$188,602

Exhibit 9 (Continued)

	1963 July	August	September	October	November	December	1963 Increase (Decrease)
LIABILITIES:							
Short-term notes payable:							
Bank borrowings	$ 217,134	$ 212,829	$ 217,416	$ 224,707	$ 230,122	$ 238,275	$ 58,275
Commercial paper	506,647	496,600	507,306	524,316	536,951	555,974	164,643
Total short-term notes payable	$ 723,781	$ 709,429	$ 724,722	$ 749,023	$ 767,073	$ 794,249	$222,918
Reserves and accruals	53,959	53,268	55,188	54,272	50,848	54,111	2,526
Wholesale in transit	25,000	25,000	25,000	25,000	25,000	25,000	(2,000)
Long-term notes – not subordinates	370,730	369,230	369,230	366,897	366,897	366,897	(38,569)
Long-term notes – subordinates and capital debt	147,767	147,767	147,767	147,767	147,767	146,767	(3,584)
Total liabilities	$1,321,237	$1,304,694	$1,321,907	$1,342,959	$1,357,585	$1,387,024	$181,291
NET WORTH:							
Preferred stock	$ 6,750	$ 6,750	$ 6,750	$ 6,750	$ 6,750	$ 6,750	$ (2,250)
Common stock	36,034	36,034	36,034	36,034	36,034	36,034	–
Paid-in surplus	11,599	11,599	11,599	11,599	11,599	11,599	–
Earned and equity surplus	122,164	123,664	122,664	124,164	125,664	126,225	9,561
Treasury stock – 21,400 shares (at cost)							
Total net worth	$ 176,547	$ 178,047	$ 177,047	$ 178,547	$ 180,047	$ 180,608	$ 7,311
Total liabilities and net worth	$1,497,784	$1,482,741	$1,498,954	$1,521,506	$1,537,632	$1,567,632	$188,602

Exhibit 10

ASSOCIATES INVESTMENT COMPANY

Maturity Schedule of Finance Receivables
December 31, 1962
(In percentages)

	Motor Vehicle and Other Retail	*Personal Installment Loans*	*Wholesale Commercial and Other Installments*
Past due (installments thirty days or more)	0.4	0.2	1.5
First month	6.1	7.2	14.8
Second month	5.8	7.0	14.3
Third month	5.5	6.7	13.1
Fourth month	5.3	6.4	12.7
Fifth month	5.1	6.2	1.8
Sixth month	4.9	5.8	2.6
Seventh month	4.6	5.6	1.7
Eighth month	4.4	5.3	1.5
Ninth month	4.2	5.0	1.4
Tenth month	4.1	4.7	1.4
Eleventh month	3.9	4.4	1.4
Twelfth month	3.7	4.1	1.4
Over twelve months	42.0	31.4	30.4
Total	100.0	100.0	100.0

The Profit Plan showed a substantial increase in the senior borrowing ratio. Without additional subordinate or equity money, it was estimated to reach 4.34 to 1 at year end.[5] This computation did not take

[5]Computed as follows: (Figures from Exhibit 9; 000s omitted)

Borrowing base		
Net worth	$180,608	
Less: Investment in wholly owned nonfinancial subsidiaries, net plant, and other assets	41,300	$139,308
Subordinated debt		146,767
Total		$286,075
Senior debt		
Short-term debt		$794,249
Reserves and accruals		54,111
Wholesale in Transit		25,000
Long-term notes – not subordinated		366,897
		$1,240,257

$$\frac{\$1{,}240{,}257}{\$286{,}075} = 4.34$$

into consideration any allowance for the Alinco matter. Mr. Coquillard felt that if the Alinco tax case went seriously against Associates, the company's borrowing base would be adversely affected. For example, if surplus were reduced by $16 million during 1963, the ratio would increase 4.59 to 1. He felt that such a possibility should be recognized in financial planning and that due allowance should be made at all times for this contingency.

Outlook for Money and Capital Markets

Mr. Coquillard thought that the market may have improved modestly since October 1962 when Associates publicly sold $50 million of senior debentures on a 4.45 percent basis. As of early 1963, he believed that such notes might go in the area of 4.40 percent at a public sale.

Mr. Coquillard had recently received a copy of *The Outlook for Business for the First Six Months of 1963* from the First National Bank of Chicago. Its chairman had predicted:

> . . . general business activity in the next six months should edge slightly higher as both consumer outlays and government expenditures continue to rise. The demand for funds by both business and consumers is likely to reflect this modestly rising trend.
>
> In my judgment, there will be an adequate supply of funds available to accommodate this slightly greater aggregate demand for credit by consumers, businesses and governments.
>
> In my judgment, therefore, interest rates in general, in the first six months of 1963, will change little from their present levels. However, a tax cut may well alter this pattern. A reduction in revenues as a result of a cut in taxes would increase the deficit of the federal government. This would oblige the U.S. Treasury to enter the market and to borrow the funds necessary to finance the additional deficit. Furthermore, if individuals spend rather than save a substantial portion of any tax cut, the demand for funds will rise without a corresponding increase in the supply of savings. In that event, a tax cut early in 1963 would put interest rates under some upward pressure in contrast to what otherwise would probably be a period of rate stability.

The predictions of the *Business and Money, 1963 Review and Outlook* prepared by the Harris Trust and Savings Bank of Chicago were somewhat different:

> Continued slow growth in economic activity in the next several months plus a further growth in savings suggests modest downward pressure on interest rates. The decline is not likely to be substantial since balance of payments restrictions will induce monetary fiscal authorities to prevent a sizable drop. A tax cut effective by midyear plus some money creation as assumed in this report is likely to promote a higher rate of economic activity in the latter part of the year. Therefore, downward pressure on interest rates should then cease and some modest upward movement might well develop. Higher private economic activity will stimulate private demands for

credit and a sizable Federal deficit will increase the volume of required government financing. Significantly, higher interest rates are unlikely pending sustained and substantial economic growth.

Mr. Coquillard believed that most of the flexibility was out of the bank prime rate and did not expect the rate to drop significantly for some time. He noted that commercial banks no longer had the supply of corporate demand deposits that used to be available to them for lending purposes; he felt that almost all corporate treasurers kept their excess funds fully invested at all times. He believed that these facts, coupled with ever-increasing overhead expense in banks and the United States balance of payments problem, tended to minimize the likelihood of a lower prime rate in the near future.

APPENDIX A

Analysis of Capital Structure[1]

Ideal Capital Structure

As a guide to future financial planning, it would be helpful to set forth as a goal an ideal form of capital structure.

The nucleus of the plan suggested below involves the employment of a capital debt instrument in place of preferred stock. This type of instrument, if properly designed, could serve as a form of equity and at the same time have the important tax advantage of interest deduction.

Despite the saving in capital cost afforded by the use of a capital debt issue instead of preferred, it would not be a suitable substitute unless it served to enhance the equity base upon which subordinated debt issues are predicated.

The capital debt form of financing is of relatively recent origin. It has been employed by GMAC, Commercial Credit, and Pacific Finance. Examination of the latter two issues (data for GMAC is not publicly available) reveals that capital debt has not been fully recognized as an equity instrument. This is evidenced by the fact that the provisions of subordinated debt issues of both Commercial and Pacific, which contain a 50 percent net worth test for the issuance of additional subordinated debt, were not adjusted to include the capital debt as part of the net worth base. From these few cases, it would seem that capital debt has served as another form of subordinated debt rather than as a real equity security such as preferred stock.

---

[1]Prepared by Financial Engineering Division of Lehman Brothers, May 25, 1953.

To gain adequate recognition of capital debt as an equity security would require Associates to undertake a major pioneering effort. A similar task was required in the establishment of subordinated debt as a base for senior debt financing. The feasibility of obtaining this recognition is uncertain in the present environment of tight money market conditions, but looking down the long road ahead, it would be a worthy objective.

With the acceptance of capital debt as a base for subordinated debt issues, a capital structure designed along the following lines would afford optimum flexibility.

A. Common stock and surplus*	$ 100
B. Capital debt (50% of A)	50
C. Subordinated debt (50% of A plus B)	75
D. Senior debt (500% of A plus B plus C)†	1,125
Total capitalization	$1,350

*Based on the consolidated balance of the company and all subsidiaries.
†This ratio applicable only as a limitation on stock payments but not as a test for the issuance of senior debt.

On the basis of the common stock and surplus of Associates as of 12/31/52, the above capitalization, if fully utilized, would appear as follows:

	Amount	*Percent of Total Capitalization*
Senior debt	$691,728,750	83.3%
Subordinated debt	46,115,250	5.6
Capital debt	30,743,500	3.7
Common stock and surplus	61,487,000	7.4
Total	$830,074,500	100.0%

In setting up the terms of the various securities, the objective would be to maintain as far as practical a uniformity of definitions to insure consistent results.

Because of the inherent nature of the finance business, involving periods of sharp decline in receivables, provision should be made for the elimination of call premiums in the event outstanding receivables fall below specified levels.

In recent issues of senior debt, full credit is given to deferred income (unearned discounts and unearned insurance premiums) and reserves for losses and contingencies in the over-all tangible asset test for the purpose of issuing additional debt or making stock payments. No recognition is given to these items in the tests contained in the existing subordinated debt and preferred stock issues. It would seem that there are sufficient grounds for exploring the possibility of including at least some portion of deferred income as part of the net worth base for the purpose of meeting tests for the issuance of additional subordinated and capital debt.

As indicated at the outset, this memorandum has endeavored to be helpful to the management of Associates Investment Company in its financial planning. The suggestions of various alterations in the company's capital structure have been made with the full realization of the difficulties of their immediate achievement in view of existing money market conditions. Nevertheless, it is hoped that they might serve as a guide in the company's long-range program.

PLANNING LONG-RANGE STRATEGY

United States Leasing Corporation

In August of 1964, Mr. Henry Schoenfeld, senior vice-chairman of the board of United States Leasing Corporation, was reviewing the company's progress and charting its future strategy. He intended to submit his findings to the board of directors in the form of specific recommendations.

Background of United States Leasing Corporation

Mr. Schoenfeld had worked at one time for a small food-processing firm in California. In 1952 when a forklift truck had broken down and the company had insufficient funds to purchase a new one, Mr. Schoenfeld had attempted to lease one. He had discovered that his only alternative to purchasing was to rent[1] the equipment. Since the cost of renting the forklift truck for two years would have been several times the purchase price, Mr. Schoenfeld had found this alternative unacceptable. Finally he had convinced a dealer to lease a forklift truck to the food-processing firm. Having decided that there was a great deal of potential connected with leasing transactions, Mr. Schoenfeld joined with three others, and shortly thereafter (in 1952) formed the United States Leasing Corporation —the first equipment leasing company—with a capital of $20,000.

From this beginning U.S. Leasing had grown very rapidly. On May 2, 1957, the first and only public offering of USL stock took place —800,000 shares at $4 per share. As of August 1964, U.S. Leasing operated nationally and in Canada through twenty-eight offices and did a larger volume of business than any other equipment leasing company.

[1]Although leasing and renting might seem synonymous, they are trade terms for long-term and short-term arrangements, respectively. Usually equipment is rented for a day, a week, or a month, while a lease covers a period of months or years.

In addition, USL held minority interest in leasing companies in England, Germany, and Japan. Although part of the company's early growth had been accomplished through merger, U.S. Leasing had not made any acquisitions since 1957. (Financial and operating information is shown in Exhibits 1–3.)

U.S. Leasing purchased all types of industrial and transportation equipment upon order of prospective lessees and then leased the equipment for most of its expected life. The usual equipment lease was a "net" lease with the lessee required to pay all property taxes, repairs, insurance, and similar costs. It was a noncancellable contract. Lease periods generally corresponded to the equipment's life and might run up to ten years; shorter terms predominated and the current average was about five years. Almost without exception the total payments in the regular lease period exceeded the purchase price of the equipment. The lessee usually had the right to a specified number of one-year renewals at a reduced rental after the regular lease period expired and in some cases had an option to purchase the equipment.

During its early years, U.S. Leasing had functioned somewhat like a broker. Its leases were individually placed with banks and were not drawn until financing had been arranged. Since U.S. Leasing had written only those leases on which it could obtain virtually 100 percent financing, the lender relied heavily on the lessee's credit. Typically, these leases had been large. It had happened that delays in obtaining approval of the lessee's credit had meant a loss of business.

As U.S. Leasing had grown, the company had tapped additional sources of funds. In 1960, U.S. Leasing had sold $5,000,000 of 6 percent subordinated notes due May 1, 1960, which were subordinate and junior in right of payment to bank and other senior debt. These notes carried warrants for purchase of 375,000 common shares at $7 to $10 per share. This subordinated debt capital enlarged the company's long-term capital base and increased temporary "warehousing capacity." USL had also obtained open bank credit lines under which leases could be financed without the necessity of bank credit approval. As of August 1964, USL management believed that the company had ample unrestricted credit lines for the temporary and/or permanent financing of its leases.

Over the years U.S. Leasing had expanded its business to include medium-sized and smaller leases as well as large individual leases. Mr. Schoenfeld believed that the smaller contracts offered several advantages to USL—namely, higher profit margins, less competition, a spreading of risks, and an increased number of customers for repeat and additional business. This change was reflected in an increase in the number of lessees at year end from 1500 in 1959 to 17,670 in 1963, and a decrease in average lease size from $26,222 to $5052 over the same period.

As of August 1964, management classified its business activities

Exhibit 1

UNITED STATES LEASING CORPORATION

Five-year Summary

(Dollar figures in thousands)

Years Ended December 31	*1963*	*1962*	*1961*	*1960*	*1959*
FINANCIAL POSITION					
Total receivables	$ 67,396	$61,199	$52,721	$48,738	$36,069
Leased equipment cost	$102,766	$90,643	$77,894	$65,855	$46,096
Residual valuation	$ 7,760	$ 6,807	$ 5,805	$ 4,876	$ 3,346
Percent of cost	7.6%	7.5%	7.5%	7.4%	7.3%
Notes payable	$ 48,537	$42,972	$38,259	$34,704	$28,929
Unearned lease income	$ 11,142	$10,416	$ 9,101	$ 8,781	$ 6,566
Long-term subordinated debt	$ 5,000	$ 5,000	$ 5,000	$ 5,000	$ -
Capital stock and capital surplus	$ 5,129	$ 5,104	$ 5,104	$ 5,104	$ 4,945
Earned surplus	$ 4,169	$ 2,874	$ 1,869	$ 1,275	$ 837
OPERATIONS					
Number of lessees – year end (in 000s)	17	11	5	2	1
Total receivables added during year	$ 31,801	$31,481	$28,565	$27,472	$19,404
Average size of lease	$ 5	$ 5	$ 9	$ 24	$ 26
INCOME					
Earned income less provision for doubtful accounts	$ 7,758	$ 6,632	$ 5,285	$ 4,612	$ 3,440
Interest and finance charges	$ 2,889	$ 2,530	$ 2,394	$ 2,074	$ 1,432
Sales, administrative, and general expenses	$ 2,588	$ 2,355	$ 1,719	$ 1,676	$ 1,393
Income before deferred federal income taxes	$ 2,279	$ 1,746	$ 1,171	$ 860	$ 614
Provision for deferred federal income taxes	$ 984	$ 742	$ 578	$ 422	*
Net income	$ 1,295	$ 1,004	$ 593	$ 438	*
Shares outstanding at year end (in 000s)	$ 2,587	$ 2,582	$ 2,582	$ 2,582	$ 2,542
Earnings per share	50¢	39¢	23¢	17¢	*
Market price of common stock:					
High	9½	8	8⅛	7	7
Low	5½	4½	4¾	4½	4¾

Exhibit 2

UNITED STATES LEASING CORPORATION

Consolidated Balance Sheet
December 31, 1963

ASSETS	
Cash	$ 3,720,576
Receivables—due in installments*	67,230,535
Residual valuation—leased equipment† (Cost of leased equipment at Dec. 31, 1963, $102,766,480)	7,760,105
Allowance for doubtful accounts	(716,136)
Unearned lease income (see Appendix A)	(11,142,649)
Advances—equipment acquisitions	511,672
Other receivables	165,874
Prepaid expenses	298,918
Investment in foreign affiliates—at cost	123,767
Office equipment and improvements (Less accumulated depreciation and amortization)	273,498
Total	$68,226,160
LIABILITIES	
Notes payable*	$48,537,489
Accounts payable	1,135,313
Accrued liabilities	488,518
Deposits—receivables collected in advance	1,093,352
Deferred federal income taxes (see Exhibit 3)	2,672,750
Long-term notes payable—subordinated notes due May 1970	5,000,000
Total liabilities	$58,927,422
Capital stock and surplus	
Capital stock	$ 2,587,500
Capital surplus	2,541,344
Earned surplus	4,169,894
Total capital stock and surplus	$ 9,298,738
Total	$68,226,160

*Receivables and notes payable: Receivables were due in monthly, quarterly, semiannual, and yearly installments over the operating cycle (number of years) of the business. Receivables of $39,958,000 were assigned as collateral to notes payable.

†Leased equipment was owned by the corporation and its subsidiaries and was located on lessees' premises. The residual values were estimated by management for each lease on the basis of such factors as renewal or purchase options and the estimated life and salvage value of the equipment. The extent by which actual realization might exceed (or fall short of) the anticipated residuals carried on the balance sheet was difficult to estimate. However, management of U.S. Leasing Corporation thought that the conservative nature of its residual valuation account was well substantiated by the fact that the company's realization on residuals had consistently exceeded original estimates.

into three main groups: sales-aid leasing, general leasing, and major leasing. Each group accounted for about one third of the dollar value of the equipment purchased for lease in 1963.

Exhibit 3

UNITED STATES LEASING CORPORATION

Consolidated Net Income
Year Ended December 31, 1963

Earned income less provision for doubtful accounts (see Appendix A)		$7,758,220
Interest and finance charges	$2,889,348	
Sales, administrative, and general expenses	2,588,907	5,478,255
Income before federal income taxes		$2,279,965
Provision for federal income taxes:		
Federal income taxes (subsidiary companies)	$ 27,279	
Deferred federal income taxes*	957,000	984,279
Net income		$1,295,686

*Deferred federal income taxes and investment credit: It is pointed out in Appendix A that U.S. Leasing used a different accounting method for tax purposes than for book purposes. The company had been accounting for Deferred Federal Income Taxes for book purposes, since the accounting method which USL used for tax purposes had in effect deferred taxable profits and hence had also deferred payment of income taxes. Hence the company had a tax loss carry forward. In addition, USL had a substantial amount of investment credit available to it which could be used to reduce income taxes payable in the year generated and at any time in the succeeding five years. This unused investment credit had resulted from the new equipment purchased in 1962 and 1963.

Sales-Aid Leasing

Mr. Schoenfeld considered sales-aid leasing, in which the company became active in 1961, to be the "bread and butter" business of USL. As of August 1964, it was the fastest growing portion of the business. It was offered through the sales force of manufacturers who sold nationally. With USL's sales-aid leasing plan, the manufacturer's salesman could offer his customers the alternative of leasing his product rather than purchasing it. If the customer desired to lease, he could sign the leasing forms carried by the manufacturer's salesmen. Upon credit approval by USL, the transaction was completed and the customer got his equipment. The results were as follows: the salesman had made a cash sale (to USL), the manufacturer had made a sale in which he did not have to assume the credit risk and collection expenses, and USL had completed a lease transaction in which it assumed the credit risk. As of 1964, most of USL's business in the sales aid leasing category was placed by the salesmen of office equipment manufacturers. Three of USL's largest associates in this category were Pitney-Bowes, Inc., National Cash Register Company, and Addressograph-Multigraph.

Company executives believed that sales aid leasing was an effective marketing tool for USL as well as for the salesman selling his product. They noted that although USL had only forty salesmen who contacted national companies, more than 4000 salesmen of various manufacturers were offering USL's lease. USL executives were convinced, as were the executives of many national manufacturing companies, that the leasing alternative increased a manufacturer's sales potential. They believed that a salesman often could make a more convincing presentation by showing that his product would save a specific amount per month and that the monthly lease payment would be something less than that. As a part of its sales-aid leasing program, USL helped train the salesmen of manufacturers in the leasing concept, provided them with printed rate cards and other merchandising tools, and supplied the actual leasing documents.

General Leasing

USL's general leasing business was obtained in several ways. The same USL salesmen that were responsible for sales aid leasing also handled general leasing. These forty salesmen were spread out over the entire country. The majority of general leasing business was obtained through cooperation with local distributors and dealers. The type of item leased varied tremendously and included such things as executive aircraft, manufacturing equipment, electronic test equipment, and office machinery and equipment. USL representatives often participated with local vendors in joint presentations to potential customers. A second source of general leasing business was direct solicitation. USL conducted an extensive direct mail campaign aimed at over 100,000 potential lessees. This campaign was also carried out on a personal basis. That is, periodically USL salesmen contacted existing lessees to ascertain whether they had additional needs that leasing might serve. In addition, representatives of USL occasionally made direct calls on firms who were not doing business with USL and who were not suggested by a national or local vendor. Finally a portion of USL's general leasing business was unsolicited. Management noted that with the spreading recognition of the U.S. Leasing name and the growth of its customer list, the amount of unsolicited business had grown steadily.

Major Leasing

Whereas Mr. Schoenfeld considered sales aid leasing and general leasing "the bread and butter" of their business, he thought of major leasing as "the icing on the cake." It produced an estimated 15 percent of net profits in 1963. It was the opinion of USL management that the company could exist without the major lease category but that the other two categories were essential to its survival.

The major lease category was substantially different from the other two categories. It was handled by a separate sales force which consisted of one man in New York and two men in San Francisco. Management likened their operations to these of a "Big Deal Group" in a major investment house. USL executives believed that in some situations leasing was the most appropriate means of financing even for corporations in the strongest financial position. They thought that special situations provided potential customers in the major lease category. For example, balance sheet considerations, government regulations, or restrictions in indentures might make leasing the most attractive or even the only feasible financing alternative; or obsolescence factors might be involved. The existing customers in this category were almost exclusively large corporations whose net worth exceeded $25 million. The size of major leases usually ranged between $100,000 and $1 million. USL had no fixed plans in this category as it did in the other two. Management believed that the ability to "tailor" lease plans to the needs of an individual customer was a vital competitive factor.

Background on Leasing Industry

Equipment leasing had grown rapidly in recent years. No central organization gathered data from the wide variety of firms engaged in the leasing business, therefore industry data on equipment lease transactions could only be estimated. One estimate placed the value of all capital equipment under lease in 1953 at about $450 million and at about $1.5 billion in 1958. These figures included all firms which carried on any leasing business. The estimate for the dollar volume of equipment on lease by leasing companies alone was $35 million in 1953 and $227 million in 1958.

There were three general types of leasing companies: the broker, the leasing firm comparable to a commercial finance company, and the lessor-maintenance company. The broker served chiefly as a money finder and assumed little or no risk in its transactions. A leasing company which functioned as a broker obtained virtually 100 percent financing from a lender, who therefore relied on the lessee for security. U.S. Leasing was such a company during its early years. The second type of leasing company was more comparable to a commercial finance company. U.S. Leasing was such a company as of 1964. These companies developed their own equity and debt base to finance a portion of their leases. Thus, they added their credit to that of the lessee in order to borrow money to finance the greater portion of their leases. The third type of leasing company, the lessor-maintenance company, maintained the equipment in addition to financing the lease. As contrasted with the financial orientation of the other two types of leasing company, many of the firms in this field were contract maintenance companies in such areas as vending machines and air conditioning.

Mr. Schoenfeld noted three main trends in the leading industry, the most significant being rapid growth. The other two tends were an increase in the competitive nature of the business and an increase in the number of different products leased. Numerous industrial companies had established their own leasing operations in order to be able to offer customers the leasing alternative. (IBM is an example of such a company.) Commercial finance companies such as Commercial Credit and CIT, which traditionally had used conditional sales contracts as their marketing tool, had established leasing divisions. Although these leasing operations were relatively new, Mr. Schoenfeld considered them as potential sources of substantial competition. Local leasing companies typically offered competition in the "brokerage" types of leasing. Commercial banks were another source of competition, since the Comptroller of the Currency had ruled in early 1963 that national banks might enter the equipment leasing field. Mr. Schoenfeld believed that the limited number of banks that had formed their own leasing departments were interested principally in large leases and were not involved in retail sales aid leasing. For the foreseeable future Mr. Schoenfeld anticipated competition only from commercial banks in the major lease category. He also believed that the entry of banks into the leasing field had furthered the prestige and development of the equipment leasing concept as well as the over-all market for leasing.

For a number of years a few leasing companies, including USL, had been expressing a willingness to lease anything but expendables. Although there had been a large increase in the number of different items leased and the number of lessees, USL executives noted that this expansion had been almost entirely within the business sector of the economy. That is, there had been very little leasing to consumers. Automobile leasing was the only major exception. USL management believed that the consumer sector represented a great source of potential business.

Opinions about the future of equipment leasing differed sharply. One school of thought held that leasing had grown as a result of special conditions existing after the war, and this school expected a decreasing volume of leasing. An opposing school believed that leasing would grow even faster in the future than it had in the past. Some writers had estimated the future quantitatively. For instance, one author wrote in 1955: "It seems safe to estimate that not more than ten percent of the output of machinery manufacturers will be channeled to leasing in the foreseeable future." On the other hand, an article in *American Business* in 1959 said that "experts" predict that one half of the nation's business will be conducted by lease rather than by purchase in the foreseeable future. Another source estimated that by 1970, 15 percent of all equipment obtained each year would be leased and that this would account for over $6 billion worth of machinery and equipment. It also predicted that the dollar volume of new leases written by leasing companies would reach $650 million annually by 1970.

Future of United States Leasing Corporation

USL management thought that processing costs set some minimum on the size of the lease with which USL should become involved. It estimated that processing costs averaged $40–50 per lease, as of 1964. The existing policy of USL was to write no leases for less than $1000. However, some leases which were less than $1000 were written provided that they made some contribution to fixed costs, that is, covered marginal costs. Those USL leases which were below the minimum ordinarily involved either large sales aid associates or major customers.

USL's return on equity had continually increased over the past few years. Management wanted this trend to continue. At worst, it did not want to make less than the current return on equity. It believed that a balanced portfolio of leases such as the company presently had enabled the company to obtain money at a relatively low cost. However, it thought that this was difficult to demonstrate since guidelines were not developed in the leasing industry as they were, for example, in the commercial finance business, and also since USL was unique in the leasing industry.

Company executives believed that U.S. Leasing should continue its expansion. This could be done, they thought, by expanding present markets, by seeking new markets, or by some combination of these two methods. USL management thought that the markets to which it directed its future attention should be sufficiently related to one another to allow the greatest possible return to USL in the long run.

During the spring and early summer of 1964, USL had established three joint ventures with commercial banks to enter the leasing business. Management knew that other banks had made similar arrangements with other leasing companies. It believed that these joint ventures would provide additional business to USL which it would not otherwise get. It thought that the chief benefit which a leasing company could provide to banks in such arrangements was its experience in the leasing business. For this reason it believed that the prestige of USL could be helpful in seeking additional business of this type. Other benefits of these joint ventures to a commercial bank, in the opinion of USL executives, included the opportunity to get into the leasing business more rapidly than might otherwise be possible and the opportunity to get into the leasing business without establishing its own organization.[2] USL management expected that commercial banks which participated in leasing, either directly or in joint ventures, would be interested mainly in very large leases.

USL management was considering an entrance into various special-

[2]USL management thought that this was significant in that it felt there were still some questions regarding the legality of banks' participation in leasing.

ized fields. One of these was the leasing of railroad cars; a second was the leasing of equipment to doctors and dentists. Mr. Schoenfeld thought that specialized areas such as these should be examined to determine their suitability to USL.

The whole area of consumer leasing had been under consideration by USL for some time. Although automobile leasing was quite prevalent, leasing of other consumer durables was virtually untried. One idea that was being considered entailed working with developers in order to lease the furniture to the purchasers of new homes. Mr. Schoenfeld thought that there were many other possible approaches to the leasing of consumer durables which should be examined. He believed that the most significant factors in narrowing the field were the credit standing of the lessees, the potential rates of return, and the durability of the asset. Although he found the consumer field attractive, he knew that USL was better grounded in the industrial market.

APPENDIX A

Accounting Procedures of U.S. Leasing[1]

The following hypothetical example will be used to illustrate the accounting procedures of U.S. Leasing:

Gross lease receivables (20 quarterly payments of $800)		$16,000
Cost of equipment		13,000
		$ 3,000
Interest costs paid by U.S. Leasing	$1,500	
Expenses in consummating lease	800	
Other overhead	200	2,500
Potential gross profit		$ 500
Residual value		$ 1,000
Potential gross profit on lease plus residual value		$ 1,500

For book purposes when a lease contract was executed, unearned lease income, representing the excess of gross lease receivables over the cost

[1]Conceptually, this sets forth the idea of the procedures generally used. This does not necessarily reflect the procedures used in all cases, however.

of equipment leased net of estimated residual valuation, was recorded. For the above example, the accounting entry would be as follows:

Receivables	16,000	
Residual valuation	1,000	
Cost of equipment		13,000
Unearned lease income		4,000

The company immediately took into earnings a portion of unearned lease income that approximately offset the expenses incurred in consummating the lease ($800 for example).

Unearned lease income	800	
Earned lease income		800

The remaining $3200 of unearned lease income was taken into earnings over the term of the lease according to the sum-of-the-digits formula, which was roughly proportional to the outstanding rentals receivable on the lease. Interest costs and other overhead were recorded as they were incurred. Thus the yearly net incomes in this example would be:

	YEAR 1	YEAR 2	YEAR 3	YEAR 4	YEAR 5
Income	$1,867	$ 853	$ 640	$ 427	$ 213
Interest costs	(500)	(400)	(300)	(200)	(100)
Initial expenses	(800)	-	-	-	-
Other overhead	(40)	(40)	(40)	(40)	(40)
Net income on lease	$ 527	$ 413	$ 300	$ 187	$ 73

For income tax purposes the company used a different accounting method. Income was recorded only as lease rentals became due, and rental equipment was depreciated over the term of the lease based on a special formula. Since interest and overhead costs were also highest at the beginning, taxable profits were deferred until the later years of a lease. Thus, in a period of rapid growth, such as had characterized the company's existence to date, the payment of income taxes was minimized or postponed.

FORMING A SMALL BUSINESS INVESTMENT COMPANY

Yerba Buena Capital, Inc. (A)

In late September 1962, Mr. Richard Sharp and Mr. Randolph Peck were trying to decide whether or not they should form a small business investment company (SBIC). (Appendix A gives brief explanations of the role of the Small Business Administration and of the formation and operation of a small business investment company.) In the time that they could spare from their present jobs they had been exploring the possibility. Both desired to reach a final decision as soon as possible.

Richard Sharp was 33 years old. He had a Bachelor of Arts in Economics and after earning a Master's Degree in Business Administration, he joined Ordinary Oil Company in St. Louis where he remained until 1959. During this time he had worked chiefly in the areas of sales and sales management. Since 1959 he had been associated with a venture capital company[1] in San Francisco that had substantial investments in twenty to thirty small businesses throughout the United States.

Randolph Peck, 32, had graduated from the California Institute of Technology in engineering and had also received an M.B.A. After two years in the Navy he joined Ordinary Oil Company, where he had held various line positions in the production area. His present job required work in the fields of labor relations, safety, quality control, and cost accounting as well as production.

Mr. Sharp and Mr. Peck had first met in 1955 shortly after both joined the Ordinary Oil Company. During the years that followed they had become close friends, as had their wives. The men had, on occasion, discussed the possibility of joining together in a business venture. However, with the exception of the idea under current consideration, they had no other formal considerations.

Mr. Sharp had first heard of a small business investment company in July 1959. At that time a friend, knowing that Mr. Sharp was planning to join a venture capital operation, showed him a prospectus of Electronics Capital Corporation. The friend inquired whether the organization Mr. Sharp was joining was such a company. (Electronics Capital Corporation was an SBIC headquartered in San Diego, California. Its 1959 public stock offering was the first made by an SBIC.) Although the firm he was joining was not an SBIC, Mr. Sharp had noted that the nature of business which the two firms carried on was very similar, that is, both financed small companies with growth potential.

Mr. Peck had first heard of a small business investment company in 1960. He recalled reading an article about an SBIC in the Midwest; its plans were to concentrate on loans rather than equity investments. This type of SBIC was more nearly a banking institution. Although this group constituted a small minority of the SBIC's, it did exist. Mr. Peck had thought that the loan business was uninteresting and therefore had no personal interest, on initial contact, in the idea of forming an SBIC.

In the months immediately after he had left Ordinary Oil Company

[1]Venture capital companies are suppliers of venture capital, which, as the term implies, is money invested in business enterprises on which the investor takes substantial chances of losses in return for chances of a multiple return on his investment within a relatively short period of time.

Mr. Sharp realized that there was in increasing number of SBIC's cropping up in the venture capital field. In the course of his work he had become personally acquainted with the management of some of them. He also knew that the number of applications to the Small Business Administration for SBIC licenses had been increasing. After being employed for two years by a venture capital company, Mr. Sharp had begun to think that he might be interested in entering this business on his own together with Mr. Peck.

In the summer of 1961, while on a business trip to St. Louis he had briefly discussed the idea with Mr. Peck. Mr. Peck had grown up in San Francisco and was interested in returning to the San Francisco Bay Area. However, Mr. Sharp's estimate that a minimum capitalization of around $1 million was essential for a successful venture capital operation had been discouraging to both men. Mr. Sharp had suggested that one source of funds might be the Small Business Administration under the provisions of the Small Business Investment Act of 1958. The two men had agreed that Mr. Sharp should talk with the SBA to get more details on small business investment companies.

Shortly after this discussion, Congress made several changes in the Small Business Investment Act of 1958 which allowed SBIC's to obtain additional money from the government. (The great majority of SBIC's had commenced with only $150,000 of private funds plus the matching SBA debenture purchase of $150,000, thus arriving at the minimum capital of $300,000.) The changes were signed into law on October 3, 1961. The SBA was now authorized to purchase the debentures of any SBIC "in an amount not to exceed the lesser of $400,000 or the amount of the paid-in capital and surplus of the company from other sources." It was also provided that the SBA could loan money within certain limits to SBIC's to increase their available funds. The amendment stated that operating loans "shall not exceed 50 percent of the paid-in capital and surplus of such company or $4 million, whichever is less." (The debentures purchased by the SBA were considered part of the capital and surplus for purposes of meeting this requirement.) In September 1961, the SBA initiated a plan to encourage banks to participate with the agency in these operating loans to SBIC's. The plan provided for the granting of a loan by the SBA and immediate assignment of the loan to a bank under an agreement whereby the bank could deliver the note to the SBA at any time and obtain the outstanding principal balance.

Mr. Sharp and Mr. Peck met again in November 1961. They reasoned that since the amendments had raised the amount of funds available to an SBIC from the Small Business Administration, they would now only have to provide one third of the capital to approach the "magic" million, that is, $300,000 of private funds plus $300,000 from a sale of debentures to the SBA plus an SBA loan of $300,000 equals $900,000.

(One of the main reasons why Mr. Sharp had felt that $1 million was necessary was that an individual SBIC's investments were limited by law to 20 percent of capital and surplus, and even for a non-SBIC venture capital firm such a policy of diversification seemed prudent. Based on his past experience Mr. Sharp felt that the typical size for the real growth potential deals was at least $200,000.)

An additional provision in the amendments allowed an SBIC to make a commitment to sell debentures to the SBA at any time in its first two years. However, the SBIC did not have to draw down the funds for one year after a commitment was made. Thus, if they decided to form an SBIC, Mr. Peck and Mr. Sharp could begin with $150,000 of private capital. They could have up to a year to draw down the $150,000, for which they would have to make a commitment at the time of organization in order to obtain the required minimum capitalization of $300,000. And, they would still be able to obtain additional funds from the SBA through the sales of debentures (up to the $400,000 maximum) provided they obtained at least an equal amount of additional private capital and made a commitment within the two year period. This would allow them to reduce the amount of uninvested funds during the process of expanding to a more economical size.

During this November meeting they had agreed that they definitely were not interested in being money lenders but that they had an interest in investing in situations with growth potential. They talked about locating in San Francisco, California, a city with which both men were acquainted. The surrounding area seemed to have many small businesses of the type which they felt had growth potential.

Mr. Sharp and Mr. Peck decided at this time to see if they could obtain enough money to start an SBIC with at least minimum capital. They also discussed the possibility of taking in additional partners. However, both men felt that even one more person might make the operation too unwieldy. In addition, they decided that they wanted more information on the SBA as regulator of the program before making a final decision. Thus, they concluded their November meeting by agreeing that further investigation was still necessary.

During the next few months, Mr. Sharp and Mr. Peck talked with SBA officials as well as the management of two publicly held SBIC's and several privately owned SBIC's. It appeared to both of them that Government officials were making every effort to make the program successful. Mr. Sharp and Mr. Peck felt that the various amendments of 1960 and 1961 to the original act were additional evidence of this. The consensus of the views of those SBIC managers to whom they talked seemed to be that although SBIC's were subject to a certain amount of red tape, this amount was not excessive.

Mr. Peck and Mr. Sharp had agreed that they should make some financial projections to determine what their needs would be and to evaluate their prospects. The two men thought that it would be a unique situation for an SBIC with minimum capitalization to have two full time managers. They felt that obtaining sufficient current income to offset operating expenses (including their salaries) might be a problem.

They could obtain a certain amount of interest income from any debentures which they purchased or from any equity-type securities which paid a dividend. SBIC's were also authorized to invest in government obligations. However, Mr. Sharp and Mr. Peck thought that efforts to maximize current interest income might cause a shrinkage in the amount of capital appreciation which they could obtain on their investments.

A second possible source of current income was available through providing advisory services ("consulting fees"). An SBIC was permitted to assist the small business concern in which it had invested or was considering investing by rendering consulting and advisory services with respect to its financial, management, and operating activities. These services could be provided before or after the SBIC made its investment. They could be rendered either on a fee or a contract basis.

On the other hand, Mr. Sharp and Mr. Peck were questioning whether most small businesses of the type in which they were interested could afford to pay consulting fees. They were wondering whether it might be better to provide their services solely for the receipt of the fee for serving on the board of directors. (As part of financing a small business concern, they intended to seek representation on the board of directors.) They might later request fees more in line with the value on the advisory and consulting services after the firm became more able to pay for the services which they were providing.

A third possible source of current income could come from "finder's fees." Based on his experiences in the venture capital field, Mr. Sharp thought that many of the most attractive opportunities required financing of $200,000 or more. Therefore, the two men had anticipated that it might be desirable to form a group in order to do deals larger than their $60,000 maximum would allow. In addition, they thought that they might derive some current income for providing investigative services for the other group members.

Investigative services, as envisioned by Mr. Sharp and Mr. Peck, consisted of a thorough analysis of the small business concern under consideration as well as its industry. They both felt it was imperative to evaluate a company's management, product, competition, and financial condition before making any commitment. They had located a number of investors (both corporate and individual) who had venture capital available and would be willing to rely largely on their judgment. Thus, Mr. Sharp and Mr. Peck would do virtually all the investment analysis and investigation for the entire group.

It appeared to Mr. Sharp and Mr. Peck that there were many ways in which they might be compensated for these investigative services. One method under consideration was to agree to perform investigative services for investors in return for a monthly retainer fee. A variation of this scheme was to charge the investors a certain percentage of the investigative costs incurred by Yerba Buena Capital, Inc. A third form of compensation for investigative services, which was based on an incentive system, was also being studied. That is, the amount of compensation might be varied depending on the success of the particular investment. Both men felt that investors were more willing to pay for investigative services when they were connected with a successful investment venture. Thus, they thought that it might be possible to obtain options to buy from the individual group members a portion of each investment which the group members had made on the basis of investigative services provided by Mr. Sharp and Mr. Peck. To be equitable to the group members, Mr. Sharp and Mr. Peck felt that such options should require that the price specified be higher than the original cost. Thus, the group member could still make some profit on the portion of its investment purchased through option by Mr. Sharp and Mr. Peck. They also felt that some time limit should be placed on the option. Specifically, they were considering a proposal of a five year option to buy 25 percent of each group member's investment at 125 percent of the group member's original cost. For example, if a group member bought 100 shares in a small business concern at $100 per share, the option would allow Mr. Peck and Mr. Sharp to buy twenty-five shares at $125 per share from the group member.

Mr. Peck and Mr. Sharp had anticipated that they would "probably" be able to liquidate their investments *on the average* after three years with a capital appreciation of 66 percent at that time. That is, an investment of $100,000 made in the first year could be liquidated in the fourth year for $166,000. They anticipated that some investments would be held longer than three years and some shorter, and that some would appreciate more than 66 percent and some less. However, they felt that they had selected reasonable averages.

On the "pessimistic" side, they figured it might take *on the average* four years to liquidate investments and that the amount of capital appreciation would be the same as over the shorter period. Namely, an investment of $50,000 made in the first year could be liquidated in the fifth year for $83,000. Built into the "pessimistic" projections was the anticipation that they would find fewer opportunities in which they might be interested. (Note that the amount of Cash Disbursements shown in Exhibit 1 is consistently lower for the "pessimistic" projections than for the "probable" projections.)

After much discussion they prepared two sets of projections, shown as Exhibits 1–5. They termed these projections "pessimistic" and "probable." Mr. Sharp had drawn on his experience in the venture capital field in making many of the assumptions necessary for the projections. But the final figures—those shown in the Exhibits—represented a joint effort.

As shown by their projections, Mr. Sharp and Mr. Peck had figured

Exhibit 1

YERBA BUENA CAPITAL, INC. (A)

Cash Disbursements (Probable)

	1st Year	*2d Year*	*3d Year*	*4th Year*	*5th Year*
OPERATING EXPENSES					
Officers' salaries	21,600	21,600	24,000	24,000	24,000
Secretary	2,400	5,000	5,000	5,000	5,000
Office rent	1,200	1,200	1,200	1,200	1,200
Supplies	240	300	300	350	350
Furniture lease	300	300	300	300	300
Auto expense	1,800	1,800	1,800	2,000	2,000
Other travel	0	500	1,000	2,000	3,000
Telephone	360	500	750	1,000	1,000
Entertainment	500	500	650	800	900
Bookkeeping	600	800	1,000	1,200	1,200
Miscellaneous	1,000	1,000	1,000	1,150	1,050
	30,000	33,500	37,000	39,000	40,000
INTEREST EXPENSE					
Commitment fee to SBA*	1,500	0	1,000	0	0
Debenture interest	0	7,500	9,500	15,000	15,000
Loan interest†	0	1,500	8,100	15,000	15,000
	1,500	9,000	18,600	30,000	30,000
CAPITALIZED FEES‡					
Organization expense	3,000	0	0	0	0
Legal and accounting fees	4,000	12,000	12,000	10,000	20,000
	7,000	12,000	12,000	10,000	20,000
Investments	100,000	300,000	300,000	250,000	500,000
Taxes (from Exhibit 4)					
Capital gain tax	0	0	0	15,500	47,000
Income tax	0	0	0	1,300	10,100
				16,800	57,100
Total cash disbursements	138,500	354,500	367,600	345,800	647,100

*Commitment fee to SBA—Charge for debentures for which the SBIC is committed to sell, but has not yet taken the funds. The rate is 1/12 percent per month.

†Loan interest—Payable on operating loans (shown on Balance Sheet) which may be obtained from banks and/or SBA. The interest rate is 5 percent per year, which is the same rate charged for debentures sold to the SRA.

‡Capitalized fees—Certain legal and other expenses directly connected with specific financing arrangements are not deductible for income tax purposes and thus are capitalized as a cost of the investment.

Exhibit 1 (Continued)

Cash Disbursements (Pessimistic)

	1st Year	*2d Year*	*3d Year*	*4th Year*	*5th Year*
OPERATING EXPENSES					
(Same as 1st year above)	30,000	30,000	30,000	30,000	30,000
INTEREST EXPENSE					
Commitment fee to SBA	1,500	0	1,500	0	0
Debenture interest	0	7,500	7,500	15,000	15,000
Loan interest	0	0	0	0	3,800
	1,500	7,500	9,000	15,000	18,800
CAPITALIZED FEES					
Organization expense	3,000	0	0	0	0
Legal and accounting fees	2,000	6,000	6,000	6,000	10,000
	5,000	6,000	6,000	6,000	10,000
Investments	50,000	150,000	150,000	150,000	250,000
Taxes (from Exhibit 4)					
Capital gain tax	0	0	0	0	1,400
Total cash disbursements	86,500	193,500	195,000	201,000	310,200

Exhibit 2

YERBA BUENA CAPITAL, INC. (A)

Cash Receipts (Probable)

	1st Year	*2d Year*	*3d Year*	*4th Year*	*5th Year*
SERVICES					
Consulting fees	0	15,000	20,000	20,000	20,000
Finder's fees	5,000	7,500	15,000	20,000	25,000
	5,000	22,500	35,000	40,000	45,000
INTEREST					
Government securities	3,000	1,500	0	0	0
Investments	1,500	13,500	33,000	48,000	58,500
	4,500	15,000	33,000	48,000	58,500
PAID-IN CAPITAL AND DEBT					
Paid-in capital	153,000	150,000	0	0	0
SBA debentures	150,000	0	150,000	0	0
Loans (SBA or bank)	0	150,000	50,000	100,000	0
	303,000	300,000	200,000	100,000	0
Sales of investments	0	0	0	166,000	500,000
Total cash receipts	312,500	337,500	268,000	354,000	603,500

Exhibit 2 (Continued)

Cash Receipts (Pessimistic)

	1st Year	2d Year	3d Year	4th Year	5th Year
SERVICES					
Consulting fees	0	5,000	10,000	10,000	10,000
Finder's fees	0	5,000	10,000	15,000	15,000
	0	10,000	20,000	25,000	25,000
INTEREST					
Government securities	3,200	2,800	2,800	2,800	1,200
Investments	1,500	7,500	16,500	25,500	34,500
	4,700	10,300	19,300	28,300	35,700
PAID-IN CAPITAL AND DEBT					
Paid-in capital	153,000	150,000	0	0	0
SBA debentures	150,000	0	150,000	0	0
Loans (SBA or bank)	0	0	0	0	150,000
	303,000	150,000	150,000		150,000
Sale of investments	0	0	0	0	83,000
Total cash receipts	307,700	170,300	189,300	53,300	293,700

Exhibit 3

YERBA BUENA CAPITAL, INC. (A)

Cash Balances at Year End (Probable)

	1st Year	2d Year	3d Year	4th Year	5th Year
Beginning balance	0	174,000	157,000	57,400	65,600
Cash receipts (Exhibit 2)	312,500	337,500	268,000	354,000	603,500
Cash disbursements (Exhibit 1)	(138,500)	(354,500)	(367,600)	(345,800)	(647,100)
Ending balance	174,000	157,000	57,400	65,600	22,000

Cash Balances at Year End (Pessimistic)

	1st Year	2d Year	3d Year	4th Year	5th Year
Beginning balance	0	221,200	198,000	192,300	44,600
Cash receipts (Exhibit 2)	307,700	170,300	189,300	53,300	293,700
Cash disbursements (Exhibit 1)	(86,500)	(193,500)	(195,000)	(201,000)	(310,200)
Ending balance	221,200	198,000	192,300	44,600	28,100

Exhibit 4

YERBA BUENA CAPITAL, INC. (A)

Profit and Loss (Probable)

	1st Year	2d Year	3d Year	4th Year	5th Year
Income (from Exhibit 2)					
Services	5,000	22,500	35,000	40,000	45,000
Interest	4,500	15,000	33,000	48,000	58,500
	9,500	37,500	68,000	88,000	103,500
Expenses (from Exhibit 1)					
Operating	30,000	33,500	37,000	39,000	40,000
Interest	1,500	9,000	18,600	30,000	30,000
	31,500	42,500	55,600	69,000	70,000
Net profit before taxes	(22,000)	(5,000)	12,400	19,000	33,500
Taxable profit after loss carry forward	0	0	0	4,400	33,500
Federal income tax (30%)	0	0	0	1,300	10,100
Net profit	(22,000)	(5,000)	12,400	17,700	23,400
Capital gains (realized)					
Sale of capital assets				166,000	500,000
Cost of capital assets (including capitalized fees)				104,000	312,000
Capital gain				62,000	188,000
Capital gain tax				15,500	47,000
Capital gain after tax				46,500	141,000
Addition to surplus	(22,000)	(5,000)	12,400	64,200	164,400

Profit and Loss (Pessimistic)

	1st Year	2d Year	3d Year	4th Year	5th Year
Income (from Exhibit 2)					
Services	0	10,000	20,000	25,000	25,000
Interest	4,700	10,300	19,300	28,300	35,700
	4,700	20,300	39,300	53,300	60,700
Expenses (from Exhibit 1)					
Operating	30,000	30,000	30,000	30,000	30,000
Interest	1,500	7,500	9,000	15,000	18,800
	31,500	37,500	39,000	45,000	48,800
Net profit*	(26,800)	(17,200)	300	8,300	11,900
Capital gains (realized)					
Sale of capital assets					83,000
Cost of capital assets (including capitalized fees)					54,000
Capital gain					29,000
Capital gain tax (after loss carry forward)					1,400
Capital gain after tax					27,600
Addition to surplus	(26,800)	(17,200)	300	8,300	39,500

*Loss carry forward is sufficiently large so that there are no federal income taxes

Exhibit 5

YERBA BUENA CAPITAL, INC. (A)

Balance Sheets (Probable)

	Beginning	*End 1st Year*	*End 2d Year*	*End 3d Year*	*End 4th Year*	*End 5th Year*
ASSETS						
Cash and government securities	150,000	174,000	157,000	57,400	65,600	22,000
Investments (at cost)		100,000	400,000	700,000	850,000	1,050,000
Capitalized expenses	3,000	7,000	19,000	31,000	37,000	45,000
	153,000	281,000	576,000	788,400	952,600	1,117,000
LIABILITIES AND NET WORTH						
Operating loans	0	0	150,000	200,000	300,000	300,000
SBA debentures	0	150,000	150,000	300,000	300,000	300,000
Capital stock	153,000	153,000	303,000	303,000	303,000	303,000
Surplus	0	(22,000)	(27,000)	(14,600)	49,600	214,000
	153,000	281,000	576,000	788,400	952,600	1,117,000

Exhibit 5 (Continued)

Balance Sheets (Pessimistic)

	Beginning	*End 1st Year*	*End 2d Year*	*End 3d Year*	*End 4th Year*	*End 5th Year*
ASSETS						
Cash and government securities	150,000	221,200	198,000	192,300	44,600	28,100
Investments (at cost)		50,000	200,000	350,000	500,000	700,000
Capitalized expenses	3,000	5,000	11,000	17,000	23,000	29,000
	153,000	276,200	409,000	559,300	567,600	757,100
LIABILITIES AND NET WORTH						
Operating loans	0	0	0	0	0	150,000
SBA debentures	0	150,000	150,000	300,000	300,000	300,000
Capital stock	153,000	153,000	303,000	303,000	303,000	303,000
Surplus	0	(26,800)	(44,000)	(43,700)	(35,400)	4,100
	153,000	276,200	409,000	559,300	567,600	757,100

their total capital requirements to be $150,000 at the company's inception and an additional $150,000 near the end of the second year. It seemed most desirable to be equal shareholders; therefore, each would need $75,000 initially and an additional $75,000 approximately two years later. Both men were able to obtain assurance that they could obtain the amounts that they were unable to provide on their own through loans from close family members.

The outstanding advantage the men saw in qualifying as a small business investment company was the leverage provided by the government funds. They felt that any tax advantages were of secondary importance. The main disadvantages seemed to them to be connected with the additional amount of regulation and restrictions to which they would be subject.

APPENDIX A[1]

Through the years a number of U.S. government agencies have had a hand in the efforts to meet the financing needs of small businesses, most notably the Federal Reserve Banks, the Smaller War Plants Corporation, and the Reconstruction Finance Corporation. After the Reconstruction Finance Corporation was liquidated in 1953, the Small Business Administration (SBA) was established by Congress by the Small Business Act of 1953. As of 1963, the SBA was the only federal government agency created and designed to render aid exclusively to small business firms.

Financial specialists of the SBA counsel small business concerns on their financial problems. If borrowing is necessary, the SBA helps them obtain funds from private sources if possible. If it is not possible for a small business to obtain financing with favorable terms from private sources, the SBA might consider making a loan on its own to the concern.

The SBA makes two types of loans—participating and direct. Because the intent of Congress was not to create a government agency that would be a competitor of private lenders, the Small Business Administration was prohibited from making direct loans if arrangements could be made for participation by a private lender. With a participating loan the SBA joined with a bank or other financial institution in a loan to a small business. The SBA might participate as much as 90 percent under the participating loan arrangement. The maximum loan that the Small Business Administration might make is $350,000.

[1]Compiled August 1963.

In its first seven years of operations (through June 10, 1960) the SBA approved over $800 million in loans. Although the total amounts involved in the loans of SBA is small compared with the volume of credit extended by private lenders, the agency has responsibilities to small business in addition to that of lending. These include giving financial counseling, certifying small firms for government orders, advising small firms on managerial procedures, providing firms with technical assistance, and providing assistance in production.

The responsibilities of the SBA were expanded in August 1958, when Congress passed a series of amendments to the Small Business Act of 1953. These amendments were known as the Small Business Investment Act of 1958. This act authorized the establishment of privately and publicly owned and operated small business investment companies (SBIC's) and delegated to the Small Business Administration the responsibility for licensing, regulating, and helping to finance these new organizations.

The following information on how to form an SBIC and how it supplies long-term funds to small business is reprinted from *The SBIC*, a booklet prepared by the Small Business Administration:

> The SBIC program is designed to stimulate and supplement the flow of private equity capital and long-term loans which small businesses need for the sound financing of their operations, and for growth, expansion, and modernization.
>
> A unique feature of this new medium of small business financing is that it brings together local capital and management talent. The organizers of investment companies usually know their own communities and industries, and are familiar with the needs of small businesses in their area. They are therefore in a good position to render needed financial and management assistance.
>
> Small business investment companies are intended to be profit-making corporations, and are either privately- or publicly-owned and -operated. The Small Business Administration encourages financial institutions to participate in the ownership of SBIC's to the extent permitted under applicable laws.
>
> SBIC's are restricted in their activities to the provision of equity capital and long-term debt financing, and consulting and advisory services, to small businesses. They may engage in other activities only if they are incidental and appropriate to those set forth above.
>
> Under the Small Business Investment Act of 1958 (Public Law 85-699), an Investment Division was established within the Small Business Administration. The powers conferred by the Act upon the Agency and its Administrator are to be carried out through the Investment Division and a Deputy Administrator for that Division.

Section 102 of the Act states: "It is declared to be the policy of the Congress and the purpose of this Act to improve and stimulate the national economy in general and the small business segment thereof in particular by establishing a program to stimulate and supplement the flow of private equity capital and long-term loan funds which small-business concerns need for the sound financing of their business operations and for their growth, expansion, and modernization, and which are not available in adequate supply: Provided, however, that this policy shall be carried out in such manner as to insure the maximum participation of private financing sources.

"It is the intention of the Congress that the provisions of this Act shall be so administered that any financial assistance provided hereunder shall not result in a substantial increase of unemployment in any area of the country."

Eligibility for Licensing

To be eligible for a license, an SBIC must meet minimum capital requirements; submit a proposal of its plan of operations to SBA, and agree to operate under SBA regulations in all its transactions with small businesses. SBA's criteria for granting licenses to SBIC's include, but are not limited to, the following:

1. The need for financing of small businesses in the area in which the proposed company is to commence operations. As far as possible, an actual, rather than a theoretical need, must be demonstrated.
2. The number of such companies previously organized in the United States, and their volume of operations.
3. The good moral character of the incorporators, the experience of management, and management's ability to carry out the proposed plan of operation.
4. The stated plans of operation of the company. These should be in such detail as to permit consideration by SBA in the light of their completeness, general feasibility, and soundness.

The general objectives of the Small Business Investment Act are paramount in the application of the criteria. Incorporators and management must be of good moral character and reputation, particularly in all their financial dealings. Management should include persons with experience in the investing, credit or similar fields. Experience requirements may vary with the size of the proposed organization, its proposed area of operations, and its ability to obtain advice and counsel from its stockholders and from others who are interested in the success of the company's operations.

The issurance of a license by SBA will depend in large measure on the Agency's determination that the applicant is able to carry out the purposes of the Act and that an SBIC is needed in its area. The SBA may, in its absolute discretion, decline to issue a license.

Any organizing group must submit to SBA for consideration the following:

1. Its articles of incorporation and bylaws whether proposed or actually adopted;
2. The amount, classes, and description of its capital stock;
3. The object for which the company is formed;
4. The name assumed by the company;
5. The area in which its operations are to be conducted;

6. The location of its principal office;
7. Names and background of its directors, officers and counsel;
8. Other items called for in an application form prescribed by SBA.

Each application for a license is subject to a full examination by the Agency's Investment Division.

Capital Requirements

Under the Small Business Investment Act, an SBIC must have, in cash, or eligible U.S. Government securities, paid-in capital and surplus equal to at least $300,000 before it receives a license and commences business. Any subsequent sales of stock in an SBIC must also be for cash, or in exchange for U.S. Government obligations.

However, additional stock may be issued as stock dividends, or under stock options for services rendered to the SBIC, or under certain conditions for payment of services to the SBIC.

To facilitate formation of SBIC's, the Small Business Administration is authorized to purchase subordinated debentures of an investment company to help it meet capital requirements. For example, SBA may purchase up to $150,000 in subordinated debentures of a company which plans minimum capital of $300,000, and in the same ratio for companies planning greater than the minimum. However, SBA may not purchase subordinated debentures of any one company for an amount in excess of $400,000.

Therefore, an SBIC planning initial capital of $800,000 may ask SBA to purchase subordinated debentures in amounts up to $400,000, if funds from other sources are not available. But if the company plans initial capital in excess of $800,000, SBA purchase of its subordinated debentures still would be limited to $400,000. A request that SBA purchase subordinated debentures beyond the minimum needed for organization purposes must be accompanied by evidence that such funds are not obtainable from private sources.

These debentures are considered part of the SBIC's paid-in capital and surplus for purposes of the Act, but must be clearly identified as debt issues on any financial statements issued by the company.

In exchange for the executed debenture, SBA will issue a commitment letter to the applicant at the time of licensing, as evidence that the amount of the debenture is required for organization and licensing. A commitment fee of 1/12 of one per cent per month will be charged by SBA on the funds so committed. These funds will be paid out by SBA in the form of a U.S. Treasury check as the Licensee may require.

In addition to the subordinated debentures, SBA may lend operating funds to an SBIC in an amount up to 50 per cent of its paid-in capital and surplus (including any subordinated debentures held by SBA), with a maximum of $4 million of loans to any one company. Before obtaining such loans, the SBIC must demonstrate that funds for operating purposes are not available from private sources, and that the funds are necessary in furtherance of the SBIC's stated investment and loan policy. Where it is deemed desirable,

SBA may resell such operating loans to banks or other lending institutions. However, the rate of interest would not be affected.

Interest Rates on SBA Financing

The rate of interest on subordinated debentures and other obligations owed by small business investment companies to SBA is 5 percent per annum. This rate may be adjusted from time to time, but adjustments will not affect the rate on debentures previously purchased by SBA or on existing loans from SBA.

Maturities and Other Terms of SBA Financing

Maturities of subordinated debentures purchased by SBA may not exceed 20 years, with amortization beginning not later than the start of the second half of the term.

Repayment of subordinated debentures may be made out of earnings of the licensee, provided the repayment does not reduce capital below the minimum requirements, or from the proceeds of the sale of additional stock, or both.

Other loans made by SBA to an SBIC will bear such repayment and other provisions as may be established by the Agency. The provisions will be in accord with the objective that funds supplied by the Agency should be retired as rapidly as is consistent with the maintenance of adequate capitalizations. Maturities shall not exceed 20 years.

The use of Federal funds for the relocation of industry is prohibited, if the relocation would result in a substantial decrease in employment in any area of the country.

Other Borrowings by SBIC's

SBIC's may borrow money from private sources. In such borrowings, the ratio of debt to capital and surplus (including subordinated debentures held by SBA) shall not exceed 4 to 1, without prior consent of the Agency.

Equity Capital Financing of Small Businesses

A major function of a small business investment company is to provide a source of needed equity capital for small business. Equity capital may be provided by an SBIC to an incorporated small business through the purchase of its equity securities—that is, stocks of any class, and bonds or debentures providing a participation in equity securities either through conversion or through accompanying warrants or options—subject to regulations of the Small Business Administration.

Where convertible debentures are used as the instrument of financing a small business they must:

1. Bear interest and contain such other terms contracted for between the SBIC and the small business. The rate of interest may not exceed the maximum rate permitted by local laws; where no State limit is fixed, the maximum cost to the borrower shall not exceed a cost approved by SBA.
2. Be callable in whole or in part upon 3 months' notice, under conditions agreed upon between the borrower and the SBIC.

3. Be convertible, at the option of the small business investment company, *or a holder in due course,* up to and including the effective date of any call by the issuer, into stock of the small business at the sound book value of such stock, determined by the parties at the time of issuance of the debentures. In determining the value of the stock, all pertinent factors are to be considered, including the actual value of the assets of the small business and the relationship of its earnings to its invested capital.

4. Limit conversion privileges to the extent that debentures may not be convertible into other equity or debt securities which carry additional conversion rights.

The SBA permits an SBIC to supply capital to a small business by means of any equity financing arrangements. However, SBA prohibits the issuance of additional stock purchase warrants or options and additional conversion privileges on stock or warrants or options obtained through conversion.

Long-Term Loans to Small Business

Small business investment companies may make long-term loans to incorporated and unincorporated small businesses in order to provide funds needed for sound financing, growth, modernization and expansion. Long-term loans, as used herein, means loans with final maturities of not less than 5 years and not more than 20 years. However, this requirement will not preclude the making of incidental shorter-term loans under certain conditions when necessary to protect the interests of the investment company. An SBIC's long-term loans must be of such sound value, or so secured, as reasonably to assure repayment. They may bear interest at rates agreed upon between the SBIC and the borrower. However, the rate of interest may not exceed the maximum rate permitted by local law; where no local limit is fixed, the interest rate charged must be within the rate limits set forth in the SBIC's proposal for a license.

Maturities of these loans may not exceed 20 years, except that the maturity may be extended or the loan renewed for additional periods not exceeding 10 years, if the investment company finds that extension or renewal will aid in the orderly liquidation of the loan.

Limitations on SBIC Financing

The aggregate amount of obligations and securities acquired and for which commitments may be issued by an SBIC for any single enterprise may not exceed $500,000 or 20 per cent of the combined capital and surplus (including subordinated debentures held by SBA) of the SBIC, whichever is the lesser, without prior consent from the Agency. And, no more than five SBIC's may join to provide financial assistance to a single small business without prior approval by SBA, unless the amount of financing is $500,000 or less.

SBA Examination and Regulation

The Small Business Investment Act provides that each small business investment company shall be subject to examinations, that it shall make such reports as are required, and that it shall be subject to regulations prescribed by the Small Business Administration.

It is SBA's intention to regulate and examine SBIC's to the end that such companies conduct their activities properly and in accordance with the Act. However, SBA assumes no responsibility to the SBIC's, their investors, small businesses, or any other parties for any consequences of the SBIC's activities.

Examinations will be made at SBA's direction by examiners selected or approved by the Agency, and the cost of such examinations, including the compensation of the examiners, will be assessed against the SBIC examined.

The Securities Act and the Investment Company Act

Organizers of small business investment companies should familiarize themselves with applicable provisions of the Securities Act of 1933, the Trust Indenture Act of 1939, and the Investment Company Act of 1940, inasmuch as an SBIC may be subject to the provisions of one or more of those Acts.

Under the Small Business Investment Act, the Securities and Exchange Commission is authorized to exempt any class of an SBIC's securities from the registration requirements of the Securities Act of 1933 if it finds that enforcement of the Act with respect to such securities is not necessary in the public interest and for the protection of investors. The Commission is authorized also to allow a corresponding exemption from the requirements of the Trust Indenture Act of 1939.

Miscellaneous

The operations of a small business investment company, including the generation of business, may be undertaken wherever practicable in cooperation with banks or other investors or lenders, incorporated or unincorporated. Any servicing or initial investigation required for loans or acquisitions of securities by the SBICmay be handled through banks or other investors or lenders on a fee basis. An SBIC may receive fees for services rendered to banks or other financial institutions.

SBIC's may make use of the advisory services of the Federal Reserve System and of the U.S. Department of Commerce which are available and useful to industrial and commercial businesses. They may provide consulting and advisory services on a fee basis to small businesses and have on their staff persons competent to provide such services.

Funds of SBIC's not reasonably needed for their current operations may be invested only in direct obligations of, or obligations guaranteed as to principal and interest by, the United States. Funds not invested in small businesses or in the Government obligations mentioned above shall be retained in cash or placed on demand or time deposit with a commercial bank which is a member of the Federal Deposit Insurance Corporation. In the case of a time deposit, maturity shall not be longer than 1 year from the date of deposit.

What Is a "Small Business Concern"?

In the regulations issued by SBA under the Small Business Investment Act of 1958, "a small business concern" is defined as one which is independently owned and operated and not dominant in its field of operation.

A parent company must be considered together with all of its affiliates in determining its eligibility as a small business. If a concern is a wholly-owned subsidiary of another concern or is under the control or the potential control of another concern other than a small business investment company, it shall be considered an affiliate; also, a concern may be an affiliate of another concern if both are owned or controlled by a third party other than an SBIC. Generally, a business will be considered small if its assets do not exceed $5 million, its net worth is not in excess of $2.5 million and its average net income, after taxes, for the preceding 2 years is not more than $250,000. If the business does not qualify under these three provisions, it may seek to qualify under certain other criteria established by SBA.

Benefits of Forming an SBIC

The benefits of forming a small business investment company are manifold, and tax exemptions granted SBIC's by Congress were enacted to provide incentive for legitimate profits.

Under the Technical Amendments Act of 1958, a stockholder in an SBIC is allowed an ordinary loss deduction (instead of a capital loss) on the sale of stock in an SBIC, or if the stock becomes worthless. Similarly, SBIC's are allowed the same loss deductions on their stock investments in small businesses provided that such stock was obtained by conversion from debentures or from the exercise of stock purchase warrants. Losses sustained in the sale of convertible debentures may also be applied against ordinary income. The Technical Amendments Act also allows an SBIC a 100 per cent deduction for dividends received from stock it holds in a small business. SBIC's which meet prescribed conditions are also exempt from the 27½ per cent tax on accumulated earnings up to $100,000 and 38½ per cent tax on such earnings above $100,000. In 1959 Congress further amended the Internal Revenue Code of 1954 to exempt an SBIC which may also be a personal holding company (within the meaning of Section 542 of the Code) from the surtax on undistributed earnings if the SBIC is "actively engaged" in supplying funds to small businesses and if a shareholder in the SBIC does not own more than 5 per cent or more equity in a business to which the SBIC provides funds.

The establishment of SBIC's was encouraged also by a series of amendments adopted by Congress in 1960. The most significant provided for equity financing of a small business through straight purchases of stock and other equity instruments as an alternative to the use of convertible debentures, required under the original statute. This gives SBIC's greater flexibility of choice in financing small businesses and makes possible the arrangement of their own portfolios of small business securities so as to improve their chances to borrow from private sources.

Another amendment made it possible for a bank which is a subsidiary bank of a bank holding company to invest capital in an SBIC (up to 2 per cent of its capital and surplus) without regard to whether the SBIC might become a subsidiary of the bank holding company.

The 1961 Congress passed additional amendments to the Small Business Investment Act of 1958. These increased to $400,000 in matching funds the amount which may be supplied by SBA in exchange for the licensee's subordinated debentures to meet organizational requirements. At the same time, the minimum capital requirement was retained at $300,000.

Funds obtained in exchange for these debentures, despite being a debt are considered part of the SBIC's capital and surplus for organizational needs and as a base for loans from SBA.

After its capital funds have been invested, an SBIC is eligible for loans totaling up to 50% of its capital and surplus, with a ceiling of $4 million on loans to any one SBIC. Such funds must be used for lending to, or investment in, small businesses.

At the same time, Congress limited to $500,000, or 20% of the capital of an SBIC, whichever is the lesser, the investment by an SBIC in any one small business, without SBA approval, as noted earlier.
Collectively, these amendments present a strong incentive to form a small business investment company.

EVALUATING AN INVESTMENT OPPORTUNITY BY AN SBIC—PART I

Yerba Buena Capital, Inc. (B)

In May 1963, Mr. Sharp and Mr. Peck were reviewing a company which has been under study for several months. They were attempting to determine whether Yerba Buena Capital, Inc. should invest in Ideal Products and, if so, what the suitable terms might be.

On October 1, 1962, Mr. Richard Sharp had submitted his resignation to the venture capital firm for which he had been working. Shortly thereafter Mr. Sharp and Mr. Peck began processing the paper work necessary for the formation of a small business investment company. Yerba Buena Capital, Inc. was organized as a California corporation on November 4, 1962, and on November 25, 1962, the Small Business Administration licensed the corporation as a small business investment company. Mr. Peck left Ordinary Oil at the end of November and henceforth both men have devoted full time to the interests of Yerba Buena Capital, Inc. Although they were seriously interested in several other investment opportunities which they had been examining, they had not yet made any firm commitments. They were particularly anxious for their first investment to be a successful one.

Ideal Products

Mr. Richard Sharp learned of the Ideal Products Company in December of 1962, when he was registering for a credit rating service with Mr. Charles Worth. During the course of their discussion, Mr. Sharp inquired about rapidly growing businesses in the San Francisco Bay Area that might possibly need outside capital. One of the companies mentioned by Mr. Worth was Ideal Products.

Ideal Products was organized as a partnership in 1953 by two young engineers—Mr. Tom Robinson and Mr. Nelson Harvey. They bought some land in San Leandro, California, and built a building on the property. The two partners purchased equipment, often in poor condition, at auctions and then made major repairs themselves to place it in operating condition. They also built some of the machinery themselves.

In 1961, the partners decided they would like to terminate the partnership arrangement. It was agreed that Mr. Robinson would buy out the partnership interest of Mr. Harvey, provided that they could agree upon a fair buy-sell price. Their accountant made the suggestion that a fair value for the company as a whole might be in the neighborhood of $480,000 or $240,000 for the one-half interest that was being sold. The partners, after further discussing this matter with their attorney, accepted this suggestion and agreed to consummate the transaction on this basis.

As of April 1, 1961, Tom Robinson undertook the operation of Ideal Products as a single proprietorship. Since the fair value of the property of the proprietorship had been determined in an arm's-length transaction, Mr. Robinson instructed his accountant to make the proper allocation of the purchase price to the respective assets of the proprietorship in order to issue "proper" financial statements. A memorandum prepared by the accountant described this task. (See Exhibit 1.)

Exhibit 1

IDEAL PRODUCTS

Accountant's Memorandum on Restatement of the Balance Sheet

In order to accomplish the restatement of values two basic principles were observed:

1. Since the cash, accounts receivable, inventories, and liabilities were already stated and carried in the accounts at actual cost which coincides with actual values, there could be no restatement of these items.

2. Any change between income tax basis and fair value had to relate to land, buildings, equipment, and patents, together with consideration of purchased good will if there were any.

Proceeding then in the area of item 2 above, a careful inventory was taken of all the equipment and patents including registered trademarks. The equipment was valued by Mr. Robinson and his staff at what they considered to be actual replacement cost in equivalent working condition. Patents were valued on an estimated income producing worth. The land was valued on the basis of a recent sale of like property in the immediate area. The buildings consisted of three units; however, two were of very recent construction and the costs were known. The cost factors existing in the new buildings were then related to the older building to reach an aggregate valuation for all buildings. In all of this work Mr. Harvey was consulted and his opinion given due weight, since he was the seller involved in the deal. When it was all done and tabulated it was found that the purchase price exceeded the fair value of the tangible assets in the amount of $31,821. This, then, was considered to be the purchase price of good will or going concern value. At this point it became a relatively simple matter to make a restatement of the cost or income-tax basis of the assets of the proprietorship as of the date of the transaction that was March 31, 1961.

Exhibit 1 (Continued)

Balance Sheet
March 31, 1961

CURRENT ASSETS		
Cash		$ 97,721
Accounts receivable—trade	$145,724	
Allowance for bad debts	9,481	136,243
Advance on commissions		2,412
Inventory—cost or market, whichever is lower		101,588
Total current assets		$337,964
OPERATING PROPERTIES		
Land	23,650	
Building	95,183	
Equipment	62,478	
	181,311	
Allowance for depreciation	16,566	
		164,745
Patents and trademarks	15,588	
Allowance for depreciation	213	
		15,375
Purchased good will		31,821
		$549,905
CURRENT LIABILITIES		
Accounts payable		$ 43,606
Salaries and wages payable		7,906
Commissions payable		16,871
Taxes payable		7,592
Deposits on sales		54,988
Harvey contract—current portion		40,000
Miscellaneous		3,223
Total current liabilities		$174,186
LONG-TERM LIABILITIES		
Mortgage payable		41,976
Harvey contract		200,000
Total long-term liabilities		$241,976
T. Robinson capital		133,743
		$549,905

After operating Ideal Products for three months as a single proprietorship, Mr. Robinson had incorporated the business, as of July 1, 1961. Since that time, Ideal Products had done business as a corporation.

A few days after first hearing about Ideal Products, Mr. Sharp called on Mr. Tom Robinson, president and sole owner of Ideal Products. Mr. Sharp's first impression of Mr. Robinson was a favorable one. Mr. Robinson appeared to be a bright, able manager who was keenly interested in seeing Ideal Products grow. While showing Mr. Sharp the plant, Mr. Robinson had pointed out that production difficulties had been minimal despite the rapid growth which Ideal Products had achieved. Mr. Sharp had observed that the physical facilities seemed to be in good order.

During this initial meeting Mr. Sharp had been extremely impressed with the product line of Ideal Products. The company manufactured heavy checkweighing and ejecting machinery for use in the canning and packing industry. (Exhibit 2 contains some information on the checkweighing industry, which appeared in a publication that Mr. Sharp considered reliable. Exhibit 3 contains articles which appeared in trade journals describing two of the major revenue producers of Ideal Products.) Four sales representatives covered a nation-wide market, with about 750 accounts sold in all.

Exhibit 2

Information on the Checkweighing Industry

Increasing concern with accurate weights of packaged consumer goods is spurring sales for a handful of firms that manufacture electronic scales called checkweighers. These high-speed machines are designed to assure that every container's contents matches the weight printed on the label.

In the summer of 1961, a subcommittee of the Senate Judiciary Committee started investigating charges of inaccurate filling or labeling of containers, drawing public attention to the problem. Now, to avoid complaints from government agencies and consumers about short weights, a growing number of packagers are installing checkweighers in their factory conveyor lines. Formerly, many of these firms just spot-checked packages at random on conventional scales.

The typical checkweigher, which is about the size of an office desk, can be adjusted to reject packages over or under a desired weight. It picks up boxes, cans or glass containers coming from a filling machine and rapidly weighs them. It automatically shifts underweights to one side, overweights to another and sends "on-weight" packages to the shipping department. Checkweighers range in price from $2000 to $15,000.

The sales vice-president of a leading scale manufacturer reports that of all his company's products, "There is none that gives us more inquiries these days than checkweighers." A company which specializes in checkweighers began production in 1953 with sales of about $50,000. Its sales last year climbed to more than $500,000 up from $300,000 the previous year. The company president estimates the current backlog of orders is more than $600,000.

Although some types of checkweighers were made before World War II, most producers say that within the past five years they have been turning out faster, more complex models.

Advanced types of checkweighers can process up to 400 filled containers a minute. Many checkweighers operate so smoothly, according to manufactures, that they can handle brimful containers of liquid products without spilling or splashing the contents. And engineers have developed accessory units that can signal the filling machine to adjust itself automatically if too many off-weight containers come down the conveyor line.

Exhibit 2 (Continued)

These technical advancements have helped make possible a variety of new applications for checkweighers. A pharmaceutical manufacturer installed a checkweigher about six months ago to "count" the number of throat lozenges in its packages. The checkweigher can detect a difference in weight if the box does not contain the desired number of lozenges. It rejects packages that are only one lozenge light, claims an official.

Other companies are learning that pin-point accuracy in weighing each container can work two ways. While helping the consumer, by eliminating underweight packages, checkweighers also aid manufacturers by ending "profit giveaway" through overweight packages. "Many companies overfill to avoid underweight," says the president of an Eastern checkweigher producer. "This is a loss of product and profit which they cannot recover."

Officials at a frozen food plant in Oregon say they had been overfilling an average of three-sixteenths of an ounce on each ten-ounce package of mixed vegetables until they installed two checkweighers on their filler lines a few months ago. Since then, they estimate they have been saving an average of more than 1200 pounds of their product in a sixteen-hour work day. A macaroni division manager says a checkweigher installed on one of his filler lines last year is reducing product giveaway by more than 450 pounds a day.

Exhibit 3

Samples of Articles from Trade Journals

1. *Automatic Checkweighers*

Solid state, modular plug-in electronics are features in a compact over-and-under weight rejector introduced by Ideal Products. This automatic checkweigher gives weight information in two channels, rejecting both under and over weights as required. The unit measures 24 × 24 inches and is also available with three-way weight status channelizer. It handles open or closed containers up to seven pounds and speeds up to 300/minute can be achieved, according to the manufacturer.

The control system is isolated in the weigh cell housing which is mounted topside so replacement with standby units can be accomplished with plug-out, plug-in simplicity for ease of maintenance.

Designed for application in either hand pack or automated lines the unit features watertight closures and fittings to accommodate washdowns. Retaining clips on external housing allow stainless steel sheeting to break away without the use of tools during sanitary maintenance procedures.

Internal vibration isolation techniques are said to contribute to a high degree of accuracy.

Single function automatic checkweighing is available in the same maker's recently introduced under weight rejector.

2. *Label Inspectors*

Use-Feature: Automatic, high-speed inspectors detect containers with twisted, torn, uneven or flapping wrap-around labels or naked cans or jars and reject them. A unit for improperly-labeled cans operates at speeds up to 1000 per minute; a unit for glass jars operates up to 300 per minute.

Description: Basically, both units inspect in the same manner, the glass jar inspector has a soft belting reject chute.

After the container leaves labeler, it is horizontally transported to photoelectric scanners. Cross beam scans for flapping, dog-eared, torn or uneven labels. Feeler fingers check for proper label alignment. Another scanner checks for naked containers.

If labeling was proper, the container continues to packaging. Improperly labeled container caused signal to open reject door.

Trap doors instantly close against rejected container as it drops into reject chute, making it impossible for properly labeled containers to follow—even when traveling shoulder to shoulder or bead to bead.

Mr. Robinson informed Mr. Sharp that the sales of Ideal Products had doubled each year for the last few years. He also stated that Ideal Products had been borrowing against receivables from a local bank. Mr. Sharp explained that this was an expensive method of financing and that what Ideal Products really needed was additional equity capital. Mr. Sharp suggested to Mr. Robinson that he make up some financial projections to determine the cash needs of Ideal Products over the next two years and that he then call him (Mr. Sharp) for a continuation of their discussion. Mr. Robinson agreed to this suggestion.

After this initial contact with Mr. Robinson and Ideal Products, Mr. Sharp began some field checking on the product line of Ideal Products. He visited some canners and packers who were using checkweighing equipment purchased from Ideal Products. Included in this group were several major customers of Ideal Products. The response from these companies was overwhelmingly favorable. "Great! No problems! I don't know how we got along before," one canning executive had said.

Having received no word from Mr. Robinson for over a month, Mr. Sharp called him in late January 1963. Mr. Robinson explained that he was just finishing up the financial projections and suggested that Mr. Sharp "come on over."

On the next day, Mr. Sharp made his second visit to the San Leandro firm. Mr. Robinson put forth financial statements (Exhibits 4 and 5) which gave the past operating results and future projections for Ideal Products. According to Mr. Robinson's calculations, the company could use new financing in the amount of $450,000. Mr. Sharp had reaffirmed Yerba Buena Capital's interest in financing Ideal Products, provided that mutually satisfactory terms could be arranged.

Mr. Robinson had initiated negotiations with the statement: "I frankly don't know what the company is worth. What do you think?" Mr. Sharp had replied that the over-the-counter market was still pretty well depressed as a result of the 1962 slump and that many promising young companies were selling at around ten times earnings. Mr. Robinson had been quick to counter that the price for some small companies was

Exhibit 4

IDEAL PRODUCTS

Assets

Assets	*Projection* June 30, 1964*	*Projection* June 30, 1963*	*Actual* Dec. 31, 1962*	*Actual* June 30, 1962*	*Actual* June 30, 1961*
Current assets					
Cash	$ 173,000	$ 270,000	$ 115,273	$ 46,253	$ 80,812
Accounts receivable	630,000	450,000	383,468	260,162	128,574
Inventory	630,000	450,000	396,125	231,124	121,346
Prepaid expenses	5,400	2,000	11,359	675	–
Total current expenses	1,438,400	1,172,000	906,225	538,214	330,732
Operating properties					
Land	36,000	36,000	36,000	36,000	36,000
Building and improvements	235,000	145,000	130,782	130,142	108,000
Equipment	180,000	125,000	129,426	98,966	92,261
Security deposits	6,300	4,500	3,637	1,800	–
Patents	28,800	28,800	28,800	28,800	28,800
Goodwill	31,821	31,821	31,821	31,821	31,821
Depreciation and amortization reserve	(80,000)	(56,000)	(40,863)	(25,609)	(1,622)
Total operating properties	437,921	315,121	319,603	301,920	295,260
	$1,876,321	$1,487,121	$1,225,828	$840,134	$625,992

*Valuation of assets is based on value determined in the purchase of the 50 percent interest of the predecessor partnership plus additions at cost.

Exhibit 4 (Continued)

Liabilities and Capital

Liabilities and Capital	*Projection June 30, 1964*	*Projection June 30, 1963*	*Actual Dec. 31, 1962*	*Actual June 30, 1962*	*Actual June 30, 1961*
Current liabilities					
Accounts payable—trade	$ 110,931	$ 61,497	$ 279,542	$106,482	$ 82,342
Salaries and wages	35,000	27,000	41,455	18,781	9,810
Commissions and royalties	45,000	45,000	57,971	53,821	30,088
Income taxes	260,000	150,000	97,168	64,350	10,988
Accrued interest	2,000	2,000	1,053	2,034	1,242
Customer deposits	70,000	45,000	56,491	5,904	12,078
Payroll taxes	27,000	21,500	25,287	14,313	–
Miscellaneous	5,500	4,500	5,365	10,401	422
Current portion of long-term debt	46,000	46,000	43,664	88,872	45,613
Total current liabilities	601,431	402,497	607,996	364,958	192,583
Long-term liabilities					
Notes payable—Officer	25,000	25,000	25,000	25,000	25,000
Mortgage payable	58,000	70,000	69,015	31,660	36,519
Harvey contract	40,000	80,000	120,000	120,000	160,000
Total long-term liabilities	123,000	175,000	214,015	176,660	221,519
Net worth					
Product guarantee reserve	45,000	27,000	23,891	10,892	–
Capital stock	211,890	211,890	211,890	211,890	211,890
Earned surplus	220,000	75,734	75,734	–	–
New financing	450,000	450,000	–	–	–
Annual net profit	225,000	145,000	92,302	75,734	–
Total net worth	1,151,890	909,624	403,817	298,516	211,890
	$1,876,321	$1,487,121	$1,225,828	$840,134	$625,992

Exhibit 5

IDEAL PRODUCTS

Income Statements
(Dollar figures in thousands)

	Projection Year Ended June 30, 1964		*Projection Year Ended June 30, 1963*		*Actual Six Months Ended December 31, 1962*	
Sales		$5,400.0 (100.0)		$3,600.0 (100.0)		$1,650.6 (100.0)
Product costs, consisting of direct costs of materials and manufacture		2,430.0 (45.0)		1,620.0 (45.0)		731.9 (44.4)
Gross margin		2,970.0 (55.0)		1,980.0 (55.0)		918.7 (55.6)
Operating expenses						
Selling	$1,540.0		$1,030.0		$353.2	
Research and development	360.0		210.0		111.8	
Administrative	280.0		215.0		110.9	
General	210.0	2,390.0 (44.3)	155.0	1,610.0 (44.7)	117.6	693.5 (42.0)
Operating income		580.0 (10.2)		370.0 (10.3)		225.2 (13.6)
Other income		20.0 (0.4)		11.5 (0.3)		9.7 (0.6)
Other expenses		(120.0) (−2.2)		(90.0) (−2.5)		(45.9) (−2.8)
Ordinary pretax income		480.0 (8.9)		291.5 (8.1)		189.1 (11.4)
Nonoperating and nonrecurring loss		- -		- -		- -
Pretax net income		480.0 (8.9)		291.5 (8.1)		189.1 (11.4)
Federal and state income taxes		255.0 (4.7)		146.5 (4.1)		96.8 (5.8)
Net income after taxes		$ 225.0 (4.2)		$ 145.0 (4.0)		$ 92.3 (5.6)

Exhibit 5 (Continued)

	Actual Year Ended June 30, 1962		Actual For Partnership Year Ended March 31, 1961	
Sales		$1,883.9 (100.0)		$946.8 (100.0)
Product costs, consisting od direct costs of materials and manufacture		790.2 (41.9)		398.0 (42.0)
Gross margin		1,093.7 (58.1)		548.8 (58.0)
Operating expenses				
Selling	$511.9		$304.3	
Research and development	104.7		47.0	
Administrative	178.6		88.0	
General	103.0	898.2 (47.7)	45.0	484.3 (51.2)
Operating income		195.5 (10.4)		64.5 (6.8)
Other income		4.3 (0.2)		3.3 (0.3)
Other expenses		(26.6) (−1.4)		(2.0) (0.2)
Ordinary pretax income		173.1 (9.2)		65.8 (6.9)
Nonoperating and nonrecurring loss		33.1 (1.8)		- -
Pretax net income		140.0 (7.4)		65.8 (6.9)
Federal and state income taxes		64.3 (3.4)		33.8 (3.6)
Net income after taxes		$ 75.7 (4.0)		$ 32.0 (3.3)

better than forty times earnings. Mr. Sharp had concluded this negotiating session by stating that he saw Ideal Products as a rather small company that (1) was subject to all kinds of risk; (2) promised probable, but by no means, sure-fire growth; (3) was too small to have a readily marketable security.

During their second meeting Mr. Sharp had told Mr. Robinson that he wanted to meet the former co-owner of Ideal Products – Mr. Nelson Harvey. Mr. Robinson arranged this for him. Mr. Robinson had said that Mr. Harvey was responsible for many of the innovations of Ideal Products. Mr. Harvey impressed Mr. Sharp as being a very creative engineer. Mr. Sharp got the feeling that Mr. Robinson and Mr. Harvey had been friendly in parting. Although Ideal Products had replaced Mr. Harvey with an experienced engineer, Mr. Sharp remained concerned that a man undoubtedly responsible for some of the past growth of Ideal Products was no longer with the company.

Mr. Sharp had also asked and received permission from Mr. Robinson to have an independent accountant examine the accounting function and other financial aspects of Ideal Products. (The accountant's report to Mr. Sharp is shown in Exhibit 6.)

Exhibit 6

Independent Accountant's Memorandum on Ideal Products

SUBJECT: Ideal Products
FROM: William Crosby
TO: Yerba Buena Capital, Inc.

On April 19, 1963, at the request of the above client I spent several hours reviewing the accounting functions and other financial aspects of Ideal Products.

Organization: The company was formed in approximately 1953 and operated as a partnership until March 1961. At this point, Tom Robinson acquired the interest of his partner and he operated the business for three months as a sole proprietorship. The business was then incorporated and Tom Robinson owns 100 percent of the stock. There are no outstanding options on any of the shares of the company.

Tax Position: I reviewed the company's state income tax return for the first fiscal year ended June 30, 1962. The Federal returns were apparently misplaced and not available for inspection. The company operated at a profit for the year ended June 30, 1962. The only reconciling item from the returns to the financial statements is the depreciation on the difference between cost and fair market value of fixed assets at date of incorporation. The unallowable depreciation is approximately $7600 a year.

Exhibit 6 (Continued)

Accounting System: I reviewed briefly the daily accounting routine. The cash receipts records are maintained on a Burroughs accounting machine, a pegboard system is used for payrolls, and the disbursements and voucher records are set up so that a local tabulating service provides voucher distribution.

I reviewed certain of the general ledger accounts and discovered the following:

A. Accounts Receivable

An aging at March 31, 1963, shows:

Current	$267,328	56.3%
February	82,663	17.5
January	64,196	13.6
December	19,314	4.1
November	5,582	1.2
Over 6 months	34,389	7.3
	$473,472	100.0%

I discussed the over six months accounts with the executive vice-president. He indicated that all the accounts were good, however, there were certain normal disputes involving performance, terms, and the like. At the end of the last fiscal year, there was approximately $26,000 in the reserve for bad debts. None has been added to the reserve this current fiscal year.

B. Fixed Assets

Fixed assets are stated at fair market value as of date of incorporation plus cost since date of incorporation. This has the effect of showing $72,000 of nondepreciable basis for tax purposes on the financial statements. The company is writing off approximately $7600 of this stated value above cost each year. The methods of depreciation are as follows:

Machinery and equipment	6 year straight line
Office equipment	7 " " "
Buildings	24 " " "
Improvements (leasehold)	8 " " "

C. Inventories

Book inventories are not maintained although the company is attempting to head in that direction. The inventory at June 30, 1962, was counted and priced at cost. The executive vice-president informed me that overhead was not added to the inventory at June 30, 1962. He also indicated that labor costs were excluded. However, I do not know the amount of inventory in process at June 30, 1962, and the labor and overhead excluded possibly could be minor in amount. The inventory figures used on the nine months statements this year were based upon an estimated cost of goods sold percentage, again excluding overhead and direct labor. Since the ending inventory on the nine months statement did not reflect labor and overhead, it would appear that they would be stated on the low side.

D. Other:

I briefly reviewed the company's work papers supporting balances in other accounts and they appeared proper.

General:

a. The company was given an unqualified opinion by its auditors on

June 30, 1962. The statements I reviewed were a balance sheet and earnings statement.

b. The nine months statement (not audited) for the period ending March 31, 1963, showed net profits of $106,662 and sales of $2,451,606.

c. The corporation assumed the note of the former proprietor on the buy out of his partner's interest. There are still three installments of $40,000 each due, on March 31, 1964, 1965, and 1966.

d. It is my feeling that, based upon a brief review, the approach to the financial accounting, with the exception of inventories, appears adequate. Although I did not study their proposals for the correction of the cost accounting problem, I feel that possibly they will need professional help in this area. I do not think that too much weight can be given to monthly operating statements until some form of cost accounting is initiated.

During the early months of 1963, Mr. Sharp continued his field investigations with customers of Ideal Products. Mr. Sharp also visited companies which were using checkweighers made by competitors of Ideal Products. He discussed the capabilities and performances of these checkweighers with company officials. Based on his own observations plus the comments of all those in the canning and packing industry with whom he had talked, by April 1963, Mr. Sharp had concluded that Ideal Products made a superior product and that the company was a leader in a rapidly expanding field.

Mr. Sharp knew of one national manufacturing company that was interested in acquiring Ideal Products. He thought that there might be others. He also felt that as of early May 1963, Ideal Products had not shopped around for financing. To the best of his knowledge Mr. Robinson had not talked seriously about additional financing for his company with any individuals or companies other than Yerba Buena Capital, Inc. In fact, in early May, when Mr. Sharp informed Mr. Robinson that he was prepared to enter final negotiations, Mr. Robinson had expressed some doubts on the desirability of obtaining additional equity capital for Ideal Products. He did, however, agree to meet with Mr. Sharp.

EVALUATING AN INVESTMENT OPPORTUNITY BY AN SBIC—PART II

Yerba Buena Capital, Inc. (C)

In May 1963, Mr. Sharp and Mr. Peck were reviewing a company which had been under study for several months. They were attempting to determine whether Yerba Buena Capital, Inc. should invest in Denver Nutronics Corporation and, if so, what the suitable terms might be. Although they had been examining several other investment opportunities, they had not made any firm commitment since they had received their charter as a small business investment company. They were particularly anxious for their first investment to be a successful one.

Denver Nutronics

Mr. Richard Sharp first met Mr. William Abbott in April 1962, when he was in Denver on a business trip. Mr. Sharp had been greatly impressed with the product of Denver Nutronics. At this time Mr. Abbott did not feel that Denver Nutronics had any immediate need for additional capital.

Denver Nutronics (DN) was organized in 1955 as a part-time activity by Mr. Abbott, who was director of a laboratory at a university. He had felt that there was a need for a consulting firm specializing in network integration. Initially the firm was in essence a "talent agency" with a reservoir of experienced scientists (for the most part university professors) with a diversity of analytical and research experience having the common denominator that the magnetic network integrator was the instrument used in the work.

About one year after it was organized, DN received a request from a government laboratory to consider building (instead of merely designing) a magnetic network integrator. After much deliberation DN somewhat reluctantly undertook the assignment, since the laboratory could not get the construction done by any competent commercial organization. However, even before this instrument was completed, Denver Nutronics was urged by the same government laboratory to consider building another of a different type. After some deliberation, this order was accepted. But almost at once, four other requests for quotations were received. Mr. Abbott felt that the company could continue to build one or two instruments per year on a part-time basis, but not more. According to Mr. Abbott, "It was at this point that our most difficult decision about the future of the company became necessary."

The decision reached was to go ahead on a full-time basis and see what the "free-growth" rate of the company might be. Since making this decision, Mr. Abbott has been devoting full-time to the affairs of Denver Nutronics. At the conclusion of their discussion in April 1962, Mr. Sharp had told Mr. Abbott, "If your company ever needs capital, I would be interested in talking further about the possibility of an investment in Denver Nutronics."

In November 1962, Mr. Sharp received a letter from Mr. Abbott stating that he was going to consider the possibility of taking in some additional outside capital. Mr. Abbott enclosed the following information about future plans:

> As a result of a considerable study of DN and other scientific enterprises of somewhat similar type, I have reached the following conclusions:

A company with the basic characteristics of Denver Nutronics delivering less than about $500,000 worth of instruments of $30,000 – $100,000 unit price can be stable and profitable. It can pick and choose among contracts and concentrate on excellence, and make those sales in which price is not the overriding consideration.

An investment company delivering above perhaps $5 million of such equipment can be fully competitive with all potential competitors, whether large or small. It can take advantage of the economies that batch or mass production offer; it can support a sales and advertising effort of significant effectiveness, and will be handling a sufficiently large number of units, at any one time, that random fluctuations in order level can always be smoothed by effective production planning.

In my view, a company of intermediate size—having annual volume in the $500,000 – $5,000,000 range, is in a more difficult position, being in fact somewhat more vulnerable to adverse external influences than either the smaller company or the larger one.

DN had grown quickly to the point where it was in the intermediate group. The company's reputation had spread to the point where both orders and requests for consideration for employment were being received from all over the world. Some of these inquiries about employment came from persons of great experience, who appeared to have the potential to assist any company they went with to become much more competitive in the field; in some cases they had already demonstrated a marked talent for invention in this area. It seemed obvious that if the company could not consider hiring the best of these candidates, it was doomed to eventual eclipse, in spite of its present commanding technical lead.

Upon consideration of these factors, the decision was made to attempt to expand the company instead of retreating to the lower stable level. A new entity, Denver Nutronics Corporation, is to be formed to facilitate financing and make possible greater profit retention than is possible in a proprietorship.

The goal of expanding to the $5 million-plus year level by 1967 was set as a lower limit with $10 million-plus in 1968 set as a target for which to shoot. A sales department was set up and some of the key scientific personnel who had approached the company were hired.

We find ourselves at the end of 1962 accepting new orders at a rate of over $100,000 per month with very good indication that 1963 orders will exceed $2,000,000, possibly very substantially. The total volume listed here is nearly $3,000,000, which of course does not include any prospects that may come to our attention after the date of writing. Historically, this company has received orders in over 80 percent of the cases in which it has bid. Of course, we have exercised strong selection as to when to bid.

Denver Nutronics has, however, reached the point where it can no longer finance its expansion at an optimum rate out of internally generated capital. Therefore, the company is presently investigating a number of proposals which have been laid before it from time to time with the objective of obtaining approximately $500,000 in additional operating funds before the end of calendar 1962 to prevent its growth from being held back due solely to a lack of adequate capital.

The funds sought will be used with self-generated funds, in the following ways (Items 5 and 6 may require additional capital later):

1. To finance work-in-process until delivery and payment. (The instruments take three months to two years to complete.)

2. To make it possible to take trade and quantity discounts rather uniformly when offered.

3. To make possible longer runs on standard parts in the company's shops, both to decrease unit cost and to enable the company to stockpile certain parts so as to be able to quote shorter delivery estimates to customers. (This seems to be the main remaining advantage big company competitors have over the company.)

4. To enable the new product development department to proceed at a reasonable speed in the completion and testing of "prototype" instruments and components, so they can be marketed as soon as possible. Denver Nutronics now has a proprietary position on many of these items and several appear to have a large market.

5. To enable the company to consider the partial or total acquisition of other companies which seem to fit well with Denver Nutronics. It is recognized that a fifteen-fold expansion in six years could in all probability be carried out more smoothly if in part accomplished by this route. In fact, the company now has several possibilities under study both in the United States and abroad.

6. To enable the company to set up network analysis facilities at its present locations and elsewhere. This, of course, requires that instruments for the purpose be produced and competent operators be trained. The potential market for such a service seems large; there is already strong indication that \$100,000–\$200,000 of such business can be had in 1963 if the network integrators are ready. Further, there is only token competition in this field.

At the same time, the company has mounted a strong effort to enter the contract research field, for government and industry. It presently appears that contracts for such research in excess of \$75,000 will be received before the end of calendar year 1962. In addition, the company is considering an exchange of stock with a "think" firm of eminent scientists which should considerably enhance its position in bidding on such projects. In the past, the company has financed all of its research and development effort out of its own funds. It presently appears that, because of great similarity of interests and goals, the government can be induced to undertake to provide support for a large portion of this effort.

I have appended hereto exhibits recording the company's growth to the present time and my personal projection of its growth potential for 1963–1968 (see Exhibits 1–3). In making my projections of the future I have included only those items for which it seems possible to make reasonable projections at this time. In other cases, no attempt to estimate the size of Denver Nutronics' possible share of the market yet seems feasible. Nor has the impact of some possible joint ventures been shown. However, it seems quite certain that substantial business and profits will result from these areas also; perhaps, enough to increase the over-all volume in 1968 or thereabouts by as much as 100 percent of that shown in the projection.

In short, the future for Denver Nutronics looks rather bright. The company has concentrated on quality and has apparently built a reputation for building the best instruments yet made in a field which many consider to be the most difficult of any instrumental analysis field. It is now preparing to exploit this reputation by an entry into other fields where there are competitors, in which we feel it can compete favorably, and to exploit to the limit by a vigorous sales effort fields in which it has pioneered. It is also ready to introduce a number of proprietary, patent-protected products for which we feel a sizable market exists. It is ready to exploit in their own right components such as magnets, power supplies and vacuum equipment which it has perfected. It is likewise prepared to expand its analysis and research activities in a major way. Also, it is ready to spread out geographically to offer better service and sales possibilities. Doubtless, a variety of "growing pains" problems will be encountered, but there is some assurance they can be solved in a satisfactory way, as the company has demonstrated an ability to attract persons of ability and to retain them thereafter.

Exhibit 1

DENVER NUTRONICS AND DENVER NUTRONICS CORPORATION

Order Record
as of December 1, 1962
(In thousands of dollars)

	1956	*1957*	*1958*	*1959*	*1960*	*1961*	*1962**
Network integrators	33	80	240	440	590	720	905
Components	0	0	0	5	15	65	135
Consulting	2	0	0	8	0	1	2
Research	0	0	0	0	0	0	75
Analysis	0	0	0	1	1	1	3
	35	80	240	454	606	787	1120

Order Projection
(In thousands of dollars)

	1962	*1963*	*1964*	*1965*	*1966*	*1967*
Equipment manufactured	1,040	2,095	3,750	5,800	7,800	10,900
Research and consulting	77	150	300	600	1,200	1,500
Analytical service	3	50	150	300	500	700
Total	1,120	2,295	4,200	6,700	9,500	13,100
Increase	333	1,175	1,905	2,500	2,800	3,600
Percent increase	42	105	83	60	42	38

Average increase 1963–1967–64%

Over-all increase–factor of 11

*Estimated.

Exhibit 2

DENVER NUTRONICS AND DENVER NUTRONICS CORPORATION

Profit Record As of October 1, 1962

	1958	*1959*	*1960*	*1961*	*1962**
Revenue from completed contracts	34,500	277,500	450,700	726,000	800,000
Cost of completed contracts	33,100	245,700	391,500	573,000	620,000
Pre-R&D profit	1,400	31,800	59,200	153,000	180,000
Amortization of R&D	8,000	20,000	43,000	59,000	70,000
Pretax profit†	(6,600)	11,800	16,200	94,000	110,000

*Figures for full year 1962 estimated from present data.
†The company has consistently made use of "incentive" depreciation rates allowed by the IRS. As of mid-1962, over $100,000 had been written off in this way.
The company has also set up a warranty reserve, which is currently in excess of $15,000. Historically, warranty cost per year has never exceeded $5000.

Coincidentally, Mr. Peck left San Francisco on a trip to the Midwest to investigate several investment opportunities for Yerba Buena Capital Inc., almost immediately after receipt of this information. On December 5, 1962, Mr. Peck visited with Mr. Abbott and others in the top management at Denver Nutronics. During their discussion Mr. Abbott had suggested that he felt the value of the company was around $2 million. This seemed high to Mr. Peck; however, no specific proposals were discussed because the company was already involved in negotiations with another investor for the funds.

Denver Nutronics employed approximately one hundred persons in Denver and Boston. The company's main plant (25,000 square feet) adjoins the campus of Denver University. Here, complete fabrication and assembly of instruments, and in-plant testing took place. Denver Nutronics' machine and welding shops were well equipped with fabricating facilities for heat testing, stress relieving, leak testing, electropolishing, and glass annealing. At the branch facility in Boston, Massachusetts, electronic circuits were designed and prototype electronic units were assembled. This office also serviced instruments in New England.

The staff of Denver Nutronics included scientists, design engineers, and technicians, experienced in network integration and allied fields, as well as a roster of university consultants, who were specialists in the varied fields in which Denver Nutronics was important. The ability to combine these talents enabled the company to design and fabricate instruments that could fulfill purchasers' particular requirements exactly.

Mr. Peck had liked the company and its management. He felt that

Exhibit 3

DENVER NUTRONICS

Comparative Statement of Financial Condition
at December 31, 1960 and 1961

Assets	*1961*		*1960*	
CURRENT ASSETS				
Cash		$ 5,759.62		$ 4,073.06
Accounts receivable—Note 5:				
Progress billing on contracts including retained percentages on contract billings—1961—$35,875.10 1960—$18,980.07	$148,648.66		$87,517.96	
Employees and affiliate	772.09	149,420.75	2,094.09	89,612.05
Inventories at the lower of cost or market:				
Materials and parts	59,166.37		37,314.87	
Finished goods	15,367.34		3,817.99	
Work in process, excluding contracts in process	24,005.38	98,539.09	22,166.14	63,299.00
Prepaid expense		2,185.20		4,671.47
Total current assets		255,904.66		161,655.58
PROPERTY, PLANT AND EQUIPMENT Net—Note 5		111,083.44		38,082.15
DEFERRED CHARGES—NOTES 1 AND 2		164,031.42		142,971.47
		$531,019.52		$342,709.20

Liabilities and Proprietor's Equity				
CURRENT LIABILITIES—NOTE 5				
Notes payable—banks		$118,500.00		$ 55,663.97
Accounts and trade notes payable		87,882.27		36,010.14
Current portion of installment contracts		8,289.89		3,094.22
Accrued salaries and wages		5,831.95		6,433.17
Payroll taxes withheld and accrued		11,054.82		6,070.17
Provision for product warranty		22,308.76		11,717.42
Total current liabilities		253,867.69		118,989.09
OTHER LIABILITIES—NOTE 5				
Notes payable—long-term	$ 64,000.00		$39,600.00	
Deferred federal income taxes—Note 3	52,511.00		5,625.01	
Installment contracts	10,122.95		1,106.82	
Other long-term liabilities	17,559.55		18,219.96	
Total other liabilities		144,193.50		64,551.79
DEFERRED INCOME—NOTE 4		94,710.59		149,646.23
PROPRIETOR'S EQUITY—NOTE 6		38,247.74		9,522.09
		$531,019.52		$342,709.20

Notes appear on p. 431.

Exhibit 3 (Continued)

Comparative Statement of Income and Proprietor's Equity for the Years Ended December 31

	1961	*1960*
Revenues from completed contracts	$726,050.09	$450,674.82
Cost of completed contracts—Note 4	576,464.27	403,435.57
Gross profit	149,585.82	47,239.25
Research and product development costs allocated to completed contracts —Notes 1 and 2	55,566.33	31,073.26
Income before federal income taxes	94,019.49	16,165.99
Provision for federal income taxes —Note 3	46,885.99	2,949.79
Income after taxes	47,133.50	13,216.20
Proprietor's life insurance premiums	1,401.25	1,894.66
Net income for the year	45,732.25	11,321.54
Proprietor's equity—beginning	9,522.09	2,545.79
Additional investments	3,742.52	900.00
Total	58,996.86	14,767.33
Proprietor's withdrawals	20,749.12	5,245.24
Proprietor's equity—ending	$ 38,247.74	$ 9,522.09

Note 1: As permitted by the Internal Revenue Code of 1954, the company has consistently deducted all research and product development costs, for Federal Income Tax purposes, in the year in which the costs were incurred.
Note 2: The company estimates that the benefits of the research and product development will continue over a five-year period. On that basis, for financial purposes, the costs incurred for research and product development during each year are capitalized and are amortized in five equal installments; one fifth in the current year and one fifth in each of the ensuing four years.

Research and product development costs which have been deducted for Federal Income Tax purposes, but which repsent deferred charges to future operations for financial reporting purposes, amounted to $142,971.47 at December 31, 1960, and $164,031.42 at December 31, 1961.
Note 3: Estimated income taxes payable in future years resulting from the excess of research and product development costs deducted for income tax purposes over research and product development costs deducted in the financial statements are reflected, for the current year, in the Statement of Income and Proprietor's Equity as "provision for Federal Income Taxes" and, cumulatively, in the Statement of Financial Condition as "Deferred Federal Income Taxes."
Note 4: As permitted by the Internal Revenue Code, the company has consistently reported on a "completed contract" accounting method for Federal income tax purposes and in its financial statements. This method recognizes income only when the contract is completed, or substantially completed. Accordingly, costs of contracts in process and current billings are accumulated, but there are no interim charges or credits to income other than provisions for losses. The activity for all contracts for the years ended December 31, 1960 and 1961 is reflected as follows:

Notes continued on p. 432.

they made good products. The controls for the network integrators were extremely technical and each instrument contained modifications, so that no two were exactly alike. Unlike some products in the electronics industry, they had both defense and nondefense applications. Their list of customers and clients included a substantial representation of industrial, government, and university laboratories. Denver Nutronics appeared to have about 20 percent of the existing market. There was a small amount of foreign competition, but their two main competitors were located in Atlanta and Boston. In short, Denver Nutronics seemed to be a leader in a scientific field which possessed a growing market.

Exhibit 3 (Continued)

	Deferred Revenues	*Deferred Cost*	*Deferred Income*	*Income*
Balance, December 31, 1959	$ 258,181.29	$123,361.48	$134,819.81	
Revenues billed – 1960	552,351.50			
Contract costs incurred – 1960		521,359.09		
Totals	810,532.79	644,720.57		
Completed contract revenues – 1960	(450,674.82)			$450,674.82
Completed contract costs – 1960		(434,508.83)		434,508.83
Balance, December 31, 1960	$ 359,857.97	$210,211.74	$149,646.23	$ 16,165.99
Revenues billed – 1961	665,398.67			
Contract costs incurred – 1961		626,314.82		
Totals	$1,025,256.64	$836,526.56		
Completed contract revenues – 1961	(726,050,09)			$726,050.09
Completed contract costs – 1961		(632,030.60)		632,030.60
Balance, December 31, 1961	$ 299,206.55	$204,495.96	$ 94,710.59	$ 94,019.49

Note 5: Assets assigned as collateral on notes and installment contracts payable aggregating $115,770.58 at December 31, 1961, consisted of the following:

Accounts receivable	$149,420.75
Plant equipment	76,310.77
Office equipment	13,757.48
	$239,489.00

Note 6: The services rendered by the proprietor for the period prior to December 31, 1961, are estimated to have a value of $96,000,000 to the company; this being the estimated costs to the company, if the services had been performed by an employee. This value is not included in the financial statements in the cost of sales, work in process, liabilities, or equity; however, net cumulative drawings of $21,374.20 have reduced equity during the same period of time.

Shortly after this December visit, Mr. Abbott notified Yerba Buena Capital, Inc. that "the calendar completions for 1962 would not reach $800,000. Several instruments which we felt earlier might be delivered ahead of schedule in 1962 will not, it appears, be shipped until January or February 1963."

Mr. Abbott gave periodic reports from time to time on the progress of Denver Nutronics. In April of 1963 he sent the financial statements of the preceding year. An excerpt from the accompanying letter follows:

> I've been so busy helping out our sales and research departments lately (they've been deluged with requests for quotations, especially on "specials" and research) that I have yet to send you the 1962 DN statement. You will note that we completed transfer of all of the assets into the corporation as of January 1, 1963[see Exhibit 7]. The 1962 figures, however, are for the proprietorship [see Exhibits 4–6].
>
> Since the first of the year we have taken in $47,000 for additional shares and expect to receive about $11,000 more from insiders very soon. We have now paid off one of our bank loans and have only an unsecured $25,000 at the bank, short-term, plus of course, the $250,000 long-term collateralized by a major stockholder. We will, however, doubtless go back to the local bank shortly with our receivables as pledge, to finance some construction

Exhibit 4

DENVER NUTRONICS

Statement of Financial Condition
at December 31, 1962

Assets

CURRENT ASSETS		
Cash		$ 13,024.24
Accounts receivable		
Progress billing on contracts—including retained percentages on contract billings—$84,939.92		153,591.69
Employee and other		821.08
Inventories at the lower of cost or market		
Materials and parts	$ 45,068.91	
Completed parts and components	15,189.55	
Work in process (excluding contracts in process)	67,363.71	127,622.17
Total current assets		$295,059.18
PROPERTY, PLANT AND EQUIPMENT		
Plant equipment	$167,048.51	
Office equipment	19,274.02	
Library	6,107.61	
Autos and trucks	2,220.00	
Leasehold improvements	93,996.07	
Total	$288,646.21	
Depreciation to date	67,005.97	
Net property, plant, and equipment		$221,640.24
DEFERRED CHARGES		
Research and development costs		270,340.38
		$787,039.80

Liabilities and Proprietor's Equity

CURRENT LIABILITIES		
Notes payable—banks	$130,441.49	
Accounts and trade notes payable	228,812.69	
Current portion of installment contracts	15,025.97	
Accrued salaries and wages	14,252.22	
Payroll taxes withheld and accrued	14,518.86	
Provisions for product warranty	11,081.78	
Other accruals	6,653.73	
Total current liabilities		$420,786.74
OTHER LIABILITIES		
Notes payable—long-term	$104,000.00	
Deferred federal income taxes	73,430.29	
Installment contracts	21,631.70	
Other long-term liabilities	26,238.14	
Total other liabilities		$225,300.13
DEFERRED INCOME		$ 26,319.49
PROPRIETOR'S EQUITY		$114,633.44
		$787,039.80

"for stock" to get our delivery times down, to eliminate our big competitors' major remaining advantage.

In reading our report please keep in mind that we are on the "Completed Contract" basis! The supplementary information sheet prepared by the Controller more accurately depicts level of operations [see Exhibit 6]. My present best guess for order volume this year is a range—$1,300,000 to $2,300,000. By June a more definite answer will be possible. Right now we have a very large number (and volume) of bids out including much activity on a very special large integrator at approximately $230,000 a piece. Here our sole competition is a Swiss firm, that can produce these for approximately $150,000. Our sales will depend on whether we can get the "Buy America" act to show any teeth.

Present backlog is, I believe (without checking), almost $600,000, up $200,000 since we last talked, I think. We are adding workers to try to chew into it faster.

I still feel we need $100,000–$250,000 during the remainder of this year, and I would prefer to have it come in for stock rather than additional debt. Not all need come in at once, however, unless we try something pretty daring.

On May 7, 1963, Yerba Buena Capital, Inc. received another report from Mr. Abbott from Denver Nutronics. An excerpt follows:

As the year has developed, and our cash position has improved, sentiment on my board had swung toward letting the price-per-share obtainable

Exhibit 5

DENVER NUTRONICS

Statement of Income and Proprietor's Equity
for the Year Ended December 31, 1962

Revenues from completed contracts		$451,486.69
Cost of completed contracts		400,437.04
Net income before provision for federal income taxes and proprietor's life insurance premiums		51,049.65
Federal income taxes (estimated)	$20,919.29	
Proprietor's life insurance premiums	1,182.50	22,101.79
Net income		28,947.86
Proprietor's equity—January 1, 1962	38,247.74	
Asset revaluation	56,000.00	94,247.74
Total		123,195.60
Proprietor's withdrawals		8,562.16
Proprietor's equity, December 31, 1962		$114,633.44

Exhibit 6

DENVER NUTRONICS

Supplemental Information
for the Year Ended December 31, 1962

NEW ORDERS RECEIVED IN 1962	$950,000	
INCOME		
Billings to customers	896,739	
Chattel loans and installment contracts	48,369	
Loans—noncollateralized	40,000	
		$ 985,108
Estimated completed portion of contracts unbilled		50,000
		$1,035,108
EXPENSE		
Salaries and wage paid	500,176	
Material purchased	300,151	
Production expense*	90,769	
Administrative and selling expense*	160,452	
		1,051,548
In addition we purchased equipment		32,194
		$1,083,742
The above expenses include:		
Research and development of new products		204,570
Improvements to the building		32,909
Equipment manufactured in our own shop		28,060
95 percent of the salaries and wages were paid to residents of the immediate area.		
Approximately $125,000 was expended in this area for materials and services.		

*Exclusive of salaries.

Note: The above figures were prepared from the records before adjustment by our auditors, to present a picture of (1) the level of operations, (2) the expenditures in the immediate Denver area, and the (3) extent of our investment in new product research.

Since our profit and loss statement is based on the "completed contract" method of accounting, these figures are not specifically comparable to the financial statements presented.

govern the number of shares released at any given time. We would be willing to release up to 25,000 shares if sold at $10/share. (As you know, there are now approximately 300,000 shares outstanding.) I am not necessarily asking you for a final decision on this now as I think you deserve to see the first and possibly the second quarter's figures and some projections before making a decision. However, I would appreciate a reaffirmation of your interest, if it still exists, and I am sure my board as well as I would likewise appreciate any comments you wish to make on the basis of your investigation on

Exhibit 7

DENVER NUTRONICS CORPORATION

Statement of Financial Condition
at January 1, 1963

Assets

CURRENT ASSETS		
Cash		$ 263,274.10
Accounts receivable		
Progress billings on contracts—including retained percentages on contract billings—$84,939.92*		153,591.69
Employee and other		750.81
Inventories at the lower of cost or market		
Materials and parts	$ 45,068.91	
Completed parts and components	15,189.55	
Work in process (excluding contracts in process)	67,363.71	127,622.17
Prepaid expenses		196.79
Total current assets		$ 545,435.56
PROPERTY, PLANT, AND EQUIPMENT		
Plant equipment	$167,048.51	
Office equipment	19,274.02	
Library	6,107.61	
Autos and trucks	2,220.00	
Leasehold improvements	93,996.07	
Total	$288,646.21	
Depreciation to date	67,005.97	
Net property, plant, and equipment		$ 221,640.24
DEFERRED CHARGES		
Research and development costs	264,840.38	
Corporation organization expenses	1,423.52	266,263.90
		$1,033,339.70

*Pledged to bank.

level of financing (and mechanisms) as a function of time *you* feel desirable for Denver Nutronics in order to permit the company to grow along the path outlined in the projection you already have. We respect your opinions on such matters very much.

In short, I hope to move these discussions from the realm of the general to the particular, so we will be able to move rapidly at a suitable time. I hope you agree with this philosophy!

Exhibit 7 (Continued)

DENVER NUTRONICS CORPORATION

Liabilities and Equity

CURRENT LIABILITIES		
Notes payable—banks	$130,441.49	
Accounts and trade notes payable	228,812.69	
Current portion of installment contracts	15,025.97	
Accrued salaries and wages	8,619.22	
Payroll taxes withheld and accrued	14,518.86	
Provision for product warranty	11,081.78	
Other accruals	6,663.63	
Total current liabilities		$ 415,163.64
OTHER LIABILITIES		
Notes payable—long-term—individuals	75,790.00	
Notes payable—long-term—banks	250,000.00	
Installment contracts	21,631.70	
Other long-term liabilities	6,695.26	
Total other liabilities		$ 354,116.96
DEFERRED INCOME		26,319.49
CAPITAL STOCK		237,739.61
		$1,033,339.70

FORMING A BIDDING SYNDICATE FOR MUNICIPAL BONDS

Bank of America National Trust and Savings Association

In January 1962, Mr. Alan K. Browne, vice-president and head of bank of America's municipal bond department, received notice of a forthcoming issue of bonds offered for competitive bids by the state of California (see Exhibit 1). He then faced the problem of forming a syndicate to bid on the issue.

Mr. Browne felt this issue held special significance for two main reasons: (1) the Bank of America's historically strong position in the underwriting of the bond financing by the state of California; and (2) the events of the preceding five months.

Text continues on p. 442.

Exhibit 1

BANK OF AMERICA N.T. & S.A.

Notice of Sale
State of California State School Building Aid Bonds
Series AA
under the
State School Building Aid Bond Law of 1960

NOTICE IS HEREBY GIVEN that the undersigned Bert A. Betts, as Treasurer of the State of California, at his office in the State Capitol, Sacramento, California, at 10 A.M. (P.S.T.) on Wednesday, January 24, 1962, will receive sealed bids for the purchase of State School Building Aid Bonds of the State of California, more particularly described below.

ISSUE: $100,000,000 principal amount, consisting of 100,000 bonds, of the denomination of $1,000 each, numbered AA1 to AA100,000, both inclusive, all dated February 1, 1962, and constituting Series AA, the second series of an issue of $300,000,000 aggregate principal amount of State of California State School Building Aid Bonds under the State School Building Aid Bond Law of 1960 (Statutes First Extraordinary Session 1960, Chapter

Exhibit 1 (Continued)

75) and Section 20 of Article XVI of the Constitution of the State of California, which was approved by the People at the special election consolidated with the direct primary election held on June 7, 1960.

INTEREST RATE: Maximum five (5) per cent per annum, payable semiannually on May 1 and November 1 in each year (except that the first coupon will represent interest from the date of said bonds to November 1, 1962). Bidders must specify the rate or rates of interest which the bonds shall bear, which must be in a multiple of one-eighth or one-twentieth of 1% per annum, payable semiannually. Bidders may specify any number of separate interest rates and the same rate or rates may be repeated as often as desired. The interest rate on each separate maturity of the bonds must be uniform for the bonds of that maturity. Only one coupon will be attached to each bond for each installment of interest thereon, and bids providing for additional or supplemental coupons will be rejected.

MATURITIES: Said bonds mature in consecutive numerical order from lower to higher, on November 1, in each of the years as follows:

$3,200,000 – 1964 to 1968, inc.
3,600,000 – 1969 to 1973, inc.
4,000,000 – 1974 to 1978, inc.
4,400,000 – 1979 to 1983, inc.
4,800,000 – 1984 to 1988, inc.

PRIOR REDEMPTION: Bonds of Series AA, numbered AA1 to AA76,000, both inclusive (maturing by their terms prior to November 1, 1984) are not subject to redemption prior to their fized maturity dates. Bonds of Series AA, numbered AA76,001 to AA100,000, both inclusive (maturing by their terms on and after November 1, 1984) are subject to redemption as a whole or in part, at the option of the State, on November 1, 1983 (but not prior thereto) and on any interest payment date thereafter prior to their fixed maturity dates at the principal amount thereof plus accrued interest thereon to date of redemption. If less than all of said bonds subject to redemption are called for redemption, they shall be callable only in inverse numerical order from higher to lower and the part of said issue so called shall be not less than all of the bonds maturing in any one year. Notice of such redemption shall be published once a week for two (2) succesive weeks in one newspaper published respectively in each of the cities of San Francisco, Sacramento, and Los Angeles, in the State of California, the first publication of which shall be not less than thirty (30) days and not more than ninety (90) days prior to the date fixed for such redemption. After the date fixed for such redemption, if the State shall have duly published notice of such redemption and shall have provided funds available for the payment of the principal and interest of the bonds so called for redemption, interest on such bonds thereafter shall cease.

PAYMENT: Both principal and interest are payable in lawful money of the United States of America at the office of the Treasurer of the State of California, State Capitol, Sacramento, California, or at the option of the holder at the First National City Bank of New York, or The First National Bank of Chicago, Fiscal Agents of the State of California.

Exhibit 1 (Continued)

REGISTRATION: Coupon bonds will be issued by the State. Bonds in multiples of $1,000 are registrable only at the office of the State Treasurer as to both principal and interest. Such registered bonds and coupon bonds are interchangeable as provided by law.

PURPOSE OF ISSUE: The bonds are authorized for the purpose of providing aid to School Districts within the State.

SECURITY: The bonds are general obligations of the State of California, payable in accordance with the State School Building Aid Bond Law of 1960 out of the General Fund of the State. The full faith and credit of the State of California are pledged for the punctual payment of both principal and interest.

LEGAL OPINIONS: The State School Building Finance Committee will at the date of delivery of the bonds deliver to the successful bidder the legal opinion of The Honorable Stanley Mosk, Attorney General of the State of California, and of Messrs. Orrick, Dahlquist, Herrington and Sutcliffe, Attorneys at Law, of San Francisco, approving the legality of the bonds, together with the usual closing proofs, including a certificate of the Attorney General that no litigation is then pending or threatened affecting the validity of the issuance of the bonds. A copy of the legal opinion or opinions will be printed on the reverse side of the bonds without cost to the bidder.

TERMS OF SALE

HIGHEST BID: The bonds will be awarded to the highest bidder. The highest bid shall be determined by deducting the premium bid (if any) from the total amount of interest which the State would be required to pay from the date of the bonds, or the last preceding interest payment date, whichever is latest, to the respective maturity dates of the bonds offered for sale, at the coupon rate or rates specified in the bid, and the award shall be made on the basis of the lowest net interest cost to the State. The lowest net interest cost to the State shall be computed on a 360-day-year basis. The purchaser must pay accrued interest from the date of the bonds to the date of delivery.

AWARD: The State Treasurer will take action awarding the bonds or rejecting all bids not later than 24 hours after the expiration of the time herein prescribed for the receipt of proposals, provided that the award may be made after the expiration of such specified time if the bidder shall not have given to the State Treasurer notice in writing of the withdrawal of such proposal.

FORM OF BID AND DEPOSIT: All bids must be unconditional (except as herein expressly set forth with respect to the delivery of Temporary Bonds) for not less than all of the bonds hereby offered for sale, and for not less than the par value thereof and accrued interest to date of delivery. Each bid must be in writing and signed by the bidder and shall be accompanied by a deposit of a certified check or cashier's check for one-half of one per cent (0.5%) of the par value of the bonds herein offered for sale, but not exceeding one hundred thousand dollars ($100,000), drawn on a bank or trust company authorized to transact and transacting business in the State of California, payable to the Treasurer of the State of California. Such bid, together with bidder's check, must be enclosed in a sealed

Exhibit 1 (Continued)

envelope addressed to the State Treasurer, State Capitol, Sacramento, California, and endorsed "Proposal for State of California State School Building Aid Bonds under the State School Building Aid Bond Law of 1960, Series AA." The deposit of each unsuccessful bidder shall be returned to him immediately upon the non-acceptance of his bid, and the deposit of the successful bidder shall immediately upon the acceptance of his bid become and be the property of the State of California and shall be credited to the successful purchaser upon the purchase price of the bonds bid for in case such purchase price is paid in full within the time mutually agreed upon between the successful bidder and the State Treasurer. If the purchase price is not so paid upon tender of the bonds, the successful bidder shall have no right in or to said bonds or by reason of said bid, or to the recovery of said deposit accompanying said bid, or to any allowance or credit by reason of such deposit unless it shall appear that the bonds would not be validly issued if delivered to the purchaser in the form and manner proposed. The State Treasurer may, with the approval of the State School Building Finance Committee, waive any irregularity or informality in any bid and may reject all bids.

DELIVERY OF DEFINITIVE BONDS OR TEMPORARY BONDS: Definitive Bonds will be delivered at the office of the State Treasurer as soon as the bonds can be prepared, which it is estimated will be about February 26, 1962. The State Treasurer is authorized to (and will at the option of the successful bidder) enter into an agreement with the successful bidder for the delivery of Temporary Bonds against payment therefor, at his office in the State Capitol, Sacramento, California, such delivery of Temporary Bonds to be made within ten (10) days after notice in writing from the successful bidder. The successful bidder shall have the right, at his option, to cancel the contract of purchase if the State Treasurer shall fail to tender such Definitive Bonds for delivery on or before said cancellation date or shall fail to deliver such Temporary Bonds within said period of ten (10) days after written notice of demand therefor, and in either of such events the successful bidder shall be entitled to the return of the deposit accompanying his bid, but without interest thereon. Temporary Bonds (if issued) will be exchangeable at the risk and expense of the owners or holders thereof but without special charge for such exchange at the office of the State Treasurer, State Capitol, Sacramento, California, for Definitive Bonds when executed and available for delivery at said office of the State Treasurer which may be subsequent to said cancellation date above specified for Definitive Bonds. Delivery of Definitive Bonds from the office of the State Treasurer shall be at the risk and expense of the owners or holders of such Definitive Bonds.

ADJOURNMENT: The State Treasurer may cancel the sale or postpone the sale to a definite or indefinite date by public announcement made prior to or at the time and place fixed for the sale of the bonds, and may give such notice of the new time and place of the sale of the bonds as he may deem advisable. If such sale is cancelled or postponed, all sealed bids will be returned unopened.

Dated: Sacramento, California, January 10, 1962
BERT A. BETTS
Treasurer of the State of California

Historical Background

The Bank of America National Trust and Savings Association had opened its doors to business for the first time in October of 1904. By the end of 1961, total resources had risen above the twelve and one-half billion dollar mark.

During this period of growth and expansion, the underwriting of municipal bonds gradually had become an important activity of the bank. The Banking Act of 1933 had prohibited the Bank of America and all other members of the Federal Reserve System from participating in the underwriting of securities other than the general obligations of government bodies. Within this constraint, however, the Bank of America had maintained a policy of entering bids on all of California's eligible municipal bond flotations, that is, those which were general obligations. Mr. Browne felt that this policy had helped assure a market for the vast financing needs of a large and rapidly growing state. At the same time, he felt this policy had greatly enhanced the prestige of the bank over the years.

The Bank of America had been unable to assume the risk of underwriting the entire amount of each of the many large issues in California. In addition, there had also been some issues outside of California which the Bank of America had desired to underwrite. Therefore, the bank had increasingly turned to syndicating over the years.

A syndicate is a group of investment bankers and/or commercial banks formed to share the risk and profit in buying a specific issue of securities. The success of such syndicates is based upon two factors. First, it has to win the right to offer the securities to the public by paying the borrower more for it than any other underwriter. Second, the syndicate has to sell the security to investors at a price high enough to pay the cost of the bonds plus other expenses, and still earn a profit. If a number of underwriting groups or syndicates are competing for an issue, each has to strike a balance between pressing hard to win the issue by paying a relatively high price to the borrower and the risk to the syndicate group that the issue cannot be sold to the public at a price to yield a profit. This task might be even more complicated by the fact that a bidding syndicate might consist of several, perhaps as many as three hundred, member firms. The Bank of America had often acted as the coordinating body in such ventures.

During 1961, groups managed by the Bank of America purchased 239 issues totaling $703,156,000 or 54.3 percent of California's municipal bond financing. Since bond financing by the state of California and its political subdivisions represented 15.5 percent of all municipal bonds sold in the United States in 1961, this was a significant portion of national sales. However, the Bank of America's role had been much more dominant when considering only the general obligations of the state of California. In fact, August 1961, marked the first time since 1956 that the state had received a bid on a major bond issue from other than a Bank of America syndicate.

As the syndicate manager, the Bank of America handled business dealings between the syndicate and the issuers, among syndicate members, and between the syndicate and the selling group. This third function was often not required since the members of the selling group were also usually members of the syndicate. Traditionally only a few other large investment banking houses and commercial banks had managed such large offerings. (Exhibit 2 shows the twenty largest managing underwriters of 1957 general obligation municipal bonds.) It had been thought that only the largest of these organizations had the capital, manpower, and market contacts necessary to promote a successful underwriting of a major security issue. As a result of recent events, which are discussed in the next section, Mr. Browne was questioning this view.

The Bank of America, as well as certain other large commercial banks and investment bankers, desired to assume the manager's role in

Exhibit 2

BANK OF AMERICA N.T. & S.A.

Principal Managing Underwriters of New Municipal General Obligation Issues, 1957
(In millions of dollars)

First National City Bank of New York*	$ 435
Halsey Stuart & Co., Inc.	367
Bank of America NT & SA*	360
Bankers Trust Company*	326
Chase Manhattan Bank*	300
Harris Trust & Savings Bank*	228
First National Bank of Chicago*	153
Northern Trust Company of Chicago*	134
Lehman Brothers	112
Kidder, Peabody & Co.	81
First Boston Corporation	80
Blyth & Co., Inc.	76
Phelps, Fenn & Co.	72
Marine Trust Co. of Western New York*	66
Harriman, Ripley & Co., Inc.	64
Glore, Forgan & Co.	61
Kuhn, Loeb & Co.	57
Chemical Corn Exchange Bank*	56
John Nuveen & Co.	56
First of Michigan Corporation	52

*Commerical bank.

SOURCE: Robinson, Roland I., *Postwar Market for State and Local Government Securities* (Princeton: Princeton University Press, 1960).

the formation and operation of underwriting syndicates. The management of the bank felt that if a firm won what the market considered a fair share of the bidding competitions in which it participated, it gained in a number of ways. Not only was its prestige enhanced, which helped in managing future syndicates, but the house was continuously proving the high quality of its market judgment and thus might be more successful in attracting additional business.

Recent Developments

On August 16, 1961, the dominance of the Bank of America group in the underwriting of the state of California major bond issues was broken when $100 million in school bonds were awarded to State Street Securities of Albany, New York, a corporate affiliate of William S. Morris & Company of New York. This marked the first time since 1956 that the state had received more than one bid on a major bond issue. Concurrent with the acceptance of the State Street Securities bid for the school bonds, the state rejected the bids (the only ones tendered) of the syndicate managed jointly by the Bank of America and Bankers Trust for $100 million veteran's and $25 million construction bonds as being unreasonably costly to the state.

William S. Morris had set up his own company in October 1959, to specialize in municipal bonds. Until the August 1961 issue, he had participated in groups organized by the Bank of America to bid for California bonds. But he felt he was not getting enough of a share in the group and decided to bid himself. The subsequent reoffering of the bonds won by his State Street Securities Corporation was extremely successful and the net profit on the issue was estimated at $1 million by a *Wall Street Journal* staff reporter.

On September 13, 1961, State Street Securities again nosed out a syndicate headed by the Bank of America and Bankers Trust for a major state issue. This time it was for $100 million of veteran's bonds—the same issue on which the state of California had rejected the Bank of America's bid in the preceding month.

After winning the bid, the State Street Securities once again successfully reoffered the bonds. The estimage of a staff reporter of *The Wall Street Journal* placed the net profit to the Morris company at better than $600,000. An article in *The Wall Street Journal on September 14, 1961 reported:*

> Some bond men believe an effect of the latest award to the Morris concern may be to spur more competitive bidding for sizable bond offerings of state and local governments than in recent years. Bond men see the possibility that big bank and investment house syndicates may lose some of the dominance they have enjoyed over the marketing of such bonds as members of the groups break away to form smaller syndicates or to submit bids entirely on their own.

> "There is no question now we're seeing a pattern take shape looking toward greater competitive bidding by an increasing number of syndicates," said the manager of the municipal department of an important New York City Bank. "States and municipalities will fare better because borrowing costs will be lower while bond dealers will have to be satisfied with a narrower margin of profit". Not all bond men, of course, believe the Morris firm's second victory in a month over the syndicate headed by Bank of America and Bankers Trust Co. will lead to any drastic change in marketing of state and local bonds.
>
> "We'll have to wait and see if what has been happening in California spreads to other states," said a municipal bond specialist whose bank was a member of the syndicate. This bond man noted factors in the California sale again working in favor of the modestly capitalized Morris concern—the relatively small size of the "good faith" deposit required by California to be made by bidders on the state's bond sales and the Morris firm's unorthodox method of reselling the bonds." Bonds are normally distributed by members of the underwriting syndicate.
>
> In distributing the $100 million bonds won yesterday as it had done on the August 16 sale, the Morris concern arranged to place the bonds through Drake & Co., a "street broker." A street broker buys and sells bonds only from and to dealers usually in the resale market, receiving a commission on the value of the transactions. The Morris company's arrangements with Drake represented the first time a street broker was used to make the initial distribution of bond issues of any magnitude. In each case, Morris agreed to pay the Drake firm 1/8 percentage point of the face value of the bonds, or some $125,000 for its services.

The next competitive bidding for a state of California issue took place on October 18, 1961. The consolidated bidding account which the Bank of America had co-managed broke up, with two strong underwriting groups (one headed by the Bank of America and the other by Bankers Trust) in addition to the single bidder (William S. Morris) submitting bids. The Bank of America syndicate submitted the winning bid. The *Commercial and Financial Chronicle* of October 26, 1961, commented upon the results of the underwriting as follows:

> The successful underwriting of the $100,000,000 State of California serial issue, which was awarded to the Bank of America N.T. & S.A. group last week, was a strong market stimulant. The speed with which a large share of the offering was placed was an impressive expression of underlying market strength.

Forming the Syndicate

When Mr. Alan K. Browne received notice of the upcoming January sale (Exhibit 1) he immediately proceeded to form a syndicate to bid on the issue. His first action was to notify previous syndicate members and others thought to be interested in such an issue. Interested institutions were asked to notify the Bank of America of the amounts of the security they would be willing to take. Five days later, on January 15, Mr. Browne sent out a notice (Exhibit 3) asking participants to confirm the formation of the syndicate and their commitment to purchase securities if the syndicate submitted the successful bid. Attached to the confirming letter was a list of some 260 syndicate members and their intended participation in the issue (Exhibit 4).

Mr. Brown felt that the presence of commercial banks in the group gave special marketing advantages to the group and added to its fundamental underwriting strength. Commercial banks, being investors as well

Text continues on p. 448, middle.

Exhibit 3

BANK OF AMERICA N.T. & S.A.
SAN FRANCISCO 20, CALIFORNIA
JANUARY 15, 1962

$100,000,000
State of California
N.E. 5% State School Building Aid Bonds, Law of 1960, Series AA
To Be Sold January 24, 1962

Gentlemen:

We confirm the formation of a Syndicate to bid for and, if purchased, to sell the above described securities (hereinafter termed "Bonds"), subject to the following terms and conditions:

1. *Participation.* The present participations of the members of this Syndicate, including yourselves, are set forth on the enclosed pages 1A through 1D; but the Manager may, at any time prior to the purchase of the Bonds, make any change in the membership of the Syndicate or in the amounts of respective participations, and any such changes will become effective notwithstanding that notice thereof may not be received by any member or members; provided, that the participation of a member shall not be increased without his consent. Your participation is for your own account, and is not to be reoffered, subdivided or transferred without the consent of the Manager.

2. *Offering Terms.* The terms of the offering, including concessions or commissions allowable to members, and to others, as well as the terms of resale of Bonds by members during the life of the Syndicate, shall be determined by the Manager with the approval of members having a majority interest in the Syndicate. Each member will be advised of such terms and of any changes therein, and each member agrees to comply with the terms from time to time in effect during the life of the Syndicate.

3. *Liability Undivided.* The Syndicate will be undivided as to selling and also as to liability. Members shall be liable in porportion to their respective participations for all obligations and expenses of the Syndicate. If this Syndicate purchases the Bonds, all sales, withdrawals and allotments from the Syndicates shall be made only upon authorization by the Manager, and all sales, withdrawals and allotments confirmed by the Manager in each case will reduce the liability of the members to take up Bonds upon termination of the Syndicate proportionately to their participation in the Syndicate. If sales are made for the benefit of the Syndicate, each member's liability will be reduced in proportion to his total participation in the Syndicate. Nothing

Exhibit 3 (Continued)

contained herein shall constitute the several members partners with one another. If, prior to all Bonds being withdrawn by members, changes are made in the offering terms, the remaining unsold Bonds may be apportioned among members on a divided liability basis, and subsequent sales and withdrawals from the Syndicate confirmed by the Manager shall reduce in like amount the liability of such members for Bonds remaining unsold and undelivered, notwithstanding prior sales and withdrawals under the original offering terms.

4. *Carry Arrangements.* Acting solely as agent for the several members, we shall serve as Manager of the Syndicate, with the customary authority and discretion, including the right to represent the Syndicate in bidding for the Bonds either directly or a delegated agent, to accept and pay for Bonds purchased, including purchasing the Bonds from the issuer in the first instance (for our own account or for our own account together with one or more members of the Syndicate) for sale to the Syndicate at cost and accrued interest, and to make arrangements to carry all or any part of the same, and for that purpose to borrow thereon from ourselves or others for account of the several members, pledging the Bonds and signing any notes or loan agreements on behalf of the members. While acting as Manager, we shall nevertheless continue to be a member of the Syndicate. Each member for whose account any such loan or other arrangement is made, shall, without the necessity of any determination, demand or notice by the Manager, be unconditionally obligated thereon directly to the lender (whether the Manager or other) for the full amount of liability incurred for his account, and no more. Upon request of the Manager at any time, the members shall contribute their proportionate share in any good faith deposit, take up and pay for their proportionate share of any unsold or undelivered Bonds at the cost thereof to the Syndicate or shall margin or make other arrangements for carrying their proportionate interest in the Bonds in such manner and to such amounts as the Manager may specify.

5. *Limit of Managers Liability.* The manager shall be under no responsibility or liability to anyone for the validity or value of the Bonds, or for the legality of the proceedings relative to the authorization or issue thereof, or for the correctness or completeness of any advertisement, prospectus or other document prepared, published or employed by the Manager or others in connection with the offering or sale of the Bonds, or for the acts of any agent selected with due care, or for anything whatever in connection with the Syndicate, except only for lack of good faith; and the Manager accepts no obligation other than those expressly assumed herein.

6. *Default of Members.* In the event of any default of any member in the performance of the obligations imposed by the terms hereof, then, without demand or notice, his interest may be terminated or transferred to another or others, but in either case without releasing him from any liability, or all or any part of his share of Bonds may be sold at public or private sale, and the Manager of any other member or members may acquire such interest or Bonds. Except as herein otherwise provided, any loss or expense resulting from any such default may be charged to the Syndicate. Default or insolvency of any member shall not terminate the Syndicate or release any other member from his obligations.

7. *Life of Syndicate.* The syndicate for a period of thirty (30) days from the date of the award of the Bonds unless previously terminated or further extended up to sixty (60) days by the Manager with the approval of the mem-

Exhibit 3 (Continued)

bers having a majority interest in the Syndicate, and after sixty (60) days by unanimous consent; provided, however, that the Manager alone may terminate the Syndicate at any time after sale and delivery of all the Bonds sold prior thereto; and provided, that the proportionate liabilities of members shall continue until final settlement is made by the Manager.

8. *Division of Profit and Loss.* Upon termination of the Syndicate, the net profit or liability for any net loss shall be divided among the members in proportion to there respective participations, except that interest accrued upon the Bonds shall be allocated to the members (including the Manager) who have advanced the capital to purchase or carry the Bonds.

9. *Member Liability for Claims.* Notwithstanding any distribution of profit or liability for any net loss shall be divided among the members in proportion to their respective participations, except that interest accrued any claim which may at any time be made against the Syndicate as such.

10. *Further Terms and Conditions.* When established by the Manager, with the approval of members having a majority interest in the Syndicate, members will be bound to observe and comply with any further terms and conditions governing the offering and sale of these Bonds.

If the foregoing terms and conditions are in accordance with your understanding, please confirm your participation in the Syndicate, upon the above terms and conditions, by signing with an authorized signature and returning to us the enclosed duplicate of this letter.

Very truly yours,
BANK OF AMERICA N.T. & S.A.
Syndicate Manager
By
Alan K. Browne, Vice-President

as underwriters, did not have to fret about the financing of their dealer inventories to the same extent that nonbank dealers did. Furthermore, the Bank of America or other leading commercial banks in the buying group might also "bank" or finance the inventories of other syndicate members if the group were not successful in selling out its offering quickly.

The syndicate which Mr. Browne was organizing consisted of an Eastern or undivided account. (See Exhibit 3—#3 Liability Undivided for details.) It was to be undivided as to selling and liability.[1]

Text continues on p. 461.

[1]Undivided as to selling meant that all of the bonds would be placed under the control of Mr. Browne, the manager of the account. Since the issue had maturity dates ranging from 1964 to 1988, to divide it would have meant that in some cases the various members would have had very few bonds from any one maturity to work on. Therefore, he felt that it was much more practical to keep all bonds together. Undivided as to liability meant that as long as any of the bonds were unsold each member would be liable for his proportionate share of the unsold amount. Each syndicate member would have a certain participation in the issue. (See Exhibit 4 for the size of each member's participation.) The syndicate member would still have this liability for his proportionate share of all unsold bonds whether he had sold considerably more than his participation or whether he had sold none.

Exhibit 4

$100,000,000
State of California
N.E. 5% State School Building Aid Bonds, Law of 1960, Series AA
to Be Sold January 24, 1962
Syndicate
Members and Participations

Members	*Office of Confirmation*	*Participation*
	Bracket No. 1	
A. C. Allyn & Co.	122 South La Salle Street, Chicago 3, Ill.	$1,500,000
Bank of America N.T. & S.A.	300 Montgomery Street, San Francisco 20, Calif.	1,500,000
J. Barth & Co.	404 Montgomery Street, San Francisco 4, Calif.	1,500,000
Blyth & Co., Inc.	2100 Russ Building, San Francisco 4, Calif.	1,500,000
The Chase Manhattan Bank	1 Chase Manhattan Plaza, New York, N.Y.	1,500,000
Crocker-Anglo National Bank	1 Montgomery Street, San Francisco 20, Calif.	1,500,000
C. J. Devine & Co.	48 Wall Street, New York 5, N.Y.	1,500,000
Eastman Dillon, Union Securities & Co.	15 Broad Street, New York 5, N.Y.	1,500,000
Equitable Securities Corporation	2 Wall Street, New York 5, N.Y.	1,500,000
The First Boston Corporation	465 California Street, San Francisco 4, Calif.	1,500,000
The First National Bank of Oregon	6th and Stark Streets, Portland 4, Ore.	1,500,000
The First National City Bank of New York	55 Wall Street, New York 15, N.Y.	1,500,000
Glore, Forgan & Co.	135 South La Salle Street, Chicago 3, Ill.	1,500,000
Goldman, Sachs & Co.	20 Broad Street, New York 5, N.Y.	1,500,000
Harriman Ripley & Co., Incorporated	63 Wall Street, New York 5, N.Y.	1,500,000
Harris Trust and Savings Bank	115 West Monroe Street, Chicago 90, Ill.	1,500,000
Ira Haupt & Co.	111 Broadway, New York 6, N.Y.	1,500,000
Hayden, Stone & Co., Incorporated	25 Broad Street, New York 4, N.Y.	1,500,000
Hornblower & Weeks	40 Wall Street, New York 5, N.Y.	1,500,000

Exhibit 4 (Continued)

Members	*Office of Confirmation*	*Participation*
E. F. Hutton & Co., Incorporated	160 Montgomery Street, San Francisco 4, Calif.	$1,500,000
Kuhn, Loeb & Co.	30 Wall Street, New York 5, N.Y.	1,500,000
Ladenburg, Thalmann & Co.	25 Broad Street, New York 4, N.Y.	1,500,000
Lazard Fréres & Co.	44 Wall Street, New York 5, N.Y.	1,500,000
Mellon National Bank and Trust Company*	514 Smithfield Street, Pittsburgh 30, Pa.	1,500,000
Merrill Lynch, Pierce, Fenner & Smith Incorporated	301 Montgomery Street, San Francisco 4, Calif.	1,500,000
R. H. Moulton & Company	405 Montgomery Street, San Francisco 4, Calif.	1,500,000
John Nuveern & Co. (Incorporated)	135 South La Salle Street, Chicago 3, Ill.	1,500,000
Reynolds & Co.	120 Broadway, New York 5, N.Y.	1,500,000
Seattle-First National Bank	Second Avenue at Columbia Street, Seattle 4, Wash.	1,500,000
Security First National Bank	P. O. Box 2097, Terminal Annex, Los Angeles 54, Calif.	1,500,000
Shearson, Hammill & Co.	14 Wall Street, New York 5, N.Y.	1,500,000
William R. Staats & Co.	111 Sutter Street, San Francisco 4, Calif.	1,500,000
United California Bank	600 South Spring Street, Los Angeles 14, Calif.	1,500,000
B. J. Van Ingen & Co., Inc.	40 Wall Street, New York 5, N.Y.	1,500,000
Weeden & Co.	315 Montgomery Street, San Francisco 4, Calif.	1,500,000
Wells Fargo Bank American Trust Company	464 California Street, San Francisco 20, Calif.	1,500,000
Wertheim & Co.	120 Broadway, New York 5, N.Y.	1,500,000
Dean Witter & Co.	45 Montgomery Street, San Francisco 6, Calif.	1,500,000
	Bracket No. 2	
Bache & Co.	36 Wall Street, New York 5, N.Y.	550,000
Bacon, Whipple & Co.	135 South La Salle Street, Chicago 3, Ill.	550,000
A. G. Becker & Co., Incorporated	120 South La Salle Street, Chicago 3, Ill.	550,000

*Added this sale.

Exhibit 4 (Continued)

Members	*Office of Confirmation*	*Participation*
Branch Banking & Trust Company	124 Nash Street, Wilson, N.C.	$ 550,000
Clark, Dodge & Co., Incorporated	61 Wall Street, New York 5, N.Y.	550,000
Fidelity Union Trust Company	755 Broad Street, Newark 1, N.J.	550,000
Gregory & Sons	72 Wall Street, New York 5, N.Y.	550,000
Paribas Corporation	40 Wall Street, New York 5, N.Y.	550,000
Wm. E. Pollock & Co., Inc.†	45 Wall Street, New York 5, N.Y.	550,000
Roosevelt & Cross, Incorporated	40 Wall Street, New York 5, N.Y.	550,000
Stone & Youngberg	1314 Russ Building, San Francisco 4, Calif.	550,000
Taylor and Company	439 North Bedford Drive, Beverly Hills, Calif.	550,000
Wachovia Bank and Trust Company†	Main & Third Streets, Winston-Salem 1, N.C.	550,000
G. H. Walker & Co.	45 Wall Street, New York 5, N.Y.	550,000
	Bracket No. 3	
Adams, McEntee & Co., Inc.	40 Wall Street, New York 5, N.Y.	400,000
James A. Andrews & Co., Incorporated	70 Pine Street, New York 5, N.Y.	400,000
Barr Brothers & Co.	40 Wall Street, New York 5, N.Y.	400,000
The Boatmen's National Bank of St. Louis	300 North Broadway, St. Louis 2, Mo.	400,000
Brown Brothers Harriman & Co.	59 Wall Street, New York 5, N.Y.	400,000
Coffin & Burr	70 Pine Street, New York 5, N.Y.	400,000
F. W. Craigie & Co.	616 East Main Street, Richmond 15, Va.	400,000
A. G. Edwards & Sons	409 North 8th Street, St. Louis 1, Mo.	400,000
First National Bank in Dallas	P.O. Box 6031, Dallas 22, Texas	400,000
First Southwest Company	Mercantile Bank Building, Dallas 1, Texas	400,000
J. A. Hogle & Co.	507 West Sixth Street, Los Angeles, Calif.	400,000
The National City Bank of Cleveland	Euclid Avenue at East Sixth Street, Cleveland 14, Ohio	400,000

†Bracket change this sale.

Exhibit 4 (Continued)

Members	*Office of Confirmation*	*Participation*
Republic National Bank of Dallas	Pacific at Ervay, Dallas 22, Texas	$400,000
F. S. Smithers & Co.	45 Wall Street, New York 5, N.Y.	400,000
Trust Company of Georgia	1 Chase Manhattan Plaza, New York 5, N.Y.	400,000
Wells & Christensen, Incorporated†	1 Chase Manhattan Plaza, New York, 5, N.Y.	400,000
Wood, Struthers & Co.	30 Wall Street, New York 5, N.Y.	400,000
	Bracket No. 4	
Anderson & Strudwick	807 East Main Street, Richmond 12, Va.	300,000
William Blair & Company	135 South La Salle Street, Chicago 3, Ill.	300,000
Blunt Ellis & Simmons†	111 West Monroe Street, Chicago 3, Ill.	300,000
Davis, Skaggs & Co.	111 Sutter Street, San Francisco 4, Calif.	300,000
Elworthy & Co.	111 Sutter Street, San Francisco 4, Calif.	300,000
The First National Bank of Memphis	Madison at Second, Memphis 1, Tenn.	300,000
First National Bank in St. Louis†	510 Locust Street, St. Louis 1, Mo.	300,000
Industrial National Bank of Rhode Island	111 Westminster Street, Providence 1, R.I.	300,000
Kalman & Company, Inc.	McKnight Building, Minneapolis 1, Minn.	300,000
Kenower, MacArthur & Co.	1824 Ford Building, Detroit 26, Mich.	300,000
A. M. Kidder & Co., Inc.	1 Wall Street, New York 5, N.Y.	300,000
Lawson, Levy, Williams & Stern	1 Montgomery Street, San Francisco 4, Calif.	300,000
Irving Lundborg & Co.	310 Sansome Street, San Francisco 4, Calif.	300,000
Mason-Hagan, Inc.	1017 East Main Street, Richmond 10, Va.	300,000
Mercantile National Bank at Dallas	P.O. Box 5415, Dallas 22, Texas	300,000
New York Hanseatic Corporation	120 Broadway, New York 5, N.Y.	300,000
The Ohio Company	51 North High Street, Columbus 15, Ohio	300,000
Shuman, Agnew & Co.	155 Sansome Street, San Francisco 4, Calif.	300,000
J. C. Wheat & Co.	1001 East Main Street, Richmond 19, Va.	300,000
Robert Winthrop & Co.	20 Exchange Place, New York 5, N.Y.	300,000

†Bracket change this sale.

Members	*Office of Confirmation*	*Participation*
	Bracket No. 5	
I. L. Brooks & Co., Incorporated	333 Pine Street, San Francisco 4, Calif.	$205,000
Julien Collins & Company	105 South La Salle Street, Chicago 3, Ill.	205,000
Dewar, Robertson & Pancoast	1100 Milam Building, San Antonio 5, Texas	205,000
Fahnestock & Co.	65 Broadway, New York 6, N.Y.	205,000
The First Cleveland Corporation	700 National City East Sixth Building, Cleveland 14, Ohio	205,000
J. B. Hanauer & Co.	140 South Beverly Drive, Beverly Hills, Calif.	205,000
Henry Harris & Sons, Incorporated	52 Wall Street, New York 5, N.Y.	205,000
The National Bank of Commerce of Seattle	Second Avenue at Spring Street, Seattle 11, Wash.	205,000
Rauscher, Pierce & Co., Inc.	1200 Mercantile Dallas Building, Dallas 1, Texas	205,000
The Robinson-Humphrey Company, Inc.	2000 Rhodes-Haverty Building, P.O. Box 1708, Atlanta 1, Ga.	205,000
Seasongood & Mayer	Security Savings Building, Fourth and Vine Streets, Cincinnati 2, Ohio	205,000
Van Alystyne, Noel & Co.	40 Wall Street, New York 5, N.Y.	205,000
The White-Phillips Company, Inc.	510 First National Building, Davenport, Iowa	205,000
R. D. White & Company	120 Broadway, New York 5, N.Y.	205,000
J. R. Williston & Beane	Two Broadway, New York 4, N.Y.	205,000
	Bracket No. 6	
American Fletcher National Bank and Trust Company*	Market and Pennsylvania Streets, Indianapolis 9, Ind.	175,000
Bosworth, Sullivan & Company, Inc.†	660 17th Street, Denver 2, Colo.	175,000

*Added this sale.
†Bracket change this sale.

Exhibit 4 (Continued)

Members	*Office of Confirmation*	*Participation*
Brush, Slocumb & Co., Inc.	465 California Street, San Francisco 4, Calif.	$175,000
John W. Clarke & Co.†	135 South La Salle Street, Chicago 3, Ill.	175,000
Courts & Co.	11 Marietta Street N.W., Atlanta 1, Ga.	175,000
Cruttenden, Podesta & Co.	209 South La Salle Street, Chicago 4, Ill.	175,000
Dreyfus & Co.	2 Broadway, New York 4, N.Y.	175,000
Field, Richards & Co.	1556 Union Commerce Building, Cleveland 14, Ohio	175,000
The First National Bank of Birmingham	17 North 20th Street, Birmingham 2, Ala.	175,000
The First National Bank of Miami*	100 Biscayne Boulevard South, Miami 1, Fla.	175,000
The Forth Worth National Bank	7th and Main Streets, Forth Worth 1, Texas	175,000
Ginther & Company	1275 Union Commerce Building, Cleveland 14, Ohio	175,000
Hayden, Miller & Co.	1840 Union Commerce Building, Cleveland 14, Ohio	175,000
Lyons, Hannahs & Lee, Inc.	79 Milk Street, Boston 9, Mass	175,000
McDonald & Company	1250 Union Commerce Building, Cleveland 14, Ohio	175,000
Wm. J. Mericka & Co., Inc.	1101 Union Commerce Building, Cleveland 14, Ohio	175,000
Merrill, Turben & Co. Inc.	1612 Union Commerce Building, Cleveland 14, Ohio	175,000
The Milwaukee Company†	207 East Michigan Street, Milwaukee 2, Wis.	175,000
Model, Roland & Stone	120 Broadway, New York 5, N.Y.	175,000
Mullaney, Wells & Company	135 South La Salle Street, Chicago 3, Ill.	175,000
Park, Ryan, Inc.	70 Pine Street, New York 5, N.Y.	175,000
Rotan, Mosle & Co.	1510 Bank of the Southwest Building, Houston 2, Texas	175,000
Stern, Lauer & Co.	120 Broadway, New York 5, N.Y.	175,000
Stockyards National Bank	P.O. Box 970, Wichita 1, Kansas	175,000
The Valley National Bank of Arizona	141 N. Central Avenue, P.O. Box 71, Phoenix, Ariz.	175,000

*Added this sale.
†Bracket change this sale.

Exhibit 4 (Continued)

Members	*Office of Confirmation*	*Participation*
	Bracket No. 7	
Bartow Leeds & Co.	One Liberty Street, New York 5, N.Y.	$150,000
Boettcher and Company	828 17th Street, Denver 2, Colo.	150,000
Curtiss, House & Company	Union Commerce Building, Cleveland 14, Ohio	150,000
J. M. Dain & Co., Inc.	110 South Sixth Street, Minneapolis 2, Minn	150,000
Dallas Union Securities Co., Inc.	1001 Adolphus Tower, Dallas 2, Texas	150,000
Dittmar & Company, Inc.	201 North St. Mary's Street, San Antonio 6, Texas	150,000
Ellis & Company	Dixie Terminal Building, Cincinnati 2, Ohio	150,000
Foster & Marshall, Inc.	1505 Norton Building, Seattle 4, Wash.	150,000
Green, Ellis & Anderson	61 Broadway, New York 6, N.Y.	150,000
Hooker & Fay, Inc.	221 Montgomery Street, San Francisco 4, Calif.	150,000
Hutchinson, Shockey & Co.	208 South La Salle Street, Suite 1225, Chicago 4, Ill.	150,000
Laird, Bissell & Meeds	120 Broadway, New York 5, N.Y.	150,000
John C. Legg & Company	22 Light Street, Baltimore 3, Md.	150,000
A. E. Masten & Company	First National Bank Building, Pittsburgh 22, Pa.	150,000
McCormick & Co.	231 South La Salle Street, Chicago 4, Ill.	150,000
McDonnell & Co., Incorporated	120 Broadway, New York 5, N.Y.	150,000
Newburger, Loeb & Co.	15 Broad Street, New York 5, N.Y.	150,000
Northwestern National Bank of Minneapolis	Northwestern Bank Building, Minneapolis 2, Minn.	150,000
Russ & Company, Incorporated	Alamo National Building, San Antonio 5, Texas	150,000
Stern, Frank, Meyer & Fox	325 West Eighth Street, Los Angeles 14, Calif.	150,000
Sterne, Agee & Leach	706 First National Building, Birmingham 3, Ala.	150,000
Suplee, Yeatman, Mosley Co., Incorporated	1500 Walnut Street, Philadelphia 2, Pa.	150,000
Sutro & Co.†	460 Montgomery Street, San Francisco 4, Calif.	150,000
Sweney Cartwright & Co.†	225 Huntington Bank Building, Columbus 15, Ohio	150,000
M. B. Vick & Company	120 South La Salle Street, Chicago 3, Ill.	150,000

†Bracket change this sale.

Exhibit 4 (Continued)

Members	*Office of Confirmation*	*Participation*
	Bracket No. 8	
George K. Baum & Company	1016 Baltimore Avenue, Kansas City 5, Mo.	$125,000
Blewer, Glynn & Co.	320 North 4th Street, St. Louis 2, Mo.	125,000
Boland, Saffin, Gordon & Sautter	64 Wall Street, New York 5, N.Y.	125,000
Burns, Corbett & Pickard, Inc.	135 South La Salle Street, Chicago 3, Ill.	125,000
Chapman, Howe & Co.	208 South La Salle Street, Chicago 4, Ill.	125,000
Cooley & Company	100 Pearl Street, Hartford 4, Conn.	125,000
Crowell, Weedon & Co.	629 South Spring Street, Los Angeles 14, Calif.	125,000
Cumberland Securities Corporation	206 Fourth Avenue, North, Nashville 3, Tenn.	125,000
DeHaven & Townsend, Crouter & Bodine	2228 Land Title Building, Philadelphia 10, Pa.	125,000
Eddleman, Pollok & Fosdick, Incorporated†	938 Bank of the Southwest Building, Houston, Texas	125,000
Clement A. Evans & Co., Incorporated	11 Pryor Street S.W., Atlanta 3, Ga.	125,000
The First National Bank and Trust Company	120 North Robinson Street, Oklahoma City 2, Okla.	125,000
First Union National Bank of North Carolina	301 South Tryon Street, Charlotte 1, N.C.	125,000
Folger, Nolan, Fleming—W. B. Hibbs & Co. Inc.	725 - 15th Street, N.W., Washington 4, D.C.	125,000
Hannaford & Talbot, a Corporation	519 California Street, San Francisco 4, Calif.	125,000
Harkness & Hill, Incorporated	140 Federal Street, Boston 10, Mass.	125,000
Harrington & Co., Inc.	1545 Deposit Guaranty Bank Building, Jackson, Miss.	125,000
Horner, Barksdale & Co.	First Colony Life Building, Lynchburg, Va.	125,000
Howard, Weil, Labouisse, Friedrichs and Company	211 Carondelet Street, New Orleans 12, La.	125,000

†Bracket change this sale.

Exhibit 4 (Continued)

Members	*Office of Confirmation*	*Participation*
Interstate Securities Corporation	Johnston Building, Suite 701, Charlotte 2, N.C.	$125,000
The Johnson, Lane, Space Corporation†	1000 Commerce Building, Atlanta 3, Ga.	125,000
Johnston, Lemon & Co.	Southern Building, Washington 5, D. C.	125,000
Poole & Co.	123 South Broad Street, Philadelphia 9, Pa.	125,000
The Provident Bank	7th and Vine Streets, Cincinnati 2, Ohio	125,000
Irving J. Rice & Company, Incorporated	202 Pioneer Building, St. Paul 1, Minn.	125,000
Saunders, Stiver & Co.	One Terminal Tower, Cleveland 13, Ohio	125,000
Stein Bros. & Boyce	6 South Calvert Street, Baltimore 2, Md.	125,000
Stranahan, Harris & Company	Owens-Illinois Building, Toledo 4, Ohio	125,000
Stubbs, Watkins & Lombardo, Inc.	615 First National Building, Birmingham 3, Ala.	125,000
Talmage & Co.	111 Broadway, New York 6, N.Y.	125,000
Westheimer and Company	326 Walnut St., Cincinnati 2, Ohio	125,000
Arthur L. Wright & Co., Inc.	225 South 15th Street, Philadelphia 2, Pa.	125,000
Wulff, Hansen & Co.	450 Russ Building, San Francisco 4, Calif.	125,000
	Bracket No. 9	
Ray Allen, Olson & Beaumont, Inc.	135 South La Salle Street, Chicago 3, Ill.	100,000
Arnold & Derbes, Incorporated	505 National Bank of Commerce Building, New Orleans 12, La.	100,000

†Bracket change this sale.

Exhibit 4 (Continued)

Members	*Office of Confirmation*	*Participation*
Carleton D. Beh Co.*	832-840 Des Moines Building, Des Moines 9, Iowa	$100,000
Beil & Hough, Inc.*	350 First Ave., North, St. Petersburg 1, Fla.	100,000
Frank & Robert Bender Co.	7817 Ivanhoe Avenue, P.O. Box 1122, La Jolla, Calif.	100,000
Herman Bensdorf & Company*	1300 Commerce Title Building, Memphis, Tenn.	100,000
Allan Blair & Company	135 South La Salle Street, Chicago 3, Ill.	100,000
Edward L. Burton & Company	174 South Main Street, Salt Lake City 1, Utah	100,000
Cavalier & Otto	301 Pine Street, San Francisco 4, Calif.	100,000
Clark, Landstreet & Kirkpatrick, Incorporated	Life & Casualty Tower, Nashville 3, Tenn.	100,000
The Continental Bank and Trust Company of Salt Lake City	2nd South and Main Streets, Salt Lake City 12, Utah	100,000
Crane Investment Co., Inc.	948 National Bank of Commerce Building, New Orleans 12, La.	100,000
Ladd Dinkins & Company	National Bank of Commerce Building, New Orleans 12, La.	100,000
Doll & Isphording, Inc.	314/316 Provident Bank Building, Cincinnati 2, Ohio	100,000
R. J. Edwards, Inc.	217 Fidelity National Building, Oklahoma City 2, Okla.	100,000
Eppler, Guerin & Turner, Inc.	Fidelity Union Tower Building, Dallas, Texas	100,000
Ferris & Company	611 Fifteenth Street, N.W., Washington, D.C.	100,000
The First of Arizona Company	342 First National Bank Building, Phoenix, Arizona	100,000
First Security Bank of Utah, N.A.*	79 South Main Street, Salt Lake City 10, Utah	100,000
First Securities Company of Kansas (Incorporated)	Schweiter Building, Wichita, Kansas	100,000
First U.S. Corporation*	Union Planters Bank Building, Memphis 1, Tenn.	100,000
Funk, Hobbs & Hart, Inc.	National Bank of Commerce Building, San Antonio 5, Texas	100,000

*Added this sale.

Exhibit 4 (Continued)

Members	*Office of Confirmation*	*Participation*
Graham-Conway Co.	1829 Kentucky Home Life Building, Louisville 2, Ky.	$100,000
Hattier & Sanford	Whitney Bank Building, New Orleans 12, La.	100,000
Hess & McFaul	American Bank Building, Portland 5, Ore.	100,000
Hess, Grant & Remington, Incorporated	123 South Broad Street, Philadelphia 9, Pa.	100,000
Investment Corporation of Virginia	215 East Plume Street, Norfolk, Va.	100,000
Janney, Battles & E. W. Clark, Inc.	1401 Walnut Street, Philadelphia 2, Pa.	100,000
Jones, Cosgrove & Miller	81 South Euclid Avenue, Pasadena 1, Calif.	100,000
Jones, Kreeger & Co.	1625 Eye Street, N.W., Washington 6, D.C.	100,000
H. I. Josey and Company*	First National Building, Oklahoma City 2, Okla.	100,000
Kaufman Bros. Co.*	P.O. Box 3235, Norfolk 14, Va.	100,000
Kay, Richards & Company	Union Trust Building, Pittsburgh 30, Pa.	100,000
Kroeze, McLarty & Duddleston*	P.O. Box 1328, Jackson, Miss.	100,000
Luce, Thompson & Crowe, Inc.	Fourth and Gold Street, Room 921, Albuquerque, N.M.	100,000
W. L. Lyons & Co.	235 South Fifth Street, Louisville, Ky.	100,000
Magnus & Company	Dixie Terminal Building, Cincinnati 2, Ohio	100,000
Mead, Miller & Co.	Charles and Chase Streets, Baltimore 1, Md.	100,000
Mid-South Securities Co.	American Trust Building, Nashville 3, Tenn.	100,000
Mitchum, Jones & Templeton	1700 Russ Building, San Francisco 4, Calif.	100,000
Moroney, Beissner & Co., Inc.	1300 Bank of the Southwest Building, Houston 2, Texas	100,000
Morrissey & Co.*	Davenport Bank Bldg., Davenport, Iowa	100,000
National Bank of Washington	P.O. Box 1631, Tacoma 1, Wash.	100,000
The National Shawmut Bank of Boston*	40 Water Street, Boston, Mass.	100,000
Nongard, Showers & Murray, Inc.	105 West Adams Street, Chicago 3, Ill.	100,000
Parker, Eisen, Waeckerle, Adams & Purcell, Inc.	1012 Baltimore Avenue, Kansas City 5, Mo.	100,000

*Added this sale.

Exhibit 4 (Continued)

Members	*Office of Confirmation*	*Participation*
J. Lee Peeler & Company, Inc.	Trust Building, Durham, N.C.	$ 100,000
Penington, Colket & Co.	123 South Broad Street, Philadelphia 9, Pa.	100,000
The Peoples National Bank of Charlottesville	300 East Main Street, Charlottesville, Va.	100,000
Pierce, Carrison, Wulbern, Inc.	1407 Barnett Building, Jacksonville 1, Fla.	100,000
Prescott & Co.	National City Bank Building, Cleveland 14, Ohio	100,000
Rambo, Close & Kerner, Incorporated	1518 Locust Street, Philadelphia 2, Pa.	100,000
Rodman & Renshaw	209 South La Salle Street, Chicago 4, Ill.	100,000
H. V. Sattley & Co., Inc.	1325 Penobscot Building, Detroit 26, Mich.	100,000
Schaffer, Necker & Co.	814 Packard Building, Philadelphia 1, Pa.	100,000
Seattle Trust and Savings Bank	804 Second Avenue, Seattle 4, Wash.	100,000
State Street Bank and Trust Company	111 Franklin Street, Boston 6, Mass.	100,000
Stifel, Nicolaus & Company, Incorporated	314 North Broadway, St. Louis 2, Mo.	100,000
Walter Stokes & Co.	1411 Walnut Street, Philadelphia 2, Pa.	100,000
Dabbs Sullivan Company*	113 East Third Street, Little Rock, Ark.	100,000
Sutro Bros. & Co.	80 Pine Street, New York 5, N.Y.	100,000
Thornton, Mohr, Farish & Gauntt, Inc.	First National Bank Building, Montgomery 1, Ala.	100,000
Tuller & Zucker	40 Wall Street, New York 5, N.Y.	100,000
Varnedoe, Chisholm & Co., Inc.	P.O. Box 203, Savannah, Ga.	100,000
Wagenseller & Durst, Inc.	626 South Spring Street, Los Angeles 14, Calif.	100,000
Walter, Woody & Heimerdinger	403 Dixie Terminal Building, Cincinnati 2, Ohio	100,000
The Weil, Roth & Irving Company	308 Dixie Terminal Building, Cincinnati 2, Ohio	100,000
C. N. White & Co.	436 - 14th Street, Oakland 12, Calif.	75,000
Robert L. Whittaker & Co.	1420 Walnut Street, Philadelphia 2, Pa.	100,000
Wiley Bros., Incorporated*	400 Union Street, Nashville 3, Tenn.	100,000
Woodcock, Moyer, Fricke & French, Incorporated	123 South Broad Street, Philadelphia 9, Pa.	100,000
Warren W. York & Company, Inc.	530 Hamilton Street, Allentown, Pa.	100,000
	Total	$100,000,000

*Added this sale.

Arriving at a Bid

On January 16, 1962, Mr. Browne sent a supplement (Exhibit 5) to the syndicate letter which described the arrangement for arriving at the syndicate's bid and detailing action to be taken by members of the syndicate. Participants were asked to fill in their bidding and selling views on a separate page of the supplement.

Mr. Browne, as syndicate manager, next turned his own attention toward arriving at a bid which would be acceptable to the syndicate as a whole and yet low enough to win the bid and provide for a successful reoffering. He viewed the determination of a bid as taking place in several steps: (1) the determination of the probable price (yields) at which the various maturities of the issue can be sold ("the reoffering scale"); (2) the selection of the gross margin or spread for which the group will work; (3) the establishment of a coupon structure that will produce enough gross revenue at the reoffering scale previously determined to cover the gross margin.

Text continues on p. 471, bottom.

Exhibit 5

BANK OF AMERICA N.T. & S.A.

$100,000,000
State of California
N.E. 5% State School Building Aid Bonds, Law of 1960, Series AA
To Be Sold January 24, 1962

Gentlemen:

1. *Selling Views and Bidding Limits.* Supplementing our Syndicate letter of January 15, 1962, we direct your attention to the following arrangements for our Syndicate's bid on the above described securities (hereinafter termed "Bonds") including action to be taken by you as a member of the Syndicate. Members should be sure to appoint their proxy as described in paragraph 4 and to make arrangements to place initial orders as outlined in paragraph 8. Your attention is also directed to paragraph 9, 11 and 20 and questions B and D on the enclosed page 2A.
On the forms on page 2A and 2B of the duplicate of this supplemental letter, please fill in your bidding and selling views, indicating under Paragraph A, page 2A, either (1) that you will abide by the bid price determined by the Manager and Advisory Committee referred to below, or (2) the bid limit beyond which you wish to withdraw from the Syndicate. This should be returned to the Bank of America N.T. & S.A. as early as possible, but not later than Monday, January 22, 1962. In addition, your reoffering price views should be wired us by 12:00 Noon (P.S.T.), Monday, January 22, 1962, if the duplicate letter will not reach us by that time. Your attention is also directed to paragraph E on the enclosed page 2A.

2. *Manager's Advisory Committee.* Because of the large membership of this Syndicate, a Manager's Advisory Committee will be set up comprising members having a participation of $1,000,000 or more in the Syndicate. This Committee or such Sub-Committee as it may appoint from among its members will have final determination of the bid and offering terms including

Exhibit 5 (Continued)

concessions and selling commissions. In addition, the Committee, or the Sub-Committee will be authorized to determine the extent to which syndicate sales may be made by the Manager for the benefit of the Syndicate. Manager's Advisory Committee members should inform the Manager if they or their representatives are unable to attend any of the meetings scheduled in paragraphs 5 and 6 below, in which event the Manager will inform such Advisory Committee members of Committee action and will act as their proxy. However, Advisory Committee members who cannot attend meetings will not accept proxies from other members as outlined in paragraph 4 below. Advisory Committee members will complete the enclosed page 2A under question C(4).

3. *Manager's Advisory Committee Voting.* Only members of the Manager's Advisory Committee authorized to vote will attend meetings. Therefore, designate on page 2A, under question C(4) of the duplicate of this supplemental letter which office will have the vote.

4. *Designation of Proxy to Represent Members in AM Matters.* Members will be required, under conditions listed in sub-headings a, b, and c below, to appoint a proxy who shall be a member of the Manager's Advisory Committee with offices in New York and/or San Francisco, other than the Bank of America N.T. & S.A. (except as noted in paragraph 2 above) or The First National City Bank of New York. The name of such member's proxy shall be indicated on the enclosed page 2A under question B(3). Please wire us the name of your proxy immediately.

a. Conditions requiring appointment of a proxy are:
   (1) Members who do not attend any of the price meetings.
   (2) Members who do not have a New York and/or San Francisco office.
   (3) Members other than the Manager's Advisory Committee.

b. Proxies so appointed will perform the following for their appointed principals:
   (1) Present members' views and inform them of preliminary details.
   (2) Inform members of final bid and offering terms.
   (3) Inform members of any increase in participation.
   (4) Inform members that they have been withdrawn from the Syndicate because the final bid exceeds their limits.
   (5) Expedite the filing of first day orders for members without New York and/or San Francisco offices.

c. Additional responsibilities of the proxy:
   (1) Will not accept more than 10 designations as proxy including all appointments accepted by branch offices of a member.
   (2) Will not drop members from the Syndicate on their own initiative without specific instructions from their appointing principal, even though proxies may themselves drop for whatever reason. Where a proxy drops from the Syndicate, he shall continue to represent his principal, as though he still remained a member of the Syndicate.
   (3) Will communicate promptly, calling collect and preferably using public wires.
   (4) Require that the appointing principal make his own decisions.

d. Responsibilities of the appointing principal:

Exhibit 5 (Continued)

(1) Proxies will be identical for all actions and should be re-appointed on similar issues.
(2) Advise the proxy well in advance of sale of his appointment.
(3) If, using a branch office of a proxy, be certain the head office is also informed of their appointment as proxy. Avoid appointing as proxy local branch offices of firms whose branch offices are widely spread geographically.
(4) Promptly inform proxy of actions to be taken including price and profit views, bid limit or willingness to accept the Manager's Advisory Committee's bid terms.
(5) Contact proxy for information if report not received in a reasonable period of time.
(6) File orders with proxy as soon as possible.
(7) Be responsible for expenses incurred by proxy in representing appointing principal or arrange for reciprocity.
(8) Observe the same discretion as members attending meetings so that information relayed will not be revealed except as authorized.

5. *Price Meetings—New York.* A preliminary price meeting of all New York City members and representatives of out-of-town members, excluding Manager's Advisory Committee members, will be held at 2:30 P.M. (E.S.T.) Tuesday, January 23, 1962, at The First National City Bank of New York, Federal Room, 55 Wall Street, New York, N.Y. In addition, for the purpose of establishing a consensus of price views in the area, presenting individual members price limits, and submitting final views for determination of the bid by the Sub-Committee of the Manager's Advisory Committee mentioned in paragraph 2 above, a New York meeting of the Manager's Advisory Committee members, including out-of-town members, will be held at 3:30 P.M. (E.S.T.) Tuesday, January 23, 1962, at The First National City Bank of New York, Federal Room, 55 Wall Street, New York, N.Y. Only one individual authorized to vote will attend to represent the respective members of the Manager's Advisory Committee. It is expected that the person to whom this letter is addressed will represent his firm at the appropriate meeting scheduled by this paragraph. If such is not the case, The First National City Bank of New York shall be advised prior to the meeting as to whom will represent his member firm.

6. *Price Meetings—San Francisco.* A preliminary price meeting of all San Francisco members and representatives of out-of-town members, and representatives of out-of-town members, excluding Manager's Advisory Committee members, will be held at 2:15 P.M. (P.S.T.) Tuesday, January 23, 1962, in the conference room, Bank of America N.T. & S.A., Municipal Bond Department, Room 950, 300 Montgomery Street, San Francisco, California. For the purpose of receiving individual price views of Advisory Committee members and consolidating all price views to establish a final bid, a San Francisco meeting of the Manager's Advisory Committee members, including out-of-town members, will be held at 3:00 P.M. (P.S.T.) Tuesday, January 23, 1962, in the conference room, Bank of America N.T. & S.A., Municipal Bond Department, Room 950, 300 Montgomery Street, San Francisco, California. Only one individual authorized to vote will attend to represent the respective members of the Manager's Advisory Committee. It is expected that the person to whom this letter is addressed

Exhibit 5 (Continued)

will represent his firm at the appropriate meeting scheduled by this paragraph. If such is not the case, the Bank of America N.T. & S.A., San Francisco, shall be advised prior to the meeting as to whom will represent his member firm.

7. *Additional Liability.* As it may be necessary for the Syndicate to take up the liability of members withdrawing before the time of sale, members are requested to indicate under paragraph E on page 2A, of the duplicate of this supplemental letter, if they are willing to take up their pro rata share of such liability, and the maximum thereof.

8. *Initial Orders.* If our Syndicate is successful in purchasing the Bonds, orders will be received by the Bank of America N.T. & S. A. in San Francisco, California, and by The First National City Bank of New York, in New York City, for a period of 4 hours following the sale time at 10:00 A.M. (P.S.T.), Wednesday, January 24, 1962. Members are requested to indicate under paragraph D on the enclosed page 2A of the duplicate of this supplemental letter whether their first orders will be filed in New York or San Francisco and with whom they will be filed. Priority orders should be phoned or wired immediately to Bank of America N.T. & S.A. or The First National City Bank of New York. During the period 10:00 A.M. to 2:00 P.M. (P.S.T.), Wednesday, January 24, 1962, while the books are open, orders will receive priority as follows:

a. First, syndicate orders from nationally and/or regionally recognized institutional investors at list prices net.
b. Second, syndicate orders from similar institutional investors at list less the dealer discount if entitled thereto. (Note: All syndicate orders must have name of purchase disclosed to the Manager and any Bonds allocated are to be confirmed by the Manager.)
c. Third, orders for specific maturities from members. Orders for specific maturities from members will be confirmed at the takedown.

In the event delivery instructions received from institutional investors request delivery of a specific bank, which in turn bills the Manager for shipping expenses beyond the point of delivery at a subsequent date, such additional expenses will not be honored by the Manager. It is suggested that the members filing such orders arrange in advance for the Manager to ship Bonds direct to the institutional investor.

Preliminary Bidding and Selling Views
$100,000,000
State of California
N.E. 5% State School Building Aid Bonds, Law of 1960, Series AA
To Be Sold January 24, 1962

Members' Bid Views

A. Please check and fill in either (1) or (2) below:
   (1) ...... We hereby agree to any bid and selling terms set by the Manager and Advisory Committee.
   (2) ...... We will withdraw from the Syndicate if the net interest cost is less than ......%.

Members' Proxy All Purposes

B. Please fill in below:
   (3) We have appointed and instructed .... (a

Exhibit 5 (Continued)

member of the Manager's Advisory Committee) through their .... office (indicate New York or San Francisco office, if in both locations) to keep us informed of the developments relating to the Syndicate and to perform for us all Syndicate member functions discussed in paragraph 4 of this letter, which we are not performing ourselves. Wire us the name of your proxy immediately.

Manager's Advisory Committee Member's Vote

C. Advisory Committee Members please fill in below:

(4) We will attend and vote in Manager's Advisory Committee meeting .... (indicate New York *or* San Francisco, not both).

Members' First Day Orders

D. Please check one of the following below (5), (6), or (7):

(5) We will file our first day orders directly through our office in New York with The First National City Bank of New York .... ☐

(6) We will file our first day orders directly through our office in San Francisco with the Bank of America N.T. & S.A. ....☐

(7) We will file our first day orders directly through our proxy as listed in paragraph B(3) above ....☐

Members' Participation Limit

E. Please check and/or fill in (8), (9) and (10) below:

(8) ...... We hereby agree to take up additional liability.

(9) ...... We do not wish additional liability.

(10) $.............. Maximum liability we will underwrite.

Dated: February 1, 1962 Due: November 1, 1964/88, incl.

Due	Offering Yield or Prices
1964	....
1967	....
1972	....
1977	....
1982	....
1984–88*	....

*Bonds maturing by their terms on and after November 1, 1984, are subject to redemption as a whole or in part, at the option of the State, on November 1, 1983 (but not prior thereto) and on any interest payment date thereafter prior to their fixed maturity dates at the principal amount thereof plus accrued interest thereon to date of redemption.

Margin of Profit ....

Suggested Bid ....% (Net interest cost)

Wire us your price views by 12:00 Noon (P.S.T.) Monday, January 22, 1962, if the duplicate letter will not reach us by that time.

Date ....

Firm Name ....

By ....

(Authorized Signature)

Exhibit 5 (Continued)

Allocation of Bonds under "priority" categories (first two) will be on the premise they are being purchased by:

a. Recognized institutional investors for their own account, including bank members of the Syndicate for their own investment account, with the understanding that any Bonds allocated to Bank members will not be reoffered during the life of the Syndicate or for 90 days, whichever is longer.
b. Trust companies and trust departments of commercial banks, including bank members of the Syndicate, for designated trust accounts.
c. Recognized investment counseling organizations for their customers.

No priority allocation will be given to institutions and organizations qualifying for priority consideration when orders filed represent:

a. Dealer orders.
b. Customer orders except as specified in Paragraphs b and c immediately above.

The Manager will further determine the priority of individual orders under the several categories as will benefit the Syndicate. Insofar as possible, the Manager will attempt to provide at least partial allocation to categories of orders, as follows: a percentage (to be determined) of the total Bonds available in all maturities combined will be set aside to fill:

a. Priority orders.
b. Member takedown orders.

Members placing orders will receive approximately their pro rata share of Bonds, within takedown category, based on their underwriting participations. Orders filled after the books are closed will be divided for priority in the same manner as those filed before 2:00 P.M. (P.S.T.) Wednesday, January 24, 1962, but will all be subordinate to orders filed while the books are open. Nothing in this agreement will be construed as entitling a member to require a pro rata distribution of Bonds in any or all maturities based on such participation of the members. After allocation of priority orders, members will receive their allotments, and in the event of oversubscription each will receive not less than his pro rata share of the Bonds remaining, to the extent that he has filed orders and that Bonds are available in the specified maturities.

Members located in New York City will use addressed order form sheets, which will be mailed to members by Bank of America N.T. & S.A. in San Francisco, upon which will be entered their initial (i.e. first day's) orders. Members located in San Francisco will use blank order form sheets furnished by the Bank of America N.T. & S.A. upon which will be entered their initial (i.e., first day's) orders. Addressed order form sheets will be mailed to New York proxies of out-of-town members and blank order form sheets will be available to San Francisco proxies of out-of-town members for the filing of orders of such out-of-town members. Each out-of-town member (i.e., having no office, either in San Francisco or New York) will file his orders through his proxy indicated in paragraph B on the enclosed page 2A. Blank order forms will be available at The First National City Bank of New York, Main Information Desk, Main Bank Lobby, 55 Wall Street, New York, N.Y. and at the Bank of America N.T. & S.A., 300 Montgomery Street, San Francisco, California.

9. *Confirmation of First Day Orders.* All Bonds allocated on initial orders will be confirmed as follows, unless another time is subsequently designated:

Exhibit 5 (Continued)

a. San Francisco—300 Montgomery Street, Room 950, 10:00 A.M. (P.S.T.) Thursday, January 25, 1962 (confirmation sheet in sealed envelope).
(1) Members whose office of confirmation is San Francisco as shown in our letter of January 15, 1962.
(2) Members who have indicated that their San Francisco office will file their orders for them as indicated under Paragraph D on the enclosed page 2A of the duplicate of this letter.

b. Los Angeles—650 South Spring Street, Room 1101, 10:00 A.M. (P.S.T.) Thursday, January 25, 1962 (Teletype message in sealed envelope).
(1) Members whose office of confirmation is Los Angeles as shown in our letter of January 15, 1962.

c. New York—41 Broad Street, 8th floor, 1:00 P.M. (E.S.T.) Thursday, January 25, 1962 (Teletype message in sealed envelope).
(1) Members whose office of confirmation is New York as shown in our letter of January 15, 1962.
(2) Members who have indicated that their New York office will file their orders for them as indicated in Paragraph D on the enclosed page 2A of the duplicate of this letter.

d. Western Union Telegram, 10:00 A.M. (P.S.T.) Thursday, January 25, 1962. Members who do not have a New York or San Francisco office, or a Los Angeles office of confirmation.

Even though advance confirmations are made in New York, San Francisco, or Los Angeles, or direct with members' offices located outside of New York or San Francisco, members' written confirmations (or "tickets") following should be addressed to the Bank of America N.T. & S.A., Municipal Bond Department, Attention Bond Cashiering Section, Room 950, 300 Montgomery Street, San Francisco 20, California.

10. *Confirmation of Unsold Balances*. Should a balance remain in the Syndicate following the confirmation of allocations on first day orders, the Bonds remaining will be split for confirmation purposes, in an amount to be determined, between the Bank of America N.T. & S.A. in San Francisco, California, and The First National City Bank of New York, in New York City. Thereby, during the hours both offices are open, Bonds will be available for confirmation in both offices. After the New York closing, all Bonds will revert for confirmation purposes to the Bank of America N.T. & S.A. and after San Francisco closing will revert to the First National City Bank of New York, until San Francisco opening.

11. *Maintenance of Reoffering Price Terms*. Members will be bound to comply with the reoffering price terms during the life of the Syndicate (see paragraph 7 of our Syndicate letter of January 15, 1962) unless released therefrom by the Manager as a result of approval thereof by the Manager and the Manager's Advisory Committee described in paragraph 2 above.

12. *Estimated Delivery*. It is estimated that the State of California will deliver the Bonds to the successful bidder on or about Monday, February 26, 1962, in Sacramento, California. Based on this estimate, should our Syndicate purchase the Bonds they will be ready for redelivery to members of the Syndicate on or about Thursday, March 8, 1962, in San Francisco, California.

a. *Delivery of Bonds to Members*. Members will arrange at their own expense to take deliver of their Bonds on the redelivery date against pay-

Exhibit 5 (Continued)

ment in funds good to the Bank of America N.T. & S.A., 300 Montgomery Street, San Francisco 20, California.

b. *Shipment of Bonds to Out-of-Town Members.* The Bank of America N.T. & S.A. will ship and will arrange delivery of Bonds upon receipt of payment in funds good to Bank of America N.T. & S.A., on the redelivery, in accordance with members' instructions, shipping cost to be at members' expense. If members' shipping instructions indicating Los Angeles, New York, or Chicago delivery are furnished on or before Monday, February 19, 1962, Bonds will be made available at Securities Department, Bank of America N.T. & S.A., 660 South Spring Street, Los Angeles 54, California; The First National City Bank of New York, 55 Wall Street, New York 15, New York; or The Harris Trust and Savings Bank, 115 West Monroe Street, Chicago 90, Illinois, on the estimated redelivery date of Thursday, March 8, 1962, for redelivery to members only against payment in funds good to the Bank of America N.T. & S.A. on the redelivery date, in accordance with members' instructions, shipping cost to be at members' expense. In case of split deliveries to San Francisco, Los Angeles, New York, or Chicago, members will arrange for full payment of total takedown at any one of the four redelivery points mentioned. In case of delivery points to members in any city other than San Francisco, Los Angeles, New York, or Chicago, payment will be made in funds good on the day of redelivery at the bank correspondent making delivery for the Bank of America N.T. & S.A.; however, no Bonds will be released at such other points until wired advice of payment in funds good to the Bank of America N.T. & S.A. has been received at the Bank of America N.T. & S.A. On request, the Bank of America N.T & S.A. will advise members the name of its correspondent bank making such delivery.

c. *Redelivery to Members in San Francisco and Los Angeles.* Members will be required to pick up their Bonds at the Securities Department, Bank of America N.T. & S.A. starting at 8:30 A.M. (P.S.T.), payment to be in funds good to Bank of America N.T. & S.A. on date of redelivery. No Bonds evidencing members' original takedowns will be delivered by messenger.

d. *Delivery of Bonds to Nonmembers.* No delivery of Bonds will be made to nonmembers of the Syndicate on instructions received from members, unless or until wired advice of payment from members in funds good to the Bank of America N.T. & S.A. on the date of redelivery has been received at the Bank of America N.T. & S.A., shipping cost to be at members' expense.

e. *Shipment of Bonds Draft Attached.* No shipment of Bonds will be made on instructions received from members requesting Bonds be shipped draft attached. Members desiring Bonds be shipped for collection must make their own arrangements or may arrange shipment through the Collection Department, Bank of America N.T. & S.A., 300 Montgomery Street, San Francisco 20, California, shipping and collection costs to be at members' expense.

f. *Retail Delivery Date.* For the convenience of members, the estimated retail delivery date has been established as Thursday, March 8, 1962. The conditions and instructions contained in this letter pertain only to original member takedowns and sales to customers and do not cover secondary market transactions between members, nonmember dealers and/or others including brokers, individual customers and institutional investors subse-

Exhibit 5 (Continued)

quent to the closing of the account by the Manager or when all Bonds have been taken down by members, whichever date is earlier. Arrangements to cover delivery of such transactions will be the responsibility of the individuals involved.

g. *Delivery on Delayed Instructions.* Bonds taken down, on which confirmation, delivery and payment instructions have not been received by the estimated instructions deadline date of February 19, 1962, will be delivered either "Regular Way" or "Delayed Delivery" from the estimated redelivery date of March 8, 1962, or such other dates thereafter as delivery instructions are received; such Bonds will not be included in deliveries scheduled for Thursday, March 8, 1962, but must necessarily follow at a later date.

13. *Instructions on Bonds to be Registered.* Members desiring registered Bonds will forward complete registration instructions two weeks in advance of the delivery date of the Bonds, which is estimated to be Monday, February 26, 1962. There will be no charge for registration. These Bonds may be registered in multiples of $1,000 and such registered Bonds and coupon Bonds are interchangeable as provided by law. Some delay in delivery beyond the redelivery date, Thursday, March 8, 1962, may result from having Bonds registered.

14. *Legal Opinion Printed on Bonds.* The Official Notice of Sale indicates that the opinion of bond counsel will be printed on reverse side of the Bonds in coupon form without cost to the bidder. In addition, one signed original legal opinion will be furnished each member of the Syndicate by the Manager against his sales as a matter of record. Members will include in their delivery instructions the number of additional copies of the legal opinion required, if any, for delivery of Bonds taken down.

15. *Member Participation in Carry.* Arrangements may be made among the members to contribute capital to pay for the Bonds upon delivery. Members desiring to contribute capital in proportion to their liability or in larger amounts for the period from the delivery date to the redelivery date, are requested to inform the Manager. Syndicate members (including the Manager) contributing capital will be entitled to accrued interest upon the Bonds at the coupon rates to the extent of funds advanced by them. In the alternative, arrangements may be made to borrow among members, or with others, to carry the Bonds at the rate prevailing generally for such loans at the time of delivery, such rates to be set at the time of delivery. In case such alternative is used, the loan interest expenses will be charged pro rata against members whose Bonds are being carried by such loans, while interest accrues on the Bonds will be distributed to the Syndicate members in proportion to their participation in the Syndicate. All arrangements for purchase and carry of the Bonds will be finally determined by the Manager.

16. *Good Faith Deposit.* Should our Syndicate purchase the bonds, members will send their share of the good faith deposit (.1% or .001% of member's participation in the Syndicate) immediately to Bank of America N.T. & S.A., Municipal Bond Department, Attention Bond Cashiering Section, Room 950, 300 Montgomery Street, San Francisco 20, California. Member's share of good faith deposits advanced will be returned as soon as possible after the estimated delivery date of February 26, 1962.

17. *Expenses.* Members will forward statements of expenses properly chargeable to the Syndicate within 7 days following the delivery of all

Exhibit 5 (Continued)

Bonds and closing of the account in order to expedite the settlement of the Syndicate. Expenses which are not considered properly chargeable to the Syndicate include wire and telephone costs incurred by members forwarding their price views and filing orders, or shipping costs from the point of delivery set by the Manager on Bonds withdrawn from the Syndicate. The Manager may in his discretion charge any such expenses to the Syndicate if the same have been incurred at the request or upon the direction of the Manager. The Manager may assess clearing fees and handling charges resulting from delivery of Bonds.

18. *Advertising*. The Manager may publish advertisements of the Bonds bearing the names of any members of the Syndicate, the expense to be charged proportionately to all members even though individually they may be nonappearing in any or all advertisements. In order to reduce advertising space costs and yet retain the advantage to the Syndicate as a whole of a reasonably wide advertising program, as well as provide better balance between that portion of the advertisement devoted to copy and that devoted to signatures, the Manager may exclude some signatures of members of the Syndicate in the lower brackets in advertisements appearing in certain areas. Members should advise the Manager as to any change in signature if at variance from the listing of members appearing on pages 1A through 1D of our Syndicate letter of January 15, 1962. Any member not desiring to appear in the advertisements should so inform the Manager. The Manager may list all or any part of unsold balances of these Bonds in the "Blue List" opposite the names of all Syndicate members who subscribe and are therefore entitled to "Blue Listing". In addition to assisting in the sale of the Bonds, such listing should provide the membership with a daily source of the unsold balance in the Syndicate as the Manager will make adjustments when Bonds are sold.

19. *Circulars*. A circular in preliminary form is being forwarded to members. Copies of this circular in final form may be ordered with your imprint and at your own expense from Benjamin H. Tyrrel, 110 Greenwich Street, New York, N.Y., Telephone WHitehall 4-9222, from Sorg Printing Company of California, 180 First Street, San Francisco, Calif., Telephone YUkon 2-9663, or from The Twentieth Century Press, Inc., 40 South Clinton Street, Chicago 6, Ill., Telephone FInancial 6-1100. In order to eliminate the additional cost of estra press runs, orders should be placed not later than the day of sale.

20. *Caution as to Release of Syndicate Details*. Members of the Syndicate are specifically cautioned not to offer Bonds, reveal prices or discuss bidding limits unless and until the Bonds are awarded to us or until it is known we are not the successful bidder.

If the foregoing terms and conditions are in accordance with your understanding, please confirm your participation in the Syndicate, upon the above terms and conditions, by signing, with an authorized signature, this copy of the Syndicate letter in the space provided immediately below and returning it to us, after completing the forms on page 2A and 2B hereof.

Very truly yours,
BANK OF AMERICA N.T. & S.A.
Syndicate Manager

We confirm our acceptance of the foregoing supplemental terms and conditions of our participation

Exhibit 5 (Continued)

Date ....
Firm Name .... By
Address ....
By ....
Authorized Signature

Alan K. Browne,
Vice President

The Reoffering Scale

A major consideration in the process of determining the reoffering scale were the terms of the new issue in light of current market factors. Mr. Browne wanted to consider the quality or market appeal of the issue as well as the over-all interest rate or yield structure. As is typical of larger issues announced for sale, the upcoming issue had been appraised by the leading investment services. On January 22, 1963, *Moody's Bond Survey* commented on the prospective sale as follows:

> . . . motivated by January's initially strong market the State of California gave just 14 days notice of an intent to sell $100 million Aa-rated school aid bonds, series AA on Wednesday, (January 24). Such opportunism is one of a number of devices which will be utilized to alleviate the vast marketing problem of the nation's most prolific tax-exempt user. Bond authorizations since 1943 alone have totaled $5.1 billion. Beginning with June 30, 1945, bonded debt has more than doubled in each five-year period: $116.1 million outstanding at June 30, 1945; $243.4 million in 1950; $767.3 million in 1955; and $1.9 billion on June 30, 1960. With the impending water financing program, the state could, if it would, have little difficulty doubling its debt again by 1965, although a big slower borrowing pace is expected.
>
> Rumor has it that California's electorate will be asked to authorize an additional $250 million school and $300 million veteran's bonds on the June primary ballot. Excluding the state's newly voted $1,750,000,000 water bond, $640,197,000 state obligations now remain authorized but unissued. However, we do not regard this impending debt as a harbinger of credit jeopardy. We reiterate our belief that enlightened debt management techniques and burgeoning resources will combine to preserve the quality of California's general obligations in the challenging years ahead.

In addition to the Aa rating assigned by Moody's, the issue was given an AAA rating by Standard & Poor's. Exhibit 6 gives an explanation of the rating scales of these investment services. These ratings attempted to designate the "intrinsic risks" which exist in a security, that is, the degree of security of principal and the likelihood of prompt payment of interest over the life of the bond.

Mr. Browne felt that the reoffering scale should be close to current market yields on similar securities. Bank of America's municipal bond department maintained charts which plotted current trends in the bond market (Exhibit 7). The Bond Buyer's Index for twenty-year bonds and the Bank of America's own twenty-year California municipal bond index were considered primary indicators of yields. The historical differences

Text continues on p. 474, middle.

Exhibit 6

Key to Moody's Bond Ratings

Aaa

Bonds that are rated Aaa are judged to be of the best quality. They carry the smallest degree of investment risk and are generally referred to as "gilt edge." Interest payments are protected by a large or by an exceptionally stable margin and principal is secure. While the various protective elements are likely to change, such changes as can be visualized are most unlikely to impair the fundamentally strong position of such issues.

Aa

Bonds that are rated Aa are judged to be of high quality by all standards. Together with the Aaa group they comprise what are generally known as high grade bonds. They are rated lower than the best bonds because the margins of protection may not be as large as in Aaa securities or fluctuation of protective elements may be of greater amplitude or there may be other elements present which make the long term risks appear somewhat larger than in Aaa securities.

A

Bonds that are rated A possess many favorable investment attributes and are to be considered as higher medium grade obligations. Factors giving security to principal and interest are considered adequate but elements may be present which suggest a susceptibility to impairment sometime in the future.

Baa

Bonds that are rated Baa are considered as lower medium grade obligations, that is, they are neither highly protected nor poorly secured. Interest payments and principal security appear adequate for the present but certain protective elements may be lacking or may be characteristically unreliable over any great length of time. Such bonds lack outstanding investment characteristics and in fact have speculative characteristics as well.

Ba

Bonds that are rated Ba are judged to have speculative elements; their future cannot be considered as well assured. Often the protection of interest and principal payments may be very moderate and thereby not well safeguarded during both good and bad times over the future. Uncertainty of position characterizes bonds in this class.

B

Bonds that are rated B generally lack characteristics of the desirable investment. Assurance of interest and principal payments or of maintenance of other terms of the contract over any long period of time may be small.

Caa

Bonds that are rated Caa are of poor standing. Such issues may be in default or there may be present elements of danger with respect to principal or interest.

Ca

Bonds that are rated Ca represent obligations which are speculative in a high degree. Such issues are often in default or have other market shortcomings.

C

Bonds that are rated C are the lowest rated class of bonds and issues so rated can be regarded as having extremely poor prospects of ever attaining any real investment standing.

Exhibit 6 (Continued)

Standard & Poor's Bond Ratings

In the Standard & Poor's bond quality ratings system, interest-paying bonds are graded into eight classifications ranging from AAA for the highest quality designation through AA, A, BBB, BB, B, CCC to CC for the lowest. Bonds on which no interest is being paid, either because of default or because of "income" characteristics, are given C, DDD, DD and D ratings. United States government bonds are not rated, but are considered as a yardstick against which to measure all other issues.

BANK QUALITY BONDS

Under present commercial bank regulations, bonds rated in the top four categories (AAA, AA, A, BBB or their equivalent) generally are regarded as eligible for bank investment.

AAA

Bonds rated AAA are highest grade corporate obligations. They possess the ultimate degree of protection as to principal and interest. Marketwise, they move with interest rates, and hence provide the maximum safety on all counts.

AA

Bonds rated AA also qualify as high grade obligations, and in the majority of instances differ from AAA issues only in small degree. Here too, prices move with the long term money market.

A

Bonds rated A are regarded as upper medium grade. They have considerable investment strength but are not entirely free from adverse effects of changes in economic and trade conditions. Interest and principal are regarded as safe. They predominantly reflect money rates in their market behavior, but to some extent, also business conditions.

BBB

The BBB, or medium grade category, is borderline between definitely sound obligations and those where the speculative element begins to predominate. These bonds have adequate asset coverage and normally are protected by satisfactory earnings. Their susceptibility to changing conditions, particularly to depressions, necessitates constant watching. Marketwise, the bonds are more responsive to business and trade conditions than to interest rates. This group is the lowest which qualifies for commercial bank investment.

SUBSTANDARD BONDS

As we move down the rating scale, beginning with BB, investment characteristics weaken and the speculative elements become progressively stronger. The fortunes of the obligors change rapidly with economic and trade conditions and in adverse periods interest requirements may not be earned. Investment in bonds in this group must be under constant surveillance. Prices fluctuate widely with changing business conditions and with little regard for the money market.

BB

Bonds given a BB rating are regarded as lower medium grade. They have only minor investment characteristics. In the case of utilities, interest is earned consistently but by narrow margins. In the case of other types of obligors, charges are earned on average by a fair margin, but in poor periods deficit operations are possible.

B

Bonds rated as low as B are speculative. Payment of interest cannot be assured under difficult economic conditions.

Exhibit 6 (Continued)

Standard & Poor's Bond Ratings

CCC-CC

Bonds rated CCC and CC are outright speculations, with the lower rating denoting the more speculative. Interest is paid, but continuation is questionable in periods of poor trade conditions. In the case of CC ratings the bonds may be on an income basis and the payment may be small.

C

The rating of C is reserved for income bonds on which no interest is being paid.

DDD-D

All bonds rated DDD, DD, and D are in default, with the rating indicating the relative salvage value.

CANADIAN BONDS
Canadian corporate bonds are rated on the same basis as American corporate issues. The ratings measure the intrinsic value of the bonds, but they do not take into account exchange and other uncertainties.

FOREIGN BONDS
Foreign bonds carry the same rating symbols as domestic bonds, but in all cases they are preceded by a * to denote a conditional rating. This is applied because the obligor is a foreign body and the bonds are sometimes affected by other than economic factors.

between various indexes and the bids on a recent major California issue are shown by Exhibit 8. In every case where the state had accepted the bid, Mr. Browne felt that the bid, in terms of yield, had been high enough to permit a successful reoffering. Considered also would be the calendar of forthcoming flotations, the current bond dealer inventory, the possibility of changes in significant market rates such as prime loan rates, and the Federal Reserve Bank discount rates during the flotation period. The January 22, 1962, issue of *Moody's Bond Survey* evaluated these factors with the following statement:

> Underwriting bidding early last week was surprisingly strong in the face of a mounting calendar for the forthcoming issues, but weakened later as many new offerings met with slower investor reception, indicative of mounting retail resistance to present yield levels. In its actions the market was almost a repetition of that of the previous week and lends credence to the view that the price rally since mid-December is topping off.
>
> The sustained drop in inventories due to dwindling new issue volume and strong demand for bonds by dealers and investors alike seems to be at an end. Inventories have risen above $300 million, which although far below the record $500 plus million, established last year, is no longer insignificant in view of the mounting forward calendar of new issues. On balance, although current developments are indecisive, it is our view that new issue supply will brake any upswing in prices and eventually produce more realistic values. Only selective buying is warranted at this time.

Exhibit 7

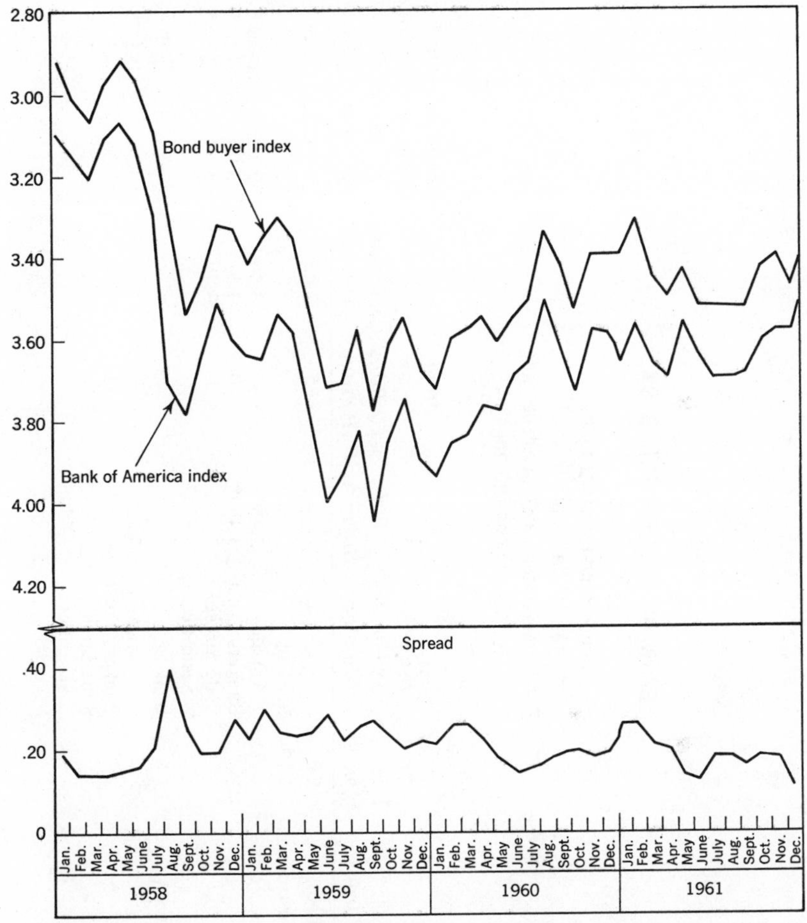

Gross Profit Margin

Mr. Browne was also faced with the selection of the gross margin. He viewed the gross margin as consisting of two elements. First of all, there was the compensation for underwriting, which was usually about 55 percent of the gross margin. From the gross margin other syndicate expenses had to be deducted. Exhibit 9 shows the closing statement for a recent issue similar to the one under examination. The gross underwriting profit was $597,582.50 and the total expenses amounted to $100,858.36. Mr. Browne considered these expenses as fairly typical for an issue and syndicate of this size.

Text continues on p. 478.

Exhibit 8

BANK OF AMERICA N.T. & S.A.

Major Bond Offerings by the
State of California in 1961
Bond Indexes for Dates Corresponding
to Major Bond Offerings

Date of Sale	*Amount*	*Purpose*	*Aver. Life Years Months*	*Bidder or Syndicate Manager*	*Bids Submitted*	*Bond Buyer 20 Bond Average*	*Dow Jones Average*	*Bank of America State of California Average 10 year*	*Bank of America State of California Average 20 year*	*Date Average Was Computed*
1/24/62	$100,000,000	(School)	15 9			3.35	3.43	2.90	3.40	1/19/62
10/18/61	100,000,000	(Construction)	14 10	Bank of America	3.461*	3.45	3.56	3.10	3.65	10/13/61
				Bankers Trust	3.4998	3.40	3.51	3.00	3.55	10/20/61
				State Street Securities	3.6247	3.39	3.49	3.00	3.55	10/27/61
9/13/61	100,000,000	Veteran	15 6	Bank of America,	3.787	3.55	3.64	3.20	3.75	9/8/61
				Bankers Trust		3.55	3.64	3.20	3.75	9/15/61
				State Street Securities	3.7596*	3.52	3.61	3.20	3.75	9/22/61

Exhibit 8 (Continued)

BANK OF AMERICA N.T. & S.A.

Date of Sale	Amount	Purpose	Aver. Life Years Months	Bidder or Syndicate Manager	Bids Submitted	Bond Buyer 20 Bond Average	Dow Jones Average	Bank of America State of California Average 10 year	Bank of America State of California Average 20 year	Date Average Was Computed
8/16/61	100,000,000	School	15	Bank of America	3.860					
				Bankers Trust		3.53	3.62	3.20	3.85	8/11/61
				State Street Securities	3.754*	3.53	3.62	3.20	3.75	8/18/61
						3.53	3.63	3.20	3.75	8/25/61
	100,000,000	Veteran	13 8	Bank of America, Bankers Trust	3.894					
	25,000,000	Construction	14 3	Bank of America, Bankers Trust	3.833					
4/5/61	140,000,000	Veteran	13 8	Bank of America, Bankers Trust	3.8723*	3.51	3.57	3.15	3.85	3/31/61
						3.51	3.57	3.25	3.90	4/7/61
	50,000,000	Construction	14 3	Bank of America, Bankers Trust	3.8474*	3.51	3.57	3.05	3.70	4/14/61
1/11/61	95,000,000	School	15 2	Bank of America, Bankers Trust	3.6838*	3.39	3.39	3.20	3.70	1/6/61
						3.41	3.41	3.10	3.70	1/13/61
						3.40	3.41	3.10	3.70	1/20/61

*Accepted by the state of California.

Exhibit 9

BANK OF AMERICA N.T. & S.A.

Closing Statement of Underwriting Syndicate

Size of issue: $100,000,000		
Issuer: state of California		
Retail offering price		$101,017,139.00
Gross selling commission		402,417.50
Proceeds to syndicate from sale of bonds		100,614,721.50
Cost of bonds sold (bid)		100,017,139.00
Gross underwriting profit		597,582.50
Less expenses:		
Advertising	$40,687.41	
Circulars	830.34	
Federal funds	396.34	
Printing	11,824.67	
Shipping	3,962.24	
Stationery and supplies	1,058.07	
Telephone, telegraph, and TWX	8,772.76	
Miscellaneous	1,626.90	
Other members	6,699.83	
Handling and clearance fees	25,000.00	100,858.56
Net underwriting profit		$496,723.94

The selling commission was the other element in the margin. When a dealer who was not a member of the syndicate got an order for the bonds, he was allowed to buy them from the syndicate at the offering price less the dealer concession. Thus the dealer (nonsyndicate member) was allowed a portion of the selling commission. The dealer concession had traditionally ranged from no concession at all on the first couple of maturities to possibly 1/4 to 1/2 point or more on the bonds of longer maturity. When the bank sold its participation to its own clients, it received its full portion of the selling commission as well as its underwriting compensation and the syndicate manager's fee.

A study by the National Bureau of Economic Research gave some data on a few winning bids, all of them handled by national houses (see Exhibit 10). These data were further limited in significance since they were mainly for deals completed in the fourth quarter of 1955. However, Mr. Browne did not feel that margins had changed significantly since that time. These tables suggested that the quality of the issue was perhaps the leading factor accounting for differences in margins. Average maturity also explained a part of the differences among margins, but less than quality.

If competitors should plan approximately the same reoffering scale,

Exhibit 10

BANK OF AMERICA N.T. & S.A.

Gross Margins on Reofferings of State and Local Government Securities Competitively Bought

(Selected accounts opened largely during the fourth quarter, 1955)

By Size

Size of Issue	*Over-all Margin per $1000 Bond**
Under $500,000	$10.86 (6)
$500,000 – $1,000,000	10.38 (17)
$1,000,000 – $2,000,000	12.71 (15)
$2,000,000 – $5,000,000	10.92 (21)
$5,000,000 – $10,000,000	10.78 (12)
$10,000,000 – $20,000,000	13.84 (8)
$20,000,000 – $50,000,000	12.28 (6)
$50,000,000 – $100,000,000	13.50 (5)
$100,000,000 and over	11.28 (1)

By Quality and Maturity
Average Margin per $1000 Bond*

	Moody's Rating		
Average Maturity	*Aaa & Aa*	*A and Lower*	*Unrated*
Less than 10 years	$8.22 (8)	$10.65 (11)	—
10 to 15 years	9.19 (10)	12.60 (10)	$14.33 (3)
Over 15 years	9.32 (4)	15.63 (6)	14.03 (3)

*Number of cases included in each average shown in parentheses.

SOURCE: Robinson, Roland I., *Postwar Market for State and Local Government Securities* (Princeton: Princeton University Press, 1960).

the critical difference among bids would probably be the profit margin planned by the various bidding groups. There were real differences with respect to price policy among the leading syndicate managers. Some firms were low margin, high volume traders; others worked to keep their margins intact.

Gross margins were, of course, what the underwriting groups *tried* to achieve. If the reoffering failed to attract buyers and price cutting became necessary, then margins would shrink or might even become negative.

Setting a Coupon Structure

The invitation to bid (Exhibit 1) permitted the bidders a great amount of flexibility in proposing coupon structures. The selection of a coupon system became a matter of considerable strategic importance to Mr. Browne. As explained, and demonstrated in Appendix A, a coupon structure which was high in the short-term end and low in the long-term end, showed the lower interest cost as computed by the traditional formula. The state of California used this traditional formula in awarding competitive bids. For this reason, the bidders had at least one good reason for shifting the high part of the coupon structure into the early maturities as much as possible.

On the other hand, this was not always good sales strategy. Since the yield curve, that is, the structure of interest rates as a function of maturity, had a positive slope, then the indicated coupon rates were just the opposite of the coupon pattern preferred for cost influencing computation. Exhibit 11 shows yield curves for U.S. government securities as of November 30, 1961, and December 29, 1961. When the coupon structure and the scale of offering yields of an issue slope in opposite directions, the early maturities will sell at premiums, the later maturities at discounts. Some bond dealers felt that many buyers prefer to purchase a bond at a price not too far from par.

The Final Decision

Mr. Browne wanted to win the bid partly because of his optimistic appraisal of the bond market and partly because he felt it was the syndicate manager's responsibility to exercise the proper persuasion in order to bring the winning bid. Prestige was also of concern to Mr. Browne, because the market apparently did not attach as much significance to membership as to leadership in a syndicate which loses the bid.

There was still concern in the mind of Mr. Browne over the recent awards to the Morris concern. He felt that the Morris system of marketing the bonds through a street broker could ultimately have a detrimental effect on bond marketing. The large syndicate headed by the Bank of America, which had traditionally purchased California bonds, had established a nation-wide market for the bonds. He thought that the Bank of America syndicate had a relationship with investment houses, institutional investors, and the buying public which was somewhat akin to that of a doctor to his patient. "We know where all California bonds are and we test the market to find out how many more it will absorb at a given price," he had said to a financial reporter some weeks earlier.

In preparing for the final price meeting, Mr. Browne knew he must plan his strategy carefully. He had to make some basic decisions about ways and means of holding the syndicate together if, during the final price meeting, any firm believing that the market risk for the proposed group bid was too great should drop out of the syndicate. If any syndicate members were to drop out, he had to be ready to absorb a greater share

Exhibit 11

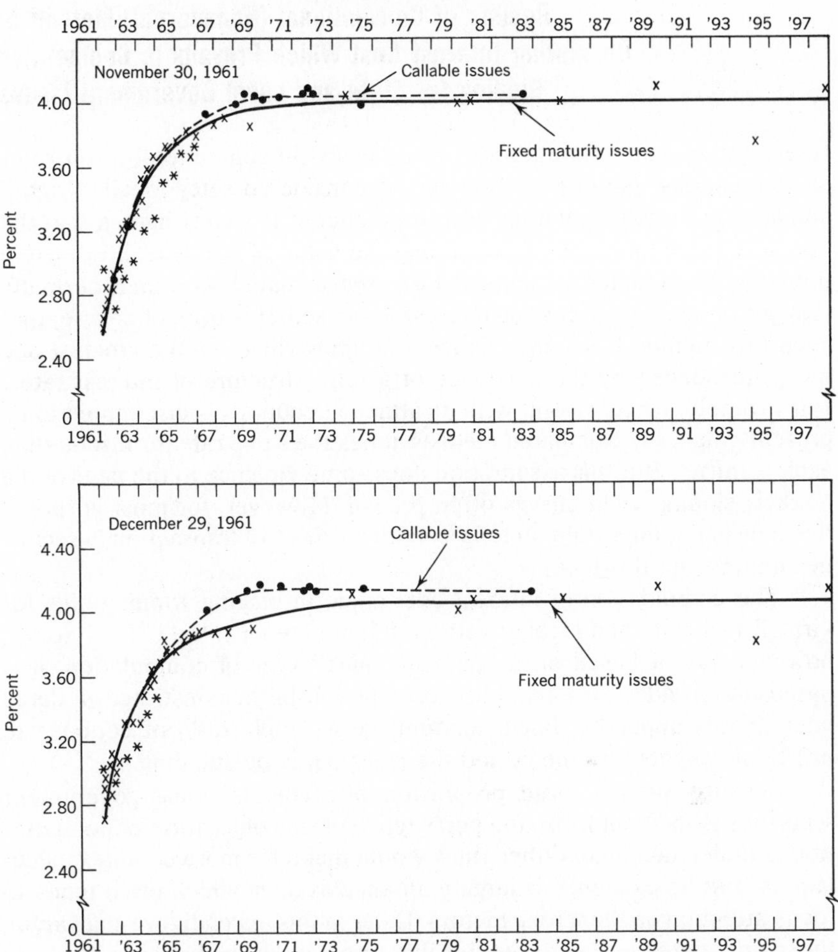

of the total underwriting in order to show his conviction to the suggested bid. That is, a strong offer to take more bonds by the manager might induce a number of potential dropouts to stay at a lower yield, partly because their share of the flotation would not be raised by a given number of dropouts since the manager was picking up the pieces. With all these thoughts in mind, Mr. Browne began to work his way toward the bid which he thought would effectively win the issue and still allow a successful reoffering.

APPENDIX A

Results of Conventional (Nonaccrual) Method of Computing Interest Cost Which Prevails in Competitive Bidding for State and Local Government Issues

Interest and cost computations are all based in some measure on rules or conventions. No one method can be considered categorically "right" and all other methods wrong. But in practice it is widely agreed that the "present value" method of computing the value of bonds as it is used in preparing bond tables presents a close approximation to what is normally thought of as interest cost or interest expense.[1] It is true, of course, that even this method has some elements of approximation, the greatest one being introduced by the existence of a term structure of interest rates. For example, when a bond with its attached coupons is discounted to its present value, the calculated yield assumes the same rate for discounting each maturity. But this assumption does some violence to the facts of the market; sloping yield curves often prevail. However, for most purposes this flaw is not important so long as both parties to a transaction in securities understand this fact.

The computation of interest cost made in picking winning bids for virtually all state and local government bond issues in the United States, however, is not based on a "present value" type of computation; it is based on an older formula. This formula will be demonstrated in detail later in this appendix, but it amounts to a simple ratio of coupons to principal weighted by the period the principal is outstanding.

Because such a large proportion of state and local government securities is in serial form, the persistence of this older form of computation is understandable. Other rules would make for more complex calculations. But its existence is largely an anachronism which often tends to focus attention on the wrong factors. Later in this appendix we shall argue this point at greater length. At this juncture it would be better to illustrate this method of computation and then to study some of its variations in practice. A hypothetical illustration has been devised and then elaborated to help in the exposition of this problem (see Exhibit A-1).

Part 1 of the illustration sets up the basic circumstances that might prevail in a very simple and uncomplicated state or local government financing. To ease the computations, small amounts have been used and all figures are rounded to the extent possible. The only departure from utter simplicity is that involved in the coupon structure assumed. In

[1]The "present value" form of calculation is also sometimes referred to as the "accrual" or "annuity" method of computing bond values.

Exhibit A-1

Hypothetical Illustration of Conventional (Nonaccrual) Method of Computing Interest Cost Prevailing in State and Local Government Borrowing

Part 1. Assume $10,000 borrowed in 1956 to mature in equal annual installments of $1000 over the next ten years and assume coupons shown in Column 5

Maturity	*Years to Maturity (Assumed)*	*Principal Maturing Each Year*	*Principal Outstanding for One Year (col. 2 × col. 3)*	*Coupon (Assumed)*	*Interest Cost (col. 4 × col. 5)*
1957	1	$1,000	$ 1,000	4	40
1958	2	1,000	2,000	4	80
1959	3	1,000	3,000	4	120
1960	4	1,000	4,000	2 1/4	90
1961	5	1,000	5,000	2 1/4	112.50
1962	6	1,000	6,000	2 1/2	150
1963	7	1,000	7,000	2 1/2	175
1964	8	1,000	8,000	2 1/2	200
1965	9	1,000	9,000	2 1/2	225
1966	10	1,000	10,000	2 1/2	250
			$55,000		1,442.5

Interest cost computation: $1,442.50 ÷ $55,000 = 2.6227 percent

Reprinted from *Postwar Market for State and Local Government Securities,* by Roland I. Robinson (Princeton: Princeton University Press, 1960).

this case, we have used three different coupon rates. Such a coupon system would not be far from those which often prevail; high for the first few maturities; that is, 4 percent; dropping back to 2¼ percent in the middle; and then up a bit again, 2½ percent in the later maturities. The so-called interest cost is simply the number of dollars that will be paid out as coupons. The "principal outstanding for one year" is each year's serial obligation, multiplied by the number of years it will be outstanding. The total of "principal outstanding for one year" is the equivalent of a single amount if it were at interest for one year.[2] The average rate of

[2]If the amounts in each maturity of an issue are equal and the period to maturity is in whole number digits, then the simple sum of digits formula could be used; that is, $n(n + 1)/2$, in this case $10(10 + 1)/2 = 55$ times $1,000 = $55,000. In practice these assumptions are quite often not true, so the more direct, even if more laborious, calculation is usually performed.

interest cost is then simply the interest cost in dollars divided by the total "principal outstanding for one year." If the bidder offers a premium, it is deducted from the dollar amount of coupons before computing the rate of interest cost. This will be illustrated in later parts.

It should be noted that this form of computation makes no distinction between a dollar of interest paid during the early years of the obligation and a dollar of interest paid in the late years near final maturity. According to a present value basis of computation, of course, the earlier dollar is worth more and correspondingly "costs" more than the later dollar. This lies back of much of the complexity in the coupon structures of many state and local government issues. Most of the sale announcements allow bidders to name the coupon or coupons to be placed in the proposed issue. Some invitations allow the bidders to name only one coupon rate; others permit varying "split coupon" arrangements. Usually only one coupon can be named for each maturity, but in a few cases more than one coupon rate for a given maturity is allowed. While the non-accural interest cost computation formula makes no distinction between early coupon dollars and later ones, the market does. In all investment markets, including that for state and local government securities, the conventions of computation are on a "present value" basis. Underwriters, therefore, can realize more from the sale of a given dollar volume of coupons on early maturities (where the discount to present value of the coupon is small) than for a similar volume of coupons on later maturities. Accordingly, there is a general disposition for the underwriters to put high coupons on early issues and lower ones on the longer maturities. The more this is done, the lower the computed interest cost, according to this archaic formula of state and municipal bidding. It is not a real saving to the borrowing governments, only a fictional one. The trouble is that this fiction has even fooled some members of the investment banking community. They speak of spending tedious hours in the price meetings held by syndicates working out coupon structures that will "save the borrowing government's money." Nothing is being saved, of course, and the market is only being made that much more complex.

This is shown in Part 2 of the hypothetical illustration (see Exhibit A-2). For the purpose of this part, one assumption has been added: that of an upsweeping yield "curve," which is a straight line in this case. Three different hypothetical cases are presented. In the first one a different coupon is put on each maturity and the coupon is made exactly identical to the assumed yield. In other words, these bonds should all sell exactly at par. This should result in as near a true interest cost at present value as any case we present here. In the second case, just one coupon has been attached to the issue, the coupon which is the average interest cost for the entire issue, according to the computations of case 1. Here, the price which would be realized for each maturity of bond is

Exhibit A-2

Hypothetical Illustration

Part 2. Same assumptions as in Part 1, with added assumptions about prevailing yields and different coupon assumptions

		Case 1	*Case 2*		*Case 3*		
	Prevailing	*Coupon-Yield*	*2.6 Percent Coupon*				
Maturity	*Yield Cost*	*Interest Cost*	*Interest Cost*	*Price*	*Coupon (percent)*	*Interest Cost*	*Price*
1957	2.00	20	26	1,005.90	108.0	1,080	2,039.20
1958	2.10	42	52	1,009.70	0.5	10	968.80
1959	2.20	66	78	1,011.60	0.5	15	950.90
1960	2.30	92	104	1,011.40	0.5	20	931.60
1961	2.40	120	130	1,009.40	0.5	25	911.00
1962	2.50	150	156	1,005.50	0.5	30	889.20
1963	2.60	182	182	1,000.00	0.5	35	866.40
1964	2.70	216	208	992.80	0.5	40	842.70
1965	2.80	252	234	984.20	0.5	45	818.10
1966	2.90	290	260	974.10	0.5	50	793.00
Total		1,430	1,430	10,004.60		1,350	10,010.90

Interest cost computations:

Case 1: $1,430 ÷ $55,000 = 2.6 percent (equivalent to "present value" cost).
Case 2: ($1,430 − $4.60*) ÷ $55,000 = 2.5916 percent.
Case 3: ($1,350 − $10.90*) ÷ $55,000 = 2,4347 percent.

*Premium.

Columns 5 and 9 were taken from yield tables using the assumed coupons of the yields applicable in each case.

shown in column 5 of part 2; the total for this column shows that the issue as a whole would sell for $4.60 more than par. If this $4.60 is deducted from the interest cost as figured in column 4 (which has the same total as column 3 but not the same amounts year-by-year), the resulting computation of interest cost by the conventional formula for awarding bids for state and local government bonds ends up slightly less than that shown in case 1. In other words, with the assumption of an ascending yield curve, a single coupon gives a computed lower average interest cost than a coupon fitted exactly to the yields of the market, which is presumably a sort of ideal case in which present value and interest cost both yield the same results.

But the extreme, and of course unreal, case would be that in which the coupon cost was moved into the first year as much as possible and as little as possible was allowed for later years. This grotesque illustration is case 3. Here a coupon of 1/2 of 1 percent for the last nine maturities was assumed; the coupon of the first year was loaded to the point necessary to make the whole issue sell for more than par, which amounted to the absurd coupon of 108 percent per annum. When the computation of interest cost according to the conventional state and local government formula is made, the presumption of lower cost is striking; the margin is much more than that which usually separates the bids of competing buyers.

In practice, of course, the buyers of issues could never go as far as case 3 assumes. The buyers are usually underwriting groups who must sell the obligations to ultimate investors, and ultimate investors have an understandable reluctance for odd and extreme coupons. A security having a coupon of 108 percent might be salable to a commercial bank with a sophisticated investment department and, what is more important, a sophisticated and understanding board of directors. But there are problems of even greater character in selling low-coupon, long-term bonds even at deep discounts. For one thing, only the initial purchaser of these bonds can use the full yield for purposes of getting an exemption from income taxation; subsequent purchasers can use only the coupon. Thus these bonds are peculiarly unmarketable obligations.

But just the same, the effects of manipulated coupon structures on the computed interest cost is material; shrewd investment bankers with sharp pencils have found that it is worthwhile to go to the extra trouble involved in marketing these securities with special coupons; they can win bids by such devices. Much of the energy of the great houses which manage the syndicate accounts that bid for these securities is devoted to just this purpose.

In Part 3 of our hypothetical illustration, we attempt to introduce a note of reality into our computations (Exhibit A-3). In the first place, the other computations assumed a market yield and any premium resulting from the "price" calculated in each case was deducted from the dollar value of the coupons or the interest cost in dollars in full. In other words, we were making no allowance for the margin of the investment banker. In cases 4 and 5 we drop this quite unreal assumption and allow a margin of a dollar a bond. For case 4 we assume a bidding group that can market some of the early maturities at a fairly high coupon, but otherwise they cannot find buyers unless they put on coupons that will "produce" prices not too far from par. The price (which multiplied by the dollar amount in each maturity is called the "production" in underwriting parlance) must yield a little margin over par since the bidding rules in most cases require a bid of par or better and the group must also work out its own margin from the sale price of the obligations. For the purpose of this case we have assumed that the second bidding group (case 5) has somewhat more aggressive salesmen; they figure that they will be able to sell the early maturities at an even higher coupon than was estimated by the first group. But their real secret weapon is assumed to be an advance deal by which they can sell the one longest maturity at a 1/2 of 1 percent coupon. They have found one investor who will buy this long-term, deep-discount bond in spite of its disadvantages.[3] The intervening coupon was doubtless arrived at during the price meeting of this bidding group at a level which was figured salable and which would "produce" a price above par for the whole issue. Using these assumptions, we find that the interest cost in case 5 is materially below that of case 4.

Exhibit A-3

Hypothetical Illustration

Part 3. Same assumptions as in Parts 1 and 2, with still different coupon assumptions and with the further exception that underwriters bidding for issues are assumed to retain a profit of one dollar a bond.

	Case 4			Case 5		
Maturities	*Coupon (Same as*	*Interest Cost Part 1)*	*Price ("production)*	*Coupons*	*Interest*	*Price ("production")*
1957	4	40	1,019.70	5	50	1,029.50
1958	4	80	1,037.00	5	100	1,056.50
1959	4	120	1,052.00	5	150	1,080.90
1960	2 1/4	90	998.10	5	200	1,102.60
1961	2 1/4	112.5	993.00	2 1/2	125	1,004.70
1962	2 1/2	150	1,000.00	2 1/2	150	1,000.00
1963	2 1/2	175	993.60	2 1/2	175	993.60
1964	2 1/2	200	985.70	2 1/2	200	985.70
1965	2 1/2	225	976.30	2 1/2	225	976.30
1966	2 1/2	250	965.40	1/2	50	793.00
Total		1,442.5	10,020.80		1,425	10,022.80

Interest cost computations:

Case 4: ($1,442.50 − $10.80*) ÷ $55,000 = 2.6031 percent.

Case 5: ($1,425 − $12.80*) ÷ $55,000 = 2.5676 percent.

*Premium less underwriters' profit.

[3]In practice they probably would have had to offer this one maturity at a yield considerably higher than the market for a more conventional issue. The low-coupon terminal maturities are usually not reoffered publicly, but underwriters report that the effective yield at which these special obligations are sold is usually from forty to sixty basis points above a comparable maturity sold at par.

BROKER MEMBERSHIP ON THE NEW YORK STOCK EXCHANGE

Stevenson, Garner & Company

In mid-February 1963, Mr. Richard Stevenson was trying to decide whether it would be advantageous for Stevenson, Garner & Company to purchase a seat on the New York Stock Exchange. He expected the firm's decision to be made at the next weekly meeting of the four partners in Stevenson, Garner & Company. As a senior partner, he wanted to have his own position clearly in mind before that meeting.

Background on Stevenson, Garner & Company

In May of 1954, Mr. Richard Stevenson and Mr. Robert Garner, as equal partners, had purchased a set on what was then the Los Angeles Stock Exchange[1] and had established Stevenson, Garner & Company. Both men had been in the investment business in Los Angeles since the late 1920s. Initially, Stevenson, Garner & Company had employed three salesmen in addition to the two partners.

As Stevenson, Garner & Company had grown over the years, it had become involved in various related financial activities.[2] As of 1963, these activities included underwriting and distributing corporate bonds and stocks and municipal issues; acting as broker for all types of corporate, government, and municipal securities; trading or dealing in various types of securities; financial advising in merger, acquisitions, and disposals; and providing other miscellaneous financial services.[3]

In its nine years, Stevenson, Garner & Company had grown substantially. At the end of its first year of operation it had total assets of

---

[1]In 1956 the exchanges of Los Angeles and San Francisco merged to form the Pacific Coast Exchange. Trading floors were retained in both cities but staff and services were centralized.

[2]Investment banking was often mixed with commercial banking prior to the Banking Act of 1933 (the Glass-Stegall Act), which specifically prohibited joint operations in both the investment banking business and the business of accepting deposits and making loans. Investment bankers were prohibited from accepting deposits and banks of deposit were prohibited from underwriting or dealing in corporate securities of any kind. Banks were allowed to continue their "investment banking" type of activities with respect to direct obligations of the United States and general obligations of any state or political subdivision thereof.

[3]When Stevenson, Garner & Company acted as a broker, it bought or sold securities for the account and risk of others. It was the agent of the customer it represented and charged a commission for its services. As a dealer, instead of buying and selling for others, Stevenson, Garner & Company bought and sold for its own account and risk.

$240,000 and gross income before expenses for the year of $105,000; at the end of 1962, it had total assets of $1,375,000 and gross income before expenses for the year of $475,000 (see Exhibit 1). In 1962 about $160,000 of gross income was derived from brokerage commissions. Most of this business was transacted on the Pacific Coast Stock Exchange. About $50,000 of this amount was reciprocal business placed by the New York Stock Exchange member who was the correspondent of Stevenson, Garner & Company. (This is discussed in detail later in the case.) Over the years Mr. Stevenson and Mr. Garner had taken in two additional partners, and as of February 1963, Stevenson, Garner & Company employed seven salesmen in addition to the four partners.

Background on the Securities Industry

Securities have been traded in one form or another in the United States since its founding. The New York Stock Exchange, the first formal marketplace in the United States for securities, was established on May 17, 1792. On that day, a group of merchants and auctioneers decided to meet daily at regular hours to buy and sell securities under an old buttonwood tree on Wall Street in New York. These twenty-four men were the original members of the exchange.

In spite of such an early beginning, securities did not become a widely accepted investment medium for the public until the sale of liberty bonds during World War I. Although the market for new securities expanded in the 1920s, it virtually disappeared between the depression years of the 1930s and the end of World War II. However, as World War II drew to a close, a shift occurred. Corporations began to raise new money through the securities markets in order to convert their facilities to meet a rising private demand for goods. Reflecting this transformation, the volume of new corporate securities offered for sale, which had declined to an annual level below $700 million in 1942 and 1943, reached $4113 million in 1946 and attained a peak of $8171 million in 1957. This expansion of new issues increased the amount of securities outstanding. Thus, during the postwar period the number of companies and stocks listed on the NYSE gradually increased, and changes in annual stock volume although more irregular were also generally in an upward direction (see Exhibit 2).

In addition to the growth in the market for securities, there was a great expansion of sales offices and selling efforts of broker-dealer firms during this period. By 1963 there were over 6000 firms engaged in some aspect of the securities business in the United States. A relatively small number of large broker-dealer firms employed a majority of all salesmen in the industry and a large number of small firms employed few salesmen.

Exhibit 1

STEVENSON, GARNER & COMPANY

Balance Sheet
December 31, 1962

Assets			Liabilities		
Cash		$ 325,608			
Securities owned at market		228,021	Accounts payable to:		
Accounts receivable from:			Brokers and dealers	$217,715	
Brokers and dealers	$189,668		Customers	642,189	$ 859,904
Customers	562,994	752,662	Accrued wages and benefits		36,797
Office equipment		17,240	Other liabilities		45,336
Prepaid expenses		3,062	Capital account		431,559
Other assets		47,003			$1,373,596
		$1,373,596			

Exhibit 2

STEVENSON, GARNER & COMPANY

Information on Stocks Listed on the New York Stock Exchange

	Number of Stocks Listed at Year End	*Total Market Value of Stocks Listed at Year End* (in billions)*	*Average Number of Shares Listed (in millions of shares)*	*Reported Annual Stock Volume (in millions of shares)*	*Annual Turnover Rate Percent*
1962	1,559	$345.8	7,374	962	13
1961	1,541	387.8	6,773	1,021	15
1960	1,528	307.0	6,153	767	12
1959	1,507	307.7	5,432	820	15
1958	1,507	276.7	4,910	747	15
1957	1,522	195.6	4,633	560	12
1956	1,502	219.2	4,149	556	13
1955	1,508	207.7	3,505	650	19
1950	1,422	93.8	2,259	525	23
1945	1,269	73.8	1,542	378	24
1940	1,230	41.9	1,445	208	14
1929	1,293	N.A.	942	1,125	119

*The market value for a stock listed at year end may be computed by multiplying the year end market price times the number of shares outstanding at year end. These figures represent the total for *all* stocks listed on the NYSE at year end.

Most of the largest broker-dealer firms had nation-wide branch operations and were members of the New York Stock Exchange. The expansion of this portion of the broker-dealer community was characterized more by a sharp rise in the size of these firms than by an increase in the number of firms. Thus, while the number of member organizations of the NYSE increased only slightly, the number of salesmen employed by these firms rose from 8000 at the end of 1945 to over 32,000 at the end of 1962 and the number of branch offices of NYSE member firms increased from 841 to 2737 over the same period.

Following the passage of the Securities Exchange Act of 1934,[4] the New York Stock Exchange had become registered as a national securities exchange on October 1, 1934. Although fourteen stock exchanges were registered under the act as national securities exchanges at the end of 1962, approximately three fourths of all transactions on national securities exchanges took place on the New York Stock Exchange.

As a membership association, the exchange was owned by the individuals who held "seats"[5] or memberships. Ownership of a seat entitled the holder to the privileges of membership and an equity interest in the assets of the exchange.

A seat had to be held personally in the name of an individual and could not be owned by a partnership or corporation. A member might be a general partner or holder of voting stock in one of the brokerage concerns which, by virtue of his exchange membership, was known as a member firm. At the end of 1962, there were 1366 memberships in the New York Stock Exchange—1101 were owned by individuals who were affiliated with 672 member firms and 265 were owned by individuals who were not affiliated with any firm or were inactive.[6]

The members of the NYSE performed various functions in connection with the market and were often classified on the basis of their principal activity. As of December 31, 1962, there were 350 specialists. A specialist executed orders in the securities in which he was registered. In addition, he also dealt as principal, thus making markets in those issues. The exchange set specific requirements for specialists regarding market experience, their dealer function, and the amount of capital they had to have. There were 666 members, affiliated with member firms, who

---

[4]The Securities Exchange Act of 1934 was designed primarily to regulate the secondary market for securities, to enforce informational requirements, and to institute trading rules. It provided an important supplement to the disclosure requirements of the Securities Act of 1933, which was aimed primarily at achieving "full and fair disclosure" of all pertinent and material facts relating to any corporate security issue publicly offered.

[5]The term "seat" originated during the early years of the exchange when the member remained seated while the president called the list of securities.

[6]From the founding of the exchange in 1792 until May 1953, member organizations had been limited to partnerships. At that time the exchange's constitution had been amended to permit corporations to become member organizations—provided such corporations were engaged primarily in the securities business as dealers or brokers. As of early 1963 about 100 of the 672 member organizations were corporations.

were either "office partners" or were on the floor of the exchange handling orders for their own firms or their correspondents. Another 150 members were floor brokers, commonly known as "$2 brokers" (although the commission they received for their services had for a long time been above that amount), who were unaffiliated with member firms dealing with the public but executed orders for them. There were 119 members involved in handling odd-lot orders; most of them were brokers working on the floor exclusively for the odd-lot dealer firms, executing odd-lot orders, and buying and selling round lots to meet the demands of odd-lot customers. There were approximately 28 individual members primarily engaged in floor trading, that is, buying and selling for their own account. Finally there were 53 inactive members. Compared with 1950, the number of floor brokers and inactive members had declined while other categories had grown modestly.

A compilation of reports filed with the New York Stock Exchange gave some information on the nature of the business of NYSE member firms. About 43 percent of total 1960 income of NYSE member firms accrued to the largest 5 percent, and only 9 percent of total 1960 income of NYSE member firms accrued to the firms in the lower half. The gross income had the following breakdown:

Commissions on NYSE	39.8%
Commissions on other exchanges	8.3
Commissions on over-the-counter sales	7.8
Trading and arbitrage	11.0
Underwriting	10.8
Interest on customer balances	13.0
Other	9.3
	100.0%

These breakdowns varied from firm to firm. Generally, New York Stock Exchange commissions were a larger proportion of total business the larger the firm and over-the-counter and trading and arbitrage accounted for a larger proportion of total business the smaller the firm. An annual survey of security commission income of NYSE members provided some additional statistical data (see Exhibits 3 and 4).

Factors Affecting the Decision

Costs of Membership

The purchase of an NYSE seat required a large initial outlay of funds. The cost of seats since 1950 had ranged from $38,000 to $225,000[7]

[7]The highest price ever paid for a membership on the exchange – $625,000 – occurred in February 1929, when there were 1100 memberships. The number of memberships was increased to 1375 in that same year and has since been reduced to 1366 by a seat retirement plan.

Exhibit 3

STEVENSON, GARNER & COMPANY

Results of 1962 Survey of Income and Expense Ratios of NYSE Member Firms

Security commission income from all sources		$1,000
Less operating expenses		
Compensation paid to others	$149	
Compensation paid to registered representatives	208	
Clerical and administrative employee costs	273	
Communications	115	
Occupancy and equipment	75	
Promotional	36	
Other expenses	54	
Total operating expenses		910
Security commission income after operating expenses		$ 90
Less allowances for "partners" compensation		82
Net profit on security commission business before income taxes		$ 8
Estimated income taxes		4
Net profit on security commission business after income taxes		$ 4

Exhibit 4

STEVENSON, GARNER & COMPANY

Survey Highlights of NYSE Member Firms

	1962	*1961*
Aggregate net profit*:		
Before income taxes	0.8%	12.0%
After extimated federal income taxes	0.4%	5.8%
Approximate industry breakeven point of daily reported exchange volume	3,700,000 shares	3,100,000 shares
Average daily reported exchange volume	3,818,077 shares	4,085,058 shares
Number of firms:		
Operating at a profit before income taxes	153	126
Operating at a loss before income taxes	193	24
Total participating in survey	346	150

*Expressed as a percentage of security commission income from all sources. Exhibit 3 shows the detail of the computation of the 1962 figure.

(see Exhibit 5). The most recent sale had been at $185,000. Mr. Stevenson estimated that the required applications to the NYSE of partners and registered representatives combined with travel, advertising, and other expenses would cost the firm about $4500. There would also be an initiation fee of $7500. Although all purchases of memberships had to be approved by the Board of Governors of the NYSE, Mr. Stevenson didn't foresee any problem in obtaining the required approval.

Exhibit 5

STEVENSON, GARNER & COMPANY

NYSE Membership Prices
for Selected Years

	High	*Low*
1920	$115,000	$ 85,000
1929	625,000	350,000
1935	140,000	65,000
1940	60,000	33,000
1945	95,000	49,000
1950	54,000	46,000
1955	90,000	80,000
1956	113,000	75,000
1957	89,000	65,000
1958	127,000	69,000
1959	157,000	110,000
1960	162,000	135,000
1961	225,000	147,000
1962	210,000	115,000

Ownership of a membership in the New York Stock Exchange would carry with it certain continuing costs. Annual costs included dues of $1500 and other annual payments and assessments of approximately $3500. In addition, Stevenson, Garner & Company would have to pay interest on any funds which it borrowed to purchase the seat. Mr. Stevenson expected the interest rate on such borrowings to be about 6 percent.

Capital Requirements

Mr. Stevenson had been advised that partnerships typically purchased NYSE seats through so-called a-b-c agreements.[8] He thought that this method was suitable for Stevenson, Garner & Company. By this method the partnership advanced the necessary funds to one of the

[8]An "a-b-c agreement" derived its name from three options provided for when the firm dissolved, the member died or retired, or when something else occurred to terminate the agreement. The member might then (a) retain the membership and pay to the firm the amount necessary to purchase another membership, (b) sell his membership and pay the proceeds over to the partnership, or (c) transfer his membership for a nominal sum to a person designated by the firm and satisfactory for membership to the Board of Governors of the exchange.

partners who became a member, releasing him from any obligation to repay the funds except under the terms of the agreement. Although the seat remained a personal franchise of the member, the risk of fluctuation was shared by the other partners in proportion to their interests in the firm.

Mr. Stevenson did not think it desirable for the firm to finance internally the entire purchase of an NYSE membership. He believed that it was advisable for Stevenson, Garner & Company to maintain a substantial cash balance to protect against contingencies. In addition, he thought that a cash purchase of the seat would reduce the "net capital"[9] of the partnership to an undesirable level. He anticipated that it would be possible for Stevenson, Garner & Company to obtain a subordinated loan at 6 percent for an amount up to $100,000 for the purchase of an NYSE membership.

Mr. Stevenson estimated the net capital of the partnership as of early 1963 at about $275,000. If the partnership used its own funds for about one half the outlay and obtained a subordinated loan for the remainder, the amount of free capital would be reduced to about $175,000; and after deduction of the minimum net capital of $50,000, the net excess capital would approximate $125,000. Since NYSE regulations provided that underwriting commitments could not exceed three times this amount, Stevenson, Garner & Company would be able to handle up to $375,000 in underwriting commitments. However, Mr. Stevenson thought that the exchange did not like to see one of its member organizations commit itself to the very limit since any drop in market value of the securities would have the effect of causing a violation. Therefore he decided that the size of underwriting commitment which the firm could handle was somewhat less than three times the net excess capital. He was bothered by the fact that a few of the underwriting deals of Stevenson, Garner & Company in the past two years had approached this amount and felt that if Stevenson, Garner & Company had to turn away a large underwriting deal, it could have a detrimental effect on future business. Mr. Stevenson expected that over the coming years the net capital of the partnership and hence the underwriting capacity would be restored by earnings. However, he knew that repayment of the loan and distributions to partners would retard this process.

NYSE Commissions

Commissions on transactions involving securities listed on the NYSE were based on the amount of money involved in the transactions.

[9]All member organizations had to maintain a "net capital" of at least $50,000. In the computation of this capital the value of the seats possessed by partners and the fixed assets were not considered. Readily marketable securities were valued from 70 percent of their market value for common stocks to 100 percent for U.S. government bonds having less than one year to maturity.

A simplified method of computing NYSE commissions was as follows:

Size of Transaction	*Commission*
Under $100	As mutually agreed
$100 – $400	2% + $3
$400 – $2400	1% + $7
$2400 – $5000	½% + $19
$5000 and over	1/10% + $39

Note: Minimum of $6 when amount involved is over $100; maximum of $75, provided the number of shares does not exceed 100.

As a nonmember of the NYSE, Stevenson, Garner & Company had to pay the same commission charges on NYSE transactions that any other nonmember (whether a broker or an individual customer) paid if he placed the order directly with a member. Mr. Stevenson thought that competition prevented his firm from charging its customers any more commission on NYSE business than the rate charged by a member. Thus, the gross income of Stevenson, Garner & Company from transactions involving securities listed on the NYSE equalled the commissions it paid to the member, notwithstanding the commissions of its own salesmen and other expenses incurred in securing and transacting the business.

The transactions were profitable to the NYSE member transacting the business and receiving the commissions. In order to obtain this business it was common in the securities business for an NYSE member to enter into a reciprocal business arrangement with a nonmember broker. Stevenson, Garner & Company and its correspondent had such an arrangement.

Under the reciprocal business arrangement the correspondent returned commission business to Stevenson, Garner & Company. This was accomplished chiefly by placing business on the Pacific Coast Stock Exchange with Stevenson, Garner & Company, which was a member of that exchange. In addition, the correspondent occasionally placed orders with Stevenson, Garner & Company for unlisted securities. This reciprocal business was placed under an arrangement involving reciprocal ratios of 2 to 1. That is, the correspondent directed $1 in commissions to Stevenson, Garner & Company for each $2 commission received. Thus, Stevenson, Garner & Company was receiving effectively 50 percent of the gross commissions on its NYSE business.[10] The correspondent also provided Stevenson, Garner & Company with free special services. These included the installation and maintenance of wire services, special research, and some promotional materials and displays.

Mr. Stevenson did not think it economically feasible for a Los

[10]There were, of course, certain costs connected with transacting the reciprocal business on the Pacific Coast Stock Exchange. These were small, according to Mr. Stevenson.

Angeles firm the size of Stevenson, Garner & Company to establish its own execution and clearance facilities.[11] Therefore, if Stevenson, Garner & Company became a member of the NYSE, he planned to continue to channel exchange orders through a member firm that possessed these facilities. He also thought that it would be desirable to continue the other special services which Stevenson, Garner & Company was presently receiving. Mr. Stevenson knew that as a member of the NYSE, Stevenson, Garner would be able to negotiate more favorable arrangements with its correspondent. The firm's correspondent had already expressed a willingness to accept an arrangement whereby Stevenson, Garner & Company would receive 60 percent of the commissions on its NYSE business rather than the present 50 percent. In addition, the costs of transacting reciprocal business would be eliminated. He thought that it might be possible to locate a correspondent, which would allow Stevenson, Garner & Company to retain 75 percent of the commissions on its NYSE business. However, he was uncertain of the quantity and quality of the free services that might be obtained in such an arrangement. (Exhibit 6 shows some computations that he performed to see what differences such arrangements would have made in past years.)

Exhibit 6

STEVENSON, GARNER & COMPANY

Share of NYSE Commissions
Under Various Assumptions

	1958	*1959*	*1960*	*1961*	*1962*
Total NYSE commissions	$72,267	$83,437	$96,712	$110,031	$98,421
Stevenson, Garner & Company share:					
50–50 (Existing Split)	36,134	41,719	48,356	55,016	49,211
60–40	43,360	50,062	58,027	66,019	59,053
75–25	54,200	62,578	72,534	82,523	73,816
Net advantage over existing split of:					
60–40	7,226	8,343	9,671	11,003	9,842
75–25	18,066	20,859	24,178	27,507	24,605

Prestige

Mr. Richard Stevenson thought that there was a large amount of prestige connected with membership in the New York Stock Exchange

[11] In order to execute a trade on the NYSE without the assistance of another member, a member firm had to have a direct wire to a partner on the floor acting as a floor broker. In order to clear a trade executed on the exchange without the assistance of another member firm, a member had to have a "back office" operating within a reasonable distance of the exchange to facilitate delivery.

and that this prestige could be beneficial to Stevenson, Garner & Company in several ways. First of all, he believed that NYSE membership would result in an increase in brokerage business, since the general public seemed to have more confidence in dealing with a firm which was a member of the NYSE. Through conversations with two recent purchasers of memberships, he had learned that the brokerage business of each had increased with membership. The commissions on the NYSE brokerage business which the firm had handled in the last five years had been:

1958	$ 72,267
1959	$ 83,437
1960	$ 96,712
1961	$110,031
1962	$ 98,421

(Under the existing reciprocal business arrangement Stevenson, Garner & Company had *received only half* of these amounts.) Mr. Stevenson felt that 1962 had been an unusual year in the securities business, which had resulted from excesses in the markets in late 1961 and early 1962. This was followed by a sharp drop later in 1962. He thought that Stevenson, Garner & Company should be able to resume the 15 percent annual growth rate in NYSE brokerage business which it had been maintaining previous to 1962. Since NYSE brokerage business did not seem to be as vulnerable as other types of business during poorer times, Mr. Stevenson thought it particularly desirable for Stevenson, Garner & Company to increase its NYSE business.

Second, Mr. Stevenson thought that the prestige of NYSE membership would be helpful in attracting personnel. In mid-1962 he had attempted unsuccessfully to hire an experienced registered representative who had moved to Los Angeles. In his opinion, one of the main reasons for his failure had been that Stevenson, Garner & Company did not have an NYSE membership.

Finally, Mr. Stevenson believed that the prestige of an NYSE membership would be beneficial to Stevenson, Garner & Company in terms of its relationships with the rest of the financial community. It seemed to him that by purchasing a seat on the NYSE a local firm could gain national recognition. He thought, for example, that as a member firm, Stevenson, Garner & Company would be invited by members of the investment banking community to participate in an increased number of underwriting syndicates.

Other Considerations

Mr. Stevenson had been told that membership in the NYSE would require additional record keeping and reports and that it would make Stevenson, Garner & Company subject to additional regulation. He had been told by other members that the exchange conceived of its regulatory role very broadly and that it regarded virtually all aspects of its members' business as being within the sphere of its concern.

Mr. Stevenson considered the purchase of NYSE membership to be a major decision. He thought that an NYSE membership should be viewed as a franchise and did not think that it was something that should be bought and sold as the market for NYSE seats rose and fell. He believed that the purchase of a seat could have many complications and felt that possibly one of his partners might object to taking on what was certainly added risk. He thought it entirely possible that NYSE membership could cause some serious differences of opinion within the partnership that otherwise might be avoided.

DEALERS IN UNITED STATES GOVERNMENT SECURITIES

This note[1] is devoted to government securities dealers. It begins with a definition of a dealer and an explanation of his relationship with the Federal Reserve. The limitations on generalizations about dealers are pointed out. It also contains a discussion of some characteristics of dealers – most significantly, their positions and financing. Since the cases to be used in conjunction with this note concern a nonbank dealer, the focus throughout the discussion of government securities dealers is on nonbank dealers.

Practically all trading in United States government securities takes place in the over-the-counter market, although the bond issues are listed on the New York Stock Exchange. Anyone may act as a dealer in this over-the-counter market if he has clients who are willing to execute their purchase and sales orders through his firm. There are certain limiting factors, however. One important limiting factor comes from the financial side. That is, a dealer has to have access to a sufficiently large amount of financing to carry his inventory of securities. A second limiting factor comes from the Federal Reserve. Although anyone may act as a dealer, to do so without "approval" from the Federal Reserve System has certain disadvantages. First of all, only "approved" dealers are invited to trade with the system account. (It has been estimated that the volume of transactions in bills between the system and the dealers averages as high as 5 percent of the aggregate bill volume of the market during some years.) Second, only "approved" nonbank dealers are allowed to enter into repurchase agreements with the Federal Reserve. (Such repurchase agreements have provided as much as 70 percent of total financing for one nonbank dealer in recent years.)

[1]Compiled September 1964.

As of September 1964, twenty-one firms were acting as dealers with "approval" from the Federal Reserve. These included six departments of large New York or Chicago banks and fifteen other firms who were involved in various phases of the securities business. Dealers maintain trading markets in treasury issues. They buy and sell for their own account and risk. Not all dealers trade in all issues, but all government securities dealers are willing to buy and sell some range of maturities —frequently in large amounts—at the prices which they quote over the telephone. As a group, the dealers are the principal (at times the only) market for outstanding treasury issues at quoted prices. They are thereby essential to an orderly market.

Payment for and delivery of government securities takes place on the next full business day following the day of the transaction, except in instances where the dealer and the investor have agreed on settlement the same day, termed a "cash" transaction, or on some later day, termed a "delayed delivery" transaction. An increasing proportion of the business in shorter government securities is being done for "cash." This development has been made possible by the physical proximity of the securities to the actual trading offices of the dealer firms, the nearness of each firm to the others, and the efficiency of the wire transfer facilities of the Federal Reserve System.

Aside from their transactions in the government securities market, there are few similarities among the dealers. Some dealers are banks; some participate in underwriting; some are members of the New York Stock Exchange; some are active in the acceptance market; and some deal in municipal, agency, and international bank bonds. These varied activities help assure a close relationship between the government market and other money and capital markets. They also create problems for comparing individual dealers.

Although government securities dealers have played an extremely important role in United States money and capital markets, particularly since World War II, virtually no information on their activities was available until the late 1950s. In 1956 *Federal Reserve Operations in the Money and Government Securities Markets* was published by the Federal Reserve Bank of New York, and in 1960 *A Study of the Dealer Market for Federal Government Securities* was prepared for the Joint Economic Committee of Congress. These two sources contained a large portion of the published material which was available as of September 1964. In addition, each week the Federal Reserve Bank of New York publishes composite figures on dealer positions, trading volume, and financing.[2] These figures also appear in the *Federal Reserve Bulletin*.

Dealers take positions in the various issues of marketable govern-

[2]Since mid-1960 the government securities dealers have been cooperating in a statistical program that includes the daily reporting of their positions, financing, and transactions to the market statistics department of the Federal Reserve Bank of New York.

ment securities. Not every dealer takes a position in every single issue; in some cases the dealer holds a "zero" position. A dealer's position (inventory) can be either positive or negative. Dealers typically maintain positive inventories of securities which allow them to accommodate purchase orders of customers. However, in some issues a dealer may take a short position at times. That is, he may sell a security which he does not own.[3] Positions are usually largest when interest rates are relatively high and are expected to fall; conversely, when interest rates are relatively low and are expected to rise, dealer positions are usually smallest.

At times some dealers maintain an investment account in addition to the regular trading position. The investment account is carefully separated, for tax purposes, from the dealer's trading position. It contains those securities (if any) in which the dealer has taken positions with the object of establishing a base for long-term capital gains. Securities which are placed in the investment account are not available for trading purposes. However, it is possible to terminate investment account transactions if the expected price change fails to develop. In aggregate, most dealers do not take large speculative positions in government securities for capital gain, and thus investment accounts (when they exist) are very small compared with the regular trading positions.

As of 1964, trading volume in the government securities market was larger than the volume of transactions on any of the organized securities exchanges. The volume figures released by the Federal Reserve include all outright purchases and sales. They do not include repurchase and resale agreements since these are not outright transactions. The customers of U.S. government securities dealers are, in order of importance, commercial banks, other financial institutions, nonfinancial corporations, the Federal Reserve System, and other government securities dealers.

Government securities dealers rely heavily on short-term borrowings to finance their positions.[4] Basically three main types of financing are used: collateral loans (a type of financing under which the dealer retains title to the securities but transfers the securities to the lender or his agent as collateral for the loan), repurchase agreements (an arrangement under which the dealer actually sells the securities but simultaneously commits himself to repurchase them at a price fixed at the time of the initial transaction), and "own bank funds" (money that is allocated to the dealer department of a dealer bank by the bank itself). This third method of financing is limited to bank dealers.

---

[3]The study prepared for the Joint Economic Committee in 1960 distinguishes between "technical shorts" and "speculative shorts." Technical short positions arise from servicing customers, whereas speculative short positions are intentionally assumed by the dealer with an expectation of a fall in the price of the security involved.

[4]An article entitled "The Financing of Government Securies Dealers" appeared in the June 1964 issue of the *Monthly Review* published by the Federal Reserve Bank of New York.

The characteristics of the dealer financing mechanism make it a primary channel for the daily redistribution of short-term funds throughout the economy and a major link among the geographical and institutional sectors of the money market. Dealer financing results in heavy daily money market activity since dealers change their positions—and hence their financing requirements—every day in response to treasury financings, Federal Reserve activity, customer needs, or their own appraisal of the market. Heavy daily money market activity is further insured by the fact that a substantial portion of the dealers' borrowings matures each day.

Government securities dealers adjust both the type of financing (for example, repurchase agreement, collateral loan) and the source of financing (for example, New York bank, insurance company) in response to the relative cost and availability of funds. Nonbank dealers shift between collateral loans and repurchase agreements and among a wide variety of lenders, including New York City banks, other banks, nonfinancial corporations, agencies of foreign banks, state and local governments, insurance companies, and a number of other financial institutions. In addition, the Federal Reserve makes repurchase agreements with nonbank dealers when it deems that open market considerations make such contracts desirable. Nonbank dealers use their own capital primarily for meeting margin requirements and maintaining the minimum balances necessary to establish credit relationships with their principal banks. Bank dealers, on the other hand, tend to rely primarily on internal funds but also utilize repurchase agreements at times to attract low-cost funds from corporations and other lenders, as well as to accommodate their customers by providing them with an investment for temporarily idle funds (see Exhibit 1).

Developments in dealer financing operations have helped lead to a more rapid adjustment by the private economy to changes in the supply of money and credit. Of particular significance has been the expanded use of repurchase agreements during the postwar period. This has made small banks and nonfinancial corporations considerably more sensitive to money and credit conditions.

As we have said, nonbank dealers finance the great bulk of their inventory by borrowing. Leverage ratios are extremely high, higher than the deposit/capital ratios of commercial banks and higher than the leverage ratios of other securities dealers. This high leverage is attainable because the credit worthiness of individual dealer firms is established and because almost all loans or other financing arrangements are collateralized or guaranteed by a deposit of government securities, thus reducing the risk of loss of principal. However, margin requirements are small when and where they exist and therefore borrowing risks are not completely eliminated. For collateral loans, margin is required generally for bonds only. It reaches a high of about 3 percent on bonds with over ten

Exhibit 1

Financing of Government Securities Dealers*

(1961–1963; annual averages of daily data)

Distribution of Financing	*Amount Outstanding (millions of dollars)* 1961	1962	1963	*Share of Total Borrowing (percent)* 1961	1962	1963
TOTAL	2,712	3,364	3,558	100.0	100.0	100.0
BY SOURCE OF FUNDS:						
New York City banks	671	890	941	24.7	26.5	26.4
Other banks	612	656	763	22.6	19.5	21.4
Nonfinancial corporations	1,171	1,462	1,467	43.2	43.5	41.2
Federal Reserve	49	59	114	1.8	1.8	3.2
Other†	208	297	274	7.7	8.8	7.7
BY TYPE OF INSTRUMENT:						
Repurchase agreements	1,716	2,132	2,242	63.3	63.4	63.0
Short‡	901	1,065	1,308	33.1	31.7	36.8
Long§	815	1,067	934	30.1	31.7	26.3
Collateral loans and own bank funds	996	1,232	1,316	36.7	36.6	37.0
BY TYPE OF DEALER:						
Bank‖	502	605	714	18.5	18.0	20.1
Nonbank	2,209	2,759	2,844	81.5	82.0	80.0

Note: Because of rounding, figures do not necessarily add to totals.
*Includes short-term financing for United States government and federal agency securities.
†Includes mainly state and local governments, agencies of foreign banks, insurance companies, and other financial institutions.
‡Repurchase agreements maturing in fifteen days or less.
§Repurchase agreements maturing in sixteen days or more.
‖Includes funds raised through repurchase agreements by dealer departments to finance their positions as well as "own bank funds."

SOURCE: *Monthly Review*, June 1964, Federal Reserve Bank of New York.

years maturity. For repurchase agreements, margin requirements vary with the source of the funds. In any case they are usually smaller than those on collateral loans. Many banks require that the value of the securities deposited against the repurchase agreement exceed the value of the contract by a small amount. Others, particularly nonfinancial corporations, do not require any margin. For any given dealer the major factors which determine the maximum amount of leverage attainable are the maturity composition of his position, the type of financing used, the source of financing, and the extent to which the dealer operates in other markets.

EVALUATION OF POSITION IN SECURITIES

Pender, Wilson & Company (A)

On Friday, September 18, 1964, the four members of the senior management group of Pender, Wilson & Company met for a review of the firm's position in U. S. government securities. Pender, Wilson & Company was owned largely (75 percent) by four senior partners—Philip Wilson, 53; Robert Tyler, 36; Lowell Sullivan, 47; and Jared Pender, 62. With them was Vincent R. Levy, who had been retained recently as a consultant to the firm. In addition to talking about the size of the position which the firm should maintain, the men had planned to discuss the maturity composition of the position.

Pender, Wilson & Company was a "recognized" U.S. government securities dealer. Its only office was in the financial district of New York City. Although the firm made markets at times in U.S. government agency securities, bankers acceptances, and commercial paper, it concentrated most heavily in the market for U.S. government securities. For example, 88 percent of its 1963 trading volume consisted of transactions in U.S. government securities. (Financial statements for Pender, Wilson & Company appear as Exhibits 1 and 2.)

Shortly after two o'clock the meeting began.

PENDER: We might as well get started. I think we should begin by discussing the outlook for business activity and interest rates. Both are important considerations in determining our position.

Personally, I think the current pace of business expansion will continue through 1965, since I don't foresee any major imbalances developing. I guess this implies two basic conclusions; one, that GNP will rise another 6 percent or so in 1965 to $675 billion or more by the final quarter and two, that no great change will be called for in discretionary monetary and fiscal policies. Therefore I am anticipating a sideways move in the yield of all government securities.

I also look for more active trading on both sides of the market. To obtain a larger portion of this increased activity, I think our firm should take a slightly higher position in both long and short maturities—say around 5 to 10 percent more. Bob?

TYLER: I see it pretty much that way too. Over the next few months we'll probably have a sideways movement in interest rates and an increase in the trading volume of government securities dealers as a whole. I think it would be profitable for us to increase our total position—particularly at the long-term end—in order to get a good share of this additional trading volume. As you know, several of our better customers have expressed an expanding interest in long-term securities.

Exhibit 1

PENDER, WILSON & COMPANY (A)

Balance Sheet
August 31, 1964

Assets

Cash balances		$ 3,475,608
Securities owned (at par value):		
U.S government securities	$386,402,713	
Obligations of U.S. government agencies	37,207,278	
Other securities	5,364,932	428,974,923
Securities sold not yet delivered (at selling price)		32,786,555
Accured interest receivable		1,894,668
Other assets		4,761,091
		$471,892,845

Liabilities and Net Worth

Collateral loans payable	$221,730,000
Unsecured loans	1,250,000
Securities of the U.S. government	
Securities sold not yet purchased (at selling price)	43,874,608
Securities purchased not yet received (at purchase price)	35,298,132
Miscellaneous accounts payable and accured expenses	2,423,389
Total liabilities	$460,514,615
Net worth	11,378,230
	$471,892,845

SULLIVAN: I can't go along with such glowing predictions. In fact, I think there is a good possibility that the economy will overheat itself during the coming months and that this will lead to a downturn in early or mid-1965. There are a number of things which point to this. First of all, the Fed has permitted our money supply to grow at a faster than normal rate. Such expansion is potentially inflationary and leads inevitably to excesses. Secondly, there have been many recent attempts to increase prices and wages. Not all of these have been successful, of course, but undoubtedly more attempts will be on the way. The generous wage settlement just signed by Chrysler may be an indication of what lies ahead. Finally, I'm concerned that the present high level of production and the anticipation of price increases, material shortages, and possible labor troubles will lead business to stockpile inventory. This inevitably leads to an inflationary spiral.

All of these factors invite monetary restraint. With higher interest rates we would incur a higher financing cost for any given position. In addition, there would be a simultaneous decline in the value of our inventory. Therefore I think we should consider reducing our present position. Since the prices of long-term securities are more sensitive to interest rate changes,

Exhibit 2

PENDER, WILSON & COMPANY (A)

Positions in U.S. Government Securities, Sept. 11, 1964

(Par value; in thousands of dollars)

Treasury Bills

Maturity Date	*Long*	*Short*	*Maturity Date*	*Long*	*Short*
Sept. 17, 1964			Jan. 7, 1965	1,806	
Sept. 24, 1964	479		Jan. 14, 1965	2	
Sept. 30, 1964			Jan. 21, 1965	1,492	
Oct. 1, 1964	2,503		Jan. 28, 1965	770	
Oct. 8, 1964	1,751		Jan. 31, 1965		
Oct. 15, 1964		212	Feb. 4, 1965	23	
Oct. 22, 1964	5,200		Feb. 11, 1965	1,769	
Oct. 29, 1964	9,772		Feb. 18, 1965	458	
Oct. 31, 1964	450		Feb. 25, 1965	2,378	
Nov. 5, 1964		12,335	Feb. 28, 1965	4,207	
Nov. 12, 1964	2,007		Mar. 4, 1965	7,212	
Nov. 19, 1964	26,880		Mar. 11, 1965	8,714	
Nov. 26, 1964	37,480		Mar. 31, 1965		
Nov. 30, 1964			Apr. 30, 1965		
Dec. 3, 1964	47,613		May 31, 1965		
Dec. 10, 1964	77,508		June 30, 1965		
Dec. 17, 1964	2,670		July 31, 1965		
Dec. 24, 1964	2,439		Aug. 31, 1965		
Dec. 31, 1964	3,588				
Total				249,171	12,547

Treasury Notes

Coupon Rate	*Maturity Date*	*Long*	*Short*
4 5/8	5/15/65		2,375
3 7/8	5/15/65	4,207	
3 7/8	8/13/65	1,542	
3 1/2	11/15/65	2,105	
3 7/8	2/15/66	4,716	
3 5/8	2/15/66	16,446	
1 1/2	4/1/66		3,000
1 1/2	10/1/66	2,701	
3 3/4	8/15/67	825	
Total		32,542	5,375

Exhibit continued.

we must be even more cautious in this area. So it would probably be a particularly good idea to get rid of some of our long-terms.

WILSON: My business forecast is less optimistic than yours Jared, and less pessimistic than yours, Lowell. I look for the present business expan-

Exhibit 2 (Continued)

Coupon Rate	Treasury Bonds Maturity Date	Long	Short
3 3/4	5/15/66		1,000
3 3/8	11/15/66		3,500
3 7/8	5/15/68	4,253	
3 3/4	8/15/68	6,786	
2 1/2	6/15/69–64	5,109	
4	10/1/69	11,673	
2 1/2	12/15/69–64	20,806	
2 1/2	3/15/71–66		4,753
3 7/8	11/15/71		50
4	8/15/72	8,263	
2 1/2	9/15/72–67		17,701
4	8/15/73	16,805	
4 1/8	11/16/73	23,784	
3 7/8	11/15/74		75
3 1/4	6/15/83–78	4,588	
4 1/4	2/15/90	1,000	
4	2/15/93–88		1,000
4 1/8	5/15/94–89	1,985	
3 1/2	11/15/98	3,612	
		108,664	28,079
RECAP OF POSITION			
Bills		249,171	12,547
Notes		32,542	5,375
Bonds		108,664	28,079
		390,377	46,001

sion to continue through the end of 1965 but at a progressively slower rate as time rolls by. I expect that we'll have a continuation of the generally easy credit conditions that have been maintained during this upswing. In the next few weeks, however, we may have a slight seasonal rise in interest rates as inventories are built up. Neglecting this minor seasonal fluctuation, I agree with you (Bob and Jared) that a sideways movement in interest rates seems highly probable for the next few months. I think there will be particular stability in long-term rates since the active participation by the Fed and the Treasury in the bond market should continue to reduce the importance of normal supply and demand factors. In other words, it looks as if the administered feature of the market will continue.

I'm not convinced, however, that there will be any change in the trading volume in government securities. It hasn't varied much over the last couple of years, you know. Therefore, I can't see any real reason why we should change either the size or mix of our total position. If anything, it seems to me that it might be wise to reduce our position in government securities —both at the long-term end where we are subject to the greatest amount of price risk and at the short-term end where the financing costs presently exceed the interest received on securities held. What's your view on all this, Mr. Levy?

LEVY: It's hard to quarrel with the forecasts which you have made. I might add a couple of factors which you all are aware of but which haven't been mentioned explicitly. First of all, the supply of floating securities[1] is higher than it's ever been. I don't think we're near the panic stage yet but it does have inflationary tendencies. And as Lowell said earlier, such tendencies may bring about monetary restraint and higher interest rates. Secondly, there has been a recent weakness in the mortgage market. This has been caused both by a slowdown in construction and by a steady increase in loanable funds. If this surplus of funds continues it will exert an upward pressure on rates.

I'd like to start talking about how your position fits into the picture. It seems to me that it should be used to meet your objectives. Perhaps we should begin with a definition of those objectives.

PENDER: I feel that Pender, Wilson & Company is in business for two reasons—to provide a service and to earn a profit. In order to be successful—as we have been in the past—we must continue to do both. Although it is difficult to attach precise weights to the importance of each objective, we shouldn't pursue either to the exclusion of the other.

WILSON: As I've said before, I think we should have only one objective. Otherwise conflicts between objectives will arise. The overriding objective which Pender, Wilson & Company should be following is to be as profitable as possible. We don't make money by just being friendly, courteous, and kind to customers. A customer, whether a corporation, a bank, or another dealer, is valuable to Pender, Wilson & Company only if we can make profitable deals with him. I am interested in profits!

LEVY: It would be helpful to me if you would explain precisely what you mean by profits.

WILSON: When I speak of profits, I mean simply revenues less expenses. The present form of our income statement divides profits into four categories: (1) trading profits; (2) profits from the investment account; (3) carry[2] on securities in which we have held or are holding positions; and (4) net income from all other sources.

LEVY: I would imagine that we all agree that the breakdown is of little significance. For example, if Pender, Wilson & Company can improve its carry by an action which reduces its trading profits by a lesser amount it should not hesitate to take that action. The main thing is to make total profits as large as possible.

PENDER: That sounds reasonable.

SULLIVAN: I'd like to get back to Phil's statement. It sounded to me like a very short-run view. How do you think the Fed would view such a short-run profit oriented policy? Pender, Wilson & Company lives on its reputation as a market maker. Obviously profits are important; however, we are well advised at times to take losses in order to maintain a market and to service customers. This is necessary to create lasting relationships between Pender, Wilson & Company and its customers. The irregular trading

---

[1]Floating securities was a term usually attached to the sum of all U.S. government securities with less than one year to maturity and commercial paper.

[2]Carry = interest received on securities held and interest paid to finance the securities held. It is possible to have a "negative carry" as well as a "positive carry."

pattern which you are suggesting would cause a loss of contact with customers. Lasting relationships with customers are the very thing necessary to enable us to be profitable over the long run. And this is what I think we should be striving for.

WILSON: I agree that it is long run profitability with which we should concern ourselves. But do you really believe that the government securities market allows any lasting relationships between customers and dealer firms? Hasn't shopping around become so prevalent in recent years that customers can be serviced only on a price basis? And if customers can no longer be serviced on a constant market making basis, it seems to me that our need for carrying a large position for trading positions is reduced. And a decrease in this position would, of course, also enable us to reduce risk. . . .

TYLER: Please excuse the interruption. But I'd like to share with you a calculation which relates to risk. To get a crude measure of risk, I took our inventory as of last Friday and computed the change in value of the inventory that would result from a change of 1/10 of 1 percent in the entire yield curve (see Exhibit 4). If interest rates fell by this amount, the market value of our inventory would increase by about $769,000. You will note that I have not included Treasury bills in my calculations. This saved a lot of time and shouldn't have much effect on the result since bill prices would scarcely change for such a small change in interest rates. For example, there would be a change in value of about $50 per $100,000 of new 182 day bills for a change in yield of 1/10 of 1 percent. For a $250 million inventory this would be $125,000. However, all of our bills mature in less than 182 days and most of them mature much sooner. Thus the change in the value of our bill inventory would probably be substantially less than $50,000. If interest rates should rise by 1/10 of 1 percent, then the $769,000 figure would represent the decrease in market value of our inventory. As I have already said, I do not expect any rise in interest rates. Nevertheless, it is important to recognize the risk which does exist, so that we can deal with it more intelligently. I think these calculations emphasize the fact that we can have a big change in the value of our inventory as a result of a small change in interest rates.

WILSON: I'd like to offer some observations on your calculations if I might.

TYLER: Please do.

WILSON: Risk is a tricky, but important problem with which we must deal. I think your approach is a good one. You have made some assumptions and then put a dollar figure on the result. However, it seems to me that these computations overlook a couple of things—namely, the financing costs and the interest earned on the securities in our position.

Since change in the level of interest rates is likely to affect our financing costs in addition to the value of our inventory of securities, this means risk is underestimated by these calculations. For example, when there is a rise in the level of interest rates, Pender, Wilson & Company incurs higher financing costs in addition to the reduction in the value of its inventory of securities. These higher financing costs are felt almost instantly because most of our financing arrangements are of such a short duration.

I also think that the interest earned on our inventory of securities should be taken into account. It diminishes the risk to some extent. We all know that a long-term security has a greater price risk than a short-term security. But let's not neglect the fact that the higher return of the long-term securities offsets some of this risk.

Exhibit 3

PENDER, WILSON & COMPANY (A)

Risk Exposure for Long Position
September 11, 1964

Treasury Notes	*Par Value ($000s)*	*Bid Price*	*Approximate Change in Price Caused by 0.10 Change in Yield*	*Approximate Change in Market Value (in Actual $)*
3⅞ 5/15/65	4,207	100.1	0.07	2,945
3⅞ 8/13/65	1,542	100.1	0.09	1,387
3½ 11/15/65	2,105	99.19	0.11	2,316
3⅞ 2/15/66	4,716	99.30	0.13	6,131
3⅝ 2/15/66	16,446	99.20	0.14	23,024
1½ 10/1/66	2,701	96.7	0.20	5,402
3¾ 8/15/67	825	99.10	0.28	2,310
Treasury Bonds				
3⅞ 5/15/68	4,253	99.15	0.34	14,460
3¾ 8/15/68	6,786	98.29	0.37	25,108
2½ 6/15/69–64	5,109	93.21	0.41	20,943
4 10/1/69	11,673	99.18	0.45	52,529
2½ 12/15/69–64	20,806	93.0	0.46	95,707
4 8/15/72	8,263	98.28	0.64	52,883
4 8/15/73	16,805	98.13	0.74	124,357
4⅛ 11/16/73	23,784	99.11	0.74	176,002
3¼ 6/15/83–78	4,588	87.20	1.20	55,056
3½ 2/15/90	1,000	88.30	1.47	14,700
4⅛ 5/15/94–89	1,985	98.4	1.67	33,150
3½ 11/15/98	3,612	88.8	1.68	60,682
				$769,092

SULLIVAN: These figures make no mention of our short position and therefore don't give the whole picture. For example, when there is a rise in the level of interest rates, the value of our inventory is decreased only in those securities in which we have a long position. For those securities in which we are short we would have an increase in the value of our inventory. Let me explain my reasoning. Wherever we have a short position, we have sold securities which we did not own. In order to deliver these securities we must borrow them from someone who does own them. Someday we will have to return these securities. A higher interest rate means that the dollar value of what we must repay is less. Thus we would have a gain resulting from those securities in which we were short. This should be taken into account in some way.

TYLER: I agree with you completely, Lowell. I have computed the immediate gain or loss that would accrue to Pender, Wilson & Company from its short positions on September 11 if there were a change of 1/10 of 1 percent in interest rates (Exhibit 5). In the event that the interest rates rose we would have a gain in all those securities where we held short position. If interest rates fell we would of course have a loss. I had not bothered to consolidate these calculations with the others although I think your suggestion to do so is a good one.

Exhibit 4

PENDER, WILSON & COMPANY (A)

Risk Exposure for Short Position

Treasury Notes	*Par Value ($000s)*	*Bid Price*	*Approximate Change in Price Caused by 0.10 Change in Yield*	*Approximate Change in Market Value (in Actual $)*
4 5/8 5/16/65	2,375	100.17	0.07	1,663
1 1/2 4/1/66	3,000	97.5	0.15	4,500
Treasury Bonds				
3 3/4 5/15/66	1,000	99.26	0.17	1,700
3 3/8 11/15/66	3,500	98.31	0.21	7,350
2 1/2 3/15/71–66	4,753	92.19	0.47	22,339
3 7/8 11/15/71	50	98.7	0.60	300
2 1/2 9/15/72–67	17,701	89.22	0.64	113,286
3 7/8 11/15/74	75	97.4	0.80	600
4 2/15/93–88	1,000	96.22	1.64	16,400
				$168,138

PENDER: It seems to me that all these ideas on risk are important ones. In fact, I think that our own feelings about risk should be major factors in determining the size and composition of our position. I want to thank you, Bob, for your extra work and let you know that we appreciate it.

LEVY: I don't want to sidetrack the discussion—but I have an idea which I'd like to throw out at this point.

PENDER: Please do.

LEVY: Perhaps we can discuss it in some detail at a later date. It hinges upon finding a suitable measure for the risk which accompanies any given position. I will use the term *risk exposure* to mean sensitivity to an interest rate change. Based on comments made earlier this afternoon, I conclude that there would be at least some support for taking the following into account in measuring risk exposure: securities in which you have a long position, securities in which you have a short position, interest received on securities held, and financing costs. Perhaps we'll come up with others.

My idea is this—given an acceptable means of measuring risk exposure, wouldn't it be possible to use the risk exposure concept more precisely in determining the size and mix of your position? Thinking out loud, let's see how this might work. To begin with, you would have to select an interest rate change. Bob used 1/10 of 1 percent in his calculations, but there's nothing particularly magical about that figure. You could use whatever existing conditions seemed to warrant. You would then have to specify a tolerable level of risk exposure for the interest rate change which you selected. The level of risk exposure would be given in dollars and could also vary in accordance with the conditions of the times. For example, in times of great uncertainty you might want to reduce substantially the level of risk exposure. Obviously, there are an infinite number of positions which would have a level of risk exposure that would be less than the amount that you selected as being tolerable. There would also be an infinite number of positions that would exceed the specified level of risk exposure. This latter group could be eliminated as possible positions for your firm. Perhaps your position at the time of analysis would exceed the tolerable level of risk exposure. This would give you a direction in which to move. Or, if your position had a level of risk exposure which was considerably less than the tolerable level, you would probably want to take steps to increase its risk exposure. I think you might find such a procedure very useful, although I have numerous questions in my mind about it at this point. For example, I'm not sure how you should choose between two positions which have an equal level of risk exposure. What are your reactions to this approach, gentlemen?

SULLIVAN: I like it, but I think the size and composition of our position should take other factors into consideration as well. Maybe we should compare the level of risk exposure with the level of benefits associated with any given position. As I said earlier, I think that there are certain benefits to be derived from such things as loyal customers and the ability to keep markets active all the time. These benefits can't be measured in dollars and cents as easily as some others but they show up in the final profit figure.

TYLER: May I break in once again? I have some facts and figures to add on the subject of trading profits (Exhibit 6), which give the relationship between trading profits and each of the following factors: total profits, average position, and trading volume. It would be possible to analyze the volume and profitability of trading in more detail, say by maturity and/or security classification, but I haven't done that here. Needless to say, such a project would require a good deal of additional work. Furthermore, I'm not sure that it would be of much use in future planning, although undoubtedly it would give us a clearer picture of the past.

WILSON: Your figures are useful, Bob. If they covered a longer time span, they would demonstrate even more clearly the extent to which trading profits are influenced by changes in monetary policy. Of course, it's a little tough for us to control changes in monetary policy, although we do try to anticipate them. Pricing strategy is probably the next most important factor in determining the amount of trading profits which we can generate. This we can control! We must avoid widening the spreads between quoted bid and asked prices or customers will buy from or sell to another dealer. On the other hand, to avoid losses, we do not want to shade our prices too much. The question here is often one of trying to decide between fast nickels and slow dimes.

LEVY: The decline in trading profits which your firm has experienced is not unique. All dealers are operating within the same environment. I have prepared an estimate of trading profits for the dealers as a group for the past few years (Exhibit 7). I would appreciate it if you would keep it under your hat since it is very unofficial. My sources include the trading volume of dealers which the Fed releases, the spreads in price quotes over this period, interest rate movements, and perhaps more important than anything else, discussions with my friends in the money market. I think that the three events most responsible for the decline in dealer trading profits are: one, an increasing difficulty in predicting interest rates; two, a decrease in the size of interest rate savings; and three, keener competition for business.

SULLIVAN: Keener competition certainly is a reality! In the last five years the Fed has added four firms to the list of those with whom it trades. This, in effect, means that there are four more dealers. In addition, most of the big commercial banks are doing quite a bit of trading out of their own accounts. For most practical purposes they might as well be counted as dealers.

WILSON: Do you have any other figures on our competition, Bob? I wonder whether we have been behaving in tune with the market.

TYLER: As you know, there are a number of statements on government securities dealers as a group which the Federal Reserve makes available each week. However, none of them contain any information on profits or costs. They contain information on the size and composition of dealer positions, dealer financing, and trading volume. I have summarized this information (Exhibits 5–7) for selected dates over the past four years. For comparative purposes, I have assembled our own data (Exhibits 8–10). We report such information to the Federal Reserve and consequently are also included in the total for all government securities dealers. Since the business of every dealer differs from that of every other dealer to a greater or lesser extent, there is a comparability problem. Nevertheless, by investigating these statements, we can speculate on the conclusions that they have drawn from the economic developments over the past four years and from the economic forecasts for the coming year.

PENDER: We're running out of time. Perhaps it's just as well. I'd like some time to work with the ideas and figures which have been presented. Is it agreeable with all of you to get together early next week?

Exhibit 5

PENDER, WILSON & COMPANY (A)

Dealer Positions in U.S. Government Securities
Averages of Daily Figures
(Par value; in millions of dollars)

		By Maturity		
Week Ending	*All Maturities*	*Within 1 Year*	*1–5 Years*	*After 5 Years*
Mar. 29, 1961	1,827	1,372	313	142
	100.0	75.1	17.1	7.8
Sept. 27, 1961	2,699	2,545	130	25
	100.0	94.3	4.8	0.9
Mar. 28, 1962	3,514	3,168	244	102
	100.0	90.2	6.9	2.9

Exhibit 5 (Continued)

Week Ending	*All Maturities*	*Within 1 Year*	*1–5 Years*	*After 5 Years*
Sept. 26, 1962	3,254	2,443	506	305
	100.0	75.1	15.6	9.3
Mar. 27, 1963	3,567	2,661	493	414
	100.0	74.6	13.8	11.6
Sept. 25, 1963	3,516	2,444	246	826
	100.0	69.5	7.0	23.5
Mar. 25, 1964	2,515	2,343	252	−80
	100.0	93.2	10.0	(3.2)
June 24, 1964	3,286	3,069	80	138
	100.0	93.4	2.4	4.2
July 29, 1964	3,773	2,652	76	1,046
	100.0	70.3	2.0	27.7
Aug. 26, 1964	3.998	2,783	567	648
	100.0	89.6	14.2	16.2

Exhibit 6

PENDER, WILSON & COMPANY (A)

Financing of U.S. Government Security Dealers
Averages of Daily Figures
(In millions of dollars)

Week Ending	*All Sources*	*Commercial Banks*		*Corporations*	*All Other*
		New York	*Other*		
Mar. 29, 1961	1,816	221	482	928	184
	100.0	12.2	26.5	51.1	10.2
Sept. 27, 1961	2,621	815	731	882	193
	100.0	31.1	27.9	33.7	7.4
Mar. 28, 1962	3,383	1,009	832	1,298	244
	100.0	29.8	24.6	38.4	7.2
Sept. 26, 1962	3,261	1,014	776	1,159	312
	100.0	31.1	23.8	35.5	9.6
Mar. 27, 1963	3,547	998	1,052	1,051	447
	100.0	28.1	29.7	29.6	12.6
Sept. 25, 1963	3,646	1,275	954	1,198	219
	100.0	35.0	26.2	32.9	6.0
Mar. 25, 1964	2,819	720	589	1,138	372
	100.0	25.5	20.9	40.4	13.2
June 24, 1964	3,433	979	797	1,455	203
	100.0	28.5	23.2	42.4	5.9
July 29, 1964	3,684	919	626	1,682	457
	100.0	24.9	17.9	45.7	12.4
Aug. 26, 1964	4,182	1,005	870	1,880	427
	100.0	24.0	20.8	45.0	10.2

Exhibit 7

PENDER, WILSON & COMPANY (A)

Dealer Transactions in U.S. Government Securities
Averages of Daily Figures
(Par value; in millions of dollars)

		By Maturity				*By Type of Customer*			
Week Ending	*Total*	*Within 1 Year*	*1–5 Years*	*5–10 Years*	*After 10 Years*	*U.S. Govt. Security Dealers and Brokers*	*Other Dealers and and Brokers*	*Commercial Banks*	*All Other*
Mar. 29, 1961	1,511	1,193	198	98	20	455	18	635	403
	100.0	79.0	13.1	6.5	1.6	30.1	1.2	42.0	26.7
Sept. 27, 1961	1,588	1,300	214	44	30	410	27	706	446
	100.0	81.9	13.5	2.8	1.9	25.8	1.7	44.5	28.0
Mar. 28, 1962	1,589	1,266	203	64	57	503	33	680	373
	100.0	79.7	12.8	4.0	3.6	31.7	2.1	42.8	23.5
Sept. 26, 1962	1,799	1,308	324	130	38	604	43	662	491
	100.0	72.7	18.0	7.2	2.1	33.6	2.4	36.8	27.3
Mar. 27, 1963	1,525	1,154	213	94	65	478	35	635	377
	100.0	75.7	14.0	6.2	4.2	31.3	2.3	41.6	24.7
Sept. 25, 1963	1,274	888	135	174	77	391	30	527	327
	100.0	69.7	10.6	13.7	6.0	30.7	2.4	41.4	25.7
Mar. 25, 1964	1,627	1,264	232	90	41	542	21	619	445
	100.0	77.7	14.3	5.5	25	33.3	1.3	38.0	27.4
June 24, 1964	1,631	1,332	180	95	23	509	20	596	505
	100.0	80.7	11.0	5.8	1.4	31.2	1.2	36.5	31.1
July 29, 1964	1,390	1,136	85	120	49	396	28	512	454
	100.0	81.7	6.1	8.6	3.5	28.5	2.0	36.8	32.7
Aug. 26, 1964	1,215	950	125	111	30	379	23	451	362
	100.0	78.2	10.3	9.1	2.5	31.2	1.9	37.1	29.8

Exhibit 8

PENDER, WILSON & COMPANY (A)

Net Positions in U.S. Government Securities
Averages of Daily Figures
(Par value; in thousands of dollars)

		By Maturity		
Week Ending	*Total*	*Within 1 Year*	*1–5 Years*	*More Than 5 Years*
Mar. 29, 1961	155,326	117,436	27,959	9,931
	100.0	75.6	18.0	6.4
Sept. 27, 1961	242,671	225,951	13,078	3,642
	100.0	93.1	5.4	1.5
Mar. 28, 1961	313,947	269,834	22,886	21,227
	100.0	85.9	7.3	6.8
Sept. 26, 1961	300,889	219,949	47,453	33,487
	100.0	73.1	15.8	11.1
Mar. 27, 1963	319,602	226,460	44,425	48,717
	100.0	70.9	13.9	15.2
Sept. 25, 1963	320,118	243,756	22,024	54,338
	100.0	76.1	6.9	17.0
Mar. 25, 1964	271,763	244,383	28,325	−945
	100.0	89.9	10.4	(0.3)
June 24, 1964	290,871	268,441	7,148	15,282
	100.0	92.3	2.5	5.2
July 29, 1964	338,704	206,002	65,421	67,281
	100.0	60.8	19.3	19.9
Aug. 26, 1964	340,876	223,233	48,130	69,513
	100.0	65.5	14.1	20.4

Exhibit 9

PENDER, WILSON & COMPANY (A)

Financing of U.S. Government Securities
Averages of Daily Figures
(In thousand of dollars)

		Collateral Loans From Commercial Banks		
Week Ending	*Total*	*NYC*	*Elsewhere*	*Repurchase Agreements*
Mar. 29, 1961	152,734	11,137	44,459	97,138
	100.0	7.3	29.1	63.6
Sept. 27, 1961	238,902	64,511	73,158	101,233
	100.0	27.0	30.6	42.4
Mar. 28, 1962	307,066	71,885	85,641	149,540
	100.0	23.4	27.9	48.7

Exhibit continued.

Exhibit 9 (Continued)

Week Ending	*Total*	*NYC*	*Elsewhere*	*Repurchase Agreements*
Sept. 26, 1962	293,951	87,007	89,108	117,836
	100.0	29.6	30.3	40.1
Mar. 27, 1963	308,573	92,871	120,268	95,434
	100.0	30.1	39.0	30.9
Sept. 25, 1963	312,658	86,057	110,680	115,921
	100.0	27.5	35.4	37.1
Mar. 25, 1964	265,515	56,431	61,895	147,189
	100.0	21.3	23.3	55.4
June 24, 1964	282,727	66,139	73,907	142,681
	100.0	23.4	26.1	50.5
July 29, 1964	328,548	72,281	86,746	169,521
	100.0	22.0	26.4	51.6
Aug. 26, 1964	330,547	76,032	86,274	168,241
	100.0	23.0	26.1	50.9

Exhibit 10

PENDER, WILSON & COMPANY (A)

Transactions in U.S. Government Securities
Averages of Daily Figures
(Par value; in thousands of dollars)

		By Maturity		
Week Ending	*Total*	*Within 1 Year*	*1–5 Years*	*More Than 5 Years*
Mar. 29, 1961	130,739	104,086	17,921	8,732
	100.0	79.6	13.7	16.7
Sept. 27, 1961	145,645	119,457	12,740	13,448
	100.0	82.0	8.7	9.2
Mar. 28, 1962	153,151	110,632	17,943	24,576
	100.0	72.2	11.7	16.0
Sept. 26, 1962	168,866	118,223	34,787	15,856
	100.0	70.0	20.6	19.4
Mar. 27, 1963	118,952	84,475	17,369	17,108
	100.0	71.0	14.6	15.4
Sept. 25, 1963	120,840	91,781	12,488	16,571
	100.0	76.0	10.3	13.7
Mar. 25, 1964	165,138	131,666	24,821	8,651
	100.0	79.7	15.0	5.2
June 24, 1964	114,774	83,672	18,718	12,384
	100.0	72.9	16.3	10.8
July 29, 1964	169,159	100,980	57,742	10,437
	100.0	59.7	34.1	6.2
Aug. 26, 1964	114,346	80,383	16,381	17,582
	100.0	70.3	14.3	15.4

BIDDING FOR TREASURY BILLS

Pender, Wilson & Company (B)

On September 21, 1964, Mr. Jared Pender and Mr. Robert Tyler were preparing tenders for Pender, Wilson & Company for 91-day treasury bills which would be issued September 24, 1964, and would mature on December 24, 1964. Mr. Pender was the head trader and confined this tracking activity to treasury bills. Mr. Tyler was in charge of the money desk. He had ultimate responsibility for the financing of his firm's position and therefore was especially conversant with current money market conditions.

During the previous week the secretary of the treasury had issued a notice inviting tenders for this issue.[1] Tenders were to be received at the Federal Reserve Banks or branches thereof up to 1:30 P.M., Eastern Daylight Saving Time, on Monday, September 21, 1964.

Mechanics of the Treasury-Bill Auction

Two types of tenders were used for treasury-bill auctions—competitive and noncompetitive tenders. Noncompetitive tenders for amounts up to $200,000 in the aggregate were always accepted and were awarded at the average price of accepted competitive tenders. Pender, Wilson & Company did not submit noncompetitive bids because for many years the firm had been bidding for amounts much greater than $200,000.

Competitive tenders gave the dollar amounts desired at various prices. (The prices had to be specified to three decimal places based on 100.000.) Thus, the bidder was not bidding for one quantity at one price *or* other quantities at other prices, but was bidding for one quantity at one price *and* other quantities at other prices. Mr. Tyler believed this technique employed in the treasury-bill auction to be unique among security auctions in that the treasury discriminated not only among bidders but also among the different prices quoted by a single bidder.

The treasury in Washington made the final decision on the tenders. After alloting the noncompetitive bids, awards were made beginning with the highest bid. The lowest accepted bid was termed the "stop out" price. When the treasury found it necessary to fill only a fraction of the tenders at the "stop out" price in order to complete its financing,[2] this

[1]Tenders were also invited for 182-day treasury bills to be issued at the same time. The two men were preparing a tender for that issue also. To simplify this case, however, there is no discussion of the 182-day issue in Pender, Wilson & Company (B).

[2]The treasury was offering $1.3 billion of 91-day bills in the September 21 auction.

fraction was prorated to each bidder in proportion to the quantity bid for at the "stop out" price. The results of an auction were announced late the same day and published by the financial press on the following day.

Competitive Bids Submitted in a Treasury-Bill Auction

Pender, Wilson & Company ordinarily submitted competitive bids for a sizable amount of treasury bills in each weekly auction. The firm submitted tenders for customers for whom it was acting as agent and also submitted tenders for its own account. (Other dealers behaved similarly and thus the combined dealer allotments had frequently run as high as one quarter of the total issue.)

Bidding as an Agent

Mr. Pender and Mr. Tyler had classified into three groups the customers for whom their firm bid as agent. This classification system was based on how the bid price was determined; that is, some granted Pender, Wilson & Company total discretion, some set certain limits, and some granted no discretion at all. In all cases, the ultimate purchaser (the individual or corporation for whom Pender, Wilson & Company served as agent) specified the quantity of bills to bid for. Thus, the classification scheme was as follows:

	Bid Quantity Determined by:	Bid Price Determined by:
Group 1	Customer	Pender, Wilson & Company
Group 2	Customer	Pender, Wilson & Company (within limits set by customer)
Group 3	Customer	Customer

Only a few customers could be classified in Group 3. They were usually major corporations who employed experts who were well versed in the government securities market and preferred to stipulate their own bid prices and quantities. Since the treasury required a 2 percent deposit on all tenders except those submitted by "recognized" dealers or commercial banks, these corporations could avoid this deposit by placing their bids through Pender, Wilson & Company. With such an arrangement they could wait longer, in many cases, before deciding on their tender prices and quantities since they could submit their tenders by a telephone call to their agent rather than by a physical delivery to the Federal Reserve Bank. They could also avoid any expense or inconvenience that might be associated with this activity. Although these corporations bought treasury bills in the auction on a fairly regular basis, only on very rare occasions did any of them submit any bids through Pender,

Wilson & Company. Mr. Pender and Mr. Tyler believed that most of these corporations submitted their bids through bank dealers because Pender, Wilson & Company and most, if not all, of the other nonbank dealers charged one basis point for this service.

Mr. Tyler noted that only in an occasional instance did a customer give limited discretion (Group 2) to Pender, Wilson & Company for submitting a tender for its account.[3] He believed that those customers who might be inclined to specify ceilings in their instructions kept in close contact with the treasury-bill market. This included conversations with personnel at Pender, Wilson & Company and other dealers on the days of treasury-bill auctions. Therefore these customers were able to get a close approximation of the bid price which Pender, Wilson & Company would submit before they gave the firm permission to use its discretion. As a result, they felt no necessity for settting limits on the bid price submitted on its behalf. Thus, Mr. Tyler thought that customers, who by their own thinking belonged in Group 2, were classified in Group 1 according to the classification method used by Pender, Wilson & Company.

Almost all of the bids which Pender, Wilson & Company submitted as an agent were in Group 1. Customers specified the amount of bills (bid quantity) on which they desired and allowed Pender, Wilson & Company to determine the bid price. Mr. Pender thought that customers submitted their bids through Pender, Wilson & Company for one or more of the following reasons: no deposit was required with their bids; it was easier and/or cheaper to submit bids in this way; Pender, Wilson & Company had exceptional judgment in the treasury-bill market; the customer did not follow the treasury-bill market closely.

Bidding for Own Account

Ordinarily Pender, Wilson & Company bid each week for a sizable amount of treasury bills for its own account. Since the bills awarded in a Monday auction did not have to be picked up and paid for[4] at the Federal Reserve Banks until Thursday, Pender, Wilson & Company had two full trading days and part of another in which to sell its new bills or to "swap" them against maturing bills before it had to put up any money at all. Mr. Pender believed that this additional leverage, as well as the short maturity of treasury bills, helped explain the fact that trading in treasury bills at times represented as much as seventy percent of the dollar volume of all trading in government securities.

---

[3]An example of such an instruction was: "Bid for $50,000 of 91-day bills for my account. Use your own discretion in determining the bid price, but do not bid higher than 99.100."

[4]Payments had to be made in either cash or maturing bills.

Types of Competitive Bids Submitted

Pender, Wilson & Company used three classifications to describe the differences in the competitive bids that the firm submitted—"to be sure" bids, "speculative" bids, and "throw away" bids.[5]

Pender, Wilson & Company usually submitted a "to be sure" bid on behalf of customers for whom it was acting as agent. In addition, the firm generally bid at this level for a few bills to insure that it would be awarded at least some bills for its own account. A "to be sure" bid was tendered at a price which reflected a slight premium in order to be reasonably sure of an award. In the 1964 market Mr. Pender noted that they had usually placed their "to be sure" bids on the order or 0.005 above their estimate of the "stop out" price. These premiums were substantially less than they had been in the 1950s. Mr. Pender believed that this narrowing had taken place because the bill market, and consequently the bill auctions, had become more stable. For example, the average range between the high and low accepted bids on 91-day bills was 0.006 in August 1964, compared with 0.020 in August 1960.

Mr. Pender thought that his firm would suffer considerable embarrassment if its bid for customers was too high. On the other hand, if Pender, Wilson & Company bid too aggressively it would run the risk of having its bid rejected. In the past, when this had happened, Pender, Wilson & Company had followed one of two policies. Either the firm sold the bills to the customer at the average accepted bid price (and bought them in the secondary market), or it told the customers that it was unsuccessful in the auction and offered to buy the issue in the secondary market for the customer without commission. Mr. Pender did not like to have his firm in the position where it had to follow either of these courses of action.

Pender, Wilson & Company regularly submitted "throw away" bids. Although, by definition, the firm did not expect an award on these bids, it was not averse to having them accepted, because it would probably be able to make a quick profit by selling in the secondary market any bills awarded on "throw away" bids. Mr. Pender and Mr. Tyler both believed that as one who made a market in government securities, Pender, Wilson & Company had a responsibility to help to insure that treasury auctions were fully subscribed. "Throw away" bids helped accomplish this, they felt. In the most recent auctions of 91-day treasury bills Mr. Pender and Mr. Tyler had been submitting "throw away" bids that were between 0.020 and 0.030 below their estimate of the "stop out" price.

Bids which were neither "to be sure" bids nor "throw away" bids

[5]These classifications served solely for descriptive purposes and had no particular significance for the auction itself. This terminology was generally used in the government securities market.

were known as "speculative" bids. To formulate the "speculative" bids for Pender, Wilson & Company, Mr. Pender and Mr. Tyler estimated the "stop out" price for the auction. Since this process provided an imprecise estimate at best, they usually made this estimate in the form of a range. As an additional risk-spreading device they typically submitted their "speculative" bids on a sliding scale. From their experience with treasury-bill auctions they knew that most, if not all, of the other dealers employed this bid-splitting technique for their "speculative" bids.

Factors Influencing Bids in the September 21 Treasury-Bill Auction

The prices and quantities for which Pender, Wilson & Company bid depended on many factors. Included among the ones which Mr. Pender and Mr. Tyler considered to be most important were the aggregate supply of and demand for the issue, the demand of Pender, Wilson & Company for the issue, general economic and money market conditions, and discussions with others who were involved in the market.

Supply of the Bill Issue

Mr. Pender believed that the total amount of bills offered in the auction had some influence on bidding. The announced (by the secretary of the treasury) supply of this particular issue was "$1.3 billion, or thereabouts." It was replacing an issue of $1.2 billion. Thus, the treasury was raising $100 million of new cash. The amount of 91-day treasury bills sold in the weekly auctions had varied between $1.2 and $1.3 billion each week for the past few years.

Aggregate Demand for the Bill Issue

Mr. Pender believed that the maturity date of the bill issue had a significant effect on the demand for an issue. Investor appetite for December maturities was typically strong as corporations sought temporary use for cash accumulated to pay year-end dividends and income taxes. The particular issue with which Mr. Pender and Mr. Tyler were concerned matured on December 24, 1964. Mr. Pender expected that this issue of 91-day bills quite possibly would have a smaller demand and would sell more cheaply than the next 91-day issue—which would mature on December 31—because of "window dressing" that took place at the end of the year. That is, he felt that some investors would accept a slightly lower return (and therefore pay a higher price) to get a security which matured (turned into cash) on the last day of the year.

Mr. Tyler thought that the influence of the maturity date on the demand for a treasury bill issue was overemphasized. He pointed out that as an investment outlet for the idle short-term capital of banks, corporations, and other large investors, treasury bills had to compete with other short-term government securities and various forms of commercial paper, including banker's acceptances, and finance company paper, as well as with time certificates of deposit and repurchase agreements. He felt these instruments, particularly the latter two, created a great deal of flexibility in the money market and virtually eliminated the effect of the maturity date on the demand for a bill issue.

One of the major factors in the demand for new bills in treasury auctions for recent years had been the Federal Reserve System. The Federal Reserve System was the only participant not allowed the choice of paying for its bills in either cash or maturing bills in bill auctions. It was required to pay in maturing bills. This limited the extent of the Federal Reserve System's participation in a bill auction to the amount of maturing bills which it owned. On the other hand, the Federal Reserve was not required to replace any of its maturing bills with newly issued bills. It could accept payment for them in cash. Thus, it could elect whether to bid to replace all of its maturing bills, only a portion of them, or none of them. Since the Federal Reserve System traditionally supplied reserves in the last week of the month, Mr. Pender and Mr. Tyler expected the system to bid to replace all of its bills which matured on September 24, 1964. In the past they had attempted to estimate the amount of bills in the open market account of the Federal Reserve System that was maturing each week. Recently, however, they had discontinued this practice since they believed that the Federal Reserve's active participation in open market operations made it impossible to make a meaningful estimate of the amount of its maturing bills.

Mr. Pender believed that the largest portion of the demand for new bills usually came from dealers, who took them into their own account and also negotiated purchases for customers. He knew that banks acquired bills for their own portfolios as secondary reserves and also negotiated purchases for their customers and that corporations bought bills as a means of employing idle capital as did government trust accounts and foreign central banks. Although Pender, Wilson & Company had no branch offices, it had both telephone and outside salesmen calling on banks, insurance companies, and the treasurers of major corporations. Mr. Pender felt that this enabled Pender, Wilson & Company to analyze the conditions in various parts of the country which contributed to the aggregate demand for a new treasury bill issue. As the 1:30 P.M. deadline for submitting tenders approached, most of these salesmen seemed to feel that aggregate demand was not appreciably different from what it had been during the most recent weeks. A few believed that it was slightly larger than for the auction of the previous week.

Demand of Pender, Wilson & Company

For the September 21 auction of 91-day bills Mr. Pender estimated that Pender, Wilson & Company, as agent, would be submitting bids for customers totaling about $22 million. This included one standing commitment that Pender, Wilson & Company had from a midwestern bank to buy in each weekly treasury-bill auction \$2.5 million of 91-day bills for its account.

Like other government securities dealers, Pender, Wilson & Company also submitted bids for its own account. Mr. Pender had thought for some time that the limit to which Pender, Wilson & Company could participate in a single auction for its own account, risk aside, depended on the firm's ability to sell the purchased bills in the secondary market and its ability to finance its purchases at a reasonable rate if it were forced to carry them. He believed that the former depended on the sales force and contacts among the corporations and banks, actively or passively seeking the issue, and that the latter was of secondary importance since Pender, Wilson & Company hoped to dispose of most of its position before the Thursday settlement date. He thought that Pender, Wilson & Company should be able to move about \$32 million of new 91-day bills from its own account at the "going rate" and probably much more than that.

Mr. Tyler thought that the cost and availability of financing had a strong influence on the amount of bills for which his firm should bid. He noted that these factors changed daily and that even in August and September, when money market conditions had been relatively stable, the source and cost of the financing of his firm's position had varied greatly. For example, collateral loans had accounted for as much as 57 percent of financing and as little as 31 percent during August and September. Over this same period the cost of collateral loans had ranged between 3.60 and 3.875; for repurchase agreements the range had been between 3.55 and 3.625. Mr. Tyler believed that the rediscount rate provided a floor for financing costs. He noted, however, that only rarely was financing available at this rate to nonbank dealers.

Mr. Tyler was concerned that because of the present yield on bills and cost of financing, any of the 91-day bills offered in this auction that Pender, Wilson & Company took into its position would have a negative carry. Furthermore, he expressed the view that the \$250 million inventory of treasury bills that the firm had was about the right amount. Although there was some difference of opinion on the most desirable amount of bills to bid for, they both believed that Pender, Wilson & Company should continue to make markets in treasury bills and therefore required some inventory of the new issue in order to serve the needs and desires of its customers. (Exhibit 1 shows the prices and quantities for which Pender, Wilson & Company had tendered in some of the recent treasury bill auctions.)

General Economic and Money Market Conditions

Each week Mr. Pender and Mr. Tyler spend part of their time reading articles and statistics on general economic and money market conditions. (Some of this material is contained in the note, United States

Exhibit 1

PENDER, WILSION & COMPANY (B)

Recent Tenders for 91-day Treasury Bills

Auction Date	Issue Date	Maturity Date	PW & Co. Bid Price	PW & Co. Bid Quantity (in millions)	Accepted Bids High	Accepted Bids Low	Accepted Bids Average	Price on Auction Date of: 91-day Bills Issued Previous Week	Price on Auction Date of: Bills with Same Maturity
Sept. 21	Sept. 24	Dec. 24						3.54	3.54
								3.52	3.49
Sept. 14	Sept. 17	Dec. 17	99.106	25	99.114	99.103	99.105	3.53	3.54
			99.104	10	(3.505)	(3.549)	(3.541)	3.51	3.51
			99.103	10					
			99.102	10					
			99.079	25					
Sept. 4	Sept. 10	Dec. 10	99.110	30	99.117	99.109	99.112	3.51	3.50
			99.109	10	(3.493)	(3.525)	(3.514)	3.49	3.47
			99.108	10					
			99.107	10					
			99.080	20					
Aug. 31	Sept. 3	Dec. 3	99.113	25	99.115	99.110	99.112	3.50	3.50
			99.112	20	(3.501)	(3.521)	(3.512)	3.47	3.47
			99.111	10					
			99.090	25					
Aug. 24	Aug. 27	Nov. 27*	99.104	20	99.106	99.100	99.102	3.50	5.51
			99.103	20	(3.498)	(3.522)	(3.513)	3.48	3.47
			99.102	20					
			99.085	20					
			99.080	50					

* 92-day bill.

Exhibit 1 (Continued)

Auction Date	*Issue Date*	*Maturity Date*	*PW & Co. Bid Price*	*PW & Co. Bid Quantity (in millions)*	*Accepted Bids High*	*Accepted Bids Low*	*Accepted Bids Average*	*91-day Bills Issued Previous Week*	*Bills with Same Maturity*
Aug. 17	Aug. 20	Nov. 19	99.115	20	99.115	99.111	99.112	3.50	3.50
			99.113	10	(3.501)	(3.517)	(3.512)	3.48	3.46
			99.111	10					
			99.109	10					
			99.100	30					
Aug. 10	Aug. 13	Nov. 12	99.112	25	99.118	99.111	99.113	3.50	3.50
			99.111	15	(3.489)	(3.517)	(3.510)	3.48	3.46
			99.110	15					
			99.100	25					
Aug. 3	Aug. 6	Nov. 5	99.118	30	99.122	99.116	99.118	3.47	3.49
			99.117	10	(3.473)	(3.497)	(3.489)	3.45	3.45
			99.116	10					
			99.115	15					
			99.102	25					
			99.097	25					
July 27	July 30	Oct. 29	99.120	25	99.124	99.119	99.122	3.45	3.48
			99.119	15	(3.465)	(3.485)	(3.475)	3.43	3.44
			99.117	25					
			99.116	25					
			99.101	50					

Government Securities, Interest Rates, and Monetary Policy.) They believed it particularly important to recognize at an early stage any trends which might be developing.

Mr. Pender thought that the prices of bills already outstanding were extremely useful as guides in formulating the bid price for a new bill issue. The 91-day bill issued the previous week provided one benchmark since the two securities were identical except for the one week difference in maturity dates. The spread between a new 91-day bill and the 91-day bill issued the previous week had varied considerably over the years. Mr. Pender believed that a spread of about one or two hundredths[6] between the two issues was reasonable in the present market. A second benchmark was provided by the bill which had been issued thirteen weeks earlier as a 182-day bill. Mr. Pender noted that it was identical to the new 91-day bill being offered in all respects, including maturity date, with the possible exception of the fact that the new bill had yet to be traded in the market. (Exhibit 1 contains the prices for these two bills as of the mornings of recent auctions. For example, as of September 21, 1964, the 91-day bill issued the previous week was quoted at 3.54 to 3.52 and the 182-day bill issued thirteen weeks earlier was quoted at 3.54 to 3.49.)

Market Opinion

Throughout the morning of September 21, 1964, both Mr. Pender and Mr. Tyler were engaged almost constantly in telephone conversations. They conferred with many others who were involved in all phases of the government securities market. The principal subject of these conversations was the treasury-bill auction. Such conversations were standard procedure before each auction.

During these discussions the participants exchanged ideas on the probable tender. For the most part participants talked about their bidding intentions in terms of rate only. On this particular morning a few of the dealers were giving only one rate, instead of a range, as was more frequently the case. Mr. Pender and Mr. Tyler agreed that the consensus of all these views lay somewhere in the 3.53 to 3.55 range. They noted that the bill market had been quite stable the past few days and believed that this phenomenon was a further indication of the narrowing range in expectations. Treasury regulations required submission of tenders expressed in price. This provided a more sensitive measure of the bidder's expectations. For example, the 3.53 to 3.55 range was equivalent to a price range of 99.108 to 99.103. As the 1:30 P.M. deadline for bid submission approached, the exchanges with other dealers, banks, and customers reverted to price.

---

[6]Bills were quoted on a discount basis.

Comprehensive Problems 14

ACQUISITION BY FINANCIAL HOLDING COMPANY

California Financial Corporation

In February 1963, Mr. John Peters, president of California Financial Corporation, had to make a recommendation to the board of directors regarding a possible acquisition. He was attempting to determine whether California Financial should acquire the Premium Finance Company and, if so, what the suitable terms might be.

Before making his recommendation, Mr. Peters planned to review the development pattern of California Financial and analyze the company as it presently existed. He also intended to study its financial condition. Mr. Peters felt that the Premium Finance Company could then be examined to see how well it would fit into the California Financial Corporation operations.

Development Pattern of California Financial Corporation

California Financial was substantially a holding company, although the parent corporation did carry on some business. Its principal subsidiary was a savings and loan association. Other subsidiaries included two title and escrow companies, a small business investment company, and a mortgage company. In addition, the parent corporation and/or its subsidiaries acted as trustee on loans made by the savings and loan association, conducted an insurance agency, and participated in the financing of real estate development projects.

Savings and Loan Business

California Financial Corporation was incorporated on December 29, 1958, with the plan of acquiring all of the outstanding stock of Surety Savings and Loan Association, which had been engaged in the savings and loan business in and around San Jose, California, since 1926. During February and March of 1959, this was accomplished.

In August 1959, California Financial acquired the assets of Sala Investment Corporation consisting principally of the stock of Security Savings and Loan Association, which had its head office in Oakland, California. Before the end of 1959, Security Savings and Loan Association was merged into Surety Savings and Loan Association, which then changed its name to Security Savings and Loan Association.

In December 1960, Security Savings merged with Provident Mutual Savings and Loan Association, which had a charter in San Francisco, but was not operating. Thus, Security Savings was able to transfer its headquarters from San Jose to San Francisco. The California Financial management felt that it would have been difficult, if not impossible, to get a new charter in San Francisco and therefore was pleased to be able to transfer its headquarters by merging with Provident Mutual. At that time, a savings and loan association was not permitted to make loans more than fifty miles from its home office. (This restriction has since been relaxed, but only to a limited extent). Therefore, this had the beneficial effect of permitting mortgage operations in Marin County and parts of Solano, Napa, and Sonoma Counties. With the addition of these, Security Savings could initiate mortgages in thirteen of northern California's growing and most prosperous counties.

Title and Escrow Business

California Financial Corporation purchased the outstanding stock of Marin Title Guaranty Company, a title and escrow company[1] in San Rafael, California, on October 2, 1961, for $250,000 in cash and a promissory note for $600,000. Marin Title had a larger share of the title and escrow business in Marin County than any other company. Management estimated that Marin Title had 30 percent of the total business in the county compared with 21 percent for the second-place company.

At the time it purchased Marin Title, California Financial also got an option to purchase a title plant in Contra Costa County, California. The company exercised this option, and established the Financial Title Company in June 1962. As of February 1963, Financial Title Company had nearly reached the break-even point. Management was extremely pleased with this performance.

Small Business Investment Company

In March 1962, Pan Pacific Investment Company, a small business investment company licensed by the Small Business Administration, was formed. California Financial purchased the initial issue of capital stock of Pan Pacific of $252,500 and the Small Business Administration was

[1]Appendix A contains some information on the activities of title and escrow companies.

committed to purchase a $50,000 debenture of Pan Pacific. It had been anticipated that Pan Pacific would invest primarily in California real estate development companies. However, under the terms of the Small Business Investment Act, and SBIC could not invest more than 20 percent of owners' equity plus SBA debentures in any single company. Thus, the limitation for Pan Pacific was 20 percent of $302,500, or roughly $60,000. California Financial executives felt that this limitation eliminated the most attractive situations from consideration. In addition, it noted that the parent corporation (California Financial) could make any of the investments which its SBIC subsidiary could make. Furthermore, the parent corporation would not be subject to regulation by the SBA Although Pan Pacific had not made any investments as of February 1963, the executives of California Financial were keeping the SBIC charter, because they believed that some day it might appreciate in value and they might be able to sell it. They noted that charters for savings and loan associations had appreciated greatly in value in recent years.

Mortgage Company

On July 26, 1962, California Financial acquired all of the outstanding stock of Duggan Investment Company and Sequoia Mortgage Company in exchange for 22,060 and 3365 shares of its capital stock, respectively. In addition, up to 13,345 shares of California Financial's capital stock will be issuable to the stockholders of Duggan Investment Company under a formula dependent upon the dollar amount of loan commitments of Duggan in process on June 1, 1962, which become loans serviced by Duggan as of May 31, 1963. The two mortgage company subsidiaries were merged under the name of Sequoia Mortgage Company[2] on September 25, 1962.

Duggan Investment Company was organized in 1956 as the result of a merger of two predecessor companies and since that date had been engaged in the business of originating and servicing mortgage loans in northern California. Since organization it had acted as an approved Veterans Administration and Federal Housing Administration mortgagee and as an authorized agent of the FHA Certified Agency Program. Duggan Investment Company had maintained its principal office at Alameda, California.

Sequoia Mortgage Company was organized in 1959 for the purpose of carrying on a mortgage loan brokerage business. The company had engaged continuously in the business of originating mortgages in the San Francisco Peninsula area centered around San Carlos, California, for major life insurance and savings institutions.

In making the decision to acquire Duggan Investment Company

[2]Appendix B contains some information on the activities of mortgage companies.

and Sequoia Mortgage, the executives of California Financial felt that the activities of a mortgage company would complement those of the parent corporation and its subsidiaries. For example, as of mid-1962, the savings and loan association relied on mortgage brokers for most of its mortgages. Although California Financial's management did not want the overhead of a large mortgage company on its payroll, it felt that the savings and loan association could provide a major portion of the business for a smaller mortgage company. In addition, they felt that a wholly owned mortgage company might be able to provide mortgages to the savings and loan association at a lower fee than it was presently paying. Management also noted that mortgage companies do a substantial amount of borrowing (Appendix B) and reasoned that a mortgage company which is a part of a strong financial enterprise would be able to get lower interest rates than it could on its own. By February 1963, much of their advance reasoning had become fact, and the executives of California Financial were generally pleased with the operating results of Sequoia Mortgage.

Other Businesses

California Financial Corporation owned a trustee company which acted as trustee on loans made by the savings and loan association. California Financial conducted an insurance agency for fire, casualty, and mortgage redemption life insurance. The agency acted for several insurance companies. The parent company also participated in the direct financing of real estate development projects which involved the purchase of land for resale.

Financial Condition of California Financial Corporation

The consolidated financial statements for recent years appear as Exhibits 1 and 2.

Borrowing of California Financial

On July 21, 1960, California Financial issued $1,000,000 of 5 1/2 percent Convertible Promissory Notes, due July 15, 1972, to a group of nine investors. In connection with the sale of the notes the company paid a commission of $15,000 to its investment bankers. All of these notes have been converted into common stock.

On October 24, 1962, California Financial issued to the public $5 million of 5 percent Convertible Subordinated Debentures, due October 1, 1977. They are convertible into capital stock on or before October 1, 1977, at $9.05 per share. In connection with the offering the company paid the underwriters $175,000. As of March 1963, none of the debentures had been converted.

Exhibit 1

CALIFORNIA FINANCIAL CORPORATION

Consolidated Statements of Financial Condition

Assets	*December 31, 1962*	*December 31, 1961*
Cash	$ 5,253,396	$ 3,034,313
United States government and other securities—at cost (market value $4,556,028 and $4,395,386)	4,685,156	4,606,716
Loans receivable	128,945,931	93,349,997
Investment in capital stock of Federal Home Loan Bank—at cost	1,512,000	1,512,000
Properties held for sale or development—at cost	6,292,103	3,674,103
Prepaid expenses and other assets	1,554,110	567,329
Property and equipment—at cost, less accumulated depreciation	2,999,839	1,899,478
Intangible excess of amount paid over net assets of subsidiary at date of acquisition	803,543	799,143
	$152,046,078	$109,443,079

Liabilities and Capital		
Savings accounts	$104,450,056	$ 82,953,894
Notes payable	8,738,828	1,575,000
5 1/2% Convertible Promissory Notes		840,000
5% Convertible Promissory Notes	5,000,000	
Advances from Federal Home Loan Bank	12,415,000	8,387,000
Loans in process	3,373,638	3,392,988
Accounts payable and accrued expenses	2,913,315	677,368
Federal taxes on income	154,189	65,274
Unearned discount interest and loan fees	435,734	779,080
Total liabilities	$137,480,760	$ 98,670,604
Stockholders' equity and general reserves:		
Capital stock, par value $1 a share:		
Authorized 5,000,000 and 1,000,000 shares, respectively		
Issued and outstanding 2,695,678 and 809, 049 shares, respectively	$ 2,695,678	$ 809,049
Paid-in surplus	5,705,777	5,594,317
Undivided profits	1,212,409	1,020,541
General reserves	9,800,193	7,186,425
	$ 19,414,057	$ 14,610,332
Less stock dividends—at approximate market values at dates of declaration	4,848,739	3,837,857
	$ 14,565,318	$ 10,772,475
	$152,046,078	$109,443,079

Exhibit 2

CALIFORNIA FINANCIAL CORPORATION

Consolidated Statement of Operations

	Year Ended December 31					
	1962	*1961*	*1960*	*1959*	*1958*	*1957*
REVENUES						
Interest on loans	$ 6,972,868	$5,172,166	$3,985,567	$2,961,524	$2,130,128	$1,714,802
Loans and other fees and commissions	3,187,962	1,669,338	1,565,780	950,873	445,265	216,404
Interest and dividends on investments	240,602	162,327	124,393	139,810	146,447	97,132
Profit on sales of real estate	229,421	308,854	37,071	81,603	84,725	88,841
Miscellaneous	47,054	188,929	44,920	12,308	54,876	64,126
	$10,677,907	$7,501,614	$5,757,731	$4,146,118	$2,861,441	$2,181,305
EXPENSES						
General and administrative expenses	$ 2,858,352	$1,778,510	$1,285,519	$ 949,838	$ 702,606	$ 667,766
Interest expense	4,984,852	3,471,347	2,761,879	1,923,703	1,518,183	1,196,227
	$ 7,843,204	$5,249,857	$4,047,398	$2,873,541	$2,220,789	$1,863,993

Exhibit 2 (Continued)

	Year Ended December 31					
	1962	*1961*	*1960*	*1959*	*1958*	*1957*
Earnings before federal taxes on income	$ 2,834,703	$2,251,757	$1,710,333	$1,272,577	$ 640,652	$ 317,312
Federal taxes on income*	120,000	65,000	16,500	21,850	10,389	8,678
Net earnings before appropriations to general reserves	$ 2,714,703	$2,186,757	$1,693,833	$1,250,727	$ 630,263	$ 308,634
Appropriations to general reserves*	2,613,768	2,110,773	1,002,851	1,205,980	578,507	276,740
Balance after appropriations to general reserves	$ 100,935	$ 75,984	$ 690,982	$ 44,747	$ 51,756	$ 31,894
Per share†						
Net earnings before appropriations to general reserves	$1.01	$0.89	$.072	$0.53	$0.27	$0.13
Appropriations to general reserves*	$0.97	$0.87	$0.43	$0.51	$0.25	$0.11
Stock dividends per share	5%	5%	5%	5%	-	-

*Earnings appropriated to general reserves are not available for payment of cash dividends unless transferred to undivided profits. Such transfers are subject to certain restrictions and are subject generally to federal income tax laws when transferred.

†Computed on basis of average shares outstanding during the year, adjusted for stock dividends and for a three-for-one stock split effective April 1962.

Adjustments were made in these statements to record the deferral of fees and discounts on loans, to record as income interest earned but uncollected, and to record accrued expenses. These adjustments were offset against general reserves and are not recorded on the books of the Association. It is the policy of California Financial Corporation to use this adjusted basis in its consolidated financial statements.

Security Savings and Loan Association, as a member of the Federal Home Loan Bank, could obtain advances from the FHLB up to 17 1/2 percent of its savings accounts. At the end of 1962 the amount of advances outstanding was $12,415,000. However, these advances could be used by the savings and loan association only and not by other subsidiaries of California Financial or by the parent corporation itself.

As of February 1963, California Financial had a line of credit of $10,000,000 with its bank. Although it was not borrowing from the bank at this time, it had used its line of credit in the past. The interest charge was the prime rate plus 1/2 percent.

Capital Stock of California Financial

The capital stock of California Financial was traded in the over-the-counter market from March 1959 to May 18, 1962. The stock was listed on the New York Stock Exchange on May 21, 1962, and on the Pacific Coast Stock Exchange on May 22, 1962. The following table shows the high and low bids for the capital stock in the over-the-counter market to May 18, 1962, and the high and low sales prices on the New York Stock Exchange from May 21, 1962, to February 18, 1963.

	March–December 31, 1959	*1960*	*1961*	*January–May 18, 1962*	*May 21, 1962–February 18, 1963*
High	8 1/4	7 3/4	22	16 5/8	13 1/2
Low	5	4 1/2	6 3/3	12 3/4	7 1/4

The above figures have been adjusted to reflect the 3 for 1 stock split in April 1962.

The closing price on the New York Stock Exchange on February 18, 1963, was 9 1/4.

Premium Finance Company

Premium Finance Company was incorporated in 1954 under the Industrial Loan law of the state of California. The financial statements of Premium Finance Company for recent years appear as Exhibits 3 and 4. An industrial loan company—such as Premium Finance—was authorized to engage in the business of making loans as permitted under Division 7 of the Financial Code. For example, an industrial loan company could lend money on a secured or unsecured basis to a person, a corporation, or an association anywhere in the state of California and, under certain conditions, out of state. Also an industrial loan company could purchase conditional sales contracts, factor accounts receivable, or generally en-

Exhibit 3

PREMIUM FINANCE COMPANY

Balance Sheets

	Dec. 31, 1958	Dec. 31, 1959	Dec. 31, 1960	Dec. 31, 1961	Dec. 31, 1962	Projected Dec. 31, 1963
ASSETS						
Cash	$ 582	$ 2,779	$ 1,577	$ 1,222	$ 250,011	$ 120,000
Loans and contracts	448,244	1,242,892	1,775,471	2,045,974	3,100,667	3,800,000
Less provision for cancellations and prepayments*	(12,376)	(47,941)	(59,618)	(57,873)	(123,522)	(135,000)
Fixed assets	6,757	16,936	28,056	30,956	33,468	33,000
Less depreciation	(792)	(1,966)	(5,333)	(9,425)	(13,024)	(16,600)
Other assets	2,101	3,436	9,588	12,072	17,016	9,000
Total assets	$444,516	$1,216,136	$1,749,741	$2,022,926	$3,264,616	$3,810,400
LIABILITIES AND OWNERS' EQUITY						
Payables – trade	$ 4,160	$ 1,236	$ 1,520	$ 160	$ 758	$ 400
companies and agents	50,379	133,600	122,252	142,833	256,607	240,000
Accruals, taxes, interest	3,263	4,552	9,283	7,912	11,106	8,000
Loans payable	260,057	778,205	1,281,199	1,522,057	2,573,967	3,009,822
Total liabilities	$317,859	$ 917,593	$1,414,254	$1,672,962	$2,842,438	$3,258,222
Long-term loans	30,361	176,361	181,160	181,160	172,800	172,800
Capital stock	80,000	80,000	80,000	80,000	80,000	80,000
Retained earnings	16,296	42,182	74,327	88,804	169,378	299,378
Total equity	126,657	298,543	335,487	349,964	422,178	552,178
Total liability and owners' equity	$444,516	$1,216,136	$1,749,741	$2,022,926	$3,264,616	$3,810,400

*See Exhibit 6 for an explanation of the accounting procedure involved with the provision for cancellations and prepayments.

Exhibit 4

PREMIUM FINANCE COMPANY

Income Statements

	Year Ended December 31					*Projected*
	1958	*1959*	*1960*	*1961*	*1962*	*1963*
Gross income	$ 86,862	$ 263,923	$ 463,276	$ 509,946	$ 705,828	$ 850,000
Less:						
Reserve*	21,958	49,669	83,178	82,393	135,189	160,000
Administration	62,051	118,882	199,632	236,860	277,744	320,000
Production		28,750	45,525	66,030	66,246	70,000
Interest	5,227	40,736	102,796	110,186	146,075	170,000
Net profit	$ (2,374)	$ 25,886	$ 32,145	$ 14,477	$ 80,574	$ 130,000
MISCELLANEOUS FINANCIAL INFORMATION						
Average loans and contracts outstanding	$640,000	$ 994,000	$1,652,000	$1,846,000	$2,540,000	$3,200,000
Premium volume	823,000	2,921,600	4,956,000	5,536,800	7,648,600	9,600,000
Number of loans processed	5,600	15,200	24,000	24,900	33,400	42,000
Average premium	149	192	209	223	229	229

*See Exhibit 6 for an explanation of the accounting procedure involved with the provision for cancellations and prepayments.

gage in any lending operations that banks could; however, certain restrictions applied to maturities and percentage of capital and surplus. Although Premium Finance was authorized to engage in any or all of the foregoing activities, it had limited itself to a special field—that of loaning money for the payment of insurance premiums to the purchasers of automobile, liability, and fire insurance policies.

Operation Procedure

To clarify the nature of Premium Finance's business a description of its operational procedure might prove helpful.

The borrower, hereafter referred to as the insured, purchased an insurance policy or policies through an independent licensed insurance agent or broker in the customary manner. Premium Finance then paid the insurance premium to the insurance carrier and notified the carrier of Premium Finance's rights to cancel the insurance policy and to receive the return portion of the unearned premium in the event of default by the insured.

In most instances the loan was repayable in ten equal monthly installments, with a down payment of 25 percent. Premium Finance operated on the basis of an "add on" finance charge which ranged from 5 percent to 15 percent, depending mainly on the size of the loan. The following outlines how a hypothetical contract would operate with an individual or business which paid out $100 per year in insurance premiums. Premium Finance would require a down payment of $25. The loan would be $75, the finance charge would be $10, which would make the total contract $85. Thus, the insured would pay $8.50 each month for ten months.

If, for example, the insured failed to make his first monthly payment, the policy would be effective for a total period of forty-seven days until cancellation.[3] According to the standard short-rate table, the premium earned for the period would have been $23; therefore, the insurance carrier would refund $77 to Premium Finance as the unearned premium (see Exhibit 5). Thus, based upon the down payment required by Premium Finance and prompt cancellation after default, the return premiums were usually sufficient to cover the unpaid balance of the loans. Any unrecovered amount was billed to the borrower.

---

[3]If the insurance payment was not received by Premium Finance within seven days of the date it was due, a late notice was sent to the insured. At the end of the fifteenth day, if payment had not been received, Premium Finance sent a notice of cancellation to the insured and proceeded to cancel the policy. Obviously a great amount of detail work was required to accomplish this. Premium Finance rented an IBM 1401 to keep track of the accounts outstanding.

Exhibit 5

PREMIUM FINANCE COMPANY

Coverage on a $100 Premium*
Calculated After Receipt of Each Payment

(1) Number of Days	(2) Short-Rate Cancellation	(3) Exposure	(4) Payments Received	(2)–(3) Coverage
0	$95	$75.00		$20.00
44–47	77	75.00		2.00
77–80	68	66.50	1	1.50
110–113	59	58.00	2	1.00
139–142	51	49.50	3	1.50
168–171	43	41.00	4	2.00
197–200	36	32.50	5	3.50
229–232	29	24.00	6	5.00
261–264	22	15.50	7	6.50
292–296	15	7.00	8	8.00
324–328	8	(1.50)	9	9.50

*Required downpayment is $25, added on finance charges are $10, and therefore total contract is $85.

Type of Business

Business was obtained from the various licensed insurance agents and brokers in the northern California area. The company had no agents of its own nor any branch office locations. According to Mr. William Bischoff, president of Premium Finance Company, "Insurance agents utilize the services of Premium Finance Company in the interest of their own business. Many agents which have clients desirous of financing their premiums attempt to carry this financing themselves. However, agents have found it to their benefit to have a financing plan such as Premium Finance's available, since the personal capabilities of any agent toward carrying financing are limited. In addition, many agents and brokers look favorably upon a plan such as Premium Finance's because it keeps the insurance company itself from dealing directly with the customer. This alleviates the fear of some agents and brokers that insurance companies may ultimately deal directly with the customer, bypassing agents and brokers altogether. As insurance agents and brokers and their employees grow accustomed to using our rate charts and loan forms, repeat business from them continues to grow. Furthermore, as a result of specializing in premium finance, every day agents and brokers not previously doing business with Premium Finance contact our company to avail themselves of our services. In addition to this growing list of active agents, several insurance companies have adopted Premium Finance's program for their agents and are promoting the program in the field as a response to their competitors. In short, the company has never been in a position where it has had to seek out borrowers for its premium finance programs; therefore, the company has had no problem in putting its money to work."

Premium Finance's lending methods differed from those customarily used in the field of consumer loans in that Premium Finance neither investigated the credit nor considered the ability of its borrowers to pay. According to Mr. Bischoff, "Although, technically speaking, Premium Finance is making loans, it is not realistic to say that it is in the loan business. Its business is that of rendering a service to the insurance industry by collecting premiums on a monthly basis. Monthly premium plans have become a generally accepted part of the insurance industry, and the requirements of such programs are now recognized by most insurance carriers. Some insurance companies have adopted their own monthly plans as well as cooperating with independent finance institutions."

Income Tax Situation

Premium Finance was presently deferring all federal income taxes.[4] Premium Finance's management believed that it was conceivable that as the business grew, the company would be able to defer income continually under the straight-line method of picking up income. It had also pointed out that if it found in any year that the method of deferring income would result in the permanent loss of a net operating loss carry forward, it could hold down expenditures, or if necessary, take the more drastic action of selling part of the loan portfolio so as to turn the deferred income into immediate income and thus utilize the expiring loss carry forward. If, on the other hand, it appeared that straight-line income pickup would result in a tax, Premium Finance could increase its expenditures (either expanding its current field or entering other lines of lending) to prevent a tax liability actually being assessed.

Exhibit 6

Independent Accountant's Explanation of Accounting Procedure of Premium Finance

Premium Finance recorded the full amount of finance charges as gross income and made a provision for whatever future losses of anticipated income would result from cancellations and prepayments. This provision has been maintained at 20 percent of the gross finance charges. To use the example stated previously, the promissory note will show a face obligation of $85 payable in ten equal payments of $8.50. Since the finance charges are $10, Premium Finance would take $8 immediately into income and put $2 into the reserve for

[4]Exhibit 6 gives an explanation of the accounting procedure employed by Premium Finance.

Exhibit 6 (Continued)

cancellations and prepayments. A ledger card would be set up showing a balance as per books of $85 and as each $8.50 payment is received it would be credited to the ledger card.

At the end of the year, the accounts which are active are separated from the accounts which are in cancellation status. The reserve is then analyzed to see if the 20 percent provision for the year has proved to be adequate. This is determined by taking 2 percent of the outstanding loan balances for all accounts in active status and 100 percent of all cancelled accounts to the extent that the money is due from the insured. An insured in cancellation status may have an unpaid balance on his ledger card of $50, of which $45 is due from the insurance carrier. Premium Finance would have to bill the insured for the remaining $5. Although the accounting treatment (a reserve of 100 percent) anticipates that none of this amount will be collected, experience shows that Premium Finance collects about 25 percent of the amount billed. When the balance proves to be uncollectible, it is written off against the reserve for cancellation and prepayment as well as against the ledger card.

The federal tax returns used a different method of picking up income. The method used is commonly referred to as the "straight-line method," that is, one tenth of the finance charge was picked up into earned income each month for the ten month period and the income allocated to the months remaining to maturity was carried as unearned or deferred income. In place of a reserve of cancellation and prepayment the standard bad debt provision to maintain a 2 percent reserve was substituted.

Except for the method of picking up income and providing for a reserve of cancellation and prepayment, all other entries on the books of Premium Finance are the same as for tax-reporting purposes.

To support its case, management noted that from 1958 to 1961, the earned surplus for tax purposes continually decreased, while, for book purposes, it continually increased. In 1962, when it became apparent that a substantial net loss carry forward would be lost unless steps were taken to earn a certain amount, Premium Finance showed a taxable net income of $14,933 (Exhibit 7). This was accomplished, according to Mr. Bischoff, by an increase in the volume of business coupled with a leveling of production expenses.

Exhibit 7

PREMIUM FINANCE COMPANY

Resume of Principal Items

		Per Books		
	Gross Income	*Addition to Reserve for Cancellation*	*Reserve for Cancellation*	*Book Net Income*
1958	$ 86,862	$ 21,958	$ 12,376	$ 2,374)
1959	263,923	$ 49,669	47,941	$25,886
1960	463,276	83,178	59,618	32,145
1961	509,946	82,393	57,873	14,477
1962	705,828	135,189	123,522	80,574

Exhibit 7 (Continued)

Per Federal Tax Returns

	Deferred Income	*Net Taxable Income*	*Retained Earnings*	*Addition to Provision for Bad Debts*	*Provision for Bad Debts*
1958	$ 29,401	($12,287)	($27,514)	$ 7,947	$26,785
1959	118,753	(33,542)	(61,056)	19,745	32,426
1960	156,922	331	(60,725)	76,823	37,748
1961	194,788	(27,532)	(88,257)	86,536	40,156
1962	302,949	14,933	(73,324)	92,669	63,275

Premium Finance's management thought that it was conceivable that the only year in which a tax liability might be incurred would be one where management decided to dimish its business efforts with a corresponding decrease in its overhead. Mr. Bischoff pointed out that, "It is not likely that management will elect to reduce its volume of business voluntarily, and in the past a reduction in the volume of business has been responded to by management with increased expenditures of advertising and promotion designed to reverse the trend, thus it is not likely that income taxes would ever be paid."

It was the feeling of Premium Finance's management that its plan of operation could be carried out for many years and that, if at some later date it would be desired to terminate the operation of the business, a plan of liquidation could be filed and the maximum tax would be limited to a capital gain tax.

Financial Condition

Premium Finance had financing arrangements with two commercial banks. It borrowed against the promissory notes and installment agreements that it held. The banks charged 6 percent interest on these borrowings. In addition, they insisted on complicated pledging procedures, which had proved to be time consuming and therefore resulted in considerable additional cost to Premium Finance. The managements of both California Financial and Premium Finance felt that this procedure and cost was unwarranted for what they considered to be gilt-edged financing.

Premium Finance also obtained a small portion (see Exhibit 3) of its financing through long-term debt. As of the end of 1962, the long-term debt consisted of notes held by several investors. The interest rates were 6 percent on the largest portion and 7 percent on the rest. As an industrial loan company, Premium Finance was also permitted to sell investment certificates to the public; however, the company had never done so.

The executives of California Financial felt that Premium Finance had great growth potential and noted that its need for funds might continue to grow. Mr. Bischoff had indicated that Premium Finance could use four million dollars immediately. In addition, he had estimated that the company might need an additional $4 million over the next two years; however, he acknowledged that the ultimate size and needs of the company were extremely difficult to estimate. California Financial executives were wondering what effect this need for funds might have on their own credit lines. They thought that it might be possible for California Financial to issue commercial paper. The company's investment bankers had indicated that they thought it might be possible for California Financial to obtain up to $20 million by issuing commercial paper.

Other Considerations

California Financial executives felt that management compatability was always an important consideration in a merger. They considered the present condition of California Financial to be a "smooth operation." They recognized that there were some differences in management philosophies between California Financial and Premium Finance, but thought that any problems which might emerge in this regard were more likely to be short run than long run.

Mr. Peters had been given the following information, which had been obtained from a report prepared by an investment banker on a company similar to Premium Finance:

> The following, which we have set up in chart form, will trace the action of $1,000 of the company's money through a period of ten months for an "add on" finance chart of 9 percent. Through the compounding and leverage factors of reloaning money which is incoming on loan payments, the investor will note that the $1,000 original money that the company has loaned out has, by the end of a ten month period, become approximately $1,253.27 in accounts receivable (see Exhibit 8). This in itself amounts to 26.3 percent interest on the company's money in ten months. When projected out to a full period of 12 months earnings this will amount to approximately 30.4 percent. Therefore, it is quite easily seen how the company can borrow money at 6–7 percent and in turn loan the money with a 9 percent "add on" finance charge and be in a very favorable position to its stockholders.

A final consideration with which Mr. Peters was greatly concerned was the earnings per share which California Financial Corporation reported to its stockholders. He felt that the terms of any merger should be analyzed carefully with respect to their effect on earnings per share.

Exhibit 8

Hypothetical Illustration of the Progress of $1000 over a Ten-month Period

	Available for Loan (Payment Received)	9% "Add-On" Charge	Loan Plus Interest	Payment
Original	$1,000.00	$90.00	$1,090.00	$109.00
1st Month	109.00	9.81	118.81	11.88
2d Month	109.00	10.88	131.76	13.18
	11.88			
	120.88			
3d Month	109.00	12.07	146.13	14.61
	11.88			
	13.18			
	134.06			
4th Month	134.06	13.38	162.05	16.21
	14.61			
	148.67			
5th Month	148.67	14.84	179.72	17.97
	16.21			
	164.88			
6th Month	164.88	16.46	199.31	19.93
	17.97			
	182.85			
7th Month	182.85	18.25	221.03	22.10
	19.93			
	202.78			
8th Month	202.78	20.24	245.12	24.51
	22.10			
	224.88			
9th Month	224.88	22.45	271.84	27.18
	24.51			
	249.39			
10th Month	249.39	24.89	301.46	30.15
	27.18			
	276.57			
Total loans made	$3,067.23			
Amount collected	1,813.96			
Accounts receivable	$1,253.27			

Gain of $253.27 on $1000 loaned for ten months, projected for twelve months = $303.92 or 30.4 percent.

APPENDIX A

The Activities of Title and Escrow Companies[1]

A title company assembles, maintains, examines, and interprets innumerable official records, laws, and court decisions, about property and people, which affect the ownership of land—and it insures that its findings are correct.

During any period, long or short, many things affecting ownership may have occurred. A title company cannot assume that nothing has happened; it searches and examines the records down to date, to disclose the current facts.

To its files are added, daily, new data from many public offices—city, county, state, and Federal District Court. Its indexes cover every parcel of land in the county, arranged so that all essential facts may be disclosed and evaluated.

A title company insures against loss and defends its clients' interests, bearing the cost of lawsuits—all as provided in its policy. In addition, it may provide escrow services. Throughout California, it is the custom when real estate changes hands, for the buyer and seller—and the lender, if any—to place their deal "in escrow" while it is being completed.

Going into escrow simply means depositing the purchase money in the hands of a responsible and impartial stakeholder, who holds all money and documents until the instructions of each of the parties to the transaction are complied with. These instructions embody the requirements of the buyer, seller, and lender, as to transfer of funds, condition of title, recordation of papers, issuance of land title insurance, and other matters.

APPENDIX B

The Activities of Mortgage Companies

Mortgage companies were first established to originate and service farm mortgages (an area in which many remain active); today they are chiefly concerned with urban mortgage investment and even more particularly with residential mortgages. They are heavily involved with the governmentally sponsored insured and guaranteed mortgage systems and have

[1]Prepared by the California Land Title Association.

originated over one third of the mortgages insured since the establishment of the Federal Housing Administration. As of 1962, mortgage companies were servicing close to $30 billion of mortgages or between one fifth and one quarter of the total outstanding home mortgage debt.

Although privately organized mortgage companies have a long and varied history, they have over the past two or three decades developed along relatively uniform lines and have assumed relatively uniform characteristics. The most common of these characteristics are those of (1) originating real estate mortgages on behalf of, or for the purpose of, selling to institutional investors, (2) arranging construction financing and interim financing of mortgages to cover the period between closing the transactions and the actual transfer of the mortgage papers to an investor, and (3) handling subsequent relations with the mortgagee and mortgagor, which involve collecting and transmittal of payment of interest and principal, dealing with delinquency when it occurs and, if need be, carrying through the processes of foreclosure and disposal of mortgaged property.

It seems important to distinguish the function of a mortgage company as described here from that of a mortgage broker, who is simply an intermediary between the borrower or originator on the one hand and investor on the other, and who maintains no continuing responsibility to either party. Many mortgage companies also engage to some degree in one or more related lines of business such as insurance, real estate brokerage, and building. Saul Klaman defines a mortgage company as "typically a closely held, private corporation whose principal activity is originating and servicing residential mortgage loans for institutional investors. It is subject to a maximum degree of federal or state supervision, has a comparatively small capital investment relative to its volume of business, and relies largely on commercial bank credit to finance its operations and mortgage inventory. Such inventory is usually held only for a short interim between closing mortgage loans and their delivery to ultimate investors."[1]

REAL-ESTATE DEVELOPMENT AND HOLDING COMPANY

Mitchell and Quinn, Inc.

In November 1964, shortly after the opening of their newest shopping center, officials of Mitchell and Quinn, Inc., a real-estate development

[1]Saul Klaman, *The Postwar Rise of Mortgage Companies,* Occasional Paper 60 (New York: National Bureau of Economic Research, 1959), p. 1.

company, were considering a number of changes in the company's basic financial policy. Previously, the company had attempted to sell each of its new development projects as soon as possible after construction had been completed and all store space had been leased. Currently, however, officials were attempting to determine whether an "optimum time to sell" could be calculated for each project. Several officials felt that the general problem of valuation was of central importance in the process of deciding when to sell a major project.

Background of the Company

Mitchell and Quinn, Inc., with headquarters in San Francisco, had been founded in 1949 by Mr. A. E. Mitchell and Mr. Brennan T. Quinn, who with their families held all of the company's common stock. The company had developed shopping centers, hotels, and retirement homes in California, Oregon, and Washington. Prior to 1949, Mr. Mitchell had been a general contractor, specializing in commercial building in the Northern California area; as executive vice-president of Mitchell and Quinn, Inc., Mr. Mitchell managed the company's activities as general contractor in construction of new projects, and supervised management of projects after completion of construction. In 1964, Mr. Mitchell was 48 years old. Mr. Quinn, age 45, had been a practicing attorney in San Francisco prior to the formation of the company. As president of Mitchell and Quinn, Inc., he spent much of his time managing the financial aspects of the business, including the acquisition of land, arrangement of mortgage financing, and negotiation of leases with new tenants.

To date, it had been the company's policy to sell each new project as soon as it had become established as a going concern. A substantial part of the firm's total income consisted of profits from the sale of major projects. The firm's record of earnings had been erratic, with high earnings in years when major projects were sold and operating losses in most other years. With the improvement in the company's cash position over the past several years mitigating the urgency to sell new projects as soon as possible, Mr. Quinn had felt that it might be advantageous to retain ownership in some major projects so that this steady rental income might help to stabilize earnings.

In the evaluation of proposed projects, it had been the company's policy to accept only those projects with an indicated after-tax rate of return to the owners in excess of 12 percent. This internal rate of return was based on the initial equity investment in the project and expected future cash flows to the equity holders, after payments of principal and interest. Mr. Quinn stated that the company probably would continue in the future to use a 12 percent cut-off rate; according to Mr. Quinn, this figure represented the company's "opportunity rate."

In July 1964, Mr. Quinn had hired Mr. Wallace C. Benjamin, a recent business school graduate, as his assistant. Shortly after joining the company, Mr. Benjamin was asked to study the firm's newest development, the Ashley-Oaks Shopping Center in San Jose, California, and to recommend a general method of determining "the optimum time to sell" major projects developed by Mitchell and Quinn.

The Ashley-Oaks Shopping Center

In August 1962, Mr. Quinn had successfully negotiated the purchase of 14 acres of open land at a total cost of $560,000 or $40,000 per acre. During the following year, plans had been completed for the Ashley-Oaks Shopping Center, and long-term financing arrangements had been made. In August 1963, construction had been started on the three buildings to be erected on the site. Early in 1964, the first building was completed and leased. The "grand opening" of the new shopping center was held in November 1964.

The cost of the new buildings and other improvements was in excess of $3.1 million, bringing the total initial investment in the project to approximately $3.7 million. A description of the types of assets in the Ashley-Oaks project is given in Exhibit 1. In 1963, Mr. Quinn had negotiated a twenty-year mortgage in the amount of $1.85 million with a large life insurance company. The balance of cash required for the initial investment was provided by private investors and by Mitchell and Quinn, Inc. The project was organized as a separate legal entity, Ashley-Oaks Shopping Center, Inc. The firm's independent auditors advised that profits from the eventual sale of the project probably would be taxed at a capital gains rate of 25 percent.

The Problems of Forecasting and Valuation

Mr. Quinn had remarked to Mr. Benjamin in their initial conversation regarding the optimum time to sell that the two biggest problems in this area were (1) forecasting revenues and expenses and (2) determining the value of the project as a going concern in later years. Mr. Quinn had said, "You have to balance what we expect to receive each year from operations, if we keep the project, against what we should get or could get for the project if we sold it."

Mr. Benjamin proceeded to gather together all available data on projected revenues and expenses for the Ashley-Oaks Shopping Center. As a first step, he talked to company officials about their expectations concerning the future of that shopping center and area in which it was located. After talking with the officers of Mitchell and Quinn, Mr. Benjamin thought it reasonable to assume that the Ashley-Oaks Shopping

Exhibit 1

MITCHELL AND QUINN, INC.

Depreciated Cost Basis: Ashley-Oaks Shopping Center

The following projected figures represent the depreciated cost basis, for tax purposes, of the shopping-center project, on the books of Ashley-Oaks Shopping Center, Inc. (dollar figures in thousands):

Year	*Period*	*Depreciation (Col. h in Exhibit 2)*	*Depreciated Cost Basis as of December 31*
1965	1	$208	$3,478*
1966	2	207	3,271
1967	3	189	3,082
1968	4	171	2,911
1969	5	157	2,754
1970	6	143	2,611
1971	7	132	2,479
1972	8	126	2,353
1973	9	124	2,229
1974	10	114	2,115

*For example, the projected cost basis as of December 31, 1965 was made up of the following assets:

I. Assets with forty-year life	
Buildings	$1,996
Administrative costs	62
Interest and other financing costs during construction	51
II. Assets with twenty-year life	
On-site improvements and landscaping	428
Commissions	123
III. Assets with ten-year life	
Fixtures	258
Total depreciable assets	2,918
IV. Land	560
Total depreciated cost basis	$3,478

Center would be physically liquidated at the end of forty years. At that time, with the projected growth in commercial development in the area of San Jose surrounding Ashley-Oaks, he felt that the fourteen acres of land would probably be cleared and sold for some better "economic use," such as high-rise apartments or office buildings. Furthermore, Mr. Benjamin thought that an estimated terminal land value of $200,000 per acre was conservative, since it was based only on the expected "upgrading" of the area and did not consider the possible effects of inflation. The salvage value of the buildings and improvements after forty years was estimated to be $200,000.

Organizing all available information, including "educated guesses" as well as objective data, Mr. Benjamin projected after-tax cash flows over a forty-year period, as shown in Exhibit 2 and discussed in the footnotes to Exhibit 2. As one of his major assumptions, he adopted Mr. Mitchell's suggestion that extensive remodeling of the shopping center would be necessary after approximately twenty years, in order to encourage major tenants to renew their leases on equitable terms. Mr. Benjamin assumed that this remodeling, including such items as repaving of the parking lot, would cost approximately \$500,000 and would be financed in full by a new mortgage.

Having completed the cash flow projections shown in Exhibit 2, Mr. Benjamin proceeded to the problem of valuation. He decided to confine his valuation analysis to the first ten years, and he hoped to be able to recommend an optimum time to sell the Ashley-Oaks Shopping Center in the decade 1965–1974.

Valuation Method A: Ashley-Oaks Shopping Center

In the past, Mitchell and Quinn had usually determined the value of a shopping-center project at a given point in time by a method which the company called "the capitalization of rents." According to Mr. Quinn, under this method, rents guaranteed by leases, less operating expenses, were generally capitalized at 7 percent, while overage rents were capitalized at 10 percent—reflecting the greater uncertainty in overage rents.[1] Mr. Benjamin was somewhat puzzled by the fact that the *current* year's rents were used in this method of valuation; he felt that the value of the project should in some way reflect expected future rents, since overage rents were expected to rise over the following fifteen years. Cash flow projections are shown in Exhibit 2. For purposes of computation, Mr. Benjamin expressed Mitchell and Quinn's existing "capitalization-of-rents" method as follows:

$$\text{Valuation Method A: } (V_A)_t = \frac{\begin{matrix}\text{guaranteed} \\ \text{rents}\end{matrix} - \begin{matrix}\text{cash} \\ \text{expenses}\end{matrix}}{7\%} + \frac{\text{overage rents}}{10\%}$$

where $(V_A)_t$ is the value of the project at the end of period t under Valuation Method A,

guaranteed rents and overage rents represent gross rent revenues in period t (columns a and b in Exhibit 2), and

cash expenses pertain to operating expenses in period t and exclude financing costs (column e in Exhibit 2).

[1]Refer to paragraphs (1) and (2) in footnotes to Exhibit 2 for a description of guaranteed and overage rents.

Exhibit 2

MITCHELL AND QUINN, INC.

Cash Flow Projections: Ashley-Oaks Shopping Center
(Dollar figures in thousands)

		a	b	c	d	e	f	g
Year	*Period*	*Guaranteed Rents (1)*	*Overage Rents (2)*	*Principal Receipts (3)*	*Cash Receipts (4)*	*Cash Expenses (5)*	*Loan Payments (6)*	*Cash Flow (BT) (7)*
1965	1	$227	$ 14	$13	$254	$154	$151	$ (51)
1966	2	337	67	14	418	68	156	195
1967	3	335	75	16	426	69	156	202
1968	4	331	99	20	450	71		223
1969	5	358	86	22	466	72		239
1970	6	356	92	24	472	73		244
1971	7	354	105	26	485	75		255
1972	8	351	116	29	496	76		265
1973	9	349	131	31	511	78		278
1974	10	347	146	33	526	79		291
1975	11	350	162	0	512	80		276
1976	12	350	178	0	528	80		292
1977	13		195		545			309
1978	14		212		562			326
1979	15		220		570			334
1980	16		220		570			334
1981	17							
1982	18							
1983	19							
1984	20							
1985	21						$ 45	$445
1986	22						45	445
1987	23							
1988	24							
1989	25							
1990	26							
1991	27							
1992	28							
1993	29							
1994	30							
1995	31							
1996	32							
1997	33							
1998	34							
1999	35							
2000	36							
2001	37							
2002	38							
2003	39							
2004	40							

Notes on facing page.

(1) *Guaranteed Rents:* Each commercial tenant signed a lease which specified an annual "guaranteed rent." Leases in the Ashley-Oaks Shopping Center had an average term of slightly less than twenty years. As of November 1964, all space in the shopping center had been leased, however, a number of tenants were not scheduled to occupy the new buildings until 1965. By the terms of the leases, total guaranteed rents for the shopping center varied to some degree in each of the first ten years. It was expected that guaranteed rents would remain constant after the first ten years.

(2) *Overage Rents:* With the exception of the bank, savings and loan association, and consumer finance company, all tenants agreed to pay "overage rents" equal to a given percentage of all sales in excess of a predetermined level of annual sales. This level is called the "sales breaker." The percentage figure varied from 1 percent to 10 percent of sales in excess of the sales breaker, depending largly on the type of store and the level of the sales breaker. For example, one tenant (a shoe store) signed a lease which provided for guaranteed rent of $9600 per year plus overage rent equal to 5 percent of all sales in excess of $192,000 per year. Aggregate overage rents were projected to increase over the next fifteen years, owing to increasing population in the area and increasing sales in the shopping center. Beyond fifteen years, sales and overage rents were expected to remain constant.

(3) *Principal Receipts from Tenants:* Two major tenants had borrowed a total of $228,000 from Ashley-Oaks Shopping Center, Inc. to finance store fixtures and working capital. The terms of the loans provided for repayment of principal over a ten-year period, 1965–1974.

(4) *Cash Receipts:*

$$\begin{aligned} \text{Cash receipts} &= \text{guaranteed rents} + \text{overage rents} + \text{principal receipts} \\ \text{(d)} &= \text{(a)} + \text{(b)} + \text{(c)} \end{aligned}$$

(5) *Cash Expenses:* Cash expenses included real-estate taxes, interest, insurance, maintenance, merchants' association dues, and management fees. The management fees—paid by Ashley-Oaks Shopping Center, Inc. to Mitchell and Quinn, Inc.—covered promotion expenses, legal and audit expenses, and general management services performed by company personnel for the shopping center.

(6) *Loan Payments:* A twenty-year mortgage in the amount of $1,850,000 with interest at 5 3/4 per cent had been negotiated with a prominent life insurance company. Terms of the loan called for payments of approximately $13,000 per month. Total payments were projected at $151,000 in 1965 and $156,000 in each of the following nineteen years. It was expected that after twenty years, a major remodeling of the shopping center would be required in order to induce major tenants to renew their leases. Mr. Mitchell indicated that, in his opinion, such a remodeling would require expenditures of approximately $500,000. Mr. Benjamin assumed that the projected expenditures would be financed by a new mortgage of $500,000 and he estimated that annual payments on the new loan would be $45,000, assuming an interest rate of 6 percent and a term of twenty years.

(7) *Cash Flow Before Tax*

$$\begin{aligned} \text{Cash flow (BT)} &= \text{cash receipts} - \text{cash expenses} - \text{loan payment} \\ \text{(g)} &= \text{(d)} - \text{(e)} - \text{(f)} \end{aligned}$$

Exhibit 2 (Continued)

h	i	j	k	l	m	n
Depreciation (8)	*Principal Payments (9)*	*Application of Tax Loss (10)*	*Taxable Income (11)*	*Income Taxes (12)*	*Terminal Cash Flow (AT) (13)*	*Cash Flow (AT) (14)*
$208	$ 54	$ 0	$(218)	$ 0		$ (51)
207	57	31	0	0		195
189	60	57	0	0		202
171	64	96	0	0		223
157	67	127	0	0		239
143	71	116	31	16		244
132	76	0	172	86		239
126	80	0	190	95		179
124	85		207	103		183
114	90		233	116		187
90	95		281	141		160
87	99		304	152		151
84	103		328	164		157
80	107		356	178		148
78	112		368	184		156
74	116		376	188		150
70	121		385	192		146
68	126		392	196		142
66	137		405	203		138
63	136		407	203		131
91	15		369	184		243
86	16		375	188		261
81	17		381	190		257
78	18		385	193		255
73	19		391	195		252
70	20		395	198		250
68	21		398	199		247
64	22		403	201		246
61	23		407	204		242
58	24		411	206		241
57	26		414	207		239
57	27		415	208		238
57	28		416	208		237
57	29		417	208		237
57	30		418	209		237
56	31		419	210		236
56	32		420	210		235
56	33		421	210		235
56	34		422	211		235
56	35		423	212	2390	2624

Notes on facing page.

(8) *Depreciation:* It was the policy of Mitchell and Quinn to use the double-declining balance method of depreciation on all new projects. In general, the company used the following figures for asset life: buildings, forty years; landscaping and other on-site improvements, twenty years; store fixtures, ten years; commissions (straight-line depreciation used), twenty years. In using the double-declining balance method, the company normally converted to straight-line depreciation at the half-life of the asset. In the case of new assets, existing tax regulations permitted the change from double-declining balance to straight-line depreciation at the discretion of the tax-payer. (The depreciated cost basis at the end of each of the first ten years is shown in Exhibit 1.)

(9) *Principal Portion of Loan Payment:* The annual principal payment was equal to the loan payment (f) minus interest.

(10) *Appreciation of Tax-Loss Carry Forward:* Mr. Benjamin estimated that Ashley-Oaks Shopping Center, Inc., would carry on its books at the end of 1964 a loss of $209,000 for tax purposes. This loss could be carried forward and applied against taxable income over the ensuing five years. Operating expenses for the partially completed center were usually high during 1964, resulting in the operating loss for the year.

(11) *Taxable Income:*

Taxable income = cash flow (BT) − depreciation + principal payments
(k) = (g) − (h) + (i)
− principal receipts − application of tax loss
− (c) − (j)

(12) *Income Tax:*

(1) = (k) × .(0.5)

It should be noted that income taxes are deducted from cash flow in the year *following* accrual. See footnote (14) below.

(13) *Terminal Cash Flow:* Total cash from liquidation of the shopping center in year 2004 (period 40).

Land: 14 acres at $200,000 per acre		$2,800,000
Buildings and improvements: salvage value		200,000
		$3,000,000
Total cash from sale (before tax)		
Depreciated cost basis:		
Land	$560,000	
Buildings and improvements	-0-	
Total cost basis		560,000
Capital gain		$2,440,000
Capital gain tax (25%)		610,000
Terminal cash flow (after tax)		$2,390,000

*(Total cash from sale minus tax)

(14) *Cash Flow After Tax:*

Cash Flow (AT) = Cash flow (ET) − income tax (for previous year)
(n) = (g) − (1)
+ terminal cash flow (AT) (in last year only)
+ (m)

Income taxes are paid in the year *following* accrual. For example, the projected accrued income tax of $16,000 in 1970 is deducted from cash flow (BT) of $255,000 in computing cash flow (AT) of $239,000 for 1971.

Mr. Benjamin found that under this method the value of the Ashley-Oaks project appeared to rise in each of the first ten years (dollar figures in thousands):

Year	Period	Guaranteed Rents	Cash Expenses	Guaranteed Rents Less Cash Expenses
1965	1	$227	$154	$ 73
1966	2	337	68	269
1967	3	335	69	266
1968	4	331	71	260
1969	5	358	72	286
1970	6	356	73	283
1971	7	354	75	279
1972	8	351	76	275
1973	9	349	78	271
1974	10	347	79	268

Year	Period	Guaranteed Rents Less Cash Expenses Capitalized @ 7%	Overage Rents	Overage Rents Capitalized @ 10%	$(V_A)_t$
1965	1	$1,040	$ 14	$ 140	$1,180
1966	2	3,840	67	670	4,510
1967	3	3,800	75	750	4,550
1968	4	3,710	99	990	4,700
1969	5	4,080	86	860	4,940
1970	6	4,040	92	920	4,960
1971	7	3,980	105	1,050	5,030
1972	8	3,930	116	1,160	5,090
1973	9	3,870	131	1,310	5,180
1974	10	3,830	146	1,460	5,290

Exhibit 3 portrays the value of the project under Valuation Method A at the end of each year through 1974. When Mr. Benjamin questioned Mr. Quinn about the rationality of this valuation method, Mr. Quinn emphasized that although the capitalization of rents might be hard to justify on theoretical grounds, it nevertheless was a method used by many syndicates and institutional investors when they were considering the purchase of a newly developed shopping center as a long-term investment.

Valuation Method B: Ashley-Oaks Shopping Center

Mr. Benjamin learned from other company employees that Mitchell and Quinn had occasionally used another "capitalization method" in valuing

Exhibit 3

MITCHELL AND QUINN, INC.

Value of Ashley-Oaks Shopping Center under Various Valuation Methods

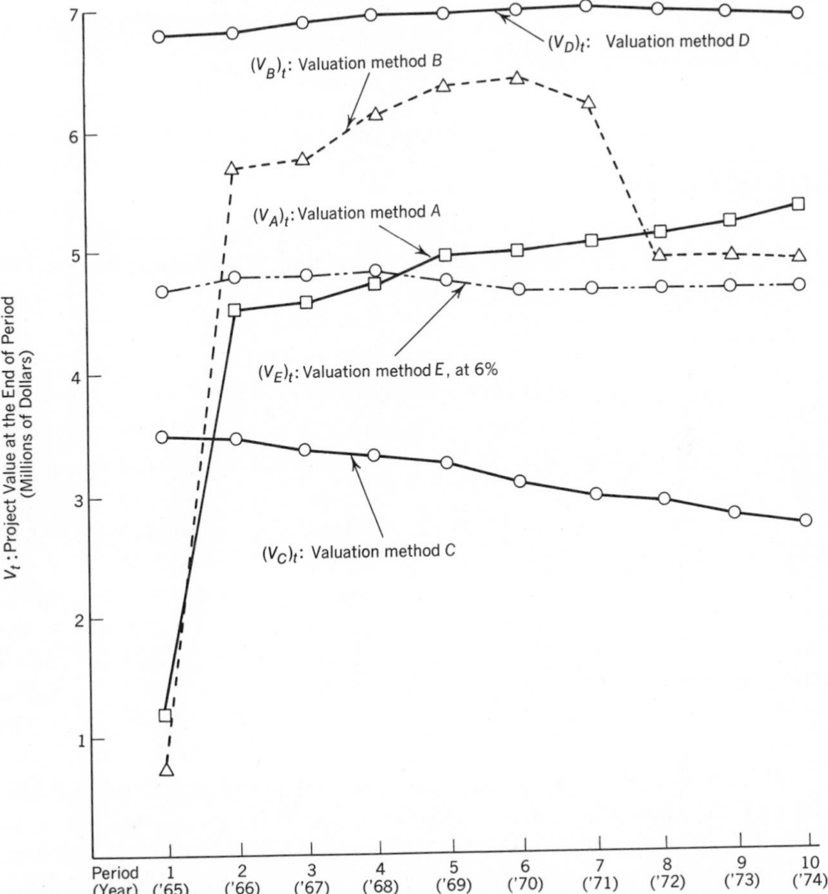

real estate projects. Under this method, the *total value* of the project at any time equalled the current value of the *equity* plus the current value of *debt* in the project; the value of the equity was assumed to be equal to current cash flow (after tax and debt service) capitalized at five per cent, and the value of debt was equal to the unpaid balance on the mortgage.

Valuation Method B: Total value = value of equity + value of debt

$$(V_B)_t = \frac{\text{cash flow (AT)}}{5\%} + L_t$$

where $(V_B)_t$ is the total value of the project at the end of period t under Valuation Method B,

Cash flow (AT) is the after-tax net cash flow to the owners in period t, after debt service (column n in Exhibit 2), and

L_t is the outstanding amount of debt in the project at the end of period t.

With this method of valuation, Mr. Benjamin found that, in the early years of the project, the value of the Ashley-Oaks Shopping Center appeared to be considerably higher than under Valuation Method A (dollar figures in thousands):

Year	Period	Cash Flow (AT)	Cash Flow (AT) Capitalized @ 5%	L_t	$(V_B)_t$
1965	1	$ (51)	$(1,020)	$1,796	$ 776
1966	2	195	3,900	1,736	5,636
1967	3	202	4,040	1,679	5,719
1968	4	223	4,460	1,615	6,075
1969	5	239	4,780	1,548	6,328
1970	6	244	4,880	1,477	6,357
1971	7	239	4,780	1,401	6,181
1972	8	179	3,580	1,321	4,901
1973	9	183	3,660	1,236	4,896
1974	10	187	3,740	1,146	4,886

With this approach to valuation, Mr. Benjamin observed that the value of the shopping center would be expected to drop after the sixth year, as cash flow (after tax) was expected to decline after the tax-loss carry forward of the early years had been fully applied. The initial tax loss is described in paragraph (10) of the footnotes to Exhibit 2.

Valuation Method C: Ashley-Oaks Shopping Center

After giving the valuation problem considerable thought, Mr. Benjamin decided that if the Ashley-Oaks Shopping Center were to be retained by Mitchell and Quinn as a long-term investment, the total value of the project in any year would be equal to the current value of the equity plus the outstanding debt in the project, as was the initial premise in Valuation Method B. However, Valuation Method C differed in its approach to determining the value of the equity. Mr. Benjamin felt that from the owners' viewpoint the value of the *equity* in any year would be equal to the present value of all *future* cash flows (after tax and debt service), discounting at Mitchell and Quinn's "opportunity rate" of 12 percent. He expressed this approach as follows:

Valuation Method C: $(V_C)_t = E_t + L_t$

where $(V_C)_t$ is the value of the project at the end of period t under valuation method C

E_t is the present value, using Mitchell and Quinn's opportunity rate of 12 percent, of cash flows (after tax and debt service) in periods $t + 1$ through 40 (column n in Exhibit 2), and

L_t is the amount of debt in the project at the end of period t.

Using the data in Exhibit 2, Mr. Benjamin calculated the required present values, and then computed the following total value of the project at the end of each of the first ten years (dollar figures in thousands):

Year	Period	E_t	L_t	$(V_C)_t$
1965	1	$1,677	$1,796	$3,473
1966	2	1,683	1,739	3,422
1967	3	1,683	1,679	3,362
1968	4	1,622	1,615	3,277
1969	5	1,662	1,548	3,210
1970	6	1,573	1,477	3,050
1971	7	1,523	1,401	2,924
1972	8	1,527	1,321	2,848
1973	9	1,527	1,236	2,763
1974	10	1,523	1,146	2,669

The changing value of the project, as calculated above, is shown graphically in Exhibit 3.

Mr. Benjamin asked Mr. Quinn for his comments on Valuation Method C. Mr. Quinn felt that the approach was an interesting one, although he emphasized that a number of the underlying assumptions in the cash flow projections in Exhibit 2 might be questioned. As an alternative to method C, Mr. Quinn suggested that it might be wise to consider the value of the Ashley-Oaks project to an outside investor. Mr. Quinn said he felt certain that a number of institutional investors were evaluating projects using present value techniques and that Mr. Benjamin should evaluate the Ashley-Oaks Center from an investor's viewpoint, using the *investor's* discount rate.

Valuation Method D: Ashley-Oaks Shopping Center

Foreseeing the possibility of computational difficulties in calculating the value of the project to an institutional investor, Mr. Benjamin decided first to approach the valuation problem from the standpoint of a nontax-paying financial institution, such as a pension fund.

He assumed that an institutional investor would finance the initial investment entirely with cash; it was not probable, he felt, that such an investor would leverage his position in the project with a mortgage or any other form of debt. As in Exhibit 2, Mr. Benjamin assumed that the investor would plan to invest an additional $500,000 for major remodeling of the shopping center in the twentieth year of the project life, and that the project would be liquidated and sold after the fortieth year, resulting in a terminal cash flow (before tax) of $3,000,000.[2] Details of the calculation of cash flows to the investor are shown in Exhibit 4. It was felt that a discount rate of 6 percent might be appropriate in a pension fund's present value computation. This approach is summarized as follows:

Valuation Method D: $(V_D)_t = C_t$

where $(V_D)_t$ is the value of the project to a non-tax-paying investor at the end of period t (hence, the price he would be willing to pay for the project, given the assumptions in the calculations), and

C_t is the present value, using the *investor's* discount rate of 6 percent, of cash flows (before tax) in periods $t + 1$ through 40 (cash flow in Exhibit 4).

(Note that there is no debt under this alternative.)

With this method, Mr. Benjamin computed the following values of the project to an investor such as a pension fund at the end of each of the next ten years; the results are also shown in Exhibit 3 (dollar figures in thousands):

Year	Period	C_t or $(V_D)_t$
1965	1	$6,744
1966	2	6,799
1967	3	6,850
1968	4	6,882
1969	5	6,901
1970	6	6,916
1971	7	6,920
1972	8	6,915
1973	9	6,897
1974	10	6,864

[2]The computation of this expected terminal cash flow is given in paragraph (13) of footnotes to Exhibit 2.

Mr. Benjamin observed that with Valuation Method D the peak value to an investor of this type appeared to occur at the end of the seventh year.

Exhibit 4

MITCHELL AND QUINN, INC.

Valuation Method D: Ashley-Oaks Shopping Center
Projected Cash Flows to a Nontax-Paying Institutional Investor
(Dollar figures in thousands)

Year(s)	*Period(s)*	*Cash Receipts (Col. d in Exhibit 2)*	*Cash Expenses (Col. e in Exhibit 2)*	*Cash Flow*
1965	1	$254	$154	$ 100*
1966	2	418	68	250
1967	3	426	69	357
1968	4	450	71	379
1969	5	460	72	394
1970	6	472	73	399
1971	7	485	75	410
1972	8	496	76	420
1973	9	511	78	433
1974	10	526	79	447
1975	11	512	80	432
1976	12	528	80	448
1977	13	545	80	465
1978	14	562	80	482
1979–1984	15–19	570	80	490
1985	20	570	80	–10†
1986–2003	21–39	570	80	490
2004	40	570	80	3,490‡

*Assumed that no mortgage or other form of debt financing would be used by the institutional investor.
†Included $500 additional investment to finance a major remodeling of the shopping center in period 20.
‡Included cash flow of $490 from operations plus the terminal cash flow (before tax) of $3,000 from liquidation of the project in period 40. The calculation of the terminal cash flow is shown in paragraph (13) of footnotes to Exhibit 2.

Valuation Method E: Ashley-Oaks Shopping Center

As a final alternative, Mr. Benjamin thought it necessary to consider a present-value approach similar to Valuation Method D from the viewpoint of a tax-paying investor, to determine the price that such an investor might be willing to pay for the project in each of the next ten years.

At the outset, Mr. Benjamin faced a problem in dealing with depreciation and the computation of annual tax charges: in a present value approach, the total value or purchase price of the project was a function of the annual cash flows (after tax); however, these cash flows were obviously dependent upon depreciation expenses, which, in turn, were a function of the purchase price. While this problem, phrased in terms of one unknown, was not conceptually difficult, it nevertheless presented a complicated task from a computational standpoint.

A friend of Mr. Benjamin's, employed as a data processing supervisor at a large insurance company in San Francisco, offered to assist Mr. Benjamin in writing a computer program to calculate the value of the project to a tax-paying investor in each of the next ten years. Using the same initial assumptions as with a nontax-paying investor in method D, they used as input data the cash flow figures (before tax) from Exhibit 4. Depreciation was then stated as a function of the unknown total value or purchase price of the shopping center. It was assumed that the investor would use 150 percent declining balance depreciation in each year up to the half-life of depreciable assets, at which time the investor would switch to straight-line depreciation.[3] With an algebraic expression for depreciation and with the initial tax-loss mentioned in footnote (10) to Exhibit 2, the program arrived at an expression for after-tax cash flow given the investor's discount rate, the program then solved for the unknown value of the project at the end of the first ten years employing a simple iteration technique.

Valuation Method E: $(V_E)_t = P_t$

where $(V_E)_t$ is the value of the project to an investor, having tax rates of 50 percent on income and 25 percent on capital gains, at the end of period t (that is, the price he would pay for the project at that time), and

P_t is the present value, using the investor's discount rate, of cash flows (after tax) in periods $t + 1$ through 40. (Given cash flows [before tax] from Exhibit 4, tax rates, and the discount rate, the program calculates depreciation, cash flow [after tax], and P_t.)

(Note that there is no debt under this alternative.)

In addition, Mr. Benjamin wanted to determine the effect of various discount rates on the present value of the project in each year. The results of his collaboration with the programmer are listed below, indicating the value of the Ashley-Oaks project at the end of each year, under a number of alternative discount rates (dollar figures in thousands):

[3]Existing tax regulations stated that second-hand or used property acquired after 1953 could be depreciated with the declining-balance method using a rate not in excess of 150 percent of the straight-line rate. Before switching to the straight-line method of depreciation, the investor would have to receive the consent of the Internal Revenue Service.

Year	*Period*	*P_t or $(V_E)_t$ at Discount Rate of* 4%	6%	8%	10%	12%
1964	1	$6,610	$4,680	$3,550	$2,850	$2,380
1965	2	6,670	4,730	3,600	2,890	2,420
1966	3	6,700	4,780	3,650	2,940	2,470
1967	4	6,620	4,790	3,670	2,960	2,480
1968	5	6,540	4,720	3,660	2,890	2,410
1969	6	6,450	4,600	3,490	2,780	2,310
1970	7	6,440	4,610	3,510	2,800	2,320
1971	8	6,420	4,620	3,520	2,810	2,330
1972	9	6,390	4,610	3,520	2,810	2,330
1973	10	6,380	4,600	3,510	2,800	2,320

Exhibit 5

MITCHELL AND QUINN, INC.

Valuation Method E: Effect of Discount Rate on Value of Ashley-Oaks Shopping Center

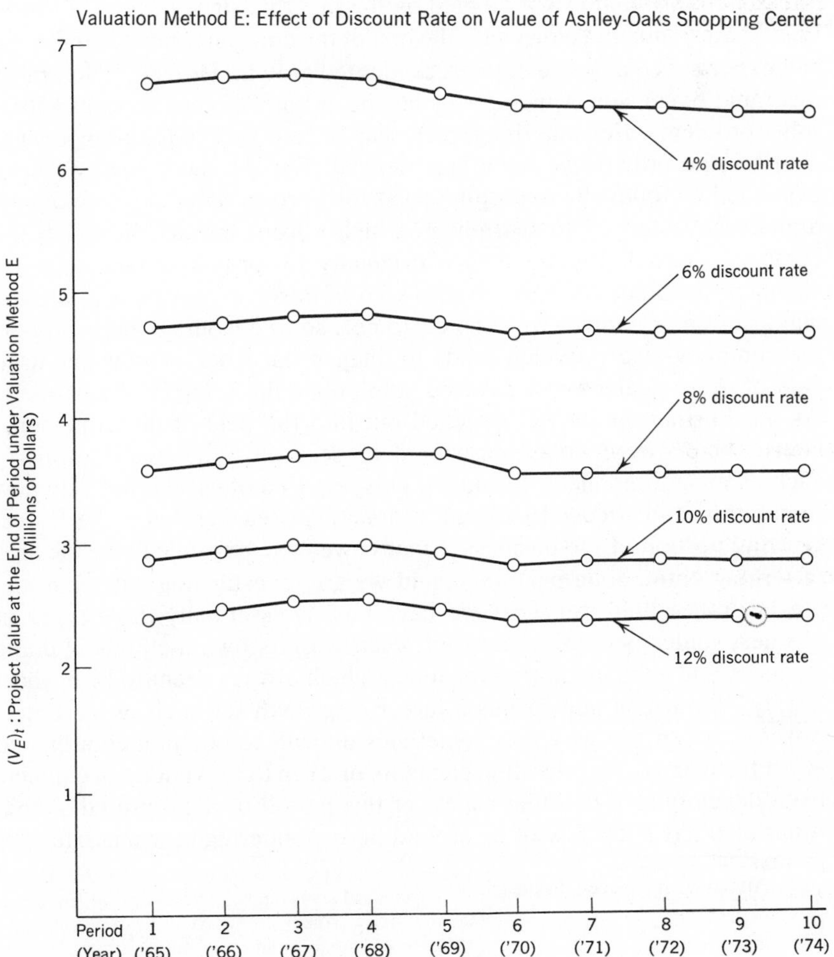

The values in each year, with each of the five discount rates noted above, are shown graphically in Exhibit 5. For purposes of comparison with other valuation methods, project values using a discount rate of 6 percent above, are shown in Exhibit 3.

ORGANIZATIONAL PLANNING

Fidelity Credit Corporation (A)

Early in 1955, Douglas A. Davis, the president of Fidelity Credit Corporation,[1] was assessing the strengths and weaknesses of his organization in order to formulate a program for improving the firm's operations. His thinking in this vein was prompted by the fact that since the end of World War II the company, along with the rest of the consumer finance industry, had experienced a period of unprecendented growth. He said, "Naturally, this rapid expansion, which for us has been fourfold, has brought with it some problems. For one thing, there has been a lack of long-range planning for the growth we have experienced. For the most part, we have expanded by following opportunities as they arose. Some of these opportunities have led us to entirely new fields from the one in which the company started. Fidelity began originally by providing consumer installment financing for cars. In that kind of business, car dealers are the main source of contact with the customer, so to encourage their support the company also provided funds to finance the stock of new and used cars of those dealers who directed automobile financing contracts to us. As our business grew we branched out into the field of direct personal loans; which were either unsecured or secured by personal property such as an automobile or furniture. This required of us a completely new orientation and focus. In recent years, this area has been the fastest growing portion of the business. Finally, we have expanded into the area of writing automobile insurance, and we are investigating entry into the life insurance field. So what we have now is essentially three types of business under one corporate roof, each with its own methods of doing business and each clamoring for funds which always seem to be in short supply. When you add to this a factor of growth for each of our enterprises you can see why it is sometimes difficult to obtain a coordinated effort from all of our operating elements or even to prevent open conflicts from developing. The other aspect of this period of rapid growth is that it has also left not a few of us around here wondering how much further

[1]All names have been disguised.

this pattern of growth will carry us and how we can effectively adjust to bigness." Exhibit 1 shows indicators of performance for Fidelity and the consumer finance industry since 1946.

The Organization

By March 1955, Fidelity, from its headquarters in Chicago, operated 253 offices located in 200 cities throughout twenty-one states. The company and its subsidiaries employed about 2700 people. In 1954, it earned $4.4 million on a total interest and premium income of $45.8 million, the highest earnings and income achieved in the history of the firm.

Fidelity's organization structure at that time is depicted in Exhibit 2. Business was conducted through three operating divisions: sales finance, consumer loan, and fire and casualty insurance. Finance, credit, law, and administrative elements carried out corporate staff work. The corporate development division carried out both staff and line duties. The functions and operations of each of these divisions are described below.

Sales Finance Division

The basic function of the sales finance division was the financing of both consumer installment purchases and dealers' inventories. Sales financing was devoted almost entirely to automobiles, although it also included some financing of mobile homes and boats. The demand for wholesale sales financing stemmed from the dealer's relationship with the automobile manufactuer, whose products he sold. The dealer's franchise usually required that he accept a minimum number of cars each year. Payment was expected when these cars were shipped. Nearly 90 percent of the automobile dealers, however, did not have the necessary capital to meet this requirement and resorted to wholesale credit from financing agencies to floor their cars. Fidelity's wholesale function was to provide a line of credit that assured the dealer the capital required to carry a thirty- to sixty-day inventory based on estimated sales of cars. As a result, the dealer was assured of being able to make direct payment to the factory at the time of shipment. Fidelity did not expect to make much, if any, profit in this wholesale phase of the business but looked at it as a service to the dealer, made to obtain his retail financing volume.

Retail sales financing (discounting) was carried on mostly through the dealers whose cars had been floored by the finance company. The automobile dealer making a new or used car sale on time originated the entire credit transaction; that is, he appraised the trade-in, he determined the downpayment, he arranged terms for the payment of the balance and he established the amount of the finance charges to be paid by the customer. To the extent that these charges exceeded the discount when he sold the contract, he had an additional source of income. On a typical deal, this

Exhibit 1

FIDELITY CREDIT CORPORATION (A)

Indicators of Performance of Fidelity Credit and Consumer Finance Industry

(Dollar figures in millions)

	Retail Installment Credit Outstanding				*Personal Installment Loans Outstanding*		*Earnings as Percent of Net Worth*			
	Automotive		*Other Consumer Goods*				*Thirteen Largest Finance Companies*			
Dec. 31	*All Finance Companies*	*Fidelity*	*All Finance Companies*	*Fidelity*	*All Finance Companies*	*Fidelity*	*High*	*Average*	*Low*	*Fidelity*
1954	$4,870	$140	$841	$15	$2,557	$77	17.6%	13.9%	9.1%	11.4%
1953	4,688	153	816	17	2,137	67	18.3	13.8	9.8	12.5
1952	3,630	142	680	14	1,866	53	18.3	13.6	9.8	12.9
1951	2,863	114	452	8	1,555	41	18.6	14.6	9.3	9.3
1950	2,956	102	532	5	1,286	21	19.2	15.9	8.6	11.3
1949	2,265	75	477	2	973	15	—	—	—	12.3
								(data not compiled)		
1948	1,333	67	287	1	854	19	—	—	—	13.3
1947	802	56	185	1	725	14	—	—	—	11.1
1946	377	24	67	—	594	10	16.0	10.3	4.1	4.7

SOURCE: Standard & Poor's, *Industry Surveys*, and compilations of casewriter.

Exhibit 2

FIDELITY CREDIT CORPORATION (A)

Earnings Comparison of Operating Elements
(Dollar figures in millions)

	1956	*%*	*1955*	*%*	*1954*	*%*	*1953*	*%*	*1952*	*%*	*1951*	*%*
OPERATING INCOME*												
Sales finance branches	$ 16.5	50.0%	$ 15.6	52.5%	$ 9.7	43.1%	$ 10.4	47.1%	$ 7.2	51.8%	$ 7.7	60.2%
Consumer loan branches	14.6	44.2	12.0	40.4	9.7	43.1	8.8	39.9	5.9	42.4	3.7	28.9
Insurance subsidiaries†	1.9	5.8	2.1	7.1	3.1	13.8	2.9	13.0	.8	5.8	1.4	10.9
Total	$ 33.0	100.0%	$ 29.7	100.0%	$ 22.5	100.0%	$ 22.1	100.0%	$ 13.9	100.0%	$ 12.8	100.0%
FUNDS COMMITTED												
Sales finance branches	$198.9	60.1%	$183.5	62.6%	$150.3	60.9%	$148.5	62.9%	$ 97.6	62.0%	$112.9	72.7%
Consumer loan branches	116.2	35.1	93.1	31.6	80.8	32.8	72.9	30.8	47.0	29.8	31.2	20.2
Insurance subsidiaries†	16.5	4.8	17.0	5.8	15.6	6.3	14.8	6.3	12.9	8.2	11.0	7.1
Total	$331.6	100.0%	$293.6	100.0%	$246.7	100.0%	$236.2	100.0%	$157.5	100.0%	$155.1	100.0%
OPERATING INCOME AS PERCENT OF FUNDS COMMITTED												
Sales finance branches		8.3%		8.5%		6.5%		7.0%		7.4%		6.8%
Consumer loan branches		12.6		12.9		12.0		12.1		12.5		11.9
Insurance subsidiaries		12.5		12.4		19.9		19.6		6.2		12.7
OPERATING INCOME AS PERCENT OF NET WORTH												
Sales finance branches†		66.4%		68.0%		52.0%		56.0%		59.2%		54.4%
Consumer loan branches‡		76.0		77.7		72.3		72.8		75.3		71.7
Insurance subsidiaries		27.8		30.9		50.0		55.8		19.7		34.1

*Before application of overhead and interest expenses (underwriting expenses for insurance subsidiaries).
†Not including life insurance subsidiary, which began operation in 1956.
‡Fidelity executives stated that sales finance companies could borrow 4 times their working capital (capital funds minus noncurrent assets), whereas consumer loan companies could borrow 2 1/2 to 3 times this amount. On the basis of this plus balance sheet figures (see Exhibit 7 Fidelity Credit Corp.(A), the casewriter calculated that since 1950 the company's equity capital would average 12.5% of funds committed to sales finance branches and 16.6% of funds committed to consumer loan branches if these functions were organized as separate companies. He then applied these percentages to the return on funds committed for each year, the only comparative measures which the company employed.

SOURCE: Company records and calculations of casewriter.

would be quite important since the sales price of the car (exclusive of finance charges) might barely cover his costs. For new cars the standard rate charged the customer by the dealer would be around $6 per year per $100 financed. This contract, when presented for sale by the dealer, would be discounted at about $4.50 per year per $100. Rates for used cars would be higher, depending on the age of the car.

Credit checks on the dealer's customers were carried out by Fidelity. If the customer was considered a good risk, Fidelity discounted the contract, that is, purchased the obligation for less than the gross contract balance and took over from the dealer the responsibility for collecting regular payments from the customer. The rate at which the contract was discounted varied somewhat depending on the dealer's volume of business, the year of the car being offered as collateral, and the amount of risk Fidelity was assuming. Fidelity first applied the proceeds from their purchase to liquidate the dealer's wholesale liability for the unit sold and then credited him with the remainder. This credit might be available to him in cash or might be restricted in a special reserve maintained to offset his contingent liability if he had guaranteed the contract.

Under Fidelity's standard plan of repurchase guarantee, if a customer defaulted and the car was repossessed, the dealer was liable for the deficiency (if any) between the amount the customer still owed and the amount for which the car was subsequently sold. The dealer's reserve was designed to help him offset such a loss. His reserve requirement was proportional to his contingent liability; whenever the balance in his reserve exceeded the required amount he could request that the difference be paid to him.

In competing for automobile contracts the sales finance division also accepted "without recourse" contracts. These were contracts which were not guaranteed by the dealer. Therefore, if the customer defaulted, Fidelity absorbed the deficiency (the difference between balance owing at time of repossession and the amount recovered on resale) without recourse to the dealer. Fidelity's discount was greater on these contracts to compensate for the company's added exposure to losses. When a dealer sold a "without recourse" contract to Fidelity, the proceeds (after liquidating any wholesale indebtedness on the unit) were immediately available to him.

Fidelity conducted its sales finance operations through fifty-three sales finance branch offices organized under four regions: north central, midwest, southwest, and west. In supervising this network the sales finance division manager was aided by two assistant division managers who divided the responsibility of managing the four regions. In March 1955, there were 712 employees in the division, broken down roughly as follows: 10 in the home office, 3 at each of the regional offices, and from 7 to 25 at each of the branch offices. Ten branches, located in the largest cities in Fidelity's territory, had staffs numbering in the upper end of this range. About 70 percent of the division's employees were women secretarial and clerical personnel.

According to Jack Phillips, the division manager, socializing with and getting to know the automobile dealers on a man-to-man basis was an important element in maintaining the close relationships which he felt were essential in his end of the business. He attributed his personal success in the company to his consistent adherence to this policy. After coming to Fidelity in 1932 he worked up through the sales finance division and was named vice-president and assistant division manager in 1944, manager of the division in 1944, and a director of the company in 1950. Phillips was 51 in 1955. As division manager, he made it a point to appear at all important dealer conferences, and both he and his two assistants spend much time traveling through the sales regions calling on the regional and branch managers and on dealers if the local managers thought that this would help cement relations between the dealer and the company.

The regional and branch managers carried out the same functions as outlined for the division within their assigned geographical areas. Each branch office was responsible for soliciting and obtaining dealers with whom they could develop a plan for providing their new and used car purchasers with financing. The branch managers were also responsible for passing on customer credit and making collections under policy guidance from the company's credit division. In conducting the wholesale end of their business, the branch managers had physical inventories made at least monthly of the cars which they "floored." These physical inventories were conducted to confirm that the dealer actually had in his possession the cars which were being financed.

Assisting the typical sales finance branch manager, who was a sales producer, was a branch operations manager who supervised the office staff and acted as second in command; a district representative who assisted in what was termed "production" work, soliciting new business among the car dealers; a collection manager; and a field representative whose job it was to call on and remedy delinquent accounts. Also assisting each branch manager were one or more insurance adjusters who represented Fidelity's insurance subsidiaries handling claims on cars which the company insured. The typical branch manager had ten or eleven years of experience with the company and had a salary of around $8500 a year. As several of Fidelity's executives described him, "He is the type of person who can sit down Monday morning, shuffle through a pile of contracts handed him by an automobile dealer, decide to buy the whole lot, and calmly write a check for $75,000. He is the salesman type of person who operates on an expense account and has a company car for his use. He has to have an ability to size up and establish rapport with the auto dealers who can make or break him since it is they who ultimately determine the quality and volume of the paper he receives." The typical sales finance branch office acquired around $6 million in retail receivables each year.

Consumer Loan Division

The consumer loan division was primarily concerned with providing direct loans to individual customers. Most loans ranged from $50 to $1500 and were made directly to individuals for the purposes of paying doctor bills, consolidating bills, education, home furnishings, and various unforeseen expenses. The money was lent for a stated period of time and paid back in monthly installments that included interest charges. Usually, the customer's car or other property was accepted as security for the loan, although some loans were made on an unsecured basis.

One of the major problems which the consumer loan division and other companies in this business had was in overcoming the stigma which the industry inherited from the "loan shark" era of the early 1900s. At that time there were no regulations governing interest rates on high risk personal loans. The interest rates allowed by the then existing usury laws did not compensate for the risk in making small personal loans to anyone who wanted money. Consequently loan brokers operated outside the law, charging, in many instances, extremely high rates. Since that time, laws regulating small loan operations had been enacted in a majority of the state legislatures throughout the United States. These acts stipulated the maximum allowable interest rates for loan brokers. For example, in 1955 in Illinois, a fairly typical state in this regard, a consumer loan company could obtain service and interest charges of 3 percent per month on the unpaid balance of the first $150 of a loan, 2 percent on the next $150, and 1 percent thereafter up to a maximum loan of $500. Such charges were all-inclusive and thus set a definite fixed price which the customer would pay for the money loaned. The small loan laws, in effect, eliminated any element of price competition between the consumer loan companies. A maximum rate of interest was stipulated by each state and all consumer loan companies charged this rate. The volume of business adjusted itself to this rate through the degree of risk a company was willing to take.

Despite the introduction of the small-loan acts, consumer loan firms continued to be thought of as charging high rates for their service. In justifying these charges, members of the industry explained that the consumer loan business was retail in nature, that is, it supplied a large number of people with small amounts of a commodity. Just as a retail storekeeper must mark up his merchandise sufficiently to cover the costs of a staff of salesmen, rent, advertising, and so forth, the same applied to the retail distribution of money. Compared with a bank or insurance company loan of $100,000 to a single borrower, where handling expenses would be negligible, the loaning of $100,000 by a consumer loan company required numerous costly transactions. For example, a typical consumer loan company in loaning $100,000 would interview an average of 832 applicants. Approximately 7 percent of these applicants would fail to qualify after the first interview. The remaining 770 required further investigation and, of these, approximately 60 percent qualified for loans. During the year, the handling of this $100,000 in loans would involve about 9600 clerical operations.

Consumer loan companies had to compete with banks and credit unions which also offered personal loans. These lending outlets usually charged lower interest rates than the consumer loan companies. They were able to do this since they generally dealt with people with better credit standings and hence incurred lower collection and credit investigation expenses.

Fidelity's consumer loan function was started in 1934. It was initially established as an outgrowth of Fidelity's sales financing business to accommodate customers who desired a personal loan. The company was thereby able to transfer such sales finance accounts to the company's own consumer loan facilities rather than have these accounts look to other companies for personal financing. The consumer loan functions were carried out initially under the sales finance organization. Subsequently a completely separate consumer loan division was established to handle a comprehensive variety of consumer loans as well as furniture and appliance contracts. The substantial geographic expansion of the consumer loan business of the company resulted in the development of a regional and district organization parallel to that of the sales finance division in order to provide effective control of such widely dispersed operations.

As of January 1955, operations in Fidelity's consumer loan division were carried out under the supervision of the division manager, 3 assistant division managers, 5 regional managers, 25 district managers, and 253 branch managers, each of whom supervised 2 to 7 people. There were 1433 people in the division. About 60 percent of the employees were women who largely held clerical and secretarial positions.

Leonard Stevens, the division manager, had seen his division expand since 1946 from 363 to 1433 people, from 91 to 253 branch offices, and from $17 million to $91 million in loans outstanding. Referring to this pattern of growth he said, "Our progress in 1954 demonstrates the value of esprit de corps and high morale. The splendid teamwork from one end of the division to the other which has resulted in our profitable expansion during the past five years is deeply appreciated." Stevens had come to Fidelity in 1938 after a number of years of experience with two finance companies in both the consumer loan and sales finance areas. He became vice president and assistant division manager of consumer loans in 1944, division head in 1946, and a company director in 1951. He was 47 years old in 1955.

There were three consumer loan assistant division managers. Two of these divided up line responsibility for the five regional areas in which the firm operated. The third assistant manager was in charge of the staff activities of the division and for handling special projects such as the development of new types of credit service.

The regional managers divided the company's territory into five regions: north central, midwest, southwest, west, and northwest. Each region was divided into districts, the managers of which had line authority over the branches in this area. The district managers typically had about ten years experience with the company and were paid an annual salary of around $8500. Therefore, they were roughly equivalent in stature to the sales finance branch managers.

Fifty-three of the consumer loan branch offices shared the same office quarters as the sales finance branches. However, they were run as completely separate operations even to the point where each operated under a different system of accounting. As one executive put it, "There may as well be a white line down the middle of the office dividing the two lending services. When a customer comes in to pay a bill he has to go to the cashier of the office who handles his type of loan even though the other cashier working for the companion division might be less busy at the time. There is little or no coordination and cooperation between the two functions."

The rest of the consumer loan branch offices were individually situated in outlying districts in contrast to the combination offices which were located near "automobile row" in large cities. A typical consumer loan branch office consisted of a manager and three or four other employees. The branch manager was responsible for initiating and passing on loans and following them through to final collection. He typically was a man who had been with the company three or four years and was paid a salary of around $5500 a year. Both he and his assistants were provided with a detailed procedure manual to guide their lending, collection, and repossession activities. As he had to make many small-size loans to build up his volume, the consumer loan branch manager had to be able quickly to size up a borrower's credit standing, ability to pay, and the value of the items which he offered as collateral. The typical consumer loan branch generated around $500,000 in loans each year.

Fidelity had been continually adding consumer loan branch offices every year since 1934 when this activity was initiated. In recent years, whole chains of offices were added at one time through the acquisition of other consumer credit companies. It had been through mergers of this type that the company obtained most of its branch offices throughout the west coast states, in Kansas, and in Nebraska. In some instances, the companies merged into the consumer loan division had directed some of their activities toward sales financing operations. When they were merged with Fidelity, the consumer loan division took it upon itself to manage the sales finance portion of the merged company as well as the consumer loan portion. In these cases the sales finance figures were submerged in the consumer loan financial reports. By 1954, an estimated 10 percent of the outstandings of the consumer loan division were tied up in sales finance contracts.

Insurance Division

The function of the insurance division was to protect the company and its customers from loss through physical damage to the automobiles the company financed. This coverage was offered to the public jointly through the sales finance branches and the auto dealers, with whom Fidelity carried on its sales finance operation. Two subsidiary companies with authorization to write insurance in the states in which Fidelity operated handled this business. In addition to the automobile dealers, a limited number of multiple-line insurance policies were written by direct agents.

The company entered the insurance field in 1945 when it undertook to provide physical damage coverage for the automobiles that Fidelity was financing. Later, this portion of the business was extended to the general public. By January 1955, the insurance organization operated in twenty-eight states. It had 277 employees including the three home office staff departments and the operating staffs of Fidelity's two insurance subsidiaries.

F. Wade Daniels, 54, vice-president and manager of Fidelity's two fire and casualty insurance subsidiaries, came to the company in 1946 after nearly thirty years of experience in the fire and casualty insurance field. He was named a vice-president of Fidelity in 1952.

Financial Division

The financial division was responsible for the financial planning, financial relations, accounting, and fiscal functions of the company. It comprised the treasurer, the controller's department, and the financial relations vice-president. The major activities carried out under these elements were as follows: The treasurer had custodial responsibility for the cash assets of the company; he was also responsible for procuring funds and handling and processing the corporate financial documents. The controller's department carried out the accounting operations of the company and maintained internal control over the company's funds and assets. The financial relations vice-president was located in New York to procure funds through the sale of commercial paper notes and to develop and maintain favorable relations with the institutions and individuals who had money to invest or who could influence or control its investment.

In January 1955, there was a total of 160 people in the division. Nine of these people were engaged in treasury or financial operations while the remaining personnel were organized under the controller's department. Coordinating the activities of each of the functional areas within the division was the division manager and company vice-president and secretary, Gordon Johnson, who was 49. He joined Fidelity in 1931 as a member of the accounting staff and became assistant secretary of the company six years later. In 1943, he was named vice-president and secretary and in 1951 was elected a director.

Credit Division

The credit division was primarily responsible for establishing the basic credit policies of the company. It provided functional guidance to the heads of the sales finance and consumer loan divisions on credit and collection matters. It also analyzed and approved new dealer accounts and maintained a continuing evoluation of the financial performance of the company's dealers. In addition, it carried out periodic examinations of compliance with company credit policies and of the effectiveness of branch collection activities. There were twenty-one employees in the division in January 1955.

S. T. Jones, 53, manager of the credit division, had come to the company in 1946 with a background in finance. He served as assistant to Fidelity's executive vice-president and as assistant division manager of sales finance before assuming his position as credit division manager in 1954.

Administration Division

It was the responsibility of the administrative division to provide administrative support for the other elements of the company. Organized under this division were departments for personnel, training, office facilities, and purchasing. The personnel department was primarily responsible for maintaining the personnel records of the company. This department provided employment services for the home office, coordinated employment standards among other departments and handled the administrative details involved with carrying out the various employee benefit programs. The formulation of personnel policies and the maintenance of salary administration plans, however, was the joint responsibility of the company's key division managers. A separately established training director within the administration division was responsible for developing and administering company training programs. The office quarters department provided for the planning and outfitting of branch offices and other physical facilities needed for carrying on the business of the company. Purchasing services for procurement of the equipment, materials, and supplies necessary for carrying out the company's operations were performed by the purchasing department.

In January 1955 there were fifty-nine people in the division broken down as follows: two in division administration, fifteen in the personnel department, three in the training department, eight in the office quarters department, and thirty-one in the purchasing department, which included the stationery warehouse function.

The manager of the administrative division, Arthur Roberts, was named a vice-president and assumed his position in 1954. He joined the company in 1945 as chief accountant and advanced to the position of treasurer in 1946 before assuming his duties as division manager. He was 63 in 1955.

Law Department

The law department provided legal counsel on matters arising from the operation of the business and rendered such legal advice and other services as needed to assure the appropriate conduct of the company's business affairs. The company's general counsel, Ralph Holms, 45, was in charge of this function. In his background as a lawyer he had specialized in federal tax law. His department consisted of eleven people in January 1955.

Corporate Development Division

Under the corporate development division there existed both corporate operating and staff functions. The line functions of the division consisted of evaluating new business activities that did not fall within the established functions of the company. If an activity looked promising, it was organized and initiated under this division. At that time a newly acquired insurance subsidiary which wrote credit life and disability policies was being directed through one department. Another of the departments in the division was exploring the possibilities of further diversification into regular life insurance operations. Public relations, advertising, and dealer services were the primary staff functions of the division. The advertising program was directed toward expanding the company's loan activities and was at that time concentrating on promotion of borrowing for travel and vacation. This work was done almost solely in support of Fidelity's consumer loan business. The dealer services department provided capital financing and specialized management counsel for automobile dealers. Under the capital financing plan the dealer furnished a part of his required investment and the company furnished the remainder. A dealer was thereby able to obtain funds to purchase a dealership or to augment his working capital. The plan provided for profit participation between the dealer and the company and was designed to permit the dealer to repay the company's investment out of profits in as short a time as possible, five years being the normal target.

As of January 1955, there were twenty-seven people in the division broken down as follows: two in administration, two in the life insurance department, seven in the credit life and disability department, four in the dealer services department, and twelve in the public relations and advertising department.

The corporate development division was organized under Frank Shoemaker, assistant to the president. Fidelity's youngest vice-president (age 42), he came to the company in 1948 following a career in the automobile industry where he held executive sales positions with two of the large producers. He joined Fidelity Credit to direct its public relations and advertising program, and was named a division manager in early 1954.

Top Management

Filling out Fidelity's top management team, were an executive vice-president, a president, and a board of directors. The executive vice-president, James Benton, had been founder and president of his own consumer loan company, with offices throughout the west coast states. He joined Fidelity in 1951 when the two firms merged. In 1952, he was named executive-vice president and director of Fidelity. With Fidelity, he performed the function of a staff officer, headquartered in San Francisco, to represent the company in the west. He was also an important contact for the company with the west coast money market. He was 57 in 1955.

Before taking over the president's position, Douglas A. Davis had had seventeen years of diversified finance experience. He joined the company in 1930, five years after its founding, after attending the Harvard Business School. His first job was soliciting new business from auto dealers in Detroit. A year later, he was placed in charge of a new department organized to handle the consumer financing of radios. Later he served as a sales finance branch manager, a new business department manager, and as manager of a division which included sixteen of Fidelity's newly established sales finance branches in the western states. When the company spread its operations to Texas, he directed the expansion of both its sales finance and its consumer loan operations there. In 1941, he was named vice-president and director, in 1944, executive vice-president and in 1945, president. He was 56 in 1955.

The sixteen-member board of directors included eleven outside directors representing various Chicago businesses. It was chairmanned by an executive representing the interest of an industrial corporation that held a substantial interest in the common stock of the company.

The committee organization of Fidelity Credit consisted of the following: An executive committee and a finance committee were established by and acted on behalf of the board of directors in the intervals between board meetings and on matters relating to the financial affairs of the corporation. Within the internal organization of the company were committees formed to handle matters of policy formulation, credit, dealer investment, personnel administration, and employee benefits.

Performance

Exhibit 3 shows measures of the company's performance in the years since 1946. A breakdown of loans and discounts outstanding at the end of selected years is shown in Exhibit 4. Exhibit 5 shows operating statements for the firm's lending operations. Operating statements for insurance operations are shown in Exhibit 6. Exhibit 7 shows a percentage breakdown of the company's balance sheets at the end of each year since 1950.

Exhibit 3

FIDELITY CREDIT CORPORATION (A)

Measures of Operations Since 1946
(Dollar figures in millions)

	Loans and Discounts Acquired	*Net Premiums Written*	*Earnings After tax*	*Net Worth*	*Ratio of Earnings/N.W.*
1954	$490	$8.6	$4.42	$38.8	11.4%
1953	473	8.4	4.76	36.8	12.5
1952	501	9.6	4.13	31.9	12.9
1951	368	7.5	2.66	28.6	9.3
1950	328	6.8	2.52	22.2	11.3
1949	270	6.1	2.27	18.5	12.3
1948	314	4.8	2.33	17.5	13.3
1947	303	3.6	1.65	14.7	11.1
1946	159	2.2	0.41	8.8	4.7

SOURCE: Company records.

Davis was described by one of his key executives as "a man with the dream of having, if not the largest, at least the most efficient and up-to-date finance company in the business. He is consistently exploring new ideas on ways to achieve this goal. While he has been president, he has

Exhibit 4

FIDELITY CREDIT CORPORATION (A)

Loans and Discounts Outstanding
at December 31 for Selected Years
(Dollar figures in thousands)

	1954	*1952*	*1950*	*1948*	*1946*
Sales finance—retail					
Automotive	$162,961	$141,037	$102,066		
Other	14,841	13,591	4,266	n.a.	n.a.
Total	$177,802	$154,628	$106,332	$ 68,794	$26,330
Percent of total	65.4%	67.6%	74.1%	62.3%	46.5%
Number of accounts	243,616	216,894	145,157	n.a.*	n.a.
Sales finance—wholesale	$ 12,257	$ 14,120	$ 12,983	$ 14,880	$11,603
Percent of total	4.5%	6.2%	9.0%	13.4%	20.5%
Consumer loans					
Automotive	$ 33,606	$ 30,281	$ 10,744		
Furniture and other security	$ 34,553	18,650	7,850	n.a.	n.a.
Unsecured	8,408	4,334	1,851		
Total	$ 77,567	$ 53,265	$ 20,445	$ 20,129	$10,172
Percent of total	28.1%	23.3%	14.2%	18.2%	18.0%
Number of accounts	241.976	152,607	70,049	n.a.	n.a.
Loans to finance companies	$ 4,054	$ 4,755	$ 3,093	$ 5,215	$ 5,066
Percent of total	1.5%	2.1%	2.2%	4.7%	8.9%
Other business loans	$ 1,439	$ 1,830	$ 701	$ 1,561	$ 3,463
Percent of total	0.5%	0.8%	0.5%	1.4%	6.1%
Total	$273,119	$228,598	$143,554	$110,579	$56,634

*n.a.—not available.

SOURCE: Company records.

seen this company grow at an amazing rate. He has maintained a warm personal relationship with all of his executives. Fortunately for a man in his position, he is not a detail man but has an excellent grasp of the big picture."

The President Views His Organization

In assessing the strengths of his organization as he then saw them, Davis pointed to the company's record of growth as an attestation of its internal soundness. He also pointed to a management group which, in his opinion, was nicely balanced as regards the attributes of youthful vigor on the one hand and experience and seasoning on the other. "Our officers have had an average of eighteen years' service with us, and our supervisory people in all divisions have had an average of over nine years'

Exhibit 5

FIDELITY CREDIT CORPORATION (A)

Financing Operations
(In thousands)

	1954	1953	1952	1951	1950	1949	1948	1947	1946
Loans and discounts acquired during year									
Sales finance division	$359,499	$356,649	$389,643	$294,271	$283,958	$232,796	$252,430	$242,149	$116,548
Consumer loan division	129,601	116,734	110,917	73,791	44,216	37,322	61,478	60,406	42,000
Total	$489,100	$473,383	$500,560	$368,062	$328,174	$270,118	$313,908	$302,555	$158,548
Earnings									
Finance charges and other income	$ 37,852	$ 35,150	$ 27,625	$ 18,969	$ 14,154	$ 13,581	$ 11,661	$ 9,943	n.a.*
Less: Operating expenses	$ 18,753	$ 16,844	$ 13,175	$ 9,405	$ 7,467	$ 7,052	n.a.	n.a.	"
Provision for credit losses	4,132	3,802	2,197	849	1,023	2,198	"	"	"
Total operating income	$ 14,967	$ 14,504	$ 12,253	$ 8,715	$ 5,664	$ 4,331	"	"	"
Less: Interest and debt expense	7,614	7,787	5,524	3,836	2,470	2,223	"	"	"
Income before federal income taxes	$ 7,353	$ 6,717	$ 6,729	$ 4,879	$ 3,194	$ 2,108	"	"	"
Less: Provision for federal taxes	3,924	3,256	2,564	2,351	1,576	860	"	"	"
Net income from financial operations	$ 3,429	$ 3,461	$ 3,165	$ 2,528	$ 1,618	$ 1,248	"	"	"
Branch operating results before application of overhead and interest expenses									
Operating income:									
Sales finance branches	$ 9,736	$ 10,396	$ 7,151	$ 7,726	$ 7,323				
Consumer loan branches	$ 9,653	$ 8,833	$ 5,991	$ 3,682	$ 2,358				
Return on invested funds†:									
Sales finance branches	6.5%	7.0%	7.3%	6.8%	8.0%				
Consumer loan branches	12.0%	12.1%	12.7%	11.6%	12.6%				

*n.a.—not available—insurance operations were lumped in with finance operations.
†These figures were compiled monthly using each month's average funds invested.

SOURCE: Company records.

Exhibit 6

FIDELITY CREDIT CORPORATION (A)

Insurance Operations
(In thousands)

	1954	1953	1952	1951	1950	1949	1948	1947	1946
Gross premiums written	$11,202	$11,056	$13,418	$9,984	$9,061	$7,866	$6,055	$4,467	$2,558
Premiums earned	7,941	8,278	8,492	7,358	5,993	5,095		not available	
Deduct: Commissions and brokerage	$ 965	$ 720	$ 1,074	$ 718	$ 605	$ 563			
Losses and adjustment expenses	4,087	4,860	6,647	5,431	3,593	2,687			
Underwriting expenses	1,020	882	931	674	539	362			
Total	$ 6,072	$ 6,462	$ 8,652	$6,823	$4,737	$3,612			
Underwriting income (loss)	$ 1,869	$ 1,816	$ (160)	$ 535	$1,256	$1,483			
Investment income	165	164	68	200	160	157			
Income before federal income taxes	$ 2,034	$ 1,980	$ (92)	$ 735	$1,316	$1,640			
Provision (credit) for federal income taxes	1,046	1,035	(51)	357	622	619			
Net income (loss) of insurance subsidiaries	$ 988	$ 945	$ (41)	$ 378	$ 694	$1,021			
Net worth of insurance subsidiaries	$ 6,191	$ 5,222	$ 4,066	$4,105	$4,162				
Net income as percent of net worth	16.0%	18.1%	(1.0)%	9.2%	16.7%				

SOURCE: Company records.

Exhibit 7

FIDELITY CREDIT CORPORATION (A)

Analysis of Condensed Consolidated Balance Sheets
December 31

	1954	*1953*	*1952*	*1951*	*1950*
ASSETS					
Cash	12.8%	15.8%	15.9%	17.3%	15.1%
Receivables (net of unearned finance charges and allowance for credit losses)	84.3	81.4	81.7	80.1	82.3
Other current assets	0.7	0.6	0.3	0.3	0.2
Other assets and deferred charges	2.2	2.2	2.1	2.3	2.4
Total	100.0%	100.0%	100.0%	100.0%	100.0%
LIABILITIES					
Short-term notes payable					
Bank loans	42.7%	48.0%	55.1%	60.2%	55.5%
Commercial paper	11.7	5.7	7.0	4.9	5.7
Other current liabilities	7.4	6.9	7.3	8.1	8.8
Long-term debt (unsubordinated)	15.0	15.4	4.7	5.8	7.6
Capital funds					
Subordinated notes	6.6	7.2	8.9	7.5	8.5
Capital debentures (junior subordinated)	3.5	3.7	4.5		
Preferred stock	0.7	1.1	1.3	4.0	4.4
Common stock and surplus	12.4	12.0	11.2	9.5	9.5
Total capital funds	23.2	24.0	25.9	21.0	22.4
Total	100.0%	100.0%	100.0%	100.0%	100.0%

SOURCE: Company records.

experience with us." Davis also expressed confidence in the company's future, "because we think we have demonstrated that we serve people in a useful and constructive way." He expected that in view of these internal and external attributes of the enterprise, the company would continue to display a strong growth pattern.

Davis, however, was concerned with a number of areas where he felt the company could improve. If his prognostication concerning future growth held true, Davis felt that in order for the company effectively to accommodate further growth, it had to strengthen itself in the area of organizational flexibility. By this he meant the ability to vary the emphasis on its various activities or to drop activities and add new ones in accordance with changing economic conditions. He thought the company was already encountering problems in this area as the consumer loan portion of the business claimed a larger and larger portion of the available lending funds. The effect of this lopsided growth in the operating divisions as he saw it was to accentuate the problem of allocating funds between the two divisions. This problem was especially apparent in a period of tight money, when it was impossible to obtain sufficient funds (at a feasible rate of interest) to meet the demands for loans that were budgeted by each of the lending divisions. It was then necessary for the company to hold back funds from some of its lending operations. For example, when tight money conditions prevailed, consumer loan branch managers were instructed not to seek out any furniture and appliance business from retailers, an activity which, while not as profitable as other activities, was an important source of direct loan business for the loan division. Another factor which intensified the funds allocation problem was the growth of Fidelity's various insurance activities. However, executives in the financial division stated that because the statements of Fidelity's casualty insurance subsidiaries were consolidated with the parent, their funds requirements did not impair the company's borrowing base.

Funds allocation was the responsibility of Gordon Johnson, the financial division manager. He was looked upon by many in the organization, and especially by those who worked for him, as a brilliant man who was able to grasp pertinent financial facts quickly and yet who could pick out flaws in the most minute details contained in the reports submitted to him. A man with experience in the organization almost as long as Davis', he was considered by most people in the company as being in a position of power through his control of funds procurement. Phillips in sales finance usually was agreeable to whatever amount of money he was allocated by the financial division, whether it agreed with his budget or not. Stevens, in the consumer loans division, on many occasions, however, expressed the opinion that the financial division should be required to raise funds sufficient to cover the budgets of the operating divisions. He also pointed to the situation where, once having been allocated funds, the sales finance division refused to release them even though they were laying idle and the consumer loan division was desperately seeking additional funds.

To resolve problems of this sort between these two divisions, the executives involved had to appeal directly to Davis since he was the only one in the company who was in a position to coordinate the activities of the divisions in accordance with the company's over-all welfare. But this in turn required of Davis a very close attention to details in order to evaluate properly the budget proposals which each of the operations divisions submitted since each division tended to play up the positive side of its argument and tone down the negative.

Davis felt that with the other demands that were placed on his time, he was not able to resolve these questions of fund allocation and activity emphasis as properly or as effectively as they should be. This situation was becoming worse, he said, as the demands on his time increased with the company's growth in size.

The disparity of growth between the two operating divisions in itself was a matter of concern to Davis. Part of this he recognized as being caused by the economic factors of increasing competition in the sales finance market coupled with a surge in the demand for credit to finance nonautomotive consumer purchases. But he thought that part of the situation was also brought about by the differences in leadership of the two lending divisions. Stevens was aggressively trying to increase the size of his portion of the business and was looking constantly for new business. Phillips, on the other hand, was more or less satisfied with maintaining the status quo and was not actively seeking expansion. Although Davis held Phillips in high esteem for his abilities, having been closely associated with him in the company for twenty-three years, he recognized that Phillips had lost some of the tremendous enthusiasm and drive of his earlier years. One manifestation of this problem was that both of Phillips' assistants were showing evidence of dissatisfaction with their roles under him. They felt he was not moving the division fast enough for them in view of the strong challenge from the consumer loan division. Perhaps the most capable of the sales finance assistant division managers was Bob Vance, a splendid salesman and promoter. But with only fifteen years of service in the sales finance division, Davis thought Vance lacked the necessary seasoning to take over as division manager. Moreover, Davis was highly reluctant to move Phillips aside in view of his excellent contributions to the company. "The man has literally sapped his energies on the company's behalf."

What concerned Davis most about the unequal growth of the operating divisions was that both he and Johnson, the financial vice-president, believed that the consumer loan portion of the business should not be expanded beyond the point where it equalled 35 percent of the company's total outstandings. The reasoning behind this was that the two executives felt that Fidelity would run into difficulties in obtaining funds should the consumer loan portion of the business be expanded beyond this point. This stemmed from the fact that ordinarily sales finance companies worked under a borrowing limitation of four times working capital as opposed to two and one half to three times working capital for consumer loan companies. Working capital under this criterion was defined as current assets, minus current liabilities, minus long-term debt, or conversely, capital funds (equity plus subordinated debt) minus fixed and other assets. While Fidelity remained predominantly a sales finance company, Davis and Johnson felt they could maintain their existing ability of borrowing up to four times their working capital.

In underscoring the importance of Fidelity's borrowing ability,

Davis pictured the company as a wholesaler of money. It purchased money in large quantities and broke it down into smaller amounts for distribution. "Both the sales and the profitability of the company," he said, "are directly related to how much money we can obtain and how much we have to pay for it."

Another problem which Johnson had brought to Davis' attention was the lack of coordination between the two principal operating divisions. For example, in some instances it had been found that the consumer loan division was financing the "front end" (downpayment) of a car, a growing practice in the small loan industry, and the sales finance division was financing the rest of the car. Yet neither division knew what the other was doing.

Still another indication of this lack of coordination was brought to Davis' attention by executives in the consumer loan division. They claimed that the branch managers were unable to elicit support from the sales finance branches in seeking out sales finance customers who might be interested in financing other types of purchases through the consumer loan division or who wished to extend the payment period on their automobile contract. When a sales finance customer wished to extend the contract period or for any reason was unable to meet his payments, it was often possible for the consumer loan division to accept a chattel mortgage on the car and thereby obtain a higher rate of interest than was obtainable on the sales finance contract. This operation, called "flipping," was an important source of new business for the consumer loan division and of higher income for the company. Yet its executives felt that the sales finance division was not cooperating with them in obtaining it.

Executives in the sales finance business countered this claim by stating that they did not want to expose the customers that they had obtained to the selling tactics of the consumer loan division. They said that the typical sales finance customer had been able to swing a sizeable downpayment for his automobile, which indicated that he had a better economic status than the typical consumer loan customer. The very fact that he was able to make this downpayment was the reason that he was able to take advantage of the lower rates of a sales finance contract. Moreover, the sales finance managers felt that if their customers were exposed to consumer loan promotion, it would have a harmful effect on the company's relations with the automobile dealers. "The word would get back to the dealers who after all are responsible for recommending our company to their customers and initiating our sales finance contracts." Sales finance managers looked upon themselves as being in a respectable business without the stigma which was attached to the consumer loan operation. "We are dealing with businessmen, reputable auto dealers, and we feel that we should see to it that there is no possibility for a stigma to be attached to our end of the business which might mar our relationship with the dealers."

Another area of concern to Davis was that the company lacked a systematic program of management development. There was a tendency under the existing organization to develop managers who were talented in the functional area in which they advanced but who lacked breadth in other areas. Davis had obtained excellent experience by working in both consumer loan and sales finance operations. The usual progression was to work up through the lines in one of the lending divisions starting from the position of branch manager or assistant branch manager. This, for example, had been the experience of Phillips, manager of the sales finance division. Although both consumer loan and sales finance activities involved similar basic lending principles there were important differences in the orientation between the two. To illustrate, consumer loan people concerned themselves primarily with the credit qualifications of individuals and dealt in many small-size loans, whereas sales finance people were concerned primarily with the credit of the automobile dealers and dealt in fewer accounts of a much larger size. For another, delinquency problems were of a much more serious nature when they arose in the sales finance business as opposed to the consumer loan. If a sales finance manager did not follow up immediately on a delinquency case, the company might be "out" some money because of the rapid depreciation on the car if it had to be repossessed. On the other hand, a consumer loan manager was accustomed to move more slowly on delinquency cases since depreciation on their secured loans was less of a factor and repossession or foreclosure was used only as the last alternative if payments could not be obtained. While the consumer loan delinquency existed, the company was entitled to interest on the money involved. These differences in orientation colored the thinking and approach used by managers in the lines of both lending divisions. The same tendency toward functional specialization also existed in the company's other line and staff elements so that management at every level below that of the president were, in most cases, specialists in only one element of the business.

Specialization by lending function provided the rationale behind the development of duplicate channels of authority for the two lending divisions in all of the regions where Fidelity was represented, except the northwest. The only reason that such duplication did not exist in the northwest was that the company maintained only consumer loan branches in that region. Another effect of this specialization throughout the company was that responsibility for coordinating all of Fidelity's functional areas fell directly on the president. It also imposed a long step which an executive hoping to advance to the presidency had to take. In all likelihood it would be some time before such a transition would be necessary since Mr. Davis was 56 and in good health. He did not contemplate retiring before he reached 65. Nevertheless, he felt that adequate preparation of his successor should be accomplished well before this time approached.

Results of the Research Firm's Studies for Fidelity Credit

In November 1955, Fidelity's board of directors was presented with a feasibility study on the use of electronic data processing by the research firm which they had retained for this purpose. The report indicated that a large capacity computer might be effectively employed in a centralized location to handle much of the company's data processing. It recommended that the company engage in a systems study which would also enable the company to select a large-scale computer.

Shortly after receiving the above report, in December 1955 the economics research division of the research firm submitted its analysis of Fidelity's ten-year market potential. On the basis of their analysis, consumer installment debt on a national basis was expected to nearly double by the mid-1960s. By 1965, Fidelity's loans and discounts outstanding were expected to reach a minimum of $648 million, nearly three times its outstandings as of December 31, 1954, if the company did no more than hold its share of the market. It was estimated that the major part of this market growth would be derived from the business available within the area the company was then serving or which could be served from existing regional centers. The study pointed out that, for the most part, the states in which the company operated exceeded the national level of population growth, per capita income, and automobile registrations, and that these states would continue to surpass the national average growth rate.

Fidelity Credit Corporation (B)

After receiving the study on Fidelity's ten-year market potential from the research firm which the company had retained for this purpose, President Davis[1] intensified his thinking about how the company might best prepare itself for the nearly threefold increase in size which was predicted. Stimulated by the economic report submitted, which supported his own forecast for the company's future, Davis first directed his atten-

[1]All names have been disguised.

tion toward developing the capability within the company to conduct its own economic forecasts.

In June 1956, Davis hired Malcolm Ritter, the man who had supervised the initial economic study for Fidelity at the research firm. Ritter was named director of economic research and he reported directly to the president. His first assignment was to establish a department, which he was to direct to carry out the economic research necessary to guide the company in planning its future development. This department was also responsible for providing functional guidance and coordination to the managers of the operating and staff divisions in developing long-range plans of the company. It was also responsible for providing data and forecasts that would assist in the preparation of the annual operating budgets. Ritter's background included an engineering degree, an MBA degree from Northwestern University, and fifteen years of experience in industry and in research. He was 36 in 1956. By early 1957 the department was staffed by four people, including Ritter.

Some measures of the company's operations from 1950 through 1956 and an industry comparison are shown in Exhibit 1. Exhibit 2 shows earnings figures for each of Fidelity's operating departments.

In a talk before a group of New York security analysts in early December 1956, Davis outlined two bench marks which the company was using to guide its planning: "Our goal is to obtain a return of 14 percent on our equity capital of $51 million, compared with a present return of 11.2 percent. Our second aim is to achieve a minimum of $752 million in loans and discounts outstanding by 1965 or more than twice our present outstandings of $370 million."

The 1956 gain in over-all earnings had been made in the face of rising interest costs. Summing up this situation, President Davis said, "Despite the problems which tight money creates, it does offer some compensating advantages. I think most business organizations are put on their mettle when they face a limiting factor like tight money, and if they weather the situation, it can have a healthy effect on the whole tone of their operation. That is what has happened to Fidelity Credit. We have, during the past year, become more selective and more critical. We've upgraded our entire level of efficiency in our operation, and we are seeking new and better methods for the way we do things. In short, spurred by the knowledge that money was getting tighter and costing more, we worked harder to manage our money better and to manage our business better."

In mid-1957 Fidelity initiated an applications study on the use of a large general-purpose computer put out by a large computer manufacturer. This firm worked closely with Fidelity on the study and was responsible for training Fidelity's personnel in the systems analysis and programming required.

Contrary to what Davis had hoped, the establishment of the long-

Exhibit 1

FIDELITY CREDIT CORPORATION (B)

Operating Measures of Fidelity Credit and Consumer Finance Industry
(Dollar figures in thousands)

	1956	*1955*	*1954*	*1953*	*1952*	*1951*	*1950*
FIDELITY CREDIT CORPORATION							
Volume of operations							
Loans and discounts acquired							
Sales finance division	$426,958	$495,770	$359,499	$356,649	$389,759	$294,271	$283,958
Consumer loan division	185,493	155,656	129,601	116,774	110,917	73,795	44,216
Net premiums written	8,520	9,731	8,542	8,306	9,629	4,532	6,870
Income from operations (before federal taxes on income)							
Financing operations	11,001	9,722	7,353	7,077	6,730	4,635	3,311
Insurance operations							
Underwriting income (loss)	–	1,030	1,869	1,815	(159)	535	1,255
Investment income	235	190	165	162	68	200	160
Income from life insurance Subsidiary	494	–	–	–	–	–	–
Total–combined operations	11,730	10,942	9,387	9,054	6,639	5,370	4,726
Less: Provision for federal taxes on income	5,974	5,481	4,971	4,292	2,511	2,709	2,198
Net income from operations	5,756	5,461	4,416	4,762	4,128	2,661	2,528
Net income as percent of net worth	11.2%	13.1%	11.4%	12.5%	12.9%	9.3%	11.4%
THIRTEEN LARGEST CONSUMER FINANCE COMPANIES							
Net income as percent of net worth							
Low	9.6%	7.6%	9.1%	9.8%	9.8%	9.1%	8.6%
Average	13.6%	13.7%	13.9%	13.8%	13.6%	14.6%	15.9%
High	16.4%	17.4%	17.6%	18.3%	18.3%	18.6%	19.2%

Exhibit 2

FIDELITY CREDIT CORPORATION (B)

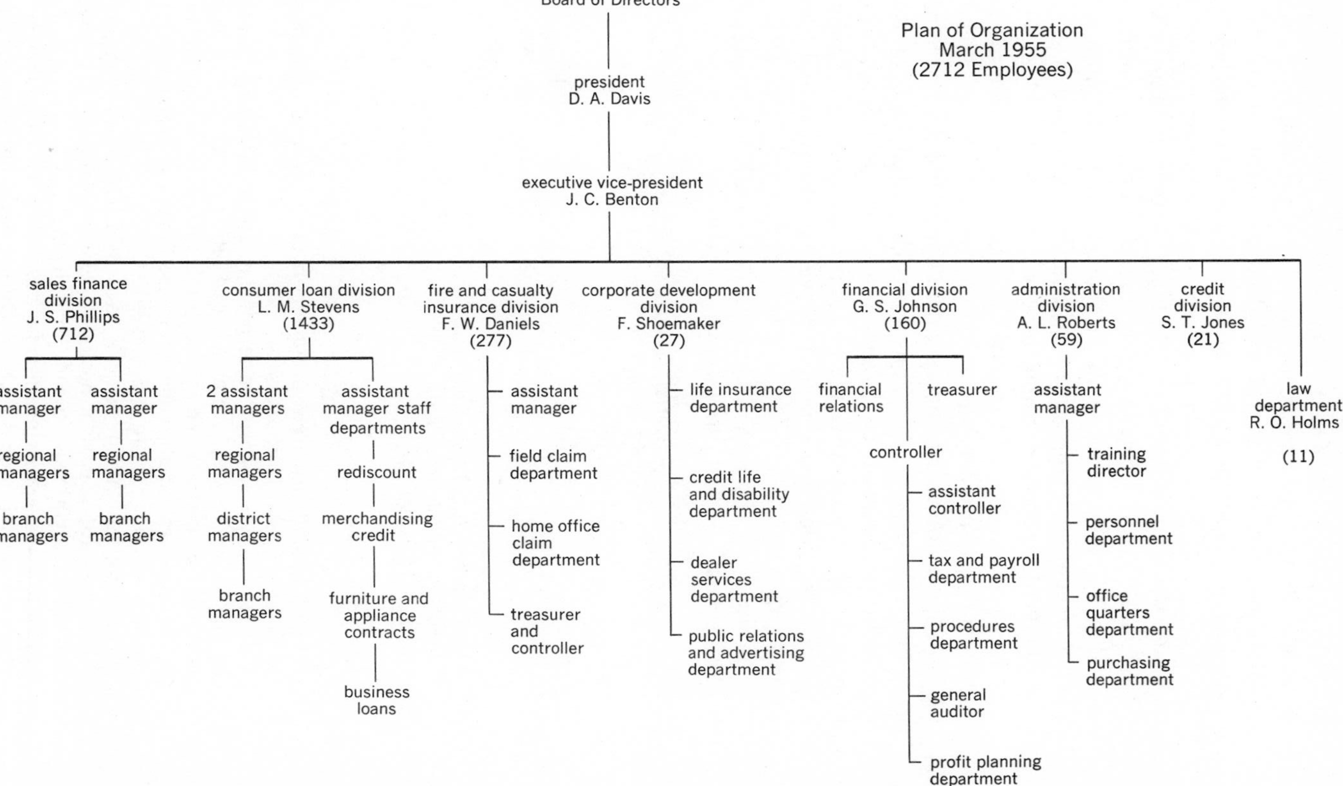

range planning and economics research department under Ritter did not alleviate the problem of allocating funds for 1957 among the operating divisions. Part of the reason for this Davis ascribed to the tight money situation and part to the newness of the department. On several occasions he had heard complaints from the operating division managers who said that the tone of Ritter's reports were such that they felt he was trying to usurp their line authority. "He's not recommending, he's telling us what to do." Davis, however, recognized Ritter as an extremely talented individual and thought he would be able to establish a better rapport with the line executives as he gained experience in the company.

Davis also recognized that for the company to achieve the growth that was predicted, it had to have an organization structure and people within that structure capable of meeting this growth. To evaluate Fidelity on both these counts he obtained the approval of the board of directors to retain the services of Consulting Unlimited, one of the nation's prominent management consulting firms. The consulting firm was asked to present its evaluation of the company and to make recommendations as to how the company should improve its operations and prepare itself for further growth.

In late 1957 the firm of Consulting Unlimited presented Davis and his key executives with the following report:

CONSULTING UNLIMITED
ADVISORS TO MANAGEMENT

Box 771
Chicago 13, Illinois
December 5, 1957

Mr. Douglas A. Davis, President
Fidelity Credit Corporation
Chicago 15, Illinois

Dear Mr. Davis:

We are submitting herewith our report of the general organization survey of Fidelity Credit Corporation.

This survey was undertaken to develop a plan or organization that would be best suited to meet the anticipated future needs, as well as the present needs of the company. The scope of this survey has covered all the positions in the organization structure, from the branch managers up through your position as chief executive officer.

In carrying out this survey we have held interviews with approximately 80 incumbents of present positions being studied. We also have reviewed and analyzed various company records, manuals and reports as were necessary to provide a sound basis for developing our recommendations on the proposed organization structure. During the initial phase of this study we established with you the objectives which were to govern the development of the ultimate organization plan for the company. During the course of this study, we developed and reviewed with you as preliminary recommendations, the optimum organization structure designed to achieve these objectives.

These preliminary objectives were subsequently examined in light of your present management personnel. A separate study was undertaken by us for the purpose of evaluating these executives against the requirements of the proposed positions. The results of this management appraisal were planned to serve a twofold purpose. The first was to provide information that would serve as a basis for establishing a program to improve and develop the management skills of executives; the second was to assist in relating management personnel to the recommended organization structure. The plan of organization recommended in this report has taken into account the results of these appraisals and in the steps of transition from the present to the proposed plan, has considered the present abilities and expected potential of the personnel who would make up the company's management organization.

In presenting the results of this study, the first section of this report briefly reviews the background of the company's history and the development of the present organization structure. The second section outlines the present plan of organization and discusses the significant features that were considered in developing our recommendations.

The third section outlines the recommended ultimate plan of organization for Fidelity Credit. Each of the objectives that were established to guide the development of the organization plan is set forth in this chapter. The top management functions are outlined and the positions that make up the organization of each of the major divisions of the company are described.

The fourth section sets forth the interim phases through which the organization structure will evolve to place the ultimate organization plan into effect.

Section 5 is a brief summary relating principally to future areas of top management interests.

Individual position descriptions for each of the positions established in the new organization plan have been developed. These position descriptions have been prepared to reflect changes that will occur during each of the three phases of installation of the recommended organization plan. These are being submitted under separate cover to serve as a basis for preparation of a new company organization manual.

This has been a stimulating and interesting assignment. We have appreciated this opportunity of working with your organization. The conduct of the study received the highest degree of cooperation on the part of all members of your organization. We wish to acknowledge particularly the efforts and contributions of Mr. Arthur Roberts and Mr. Malcolm Ritter. Their interest and enthusiasm played a large part in bringing this assignment to a successful conclusion.

We look forward to be of any assistance in carrying out the recommended program.

Very truly yours,

s/ John A. Govern
for Consulting Unlimited

The first section of the report describing the company's historical background and the portion of the second section that outlines the present plan of organization have been omitted. The material contained in these sections has been covered in Fidelity Credit Corporation (A) in much greater detail than in the consulting firm's report. Portions of the third section have also been omitted, which describe the functions of various subelements in the divisions whose functions remained unchanged from the existing organization. Fidelity's organization as it appeared in November 1957 is shown in Exhibit 3.

Section Two: Present Plan of Organization

The present plan of organization has evolved in a sound and logical manner as the company has grown over the past years. It is basically organized around the major operating activities of the company. The necessary staff services to provide effective support to their operations have been appropriately provided.

There are several aspects of the present organization, however, that should be considered in establishing the future organization objectives of the company.

1. *There is an excessive number of positions reporting directly to the president.* There are eleven positions that report to the president. This results in an unusually heavy burden of administrative detail falling directly upon him. His is the task of coordinating each of the division's activities and giving management direction to each of their operations. This, added to the responsibilities of carrying out the basic function of his position, to plan and direct the over-all course of the company's affairs, creates an excessive span of control.

2. *Many management functions are duplicated between the sales finance and consumer loan divisions.* The administration and coordination of the lending activities of the company are made more difficult as a result of being organized into two separate organization units reporting directly to the president. Under this arrangement, duplicate regional organizations exist in the areas in which these lending activities are being conducted. Being separately organized, the coordination of their activities and direction of their efforts in conformance to the company's over-all policy falls directly upon the president. The allocation of funds and the emphasis to be placed on the company's various types of lending operations cannot always be accomplished as effectively or as promptly as they should be.

3. *The coporate development division contains too many unrelated functions.* The corporate development division at present is responsible for several important but unrelated types of activities. The major function of this division has been the development and administration of effective public and financial relations programs. However, as steps have been taken to place new operating activities

Exhibit 3

FIDELITY CREDIT CORPORATION (B)

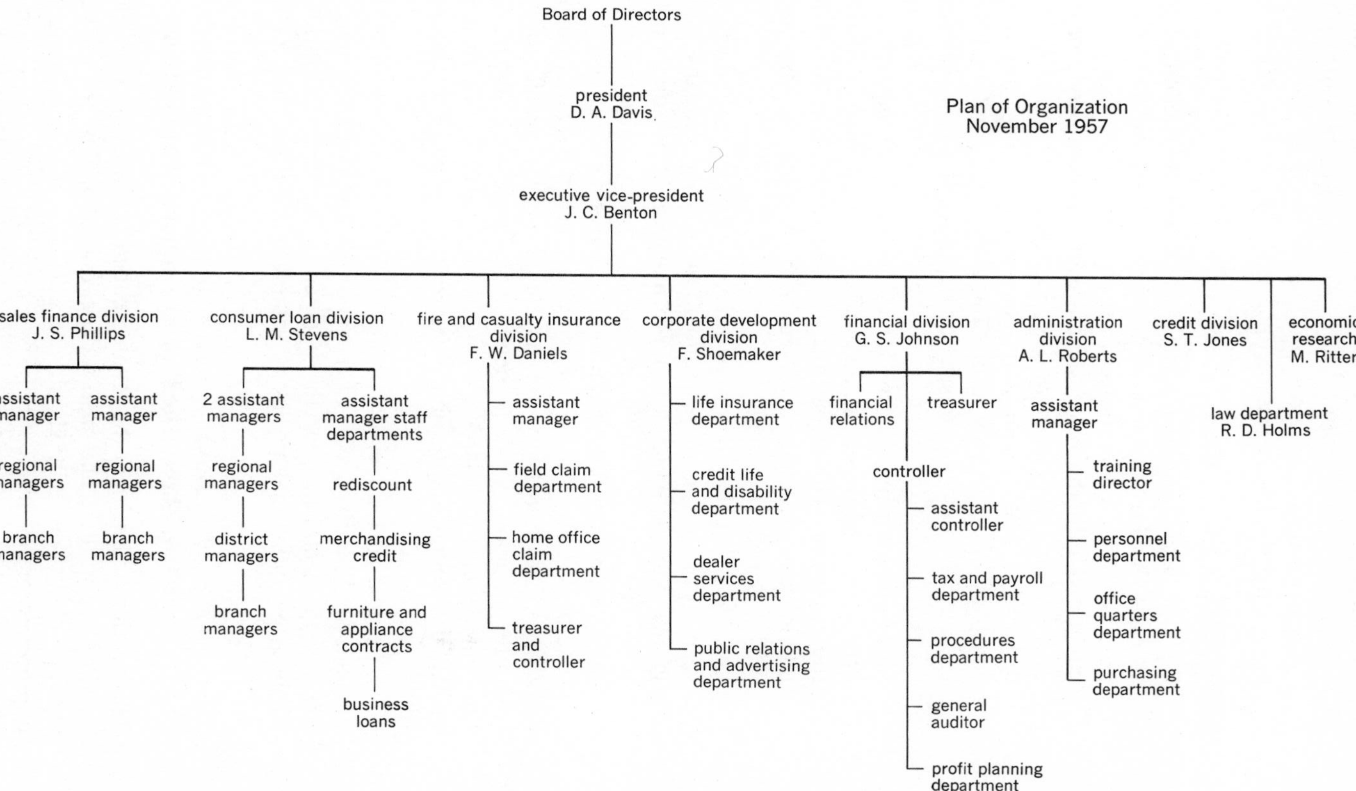

into effect, the task of developing and organizing them has been assigned to this function. At the present time the supervision of the company's dealer services program as well as the initial steps in organizing the life insurance operations are assigned responsibilities of this position.

This arrangement has made it possible for these activities to obtain the full attention and management direction needed at the initial stage of the development. However, as they grow and become more fully established operations of the company, they should be properly integrated into the basic structure of the company's organization.

4. *The employee relations function of the company is not fully organized.* The various activities related to the employees of the company are not given a fully integrated organizational status. The present personnel administration department is primarily responsible for maintaining the basic personnel records of the company. It provides employment services for the home office department and coordinates employment standards between the other departments for the company. This department is also responsible for handling the administrative details involved with carrying out the various employee benefit programs.

On the other hand, a separately established training director is responsible for developing and administering company training programs. For the most part, the formulation of personnel policies and programs and the maintenance of salary administration plans are the joint responsibility of the principal division executives.

The organization of the company has served the requirements of the company's growth up to the present time; however, the effectiveness with which the company is able to meet the challenges of its future opportunities will depend to a large extent on the degree to which it will have provided a sound and flexible organization structure to accomodate its future growth.

The next section sets forth the ultimate plan of organization recommended for Fidelity Credit Corporation. It discusses the objectives that have been established for the company's future organization and describes the individual positions established within each of the major divisions.

Section Three: The Proposed Ultimate Organization

This section will present the recommended organization plan for Fidelity Credit Corporation. This plan was developed against the background of specific objectives that should be achieved in establishing the most appropriate organization structure to meet the company's long range requirements; these objectives are outlined initially. Each of the positions as they have been established within the recommended plan is described in subsequent parts.

Objectives of the Recommended Organization Plan

The development of a recommended organization plan for Fidelity Credit has sought to obtain a number of objectives which are essential to providing the type of organization structure that will serve the company's needs during the years ahead. These objectives are outlined in the following paragraphs.

1. *Reduce the administrative burden of the president.* As the chief executive officer of the company, the president is responsible for the over-all planning, directing, and controlling of its operations. These are functions that only he can perform; consequently the organization structure should provide for the maximum delegation of all detailed administrative and operating duties.

2. *Provide flexibility to accommodate the future pattern of operation.* The organization plan of Fidelity Credit should be designed to accommodate the projected growth of the company's operations. Consideration should be given not only to the expansion and the size of the company but to the nature of the growth and to the characteristics of its operations and the location in which it will be conducted.

   The basic organization structure of the company should also be sufficiently flexible so that when new activities are engaged in by the company, or as existing operations may be eliminated or modified, it would not be necessary to make any changes in the basic organization structure to accommodate these varying circumstances.

3. *Establish the basic organization framework around the main corporate functions.* The basic organization framework would recognize the four main corporate functions which comprise Fidelity Credit's business. These functions are the procurement of funds which are needed to carry on the ever-expanding business of the company; the employment of these funds in the various types of lending purposes and other operations of the company; the scorekeeping needed to manage and control the company's business; and other corporate-wide staff activities necessary to provide adequate services to the company's operations.

   In setting up the basic organization plan to recognize these primary functions, identification and emphasis should be given to the need for greater specialization in fund procurement. It should provide for the most effective coordination of the company's lending activities, particularly in the allocation and transfer of funds among the various lending activities in response to both the physical plans and current operating opportunities. Management direction over all the various types of insurance activities of the company should be centralized.

4. *Identify and give emphasis to forward planning.* Long-range planning is one of the major responsibilities of top management. This planning function is of prime importance in assuring the perpetuation of the company and requires a qualified staff function to coordinate the planning activities of management and organize them into over-all long-range plans for the company.

5. *Provide for the development and progression of qualified management personnel.* The organization structure should provide for logical progression of management talent up through the organization in order that executive positions, including the presidency, can be provided with fully qualified candidates. The important functional areas of the company should be strengthened organizationally so that there will be individual competency available in the particular area that will be of greatest importance to Fidelity Credit in the future.

6. *Provide the basis for a sound salary-administration plan.* The organization structure should be established in such a way that a sound position evaluation program and a plan of salary administration will provide balanced and fair compensation for all mangement and staff positions.

7. *Identify and give emphasis to the total personnel function.* The organization plan should give particular attention to the function of personnel administration and employee relations within the company. It should facilitate the company's management inventory and development program now underway and provide for effective administration of its employee relations program.

8. *Provide for the development and accommodation of electronic data processing procedures.* The organization structure of the company should be determined in such a way that it can accommodate the objectives of electronic data processing and enable the maximum benefits and economies to be realized from its installation.

The foregoing objectives have been developed and established as the criteria around which the development of an appropriate organization structure for the company's future operations has been determined. The ultimate organization plan that is discussed in the following paragraphs of this chapter has been designed to achieve the results for which these objectives were established.

Top Management Functions

The top management function of Fidelity Credit has been established in the positions of the president, the executive vice-president, and the senior consultant to the president. The chart of organization showing these positions and those subordinate to them appears as shown in Exhibit 4. The basic functions of each of these positions under the proposed organization plan are presented in the following paragraphs.

1. *President.* The fundamental responsibility of the chief executive officer of Fidelity Credit is his obligation to perpetuate the enterprise on a sound and profitable basis. He is responsible for the board of directors, for determining the company's objectives, and for developing a long range plan of action that will accomplish them. He is also responsible for formulating the basic policies governing the operation of the company and for maintaining a sound organization structure to carry them out. He is responsible for selecting and developing the talent needed to fill the needs of the company for its key positions and for establishing an effective means of control to appraise current performance to take corrective action on significant deviations from plans. Last but not least he is jointly responsible with the board of directors for managing the corporate income in such a way as to maintain the financial soundness of the company and the efficient utilization and development of the company's assets.

2. *Executive Vice-President.* The position of executive vice-president reporting directly to the president has been established to accomplish one of the principal objectives of the organization plan. This is to reduce the present excessive span of control of the president and to provide for the greater delegation of detailed administrative and operating management duties. Under this arrangement the executive vice-president will be directly responsible for all of the operating functions of the company. In addition, the controllers activities and other staff functions which serve principally the operating position will also be placed under his direction.

This will leave the president with only the financial, investment, public relations, and planning functions of the company under his immediate direction, in addition to the executive vice-president. These are the functions with which the president is most directly concerned in carrying out his over-all responsibility for the planning and direction of the company's operations. The administrative burden of directing the company's operations and related staff services will fall directly on the executive vice-president.

3. *Senior Consultant to the President.* A substantial growth of the company has been forecast for the future. The increased management load will create a need for a seasoned executive to manage the expanding investments of the company and to provide counsel and assistance to the president in the formulation of policies and plans for the company's operations. The position of senior consultant to the president is established to provide this capacity within the top management of the company. This position will be directly responsible for administration of all the company's investments in real estate, in other property, and in automobile dealerships. The incumbent will also carry out important top management assignments as delegated by the president.

Funds-Procurement Functions

The management of the capital structure of the company in such a way as to provide ample supply of low cost money is the company's major financial responsibility. The position of vice-president—financial division has been established to carry out this function. This position is responsible for planning the acquisition of funds needed to meet the projected money requirements of the company for putting approved plans into effect and for administering the company's relationships with banks, investment houses, and other investors. This position is also responsible for providing counsel to the president on conditions in the money market, on timing of proposed changes in capital and debt structure of the company, as well as on the financial implications of the company's lending and investment program.

Funds-Employment Functions

The employment of funds is the company's basic business. It is accomplished through various lending services offered by the company as well as through the underwriting of both casualty and life insurance risks and other specific investments made by the company. Reference to Exhibit 4 will show those divisions of the company that perform this major corporate function.

1. *Vice-President—Investment Division.* This position is responsible primarily for the management of the company's major investments. It is responsible for formulating and recommending policies and programs in connection with the marketing or liquidating of company investments in real estate and other properties or businesses.

2. *Vice-President—Insurance Division.* The company is engaged in various types of insurance operations. One of the principal objectives of the organization plan was to centralize the direction and management of this type of business. To accomplish this the position of vice-president—insurance division has been established for planning and directing all insurance operations carried on by the company. This position is responsible for the management of the specific subsidiary insurance companies that have been and will be formed in the future to carry on this type of business.

3. *Vice-President—Lending Operations.* The lending operations of the company represent the principal business of Fidelity Credit. The employment of the majority of the capital funds of the company takes place within the various types of lending activities and services that are conducted by the company.

To provide effective management of this important function the position of vice-president—lending operations has been established.

The consolidation of all the lending activities of the company under a single principal executive is expected to achieve several significant objectives. The principal advantages to gain from this consolidation are discussed in the following paragraphs.

A conflict of interest is always inherent in a situation where more than one responsible unit of the organization is carrying out similar types of activities within the same area of the company's operations. Under a single organization, these conflicts can be largely eliminated by establishing a single responsibility at a high management level for administration of these various types of activities.

The allocation of funds to provide optimum yield from the company's lending activities is the prime objective of the lending operations. If these activities are carried out under separate organizations, each, in seeking fair advantage under the allocation of available funds, will resist transfers of funds from their own organization. By establishing a single management responsibility for these lending activities, it will be possible to coordinate the allocation of funds between the various lending activities with greater flexibility in order to secure optimum yield from current operating opportunities.

The consolidation of the management of the lending activities will provide for the utilization of both the facilities and the location of the consumer loan offices to increase the volume and profitability of sales financing business. Properly coordinated, the individual consumer loan offices can provide better service to sales finance customers located within their areas and create new sources of sales finance business that, under the present organization plan, would not be profitable for the more centrally located sales finance offices to handle.

The servicing of sales finance business by the individual consumer loan offices would also provide for an increase in the number and quality of consumer loan customers available in each of those offices as a result of the increased potential of "flips" that would be generated from the sales finance collection activities in their area.

The reduction of acquisition service and operating costs in the combination offices where sales finance and consumer loan activities are carried on jointly would be made possible through the consolidation of certain administrative activities and clerical procedures that are common in both the sales finance and consumer loan businesses.

One of the major requisites for the application of electronic data processing procedures is the standardization of operating policies and procedures. Looking ahead to the time when Fidelity Credit will be able to achieve the benefits that are available from the installation of electronic data processing procedures, the administration of coordination of all of the data originating activities can be carried out more uniformly and effectively within a single operating organization structure.

Under the present organization plan the separation of the sales finance and consumer loan activities, all the way up to the top management levels, to the president, results in the development of management talents along a specialized type of lending operations that are carried on within each of the separate organizations. The consolidation of the management structure for all the lending operations of the company will require a broadening of interests and scope of persons progressing through the lower management levels. Consequently, their eventual experience and development in the upper levels of lending management will provide more effective and well-rounded candidates for top management positions.

The over-all results of establishing a single major organization unit of the company within which the lending operations will be conducted will provide a structure that will accommodate the projected growth and expansion of these operations both geographically and in the nature and volume of operation. The administration of these functions can be subdivided into major geographical areas which can be managed as smaller but completely integrated operations. This has the further advantage of establishing another mangement level where profit and loss accountability will provide a strong motivation as well as a control device.

Scorekeeping Functions

The scorekeeping function of Fidelity Credit represents the top management activities that are responsible for the primary recordkeeping and control activities needed to provide management with the information essential to direct the operations of the company in accordance with established policies and plans. The recommended organization plan establishes one position under which this function is carried out—the controller's position. The controller is responsible for maintaining adequate accounting records of the company's operation and its financial position and for maintaining adequate internal control over the company's funds and other assets. This position is responsible for providing the operating supervisors, officers, and directors of the company with adequate financial and operating information that will afford a sound basis for their effective planning and controlling of the company's operation.

Other Corporate-wide Staff Functions

The remaining management functions established under the recommended organization plan comprise the corporate-wide staff services needed to support effectively the company's operation. Reference to

Exhibit 4 will show that three of these functions are primarily related to the operating activities of the company and report to the executive vice-president. They are the credit and facilities division, the legal department, and the employee relations department. Two other departments are staff activities that are concerned with the major responsibilities of the president's position and are the public relations department and the director of planning. The basic function of each of these staff divisions under the proposed organization plan is discussed in the following paragraphs.

1. *Vice-President—Credit and Facilities Division.* This position is responsible for the staff activities that are necessary to formulate, interpret, and enforce the company's credit policies. In carrying out this function, this position will recommend credit policies that are designed to achieve an optimum balance between the company's loan volume and profit objectives. It will also advise and assist the operating executives in applying these policies to their specific operation and will review operating credit practices and files to assure adherence to established policy. This position is also responsible for administering the office facilities and purchasing services of the company.

2. *General Counsel—Legal Department.* The general counsel is responsible for providing the legal services needed to maintain the company's optimum operation and transactions in a sound legal position. Under the recommended plan the general counsel will also be designated as secretary of the company and as such will be responsible for maintaining the minutes for the stockholders and directors meetings and for maintaining and executing other official corporate records.

3. *Director—Employee Relations Department.* This position is responsible for administering the personnel program for the company and for providing the necessary personnel staff services for all levels of management. This position will formulate and recommend the personnel policies and programs of the company. It will establish and administer the procedures necessary for carrying out an effective and well-balanced management development and training program in order that a continuous backlog of promotable executives are being developed at all levels to fill the needs for management talents that the company's future growth will require.

4. *Director—Public Relations and Advertising Department.* The primary responsibility of this position is for the planning and coordination of activities throughout the company to tell a consistent and effective story to stockholders, employees, government officials, and the general public in the community it serves. This position is also responsible for coordinating the planned public relations activities and for planning and administering the advertising and

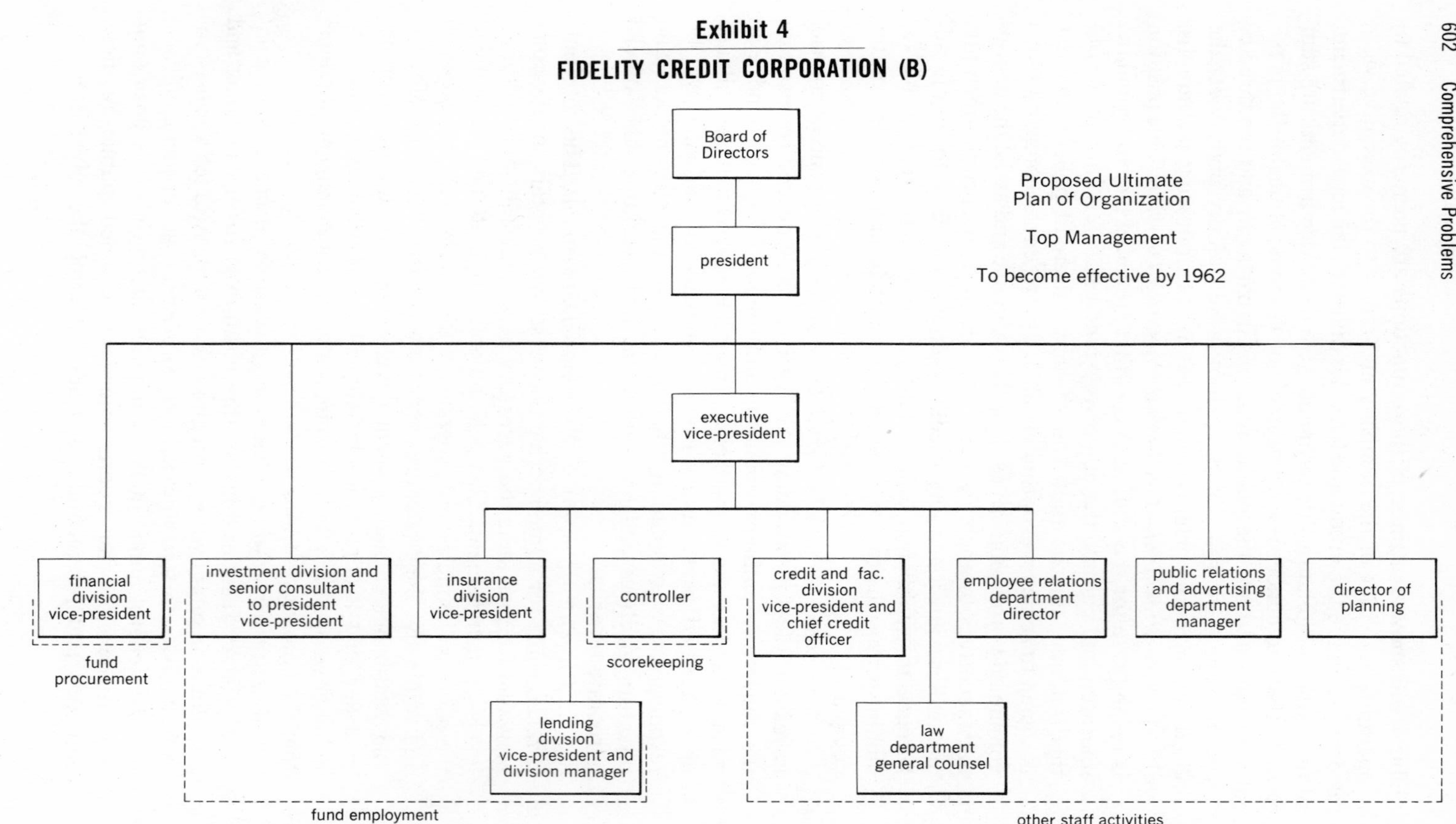
Exhibit 4
FIDELITY CREDIT CORPORATION (B)
Board of Directors
president
Proposed Ultimate Plan of Organization
Top Management
To become effective by 1962
executive vice-president
financial division vice-president
fund procurement
investment division and senior consultant to president vice-president
insurance division vice-president
lending division vice-president and division manager
controller
scorekeeping
fund employment
credit and fac. division vice-president and chief credit officer
law department general counsel
employee relations department director
public relations and advertising department manager
director of planning
other staff activities

merchandising program needed to supplement the company's selling efforts.

5. *Director of Planning.* This position has been established to achieve one of the more important objectives established for this organization plan. The importance of long-range planning to the successful growth and operation of the business makes it necessary to identify and give emphasis within the organization to those activities which comprise this function. The director of planning is responsible on a staff basis for the economic research to guide the company in planning its future development. This position also coordinates the planning activities in all areas of the company, out of which is developed a sound and complete over-all long range plan for the company.

The foregoing paragraphs have presented the top-level management organization that comprises the four major corporate functions. The following paragraphs will describe the recommended organization plan for each of the major divisions.

The report then went on to describe the basic functions of each of the elements of the financial division, investment division, insurance division, credit and facilities division, and controller's division. Each of the elements described had the same function as it had had in the previous organization, with the exception of the controller's division. In the controller's division an electronic data processing department was added. This department was to be responsible for the programming, maintenance, and operation of the electronic data processing equipment installed by the company. It was to be responsible on a service basis for the timely and accurate production of reports and other data to be produced by the electronic data processing system. Following are the parts of this section that describe the functions of various elements where radical changes in functions were recommended over the existing organization.

Lending Division Organization

The departments that comprise the lending operation's organization are shown in Exhibit 5. The basic functions of each of the departments are discussed in the following paragraphs.

1. *Development and Planning.* This department is responsible for all of the staff activities necessary to create, implement, and promote aggressive lending programs. This department will be responsible for developing new types of lending activities with significant volume and profit potentials and for developing the volume and profit objectives for both new and existing lending programs.

A separate department is established for each of the major types of lending activity being carried out by the company. Each of these specialized loan departments is responsible for all the staff activities that are necessary to develop, plan, and promote the company's program for each of the lending activities for which they are specifically responsible.

Each manager will also be responsible for providing technical assistance to the field organization in his speciality. He will also be responsible for developing individual programs and selling procedures to assist the field organization in the promotion of each of the company's lending activities.

2. *Field Organization—Area Managers.* Reference to Exhibit 5 will show that the field operations of the lending division are organized on a regional basis with the branch operations for each of the sales finance functions and the consumer loan functions being separately administered by their respective regional managers. Each of these regional managers reports to a single area manager who is responsible for all of the lending activities of the company being carried out within his assigned area.

The vice-president—area manager of the lending division is the line executive responsible to the vice-president—lending division for the field operations for all the lending activities within his assigned geographical area. He will be responsible for planning, organizing, and directing the activities of the regional and district managers for each of the sales finance and consumer loan organizations within his area. The regional and district managers in turn will be line managers responsible for directing, respectively, the sales finance activities or consumer loan activities as they are assigned within each region.

Within each of the combination offices where both sales finance and consumer loan activities are conducted, the branch operations manager will be responsible for supervising the clerical activities and internal recordkeeping operations for the entire combination office. In this position the branch operations manager will be responsible to the vice-president—lending administration for conducting the internal operations of his branch in accordance with the established policies and procedures. He will also be responsible to each of the sales finance and consumer loan managers in his branch for maintaining adequate operating and clerical facilities of the branch location.

3. *Lending Administration.* This position is responsible for all of the administrative and staff services and activities in the lending division. They are organized as follows:

(a) *Under regional supervisors* there would be provided a program of systematic staff assistance and review of the credit practices of the branch offices to implement the company's policies in the lending division.

(b) *Under an operations analysis supervisor* the program

Exhibit 5

FIDELITY CREDIT CORPORATION (B)

Proposed Ultimate Plan of Organization

Lending Division

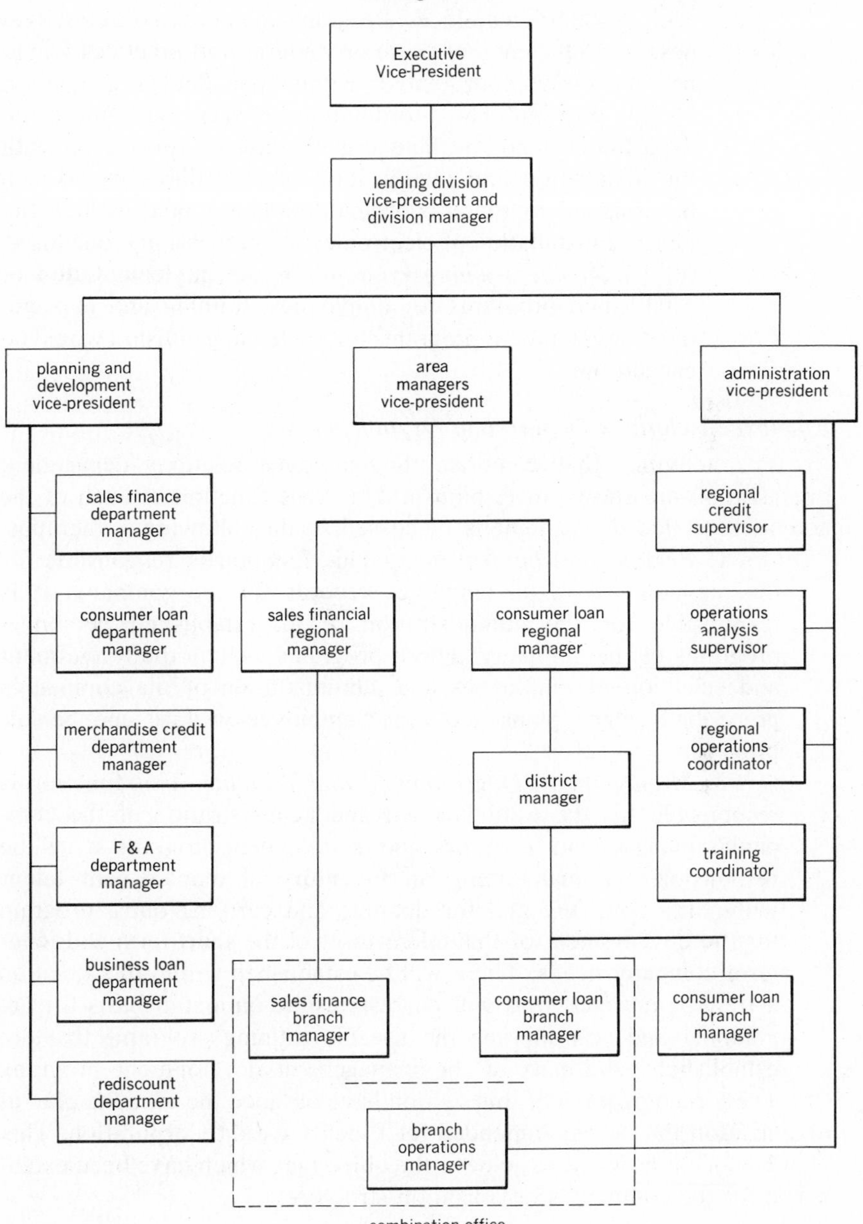

and procedures governing the preparation of budgets, budgetary control, and cost analysis would be accomplished.

(c) *Under operations coordinators* assigned to each area, staff follow-up would be provided to see that established operating procedures and methods are being followed in each of the branch offices. Programs to improve the effectiveness and efficiency of these procedures and practices would be uniformly coordinated within the field organization by this position. The coordination between the home office departments and the field organization in connection with the installation and modification of procedures would also be assigned to these coordinators. This would include the planned installation of electronic data processing procedures.

(d) *Under the training coordinator* the implementation of established programs for employees' training and management development programs for the lending division would be carried out.

Employee Relations Department Organization

The activities that comprise the employee relations department organization are shown in Exhibit 6. The basic function of each of the activities of this department is discussed in the following paragraphs.

1. *Personnel Administration.* This function is responsible for the maintenance of all employee records for the company. It is responsible for the administration of all established personnel programs of the company. These programs include the recruitment and selection of employees and administration of the company's prescribed salary plans and other employee welfare and benefit programs.

2. *Management, Development, and Training.* This function is responsible for the establishment and administration of the company's management inventory and development program. It will be responsible for maintaining an inventory of management talent within the company and for defining and carrying out a program for the development of this talent to meet the short-term and long-term company needs. There will be established within this function a training director who will be responsible on a staff basis for developing and coordinating the specific training programs that are established as a part of the management development program.

The foregoing parts of this section have outlined the ultimate plan of organization that is recommended for Fidelity Credit Corporation. This plan has been designed to achieve the objectives which have been established for the company's organization structure.

Exhibit 6

FIDELITY CREDIT CORPORATION (B)

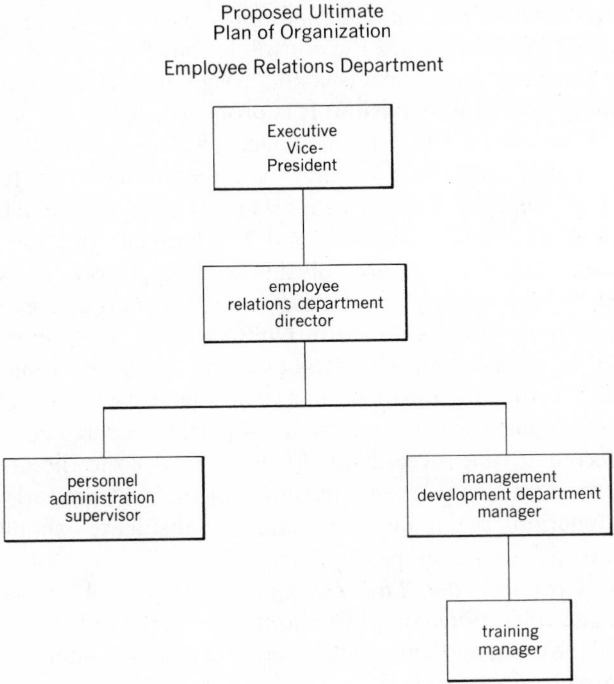

The next section will outline the successive steps that will be required to place the ultimate organization structure in effect.

Section Four: Installation of Organization Plan

The recommended ultimate organization plan represents several significant changes from the present organization structure of the company. The successful accomplishment of organization changes must recognize the human element involved. Thus the changes should be made in a planned and orderly fashion to provide adequate time for growth and adjustment of management personnel to newly assigned positions.

This section will outline the recommended steps for installing the ultimate organization plan. It will describe the steps that should be taken immediately to place this plan into effect and will outline the subsequent phases through which the organization structure should evolve in order to accomplish successfully the ultimate plan.

Immediate Steps

It is recommended that the action necessary to place the initial phase of this organization plan into effect be carried out in the following steps:

1. *Combine the lending functions under a single major executive.* The first step toward the consolidation of the lending operations of the company is the selection and assignment of the vice-president—lending operations division. It is proposed that in this initial phase each of the assistant division managers in charge, respectively, of the sales, finance, and the consumer loan operations report to the vice-president—lending division without any change in the existing organization or duties. The planning and development function as well as the administrative function of this division, however, should be established immediately by the assignment of appropriate executives.

2. *Create the Investment Division.* The investment division should be created and the establishment of the position of senior consultant to the president made at the same time. The dealer services department and the real properties department should be transferred to the investment division. Under the direction of the vice-president—investment division, all the real property management functions of the company and its subsidiaries should be consolidated as quickly as practicable.

3. *Establish the Life Insurance Division.* The planned life insurance operations should be identified as an independent operation of the company and established as a separate operating division reporting to the president.
Since the life insurance activities are presently under the vice-president—corporate development, who has also been principally responsible for the public relations function, it is proposed that he would be set up as the vice-president in charge of the life insurance division, and that public relations and advertising would continue to receive his administrative direction.

4. *Establish the Management Development Department.* The management development department should be set up to administer the company's management inventory and development program. The present training function should be transferred to this department.

5. *Eliminate the Administrative Services Division.* The existing administrative services division should be dissolved. The management development department and the personnel administration department should be established to report directly to the president through the employee relations advisor. The office quarters department should be transferred to the credit and facilities division to

become the office facilities department. The purchasing department should also be transferred to the credit and facilities division.

The foregoing steps will complete the installation of the initial phase of the organization plan. Exhibit 7 shows the organization as it will exist when these steps have been completed. It is recommended that the foregoing steps be made effective January 1, 1958.

Subsequent Steps

The remaining steps required to place the ultimate organization plan completely into effect should take place during the period 1958–1959. The timing of these steps depends to a large extent upon the ability of the individual executives to develop the capacities necessary to carry out the responsibilities under the recommended organization plan. These remaining steps are outlined in the following paragraphs and should be taken when the requirements of each individual involved have been fulfilled.

1. *Transfer Controller from Financial Division and Establish as a Separate Function Reporting to the President.* Appropriate steps should be taken as soon as practicable to separate the controller function from the financial division and set it up as a separate staff division reporting directly to the president. This step should be taken as soon as it is felt that the controller can assume the responsibility for managing this function without the direction of the vice-president—financial division.

2. *Combine the Insurance Divisions under a Single Major Executive.* In the initial organization phase the life insurance division was established reporting to the president separately from the fire and casualty division. As soon as the life insurance activities have been completely organized and established, each of these two major insurance divisions should be set up to report as major subdivisions of a single insurance division reporting to the president.

3. *Establish the Field Operation of the Lending Division under Area Managers.* The establishment of the position vice-president—area manager in the lending division should be accomplished as soon as the management activities and capacities of the present sales finance and consumer loan assistant division managers can be developed to take over the management of both types of lending operations in the field. At the same time the necessity to combine all of the recordkeeping and clerical functions in the combination offices should be carried out by the vice-president—lending administration. Two departments under the vice-president—planning and development should be created for the sales finance and the consumer loan activities.

Exhibit 7

FIDELITY CREDIT CORPORATION (B)

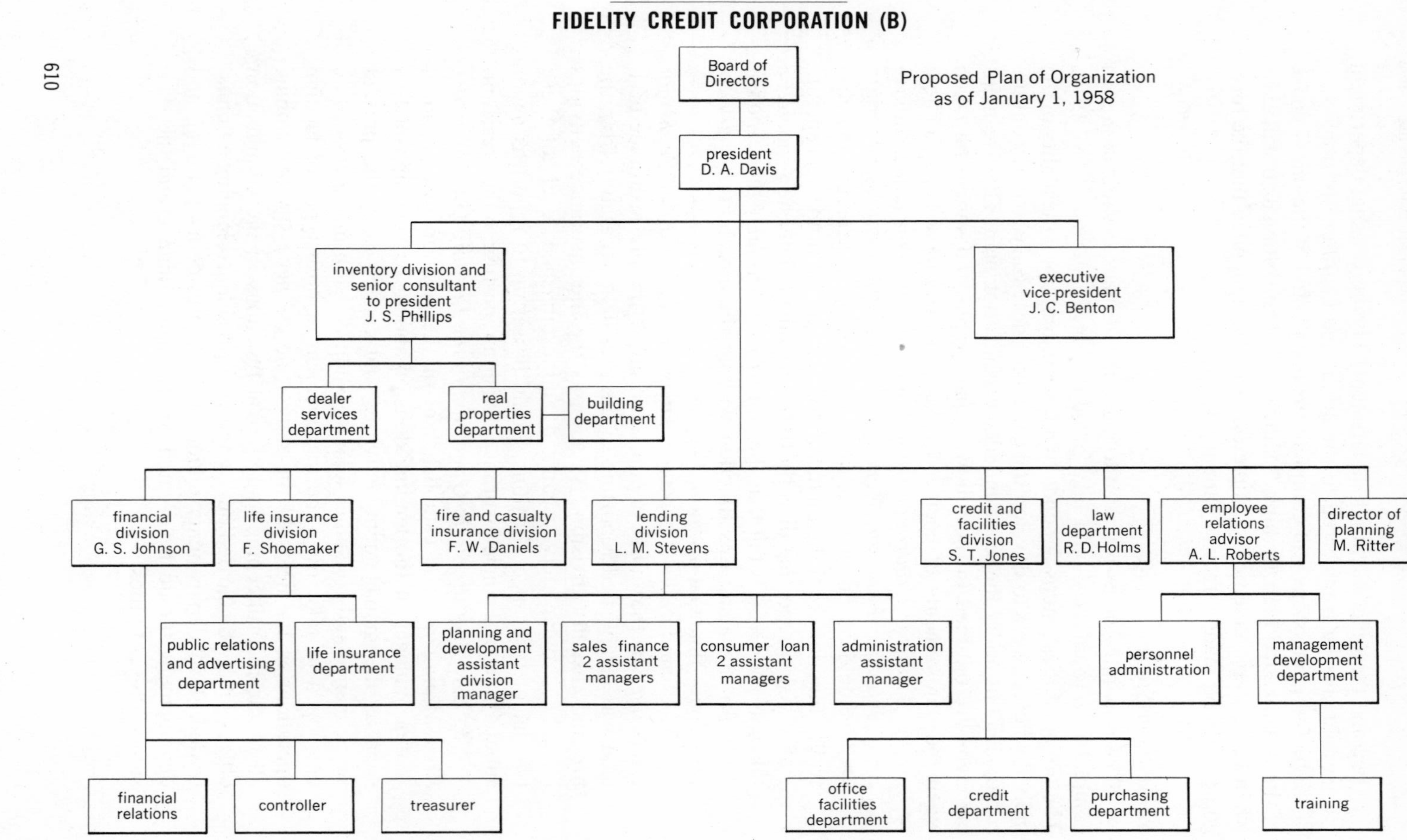

4. *Establish Public Relations and Advertising Department under the President.* The public relations and advertising functions should be established to report directly to the president at the time that the life insurance division is transferred to the newly established division.

5. *Create the Position of Executive Vice-President.* As a final step in placing the ultimate organization plan into effect, the position of executive vice-president should be established. As previously described in this report, it is the intention to place all of the operating and related staff operations under the executive vice-president. Under this arrangement the following positions would then report to the president:

financial division
investment division
public relations and advertising
director of planning
executive vice-president

Reporting directly to the executive vice-president would be:

controller's division
insurance division
lending division
credit and facilities division
law department
employee relations department

With the completion of this step, the ultimate organization plan recommended for the company will be completely in effect, and a major objective of reducing the operating load on the president will have been achieved. The establishment of the position of executive vice-president will also provide for the development of a candidate to succeed to the position of president. In order to provide ample time for the development and experience in this position this move should be accomplished at least by 1962, at which time the complete organization plan of Fidelity Credit Corporation will be that shown in Exhibit 8.

The steps that have been described in this section have been established in order to bring about a smooth transition from the present management organization plan to the one ultimately recommended. An ingredient essential to the successful operation of any organization plan is the result of staffing it with adequately trained management talent. The satisfactory accomplishment of the recommended steps must therefore depend upon the success with which the company can develop the capacities and skills that are necessary to carry out effectively the responsibilities of each management position.

A complete inventory of the company's key management talent has been completed and a comprehensive management development program

Exhibit 8

FIDELITY CREDIT CORPORATION (B)

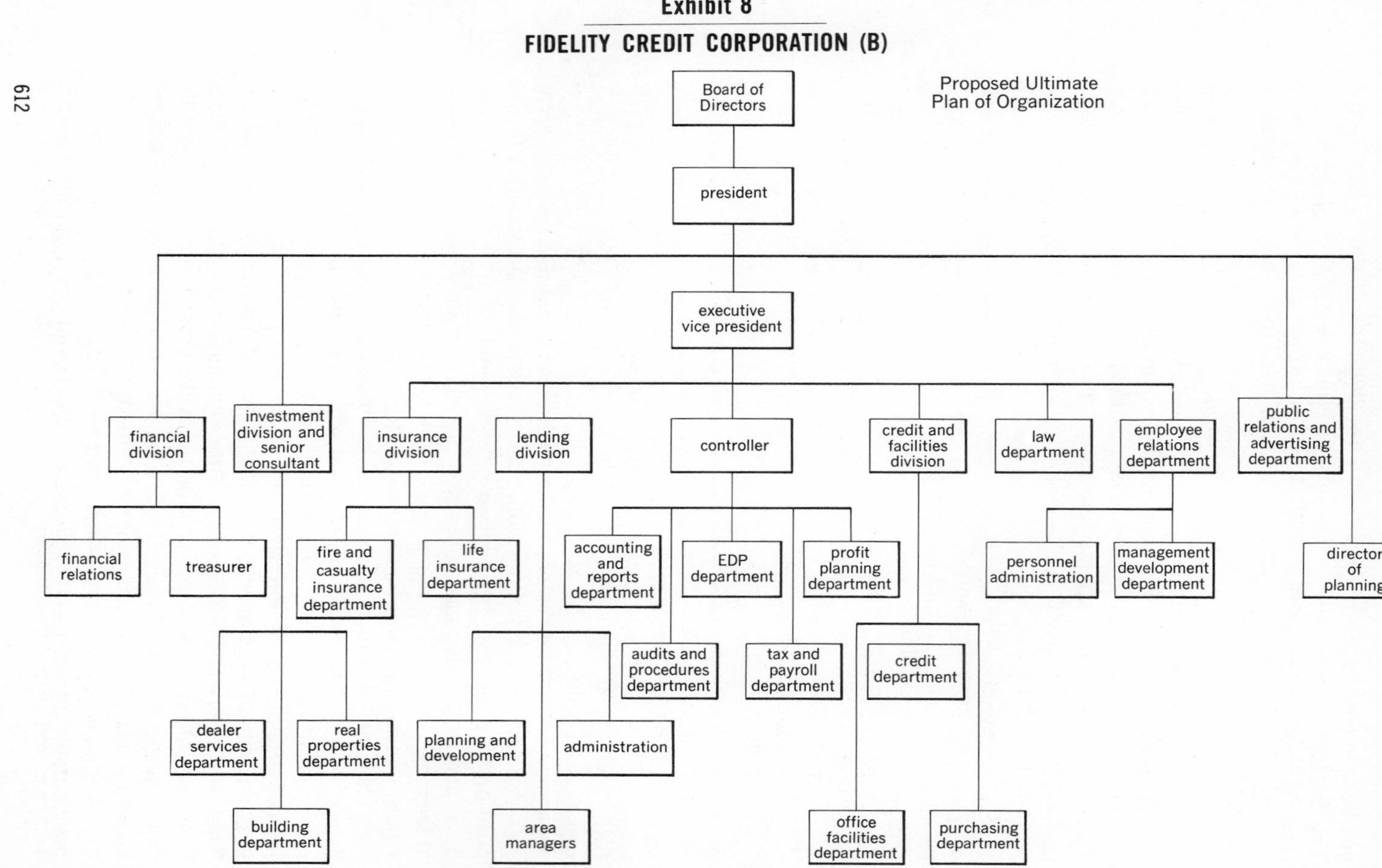

has been recommended and outlined in a separately submitted report. The implementation of the management development program is currently getting underway and its emphasis is being geared not only to the over-all development of management skills but to the specific needs of the individual managers to develop themselves to fulfill their planned responsibilities under the recommended organization structure.

Section Five: Summary

The organization plan that is set forth in this report and the accompanying position descriptions which describe the activities, responsibilities, and the fundamental relationships of each position in the organization's structure provide the basic management tools for establishing an effective organization structure that will meet the objectives of the company's future plans. A companion study has provided Fidelity Credit with the complete inventory of its existing key management talent, from which a development program can be constructed to staff the organization's structure with capable executives possessing the potential to grow and thus meet the challenges of managing a successful and expanding company.

Top management should continue to direct its attention to the environment in which the total organization plan will operate. Consideration should be given to the development and maintenance of an up-to-date and well-balanced compensation plan for all its management people which is capable of keeping pace with the growth and changes that will occur in the organization in the years to come. Continuing emphasis on the management development program and on the maintenance of clear channels of communication will provide the interest and vitality necessary to insure the successful operation of the company's organization plan.

Fidelity Credit Corporation (C)

In February 1958 the president and board of Fidelity Credit Corporation[1] decided to put into effect the first stage of an organizational realignment which differed only slightly from the one proposed by the firm of Consulting Unlimited. Commenting on his reaction to the report, president Davis said, "Although the study substantially verified my thinking at the time, I felt greatly relieved to gain concurrence with my ideas from an objective and competent source."

[1]All names have been disguised.

The study marked the beginning of a close relationship between Fidelity Credit and the consulting firm. Consulting Unlimited was subsequently engaged to perform studies on Fidelity's committee system, its salary administration, and on the formation of a company policy manual.

Implementation of the Change

The first phase of Fidelity's organizational realignment was announced by a memorandum to all employees signed by President Davis. The substance of this memorandum was also reproduced in the company's employee magazine. In stating the purpose behind the change President Davis said, "Our organization has evolved in a sound and logical manner as the company has grown over the past years, and has served the requirements of our growth up to the present time. However, the effectiveness with which the company is able to meet the challenges of its future opportunities will depend to a large extent on its having provided an organization structure that is adaptable." The memorandum then went on to list the objectives of the change as they appeared in the consulting firm's report [see Fidelity Credit Corporation (B)]. The bulk of the memorandum was devoted to stating the reasons given in the consulting firm's report for combining the sales finance and the consumer loan divisions. Fidelity's new formal organization as it appeared in this memorandum is shown in Exhibit 1.

Actually several of the changes that appear in Exhibit 1 were accomplished or had been prepared for before the firm of Consulting Unlimited submitted its final report. The first of these changes was the creation of the employee relations division under Roberts, who had previously been the manager of the administration division. The administration division was eliminated; its purchasing and office quarters departments were placed in the credit division, which was subsequently renamed the credit and facilities division. John Meany, who was selected by the consulting firm for this purpose, was hired to replace Roberts, who had reached the company's compulsory retirement age of 65. Meany, who was 37 years old, had been a management development and training director for a large auto company. The employee relations division was instrumental in assisting the consulting firm in its assessment of Fidelity's management and in carrying out the management counseling program which followed from this assessment.

Phillips, head of sales finance, in a series of meetings with members of the consulting firm, discussed the importance of the company investments and Davis' need for consultation and agreed to become investment division manager and senior consultant to Davis.

Having completed these initial changes, in its top management

Exhibit 1

FIDELITY CREDIT CORPORATION (C)

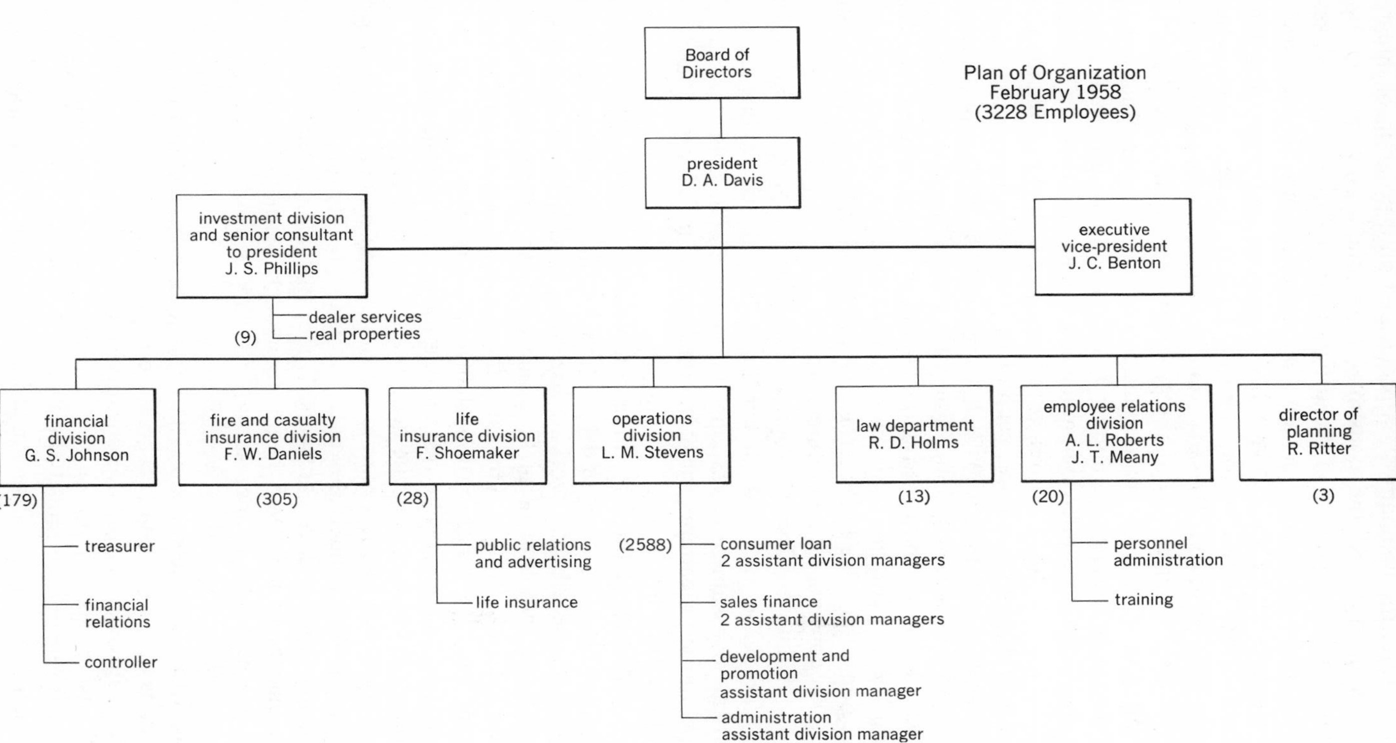

structure, the company then proceeded on a program of integrating the sales finance and the consumer loan functions within the operations division. The first part of this program consisted of a series of sessions in which the operations division manager and his six assistant division managers wrote their own job descriptions and those of each position below them in the division as it would function when complete integration had been achieved. These sessions took place over a 2 1/2 month period.

Next a series of training programs were undertaken, starting in the spring of 1958, to prepare managers of both lending functions to handle integrated lending operations. The first of these programs was directed toward the consumer loan and sales finance assistant division managers who were to become area managers in the new organization. Training was on-the-job in nature; each of the two sales finance assistant division managers was paired with his consumer loan counterpart and began working closely with him. While this was taking place, a similar program was directed toward the regional manager of both lending functions. Here on the job training was also possible since in most of the company's regions, the sales finance regional manger was located in the same office as his consumer loan counterpart.

A ten-week formal program of training was given in each of Fidelity's geographical areas, to all consumer loan district managers to prepare them to assume the responsibilities for credit, collection, and general operating procedures for both consumer loan and sales finance activities in the branches assigned to them.

In each of the fifty-three combination branch offices the consumer loan branch manager and the sales finance branch operations manager located there began working together. Fidelity conducted this training with the intention of picking one of these as over-all manager of the combination branch. The sales finance branch managers were informed that when the organization change was completed they would become district sales managers responsible for generating sales finance business for all the branches in the district assigned to them.

At each of the separate consumer loan branch offices, a procedure manual was handed down to the manager instructing him on how to handle sales finance contracts. Under the guidance of this manual, these managers in mid-1958 began to accept "without recourse" contracts, a phase of sales finance activity which was similar to the consumer loan work with which they were familiar. The final objective of this training was to make these managers capable of handling all sales finance contracts as well as dealer wholesale financing.

Stevens, the operations division manager, cited two reasons for focusing this training on the consumer loan branch managers. The first was to be able to offer both consumer loan and sales finance services to Fidelity's customers at each of its branch offices. This was seen as a way to improve Fidelity's competitive position. At that time the company was offering both services at only 53 combination offices; however, there were 315 consumer loan offices that offered no automobile sales finance services. The second reason was to offset somewhat the fall off of sales finance business which the company was experiencing as a result of an economic downturn in 1958. The effects of this recession had been felt greatly in the auto industry to which the sales finance portion of the business was strongly tied. By making it possible for its consumer loan branches to purchase retail automobile sales contracts, the company hoped to at least maintain its auto sales financing volume.

All these training programs were described by top executives in the operations division as being completely adequate in their content, "All of the information was there," he said. "The programs covered the project if a man wanted to pick it up."

Besides assisting with these training programs, Fidelity's employee-relations division was at the same time conducting personnel evaluation and guidance programs at the branch level of the operations division. Instrumental in conducting these programs was Richard Linholtz, a psychologist by training, who was hired in early 1958 to replace the former training director in the employee relations division. As Linholtz described it, "Our assessment of managerial talents in the operations division was a continuation of the study which was made by Consulting Unlimited. In conducting this study we first had to alleviate the uncertainty which people throughout the division had concerning this type of program. A lot of people had developed strong reservations about it from the way the consulting firm conducted its study." Linholtz said that Fidelity's study concluded that roughly out of every one hundred managers in the operations division there were ten really good sales managers, sixty good consumer loan managers, and twenty managers who could adequately handle a small combination branch.

In November 1958, Fidelity's territory was divided into four areas and an assistant division manager was assigned to each. Care was taken to see that each of the two consumer loan assistant division managers was backed up by a strong sales finance regional manager, and that the two sales finance assistant division managers were placed in areas where they were backed up by strong consumer loan regional managers.

Near this same point in time in November 1958, Fidelity's top executives were faced with the decision of whether or not to implement a program for the installation of electronic data processing. An applications study on the use of a large general-purpose computer had been completed by members of Fidelity's newly organized data processing department, which reported to the controller. This study indicated that not only would such a system facilitate further growth of the company through faster and more complete processing of information but that it would also pay for itself through savings of clerical labor costs. The decision was made to go ahead with the installation program. Commenting on this decision, President Davis said, "We made the decision fully aware of the risk that we were taking in light of the organizational changes that were being made at the time. What convinced me to go ahead was primarily that Stevens was highly enthusiastic about carrying out the program. A second reason was that conversion to electronic data processing would short cut the steps we had to take anyway in integrating the different accounting procedures being used in our sales finance versus our consumer loan activities." A large general-purpose computer was ordered for one year delivery. The year 1959 was spent putting together the necessary computer programs.

In February 1959, Fidelity's employee relations division put into effect a new salary administration program which had been recommended to the company by the firm of Consulting Unlimited. The salient features of the new program were that a salary range was designated for each position in the company, each employee in the company was informed of his salary range, and each manager was informed of the salary ranges of each position below him in the organization. Responsibility for administering the new salary plan was delegated to the lowest managerial level in each division. Previously all salary adjustments had been handled by a committee of seven of the company's vice-presidents. Initially there was a good reaction to the new program according to the employee relations division manager. "However," he said, "dissatisfaction began to arise when people found that there was definite limit to the salaries they could obtain in the job they were holding. Some people were already above this upper salary limit. However, we made no downward adjustments. Another thing that happened was that some of our branch managers put through excessive raises for their people and these decisions had to be reversed. Despite the problems that arose, the new program did much to eliminate salary inequities and was a major stride forward for the company."

While the above programs were being carried out in early 1959, Stevens, the operations division manager, became aware of some changing economic developments which he thought would adversely affect the company's future credit losses. The economy was recovering from the 1958 recession, the demand for credit was high and interest rates on the company's borrowed funds were increasing. According to Stevens, he began to institute measures to have his division become more selective on the credit risks it was taking, especially in its sales finance activities. He said, however, that with all the changes that his division was undergoing, these measures did not become effective until mid-1959 and by that time a considerable amount of poor-quality automobile paper had been purchased.

In July 1959, Fidelity completed the final stages of the integration of its two lending functions. The consumer loan district managers were generally delegated the duties of district operations managers while the sales finance branch managers were promoted to the positions of district sales managers. At each sales finance branch office, a new manager was appointed to be responsible for combined sales finance and consumer loan activities. In addition, Bob Vance, one of the division's area managers, interchanged jobs with the manager of development and promotion activities. According to the division manager, this change was made to give Vance staff experience to groom him for the post of assistant to the division manager and also to give the staff manager line experience. Ex-

Exhibit 2

FIDELITY CREDIT CORPORATION (C)

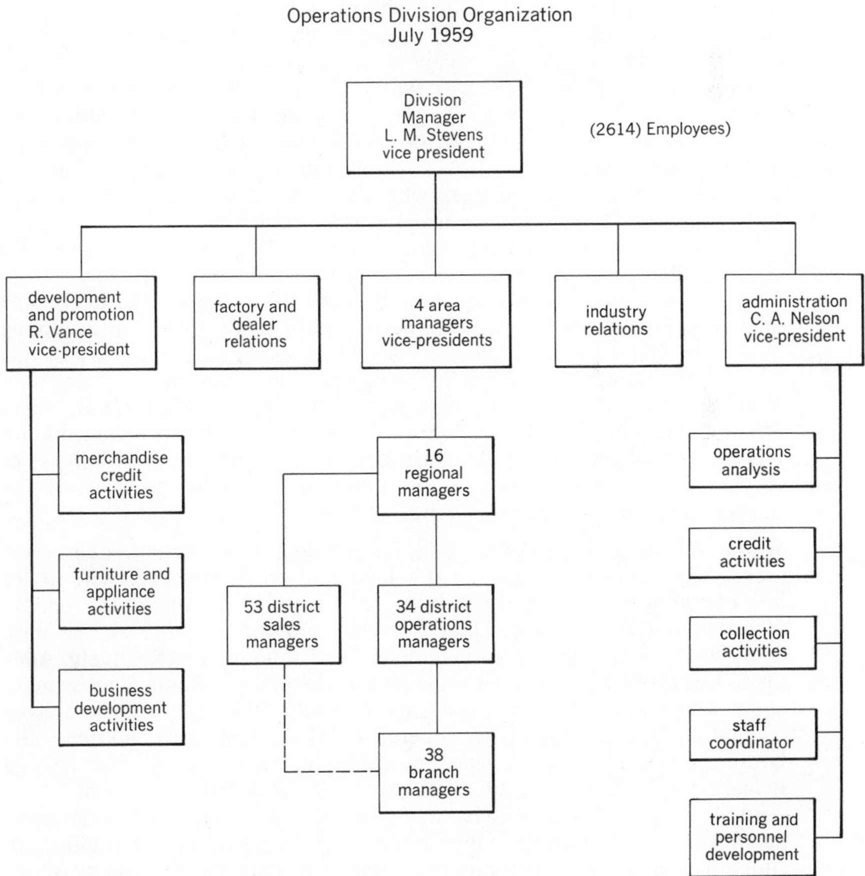

hibit 2 shows the formal organization of the operations division as it appeared after these changes.

Difficulties in the Operations Division

Once the integration of the company's sales finance and consumer loans functions had been carried to the point where the consumer loan branch managers were handling sales finance contracts in addition to their consumer loan responsibilities, some serious difficulties began to develop. Following is how one staff executive of the operations division in retrospect described what had happened:

> Real friction began to develop when we took our old sales finance branch managers and made them district sales managers. These "production men" were told that it was their job simply to generate business and that the branch managers would have the responsibility for judging the quality of the new business which was brought in and for collecting it. So generate business they did. What happened was that with all of our best line people concentrating on "production" work, the people left in charge of the branches couldn't handle the job, especially with the tremendous quantity of new business coming their way. Those who had previously been consumer loan managers did not always have the ability to judge on the quality of the new auto business they received. On top of this, some car dealers, sharp operators in their own right, began to take advantage of some of our "green" consumer loan branch managers who were just learning the sales finance business. Furthermore, these consumer loan branch managers became enraptured with the idea of how easy it was to build up their volume in $1000 and $2000 increments through sales finance contracts as opposed to an average consumer loan of around $550. Our branch and district operations managers just did not recognize the problems associated with accepting new sales finance volume without closely checking on the quality of this volume. Even when they finally recognized that they were getting into difficulty, most of these managers were reluctant to appeal for help and attempted to work out the situation themselves. When they tried to work out their own problems, many demonstrated that despite the thoroughness of their training in sales finance operations, they had not retained the knowledge of these operations that was required of them.
>
> At the regional level of the division, the problem of inadequate supervision arose. Most of our managers at this level had previously been able to get into operating details when they were in charge of only one of the lending functions. After the change, however, they refused to recognize that they could not concern themselves with details and still operate effectively. Adding to this problem at the regional level was the fact that some of these managers who had a sales finance background refused to concern themselves adequately with consumer loan operations. They tended to look upon the consumer loan end of the business as a shoddy, low-status job. The regional managers of Texas and California never really accepted integration.
>
> And then there was the problem that some of our regional and district managers were not qualified to take on the greatly increased responsibilities in running an integrated operation. This was especially true with some of our

> people who had been consumer loan managers. At one time, in the company's previous history, we had hired a group of consumer loan managers in a block after they had walked out on another consumer loan company. Many of these people couldn't measure up to their new responsibilities with us.
>
> The problem of incapable management was present in one instance even at the area level of the organization. This man was made an area manager after he had served a number of years in a staff capacity. Even though he had previous line experience, he had difficulty in measuring up to the new job and had to be transferred back to a staff position.
>
> The net result of all these conditions was that we saw a real delinquency problem building up. At the same time, our available lending funds were pretty well committed and we had to step in and tell our "production" people to ease up on their activities. This, in turn, didn't do much to bolster the morale of these people. Many of them requested that they be put back into their previous positions as branch managers.

As a part of the corrective action being taken to alleviate these difficulties, Vance was moved from the position of development and promotion manager to the newly created position of field operations manager. In this capacity the four area managers reported to him. Vance had been a sales finance assistant division manager under the company's old organization. He was described throughout the company as a good salesman, a good straw boss, and the most effective manager under Stevens.

Further Modifications in Fidelity's Top Management Structure

By the end of 1959 a number of changes had taken place in Fidelity's top level organization. The controller's department and the public relations and advertising department were given divisional status and a direct reporting relationship to the president. A new division, the commercial financing division, was formed to explore the possibilities of expanding this phase of the company's activities. Three executives were named senior vice-presidents. These were the financial vice-president, Johnson; the vice-president of operations, Stevens; and the insurance vice-president, Shoemaker. Both the fire and casualty and insurance division and the life insurance division were placed under Shoemaker's control. According to President Davis, Shoemaker was chosen over Daniels of the fire and casualty division because Shoemaker had given evidence of greater flexibility in administrative ability. Daniels was considered to be more of a functional specialist.

Line and Staff Relationships

After the above changes had been put into effect, many company executives felt that the friction points which had existed between Fidelity's line and staff elements continued in effect. In fact, many of these executives believed that these types of conflicts had increased. The main point of friction cited was between the operations division and the controllers division. The controllers division executives said that they were unable to obtain any cooperation from the operations division when it came to obtaining financial information necessary for their analysis and information. Executives in the operations division claimed that the manager of the controller's division refused to look upon his organization as a service division. They said, "He is reluctant to give financial information voluntarily to any of our operating managers, and yet he feels that he should be able to call the shots whenever he needs information from us."

One executive in the operations division, who had been known to make extensive use of Fidelity's staff services, played down the importance of conflicts between the company's line and staff elements. He said that he had always attempted to make use of a number of staff people whom he would directly contact for the information he needed. "The conflicts that did develop," he said, "were, in many cases, the fault of the staff man himself. For example, Fidelity's planning department had a habit of presenting its reports in a manner which seemed to usurp some of the decision-making responsibility of the line managers. This did not help sell the planning department's ideas. I personally found, however, that this department contains a number of very talented people and that they can be very helpful to me." This executive mentioned, however, that the operations division seldom made use of the credit department. As he put it, "The credit department is a boiled-down department, having only the skeleton remains of a group most of which had been taken into the operations division. It is more or less bypassed in the organization now that the operations division has its own credit personnel."

Another highly placed executive in the operations division was of the opinion that outside staff assistance was unnecessary and was a drain on the profitability of the company.

The Use of Human Relations Laboratories

In early 1960 executives in Fidelity's employee relations division were concerned with the breakdown in communications which they observed had taken place throughout the company. This they attributed to the many changes in organization and procedures which had been put into effect. Moreover, they were dissatisfied with the lack of effectiveness of the formal, lecture-type vocational training that was being employed as a part of the company's executive development program. Consequently, it was the idea of Meany, the division manager, and Linholtz, who had been advanced to the post of executive department manager, that Fidelity should experiment with an unstructured training group program. This training concept had been developed by Leland P. Bradford, a social psychologist, and his associates at the National Training Laboratory in Group Development.

Linholtz referred to this program as a human relations or leadership laboratory. The program was presented to Fidelity's managers in the following manner: "For the first time anywhere, a group of the nation's top authorities on motivational counseling will be gathered together to *help you help others* get things done." The "laboratories" were designed to achieve this end by isolating groups of up to a dozen executives on a "cultural island," such as a hotel, removed from their work environment, and letting them observe and experiment with how their behavior affects other people. Participants in this training were assigned to discussion groups, but no formerly designated leaders were appointed and there was no predetermined agenda. Each group was presented with the idea that its members were not only scientists in the "laboratory," but also that they were their own subjects. The members were encouraged to discuss frankly one another's behavior and the feelings that might be causing that behavior. A psychologist was assigned to each group and participated in the discussions, but his role was only to point out from time to time the behavioral aspects of what was taking place when he felt that this knowledge would be helpful to the group process. The discussion sessions took up about four hours of each day's training. They were interspersed by lectures dealing with the psychological aspects of a manager's job and by various training exercises, such as role playing and communication experiments.

After a number of these sessions had taken place, according to Linholtz, the participants had largely abandoned their defense mechanisms and were more freely expressing their feelings to one another. "These unstructured group sessions," he said, "for the first time for most of these executives, placed them in a favorable environment for communicating with, listening to, and understanding others."

Initially four human relations laboratories were held for Fidelity's executives throughout 1960 and were of one week duration. The first phase of each "laboratory" focused on personal and interpersonal relationships throughout the top management level of the company. Its object was to get these executives together simply to understand what each was doing and what problems they were facing. The second phase had a functional orientation. Here the executives were divided into groups which regularly worked together in performing day to day operations for the company. The purpose of the functional groupings was to have these executives work out methods by which they could solve problems which they held in common. In the words of one executive, "This was the first time that some of our people had been asked to contribute ideas on how they should organize themselves and their work. I personally didn't get very much out of these meetings, since I have been working pretty well with people from other divisions all along. But I noticed a tremendous effect on some of the other people in the organization."

Reactions to the program among the managers who had participated, however, were mixed. One reaction was expressed as follows: "I went along with the program strictly because I knew it had top management sanction. It seems to me that we ought to concern ourselves with how to make a profit instead of worrying about being nice to people." Another reaction was that the program had definitely served to open up channels of communication. A third was, "I think the program needlessly caused us to expose our personal feelings to the people we work with."

According to Linholtz and Stevens, the human relations laboratories worked so well that a modified version was developed for use at the lower managerial levels of the operations division at the end of 1960. The program was condensed into a three-day period and focused entirely on a functional, problem-solving orientation. The purpose of the program, said Linholtz, was threefold: "First, get rid of barriers to communication; second, reveal and identify common problems throughout the company; and third, reveal problems which the group attending the session couldn't deal with." At the end of each of these sessions, the group was asked to submit a report pointing out to top management the problems that it could not cope with. Linholtz said that in the past these sensitivity meetings had encompassed only two levels of the organization at a time. In the future, he said that he envisioned that similar meetings would be set up which would encompass all five levels of the operations division at the same time.

To ascertain the results achieved by the human relations laboratories, Linholtz made a questionnaire survey. In a memorandum reporting on the findings of this survey Linholtz said that he had received nearly a 70 percent return on the 215 questionnaires he sent out, and of those returned, 80 percent indicated a favorable response, and 60 percent reported that they had changed some of their policies, procedures, and practices as a result of the program.

The Installation of Electronic Data Processing

A large general-purpose computer was delivered to Fidelity's headquarters in early 1960. Before conversion of its branch data handling was started, the computer was tested out on one of the company's lending districts. Full scale conversion of the branch offices was started in mid-year and by the end of 1960 the data processing of two thirds of the branch offices was being handled by the computer.

Fidelity's data processing system was a highly complex one. There was a large number of branches to be serviced and they were spread over many states, each with different laws regulating consumer loan activities. Moreover, legal regulations required different techniques for handling sales finance as opposed to consumer loan business. Consequently, many bugs had to be ironed out of the programs during the conversion process. According to Stevens, the operations division manager, late and erroneous information was being fed back to the field.

Fidelity's primary purpose in employing electronic data processing was to be able to obtain more information and to facilitate further growth of the company. But it was also agreed upon by top executives throughout the company that the number of clerical employees in the field would be reduced as the computer took over more of the recordkeeping operations. The applications study had indicated and a subsequent field test had demonstrated that it would be possible for the company to handle 350 accounts per branch employee with electronic data processing as compared with a normal rate of around 270 accounts per employee without using a computer. It was also shown that the computer could begin to pay for itself at the point where it had achieved a productivity of about 325 accounts per employee. In the long run, therefore, it was indicated that the computer could pay its own way. But to do this it was necessary for the company to reduce its field working force as the computer took over more and more of the processing of field records.

In actual practice, as branches were put on to the computer there was no corresponding reduction in the field working force. The field managers argued that they could not cut down the size of their staff until EDP improved. In fact, many of them added still more people to their organizations, claiming that the EDP system had added to their work load. Many managers found themselves working for twelve hours six or seven days a week while their branch was in the conversion process. As the manager of one large branch office put it, "How can we cut down on the size of our working force when every week a different staff man from company headquarters drops in on us to tell us of a new change that has to be put into effect in our accounting records? In the last three weeks we must have put through three major changes in these records which have involved going through the complete file of ledger cards." The increase in the field working force had taken place during a period when the number of accounts had actually been falling off. The effect of this increase in field personnel was that operating costs rose sharply. Behind this, as one executive pointed out, was the fact that labor accounted for 50 percent or more of the company's operating costs.

Another problem which appeared with the introduction of electronic data processing was that line managers in the operations division began blaming the machine for adding to their problems. In some cases these accusations were justified, since through lack of proper programming the computer output was frequently in error. For example, two payments might be credited to an account for every one payment that came in. But top executives in the operations division also felt that many of the accusations stemmed from the fact that field managers were unfamiliar with and were unwilling to go out of their way to acquaint themselves with the new format in which the data output from a computer was presented to them.

Adding to the doubts of the line managers concerning the usefulness of the computer was the introduction of new definitions for terms to which these managers had become accustomed. For example, the programmers did not take into account the fact that there were two definitions of such terms as "delinquency." The controller had one definition and the field managers another. According to the controller's definition, if a payment is thirty days late from the date of the last payment the account is labelled "delinquent." The field managers, on the other hand, followed the former company and industry practice of aging as of a month-end cut-off date and were not aware of the controller's definition. For example, if a branch manager knew that the customer was prone to be tardy in his payments but that he would eventually make good his payments, this account might be properly extended and it would not show on the monthly delinquency report. As might be expected, the programmers who were organized under the controller's division used the controller's definition of this term. The net effect was that as the company rapidly put its branches on to the computer, its delinquency figures nearly doubled in size. One reaction of some top executives in the company on seeing this report was that the branch managers had been withholding information. Therefore pressures were brought to bear on the branch managers. Adding to the problem was the fact that the computer had been programmed to address a form letter notifying each delinquent customer that his payment was overdue. These letters were then sent to the branch in batches to be mailed to the customer. There were cases of fifteen days delay between the time that the delinquent accounts had been identified and the delinquency notices had arrived in the hands of the customers. By this time, many of the customers would have made their payment. Even after the different definitions of "delinquency" had been spotted, the branch managers pointed to the harm that was done to their relationship with their customers and used this as an example of why they felt the EDP system was harming, rather than helping, their operations.

The problem of adversely affecting customer relations was later resolved to some extent by mailing delinquency notices directly from the computer center. The letter asked customers to ignore the notice if payment had been made. The branch managers, however, were still reluctant to give their support to the new system, according to a staff executive in the operations division.

Economic Conditions in 1960

Throughout 1960 an economic recession and the advent of the American-built compact car made their impact on Fidelity's market. Because of the competitive advantages of compact cars versus standard-size used cars, a traditional used car purchaser was attracted to the compact car with the net effect of deflating the used car market. Depreciation on used cars consequently was accelerated at a time when down payments were decreasing. Therefore, when a sales finance customer defaulted, his equity build-up had not kept pace with the depreciation of his car and the company took a loss on repossession, if this was a "without recourse" contract. Stevens, of the operations division, said that many customers deliberately defaulted on their payments in order to purchase compact cars, which required lower monthly payments. "Many of our collection men," he said, "were not capable of handling this situation. Moreover, we had lost some of our flexibility in coping with this difficulty because of the internal changes we were making."

Effect on Fidelity's Operations

By the time the year-end financial statements for 1960 were in, the full implications of the internal and external conditions which Fidelity was facing were seen. The 1960 operating results for Fidelity's lending operations are compared with other years in Exhibit 3. Exhibit 4 shows a six-year consolidated income analysis for Fidelity and a comparison with the earning records of the thirteen largest consumer finance companies.

Further Changes in the Operations Division

In early 1961 Stevens, the division manager, instituted a modification in the program to achieve a fully integrated lending operation. After experimenting with the idea in one of Fidelity's regions, he established what were called "service centers" in twelve of the largest metropolitan areas in the company's territory.

Each of these offices was located centrally in relation to a large number of branch offices, its function being to generate sales finance accounts

Exhibit 3

FIDELITY CREDIT CORPORATION (C)

Ten-year Comparison of Financing Operations
(Dollar figures in thousands)

	1960	*1959*	*1958*	*1957*	*1956*	*1955*	*1954*	*1953*	*1952*	*1951*
Loans and discounts acquired										
automobile and other retail	$287,500	$388,811	$266,392	$257,715	$269,432	$269,141	$209,946	$204,797	$233,200	$157,340
Percent of total	37.6%	39.9%	39.2%	40.2%	44.0%	40.7%	42.9%	43.3%	46.6%	42.8%
Automobile wholesale	195,974	305,970	183,300	179,291	157,515	230,617	149,544	151,854	156,435	136,892
Percent of total	25.7%	31.9%	27.1%	28.0%	25.7%	35.4%	30.6%	32.1%	31.3%	37.2%
Consumer loans	250,400	253,687	213,547	192,398	170,583	145,719	120,688	105,341	98,417	64,551
Percent of total	32.7%	26.4%	31.6%	30.0%	27.9%	22.4%	24.7%	22.3%	19.6%	17.5%
Commercial loans	30,741	17,369	14,212	11,501	14,907	9,933	8,910	11,423	12,551	9,217
Percent of total	4.0%	1.8%	2.1%	1.8%	2.4%	1.5%	1.8%	2.3%	2.5%	2.5%
Total	$764,615	$965,837	$677,451	$640,905	$612,437	$655,410	$489,088	$473,415	$500,603	$368,000
Credit losses (net of recoveries)	$ 12,026	$ 6,209	$ 4,661	$ 3,198	$ 2,206	$ 2,023	$ 3,854	$ 3,429	$ 1,674	$ 691
Ratio to loans and discounts liquidated	1.55%	0.74%	0.74%	0.52%	0.39%	0.35%	0.81%	0.75%	0.38%	0.20%
Operating results of branch offices (before deduction of overhead and interest)										
Operating income										
Sales finance branches			$ 19,294	$ 19,841	$ 16,527	$ 15,624	$ 9,736	$ 10,395	$ 7,151	$ 7,726
Consumer loan branches	45,538	46,921	$ 18,265	$ 17,011	$ 14,551	$ 11,992	$ 9,654	$ 8,833	$ 5,991	$ 3,682
Return on available lending funds										
Sales finance branches			8.26%	8.93%	8.32%	8.53%	6.50%	7.02%	7.33%	6.81%
Consumer loan branches	8.90%*	9.93%*	12.87%	14.26%	12.80%	13.06%	11.96%	12.14%	12.72%	11.62%

*Includes both sales finance and consumer loan operations. Figures are not perfectly comparable due to shifts of some expenses from the branch to the district levels, especially in 1960.

SOURCE: Company records.

Exhibit 4

FIDELITY CREDIT CORPORATION (C)

Six-year Comparison of Consolidated Income
and Earnings Comparison with Thirteen Largest Consumer Finance Companies
(Dollar figures in thousands)

	1960	*1959*	*1958*	*1957*	*1956*	*1955*
INCOME						
Finance charges	$73,502	$66,387	$56,724	$54,838	$47,499	$42,082
Insurance premiums net of commission, losses, and adjustments	4,447	5,387	3,794	3,542	2,072	2,301
Other income	1,028	901	692	593	680	733
Total income	$81,872	$75,291	$61,210	$58,973	$50,250	$45,116
EXPENSES						
Salaries (except insurance adjustors)	$19,205	$17,406	$14,946	$14,184	$12,571	$11,184
Other operating expenses	17,312*	14,869	12,939	12,476	10,816	9,786
Provision for credit losses†	12,230	7,043	5,273	3,690	3,074	3,588
Total expenses	$48,757	$39,317	$33,158	$30,349	$26,460	$24,558
Operating income (before interest)	$32,928	$35,974	$28,052	$28,614	$23,790	$20,570
Interest and debt expense	23,623	21,420	14,500	14,766	12,659	9,629
Income before federal income taxes	$ 9,491	$14,554	$13,553	$13,848	$11,731	$10,940
Provision for federal income taxes	3,712	6,409	5,602	6,414	5,973	5,481
Net income	$ 5,780	$ 8,145	$ 7,950	$ 7,434	$ 5,757	$ 5,459
Net income as percent of net worth						
Fidelity Credit Corporation	7.5%	10.7%	12.3%	12.1%	11.2%	13.1%
13 Largest consumer finance companies						
Low	7.5	10.3	8.6	10.1	9.6	7.6
Average	12.2	12.4	12.4	13.6	13.6	13.7
High	14.9	15.2	15.3	15.9	15.8	17.0

*Includes $1,230,000 in nonrecurring costs for conversion to electronic data processing.
†This provision was based on Fidelity's estimate of possible credit losses in the loans outstanding at the end of each year.

SOURCE: Company records and compilations of casewriter.

and to handle deliquent sales finance accounts. The branch offices, which were in the service center's territory, were left the responsibility of routine servicing of sales finance contracts sold to them by the service center in addition to their function of both generating and collecting on direct consumer loans. But such branch offices would no longer solicit sales finance business. A number of branch offices remained in the organization, however, which were outside the territories of the service centers. These offices maintained all the functions required to conduct both sales finance and consumer loan business. Stevens cited two reasons behind the introduction of the service center concept. The first was to place responsibility for judging the quality of new business on those people who generated the new business, since quality and volume were directly interrelated. The second reason was to utilize more effectively Fidelity's available managerial talent. In commenting on the implementation of the service center idea, Stevens said, "The whole idea would have been impossible without a computer. By having an electronic data processing system we can now transfer a customer's account to the branch nearest his home no matter where he bought his car. And yet we can still keep track of the quality of the paper which each car dealer passes on to us."

Along with the service center concept, a number of other changes were made in the operations division. Fidelity's territory was redivided into six areas, thereby adding two more area managers to the operations division. One third of the regional managers were either shifted to new positions or were terminated. As one operations executive put it, "The firing of several regional managers set a precedent in our company. Up until this time the company had been pretty soft-hearted when it came to firing people."

Vance retained his responsibilities as field operations manager but was advanced to assistant division manager and was given additional responsibilities. Exhibit 5 shows the organization of the operations division after these changes were made.

In early 1961 conversion of the branch accounting systems to electronic data processing was temporarily held up to allow the company time to adjust some of the difficulties which the conversion had created. To check the upswing in the number of clerical employees, several staff executives in the operations division tried to reason with the branch managers to make them more conscious of their profitability and of the effect which labor costs had on this profitability. However, one of these executives commented, "We can't seem to drive this message home with the branch managers. They are solely volume orientated." Finally, Vance, the assistant division manager, sat down with each area manager and told him, "From now on, I'll tell you how many people you can have."

By mid-1961, the operations division had achieved a cut-back of

Exhibit 5

FIDELITY CREDIT CORPORATION (C)

Operations Division Organization
July 1961

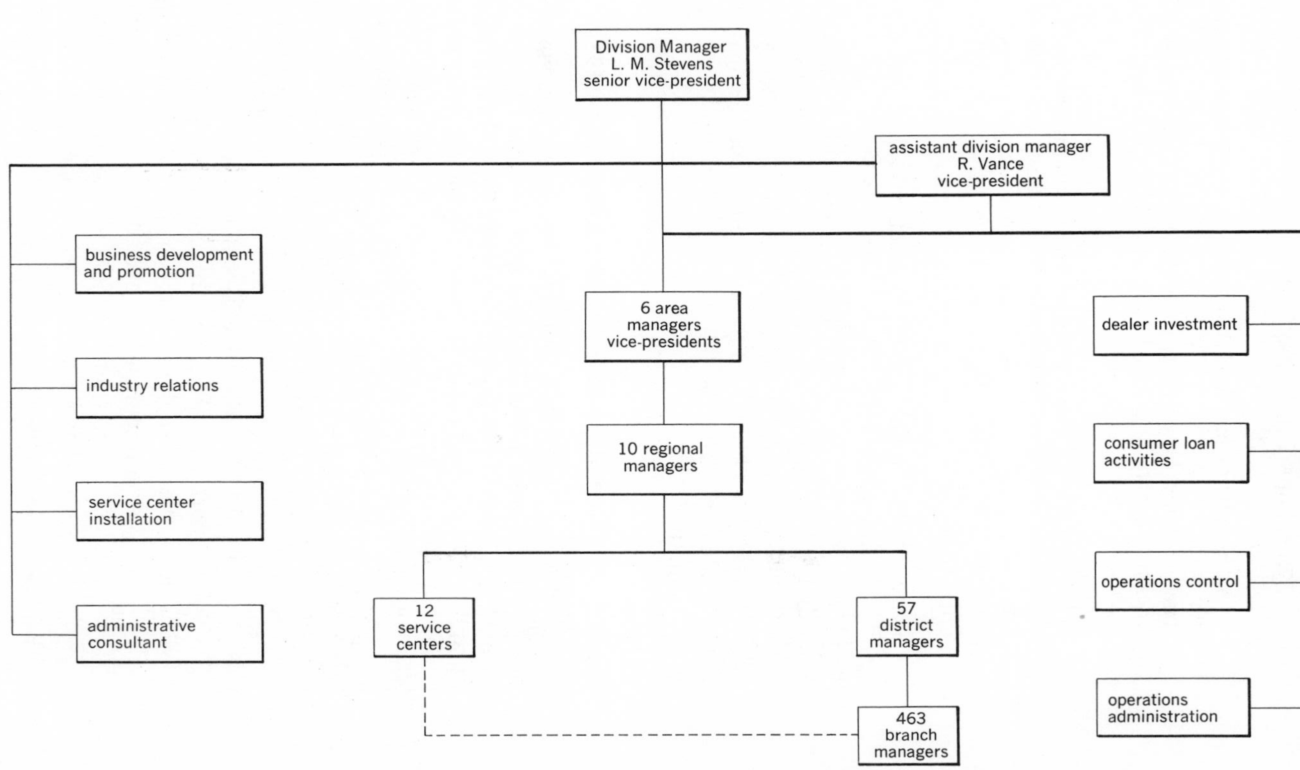

10 percent in its field working force. Even at that time, one staff executive in the operations division commented that productivity was only at a level of 270 accounts per employee.

> "As recently as last week," he said, "I heard discussions by some of our area managers saying, 'we need more people.' I don't think any of our line managers know how to make a profit. We tell our branch managers that in order for Fidelity to earn a 12 percent return on its equity capital, which is about average for the consumer finance industry, the branches have to earn a return of 10 percent on their average funds invested. We figure this return by deducting only those costs which are controllable by the branch manager, that is, before we deduct administrative expenses of the elements above them in the organization and before interest charges. Right now our branches are earning an average of 8 percent on their average funds employed."

In resuming the conversion to electronic data processing the managers of the branches yet to be converted were asked to name a time for the change-over which would least interfere with their lending activities. According to an executive in the employee relations division, this helped elicit the branch managers' cooperation. "It was amazing," he said, "how easy it was to put a branch on the computer once the manager's cooperation was obtained." By the fall of 1961 all of Fidelity's branches were on the computer.

Top Management Organization in July 1961

By mid-1961, Fidelity had seen two important personnel changes outside of the operations division. The first was that Daniels of the fire and casualty insurance division left the company. This left the presidents of Fidelity's two fire and casualty insurance subsidiaries reporting directly to Shoemaker, the senior vice-president of insurance. The second was that the controller had left the company for a position elsewhere. Lacking a man with the immediate capabilities of running the controller's division, this division was placed under the supervision of the senior vice-president of finance, where it had originated. In addition to the above changes, the division under Phillips, senior consultant to the president, was reorganized to include Fidelity's office facilities department and its purchasing department. Removed from his responsibility was the dealer services department which handled Fidelity's investments in automobile dealerships. This department was placed under the operations division. The reorganized division, under Phillips, was renamed as the facilities division. Exhibit 6 shows Fidelity's top management structure as it appeared after these changes.

Exhibit 6

FIDELITY CREDIT CORPORATION (C)

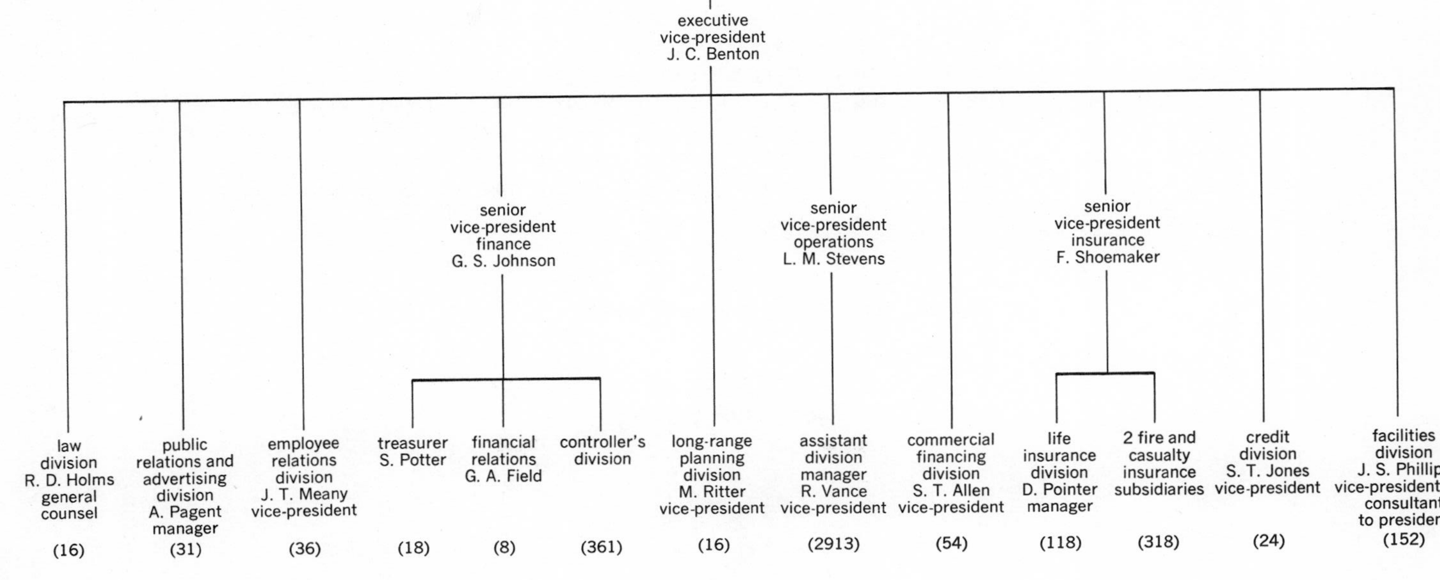

Present Value Tables

TABLE I

Value of $1 n Periods Hence with Interest Rate i per Period

$$S(i,n) = (1 + i)^n$$

n	1%	2%	3%	4%	5%	6%	8%	10%	15%	20%
1	1.0100	1.0200	1.0300	1.0400	1.0500	1.0600	1.080	1.100	1.150	1.200
2	1.0201	1.0404	1.0609	1.0816	1.1025	1.1236	1.166	1.210	1.322	1.440
3	1.0303	1.0612	1.0927	1.1249	1.1576	1.1910	1.260	1.331	1.521	1.728
4	1.0406	1.0824	1.1255	1.1699	1.2155	1.2625	1.360	1.464	1.749	2.074
5	1.0510	1.1041	1.1593	1.2167	1.2763	1.3382	1.469	1.611	2.011	2.488
6	1.0615	1.1262	1.1941	1.2653	1.3401	1.4185	1.587	1.772	2.313	2.986
7	1.0721	1.1487	1.2299	1.3159	1.4071	1.5038	1.714	1.949	2.660	3.583
8	1.0829	1.1717	1.2668	1.3686	1.4775	1.5938	1.851	2.144	3.059	4.300
9	1.0937	1.1951	1.3048	1.4233	1.5513	1.6895	1.999	2.358	3.518	5.160
10	1.1046	1.2190	1.3439	1.4802	1.6289	1.7908	2.159	2.594	4.046	6.192
11	1.1157	1.2434	1.3842	1.5395	1.7103	1.8983	2.332	2.853	4.652	7.430
12	1.1268	1.2682	1.4258	1.6010	1.7959	2.0122	2.518	3.138	5.350	8.916

Present Value Tables (Continued)

n	1%	2%	3%	4%	5%	6%	8%	10%	15%	20%
13	1.1381	1.2936	1.4685	1.6651	1.8856	2.1329	2.720	3.452	6.153	10.699
14	1.1495	1.3195	1.5126	1.7317	1.9799	2.2609	2.937	3.797	7.076	12.839
15	1.1610	1.3459	1.5580	1.8009	2.0789	2.3966	3.172	4.177	8.137	15.407
16	1.1726	1.3728	1.6047	1.8730	2.1829	2.5404	3.426	4.595	9.358	18.488
17	1.1843	1.4002	1.6528	1.9479	2.2920	2.6928	3.700	5.054	10.761	22.186
18	1.1961	1.4282	1.7024	2.0258	2.4066	2.8543	3.996	5.560	12.375	26.623
19	1.2081	1.4568	1.7535	2.1068	2.5270	3.0256	4.316	6.116	14.232	31.948
20	1.2202	1.4859	1.8061	2.1911	2.6533	3.2071	4.661	6.727	16.367	38.338
21	1.2324	1.5157	1.8603	2.2788	2.7860	3.3996	5.034	7.400	18.821	46.005
22	1.2447	1.5460	1.9161	2.3699	2.9253	3.8035	5.437	8.140	21.645	55.206
23	1.2572	1.5769	1.9736	2.4647	3.0715	3.8197	5.871	8.954	24.891	66.247
24	1.2697	1.6084	2.0328	2.5633	3.2251	4.0489	6.341	9.850	28.625	79.497
25	1.2824	1.6406	2.0938	2.6658	3.3864	4.2919	6.848	10.835	32.919	95.396
26	1.2953	1.6734	2.1566	2.7725	3.5557	4.5494	7.396	11.918	37.857	114.475
27	1.3082	1.7069	2.2213	2.8834	3.7335	4.8223	7.988	13.110	43.535	137.370
28	1.3213	1.7410	2.2879	2.9987	3.9201	5.1117	8.627	14.421	50.065	164.845
29	1.3345	1.7758	2.3566	3.1187	4.1161	5.4134	9.317	15.863	57.575	197.813
30	1.3478	1.8114	2.4273	3.2434	4.3219	5.7435	10.063	17.449	66.212	237.376
35	1.4166	1.9999	2.8139	3.9461	5.5160	7.6861	14.785	28.102	133.175	590.668
40	1.4889	2.2080	3.2620	4.8010	7.0400	10.2857	21.725	45.259	267.862	1469.771
45	1.5648	2.4379	3.7816	5.8412	8.9850	13.7646	31.920	72.890	538.767	3657.258
50	1.6446	2.6916	4.3839	7.1067	11.4674	18.4202	46.902	117.391	1083.652	9100.427

Present Value Tables

TABLE II

Present Value, P, of \$1 to be Received, n Periods Hence, with Interest Rate i per Period

$$P(i,n) = (1 + i)^{-n}$$

n	1%	2%	3%	4%	5%	6%	8%	10%	15%	20%	25%	30%	35%	40%	45%
1	0.9901	0.9804	0.9709	0.9615	0.9524	0.9434	0.9259	0.9091	0.8696	0.8333	0.8000	0.7692	0.7407	0.7143	0.6897
2	0.9803	0.9612	0.9426	0.9246	0.9070	0.8900	0.8573	0.8264	0.7561	0.6944	0.6400	0.5917	0.5487	0.5102	0.4756
3	0.9706	0.9423	0.9151	0.8890	0.8638	0.8396	0.7938	0.7513	0.6575	0.5787	0.5120	0.4552	0.4064	0.3644	0.3280
4	0.9610	0.9238	0.8885	0.8548	0.8227	0.7921	0.7350	0.6830	0.5718	0.4823	0.4096	0.3501	0.3011	0.2603	0.2262
5	0.9515	0.9057	0.8626	0.8219	0.7835	0.7473	0.6806	0.6209	0.4972	0.4019	0.3277	0.2693	0.2230	0.1859	0.1560
6	0.9420	0.8880	0.8375	0.7903	0.7462	0.7050	0.6302	0.5645	0.4323	0.3349	0.2621	0.2072	0.1652	0.1328	0.1076
7	0.9327	0.8706	0.8131	0.7599	0.7107	0.6651	0.5835	0.5132	0.3759	0.2791	0.2097	0.1594	0.1224	0.0949	0.0742
8	0.9235	0.8535	0.7894	0.7307	0.6768	0.6274	0.5403	0.4665	0.3269	0.2326	0.1678	0.1226	0.0906	0.0678	0.0512
9	0.9143	0.8368	0.7664	0.7026	0.6446	0.5919	0.5002	0.4241	0.2843	0.1938	0.1342	0.0943	0.0671	0.0484	0.0353
10	0.9053	0.8203	0.7441	0.6756	0.6139	0.5584	0.4632	0.3855	0.2472	0.1615	0.1074	0.0725	0.0497	0.0346	0.0243
11	0.8963	0.8043	0.7224	0.6496	0.5847	0.5268	0.4289	0.3505	0.2149	0.1346	0.0859	0.0558	0.0368	0.0247	0.0168
12	0.8874	0.7885	0.7014	0.6246	0.5568	0.4970	0.3971	0.3186	0.1869	0.1122	0.0687	0.0429	0.0273	0.0176	0.0116
13	0.8787	0.7730	0.6810	0.6006	0.5303	0.4688	0.3677	0.2897	0.1625	0.0935	0.0550	0.0330	0.0202	0.0126	0.0080

Present Value Tables (Continued)

TABLE II

n	*1%*	*2%*	*3%*	*4%*	*5%*	*6%*	*8%*	*10%*	*15%*	*20%*	*25%*	*30%*	*35%*	*40%*	*45%*
14	0.8700	0.7579	0.6611	0.5775	0.5051	0.4423	0.3405	0.2633	0.1413	0.0779	0.0440	0.0253	0.0150	0.0090	0.0055
15	0.8613	0.7430	0.6419	0.5553	0.4810	0.4173	0.3152	0.2394	0.1229	0.0649	0.0352	0.0195	0.0111	0.0064	0.0038
16	0.8528	0.7284	0.6232	0.5339	0.4581	0.3936	0.2919	0.2176	0.1069	0.0541	0.0281	0.0150	0.0082	0.0046	0.0026
17	0.8444	0.7142	0.6050	0.5134	0.4363	0.3714	0.2703	0.1978	0.0929	0.0451	0.0225	0.0116	0.0061	0.0033	0.0018
18	0.8360	0.7002	0.5874	0.4936	0.4155	0.3503	0.2502	0.1799	0.0808	0.0376	0.0180	0.0089	0.0045	0.0023	0.0012
19	0.8277	0.6864	0.5703	0.4746	0.3957	0.3305	0.2317	0.1635	0.0703	0.0313	0.0144	0.0068	0.0033	0.0017	0.0009
20	0.8195	0.6730	0.5537	0.4564	0.3769	0.3118	0.2145	0.1486	0.0611	0.0261	0.0115	0.0053	0.0025	0.0012	0.0006
21	0.8114	0.6598	0.5375	0.4388	0.3589	0.2942	0.1987	0.1351	0.0531	0.0217	0.0092	0.0040	0.0018	0.0009	0.0004
22	0.8034	0.6468	0.5219	0.4220	0.3418	0.2775	0.1839	0.1228	0.0462	0.0181	0.0074	0.0031	0.0014	0.0006	0.0003
23	0.7954	0.6342	0.5067	0.4057	0.3256	0.2618	0.1703	0.1117	0.0402	0.0151	0.0059	0.0024	0.0010	0.0004	0.0002
24	0.7876	0.6217	0.4919	0.3901	0.3101	0.2470	0.1577	0.1015	0.0349	0.0126	0.0047	0.0018	0.0007	0.0003	0.0001
25	0.7798	0.6095	0.4776	0.3751	0.2953	0.2330	0.1460	0.0923	0.0304	0.0105	0.0038	0.0014	0.0006	0.0002	0.0001
26	0.7720	0.5976	0.4637	0.3607	0.2812	0.2198	0.1352	0.0839	0.0264	0.0087	0.0030	0.0011	0.0004	0.0002	0.0001
27	0.7644	0.5859	0.4502	0.3468	0.2678	0.2074	0.1252	0.0763	0.0230	0.0073	0.0024	0.0008	0.0003	0.0001	0.0000
28	0.7568	0.5744	0.4371	0.3335	0.2551	0.1956	0.1159	0.0693	0.0200	0.0061	0.0019	0.0006	0.0002	0.0001	
29	0.7493	0.5631	0.4243	0.3207	0.2429	0.1846	0.1073	0.0630	0.0174	0.0051	0.0015	0.0005	0.0002	0.0001	
30	0.7419	0.5521	0.4120	0.3083	0.2314	0.1741	0.0994	0.0573	0.0151	0.0042	0.0012	0.0004	0.0001	0.0000	
35	0.7059	0.5000	0.3554	0.2534	0.1813	0.1301	0.0676	0.0356	0.0075	0.0017	0.0004	0.0001	0.0000		
40	0.6717	0.4529	0.3066	0.2083	0.1420	0.0972	0.0460	0.0221	0.0037	0.0007	0.0001	0.0000			
45	0.6391	0.4102	0.2664	0.1712	0.1113	0.0727	0.0313	0.0137	0.0019	0.0003	0.0000				
50	0.6080	0.3715	0.2281	0.1407	0.0872	0.0543	0.0213	0.0085	0.0009	0.0001					

Present Value Tables

TABLE III

Value of $1 per Period, n Periods Hence, with Interest Rate i per Period

$$S(i, n) = \frac{(1 + i)^n - 1}{i}$$

n	1%	2%	3%	4%	5%	6%	8%	10%	15%	20%
1	1.0000	1.0000	1.0000	1.0000	1.0000	1.0000	1.000	1.000	1.000	1.000
2	2.0100	2.0200	2.0300	2.0400	2.0500	2.0600	2.080	2.100	2.150	2.200
3	3.0301	3.0604	3.0909	3.1216	3.1525	3.1836	3.246	3.310	3.472	3.640
4	4.0604	4.1216	4.1836	4.2465	4.3101	4.3746	4.506	4.641	4.993	5.368
5	5.1010	5.2040	5.3091	5.4163	5.5256	5.6371	5.867	6.105	6.742	7.442
6	6.1520	6.3081	6.4684	6.6330	6.8019	6.9753	7.336	7.716	8.754	9.930
7	7.2135	7.4343	7.6625	7.8983	8.1420	8.3938	8.923	9.487	11.067	12.916
8	8.2857	8.5830	8.8923	9.2142	9.5491	9.8975	10.637	11.436	13.727	16.499
9	9.3685	9.7546	10.1591	10.5828	11.0266	11.4913	12.488	13.579	16.786	20.799
10	10.4622	10.9497	11.4639	12.0061	12.5779	13.1808	14.487	15.937	20.304	25.959
11	11.5668	12.1687	12.8078	13.4864	14.2068	14.9716	16.645	18.531	24.349	32.150
12	12.6825	13.4121	14.1920	15.0258	15.9171	16.8699	18.977	21.384	29.002	39.580
13	13.8093	14.6803	15.6178	16.6268	17.7130	18.8821	21.495	24.523	34.352	48.497

Present Value Tables (Continued)

TABLE III

n	1%	2%	3%	4%	5%	6%	8%	10%	15%	20%
14	14.9474	15.9739	17.0863	18.2919	19.5986	21.0151	24.215	27.975	40.505	59.196
15	16.0969	17.2934	18.5989	20.0236	21.5786	23.2760	27.152	31.772	47.580	72.035
16	17.2579	18.6393	20.1569	21.8245	23.6575	25.6725	30.324	35.950	55.717	87.442
17	18.4304	20.0121	21.7616	23.6975	25.8404	28.2129	33.750	40.545	65.075	105.931
18	19.6147	21.4123	23.4144	25.6454	28.1324	30.9057	37.450	45.599	75.836	128.117
19	20.8109	22.8406	25.1169	27.6712	30.5390	33.7600	41.446	51.159	88.212	154.740
20	22.0190	24.2974	26.8704	29.7781	33.0660	36.7856	45.762	57.275	102.443	186.688
21	23.2392	25.7833	28.6765	31.9692	35.7193	39.9927	50.423	64.002	118.810	225.025
22	24.4716	27.2990	30.5368	34.2480	38.5052	43.3923	55.457	71.403	137.631	271.031
23	25.7163	28.8450	32.4529	36.6179	41.4305	46.9958	60.893	79.543	159.276	326.237
24	26.9735	30.4219	34.4265	39.0826	44.5020	50.8156	66.765	88.497	184.167	392.484
25	28.2432	32.0303	36.4593	41.6459	47.7271	54.8645	73.106	98.347	212.793	471.981
26	29.5256	33.6709	38.5530	44.3117	51.1135	59.1564	79.954	109.182	245.711	567.377
27	30.8209	35.3443	40.7096	47.0842	54.6691	63.7058	87.351	121.100	283.568	681.852
28	32.1291	37.0512	42.9309	49.9676	58.4026	68.5231	95.339	134.210	327.103	819.223
29	33.4504	38.7922	45.2189	52.9663	62.3227	73.6398	103.966	148.631	377.169	984.067
30	34.7849	40.5681	47.5754	56.0849	66.4388	79.0582	113.283	164.494	434.744	1181.881
35	41.6603	49.9945	60.4621	73.6522	90.3203	111.4348	172.317	271.024	881.168	2948.339
40	48.8864	60.4020	75.4013	95.0255	120.7998	154.7620	259.057	442.593	1779.1	7343.9
45	56.4811	71.8927	92.7199	121.0294	159.7002	212.7435	386.506	718.905	3585.1	18281.3
50	64.4632	84.5794	112.7969	152.6671	209.3480	290.3359	573.770	1163.909	7217.7	45497.1

Present Value Tables

TABLE IV

Present Value of $1 per Period with Interest Rate i per Period

$$P(i, n) = \frac{1 - (1 + i)^{-n}}{i}$$

n	1%	2%	3%	4%	5%	6%	8%	10%	15%	20%	25%	30%	35%	40%	45%
1	0.9901	0.9804	0.9709	0.9615	0.9524	0.9434	0.9259	0.9091	0.8696	0.8333	0.8000	0.7692	0.7407	0.7143	0.690
2	1.9704	1.9416	1.9135	1.8861	1.8594	1.8334	1.7833	1.7355	1.6257	1.5278	1.4400	1.3609	1.2894	1.2245	1.165
3	2.9410	2.8839	2.8286	2.7751	2.7232	2.6730	2.5771	2.4869	2.2832	2.1065	1.9520	1.8161	1.6959	1.5889	1.493
4	3.9020	3.8077	3.7171	3.6299	3.5460	3.4651	3.3121	3.1699	2.8550	2.5887	2.3616	2.1662	1.9969	1.8492	1.720
5	4.8534	4.7135	4.5797	4.4518	4.3295	4.2124	3.9927	3.7908	3.3522	2.9906	2.6893	2.4356	2.2200	2.0352	1.876
6	5.7955	5.6014	5.4172	5.2421	5.0757	4.9173	4.6229	4.3553	3.7845	3.3255	2.9514	2.6427	2.3852	2.1680	1.983
7	6.7282	6.4720	6.2303	6.0021	5.7864	5.5824	5.2064	4.8684	4.1604	3.6046	3.1611	2.8021	2.5075	2.2628	2.057
8	7.6517	7.3255	7.0197	6.7327	6.4632	6.2098	5.7466	5.3349	4.4873	3.8372	3.3289	2.9247	2.5982	2.3306	2.109
9	8.5660	8.1622	7.7861	7.4353	7.1078	6.8017	6.2469	5.7590	4.7716	4.0310	3.4631	3.0190	2.6653	2.3790	2.144
10	9.4713	8.9826	8.5302	8.1109	7.7217	7.3601	6.7101	6.1446	5.0188	4.1925	3.5705	3.0915	2.7150	2.4136	2.168
11	10.3676	9.7868	9.2526	8.7605	8.3064	7.8869	7.1390	6.4951	5.2337	4.3271	3.6564	3.1473	2.7519	2.4383	2.185
12	11.2551	10.5753	9.9540	9.3851	8.8633	8.3838	7.5361	6.8137	5.4206	4.4392	3.7251	3.1903	2.7792	2.4559	2.196
13	12.1337	11.3484	10.6350	9.9856	9.3936	8.8527	7.9038	7.1034	5.5831	4.5327	3.7801	3.2233	2.7994	2.4685	2.204

Present Value Tables (Continued)

TABLE IV

n	1%	2%	3%	4%	5%	6%	8%	10%	15%	20%	25%	30%	35%	40%	45%
14	13.0037	12.1062	11.2961	10.5631	9.8986	9.2950	8.2442	7.3667	5.7245	4.6106	3.8241	3.2487	2.8144	2.4775	2.210
15	13.8651	12.8493	11.9379	11.1184	10.3797	9.7122	8.5595	7.6061	5.8474	4.6755	3.8593	3.2682	2.8255	2.4839	2.214
16	14.7179	13.5777	12.5611	11.6523	10.8378	10.1059	8.8514	7.8237	5.9542	4.7296	3.8874	3.2832	2.8337	2.4885	2.216
17	15.5623	14.2919	13.1661	12.1657	11.2741	10.4773	9.1216	8.0216	6.0472	4.7746	3.9099	3.2948	2.8398	2.4918	2.218
18	16.3983	14.9920	13.7535	12.6593	11.6896	10.8276	9.3719	8.2014	6.1280	4.8122	3.9279	3.3037	2.8443	2.4941	2.219
19	17.2260	15.6785	14.3238	13.1339	12.0853	11.1581	9.6036	8.3649	6.1982	4.8435	3.9424	3.3105	2.8476	2.4858	2.220
20	18.0456	16.3514	14.8775	13.5903	12.4622	11.4699	9.8181	8.5136	6.2593	4.8696	3.9539	3.3158	2.8501	2.4970	2.221
21	18.8570	17.0112	15.4150	14.0292	12.8212	11.7641	10.0168	8.6487	6.3125	4.8913	3.9631	3.3198	2.8520	2.4979	2.221
22	19.6604	17.6580	15.9369	14.4511	13.1630	12.0416	10.2007	8.7715	6.3587	4.9094	3.9705	3.3230	2.8533	2.4985	2.222
23	20.4558	18.2922	16.4436	14.8568	13.4886	12.3034	10.3711	8.8832	6.3988	4.9245	3.9764	3.3253	2.8543	2.4989	2.222
24	21.2434	18.9139	16.9355	15.2470	13.7986	12.5504	10.5288	8.9847	6.4338	4.9371	3.9811	3.3272	2.8550	2.4992	2.222
25	22.0232	19.5235	17.4131	15.6221	14.0939	12.7834	10.6748	9.0770	6.4641	4.9476	3.9849	3.3286	2.8556	2.4994	2.222
26	22.7952	20.1210	17.8768	15.9828	14.3752	13.0032	10.8100	9.1609	6.4906	4.9563	3.9879	3.3297	2.8560	2.4996	2.222
27	23.5596	20.7069	18.3270	16.3296	14.6430	13.2105	10.9352	9.2372	6.5135	4.9636	3.9903	3.3305	2.8563	2.4997	2.222
28	24.3164	21.2813	18.7641	16.6631	14.8981	13.4062	11.0511	9.3066	6.5335	4.9697	3.9923	3.3312	2.8565	2.4998	2.222
29	25.0658	21.8444	19.1885	16.9837	15.1411	13.5907	11.1584	9.3696	6.5509	4.9747	3.9938	3.3316	2.8567	2.4999	2.222
30	25.8077	22.3965	19.6004	17.2920	15.3725	13.7648	11.2578	9.4269	6.5660	4.9789	3.9950	3.3321	2.8568	2.4999	2.222
35	29.4086	24.9986	21.4872	18.6646	16.3742	14.4982	11.6546	9.6442	6.6166	4.9915	3.9984	3.3330	2.8571	2.5000	2.222
40	32.8347	27.3555	23.1148	19.7928	17.1591	15.0463	11.9246	9.7791	6.6418	4.9966	3.9995	3.3332	2.8571	2.5000	2.222
45	36.0945	29.4902	24.5187	20.7200	17.7741	15.4558	12.1084	9.8628	6.6543	4.9986	3.9998	3.3333	2.8571	2.5000	2.222
50	39.1961	31.4236	25.7298	21.4822	18.2559	15.7619	12.2335	9.9148	6.6605	4.9995	3.9999	3.3333	2.8571	2.5000	2.222